Getting
the
MBA
Admissions
Edge

What the applicants say:

This book has helped me throughout the entire process, from choosing the right school to getting admitted to the school of my choice.

I purchased 3 books about applying for an MBA and your book was by far the best.
Reader from Goldman Sachs

My thanks and congratulations. You have assembled a great book of information that is invaluable to someone like myself. I have been in Investment Banking for close to four years and feel that it is the right time for me to obtain an MBA. Your book has given me so much, it has allowed me to consider aspects of the admission process that I otherwise would have never thought of and the book has also given me some much needed confidence that I can really succeed in such a competitive process.
Analyst with Salomon Smith Barney

Loads of useful information and insider tips. You can tell it was written by successful candidates – the writer of each chapter gives the tips he used to get admitted to his school. this is the only book I've come across where the writers are in a position to share a lot of insider views and information about a whole range of schools.

I was admitted to Harvard, Columbia and Chicago and a lot of it is probably due to this book. Decided to write a quick review just in case it can help you in the MBA battlefield! This book is very comprehensive and takes a while to wade through all the info - good stuff though. (V good interviews with Admissions directors , a stack of example essays - but don't copy them - everyone seems to be using this book! also, a really good bit on the secrets of "how to market yourself to be the 'one'". A lot of people on campus said they went with this one.
Reader from Atlanta

I went to a great school for undergrad and now have the privilege of working for a large US investment bank... I would strongly recommend this book to anyone thinking about applying to a Top 10 school on account of the general, as well as school-specific, insider tips on applying.
reader from Goldman Sachs

Great general information on the MBA admissions process. Very detailed school reviews and tips.
Reader from Saddle Brook, NJ

Well written, lots of ideas, clear strategies. Takes you through the selection process with some very sophisticated analysis that I haven't seen in other MBA books. There are very few books on applying to business school anyway, but this is a "must buy".
Reader from a major investment bank

The MBA Site Ltd

The MBA Site Ltd is a publishing and advisory firm established to help individuals in their choices and applications to business schools.

©The MBA Site Ltd Limited 2001. All rights reserved.

First Edition US Published 2002

ISBN 0 9714822 0 9

Typeset by Maïté Rameil and Franck Desplats.
Cover designed by Chris Evans and Laurent Philton.
Printed and bound by Mackays.

US Congress Library Cataloguing in Publication Data
A catalogue record of this book is available from the US Congress Library.

Getting the MBA Admissions Edge

Alan Mendonca
Matt Symonds

The MBA Edge Team

As business school is quick to reinforce, great ideas require great people. Alan and I have been lucky to work with such a talented team...

Student Authors

F. Aloisi (MIT): Summer internship with Bain. Pre-MBA: Project manager for a major telecommunications company and a major bank.

A. Boureghda (Columbia): Consultant with AT Kearney. Pre-MBA: Trader with Deutsche Bank for 3 years.

Tim Chang (Stanford): Pre-MBA: Directed product launches at Gateway 2000; worked for General Motors in Japan.

Ralph Czuwak (INSEAD): Consultant with McKinsey before and after MBA.

A. Debane (Haas-Berkeley): Consultant with Booz Allen. Pre-MBA: With Alstom for 4 years.

J.F. Dieudonné (Northwestern - Kellogg): Internship with gap.com. Pre-MBA: Marks and Spencer and Vivendi.

Joshua Greenhut (Columbia): Pre-MBA: Publishing industry.

Everett Hutt (Wharton): Consultant with McKinsey.

S. de Longeaux (Chicago): Summer internship with Bain. Pre-MBA: Accenture.

Jessica Jensen (INSEAD): Pre-MBA: Consultant with BCG.

Shana Johnston (Wharton): Manager in the Staff Associate program at Sprint Corp. Pre-MBA: Swiss Re Life.

Eric Michel (Stanford): Worked for government in environmental policy and with Accenture.

Adrian Mitchell (Harvard): Pre-MBA: Business Analyst with McKinsey.

Phil Silberzahn (NYU): CEO of start-up. Pre-MBA: Started computer firm and sold it 4 years later. Post-MBA: Accenture; ran computer firm in India.

Patrick Sommelet (NYU): Pre-MBA: Capital markets. Post-MBA: Investment banker with Merrill Lynch.

JENNIFER DONNELLY
Senior Editor and Contributing Author

According to our editor, revamping colleagues' business school essays at KPMG Consulting proved perfect preparation for *The Edge*. Outside of www.theMBAsite.com, Jennifer works on special projects for the former cultural counselor to the U.S. from France, directs a creative writing program, and translates from French. During the 1996 U.S. presidential election, she researched editorials for a political journalist in Washington D.C.

TIM BIRD
Marketing and Public Relations Manager

Tim has been at the heart of the development of The MBA Site, conducting preliminary research on the business schools, overseeing the publishing process, and providing both content and architecture for the website. In addition to managing the worldwide distribution of the book, Tim handles corporate relations, and tirelessly responds to inquiries from readers the world over.

Contents

OUR THANKS

Creating this book has taken us nearly two years. The authors and the MBA Site team would like to thank all of you that have made such a valuable contribution:

- The Deans who shared their vision of the MBA and the future of their schools:
  Kim Clark (Harvard), Georges Daly (NYU), Bob Hamada (Chicago), Patrick T. Harker (Wharton), Donald P. Jacobs (Northwestern-Kellogg), and Richard Schmalensee (MIT).

- The various Admissions Directors and Personnel who took the time to explain the admissions process and the main criteria for selection at their schools:
  Rod Garcia and Julie Strong (MIT), Pete Johnson, Cherie Scricca, Fran Hill (Haas-Berkeley), Don Martin, Jessica Pounds, Myriam Fisas, and Akieva Harrell (Chicago), Linda Meehan, Keshia Mark, Maria Graham, and Rosy Nograles (Columbia), Mary Miller, Joanne Hvala, and Mark Truscinski (NYU), Marie Mookini (Stanford), Kirsten Moss, Eileen Chang, and Maura Byrne (Harvard), Sharon Hoffman, Lisa Park, Maureen Phelan, and Elvira Prieto (Stanford), Julia Tyler, Mary Ferreira, and Olivia Hutton (London Business School), Myriam Pérignon, Nick Barniville, and Joelle Dulac (INSEAD), Michele Rogers and Richard Honack (Northwestern-Kellogg), Meghan Laska and Eric Chambers (Wharton), as well as Lynne Reynolds (Alumni Director at Stanford) and Loretto Crane (Communications Director for the Harvard MBA).

- The current students and alumni who provided so much help for the book:
  Luc Andriamampianina, Olivier Aries, Hillary Beard, Isabelle Bonneau, Olivier Cardon, Dr Stefan Culen, François de Borchgrave, François Desné, Hala et Robert Frangie, Olivier Glauser, Daniel Ghiotti, Sara Green, Frédéric Jannin, Homayoun Hatami, Sophie Kerob, Jane de Larderel, Stéphane Panier, Jacques-Olivier Quilghini, Alberto Sanz, Serge Vidal, Didier Vilain, Katherine White, Pete Zehnder and Sven Zehnder.

- A thank you to all of you who provided so much talent, support and encouragement: Ranjith Abeyranta, Maïté Rameil, Franck Desplats, Christopher Davies, Dawn Bournand, Spencer Matheson, Catherine Wallace, Rachel Gorney, Gail Rosecrance, Abhaya Kaufmann, Isabelle Pasmantier, Helen Giudici, Laurent Philton, Bill Stephens, Tony Kendrick, Meg and Jim Symonds, Elise Zelechowski.

- Much appreciation for those who lent knowledge and expertise on everything from résumés for Harvard to shuttle buses at Chicago: Julian Jordan, Ariel Kelman, and Ravi Rajagopalan.

PART FOUR: The Schools Close-Up

Unique research tools at

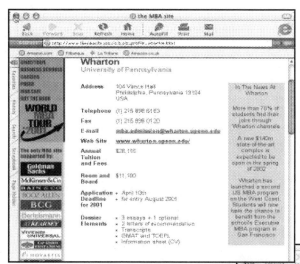

> *Find out where and when the top business schools are presenting around the world*

> *Review every FAQ collected from the admissions offices*

www.theMBAsite.com

> *Fast link direct to specific school web pages, application downloads*

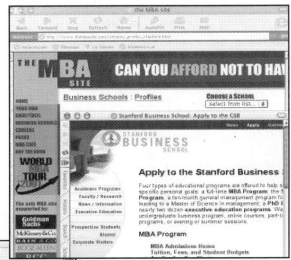

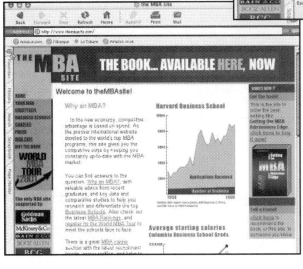

> *Ace the tests, research the careers, join the forums...*

Till min älskling Linn af Geijerstam
. . . för alltid

Maria, Max et Theo
Love's energy into life

Harvard Business School

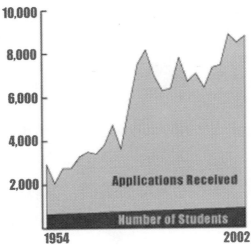

SOURCE: HBS reports and archives, HBS Registrar's Office, and HBS Class of 2000 Prospectus

FOREWORD

As the graph on the previous page indicates, getting admitted into MBA programs is becoming more and more competitive. Over the last five years, the numbers of candidates has increased by as much as 66% at Wharton, 45% at Stanford, and 85% at INSEAD. The current downturn in the U.S. economy is encouraging even more young professionals to return to school.

The stakes are high, as the Masters in Business Administration has become the only degree qualification to gain worldwide recognition, whether that be in the US, Asia, Europe or Latin America. A graduate from a prestigious business school thus has the chance to work anywhere in the world, from Rio to Bangkok, San Francisco to London. Apart from the international mobility that it offers, a great advantage of the MBA is the wide range of career possibilities that it opens up. The main difficulty for graduates is to determine the professional field best suited to their personalities, as the choice is so great: Wall Street trader, strategy consultant, investment banker, entrepreneur, multinational executive, marketing director, venture capitalist, etc. Once admitted to an MBA program, you will have around two years to decide in which sector you wish to work and which job appeals to you the most. An MBA gives you the possibility of doubling, even tripling your salary, as the packages offered to MBA graduates are extremely attractive (three years after graduation from Harvard, the average salary is in the neighborhood of $175,000/year):

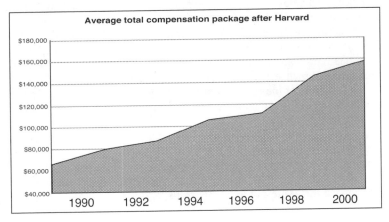

An MBA can also be the beginning of a prestigious career, as testified by the number of leading businessmen and women who have attended the top schools: Philip Knight (Nike), Alan Greenspan (Federal Reserve Bank), J.D. Power III (J.D. Power and Associates), Meg Whitman (EBay), Christopher Galvin (Motorola), Tony Wheeler (Lonely Planet), Franck Schrontz (Boeing), Scott McNealy (Sun Microsystems), James Bankoff (Netscape), Michael Porter (E*TRADE), Louis Gerstner (IBM), Raymond Gilmartin (Merck), Lawrence Weinbach (Unisys), Richard Fuld (Lehman Brothers), Carly Fiorina (Hewlett Packard), Jeanne Jackson (Walmart), Donna Dubinsky (Handspring), Alan Lafley (Procter & Gamble), Richard Wagoner (General Motors), Robert Louis Dreyfus (Adidas), Donald Fisher (Gap), Ron Perelman (MacAndrews & Forbes Groups), John Browne (British Petroleum), Lukas Muehlemann (Crédit Suisse First Bank), Michel Bon (France Telecom), Grit Gadiesh (Bain), Lindsay Owen-Jones (L'Oréal)...

The MBA is an investment of your time and money. Everything possible should therefore be done to ensure that you get into the best program to guarantee the best return on your investment. Completing the MBA admissions applications can be a long and arduous task. Over this period, it is often tempting to consider giving in, faced with such uncertain odds of achieving success. However, the workload deserves sustained and meticulous attention, and it is with this in mind that we compiled this book, with the goal of significantly improving your chances of admissions to the top MBA programs.

Over more than 600 pages, we have carried out a thorough study of the MBA applications dossiers of the top business schools. For eleven of the very best programs, we tracked down recent graduates to create individual chapters packed with insider advice that takes you beyond the glossy brochures and the websites. You will find detailed analysis of the essay questions, as well as a selection of the best sample answers for every question (in total, over 100 essays). The authors of each chapter come from extremely varied backgrounds, both in terms of their former education (business, engineering, political sciences, humanities) and professional experience (consultant, trader, engineer, marketing director, entrepreneur). This diversity is reflected in the advice, and you will no doubt find of most interest the words of authors whose educational and professional background is most similar to your own. Each of the authors speaks with authority, having successfully completed an MBA at these prestigious schools.

This is one of the major strengths of the book, as, until now, most books dealing with MBA admissions have been written by journalists who have never completed an applications dossier. We believe that there is no substitute for experience in giving concrete and reliable advice. This is all the more true considering the complexity of the applications process, and differences between the MBAs are often difficult to spot for someone who has not spent two years in the school. However, it is essential to fine-tune your application according to the specifics of the chosen school. To complement our own experiences, we have also called upon the opinions of insider experts, such as the Admissions Directors of the major business schools. Furthermore, each chapter includes an interview with the Dean outlining their vision of their MBA program's future in the coming years.

This publication aims to give an exhaustive overview of the MBA. When we were applying for our MBAs, we often remarked upon how useful it would be to have access to first-hand commentary from the real insiders -- the graduates of the MBA programs, and the professionals who direct these institutions. We sincerely hope that the results of our work will provide applicants with the information and advice that were not available to us, and act as a guide along the path towards MBA success.

We welcome you to share with us any comments on our publication.

Alan Mendonca
alain@theMBAsite.com

Matt Symonds
matt@theMBAsite.com

How to Choose your MBA

HOW TO CHOOSE YOUR MBA

Applying to Business School is rarely an easy process. An MBA represents a considerable investment, measured not only by time and money, but also the interruption of your current career and the upheaval in your personal life. It is to be hoped, therefore, that your MBA experience lives up to your expectations, and gives you a strong return on your investment long after you graduate.

In order to achieve this goal, the first step is to carefully choose the schools to which you should apply. The second step, of course, is to get accepted! We encourage you to be as thorough as possible when coming up with your target list of schools by taking the following steps:
1) List the specific benefits you hope to gain from your MBA, including financial gains, career advancement, personal development, etc.
2) Consider the teaching methods and the learning environment that best suit your learning style and personality.
3) Identify the MBA programs best corresponding to your expectations listed above, taking into account their reputations, alumni networks, and academic strengths and weaknesses.

Many students make the mistake of selecting schools entirely on the basis of the most recent rankings published by well-known newspapers and magazines. We suggest that you be wary of such an approach, given that the rankings change from one year to the next, and from one newspaper to another. Furthermore, the overall rankings tend to be very general - so a school could be very well placed in the overall ranking, but may be fairly weak in the particular area that interests you.

If your choices are based solely on the rankings, you might end up being disappointed. For instance, we once met a candidate who had applied to INSEAD with the idea of then working in a number of Asian countries. The excellent reputation enjoyed by the school was a selling point for this candidate, but the reality is that the school is far better known in Europe than in Asia (though this will no doubt soon change following the recent opening of the Singapore campus). If the candidate had taken the time to more closely analyze which school best fit his specific set of criteria, he might well have prioritized certain top US schools that are very well regarded in Asia.

To avoid making similar oversights, try following this step-by-step analysis of which MBA program is right for you:

WHAT BENEFITS DO YOU HOPE TO GAIN AFTER YOUR MBA?

Take some time to make a list of all the things you are looking to gain from your MBA. Studies show that the main benefits are typically:
- An increase in salary and earnings potential
- Development of skills in specific fields (finance, marketing, strategy, etc.) in order to have access to certain positions (consultant, investment banker, venture capitalist, etc.) and certain

companies (McKinsey, Goldman Sachs, etc.)
- Access to a network of alumni
- Greater opportunities to work in a country or geographical region of your choice
- Development of the skills needed to set up your own company
- Increased recognition based on the reputation of the school

Obviously the anticipated benefits will be numerous, but you should try to think about them in relation to one another. For example, just how important to you is the alumni network as compared to the average graduating salary? Graduates from Stanford are among the best paid, but there are fewer alumni than at Wharton and Columbia.

The analysis of these benefits should be considered over both the short and the long-term. Many candidates hope to work in consulting or investment banking, but these are often short or medium-term goals. Included in your thinking should be what you intend to do 5 or 10 years after graduation, and you need to bear this in mind when choosing schools (this process will also prove essential in the essay writing process). It is necessary from the very beginning of the application process to compare the schools' reputations and the extent of their alumni networks in the professional fields and in the geographical locations where you hope to work.

WHAT ARE THE TEACHING METHODS AND THE SCHOOL ENVIRONMENT THAT BEST SUIT YOUR LEARNING STYLE AND PERSONALITY?

Business School should enable you to achieve a number of goals after graduation, but the MBA program is an experience in and of itself, and each school has a very distinct profile. For example, some schools are well-known for their constant promotion of teamwork, while others place greater emphasis on individual achievement. Similarly, schools vary greatly in their mix of teaching methods (case study, lectures, group projects, etc.) Such qualitative factors will clear bear significantly on your appreciation of the MBA experience, and should be taken into account as you draw your list of schools. Reflect upon the respective merits of:
- working and being evaluated as part of a team versus as an individual
- learning through case studies versus lectures
- the competitive nature of the school (the grading system)
- the flexibility to adapt the academic program according to individual needs
- the reputation and availability of the professors
- importance that the school attaches to the "big picture" versus technical details
- the social life at the school
- the international nature of the school (students, faculty, course material, recruitment)
- the quality and diversity of recruiters

You shouldn't underestimate the importance of these factors, as they are key for your own satisfaction. We have met Harvard students who didn't enjoy their two years at the school because they hadn't realized how uncomfortable they would feel in such an individually competitive environment. On the other hand, certain students from Kellogg sometimes suffer from the ever-present team approach, and they complain that they have to work in groups for even the most minor projects.

Another reason to pay close attention to these qualitative factors is that they are sometimes helpful in differentiating one school from another. We've said that the main reason for choosing a particular MBA is the benefits gained after graduation (the factors from Step 1: salary, career opportunities, alumni network, etc.). But when you compare the top schools it's often hard to see much difference among them because they all lead to very similar opportunities. On the other hand, the qualitative factors (teaching methods, atmosphere, etc.) vary far more from one school to another, and can thus be of great use in making your choice.

For example, MIT and Harvard both offer tremendous opportunities after graduation, in terms of salary, alumni network, and reputation. However, the schools are very different in their pedagogical approach: Harvard places greater emphasis on general discussion and case studies, while MIT insists on a more technical approach.

IDENTIFY THE SCHOOLS WHICH BEST CORRESPOND TO YOUR EXPECTATIONS AFTER GRADUATION, AND THE ENVIRONMENT YOU'RE LOOKING FOR DURING THE MBA.

Once you have worked out what you want both during and after the MBA, you need to 1) obtain information on the different MBA programs; and 2) intelligently use this information to choose schools that fit your selection criteria.

The main sources of information available to you are;
- this book (given that we've done a lot of the research for you!)
- the schools' websites
- presentations organized by many of the schools in various geographical locations, and MBA Fairs such as the World MBA Tour (see www.worldmbatour.com for details of dates and locations)
- the alumni of the schools, including friends and colleagues (check our website, www.thembasite.com, for the contact information for the top schools' alumni chapters)
- the teachers at GMAT test prep centers - they are often well-informed and very objective
- the companies in the areas that interest you
- the online business school sections of newspapers and magazines such as Business Week (http://www.businessweek.com), US News (http://www.usnews.com) and The Financial Times (http://www.ft.com). This information can be accessed for free
- if you have the time and the money, you might consider campus visits to the schools that interest you

It is crucial to do this research because, as we've noted, on the surface schools look very similar in terms of their reputations for bankers and consultants, their curricula that alternate between core courses and electives, and their much vaunted student diversity (each school has its fighter pilot, Olympic medalist, and the flags of over 40 countries in the entrance hall). If you just stick to the beautifully designed school brochures, you may not notice the subtle differences between each institution. And think about how much time you spend deciding which car or which portable computer to buy. The total cost of your MBA will probably be at least five times greater than the cost of your car, so it really is in your interest to take the time to thoroughly research the schools!

Advice for your research
First of all, bear in mind that some of the sources of information listed above are by no means objective. For example, if you attend a presentation at a certain school, don't forget that the presenter is there to sell his or her school. Their goal is to increase the number of applicants to the school, because this, in turn, increases the selectivity of the school (which is taken into

account in some of the rankings). Don't be surprised to be seduced by a very smooth marketing operation. The schools are particularly good at this game, with Powerpoint presentations, impressive testimonies from former students, unbelievable salary figures from last year's class, and a smattering of beautiful photos which are enough to make you want to give everything up to join this student nirvana! But keep your eyes open and listen with a critical ear to what you hear. Don't hesitate to ask very direct questions like:

"I'm having a hard time understanding the differences between school X and school Y. Can you clearly explain the differences?"

"What are the weaknesses of your school?" This can be worded along the lines of, "Given that no institution is perfect, can you let me know which are the areas for improvement at your school?"

We strongly recommend that you get in touch with alumni. Even if the majority of them provide a ringing endorsement of their school, they are sufficiently detached to give you useful information about the school. Preferably try to contact former students who have graduated recently- they are probably more in tune with the latest initiatives at their alma mater. If you don't know anyone from the schools that interest you, go right ahead and contact the local alumni club (see www.thembasite.com). Most of the clubs have a designated member who handles inquiries from potential applicants, so they are waiting to hear from you.

If one of your goals in doing the MBA is to gain access to particular companies, we recommend that you call the companies in question and ask them which business schools they recruit from, as well as starting salaries for MBAs (if these issues interest you). Some companies are more courteous than others - it's better to find out before rather than after. If you're polite, the human resources managers are more often than not delighted to answer your questions - you may one day be a future recruit for them!

Some kinds of information about the schools are easier to get hold of than others. If your chief considerations are starting salary and the number of alumni in Europe, this information is easy to obtain because it can be quantified. However, if your selection criteria include the liveliest social life, or the lack of fierce competition between students, then you'll have to undertake more in-depth investigations. The surveys that we've conducted should help you to better understand these more qualitative aspects.

Finally, we suggest that you take a look at the major rankings. You could limit yourself to Business Week, US News and the Financial Times, since these journalists have researched their work very thoroughly. Bear in mind what we said about the overall rankings, and take a close look at the specialized rankings according to areas of interest (salary, international, alumni network). The following pages provide a summary of these rankings.

OVERALL RANKINGS

Be careful!

We have a long tradition of rankings in the United States. American magazines were the first to compile lists of the top 500 companies, the 100 richest people, the 50 best places to live and even the 10 worst-dressed movie stars. Rankings are entrenched in popular culture and classifying the products of the free market keeps the wheels of capitalism turning. But you need to take rankings with a big grain of salt!

Business Week, US News & World, and only fairly recently the Financial Times publish Business School Rankings every year or two. The results are eagerly awaited and are the subject of much debate amongst the schools, alumni, recruiters and MBA candidates. The results of the rankings change from one year to the next, and from one publication to another. For example, Stanford is ranked number one by US News, but is placed number eleven in the Business Week rankings of the same year.

One of the explanations for such disparities is the lack of a single, objective method for compiling the ranking of the best MBAs. The aim is to compare different institutions according to a number of pre-defined criteria. It's easy to compare the respective heights of Al and George because height is an objective measure that provides easy comparative data. But things get a little trickier when you are trying to establish whether Columbia is better than MIT. Imagine that you are a journalist at Business Week, and that your boss has just asked you to come up with a methodology for business school rankings. What are the criteria you'll use? Graduating salaries, or the number of Nobel Prize-winning professors, GMAT scores or recruiter satisfaction? The Business Week, US News and Financial Times rankings are the result of a number of journalists' subjective selection of data for defining the top schools. Furthermore, the criteria change from year to year in some publications. This explains why the rankings differ from one publication to the next and, even within the same publication, from year to year. Naturally the different methods inspire heated debate. There are many who feel that the criteria used by the journalists and their influential publications are highly contestable.

So how do we work our way through this apparent minefield? First, it's a good idea to better understand how the rankings are compiled, taking into account the strengths and weaknesses of each. For the candidate, the rankings are only useful if they help in deciding which schools to apply to. Rather than just blindly accepting the rankings themselves, use them to compile your own list. The bottom line is to choose the schools that best match your goals.

OVERALL RANKINGS

We thought it would be a good idea to show the overall rankings of the past 10 years, to give you an idea of how things change. The chart on the following page shows the trends from year to year and from publication to publication; this helps you see which schools are on the way up or on the way down. One rule of thumb for slogging through the numbers: if the school is consistently in the top ten, don't worry -- it's a good school.

	US News & World Report							Business Week						Financial Times		
	1990	1994	1996	1998	1999	2000	2001	1990	1992	1994	1996	1998	2000	1999	2000	2001
Berkeley	13	12	10	10	14	10	7	18	18	19	13	16	18	14	12	14
Chicago	8	6	6	6	6	6	9	2	2	3	8	3	10	6	6	4
Columbia	10	11	8	3	7	6	6	9	9	8	6	6	7	2	5	5
Cornell	12	15	15	20	16	15	16	14	14	15	18	8	8	12	10	15
Dartmouth	6	7	7	8	12	11	11	6	6	13	10	10	16	9	15	13
Duke	9	9	9	10	9	8	8	12	12	11	11	7	5	15	17	18
Harvard	2	3	5	1	2	1	2	3	3	5	4	5	3	1	1	2
Insead	not applicable							not applicable						11	9	7
LBS	not applicable							not applicable						8	8	8
Michigan	7	8	12	10	7	9	10	5	5	6	2	4	6	16	16	16
MIT (Sloan)	5	2	2	3	5	4	5	13	13	10	9	15	4	5	4	6
Northwestern	4	5	4	6	2	5	3	1	1	2	3	2	2	7	7	9
NYU	18	17	13	14	13	14	12*	15	15	16	14	13	13	17	13	10
Stanford	1	1	1	1	1	1	1	7	7	4	7	9	11	3	3	3
UCLA	15	10	16	8	10	11	12*	16	16	9	12	12	12	10	14	12
Virginia	11	13	11	10	11	11	15	11	11	12	5	11	9	19	19	22
Wharton	3	4	3	3	2	3	4	4	4	1	1	1	1	4	2	1
Yale	25	19	18	15	15	16	12*	n/a	n/a	n/a	22	20	19	20	18	20

Business Week and US News only feature American schools, so if you're interested in programs outside the US, bear in mind that you won't see INSEAD or LBS on these lists, although Business Week now publishes a list of top international MBAs, which is separate from its primary, U.S.-based list. The Financial Times was the first newspaper to compile a worldwide ranking, which compares European schools with their US counterparts.

US NEWS
Since 1990, US News & World has produced an annual rankings edition of the top 50 business schools. It hits the newsstands in March. The rankings are calculated according to the following weighted averages.
- 40%: reputation of the school, broken down to
  - 25% from the opinions of the schools' Deans on the academic quality of the other schools (five categories rated from weak to outstanding). The survey is sent out to around 320 Deans, more than half of whom respond.
  - 15% from a company survey of regular MBA recruiters, who provide their list of the top 25 MBAs. The response rate is typically around one third of those polled.
- 35%: employment after the MBA, specifically
  - 14% from average salaries upon graduation (this information is provided by the schools). This includes base salary as well as signing bonuses, but does not include bonuses occasionally conferred for expenses such as tuition or relocation.
  - 7% from the percentage of students who had already found a job before the end of the MBA program (schools provide this information).

- – 14% from the percentage of students who found a job within three months of completing the MBA program (schools provide this information).
- 25%: school selectivity, made up of
  - – 16% from average GMAT scores (schools provide this information).
  - – 7.5% from average GPA and grades from undergraduate study (schools provide this information).
  - – 1.5% from admissions selectivity, based on the percentage of students accepted out of the total number of applicants (schools provide this information).

Analysis of the US News Rankings

Strengths
- The defining characteristic of the US News methodology is its reliance on objective data such as average GMAT scores and graduating salaries. This approach avoids the dubious situation of students being asked to "impartially" evaluate their own schools (see Business Week). The US News approach places greater emphasis on the quality of students and their success after school rather than the image that they and employers have of them. To make an analogy with laundry detergent, a US News survey would rank detergents based on the quality of the ingredients and the sale price, rather than the feedback of retailers and consumers (as is used by Business Week).

Weaknesses
- One limitation of this methodology is that almost 60% of the assessment relies on data provided by the schools. It is obviously in the schools' interest to portray themselves in the best light possible, while continuing to uphold standards of ethics and honesty. The figures can be altered in subtle ways. For example, the schools must provide their MBA students' undergraduate GPAs. It is possible that a school may provide only the grades of US students and not those of the international students (which typically suffer in the conversion), thereby appearing more favorably against a school that provided GPAs for all its students. Around 14% of the evaluation is also based on median starting salaries of graduates, but each school is free to choose how this information is collected. By highlighting these issues, we are not pointing a finger at the highly-ranked schools, all of which have excellent reputations, but merely trying to point out some potential drawbacks of the US News method.

- One part of the ranking reflects the preferences of MBA employers when recruiting at the schools. These opinions are based on the US market, and are unlikely to take in to account the reputation of these MBAs in other countries. This is something to bear in mind if you are thinking of working abroad after your MBA.

- The US News' use of average starting salaries after graduation means that the higher the starting salaries, the better the ranking of the school. But even if many MBAs work in the same sectors, the distribution between sectors might be very different. Some schools are very much oriented towards financial services (investment banking, trading and so on) while others may produce more entrepreneurial graduates. Finance is certainly more immediately lucrative for young graduates. In the most recent graduating class at Harvard, the average base salary for corporate finance was $142,000, compared to an average of $90,000 for entrepreneurs. Schools with a high percentage of students going into finance and consulting (the two highest paying sectors) will thus fare better in the US News

Ranking than schools with more marketing, manufacturing and start-up recruits. It is also possible that students who attend schools claiming high starting salaries but do not go into finance or consulting may be disappointed after graduation. It is perfectly understandable why salaries are a factor in compiling the rankings; many candidates judge the quality of the schools by the financial returns they can expect to enjoy after earning their degrees. However, the returns should be measured over a period of several years to avoid any artificial inflation in certain industries. In the case of entrepreneurs, starting salaries may be lower, but if their start-ups take off, they can end up millionaires. Any ranking that takes into account the progression of MBA graduates' salaries over a number of years would give a better sense of the earnings potential a school can offer.

Strengths and weaknesses
- Nearly 16% of the overall rating of a school is linked to average GMAT scores of the admitted students. The higher the average, the higher the school rating. This explains in part why Stanford has been sitting at the top of the US News rankings for the past ten years. The thinking is that student quality can be measured by GMAT scores. Though high GMAT averages would suggest smarter students, beyond a certain score the differences don't mean very much. Does the 27-point difference between Stanford (727) and Kellogg (700) really mean that the quality of students is greater at Stanford? If you assume that there is a statistical significance, it might simply mean that Stanford students have stronger verbal logic and math skills, but ignores qualities such as leadership or charisma. There are even those who think that the verbal and math skills may be acquired at the expense the other "soft skills." Opinions are divided, so you need to make up your own mind.

BUSINESS WEEK

The Business Week rankings have made the front cover of the magazine since 1988. They are usually published in October, every two years. The whole approach of this ranking system is very different from that of US News. Instead of using school selectivity data and MBA Deans' opinions, Business Week believes that the quality of an MBA is measured by client satisfaction. This means both the opinions of students (who have paid a lot in tuition) and employers (who pay a lot to recruit the MBAs)!

Business Week conducts two surveys to measure satisfaction levels:
- The graduate ranking: More than 10,000 questionnaires are sent out at random to students from the schools' most recent graduating classes. In order to avoid major swings in the results from one year to the next, Business Week uses a weighted average: the results are calculated according to specific proportions. 50% is based on the results from the current year's study (n), 25% from the preceding year's results (n-1), and 25% from results of the study conducted two years before (n-2).

- The corporate ranking: Business Week surveys close to 350 companies that actively recruit on MBA campuses (around 260 companies responded to the last survey). The company recruitment officers are asked to rank the MBAs according to the quality of their graduates. The ranking is done on a sliding scale from 1 to 20: the school ranked top gets 20 points, the next one down gets 19 points, etc. and the school placed 20th receives only 1 point. The schools' ranking table is calculated from the cumulative number of points obtained.

To arrive at the overall ranking, Business Week doesn't use the sum of the two rankings (e.g. by combining a 1st in the graduate ranking + 3rd in the corporate ranking to award second place in the overall ranking). In fact, Business Week looks at the score obtained in each individual ranking and then positions the schools according to the sum of these scores. This avoids giving too much weight to very slight differences between schools in one of the rankings. For example, Harvard is ranked 6th in corporate and 13th in graduate, as opposed to Cornell, which is in 11th position in corporate and 4th in graduate. On the face of it, Cornell should end up with a better overall position than Harvard, given that Cornell carries an 11th and a 4th position, whereas Harvard only gets 6th and 13th place. However, Harvard will get the better overall ranking because the differences between the individual scores in the graduate ranking are very slight (there are only slight differences between 4th and 13th place), whereas there is a big difference in the corporate ranking individual scores.

Analysis of the Business Week Rankings

Strengths
- The defining characteristic of the Business Week rankings is that they're based on the satisfaction of the two main MBA 'clients': the students and the recruiting companies. For Business Week, GMAT averages and undergraduate GPAs (see US News) are not real measures of the quality of an MBA. What matters is being able to gauge the students' degree of satisfaction with their commitment to their MBA and the opinion of the main recruitment officers on their new hires (corporate ranking). To continue the analogy with laundry detergent, the Business Week approach would measure the product by user satisfaction (i.e., that of the MBA students and the companies who hire them) rather than by the quality of the raw materials used to make the product (i.e., GMAT scores, undergraduate grades, etc.).

Weaknesses
- Students are not entirely objective in their assessments, hence the main limitation with this kind of ranking. The more students speak favorably about their school, the higher it will climb in the ratings, and this is in the students' interest, given that the school's reputation is an important element in the recruitment process (most companies lock you into salary grids depending on the category of school you went to). This is especially true of the lesser known schools, since the rankings have very little impact on the big names like Harvard or Stanford, given that these schools are very well established. I found some newspaper articles that reported on students' opinions on Business Week's surveys. One student remarked,
  "I wonder why Business Week uses a methodology for its rankings that is so clearly flawed. Every student responding to the survey is presented with a conflict of interest. Business Week's rankings are visible throughout business, and it clearly helps a student's career (as well as his self-esteem) to have his school perform well in the ranking. When I had to fill out your survey, I struggled with this issue, torn between answering honestly to the survey and presenting my school favorably. While I recognize the value of measuring the quality of the program from those closest to it, student surveys are just not an objective enough measure."
- What's more, this problem has finally been brought to light. Upon the publication of its last ranking table to date, Business Week pointed out that some students had been deliberately overenthusiastic about their schools in order to improve the ranking. The article claims that some students even went to the length of circulating leaflets asking students to be less critical of their school. Business Week was able to handle these cases of manipulation, but they

haven't yet found a ranking method which can take into account this latent tendency for exaggerated evaluations.

- The second weakness of the Business Week method is that it ignores the fact that students in one school have very different expectations from those in another. In general, the greater the school's reputation, the more ruthless the students are in their assessment. Students who get admitted to the MBAs with the best reputation usually have very successful starts to their careers, and so are very aware of the sacrifice that these two years of study represent. A student from Thunderbird or Georgetown University doesn't have the same expectations as a student from Stanford of Harvard. With this in mind, it seems reasonable to ask whether it is a good idea to rank schools according to the level of student satisfaction since using this measurement criteria can lead to lesser-known universities being ranked as top MBAs in the 'student ranking' tree.
- As is the case with the US News survey, Business Week focuses on US programs. Although it accounts for international students, the proportion of European students questioned rarely goes beyond 10%. Therefore, for international students, the graduates' evaluations are not indicative of the program's reputation. If you want to base your career abroad, you should bear this in mind. The best example is perhaps that of Northwestern (Kellogg), whose reputation in the United States rivals that of Harvard or Stanford, but is little known in Europe.

FINANCIAL TIMES

The fact that the renowned London daily has been publishing MBA rankings since 1999 is a good sign that MBAs are increasingly becoming a reality outside of the United States. This ranking is the only one to be global in its scope, i.e. that compares American and international MBA programs. Its methodology is based on two surveys: one of the business schools themselves, and another of alumni three years following graduation.

Through these studies, the FT gathers data according to about twenty assessment criteria including: the salary of former students three years after graduation, the percentage of students who found jobs within three months after graduation, the quality of research projects undertaken at the school, the percentage of international students at the school, the percentage of salary increase after the MBA as compared to before the MBA, etc.

For each of these categories, the FT ranks the schools and assigns 100 points to the best school in its category. The other schools are then given a number of points according to their performance relative to that of the best school. For example, Harvard gets 100 points in the category for "salaries three years after graduation" with $173,120. Wharton comes in second with $162,610, so it gets 95 points ($=162,610/173,120$). By this method, each school gets assigned a number of points for each of the twenty criteria considered.

To arrive at an overall ranking, the Financial Times averages the number of points each school gets, weighted according to the following proportions of the various criteria:
- 20%   for the salary level three years after graduation
- 20%   for the percentage of the increase in salary compared to before the MBA
- 10%   for the research conducted at the school

- 6%   for the percentage of graduates who neither work in their country of origin nor in the country where they completed their MBA.
- 5%   for the percentage of professors holding PhDs.
- 5%   for the number of PhDs conferred by the school each year.
- 4%   for the percentage of international students.
- 4%   for the percentage of international professors.
- 3%   for the level in terms of company hierarchy attained by graduates three years after graduation.
- 3%   for the difference between the cost of the MBA and the recorded salary gains three years later.
- 3%   for the percentage of alumni who consider themselves satisfied three years after graduation.
- A dozen other criteria with a weight of about 1 or 2%, including: the number of languages candidates have to master in order to be admitted, the percentage of women professors, the percentage of graduates who find employment within three months of graduation, etc.

Analysis of the Financial Times Rankings

The principles of the Financial Times rankings are much more quantifiable than those of US News. In effect, the Financial Times isn't looking to rank the MBAs according to their image in the eyes of students or companies (like Business Week). Rather, it seeks to rank according to a specified set of certain objective and quantifiable criteria to define the quality of the various MBA programs. The only difference between US News and the Financial Times is in regards their respective manners of weighting the various criteria against one another.

While US News employs numerous criteria to measure the "quality" of students and their admission to the programs (by GMAT, GPA, etc.), the Financial Times seeks more to measure the quality of the instruction during the MBA (for example by looking at the percentage of professors holding PhDs, the number of international students, or the quality of research projects undertaken at the school). The common denominator between US News and the FT is the weight accorded to the performance of graduates after completing the MBA (measuring salaries, for example). This counts for nearly 40% in both publications.

Strengths

- As with US News, the major dawing point of the FT methodology is its reliance on objective measures, such as the salaries obtained by graduates three years after graduation. This method thus prevents results that are biased due to unreliable responses to less objective methods, as with surveys that ask recent graduates to "impartially" judge their own schools (see the Business Week section).

- To obtain objective and quantifiable data, the Financial Times surveys the schools and then alumni three years after graduation. As with US News, one must assume that all the schools gather the information with the same thoroughness, rigor, and by the same ethical standards. On the other hand, the alumni surveys still have to be approached with caution. In our opinion, the risk is considerably lessened by the fact that the FT surveys alumni three years after they've left the school; since they are already well-established in their professional careers, they are more disposed to reflect on their MBA programs with more perspective. They will therefore come across less like die-hard fans, and will be more objective in regards to their MBA experience.

- Considering the strong reputation of the Financial Times in Europe, it would seem likely that most of the responses to the FT survey would come from alumni established in Europe. They allow for the assessment of MBAs in Europe, which is interesting for candidates who want to work in Europe after graduation. It is useful to remeber that U S News and Business Week rank only programs in the US, which can sometimes lead to a discrepancy between the value of an American MBA versus an international MBA in the survey results. It was noted above that Northwestern (Kellogg) doesn't have the same reputation yet in Europe that it does in the States. The FT rankings make this discrepancy quite clear: Kellogg ranks only seventh, while it is always among the top few MBAs in the American magazines, US News and Business Week.

- The salaries measured by the Financial Times are readjusted according to the cost of living in the country of residence. In fact, the FT normalizes the salaries according to the PPP (purchasing power parity) indices established by the World Bank. That allows for comparison of graduates' real buying power, no matter what country they live in. This helps avoid certain schools appearing to be more advantageous simply due to the fact that their graduates live in cities where salaries are especially high, but without any increased purchasing power.

Weaknesses
- It must be assumed that all the schools provide data with the same level of rigor and honesty (see the section on the weaknesses of the US News methodology).

- In its calculations of the weighted averages, the Financial Times assigns different coefficients to each of the school evaluation criteria. Nearly 50% of the coefficients are for salary performance categories (salary level three years after graduation, the increase in salary compared to before the MBA, return on investment, etc.), 20% for international aspects (the number of international students and professors, etc.), 5% for the representation of women (percentage of female students and professors), and 5% for various other categories. If you conclude that this distribution of percentages correctly corresponds to the relative weight of the main factors determining the performance of an MBA, then this general ranking system is truly legitimate. However, if you think that the weighting of these categories is not accurate (because, for example, perhaps you don't think the percentage of professors holding Ph.D.s is important), you'll have to interpret this overall ranking system more carefully.

CONCLUSION

So now you understand that the rankings have to be analyzed very carefully. There will never be one perfect methodology. For its part, Business Week's approach seems interesting because it directly surveys the students (who have tested the product for you) and the companies, who will evaluate you upon your graduation from an MBA. However, the value of such surveys assumes a degree of impartiality on the part of the students and companies questioned. It seems like students would struggle to be both participant and judge at the same time.

Moreover, the US News approach, and to lesser degree that of the FT, aren't completely satisfactory. To avoid ending up with uniformly positive responses from students, these publications collect more objective and quantifiable data (average GMAT scores, salary, school selectivity, etc.). In this case, it's the schools that provide the bulk of the information, but that assumes that they all communicate with the same level of rigor and honesty. In an ideal world, there would be an organization to control the accuracy of the information provided by each of the schools!

So what lesson can be drawn from the overall rankings? Above all, we suggest that you get an idea of the average positioning of schools in the different rankings. The figures indicated in the table below are the mathematical averages of the rankings for each school from US News, the Financial Times and Business Week. Business schools may be divided into two fairly easily distinguishable groups:

1. Harvard, Wharton, MIT, Stanford, Columbia Kellogg, and Chicago are always ranked, on average, in the top ten best schools.

2. Duke, Michigan, Cornell, UCLA, Virginia, NYU, Berkeley, Dartmouth and Yale are always ranked, on average, below tenth place. In some publications, certain of these schools place in the top 10, but when averaging all three publications, they all rank below that.

INSEAD and the London Business School are not included in these calculations because they are not ranked by US News and Business Week.

Besides these combined rankings, we encourage you above all to study the rankings by specialization. Rather than relying on the overall rankings, whose composition do not reflect the importance of your own selection criteria, it is far better to establish your own general ranking system, according to what is most important to you.

	Average of the rankings	US News	Business Week	FT
Harvard	2.3	2	3	2
Wharton	2	4	1	1
MIT (Sloan)	5	5	4	6
Kellogg	4.7	3	2	9
Stanford	5	1	11	3
Columbia	6	6	7	5
Chicago	5.8	9	10	4
Duke	10.3	8	5	18
Michigan	10.7	10	6	16
Cornell	13	16	8	15
UCLA	12	12*	12	12
Virginia	15.3	15	9	22
NYU	11.7	12*	13	10
Berkeley	13	7	18	14
Dartmouth	13.3	11	16	13
Yale	17	12*	19	20

RANKING BY SALARY

One of the first things you look for in choosing an MBA is the job prospects it will open up for you, because this is what's going to help you judge the level of return on your investment of time and money. An objective way of choosing the most 'profitable' MBAs is to take a close look at the exit salaries for each school.

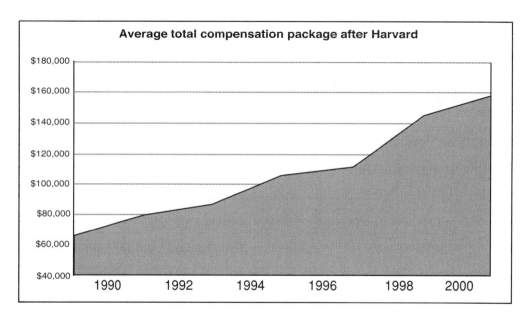

Average total compensation package after Harvard

First of all, it must be said that there has been a phenomenal rise in MBA graduates' salaries over the last few years. Defying all growth indices, graduate salaries have more than doubled in the space of 10 years. To put this into context, the graph above gives Harvard's exit salaries (note that similar growth rates have been documented in all the other MBAs). Most of the graduates from the best MBA programs receive total compensation packages higher than $100,000 directly upon graduation.

Why such a massive increase in companies taking on these young MBA graduates?

- The persistent good health of the American economy provides a very favorable climate for companies on the lookout for young talent to manage their strong growth. Their weighty profits give them ample margins and they don't have to count pennies in attracting MBA graduates.
- Many non-American companies are now faced with the globalization of markets, and are now active in all of the principal economic areas of the world (the Americas and Asia). As companies become increasingly international, they look for young managers who have a global vision as well as access to a network of former students on each continent. In the last

few years, therefore, we have seen the emergence of European employers such as Bertelsmann, Vivendi and Novartis. These companies help increase the number of job offers made to MBA graduates, while the number of diplomas remains the same. So the laws of supply and demand push up salary levels.

- Lastly, the internet has also had an impact on MBA graduate exit salaries. Despite the current downturn, more graduates are setting up or working for start-ups, getting the opportunity to run fast-growth companies, or even becoming millionaires. In order to attenuate the effects of this trend, some large companies – consulting firms and investment banks – waste no time stepping in and raising employees' starting salaries still higher.

The school rankings by salary can sometimes seem a little arcane. Indeed, different publications have different approaches:

1) US News and Business Week look at the financial package that students receive upon leaving their school.

The reason for this is that companies use several kinds of financial compensation incentives to attract MBA students:

- annual salary
- signing bonus (to get the applicant to sign his contract quickly - the earlier in the year he signs, the higher the bonus)
- reimbursement of part or all of the candidate's MBA tuition
- guaranteed year-end bonus
- relocation bonus
- other perks, such as reduced mortgages, housing, automobiles, etc.

Each of the tables below include some aspect of these various financial incentives: post-MBA annual salary (left hand column), salary + signing bonus (middle column), and total financial package (right hand column). If you want to find the total financial amount offered at the moment you walk out fresh from an MBA, spend some time looking at the right hand column (total compensation package).

Source: Business Week 2000 *	Average starting salary $
Harvard	99 274
Columbia	88 273
Stanford	98 162
Northwestern	90 000
MIT	92 343
Wharton	92 081
Dartmouth (Tuck)	91 223
Chicago	88 727
Virginia (Darden)	80 000
Duke (Fuqua)	86 450
Berkeley (Haas)	90 000
Cornell (Johnson)	87 700
Michigan	73 047
UCLA	84 518
Yale	85 371
NYU (Stern)	82 861

Source: US News 2001 *	Average starting salary + signing bonus ** in $
Harvard	117 180
Northwestern	112 994
MIT (Sloan)	112 741
Wharton	111 747
Columbia	110 556
Dartmouth (Tuck)	109 543
Stanford	108 441
Chicago	107 895
Cornell (Johnson)	107 283
Duke (Fuqua)	106 761
Michigan	105 282
Virginia (Darden)	103 820
NYU (Stern)	103 462
Yale	102 383
Berkeley (Haas)	104 159
UCLA	99 973

Source: Business Week 2000*	Total package *** in $
Harvard	145000
Stanford	138000
MIT	130000
Dartmouth (Tuck)	127000
Wharton	125500
Columbia	125000
Northwestern	125000
Chicago	120000
NYU (Stern)	120000
Berkeley (Haas)	117000
Yale	116000
Cornell (Johnson)	115000
Michigan	115000
UCLA	115000
Virginia (Darden)	115000
Duke (Fuqua)	109000

*data on INSEAD, IMD, LBS and McGill were not inclued in US News'and Business Week's ** school survey *** basic salary +signing bonus + reimbursement of tuition fees + guaranteed year-end bonus + perks: car, relocation bonuses (student survey)*

It must be said that the size of these compensatory incentives (besides the salary) are proportional to the school's prestige. The US News salary ranking shows that there is very little difference between the schools in terms of exit salary and signing bonus levels (there's a mere $10,000 gap between 1st and 10th place). However, companies seem to have different school policies for the other financial incentives (reimbursement of tuition fees, for example). The difference between Harvard (1st place in the ranking) and Berkeley (10th) is close to $30,000.

US News and Business Week's rankings obviously have weaknesses. In the first place, they compile all the salaries of MBA students who, in the majority of cases, remain working in the United States. If you wish to work outside of the States, these salaries would have to be adjusted in order to be relevant to the continent concerned. You'll notice that it isn't in the United States that salaries are highest (be careful to note, however, that this data doesn't take into account the cost of living, which differs from one city to the next).

source: Harvard	Index of salaries/continent
Base = salaries US	100
Asia	-93
Europe	(111)
Canada + Mexico	(112)
Latin America	(98)

Furthermore, the US News and Business Week rankings don't provide any information about the distribution of graduates across the various business fields. It must be stressed that there are big salary differences depending on the given field of activity. To give you an idea, here is the salary index per sector upon leaving Harvard:

source: Harvard	Index of salaries/sector
Base	100
Private Equity	(170)
Trading	(165)
Venture Capital	(155)
Investment Banking	(140)
Consulting	(135)
Marketing	(106)
Entrepreneur	(100)

Therefore, a school's average salary level will heavily depend on its graduates' choice of sectors of activity. Schools that have a reputation for finance (e.g. Columbia) will therefore have an advantage over schools whose strength is in entrepreneurship (e.g. Berkeley).

2) The Financial Times looks at graduates' salaries three years after leaving their school.
The FT performs an exhaustive survey of former students who obtained their MBA three years before. Unlike US News or Business Week, its objective is not to measure the amount of money a student will receive upon finishing an MBA program (salary + reimbursement of tuition fees + signing bonus, etc.), but the salary he or she will receive three years further down the road. Furthermore, the FT compares all MBA students, especially at European institutions, against their American counterparts.

The FT method is very rigorous, because salaries are standardized according to PPP indices (purchasing power parity – established by the World Bank). The salaries from one country to another are analyzed on a comparable scale (salary standardization and cost of living). This allows the reader to compare the true purchasing power of graduates wherever they are in the world. This information is featured in the column headed "Salary after 3 years."
Furthermore, the FT goes back over its data to tackle the problems posed by the range of business activity across different fields (see the US News and Business Week rankings weaknesses). Since some sectors (such as finance) are more profitable for employees than others, schools may see their graduates' average salaries fall depending on the distribution of graduates across different sectors.

In order to avoid this, the FT calculates average salaries by imposing the same standard range for all sectors for all the schools. This range corresponds to an average range of 100 MBA graduates surveyed by the FT (22.7% in finance/banking; 19.1% in consultancy; 11.6% in industry; 15.7% in IT/Telecom; 30.9% in remaining sectors). The results are given in the "weighted salaries" column.

Source : Financial Times 2001	Salaries 3 years after graduation $	Source : Financial Times 2001	Salaries $ weighted/sectors
Harvard	173,120	Stanford	171,318
Stanford	168,318	Harvard	164,152
Wharton	162,610	Wharton	151,714
Chicago	157,872	MIT	148,986
Columbia	157,775	Dartmouth (Tuck)	148,393
Dartmouth (Tuck)	152,799	Chicago	143,935
MIT	149,934	Columbia	140,886
Northwestern	134,341	Northwestern	130,101
UCLA	131,494	Insead	127,910
IMD	130,367	IMD	126,656
Insead	129,272	UCLA	125,396
NYU (Stern)	127,255	Berkeley	124,665
Berkeley	126,780	Virginia (Darden)	120,094
Yale	123,046	Yale	119,850
Virginia (Darden)	121,736	NYU (Stern)	119,780
Cornell (Johnson)	117,507	Cornell (Johnson)	116,426
LBS	115,577	LBS	113,538
Duke	113,524	Duke	111,514
Michigan	113,106	Michigan	108,005

It's worth noting that schools like Harvard, Wharton, Columbia, Chicago and NYU have slightly dropped in this ranking because they have a tendency to be overrepresented in finance and consulting, which is corrected by the salary weighting. However, schools like Stanford, MIT and Northwestern are climbing because they tend to make their presence felt in marketing and entrepreneurship (less lucrative sectors).

This weighting by area of activity is useful since you can compare the schools without knowing which sector you are interested in (the typical behavior of an MBA graduate is being used as a standard measure for all the schools). In the interests of thoroughness however, it must be said that the chance of being employed in a given sector varies from school to school. The correction by the weighting of the sample by the FT seems to assume that schools with an identical range are comparable since it doesn't depend on the school so much as on the students. But going into investment banking or strategic consultancy is made easier at some of the very prestigious schools. So an improvement in the ranking of weighted salary averages for some schools (vs. the non-weighted salary after three years) is sometimes more the result of the schools' difficulty in entering the most lucrative sectors, than a result of students choosing other, less profitable fields. It must be said that these subtleties vary from one school to the next. You should therefore look closely at the schools which interest you in order to understand whether the salary range is linked to the students' choices or to the schools' reputation in the eyes of the appropriate companies.

3) Forbes magazine looks at the return on the MBA graduates' investment relative to the school tuition fees and the difference to be made up in future salary.

Forbes magazine's study will appeal to lovers of finance, because its very rigorous method is linked to Net Present Value. Forbes sent close to 14,000 questionnaires to every graduate from 80 MBA programs (in the United States!) in order to measure their financial compensation over the four years after their MBA as well as their pre-MBA salary.

With this information in hand, Forbes estimates the salary the applicant could have been earning, had he not done an MBA. Depending on this estimate, Forbes applies the following formula:

+   salary obtained over the four years after the MBA
−   estimated salary obtained without having done the MBA. That is, the income lost during the MBA plus over the four years after the MBA). For this, Forbes estimates the pre-MBA salary including an annual growth estimate.
<u>−   tuition fees.</u>
=   the net gain thanks to the MBA

In order to bring the net gains up to date, Forbes even goes to the extent of discounting annual gains which give an average return rate from the financial markets. That said, their model doesn't cope with certain subtleties such as the tax differentials between the various salary levels.

This ranking doesn't aim, therefore, to categorize MBA programs by graduate exit salary, but rather by 'quality/price ratio.' Using this approach, an MBA program whose tuition fees are low could expect to be extremely favorably placed in the ranking even if the salaries are not among the highest. For example, Berkeley is ranked 4th with an average salary after four years of

$110,000, but with $40,000 worth of tuition fees. On the other hand, Kellogg holds only 12th position, in spite of an average salary of $138,000, but with heavier tuition fees of $54,500.

It's a shame that the Forbes ranking doesn't take into account European MBAs like INSEAD or IMD. This is because their one-year duration limits tuition fees, so there is less of a salary gap to fill without lowering the salaries by too much. It is more than likely that these MBA programs offer an excellent quality/price ratio.

Source : Forbes' 2000	Net gain over 5 years $	Pre-MBA salaries $	Tuition fees of MBA $	Average salaries 4 years after graduation (1998 figures) $
Harvard	101 000	50 000	52 500	171 000
Dartmouth (Tuck)	87 000	45 000	53 000	160 000
Stanford	74 000	47 000	52 200	140 000
Berkeley	64 000	38 000	40 100	110 000
UCLA	63 000	42 000	42 700	140 000
MIT	59 000	45 000	54 200	136 000
Columbia	58 000	40 000	54 300	125 000
Wharton	56 000	45 000	52 600	150 000
Chicago	55 000	44 000	52 400	122 000
Virginia (Darden)	54 000	38 000	44 100	112 000
Carnegie Mellon	49 000	34 000	49 000	100 000
Northwestern	41 000	45 000	54 500	138 000
Cornell (Johnson)	37 000	35 000	50 000	107 000
Washington (Olin)	35 000	26 000	48 900	85 000
Duke	29 000	40 000	51 500	108 000
Texas (Austin)	26 000	29 000	27 200	95 000
NYU	23 000	21 000	54 000	110 000

RANKINGS
BY JOB

In addition to salary, it's useful to look at the other opportunities offered by each of the business schools. At first glance, the top schools all offer the same career options and access to the same companies. The profiles of recently graduating students all testify to the diversity of career opportunities: investment bankers, consultants, venture capitalists, entrepreneurs. And the list of recruiting companies is pretty much the same from one school to the next.

However, a more detailed analysis reveals significant differences between the schools. A breakdown by sector reveals four distinct groups of schools:

1) The heavyweights of finance: NYU, Columbia, Wharton and UCLA. In these schools, around 50% of the graduates head towards positions in financial services, for the most part investment banking. With the exception of UCLA (Los Angeles), all these schools are on the East Coast, and in the case of NYU and Columbia, the proximity to Wall Street gives them an added advantage for well-placed financial positions. It also means that the stars of Wall Street can often be found giving a guest lecture or even teaching certain classes.

2) Graduates from Duke, Kellogg and Michigan are fairly evenly spread between consulting, finance and marketing. The open balance means that these programs are well suited to students who have yet to decide on their career path.

3) Tuck, MIT, INSEAD and Darden would seem to be more consulting oriented, given that as many as 40% of the students start in this field post-MBA.

4) Stanford and Harvard are very well represented in consulting and finance, and to a lesser extent in marketing, entrepreneurship and general management. More than other programs, these two seem to be breeding grounds for start-up ambitions, with more than 10% of students trying their luck with their own company upon graduation. The following graph very clearly illustrates the fact that many Harvard and Stanford graduates are currently turning their backs on big companies in favour of joining or launching a start-up.

Source : Placement reports**	Consulting	Finance			Marketing	Business Devel or Strategic planning	General management	Entrepreneur
		Investment banking	Other Finance*	Total				
1) NYU	21%	36%	18%	54%	12%	7%	2%	n/a
Chicago	33%	21%	30%	51%	8%	3%	1%	n/a
Columbia	31%	31%	19%	50%	9%	n/a	3%	n/a
Wharton	32%	21%	24%	45%	9%	3%	5%	n/a
UCLA	30%	10%	28%	38%	10%	2%	3%	n/a
2) Duke	31%	12%	23%	35%	19%	3%	6%	n/a
Kellogg	39%	11%	12%	33%	18%	11%	6%	n/a
Michigan	34%	8%	20%	28%	21%	3%	5%	n/a
3) Tuck	45%	14%	17%	31%	-	-	3%	4%
MIT	40%	10%	17%	27%	14%	7%	2%	1%
INSEAD	40%	-	-	17%	9%	8%	7%	n/a
Darden	33%	13%	10%	23%	11%	5%	8%	3%
4) Harvard	23%	9%	20%	29%	10%	12%	11%	12%
Stanford	18%	7%	18%	25%	12%	11%	2%	10%

* *Venture capital, sales & trading, commercial banking, private equity, portfolio manager, private banking*
** *Figures for the main functions of graduates. Data obtained from 95% of the graduation class.*
n/a = not applicable

The next tables show the sizes of the companies (by number of employees) that are recruiting at Harvard and Stanford.

Staff	Distribution of graduates (Harvard)		
	1996	1997	2000
< 50 people	14%	22%	27%
51 to 1000	24%	20%	26%
1001 to 10000	35%	34%	29%
>10000	27%	24%	18%

Staff	Distribution of graduates (Stanford)		
	1996	1997	2000
< 50 people	15%	21%	29%
51 to 1000	23%	23%	23%
1001 to 10000	39%	33%	28%
>10000	23%	23%	20%

	1	2	3	4	5	6	7	8
Berkeley (Haas)	AT Kearney	Accenture	Bank of America	Booz Allen & Hamilton	Ford	Hewlett Packard	Intel	McKinsey
Columbia	Goldman Sachs	Morgan Stanley	McKinsey	Lehman Brothers	American Express	Citigroup	Booz Allen & Hamilton	JP Morgan
Chicago	McKinsey	Lehman Brothers	Booz Allen & Hamilton	Goldman Sachs	Merrill Lynch	Accenture	Chase	BCG
Cornell (Johnson)	Pricewaterhouse Coopers	Salomon Smith Barney	Bain	Hewlett Packard	Pittiglio Rabin Todd & McGrath	American Express	Accenture	McKinsey
Dartmouth (Tuck)	Bain	McKinsey	Goldman Sachs	Mercer	Accenture	Bow Street	Booz Allen & Hamilton	Wheelhouse
Duke (Fuqua)	Booz Allen & Hamilton	Pricewaterhouse Coopers	Deloitte Consulting	Johnson & Johnson	McKinsey	Dell	Lehman Brothers	Goldman Sachs
Harvard	McKinsey	Bain	Goldman Sachs	Siebel	BCG	Lehman Brothers	Monitor	Dell
Insead	McKinsey	BCG	AT Kearney	Bain	Booz Allen & Hamilton	Lehman Brothers	Merrill Lynch	Morgan Stanley Dean Witter
LBS	McKinsey	DLJ	Goldman Sachs	Merrill Lynch	Deutsche Bank	Salomon Smith Barney	Credit Suisse First Boston	Bain
Michigan	McKinsey	AT Kearney	Dell	American Express	Diamond Technology	Ford	Chase	Accenture
MIT (Sloan)	McKinsey	Goldman Sachs	Bain	Intel	Morgan Stanley Dean Witter	BCG	Intel	Diamond Technology
Northwestern (Kellogg)	McKinsey	BCG	Bain	Goldman Sachs	Mercer	Booz Allen & Hamilton	Lehman Brothers	Siebel Systems
NYU (Stern)	Lehman Brothers	JP Morgan	Chase Manhattan	DeutscheBank	McKinsey	Salomon Smith Barney	American Express	Bear Sterns
Stanford	McKinsey	Goldman Sachs	Bain*	BCG*	Siebel Systems*	Intuit*	Loudcloud	Morgan Stanley Dean Witter
UCLA (Anderson)	Intel	Goldman Sachs	Lehman Brothers	Morgan Stanley Dean Witter	Robertson Stephens	McKinsey	Salomon Smith Barney	Diamond Technology
Wharton	McKinsey	Bain	Goldman Sachs	BCG	JP Morgan	Credit Suisse First Boston	Morgan Stanley	Deloitte Consulting
Yale	Booz Allen & Hamilton	Lehman Brothers	Intel	marchFIRST	McKinsey	DLJ	Fleet Financial	Goldman Sachs

The table above shows the main recruiters at the top MBA programs. The most prestigious consulting services are very well represented (Mckinsey, BCG, AT Kearney, Bain, Booz Allen & Hamilton) as are the leading investment banks (Goldman Sachs, JP Morgan, Merrill Lynch, Morgan Stanley, Credit Suisse First Boston, Lehman Brothers, etc.). In addition to giving high salaries, these companies enable recent graduates to apply their learning on projects that are as varied as they are intense. Such professional experiences may then prove very useful to vault students into executive positions in multinationals.

Beyond the traditional banks and consulting firms, in the past few years an increasing number of hi-tech firms has made their presence felt: IBM, Intel, Hewlett Packard, Dell, Yahoo, Siebel, in addition to a number of small, dynamic start-ups seeking MBA graduates to help manage their rapid growth. However, in light of the economic climate of 2001-2, this trend is rapidly becoming a thing of the past.

RANKING BY SPECIALITY

If you know what skills you want to acquire during your MBA, it is interesting to take a look at the MBA rankings by subjects taught. This way, you can identify the schools which have a reputation in the areas that interest you (the survey focuses on General Finance, Marketing, Accounting, Information Systems, Operations, Entreprenership, International Business and Quantitative Analysis).

A few remarks:
- first of all, it is a pity that Business Week and US News only rank American MBAs, because it would have been interesting to compare European MBAs (INSEAD, LBS, IMD, etc.) with the American MBA programs.
- once again, the methods adopted by Business Week and US News are different: Business Week asks companies to rank the MBAs according to their strengths in each discipline, whereas US News conducts a survey of the people who run the MBAs. We feel that Business Week's way of going about things is more appropriate here because it's the companies who will be recruiting you, and not the MBA faculty.

General Management	
Business Week	US News
1. Harvard	1. Harvard
2. Kellogg	2. Stanford
3. Michigan	3. Kellogg
4. Wharton	4. Michigan
5. Chicago	5. Wharton
6. Stanford	6. Darden
7. Virginia	7. Tuck
8. Duke	8. Berkeley
9. Columbia	9. Duke
10. Dartmouth	9. UCLA

Finance	
Business Week	US News
1. Chicago	1. Wharton
2. Wharton	2. Chicago
3. Harvard	3. NYU
4. Columbia	4. Stanford
5. Michigan	5. MIT
6. Kellogg	6. Columbia
7. NYU	7. Kellogg
8. Indiana	8. UCLA
9. Duke	9. Harvard
10. Stanford	10. Berkeley

Marketing	
Business Week	US News
1. Kellogg	1. Kellogg
2. Harvard	2. Wharton
3. Michigan	3. Harvard
4. Wharton	4. Duke
5. Duke	4. Michigan
6. Chicago	6. Stanford
7. Stanford	7. Columbia
8. Columbia	8. Berkeley
9. Cornell	9. UCLA
10. UCLA	10. Chicago

Accounting	
Business Week	US News
1. Wharton	1. Illinois
2. Chicago	2. Wharton
3. Michigan	3. Texas (Austin)
4. Columbia	4. Chicago
5. Indiana	5. Michigan
6. Kellogg	6. Stanford
7. Harvard	7. NYU
8. Cornell	8. USC
9. NYU	9. Kellogg
10. Texas	10. Harvard

Operations	
Business Week	US News
1. Michigan	1. MIT
2. Carnegie Mellon	2. Purdue
3. Kellogg	3. Carnegie Mellon
4. MIT	4. Stanford
5. Cornell	5. Michigan
6. Purdue	6. Harvard
7. Chicago	7. Wharton
8. Harvard	8. Kellogg
9. Wharton	9. UCLA
10. Stanford	10. Indiana

Technology/Information Systems	
Business Week	US News
1. MIT	1. MIT
2. Carnegie Mellon	2. Carnegie Mellon
3. Michigan	3. Texas
4. Wharton	4. Arizona
5. Chicago	5. Stanford
6. Stanford	6. Minnesota
7. Kellogg	7. Wharton
8. Harvard	8. NYU
9. Duke	9. Maryland
10. Purdue	10. Michigan

Quantitative Analysis	
Business Week	US News
1. Chicago	1. MIT
2. Wharton	2. Carnegie Mellon
3. MIT	3. Chicago
4. Harvard	4. Stanford
5. Kellogg	5. Wharton
6. Michigan	6. Michigan
7. Carnegie Mellon	7. Purdue
8. Columbia	8. Berkeley
9. Stanford	8. Kellogg
10. Cornell	10. Duke

Entrepreneurship	
Business Week	US News
	1. Babson
	2. Wharton
	3. Harvard
data	4. Stanford
not available	5. UCLA
	6. USC
	7. Texas (Austin)
	8. MIT
	9. Kellogg
	10. Berkeley & Michigan

International	
Business Week	US News
	1. Thunderbird
	2. South Carolina
	3. Wharton
data	4. Columbia
not available	5. Harvard
	6. NYU
	7. UCLA
	8. Michigan
	9. Kellogg
	10. Duke

RANKING BY TEACHING METHODS

On the face of it, the teaching seems to be pretty much the same at the various MBAs. No matter where you go, you'll hear about the "global economy," "Net Present Value," "core skills," the all-important "shareholder value" and more recently "consumers lifetime value." But while the subjects taught may be identical, the way they are taught differs greatly from one school to the and it is easy to distinguish the different methods: lectures, case studies and group projects.

Lectures

These classes are equivalent those in many undergraduate programs: content is mainly conveyed to students by a professor who identifies the main points on a given subject. We should point out, however, that these lectures tend to be very interactive because students often spend between two and four hours preparing for the lecture the day before, and they have no qualms about getting involved in the lecture and asking the professor questions about things that are still unclear.

Case studies

Harvard has built its entire reputation on case studies. The idea is to convey knowledge by examining detailed real-life examples. Knowledge here is therefore inductive, whereas the lectures are deductive and based on theory, which is then illustrated with examples. Performing case studies is a little unsettling at first because the professor steps aside to leave the floor open for discussion among the students. The teacher's effectiveness lies in his or her ability to structure the group discussion so that it leads to certain principles. This being the case, teaching quality depends on student quality and on students' desire to be fully involved in the discussion. So you learn to overcome your shyness and to express yourself in a convincing way in a crowded lecture hall!

Group projects

Group projects, as opposed to work done on an individual basis, revolve around the group preparation of papers, which are pretty much like research work on a given subject or company. It generally involves bringing together a lot of information on the subject at hand, analyzing it, and if necessary, talking about it in the group. This leads up to writing a report and/or a class presentation of the salient points to be learned from a particular case. Given that these projects are performed in groups, it's an excellent chance to apply your teamwork skills right from day one of the academic year. In addition to this, the information gathering and analysis stages are good exercise for jobs like consultancy or business plan writing, because the information gathered and the analysis performed are usually key factors for success.

It goes without saying that some people are more comfortable with one or another of these methods. Pragmatists are generally very comfortable with case studies, whereas others prefer theoretical discussions. If speaking in public is a source of anxiety for you, Harvard won't be very restful for you, though it may be your chance to get the better of one of your weaknesses. It's up to each person to choose the schools that correspond to his or her preferences or to weaknesses he or she wants to work on, because the aim of an MBA is to learn something, even if it involves a little bit of suffering.

Below, all the MBAs are been divided into four groups according to the teaching methods used most often:

1. Lectures: UCLA, Yale, Wharton and Chicago (we advise you to read the chapter on Chicago because the advantages and disadvantages of the lectures are well analyzed)

2. Group projects: INSEAD, Northwestern

3. Mix of the three methods: Duke, NYU, LBS, Columbia, MIT, Dartmouth, Michigan

4. Case studies: Cornell, Berkeley, IMD, Stanford, Darden, Harvard

	Lectures	Case Studies	Others *
1) UCLA	60%	30%	10%
Yale	60%	30%	20%
Chicago	50%	25%	25%
2) Insead	30%	30%	40%
Northwestern	30%	30%	40%
3) Duke	33%	33%	34%
NYU	33%	33%	34%
LBS	33%	33%	34%
Columbia	40%	40%	20%
MIT	40%	40%	20%
Dartmouth	40%	40%	20%
Michigan	40%	40%	20%
4) Cornell	30%	40%	30%
Wharton	30%	45%	35%
Berkeley	30%	50%	20%
IMD	20%	50%	30%
Stanford	30%	55%	20%
Virginia	20%	65%	15%
Harvard	15%	80%	10%

* group projects, individual research

Source: student survey

RANKING
BY INTERNATIONAL DIMENSION

Of great importance today is an MBA's international scope, because one of the advantages of the MBA qualification is essentially getting a passport to work in many different countries. The international scope of an MBA can be measured in many ways: percentage of international students, percentage of international professors, range of graduates' geographical locations, the percentage of courses dealing with international companies, etc.

Source : Business School	% international students
IMD	96
INSEAD	90
LBS	80
Cornell (Johnson)	37
MIT (Sloan)	37
Berkeley (Haas)	35
Harvard	34
Michigan	33
Yale	33
NYU (Stern)	32
Chicago	31
Duke (Fuqua)	31
Northwestern (Kellogg)	31
Dartmouth (Tuck)	30
Stanford	29
Columbia	27
Virginia (Darden)	26
UCLA (Anderson)	24
Wharton	21

The tables above and on the following page enable you to gauge the international scope of the various MBAs. European MBAs set themselves apart from the rest by their high percentage of international students and professors. However, this figure needs to be put into perspective because international students are defined as non-natives of the country where the MBA is located. For example, at INSEAD, all non-French students are expressed in the table as international students. But most of these come from other European countries (61% of the student body), and the great majority of the student bodies of the American MBA programs are American. In fact, European MBAs may only seem to be more international because Europe is made up of many nationalities whereas the USA is one and the same country. If you look at the percentage of students from other continents (South America, Asia, Africa and the Middle East), you soon realize that the European MBAs are no more international than American MBAs. The tables that compare the origin and geographical range of INSEAD graduates with graduates from Kellogg (which is typical of American MBA programs) show that European and American MBA graduates tend to be based on their home continent.

Sources: Schools Profile class of 2003	Student origins	
	INSEAD	Kellogg
Western Europe	47% 10%	7%
Eastern Europe	6%	1%
North America	9%	73% 69%
Latin America	6%	7%
Asia & Pacific	18%	11%
Others**	7%	1%

Sources : Schools Placement data, class of 2001	Geographic distribution of graduates	
	INSEAD	Kellogg
Western Europe	60%	5%
Eastern Europe	4%	1%
North America	12%	87%
Latin America	2%	3%
Asia & Pacific	8%	4%
Others**	4%	0%

*USA, Canada and Mexico - **Africa, Middle East*

The MBA brochures proudly rattle off the numerous nationalities which make up their student body, but international students are still a minority. This helps put into perspective the teaching method of these programs, which tends to bear the stamp of the culture of their home countries. The opening of INSEAD's Singapore campus, and the chance of taking courses there, offer an interesting opportunity. Perhaps INSEAD will then offer the first full-time program which can legitimately claim international MBA status. The alliance between Wharton and INSEAD will be another international trend to watch.

RANKING
BY ACADEMIC RESEARCH

Whatever career you are interested in, it's useful to be in an environment where professors are on the cutting edge of their field. This way you'll be the first to hear about the latest breakthroughs in specific fields, such as in derivative instrument pricing (market finance), or new theories in organizational behavior.

Most schools require or encourage professors to devote part of their time to academic research. Moreover, some schools even count some Nobel prize winners in their ranks, which is the case for Chicago, MIT, Harvard and Stanford.

In its MBA rankings, the Financial Times has undertaken to rank schools according to the excellence of their academic research. This ranking is based on the following criteria:
- The number of research publications in specialized journals. This holds true for 11 research fields related to business.
- The number of professors holding PhDs.
- The number of PhDs the school grants each year, plus a particularly favorable weighting for new PhDs who obtain a tenure-track position at one of the 50 best schools.

This general ranking gives you an idea of the schools that are at the cutting edge of the various disciplines taught. A score of 100 is awarded to the most active school in research. Grading the schools (in points) is done relative to the top school, which enables you to measure the size of the gaps between the various schools. There are of course variations depending on the discipline. We advise you, therefore, to get in touch with the schools so you can receive more information on the subjects of interest to you. The Financial Times study demonstrates Harvard's reputation as a cutting edge research center. Wharton, Chicago, and Stanford also stand out. In contrast, you'll notice MIT's 9th place position (down from no. 2 in 2000), and INSEAD's notable absence (no.24).

Source: Financial Times 2001	Research ranking
Harvard	100
Wharton	91
Chicago	86
Stanford	85
Columbia	72
University of Maryland	71
Michigan	71
Berkeley	70
MIT	70
UCLA (Anderson)	69
LBS	63
NYU (Stern)	62
Irvine	62

RANKING BY LOCATION

In selecting a school, location often becomes a key issue. This decision involves more than just choosing the sandy beaches and blue skies of California over the icy winters on Lake Michigan (though many a student has come to rejoice or regret the climate during their two years at business school). The reality is that both the culture of the school, and the job offers during summer internships and upon graduation are heavily influenced by the location of your MBA.

California schools and their students led the way in the mid 1990s to embrace the internet and its business opportunities, and this was reflected in course content, campus computer facilities, and recruitment in the bay area. Schools on the east coast have since moved to bridge the gap (students at MIT are quick to point out that the school is no slouch when it comes to technical innovation!), and generally the top schools have integrated e-learning and e-business into their core curricula. Many in fact now include study trips to Silicon Valley to look more closely at the opportunities and business models as they develop. The careers offices are also working harder to attract recruiters from the Valley and other high-tech areas around the world to campuses on the other side of the country, while many students think nothing of crossing the country for interviews, or approaching California-based venture capitalists for initial funding and support.

For those MBA students looking at a career in financial services, location will again push many to consider schools in the money markets of New York and Chicago. NYU, Columbia and Chicago all have world-class reputations for finance, and the schools are able to attract outstanding faculty who are otherwise consulting with banks and financial institutions. Students also appreciate having the CEO of a top investment bank as a guest lecturer, and are keen to reinforce their learning through a summer position between year 1 and year 2. Wharton provides a notable exception to this model – a good two hours from Wall Street, the school is considered by many to be the number one school for finance. This reputation ensures that students are not lacking offers when they leave school.

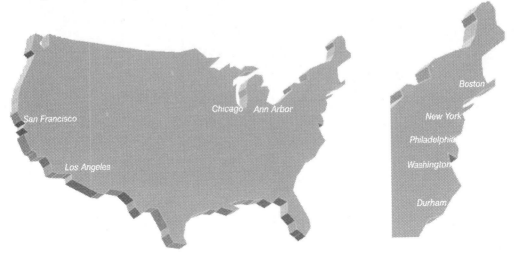

RANKING
BY SCHOOL SELECTIVITY

Before throwing yourself into the (lengthy) preparation of the application dossiers, you should take a look at the selectivity of a school to get an idea of your chances of admission. Certain MBAs are highly selective. Stanford is a good example, accepting fewer than 10% of the candidates that apply. The figures below indicate the numbers of applicants in a given year, as well as the class size. Just comparing the two figures doesn't give you the selectivity of the school, because certain candidates accepted into a program don't necessarily accept, having been accepted elsewhere, or having decided to postpone their decision to do their MBA. Thus all the schools end up offering places to more candidates than the actual class size.

Over 7200 candidates applied to Wharton for the 789 places available, and nearly 1060 candidates were offered a place in the program. Of them, about 270 candidates chose to go to another school or pursue another project. The admissions rate at Wharton is therefore around 14%, and not 10.6%. There is hope! Obviously the rate of non-acceptance is inversely proportional to the reputation of the school. Only 19% of those accepted into Harvard and 22% at Stanford didn't accept the offers made, while the figure is closer to 50% at schools like Cornell and Michigan. Such yield figures are difficult to obtain from the schools, and they do not figure below.

Source: Business Schools	Total number of candidates	Admitted students
Harvard	8893	880*
Wharton	7273	789*
Kellogg	6039	900
Columbia	5637	704
Stanford	5431	365*
UCLA (Anderson)	4926	330
NYU (Stern)	4039	435*
Michigan	3987	429
Chicago	3871	487*
INSEAD	3500	975
Duke (Fuqua)	3276	330
Berkeley (Haas)	3265	473
MIT (Sloan)	3000	470
Cornell (Johnson)	3038	280
Dartmouth (Tuck)	2689	190
Virginia (Darden)	2682	240
Yale	1897	225
LBS	1344	246
IMD	785	83

* # entering students

The table below gives GMAT averages at some of the top schools. The averages have increased significantly in the last few years as the number of candidates to the schools has increased. However, keep in mind that these scores represent an average -- not every applicant to Stanford has scored a 720, and your application won't be rejected solely because your GMAT doesn't soar into the upper stratospheres of the 700s. Take a look at the ranges of applicants' GMAT scores, listed in the Key Data sections under the schools chapters in this book; these figures will give you a good idea of the ballpark in which you should aim to score.

Nonetheless, it is very important to prepare yourself for these tests and obtain scores that will keep you competetive at the schools of your choice.

Source: Business Schools	Average GMAT Class of 2001
Stanford	727
Columbia	704
Harvard	703
Wharton	703
MIT (Sloan)	700
Northwestern (Kellogg)	700
UCLA (Anderson)	690
NYU (Stern)	689
Yale	689
Berkeley (Haas)	688
Insead	685
Virginia (Darden)	685
Chicago	684
Dartmouth (Tuck)	682
LBS	680
Duke (Fuqua)	677
Michigan	675
Cornell (Johnson)	675
IMD	650

A EUROPEAN MBA
PROS AND CONS

The global economy is as much a reality in the classroom as it on your desktop or in your company's mission statement. But how far are you prepared to travel to gain an intenational edge? The top US schools all provide exchange programs or international study options, and the impact of program alliances in executive education between the likes of Wharton and INSEAD, or Columbia and LBS, will no doubt be felt in the full-time MBA, with increasingly international faculty, case study material and students.

To help you decide whether an international MBA makes sense for you, we surveyed both European and American MBA graduates of programs in Europe and the US. Based on these interviews, we have set out below the main advantages and disadvantages of the European MBA option.

The Pros of a European MBA:

- Cost: MBAs in Europe are cheaper than their American counterparts. On average, one year of tuition fees in Europe costs $23,000 (INSEAD, IMD, LBS, and Rotterdam average), whereas these costs now often rise above $30,000 for American MBAs. This includes tuition fees only; it would be difficult to include figures for the cost of living in this comparison, given that this varies from city to city and from continent to continent.
- The European Old Boys networks: a significant number of European MBA graduates remain in Europe, whereas the great majority of American MBA graduates remain in the United States. The only exceptions to this rule are Harvard with nearly 7000 alumni in Europe, and IMD with far fewer MBA graduates in Europe due to the very small size of its student body (nearly 80 students in any given academic year).
- Contacts with European companies: if your goal is to work for a large European industrial group, contacts can be easier to obtain at European MBA campuses. Many European companies don't bend over backwards to recruit MBA graduates from the States, who are worth their weight in gold in the eyes of American consultancy firms, investment banks and the like. However, major European companies are becoming more and more interested in the MBA profile, and are starting, quite naturally, by looking at the European MBA campuses.
- Cultural experience: going abroad gives you the chance to spend one to two years in a new country. Whatever your area of work after your MBA, you will certainly encounter people from around the world, so spending a few years in a new cultural and, perhaps, linguistic environment can prove to be a valuable experience.

The Cons of a European MBA:

- Geographical flexibility: a degree from one of the best American MBA programs is (at least for the moment) the best passport for working in the country of your choice - not only in Europe, but also in Asia, South America and of course in the United States.
- The Old Boy Networks in the rest of the world: if you are planning on working in the Americas or in Asia, the alumni from the prestigious American universities are much more present and influential there than the European MBA networks.
- Practical considerations: if you have a family or a very absorbing social life, a European MBA can mean a major upheaval and an exhausting move.

MBA IN ONE YEAR
VS. TWO YEARS

During the IT-industry boom of the late 1990s and early 2000s, business schools were faced with pressure to shorten their MBA programs to one year, thus allowing students to return more quickly to the fast-moving job market. Many schools resisted, maintaining that the management tools necessary to succeed in both the old and new economies over a 40-year career are better provided over a two year period. On the other hand, schools such as INSEAD, IMD and Northwestern offer the possibility of obtaining the precious MBA certificate in twelve months or less, and Columbia offers an eighteen-month format which skips the standard summer internship. As with the question of staying in the US versus going abroad, we talked with supporters of the one-year MBA as well as graduates from two-year programs to get first-hand reports on the ups and downs of both models. Below are our findings on the one-year option.

The advantages of one year:

- The cost: logically, tuition fees for a one-year MBA as well as the loss in income to make up later are lower than for a two-year MBA. It's an indisputable advantage given the high cost of MBAs. Nevertheless, we urge you to not let your decision be based purely on financial considerations, as there are many loan possibilities open to you that can give you much more flexibility in your choice of MBA (One of the authors of this book was in debt to the tune of $70,000). Don't forget that exit salaries are very high and that many companies offer to reimburse your tuition fees.
- Time: to spend two years studying again can seem like an eternity for some people, impatient in year two. It all comes down to each person's individual situation. The most common of these are:
  - you think you're too old and don't want to waste two years doing an MBA.
  - you have a family or a social life that won't allow you to spend two years on a campus.
  - you have a very clear idea about what you want to do after your MBA and your goal is therefore to rapidly get your diploma in order to attain this objective.

The disadvantages of one year:

- Not enough time to choose the career you're going to pursue after your MBA. In the essays, the great majority of applicants proudly proclaim their clear idea about what they want to do after their MBA. But once on campus, you see that every student falls prey to hesitation in the face of so many career opportunities. If you do visit a campus, you will definitely have ample time to hear a student sigh:

I went to a breakfast meeting with partners from BCG London: I'm attracted by the intellectual aspect of consultancy jobs as well as by the diversity of their tasks, and that convinced me to apply for a job with them... well, right up until midday when I ate with a former student who works for Morgan Stanley, who couldn't contain himself any longer about the fact that he'd worked with the CEO of XX to engineer a hostile takeover over YY and, what's more, he gave me an inkling of the size of end of year bonuses. It's really tempting... So I set off again pen in hand to draft a letter to Morgan Stanley. On the way I met Andres, who's done a year's internship helping the president of one of the largest

Bertelsmann divisions. He told me he'd been involved in defining the new Internet strategy for the subsidiary and that Bertelsmann had offered him to take up the directorship of one of their units… with a great salary, and without having to work too late in the evening and on the weekend! He was kind enough to offer to introduce me to the Director of Human Resources for Europe! I set off again thinking about what happened to Andres… he too had hesitated between consultancy and merchant banking and in the end had opted for a large industrial group. Once home, I settled into my sofa with the school's paper and a big sandwich. The paper had done an editorial on Internet IPOs and on former students who had become millionaires in the space of a few months… and I couldn't help thinking that I should perhaps start looking into this…!

This anecdote is fairly representative of MBA student dilemmas. We don't think two years is too much time to spend looking much more closely at potential jobs that appeal to you. Indeed, the first year is often so intense that the main goal is just to survive. In contrast, the second year is designed to give students time to explore the various opportunities that are open to them. Aside from this, the chance of doing an internship is a unique opportunity to see for yourself what certain jobs are really like, and sometimes they're very different from the way they're presented in the glossy company brochures. One of my fellow students who was in the same year as one of the authors of this book did two internships because he was hesitating between the idea of working as a consultant and working for a start-up. Try thinking about it this way: how many times in your life will you have the opportunity to experiment with one or two jobs, with no real potential downside? This singular opportunity mustn't be underrated.

- The social life: spending two years on a campus really helps you discover and build friendships with some of the people you meet. Some will be people you can depend on long after you have your MBA degree in hand.

HOW MANY SCHOOLS SHOULD I APPLY TO?

Having carefully examined your personal goals and gathered together a wealth of information on various MBA programs, you should be able to identify which MBA would be best for you. In most cases, an initial list of business schools is too long, and many applicants wonder how many is too many MBAs to apply to.

It's clear that there is no one answer, because it really depends on how much time you have to prepare your applications as well as on your chances of getting in. Below are a few things to think about:

Usually, the MBA programs to be kept on your list can be assessed in two ways:
- The strength of your preference for this school: you've noted several MBAs which meet your various criteria but there are clearly some on your list that are much better suited than others.
- Your perceived chances of getting in: even before applying, each applicant has some idea of his/her chances of success. Typically, this assessment of your chances is fairly unscientific. We talked with a number of applicants to understand the basis for this judgment call. On the one hand, applicants compare themselves with the average profile of those admitted to the school they're aiming for (GMAT, professional experience, previous education, etc.). On the other hand, every applicant has a degree of self-confidence. Based on these factors, applicants assess their chances of getting in, so there may be some logic to it. However, some told me that they had no chance of getting into Harvard, but that they had a good feeling about Wharton!

In making your final decision regarding which MBAs to apply to, we urge you to focus on the programs that appeal to you the most, and not to worry too much about your likelihood of being accepted. Indeed, your greatest enemy is none other than yourself. You will simply knock yourself out of the running if you don't have confidence in yourself or if you feel you can't compare with the average profile of applicants who do get in to the school you're aiming for. Don't let bad grades from previous studies get in your way, or get caught up in thinking that only employees from McKinsey and Goldman Sachs can claim to have professional experience of any importance.

The perfect application doesn't exist. We have met applicants with diplomas from the top universities, 720 on the GMAT and three years experience in the most prestigious consultancy firms in the world, who didn't get in to any of the schools they applied to. That said, we met an Italian at Harvard who was admitted despite his 600 on the GMAT and his degree from a little known university where he got average grades. Each school has its own admissions process. But generally the first and foremost selection criteria are personality and leadership potential, which will be evident in your application. The only exception to what we've said are your GMAT scores (and TOEFL scores, if applicable): if you get a GMAT score lower than 600 (and a TOEFL score lower than the school's requirement -- see its prospectus), then we encourage you to take them again (one of my friends took the GMAT three times and now he's at Kellogg).

We very much hope that reading the previous paragraphs has boosted your confidence to apply to the schools you most want to attend. However, what we've said still doesn't help you determine the maximum number of schools to apply to. Our best advice is to first apply to your first choice schools and to send your application as early as the first round in October or November (which means that you'll have prepared the various parts of your application over the spring and/or the summer). Replies are generally sent out in January. In case of rejection, you can then apply to your second choice schools. In this way, you'll be able to concentrate completely on the three or four schools which appeal to you the most.

Given that you are limiting yourself to a few schools (at least for the first round), you must maximize your chances of being admitted to these schools. So be professional, take the time to truly understand what the schools are looking for and to tailor your essays to match these expectations. We'll talk more about this in the sections on essays, but we'll tell you right now to avoid the quick 'cut and paste' method for your essays. The same themes are often addressed by the different schools, and even though your answers may sometimes be the same in terms of content, the way you present this content must be custom-tailored for each school's individual profile.

General advice for the ADMISSIONS Application

THE IDEAL TIME
TO APPLY TO SCHOOL

GETTING THE TIMING RIGHT

When should you apply to business school? We've seen thousands of candidates go through this process and very often the proper timing makes or breaks their quest. Once you've made the decision to pursue an MBA, and drawn up your shortlist of schools, you are then confronted with the deadlines used by the schools in the application process. Despite the claims from certain schools that there is no ideal time to apply, the majority of schools admit that timing can play an important role in the admissions process.

Many schools use what they call a rolling admissions process. This means quite simply that they are constantly receiving and reviewing applications throughout the academic year. They accept or reject the applications as they are reviewed (including a waiting list option for borderline applications), and provide a response within four to six weeks of reception. Other schools use rounds of application, whereby they determine three rounds of deadlines, typically in November, January and March for a September class start (see chart below). At this stage they gather together all the applications that are of interest to them and start to make decisions whether you are in, out, or placed on a wait list. These decisions are typically made by an Admissions Committee which can be made up of Admissions Officers, professors, and students.

But before the Admissions Committee gets to decide between the New York investment banker, the California hi-tech whiz and the Boston management consultant, applications are checked over to make sure that they are complete (GPA, test scores, essays, letters of recommendation etc.). If any elements of your application are missing you can expect the file to sit on a desk and start to collect dust – or at least get overlooked. Being organised at this stage is crucial, to make sure that both you and your recommenders have provided the school with all that they need to make a decision.

So which deadline should you aim for? And what goes in that Express Pack that you hand to Mr Fedex? The deciding factor must be to apply to school when you have prepared a top-notch application. If meeting the November deadline means a poorly prepared GMAT test, with hurried essays that lack definition and impact, you'd be better waiting for the next round. If however you are preparing well ahead of the game and feel that your application is as strong as it can be, apply early. The reason for this lies in the numbers game.

A top school such as Wharton may receive over 7000 applications in a year for 785 places in the program. For the first round deadline in mid-November all 785 places are typically available (perhaps a small handful of places have already been filled by students with deferrals or exceptional circumstances). The Admissions Committee then starts to offer places to the best candidates, and by the time you reach the second round deadline in January there may be 400 or so places left (my figures are purely illustrative). Continue to the third round deadline in March and you may be left with only 100 to 200 places still to be filled. Also bear in mind that Wharton has received as many as 2000 applications in the last 24 hours before the final deadline – at a time when there are only a handful of places left. It's great business for UPS, DHL and the rest, but makes your chances for success very slim indeed.

The chart below is drawn from a presentation made by Sharon Hoffman, Associate Dean and Admissions Director at Stanford. She is very candid about the timing of applications to a school that rejects fourteen applications for every one that it accepts. And no, there is not a printing mistake for the number of places still available in the third round in 1999.

	1st Round November	2nd Round January	3rd Round March
# places available at beginning of round (1999)	360	120-180	3
% of places normally allocated per round	40-50%	30-40%	10%
Description of timing	Excellent	Very good	Catastrophic

This is a school to which it is always exceptionally difficult to be admitted, but in Round 3 it is nearly impossible - the school typically only takes a handful of candidates at this stage of the admissions process. Of course there are always candidates who are accepted in the third round, but if you're trying to maximize your chances of success, apply early.

So what exactly are you trying to pull together to complete the application?
The admissions process for MBA programs is a lot like that for undergraduate admissions: you must produce essays, letters of recommendation and transcripts, and take standardized tests. However, the MBA application should reflect the maturity and experience that you've gained in the ten years since applying to college, and show a clear focus on career goals.

The format of the GMAT is typical of standardized tests that evaluate basic quantitative and verbal skills. It should be remembered that the GMAT does not guarantee acceptance for those with the highest scores. In fact, maybe you should avoid the perfect 800 score on the test, because the seven or eight students that achieve this out of the 210,000 GMAT test takers every year may get the label of "weirdo"! Our advice is to deliberately get the last question wrong. Even if you know from Pythagorus that the square of the hypotenuse should be answer choice 4, select 2 instead – believe us, 780 or 790 looks great on your application! Seriously though, a great score on the GMAT does not guarantee acceptance (though a poor score makes admittance very difficult).

The following chapters of this book reinforce the idea that the schools are looking for a wide variety of profiles, with different achievements, goals and ambitions. There may be a common thread of leadership, or high-potential, but there is no magic formula for getting into school. To get a better sense of the abilities and characteristics of a candidate, schools look at four areas:

Academics.
Remember that the M in MBA is for Masters. Do you have the academic aptitude to get you through school? You need to provide:

- Undergraduate and other transcripts, including GPA
- GMAT score (and TOEFL, if applicable)

Professional Experience.
The top programs all require a minimum of two years professional experience (unless perhaps you have been studying for a PhD). You need to provide:
- Résumé of your career to date
- Essays that provide examples of professional achievements
- Letters of Recommendation
- Interviews to share goals and objectives

Personal.
All those mountains you have climbed, pianos you have played, winning goals you have scored. You need to provide:
- Essays that provide examples of personal achievements
- Interviews to convey your values and sense of self

Attention to Details.
As the admissions staff reviews thousands of application, every last detail counts:
- Did you apply early? Did you thoroughly proofread? Did you spell the school's name right?
- Did you pro-actively seek interviews? Were you polite to the receptionists on the phone?

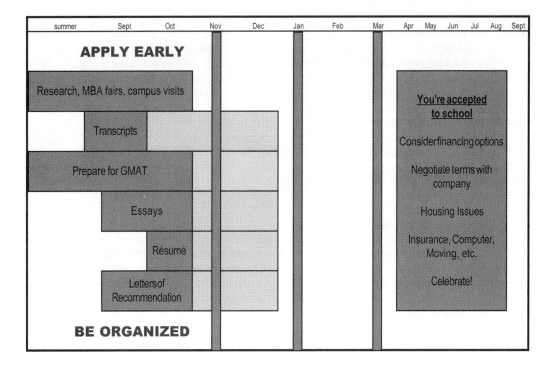

Pulling the different pieces of the application together requires you to be on top of things from the beginning. The timeline below indicates what you need to be tracking throughout the application process, and when you need to complete the various components to respect the first or second round deadlines. However long the initial process of selecting schools, certain candidates spend months, sometimes even years, nurturing and refining their profile and subsequent application, while others complete the entire process in a frenzy of esssay writing and test taking. Whether you are applying to one school or several, you will need to devote time and energy to produce a polished marketing document that features you as the product. As you prepare your application to business school, pay particular attention to the elements of the application on which you can still have an impact.

1. Request applications from your schools of interest
- at the World MBA Tour
- on-line

2. Prepare for the GMAT (and TOEFL, if applicable).
- Anywhere between 1 and 6 months of prep, depending on your initial level
- Remember that this is an element of the application that you can still influence

3. Start work on your essays
- brainstorm achievements, strengths and weaknesses
- define your goals and objectives in choosing to do an MBA

4. Get your letters of recommendation
- Select & approach the right individuals
- Propose having lunch to:
  - discuss your project and remind them of your achievements
  - provide them with a draft of your Application as a guide for continuity
  - establish clear and reasonable deadlines for completion (six to eight weeks)
  - Give them a call after three or four weeks to find out how the letters are progressing

5. Request your undergraduate transcripts
- Allow at least two months
- Check with the business schools whether they require translations

6. Take the GMAT (and TOEFL, if applicable)
- Have scores sent to the schools

7. Complete work on your essays
- Have friends and colleagues whose opinions you value re-read for an honest evaluation
- Consider working with a professional admissions counselor to sharpen the focus of your work

8. Mail all completed applications
- Allow time to arrive by the school deadline (postmarks don't count)
- Always request return receipt
- Keep photocopies for your records

Apply early, and be organized. As we have already stressed, the earlier you complete your application the better your chances of admission.

DEFINING AN OVERALL POSITIONING STRATEGY

STEP 1: IDENTIFY NEEDS

Understand exactly what those needs are and their order of importance.

The basic rules of marketing at Procter & Gamble, as in all such companies, begin by studying the consumer (the target) and his needs. In your case, the consumer is the school, because it's the school that chooses the applicants. Just like a consumer of laundry detergent, a business school has criteria it needs to fulfill in order to reach its desired end.

To draw out the analogy:

- A family needs a laundry detergent that removes stains without fading a garment's colors, because their goal is to get the clothes spotless. Their profit is to gain pleasure from really looking after each other.
- The business schools need intelligent applicants, potential leaders with a sense of ethics, because their goal is to teach them to be the leaders who will gain renown in their area. Their profit is thereby to enhance the school's reputation as well as to generate donations from former students, who generally bolster the school's budget with significant contributions.

Your job is to identify each school's needs. On the surface, the glossy brochures for every institution describe the ideal applicant as intelligent, a leader, a team player, ethical, able to learn from his or her mistakes, open to an international perspective and modern technology, etcetera, etcetera. However, a careful study will reveal subtle differences amongst the profiles sought after by each school. These nuances can be seen on two levels:

Before anything else, you must isolate as precisely as possible the qualities sought by the schools, as they sometimes have a rather rarefied way of expressing themselves. For example, the brochures mention leadership qualities, team spirit, and so forth, which are ostensibly very familiar territory -- but are you capable of defining more closely what leadership or team spirit is? If you are unsure of your definition, you must continue with your research to enable you to articulate the precise skills and behavior associated with leadership, team spirit, international mindedness, ethics, innovation, and so on. Waste no time in visiting the school's website, asking questions by phone or meeting the admissions staff at open house events.

To give you an idea of what we mean by specifying the qualities required for successful applicant: leadership can be broken down into certain aptitudes -- the capability to:

- Define a relevant vision (goals & strategies). In order to define their vision, leaders must be able to analyze quantitative/qualitative data so that they can see the big picture.
- Communicate this vision to the people who work with/for you.
- Motivate employees around these goals, that is, know in particular how to listen to them and to find the right way to deal with them.
- Train others to help them achieve the objectives set according to the strategies chosen (and also be able to do it oneself!)

It is up to you to track down the appropriate definition of the principal qualities sought by the schools; if you're not entirely sure what the school is looking for, you have little chance of meeting their needs!

You must also understand the relative importance of the qualities sought by the school because this differs from school to school. Some schools place particular emphasis on qualities which are less prized by others. The reason is simple: there is no 11th Commandment which has exactly set down the order of the qualities you need in order to excel in the business world. There is of course a concensus of opinion for the desired qualities (i.e., the "ideal applicant") but not for the order of importance of these qualities relative to one another: Harvard puts individual leadership at the top of the list, whereas Kellogg holds that team spirit is the primary quality!

In short, you must exactly define the meaning of the qualities that the schools are looking for and rank them in order of importance. The schools say it loud and clear that before anything else they are looking for a diversity of profiles amongst students. But don't confuse profile with qualities. The schools are looking for certain qualities that it could find just as easily in a British consultant, an American naval officer, a Brazilian engineer or a Japanese banker.

To help you understand the qualities the schools are seeking, you have at your disposal:
- this book, as we've done a lot of the legwork for you
- the essay questions on the application, because they reflect what the school is looking to find out from the applicant.
- the schools' websites
- the presentation sessions that the schools regularly organize around the world (for an up-to-date list of off-campus information sessions, consult www.theMBAsite.com).
- former MBA students
- the teachers at GMAT preparation test centers, because they're generally well informed and very objective.
- Online articles about the business schools, notably at the websites of Business Week (http://www.businessweek.com) and US News (http://www.usnews.com), and to a lesser extent, the Financial Times (http://www.ft.com). This information is free of charge.
- If you've got the time and the money, a visit to the campuses of the schools which interest you.

You will have to demonstrate a great capacity for listening to people, as well as the critical thinking skills in order to get behind the often very long, sometimes vacuous sentences (eg: "we are looking for outstanding candidates who will lead the economy in the new millenium") which is in every brochure.

The consumer study is the first marketing step in your application. The large majority of the applicants fall at this first hurdle because they haven't been able to specifically identify the differences between each school. Their greatest error is thus to send standardized essays, which serve only to fill the admissions office's circular file, because they don't appeal to the specific nature of a school. If you've successfully passed this first stage, the next step is to meet with maximum impact those needs that you have identified.

STEP 2: MEET THESE NEEDS USING YOUR PAST EXPERIENCE
You should by now have defined for each school the precise meaning and the order of importance of desired qualities. For example, imagine that School X seeks, in order of importance:
1 - leadership, which for this school means the capacity to innovate and to motivate others to achieve the goals of the innovation.

2 - a very analytical mind.

3 - openness to an international perspective, which translates as being able to work in different cultural contexts.

Note that general terms such as leadership or international perspective were carefully defined.

From this point on, you must select from your past experiences those which best illustrate the qualities that the school is seeking from potential students. In other words, the experiences that you choose to relate must demonstrate that you possess these qualities. The difficulty with Step 1 is listening to and understanding the needs of each school, whereas the challenge with Step 2 is in relating your most relevant experiences in the light of the desired qualities. It's a significant feat of memory: for each of the desired qualities, you will have to think of numerous situations and analyze how they show that you possess this quality. Many students make mistakes at this stage because:

- they don't devote enough time to looking for the right experiences
- they limit their search to professional situations and neglect outside activities (sports, culture, community involvement, etc.); or, conversely, they focus only on personal accomplishments and neglect to mention professional situations.

If you have problems pinpointing suitable experiences, don't hesitate to talk about these issues with people who know you well. Ask them for examples of situations where you have shown such and such a quality. In general, this process should prove very fruitful, as memory can be selective and other people sometimes recall experiences that you yourself have forgotten, or can see things in a different light.

STEP 3: ANSWER CONVINCINGLY BY CHOOSING YOUR MOST RELEVANT EXPERIENCES AND PRESENTING THEM WITH MAXIMUM IMPACT

After step 2, you will probably have gone through a large number of experiences which should correspond to the qualities sought by the school. In order to be convincing, you must select the experiences which in themselves convey the idea that you possess the qualities required. Experiment with different ways to express this, so as to be as persuasive as possible.

a) Choose your most relevant experiences for each of the desired qualities.

For each quality, we recommend that you set down in front of you the list of experiences that you've drawn up. Then let your common sense decide: put yourself in the reader's position and ask yourself whether you would be convinced that the applicant possesses a given quality upon reading about a certain experience. Do this test and there's a strong possibility that one of these experiences will stand out from the rest. If however you still can't see the right choice, we would encourage you to sound out people around you, describe your experiences and ask them which experience best conveys the quality in question (this way you leave nothing to chance - it's the art of marketing in all its glory!).

For example, imagine that you are looking to highlight your leadership qualities. After the work done in Step 2 (cf. p.67), you have defined leadership as the ability to:

- Define a relevant vision (goals & strategies). In order to define their vision, leaders must be able to analyze quantitative and qualitative data in order to see the big picture.
- Communicate this vision to the people who work with/for you.
- Motivate employees around these goals, that is, know how to listen to them and to find the right way to deal with them.
- Train others to help them achieve the objectives set according to the strategies chosen.

You have identified three experiences as potential illustrations:
- In your capacity as a consultant for the consulting firm X, you were responsible for one part of a mission undertaken for a very important client. The goal was to help your client make a decision about the closure of a division. You defined the objectives and methodology of your part of the study which you then checked with your task leader. A junior consultant was working for you, which enabled you to worker faster and to conduct a more in-depth analysis. Your work was very much appreciated by the client, who publicly congratulated you at the final presentation.
- You organized your school's year-end ball five years ago. In this capacity you defined certain objectives and persuaded the other organizing members to agree to them. You then drew up a plan detailing the sequence of events at the ball, as well as the distribution of tasks among the various members. You were conscientious in supporting and motivating the members of the organizing team because it's not easy to organize an event while studying for final exams. The end result: the ball was a financial success, as you sold 30% more invitations than the year before, and the evening was a social success, as the hall was still full at four in the morning. The Dean personally noted your contribution.
- You are president of your local tennis club. In this capacity you recommended to your local council the construction of three new tennis courts. The goal was to enable more young people from underprivileged areas to discover the joys of tennis. With the help of another member, you put together a convincing application, which you personally presented to the mayor. The courts were built, and thanks to your efforts many young people were thus able to discover tennis.

At first glance, these three examples convey the idea that the applicant has certain leadership qualities. Nevertheless, only the second example gives the impression that the applicant possesses all the aspects of leadership defined at the beginning of this example. Indeed, the ball experience clearly shows the person's leadership potential given that at the beginning he had no hierarchical superiority over the other organizing members, and it was only because of the relevance of his/her goals and communication skills that he/she rallied the other members around them. Furthermore, in reading between the lines, one can see the presence and the daily motivation that the applicant was able to provide for the other members.

b) Once you have selected the experience which best conveys the fact that you have the desired quality, you must work on the way you put this down on paper, in order to be as convincing as possible.

For this, we recommend you use the communication methods similar to those developed by Procter & Gamble, because they are very persuasive. They can be summarized in four sequences: drama, profit, demonstration, results. If you pay attention to advertisements for personal hygiene products (shampoo, soap, toothpaste, etc), you realize that every one of these advertisements generally follows this way of thinking.
- Drama: a greasy stain has appeared on the favorite garment of a girl who was getting ready to go to school for an important event (for your information, greasy stains are amongst the most difficult stains to remove!).
- Profit: X laundry detergent claims to wash away even the greasiest of stains.
- Demonstration: thanks to its chemical agents which penetrate right down to the heart of a stain, detergent X cleans even the most difficult stains.
- Results: the young girl's garment is as good as new and she'll look dazzling for school.

These advertisements may not be renowned for their creativity, but remind yourself that you may not be part of the target audience (they're aiming at homemakers). In this case, these advertisements are unarguably effective, to such an extent that Procter & Gamble has been driving the message home, using the same format, for decades. It's one of the secrets of their supremacy in marketing.

It simply remains for you to capture the spirit of this method of communication when writing your essays. Let's go back to the example of the school ball, for the essay on leadership.

Drama: The goal is to explain the difficulty of the task you've set for yourself, which will enable you to highlight your accomplishments with even more panache. This part is all the more important given the lack of context for the admissions committee - they don't know if the organization of a university ball is harder than managing a military unit or overseeing a construction site. So you have to help them understand the context in which you are operating because that way they can better compare your qualities against those of other potential students. In the ball example, you must list all the contextual information which made leadership such a challenge:
- It's the year-end ball, for which people have high levels of expectation.
- For the first time, the Dean of the university will be attending and will give an opening speech.
- The difficult final exams present a major distraction from the management of this project as the members of the organizing team cannot commit much of their time.
- The ball's budget is very limited

Profit: You have to explain exactly what you did. Generally, one line is enough. In the ball example, you "led the organization of the ball from beginning to end".

Demonstration: You must set out the methods you used to deliver the profit you mention above. In the case of the essay on leadership and the organization of the ball, you must therefore make it clear that you:
- clearly defined your vision of the way you counted on organizing the ball (objectives & strategies)
- successfully presented this vision to the other members of the team
- organized the distribution of the workload between the various team members and the scheduling of the preparation
- motivated and supported the team members to help them in their tasks and at the same time managed the revision for their exams (for example, you organized collective revision sessions).

Results: the goal is to quantify the results gained, be they numerical results ("hard data", for example the rise in sales) or human results ("soft data", for example the improvement of the work atmosphere). Indeed, it's important you show you can "make the numbers" but not to the detriment of people! In the ball example, you should mention:
- the 30% rise in ticket sales compared with the previous year
- the success in the event's popularity, to the extent that the hall was still full at four in the morning (an unprecedented achievement!)
- the personal thanks from the Dean in the school newspaper, and the fact that you received recognition of your contribution to the school.

Once you have done this work, you then have to make the connection between the four parts, but that shouldn't pose too much of a problem by this stage. Note that this presentation method applies just as well to essays as to letters of recommendation and the interview.

STEP 4: REPLY IN A DISTINCTIVE AND PERSONAL WAY (ENGAGINGNESS)

It is important to be convincing, but that alone won't guarantee you a place; there remains a final stage before concluding your personal marketing in line with the Procter & Gamble method: you must be distinctive in order to differentiate yourself from the other applicants. This means that you must a) relate an experience which is out of the ordinary; b) open yourself up to the admissions panel using a personal and sincere style; and c) bring out an overall "marketing position" for your application. If you get it right, then what you put down will be engaging, and will hold the attention of the reader, ensuring that your application distinguishes itself from the others.

a) Choose some out of the ordinary experiences

You must not only select experiences that best convey certain qualities, as well as set them down in a persuasive manner (cf Step 3). It is to your advantage to have atypical experiences. If your application bears only examples of your latest projects at work, or run-of-the-mill activities during your school career, you stand a strong chance of going unnoticed among the 7000 other candidates. The solution is to ensure that some of your experiences are not run-of-the-mill: if you have a passion for digital photography, or you have helped with humanitarian aid to Africa, or even a passion for acid jazz or a pronounced taste for cooking, make sure to mention them. This piece of advice is all the more important for those of you who with backgrounds such as consulting, investment banking or marketing because a lot of applicants will, on the surface, have a profile similar to yours.

b) Open yourself up to the admissions panel using a personal and sincere style

It is vital that you reveal your personality through your application, so that the admissions committee can better appreciate the richness of your personality. Above all, don't box yourself into the cliché of the ideal applicant. Each one of us has his strengths and weaknesses, his good and his bad experiences. Also, if you want to talk about your family, about your community or about a person or experience that has made a particular impression on you, it may work to your advantage because in this way you will draw the attention and often gain the empathy of the reader.

Aside from this, you should try to avoid wording that seems too cold, indifferent, and impersonal. It is true that such wording allows you to avoid taking risks, as the formulae are familiar to everyone, but an overabundance of formulaic expressions will prevent your personality from coming through. Therefore, use "I" instead of "one/we", and use "active" rather than "passive" phrasing. Be natural in your writing; don't borrow anyone else's style.

c) Bring out the strong themes in your application

Some people refer to this process as "positioning" because it involves arranging your various experiences around a limited number of themes. It could be certain aspects of your personality, some passion, or areas where you show a high level of skill. An applicant's positioning must be able to be summarized in three or four chosen themes. The advantage of having these load-bearing themes is that they help the admissions committee to synthesize your various experiences. If you don't put any work into positioning, it's possible that the admissions committee will have difficulty seeing the link between your various experiences, giving the impression that your personality is a little too "disparate".

A few examples of positioning, as reported by one of the authors of this book:
- For me, my positioning was around my initiative-taking mentality (my extensive experience in

initiating and leading team projects) and my marketing expertise (close to five years, three of which were in consumer goods (Procter & Gamble, Kraft) and two years in the service sector (with a major airline).

- One of my colleagues, a consultant, had chosen to position himself around the following themes: 'multi-cultural' (he grew up in three different countries, did his national service in a fourth country and he speaks four or five languages); 'analytical' (he has always had a passion for numbers and for thorough analysis); and finally, 'cultural sensibilities' (15 years of piano playing and a recent passion for painting).
- Another of my colleagues, an audit officer in a large firm, chose the following as his themes: Europe (he worked in Brussels on a number of European matters), his academic excellence (he picked up top grades and first places throughout his education) and lastly his generosity in helping others (he was a tutor to children from under-privileged districts and involved in a humanitarian project to Africa).

Don't confuse themes with experiences: the themes are the points of focus around which to organize those particular experiences which demonstrate that you possess certain of the qualities sought by the school.

STEP 5: ORGANIZE YOUR APPLICATION TO MEET THE NEEDS OF THE SCHOOL

Finally, you must now organize your application to be sure that you are making good use of the various opportunities to reveal your personality (essays, references, interview) and are communicating your 'load-bearing' themes, as well as your corresponding personal experiences. I advise you to be rigorous, because your application must correspond as precisely as possible to the order of importance of the qualities sought after by the school (cf. step 1).

To summarize, if you have identified that the school is looking for, in order of importance:

- leadership, i.e. the ability to initiate projects, give them structure and motivate a team so as to make the projects successful;
- openmindedness and an international perspective, i.e. the ability to work in a different cultural context;
- humility, that is, the aptitude to recognize and to learn from one's failures;

... then you must plan the messages and the framework of the various pieces of your application to express precisely these qualifications. And you must explain in detail to your recommenders this method of organization.

Now you know everything about the fine art of personal marketing. It's the method used by one of the co-authors of this book on his application to Harvard. And if you don't get a place at the MBA of your choice, you can always switch to marketing!

THE INTERVIEW

Increasingly, schools use the interview as a part of the admissions process. The policies differ from school to school:

- Obligatory for all applicants (eg: Kellogg)
- On invitation: after studying the applications, the school invites some applicants to interview (eg: Harvard, Columbia, and now Wharton)
- No interview in the admissions process, which is done only by written application (eg; Stanford).

Interviews last between 30 minutes and one hour. The majority of schools offer the possibility of having the interview conducted by a member of the admissions committee (at the school or at presentation tours organized by the schools in the principal cities across the world) or with former students specially selected for this purpose.

There are numerous reasons to explain the growing importance of interviews in the admissions process. First of all, it's an excellent opportunity to test your 'soft skills', which are becoming more and more important in the business world. These 'soft skills' consist of your aptitude to communicate, your charisma and your strength of character. In your application, these elements appear only implicitly; in an interview, on the other hand, these qualities become more evident. Another reason for the expanding use of interviews lies in the fact that the schools are seeking more and more to sell themselves to certain applicants. Each school seeks to attract the best applicants because it is they who will later carry the reputation of the school. Competition is therefore intense and the schools use the interview to show themselves in the best light to the best applicants.

QUESTIONS AT THE INTERVIEW

Even if each interviews is unique, there is great similarity in the subjects touched upon. The principal things your interviewer will be looking at are:

- your previous education
- your professional experience
- your extra-professional activities
- your character and your values
- your motivation for doing an MBA and, more specifically, at the school with which you're interviewing.

We polled numerous MBA students in order to gather a list of the questions most frequently posed in each of these categories. The great thing about this list is that it gives you the wording of most of the questions you will be asked. This list is very exhaustive, and you certainly won't have to answer even a tenth of these questions. The problem is that you don't know which ones you will be posed. We therefore suggest that you prepare a response to most of these questions so that you can be convincing on the spot.

Your previous education:

- Which school did you attend and why that one?
- Would you choose the same studies again if you could do it over again?

- What was your major and why?
- What overall grades did you get? Did you get honors?
- Which courses were you best at? Why?
- What did you like most about this part of your education?
- What did you least like about this part of your education?
- What extra-curricular activities did you participate in? Why and what was your contribution?
- How did you pay for your education?

Your professional experience:
- Can you briefly describe your career progress to date?
- What are your long term career aspirations and why?
- Please discuss the factors, both professional and personal, influencing the career decisions you have made so far.
- Can you briefly describe the key responsibilities of your current job?
- What are the key challenges of your job?
- While recognizing that no day is typical, please describe a representative working day.
- Why did you choose this profession? Why this company?
- What do you like best/about your current job?
- Describe your most successful accomplishment at work.
- Describe a failure on the job.
- What could you do to be an even more effective member of your organization?
- Describe a situation in which you have been in the position of leading a group.
- What have you done to develop those under your responsibility?
- What specifically have you done to help your company change?
- How does your performance compare with that of your peers at a similar level?
- Describe your relationship with your boss. What is good and bad about it?
- Where is your industry heading in the next five years? (all the more important if your interviewer works in the same domain).

Your extra-professional activities:
- How do you spend your time outside of work? What activities do you enjoy most and why?
- Describe a situation where you have been in a position of leading a group in those activities.
- Describe your key accomplishments in these activities.
- Describe any failure in these activities.
- What is the last book you read? What did you think of it?
- What is your favorite sport? What aspect of it appeals to you?

Your reasons for doing an MBA and more specifically the reason you are doing this interview:
- Why do you want to do an MBA? Why now?
- Where do you expect to be in 5 years?
- What do you expect to get from an MBA?
- Why do you want to come to our school in particular?
- Which other schools are you applying to?
- How did you choose these schools? Why so many/few?
- Which school is your first choice?
- What if you are not accepted in the schools you are applying for? if you didn't get into any programs?
- What specific questions do you have about our school?
- What would you contribute to our school that is distinctive?

Your character and your values
- Tell me about yourself.
- How would your friends describe you?
- What are your main strengths and weaknesses?
- What have you done that you are proud of?
- Who are your heroes? Why?
- Describe any significant experience abroad. What did you learn from this?
- Describe an ethical dilemma that you faced. How did you resolve it?

GENERAL ADVICE FOR THE INTERVIEW

This book brings together a tremendous amount of advice on the interview: in the chapters on the various schools (Harvard, MIT, Stanford, NYU, Kellogg, Columbia, Wharton, INSEAD, Berkeley, Chicago and LBS), their authors will give you some great advice for successfully passing the interview. Their advice has been tested and proven, because each of these authors was admitted! However, there are *four* key pieces of advice to really underline:

1. Set your communication objectives

Like a politician or an advertising professional, you should define, prior to the interview, pertinent communication objectives. We mean by this that these communication objectives must enrich the overall positioning that you have developed for your application (cf section on general strategy for the application). You will also have to adapt these objectives depending on the school with which you have an interview, as each one has different buttons to press.

For example, the communication objectives of a Harvard colleague were:
- that he is a self-made man with a sense of initiative
- his openmindedness and international perspective
- his human qualities

Another of my fellow students had as his objectives
- his academic excellence
- his hi-tech expertise, in particular the internet
- his team spirit

You must not only take the time to pinpoint these objectives, but also to specify personal experiences which will illustrate the qualities on which you wish to place special emphasis.

2. Prepare your interviews until you are blue in the face

The key to success is not only to think about the answers to standard questions, but also to train yourself in getting these replies across. The secret of success is none other than doing 'mock' interviews. Try to get interviews from former MBA students or, failing that, with office colleagues or friends. One of the best-known professors at Harvard describes the three degrees of an applicant's preparation as the following:
- 'The sputterer': the applicant has very vaguely prepared the contents and the shape of what he's going to say. The only advantage of this level is that the applicant is spontaneous!
- 'The record': the applicant has adequately prepared the contents -- but not enough to avoid giving the impression that it sounds overly prepared.
- 'The actor': the applicant has so well prepared the contents and the shape that he has the opportunity of concentrating on interacting skillfully with his interviewer. The latter will therefore not realize that the whole thing was prepared!

Studies have shown that the worst thing that can happen to you is that you fall into category 2 and that the best situation is to be 'the actor' (category 3). For once the best option is not the enemy of perfection, so you can give full rein to mock interviews until you feel that your mind is no longer busy rummaging around in the pigeon holes of your memory, but rather interacting with your environment.

3. Plead your case with eloquence!

We recommend that you be eloquent in the way you express yourself because one of the primary objectives of the interview is to see if you are a communicator. On the one hand, this means that you prepare answers for each of the questions (cf above). On the other hand, you must put passion into what you're saying because it will give you that extra something to make you stand out from the rest. In the first year at Harvard, one of the courses studies the origin of the charisma of certain great business leaders. It emerges that the most charismatic leaders are those who feel a true passion for their work. This of course shines through in what they say... passion is contagious and an impassioned speaker speech arouses far more interest from an audience. So give full voice to your deepest desire to do an MBA and to your career plans.

4. At no point should you lower your guard

Interviews with former students can become particularly friendly (one of my school friends told me that he had his interview in a former student's winter chalet). One of the greatest mistakes to make is to lower your guard because the friendly atmosphere can make you feel like admitting to and sharing certain doubts. Don't let yourself go right up to the end of the interview. If you are still wondering whether the MBA corresponds to your personality and objectives, this is certainly not the place to discuss it.

ADVICE FROM THE INTERVIEWERS

We have interviewed some former students who are used to doing admissions interviews. We felt it useful to see things from their perspective in order to better understand the way the interview works. We chose former students from different schools in order to get diverse and complementary opinions.

Can you briefly introduce yourself?

(name, where you live, MBA and class of graduation, main companies you have worked for, how many MBA candidates you have interviewed...)

> *Harvard Business School: Charles Ullens, MBA 1957: "My first job was at J. Walter Thompson, at the time the largest advertising agency. I moved then to the food industry and finally to M&A. I have interviewed over 100 MBA candidates."*

> *MIT: Rod Garcia, Director of Admissions: "You can contact me if you do not find all the information you need here (rgarcia@mit.edu)."*

> *Wharton: Everett Hutt, MBA 1999: I work for McKinsey and have also worked in advertising, in law, at UNESCO. I have interviewed over 80 candidates, mostly as a student interviewer.*

> *Kellogg: Sven Zehnder, MBA 1996: "I have worked for Adidas and Nike full-time and had a short stint at Coca-Cola for my summer internship during my MBA studies. Since I graduated, I have interviewed about 15–20 candidates."*

LBS: Philippe Silberzahn, MBA 1997: Worked for Andersen Consulting and now Digital Airways, a start-up focusing on mobile Internet technologies.

INSEAD: Stefan Culen, MBA 1975: "I am self-employed and work as a designer and product developer. I have interviewed approximately 150 candidates.

What are typical questions you ask in an interview?

MIT:

Typical questions you will be asked range from your professional background (which companies have you worked for? What were your responsibilities? What did you get out of it?), to your motivations for joining MIT (what motivated your application?) and your ambitions for the future (what will you be doing in 10 years?)

But remember that the interview is not an interrogation! You must make sure it is a dialogue by asking questions yourself.

Wharton:

I usually start with the person's current job and work back to his first job. Then I switch to the future -- his goals, and why and MBA fits in now. I move on to teamork examples and finish up with personal interests. I always ask if there is any important information he wanted to convey that he hasn't yet.

Kellogg:
- What has been your biggest professional challenge so far and why?
- What did you do to overcome it? Why exactly do you think you failed? What did you learn from it?
- Biggest accomplishment? Why are you proud about it? What difficulties did you have to overcome?
- Tell me about a leader you admire, and why?

London Business School
First I ask the candidate to introduce him/herself. My initial set of questions is very basic; its purpose is to clarify, if necessary, what is contained in the application about education, experience, employment history. This part aims at understanding where the candidate comes from. Then I am interested in the objectives: why an MBA, and why LBS. This is more future-oriented.

INSEAD:
- Why INSEAD?
- Where do you come from and where do you want to go from now on?
- What do you like in your present job and what do you dislike?
- What are your strengths and what are your weaknesses?
- What are the alternatives in case you are not accepted?
- What books do you read, music do you listen to, what sports do you do?
- What are your favorite countries to live and work in?
- Do you have dreams you want to make come true?

What are unusual questions you ask in an interview?

MIT:
Questions really do flow in the conversation. There are no real unusual questions but you must be ready, for instance, to talk in depth about what you think you can bring to MIT both academically and socially. You will not only be selected for your diplomas but also for your personal interests and achievements (sports, associations, etc.).

Wharton:

I usually ask the range of questions, but often I will probe very deep, searching for real insight, especially if I think the response is 'canned.' Other times; I will change the order, asking questions that don't necessarily follow each other, to see how the person reacts to instability. Or, I may sit quietly for 15-30 seconds when a person has responded to see how they react.

Kellogg:

- *Why should Kellogg accept you, considering there are thousands of qualified candidates who are dying to get in?*
- *How would your department's assistant describe you?*
- *Analyze the pros and cons of a matrix organization.*

London Business School:

It depends a lot on whom I am interviewing. It is generally linked to the candidate's profile, and based on the potential weaknesses I can detect. For instance, a computer programmer might be a bad team player, and a bond trader may not have any involvement in charities, etc.

INSEAD:

- *How has the element of luck been influential in your life?*
- *"When you are young, you think, justice is the least you can expect, when you are old, you know, it is the utmost." What is your opinion?*
- *Have you ever deeply regretted one of your decisions and why?*
- *The famous German film director Hans-Jürgen Syberberg once said: "To understand the success of Adolf Hitler, one has to acknowledge that he was an eminent artist." What are your feelings towards this statement?*
- *What do you think about the boycott against Iraq?*
- *Any other question resulting from the news of the day, death of the Princess of Wales, Formula One driver Schumacher again caught cheating, Austria's right wing party in government, anything about which the candidate should be able to have a sound and well-developed idea.*

What qualities are you looking for during an interview?

Harvard:

The candidate must:
- *be very intelligent and ambitious*
- *be a leader who can communicate with and influence all people he works with*
- *have worthwhile experiences which he will bring to class discussions*

Wharton:

A person who can pass the 'Pittsburgh Airport Test': that is, someone whom I would enjoy spending long hours with regardless of whether I was obliged to due to work or school. This is a combination of factors, probably best defined as sociability or likability.

MIT:

We are not looking for specific and identical qualities in each of our prospective students but we try to put together a group of young men and women with different strengths and weaknesses. That is what makes the strength of each class. If I had to give one or two examples of what specific qualities we are looking for, I would say capacity to work hard and a degree of initiative. In fact, MIT requires a commitment to hard work and it would be a shame to recruit someone who would not be able to handle it. You will therefore have to prove to your interviewer that you are a hard working person as well as a self-starter.

Kellogg:

> *This is my personal preference and potentially is not perfectly in line with the school's criteria. Personality, intellect, team player, leadership potential, career focus, what they do on the side. Also, the ability to answer a few questions; if I asked one or two followup questions, I expect them all to be answered in a row, without me having to raise the questions again!*

London Business School:

> *Honesty, consistency, simplicity. I appreciate somebody who strikes the right balance between ambition, personality and openness, who is aware of his/her weaknesses and not afraid to display his/her strengths. Overall, it's an attitude. More basically, a candidate should not dodge questions. Answer a question, even if it has to do with a weakness. There is no perfect candidate, and the easier it is to spot weaknesses, the better.*

INSEAD:

> *Verbal intelligence, style, fantasy, humour, personality, awareness, enchantment, seriousness of purpose, versatility, social responsiblity, ambition, manners*

What makes a candidate outstanding?

Harvard:

> *The candidate must demonstrate the qualities I have mentioned above and also a well-balanced personality.*

Kellogg:

> *If he does well on all of the above. Besides, Kellogg has a very unique student profile and there should be a great fit. I would define this profile as the following: Kellogg is like a big happy family. People are very much working together as a team: in academics and extra-curricular, most activities are run by students and many contribute tremendously, in various forms and degrees of involvement, on the overall experience one goes through at Kellogg. Most students have a common goal, and that is to learn from others and at the same time make this a better place. As a result we have students who like to initiate things, come up with new ideas and execute: characteristics I found tremendously important also in the business world. Most students in my opinion have a strong, yet pleasant personality. The students know what they want, but never have a touch of arrogance. Strong character, intelligent and humble.*

MIT:

> *Obviously, a very good understanding of the global economic environment is a strong asset. A thorough reading of the Financial Times or the Wall Street Journal can help you understand at the same time the actors and the dynamics of the economic world. I will just give one example: it is not enough to know that AOL bought Time Warner. MIT Sloan will force you to understand the logic behind this acquisition, the mechanism and the implications for the rest of the industry. Be smart!*

Wharton:

> *Beyond likability and sociability, to be outstanding he or she must be quick, witty, well-rounded, articulate, and focused.*

INSEAD:

> *A good combination of the above mentioned properties plus one or two exceptionally strong virtues.*

London Business School:

> *I would say it's personality. The interviewer is looking for somebody who is not an android. Somebody you would like to invite for dinner after the interview, to pursue the discussion. He/she must be able, while responding precisely to questions, to broaden the discussion, without unnecessary speculation and sidetracking. This requires an attention to the interviewer.*
>
> *Typically, an outstanding candidate has already achieved impressive results in his early career, one way or another, by showing determination, ambition, sense of risk and ability to master his own destiny. An MBA would fit perfectly and allow him to pursue on the same track with renewed strength.*

What are the main mistakes candidates make during an interview?

Harvard:

> *They forget the essential -- describe themselves as they are -- because they try to project an 'ideal personality'. One more time, there is no 'ideal candidate': we value all kinds of background and experiences.*

Wharton:

> *- Nervousness. On the flipside, arrogance.*
> *- Lack of preparation.*
> *- Lack of humor.*

Kellogg:

> *They are not being themselves. If there are inconsistencies and if they are too egocentric.*

MIT:

> *There is nothing worse for an interviewer than to have the impression of having an actor in front of him or her. Be relaxed and be yourself!*

London Business School:

> *i) lack of preparation – It shows inconsistencies in the application, lack of knowledge about the school. As a result, you get generic answers on why an MBA, why LBS... and ii) defensiveness – the interviewer wants to see a candidate who is confident, although not arrogant. Don't be apologetic on a weakness. It's a weakness, period.*

INSEAD:

> *She/he should just be herself/himself. The worst mistake is to try to fool the interviewer or the admissions committee altogether. Absolutely deadly. No other mistakes are really bad.*

How do you think an applicant can best prepare for an interview?

Kellogg:

> *Think about what they have done and what they want to do. Be themselves, firm and calm. Show their personalities and be proud of them.*

MIT:

> *One of the criteria on which you will be judged is your ability to communicate. Be concise and clear when you make a point. Use short sentences. Do not hesitate to train with a friend or a colleague in presenting yourself.*

Wharton:

> *Practice, practice, practice! If you're nervous, you'll get better. If you are arrogant, hopefully the mock interviewer will tell you.*

London Business School:
> *1. Do the homework: know what's in the application you sent to the school, know the school and what differentiates it from others*
> *2. Prepare. Find a friend to interview you several times. Do it seriously.*
> *3. Be yourself - don't try to be what you are not. Remember there is no perfect candidate.*

INSEAD:
> *Have the answers ready for the usual set of questions and keep an open mind for the rest. Since the interview is about motivation and personality, nothing serious can be prepared.*

At some stage of the interviews, prospective candidates are given the chance to ask questions. Can you give us examples of good questions you have been asked?
Wharton:
> *Any question is good so long as it is a) sincere, and b) also posed to the other schools, to compare responses.*

Kellogg:
> *I have to admit that this is very much towards the end of an interview and I assume that most interviewers will already have pretty much set their mind on their evaluation. However, it does show some intellectual curiosity if you ask a great question. Obviously if you don't ask any question that's bad and it shows a lack of interest. Personally, I like the personal questions: how I felt about my experience, how did Kellogg add value in my current job – these kind of questions.*

Harvard:
> *The candidate must take time to define his short and long-term objectives and how an MBA degree fits in them. A lot of candidates have short-term objectives but they do not take time to think about what they want to do in 10 or 20 years. This is very important. The candidate must also demonstrate that he has gathered information on the program he is applying to.*

MIT:
> *As I said, the interview is not an interrogation. You must make sure it is a dialogue and ask questions. But do not ask questions for the sake of asking questions. Do not repeat the school brochure. Be sincere and do not hesitate to discuss personal problems for instance. If you are worried because your wife is coming with you and is going to lose her current job, say it! Last year, a Belgian candidate whose wife was working for a large law firm in Brussels, shared his concern in finding an activity for his wife in Boston. She is now working in an MIT department. But you can also ask questions regarding research opportunities (as a Research Assistant for instance).*

London Business School:
> *Generally, these questions come from candidates who are genuinely hesitating between different schools. They ask for advice, in particular suited to their own background, situation and objectives. They ask about strengths and weaknesses of LBS.*

INSEAD:
> *- How do I best prepare for INSEAD? How about language abilities?*
> *- Should I travel to Fontainebleau beforehand?*
> *- What are the best experiences you had in your year?*

At the end of interview, what kind of report do you make to the Admissions committee? (Do you formally recommend yes, no, maybe or do you rate candidates on various skills? Be specific.)
Kellogg:
> *We will evaluate the candidate on multiple characteristics (which I am not willing to outline here)*

and in the end I have to give an overall impression. The choices I have are: Outstanding/Strong/ Average/Below average/Poor

MIT:
A positive or negative recommendation is made after the interview.

Wharton:
I make recommendations on a sliding scale from 'outstanding' to 'no way'. I also give a yes or no recommendation. Moreover, I must make comments on several criteria: education, professional experience, teamwork, desire to attend Wharton, personal qualities.

London Business School:
LBS interviewers have to fill a detailed questionnaire where all aspects of the candidate are described, and then make a final recommendation. Based on this, and on the application, the admissions committee makes their decision, which is not necessarily what the interviewer may have recommended (this happened to me once).

INSEAD:
I have to fill out an interview report to INSEAD with specific examples including:
- *A recommendation of admission (probable admit, unlikely admit, do not admit, to be postponed)*
- *Overall assessment: what are my impressions of the candidate and why? Qualities such as leadership, interpersonal skills, judgement, goal orientation, creativity, motivation, entrepreneurship are of high importance.*
- *Assessment of candidate's personality: communication and interpersonal skills, leadership potential, charisma, teamwork.*
- *Evaluation of candidate's main achievement, evidence of responsibility and achievement*
- *Motivation: candidate's main rationales for applying to INSEAD*
- *Career analysis: candidate's plans for after INSEAD.*

HOW TO MAXIMIZE YOUR RESUME

The author of the following suggestions, Jack Quilghini, received his MBA from Harvard Business School in June 2000. Previously, had worked for five years in the tax division of a major bank. As part of his activities in retail and investment banking, he took part in, and then directed himself, strategic audit assignments and risk audits. He currently works at McKinsey in New York.

AN IMPORTANT PART OF YOUR APPLICATION
For many weeks, you have spent endless hours every night, after coming home from your office, revising your essays. You have done so by carefully studying the programs for each school you are

Jason Johnson
100 Fifth Avenue, New York, New York 10012
Tel: (212) 867-5309 johnson@hotmail.com

EDUCATION *1997*	WHARTON SCHOOL UNIVERSITY OF PENNSYLVANIA

Bachelor of Science in Economics. Concentration in Finance.
Semester abroad in Madrid, fall 1992. Captain, Varsity Golf Team 1992-93; All-Ivy Golf Team, 1992; Resident Advisor, 1992. ∎

EXPERIENCE

1999- present

THE PARTHENON GROUP   BOSTON, MA LONDON, UK

Consultant

- Led market entry analysis of water desalination industry for $200MM pump manufacturer. Developed, executed customer surveys, analyzed competitive structure of market; assessed margin sustainability and forecast market demand. Presented findings to division president.
- Provided financial appraisal, strategic recommendation for sale of UK electronic publishing division of $200M content aggregator. Coordinated due diligence, interviewed division CEO; designed analysis to highlight key revenue, cost drivers; built DCF valuation model, delivered recommendation to Managing Director of acquiring firm.
- Member of market entry strategy team working with client management in $30M electronic content business. Heavily involved in designing, executing market analysis, customer surveying; evaluating potential business models; assessing growth/profitability prospects, competitive threats. Presented findings, resulting in $280M acquisition of competing firm.

1997-1999

THE INTERNATIONAL FINANCE CORPORATION (IFC)   WASHINGTON D.C.

Private equity/Commercial lending arm of the World Bank Group
Investment Analyst, Latin America and Caribbean Department

- Managed $12M IFC debt/equity investment in São Paulo-based small appliance manufacturer. On-site due diligence, extensive interviews with management team. Developed cash flow model and proforma financial statements. Heavily involved in preparation of term sheets, information memoranda; structuring, negotiating legal agreements in Portuguese and English.
- Member of two-person investment team on $115M Brazilian textile deal. Participated in on-site due diligence in northeastern Brazil and built integrated cash flow spreadsheet model. Designed and led in-depth textile market study in São Paulo, Rio de Janeiro: interviewed local raw material, fabric and garment vendors. Aggregated information on trends and structure of market. Participated in structuring, negotiating investment agreements.
- Prepared annual assessment report of $100M investment in Colombian polyester manufacturer. Conducted individual on-site research in Medellín, interviewed CFO, senior executives and operating personnel. Built model of financial returns, presented to senior IFC management. Report cited as Best Demonstrated Practice and incorporated into template for future reports.
- Screened investment proposals in electronics, retail, consumer products industries.
- Prepared, delivered equity sale documents; option valuation for stake in pulp/paper portfolio company; monitored portfolio company compliance with financial covenants.

OTHER

Native English speaker; fluent in Portuguese, Spanish. Youngest-ever Barbados National Men's Golf Champion; national golf team member. Student of military, economic history.

applying to and by getting lots of advice and recommendations. Now the writing is finished, but the application deadline is fast approaching. But that's no problem; there's nothing left to do except fill in the application forms and update your résumé, which shouldn't take more than an hour. You have already thought about this and decided that the easiest way is to revise the most recent version of your résumé, which you drafted to get your last job.

Without a doubt, you could content yourself with a quick revision of that document. But in doing so, you risk passing up an opportunity that could perhaps make that crucial difference between your application and the 8,000 others, or at least keep you in the running. By illustrating and reinforcing the messages and examples developed in your essays, your résumé can add more weight to your candidature and improve your chances for success.

CHARACTERISTICS OF A GOOD RESUME FOR AN MBA APPLICATION
To measure the potential role of the résumé as a supporting document for your MBA application, it's useful to recall briefly what the admissions panels are looking to evaluate in it, beyond its informative function (the number of years of professional experience, jobs and posts held, previous employers, etc.). In fact, what admissions officers are most commonly looking for in a résumé is usually based on three specific elements of the candidate's professional background: coherence, diversity and success.

- A relatively coherent background. Ideally, the different stages of a young professional's career will be connected to one another by the opportunities that the candidate will have known how to create for himself, either within or outside of his company, in line with his long-term career goals. Thus an engineer's experience in technology will lend more credibility to a start-up project.

- Diverse experiences. The richness of your background is every bit as important as its coherence. The admissions officers therefore expect to find experiences in a candidate's background that will allow him to better grasp the teachings offered by the MBA curriculum. Thus some of the programs have established a formula of previous international and multidisciplinary training experience for managers and leaders. This includes experience in managing teams, responsibility for projects, the experience of setting up a business (even in a limited sense). All of these will undoubtedly reinforce your application to one of these programs.

- Visible signs of success. In order to evaluate your professional performance, the admissions officers will measure the duration of each of your jobs, the evolution of the responsibilities you have had, and the progression of your salaries and bonuses, as well as the results you got both individually and as a member of a group, or better even, as a manager of a team.

SOME PRACTICAL TIPS FOR WRITING YOUR RESUME
Procedures vary from one institution to another, but most of them ask you to provide a list of your previous jobs (employment history) and/or a copy of your résumé. The following paragraph is not meant to explain how to write your résumé - there's no shortage of good books on that subject. On the other hand, writing the employment history part of the résumé can prove to be a more delicate exercise.

Don't forget the rest of your application! If you draft your employment history (or even your resume) before the rest of the application, it will be easy to loose sight of two essential points:

- Adapting to the programs concerned: as with the essays and the other parts of your application, it's important that the employment history highlights aspects of your professional background that are particularly relevant to the subjects taught in the programs. It's a matter of reinforcing your past experiences in, for example, team management, or project management for the applications to those programs especially oriented towards the development of these leadership characteristics.

- Maintaining coherence with the rest of your application, especially with the essays and letters of recommendation. Your employment history should mention important examples from your professional experience that are mentioned in your essays. Likewise, it's best for your letters of recommendation, especially those from your coworkers and supervisors, to be in line with the descriptions of your professional responsibilities. For that reason, it might be useful to discuss your employment history with the authors of your letters of recommendation; you could even give them a copy of your résumé, or better yet, a draft of your employment history. These things are absolutely essential to bear in mind! Of course, don't forget to include:

- A succinct descriptive list of your employers: just like the presentation of your previous studies, don't hesitate to describe the activities of your employer (sector or industry, products, location, etc.). You may also include, if need be, some figures documenting the company's exports and its rankings in lists like the Fortune Global 500. Doing this can only improve the credibility of your application.

- A dynamic and original description of your career: in case you haven't already been explicitly asked to provide this according to a specific format on the application, it is best to do so in the résumé. A description of your successive jobs should ideally include a summary of your responsibilities, the results you achieved during the time you held the position (with figures, if possible), as well as the main challenges that you faced and were able to overcome.

- Concrete examples: it is essential to provide concrete evidence of aspects of your professional experience to ensure the success of your application. Give examples of results you achieved, such as an increase in sales figures, a reduction in costs, or a positive procedural change instigated by your actions, etc. Conversely, if you limit yourself to general descriptions of your jobs, it will be difficult to be original. In being concrete, you will be able to narrow the gap between yourself and the other candidates, even if they have held similar jobs with comparable responsibilities. Your résumé will carry weight and credibility such that it will be difficult for the admissions officers to ignore your application.

SUBMITTING YOUR APPLICATION A SECOND TIME

Some of you may have already applied to MBA programs, but didn't get in to the schools you aimed for. While the admissions process is very selective, you should know that rejections are rarely definitive.

Should you re-apply?

If you are convinced (after a lot of reflection) that an MBA will allow you to attain the professional objectives you've set for yourself, then I strongly advise you to apply again for an MBA. It's hard to get accurate statistics on the number of candidates who are admitted following their second attempt. However, be aware that 10% of the candidates who apply to Wharton have been rejected the first time, and that 21% of these "re-applicants" are admitted, even though the overall average admissions rate for the school is 14%. Therefore, the chances for admission are much greater for the second attempt.

What should your strategy be?

It's difficult to write this part after having given you the most relevant advice. Real-life experience is always the best source of instruction, so we asked a Harvard graduate who had been rejected after his initial application, and then admitted the second time around. After having had this experience, he has helped several other candidates in the same situation. The following suggestions will definitely help you ask yourself the right questions, and then redefine the overall positioning of your application.

AN INITIAL REJECTION MAY NOT BE THE LAST WORD

You have worked night and day for three months, writing and re-writing your essays, feverishly preparing for and taking the GMAT, harassing the writers of your letters of recommendation to respect the application due dates, obtaining transcripts from your schools and universities as well as getting certified translations of all of your transcripts and diplomas. In enough time before the application deadline, you have sent your completed application along with a check for a not insignificant amount, and all this for each one of the schools you've chosen to apply to. So, you now realize that these applications have taken up so much energy and attention that perhaps what once seemed to a simple exploration of an alternative for your professional development has little by little become an all-consuming project; even a dream. Despite yourself, you already imagine yourself sitting on the steps of the Baker Library at Harvard, or wearing a Stanford T-shirt under the California sun while thinking about the business plan for your future start-up…

Nevertheless, a few weeks later, coming home from a long day at the office, your heart pounding, you open the first response letter: a rejection. Your disappointment grows with each new letter, all just as polite but as negative as the previous one. Even so, there is some good news: you can re-apply with strong chances for success, and you can turn your initial failure into a strong point for your new candidature. That being so, to this end you have to dedicate yourself to a difficult exercise: understanding the reasons for your initial failure and developing a completely new application strategy.

THE NECESSITY FOR AN OBJECTIVE DIAGNOSIS:
Most of the schools offer neither reasons for a rejection, nor the possibility for getting personalized feedback, even if you call them. The rejection letters, to avoid being hurtful, are usually very vague. Nevertheless, they usually insist on a common point: the decision is by nature subjective, relative to the quality of the other candidates, and a rejection is usually not due to one single element of the application. Most of the time, a rejection is really a result of a combination of factors, of an overall impression that you will have to identify and correct in your new application.

Avoid hasty and simple conclusions
After such a letdown, it is tempting to attribute the rejection to other factors, rather than to the quality of the application itself: the application was too late, there were quotas working against me, the admissions officers don't understand the significance of my undergraduate work, etc. The reality is that only those applications of the highest caliber will be most often accepted. The truth, therefore, lies elsewhere. Without a doubt there is something serious to correct in your application. And you have to find out what it is.

Asking yourself the right questions
Here are some suggestions for reviewing your application as a whole. They are basically a mini-marketing plan, where the universities play the role of client, you are the product and the application is your promotion medium.
- For the client: Have I really understood the recruitment criteria for each of the school I applied to? What about in terms of academics (GMAT, GPA, reputation of undergraduate school, etc.)? In terms of professional realm (quality and duration of professional experience, proven leadership potential, etc.)? Have I really understood the objectives for each of the programs?

- For the product: do I have what it takes – the raw materials – to produce an application that represents a well-crafted profile? How does my profile differ from that of the thousands of other applicants?

- Promotion: have I tailored my application according to the specific demands of school (for example, using words and themes from the program's brochure in my essays, referring to specific courses, etc,)? Does my whole application convey an original, clear and coherent message that conforms to the objectives of the program?

Some practical tips
Though it's crucial, this stage in the diagnosis process requires doing some difficult introspection. Here are four tips to help direct you and manage your feelings:
- Wait. Doing a diagnosis in the heat of the moment, just after receiving rejection letters can't possibly be completely objective. A few weeks of rest and thinking about other things will only sharpen your ability to generate constructive criticism afterwards.

- Concentrate your efforts as much on the product as on promotion. It's a matter of understanding and correcting not only the discrepancies between your application (your promotion medium) and the schools' selection criteria, but also between your entire profile (your product) and these criteria. Maybe you can voluntarily do something at work for a certain project that will give you some real leadership experience?

- Look in from the outside. The ideal situation would be to ask someone from a different background to offer a critical look at your application from the beginning of the application on. Even in that situation, the person would have to know the target schools really well. This person may be rather difficult -- or even impossible -- to find! If you know such a person, you have most certainly already asked him or her to help you with your initial application, so now he or she would have lost a degree of objectivity. To complement and/or replace such a person, some books can help you. For example, reading essays written by admitted students can allow you to see easily enough what might be missing from your own work.

- Think of this exercise as an opportunity, rather than a chore. It's always difficult to accept criticism, even when it's constructive, or to initiate a critique of your own work. That being said, most of the courses in MBA programs are concerned with leadership, and being able to do this is key. MBA or no, you will get something out of this process.

THE ADMISSIONS APPLICATIONS: DO THEM OVER!

To better define your new application strategy, it's useful to understand how the admissions officers review applications from 'reapplicants'. In fact, most schools ask you to indicate if you have already submitted an application in the past. The procedure can vary from one school to the other, but this information allows them to look at your old application (or a summary of it) and compare it with your new one. So it is important to make evident as many changes and improvements as possible.

Standardized tests

Retaking the GMAT to improve your scores may be an option to consider, especially if your initial scores were significantly lower than the average scores of students admitted to your target schools. Likewise, getting a very high GMAT score can help offset a mediocre GPA. Don't worry about retaking these exams - even in the best programs, students who have taken the GMAT two or three times are not uncommon.

Letters of recommendation

The instructions for the applications contain specific guidelines for re-applicants. Though they may vary from one school to another, the options you have available are usually the following:

- Only one new letter: this is the option suggested by many of the schools, such as Harvard Business School. The idea is to provide one new letter of recommendation to update your application, so it should describe the period of time between the two application attempts. This makes sense, since the initial letters of recommendation should have adequately covered the various academic, professional and personal aspects of your candidature. Though it can be difficult to obtain, it is advisable to get a letter from someone in an even higher position, or at least from someone on the same level.

- More than one new letter: admissions offices often allow candidates the freedom to produce more than one new letter. This is the option to take if, at the end of your diagnostic process, you conclude that your initial letters proved to be insufficient. The new letters have to be rewritten by the same authors, to emphasize certain specific points, if need be. That being the case, one single letter of recommendation from an author who can attest, in a credible and eloquent manner, to the quality of your candidature will usually have more impact on the admissions officers than three new letters.

The essays

The quality of your essays is a measure of the coherence of the overall image you present relative to the demands and objectives of a given program. For example, don't talk about leadership in every essay if the program has the goal of developing leaders. It's a matter of not only convincing them that you are capable of successfully completing the program, but also that you can contribute and share your experiences with other students. For re-applicants this first objective is coupled with a second, equally important point: to demonstrate what makes you a better candidate now. The conclusions from your personal diagnostic process are extremely useful for this.

Just as for your letters of recommendation, it is best to give priority to recent examples and situations in order to convince the reader that you have gained new wisdom from the additional experiences you have acquired since the first time you applied. The better option is to therefore completely rewrite your essays, at least as much as you can. Of course, it's hard to imagine how your greatest accomplishments could be completely different from one year to the next. But if you decide to re-use all or part of an essay from your initial application, you still shouldn't hesitate to rewrite it to better integrate everything you need to include, since your essays have to constitute a coherent whole.

Several schools have essays topics about failure. Like any leader, a manager has to be able to learn from his failures. Show what you have learned: the conclusions from your diagnostic, as personal as they may be, can help you write very original essays. Don't hold back! A lot of schools offer the option of writing an extra free-form essay. Don't hesitate to do it as a conclusion where you summarize why - more than you did in your first application - you think you are a worthy applicant. A little boldness won't hurt your chances for success and will allow you to differentiate yourself yet again, turning your initial failure into an advantage and something that sets you apart.

PATIENCE IS A VIRTUE; HASTE AND BLINDNESS AREN'T

Avoid haste. If you have endured a rejection this year (class n), go ahead and wait a whole year before resubmitting your application for the class (n + 2) the following year. Take advantage of this year to do the diagnostic work at your own pace, improve your GMAT scores , do some research (media, books), ask for more advice (at school presentations, from alumni networks and mentors), and above all to further your professional experience. Continuing to gain work experience is without a doubt THE most important aspect of the admissions application and the main reason many candidates are initially rejected. The more you can accumulate professional experience that is both interesting and usable for your essays, the more you improve your chances. A new application sent in October after an initial refusal in February of the same year is only rarely based on much richer professional experiences.

Don't let your eyes be bigger than your stomach. After a series of rejections, some applicants may want to submit applications to a larger number of less prestigious and less selective schools than their first choice schools. Such a strategy may be advantageous if, for example, management training seems indispensable to your future professional success. That being the case, it may, paradoxically, be more reasonable to reduce the number of target schools, in order to maximize the amount of time you can really tailor the components of the applications to the specific demands and goals of the various programs. In concentrating your efforts, you can also concentrate your chances for success.

Avoid endless efforts in vain. By the third rejection, the message from a university is clear, and is not going to change. Reassure yourself - lots of very happy company directors don't have MBAs, even if they have tried to get one!

Getting
the
GMAT
Edge

GMAT
Graduate Management Admissions Test

Creator	Education and Testing Services
Address	GMAT Educational Testing Services PO Box 6103 Princeton, New Jersey 08541-6103
Telephone	(703) 749-0131/1-800-GMAT-NOW
Website	www.gmac.com
E-mail	gmat@ets.org

about the test

Format	Computer Adaptive Test
Length	Three and a half hours Quantitative 37 qs. - 75mins Verbal 41 qs. - 75 mins 2 essays x 30 mins
Scoring	200 - 800 points % ranking for math and verbal 0 - 6 points for essays
Score Reporting	Results given on test day Official record sent to schools within 2 weeks

the registration process

Registration Dossier	By mail or downloadable from ETS website
Schedules & Deadlines	Year round Monday - Friday, last 3 weeks of every month, and second Saturday of every month Register at least 48 hours before test
Test center Locations	In Sylvan Learning Centers in all major cities; contact GMAC for details.
Tuition fees	$200 in 2001

average scores

	Averages for the top MBAs			
	1998	1999	2000	2001
GMAT Scores	681	688	689	689

schools average

Stanford	727
Columbia	704
Harvard	703
Wharton	703
MIT (Sloan)	700
Northwestern (Kellogg)	700
UCLA (Anderson)	690
NYU-Stern	689
Yale	689
Berkeley (Haas)	688
Insead	685
Virginia (Darden)	685
Chicago	684
Dartmouth (Tuck)	682
LBS	680
Duke (Fuqua)	677
Michigan	675
Cornell (Johnson)	675
IMD	650

THE GMAT INTRODUCTION

RETURN ON INVESTMENT

The sage knows to benefit often from the lessons of an enemy.

Aristophanes

Alan and Matt are best friends and prospective MBA students. Recently, they took a hiking trip together in the Alaskan wilderness. One day, after marching through dense forest all morning, they entered a broad clearing covered in tall grass. Halfway across it, they were stopped in their tracks, terrified, when a huge grizzly bear rose up from the grass only 20 meters from where they stood. The bear was about to attack, and both friends knew enough about the wilderness to know that hikers, wearing backpacks and boots, never outrun charging bears. In short, the closest tree was too far away…

With death, then, only seconds away, Alan turned to Matt and said, "Matt, my friend, I regret that fate has kept us from Harvard Business School and long, happy lives. I only wish to say it has been an honor being your friend."

"Yeah," Matt replied, "Me too." He then quickly dropped his pack and started sprinting for the trees.

"Matt! What are you doing?" Alan shouted after him. "You're a fool to think you can outrun that bear!"

"I don't have to outrun the bear," Matt yelled back. "I just have to outrun you!"

You and 225,000 others…

This case study in competition aptly illustrates the intensity of the admissions process at the top business schools. And nowhere is it more relevant than in the Graduate Management Admission Test, the GMAT. This three and a half hour standardized exam is a required element in your dossier, and your results are among the first pieces of information consulted by admissions officers. A strong score on the GMAT will not by itself get you in, but without a strong score, your chances are greatly reduced.

A few statistics provide a vivid picture of the competition. This year, close to 230,000 people will take the exam. Fewer than 15,000 will score high enough to match or exceed the average GMAT scores for candidates accepted to Harvard, Wharton or INSEAD. And only a stunning 5,000 will match or exceed the average at Stanford. More broadly, the top programs benchmark scores placing candidates in the top 10% of the test-taking pool. Thus, to consider yourself a competitive candidate, you'll need to "run faster" on the GMAT than 225,000 other young professionals.

The chart below shows the annual number of GMAT test-takers, and the proportions who have matched or exceeded both the top 10% taking the test, and the average incoming score for Stanford:

Total number of GMAT test-takers

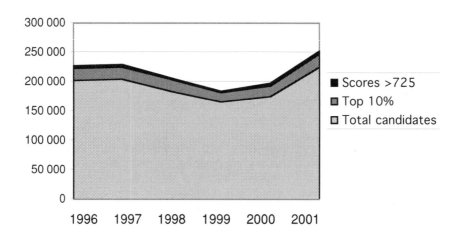

In this chapter, we'll demystify the GMAT, show you how it's scored and applied by the programs, and suggest ways you can prepare, adjust to and succeed at this exam. Also, we'll advise you on how to fit your GMAT preparation (yes, you'll have to prepare!) into your overall admissions game plan. And finally, for applicants for whom English is not a native language, we'll fill you in on the TOEFL, the Test Of English as a Foreign Language, less important than the GMAT but nonetheless a required component of your dossier if you did not grow up in an English-speaking country.

Register now to win cash and prizes!
Your first step in taking the GMAT is to obtain the GMAT Bulletin, a brochure that introduces the exam, provides registration information and explains score reporting procedures. You can request one directly from the publisher ETS, pick one up at nearly any business school admissions office, test preparation center or other business education institution, or access the bulletin via the Internet www.gmac.com/gmat.

It is easy to register for the exam. Simply call ETS at 1-800-GMAT-NOW, let the operator know you wish to schedule a GMAT exam, tell him or her your preferred date and time (morning or afternoon) and have your credit card handy. You'll be given a date and time to show up for the test, and a confirmation number. The test can be taken at any test center year-round, but note that centers are closed the first week of each month. Also, Saturday dates are often booked far in advance, particularly during the busy months of October through February. Taking the GMAT is not cheap; expect to pay around $200 for the privilege.

A short business case in Supply Chain Management

It's expensive largely because the exam is delivered via a long supply chain. Ultimate authority over the exam rests with GMAC, the Graduate Management Admissions Council, which represents most American MBA programs and coordinates business school admissions, promotions and communications. GMAC contracts the nuts and bolts of the GMAT to the Educational Testing Service (ETS). In America, one grow up with ETS, because this organization develops and administers nearly all of the nation's standardized undergraduate, graduate and professional exams. By the time you've finished your MBA school applications, you'll know ETS well. But you'll never meet them because when you walk into a test center to sit the exam, you'll be serviced by yet another link in the chain, Sylvain Learning Centers, who are contracted by ETS to develop and operate the exam computer network and test centers.

The point of this testing industry "value chain" case is to drive home a key fact: despite the steep price you pay for the test, you are not the "client" of Sylvain, ETS or GMAC. Your money gives you the right to expect quality service, a good testing environment, and accurate, timely reporting. But the real "clients" are the MBA programs represented by GMAC. They are ultimately responsible for how the test works, what material it covers, and how the results are used. So what do business schools want from the GMAT? What do they want to learn about you when they examine your results?

GMAT results - Keeping the customer satisfied

Officially, the GMAT is designed to achieve two main goals:
- provide business schools with a user-friendly, quantified means of comparing individuals from widely differing educational backgrounds
- statistically predict an individual's chances of success during the rigorous first year of an MBA program, i.e. indicate to what degree you possess the intellectual skills considered central to success in an MBA program

In terms of your overall dossier, admissions directors tend to consider the GMAT in conjunction with your academic record, lumping the two together to comprise the major components of the criterion of "academic potential". If your university education is atypical – you didn't study business or engineering, or you attended a school no one has ever heard of – or you have been out of school for more than five years, the GMAT takes on added importance.

Unofficially, the GMAT is also often used as part of the "first look" that admissions officers give applications. Imagine you work in the Stanford admissions office and you have to evaluate 6,000 applications a year (probably half of which arrive the week before the final deadline). You're going to need a fast way to prioritize them. A quick peek at that handy three digit GMAT score, and you will know which files go in the "highly interested" stack, the "somewhat interested" pile, or the "to be recycled" pile.

Top programs are sensitive to GMAT results in one final way. Their prestige is partly based on the excellence of their student body and the rigor of the admissions process. One of the easiest, most widely-recognized ways to ensure both is to demand high GMAT scores. In fact, many of the rankings conducted by newspapers and business magazines use a program's average GMAT score as a factor in their calculations. And so prestige-minded programs (aren't they all) are given even greater incentive to value and demand high GMAT scores.

If Greenspan knew, he'd push up interest rates

The pool of applicants has responded remarkably well to such demands. As more and more talented professionals choose to pursue an MBA, and thus prepare vigorously for the GMAT, we've witnessed a sharp increase in the average incoming GMAT scores reported by the top programs. For example, only four years ago INSEAD's reported average was about 650 (or the top ten percent) and some applicants with strong professional backgrounds were gaining admission with scores as low as 590. Today, Insead's reported GMAT score average is 685 (about the top five percent) and even the most highly qualified candidates are expected to post very strong scores. At Kellogg, Duke, Darden, in fact throughout the Top 20, this same "score inflation" is a fact of life.

The following table shows score inflation among the Top 20 over the past three years:

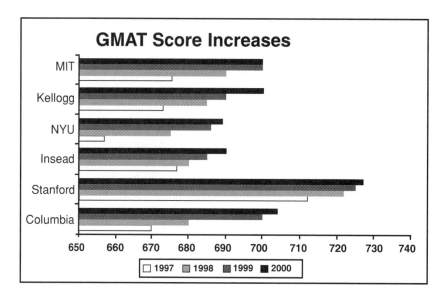

The real value-added

All of this may sound rather pessimistic and cynical and doesn't give just due to the subtleties of the admissions process. Admissions officers are by and large experienced people who indeed read all applications that meet the deadline and consider many, many factors when making admissions decisions. As we said before, a high score doesn't guarantee admission, and from time to time people with relatively low scores do get in. Perhaps the most constructive way to think about the GMAT is as an opportunity, in fact, one of the rare opportunities left to you to make your candidacy stand out.

Think about it. What are the most important factors in the admissions process? Your work experience? This isn't likely to change much during the time you prepare your dossiers. Your education? Ancient history. Your recommendations? Not entirely under your control. So what is under your control? Your application essays…and your GMAT.

A score in excess of your program's reported average will do much to offset any "risk" posed by a lackluster academic record or a "non-business" academic or professional background. Instead of being seen as a candidate who doesn't belong, you'll more likely be viewed as a welcome dose of class diversity. Finally, whether or not other parts of your dossier pose a risk, a great score on the GMAT helps ensure your application sparks interest and above-average care. Adequate test preparation is therefore crucial to help you achieve the score you'll need. In short, excellent GMAT preparation should be an integral part of your admissions strategy. It's simply the best way to add maximum value to your applications.

Testing potential top managers

By now you're probably on the phone to Mom to ask her to dig through your old stuff for those long-forgotten high school math and English books. Not so fast! Your first step in GMAT preparation is to ask yourself, if MBA school is the gateway to top management, shouldn't the GMAT test a person's potential to master top management skills?

Of course it should. In fact, the test makers have designed the GMAT to test a very specific battery of skills effective senior executives use every day. And guess what: You already know these skills. Brainstorm a bit. What do top managers do? They:

- think strategically
- manage time well
- set priorities (and stick to them)
- communicate clearly, concisely and persuasively
- build analyses based on facts and observation, not on thin air
- evaluate critically the work of others
- make the most of resources (including themselves)
- simplify complex issues
- make decisions
- tolerate risk
- understand that business success isn't about being perfect, but about being better

The GMAT's 78 questions and two essays will challenge you on each and every point. So as you read the rest of this chapter, try to connect what you learn about the exam with the points above - and with your own managerial skill set. Every connection you make will help demystify the test and increase your score.

GMAT MINI-DIAGNOSTIC

Before we go any further, how about testing your current GMAT level? The mini-diagnostic below will give you an idea of what is tested. You will see problem solving, data sufficiency, sentence correction, critical reasoning and reading comprehension - all the question types that make up the GMAT multiple choice sections. Give yourself ten minutes to answer the six questions on the maths section and ten minutes for six questions on the verbal section, and then we'll go through the questions with strategies and approaches to score even higher on test day.

QUANTITATIVE SECTION

1. Which is the closest approximation of five billion divided by 397,264?
    (A) 12.5
    (B) 1,250
    (C) 2,250
    (D) 12,500
    (E) 20,000

2. A jet airplane approaching the town of Springerville, which lies at a straight line distance of six miles from Tombstone, reads on its radar a distance of six and one half miles between the airplane and Tombstone's airport at the instant the airplane passes directly above Springerville. At that instant, what is the airplane's altitude, in miles?
    (A) 1.5
    (B) 2.5
    (C) 3.4
    (D) 5.0
    (E) 6.5

3. For any non-prime integer q, the "proverbial" of q is the product of the largest and smallest prime numbers that divide evenly into q plus the difference of the largest and smallest prime numbers that divide evenly into q. Which of the following, if increased by five, has the greatest proverbial?
    (A) 9
    (B) 15
    (C) 19
    (D) 21
    (E) 49

4. Two automobile manufacturers, Nash and Tucker, declared profits on the sales of their cars for the year 1998. Which manufacturer posted the greatest profit?
    1. Nash's total cost per automobile is 78% of the sales price, and in 1998, it sold 250,000 automobiles.
    2. Tucker's total cost per automobile is 85% of the sales price, and in 1998, it sold 200,000 automobiles.

(A) Statement 1 BY ITSELF is sufficient to answer the question, but statement 2 by itself is not.
(B) Statement 2 BY ITSELF is sufficient to answer the question, but statement 1 by itself is not.
(C) Statements 1 and 2 TAKEN TOGETHER are sufficient to answer the question, but NEITHER statement BY ITSELF is sufficient.
(D) Either statement BY ITSELF is sufficient to answer the question.
(E) Statements 1 and 2 TAKEN TOGETHER are NOT sufficient to answer the question. More data pertaining to the problem is necessary.

5. Is the integer x an even number?
　　　1. x/3 is greater than 1
　　　2. x has only two factors

(A) Statement 1 BY ITSELF is sufficient to answer the question, but statement 2 by itself is not.
(B) Statement 2 BY ITSELF is sufficient to answer the question, but statement 1 by itself is not.
(C) Statements 1 and 2 TAKEN TOGETHER are sufficient to answer the question, but NEITHER statement BY ITSELF is sufficient.
(D) Either statement BY ITSELF is sufficient to answer the question.
(E) Statements 1 and 2 TAKEN TOGETHER are NOT sufficient to answer the question. More data pertaining to the problem is necessary.

6. What is the value of x?
　　　1. $y(x^2-9)=0$
　　　2. y does not equal zero
(A) Statement 1 BY ITSELF is sufficient to answer the question, but statement 2 by itself is not.
(B) Statement 2 BY ITSELF is sufficient to answer the question, but statement 1 by itself is not.
(C) Statements 1 and 2 TAKEN TOGETHER are sufficient to answer the question, but NEITHER statement BY ITSELF is sufficient.
(D) Either statement BY ITSELF is sufficient to answer the question.
(E) Statements 1 and 2 TAKEN TOGETHER are NOT sufficient to answer the question. More data pertaining to the problem is necessary.

VERBAL SECTION

1. Like many marriages between Hollywood celebrities, grave difficulties in mergers between well-known companies are often experienced due to jealousy over which partner will receive more attention, both within the partnership and from the outside public.

(A) grave difficulties in mergers between well-known companies are often experienced due to jealousy over which partner will receive more attention
(B) grave difficulties in well-known company mergers are often experienced due to jealousy over which partner will receive more attention
(C) mergers between well-known companies often experience grave difficulties due to jealousy over which partner will receive more attention
(D) mergers between well-known companies often have been experiencing grave difficulties due to jealousy over which partner will receive more attention

(E) well-known company mergers often have been experiencing grave difficulties due to jealousy over which partner will receive more attention

2. Each and every one a Nobel Laureate, Toni Morrison, William Faulkner, Albert Camus and Gunther Grass, these writers' novels have been sharp social critiques and have been seeking ways to create new spaces wherein communities can probe societal ills and lay the basis for social healing to take place.

(A) Each and every one a Nobel Laureate, Toni Morrison, William Faulkner, Albert Camus and Gunther Grass, these writers' novels have been sharp social critiques and have been seeking ways to create new spaces wherein communities can probe societal ills and lay the basis for social healing to take place.

(B) Each and every one a Nobel Laureate, Toni Morrison, William Faulkner, Albert Camus and Gunther Grass, they have been sharp social critics in their novels and seekers of ways to create new spaces in their writings wherein communities can probe societal ill and lay the basis for social healing to take place.

(C) Toni Morrison, William Faulkner, Albert Camus and Gunther Grass, each and every one a Nobel Laureate, these writers have been sharp social critics in their novels and have been seeking ways to create new spaces in their writings wherein communities can probe societal ills and lay the basis for social healing to take place.

(D) The novels of Nobel Laureates, Toni Morrison, William Faulkner, Albert Camus and Gunther Grass, sharply criticize society and seek to create new spaces wherein communities can probe societal ills and lay the basis for social healing to take place.

(E) Communities can probe societal ills and lay the basis for social healing to take place in Nobel Laureates', Toni Morrison, William Faulkner, Albert Camus and Gunther Grass, novels sharply critical of society and seeking to create new spaces.

3. Some advisors to the American President urge that next year's Federal budget include sizeable provisions for foreign aid to the Asian countries worst hit by the economic crisis. A number of American senators, however, have vowed to vote down this measure, saying a large influx of American funds will only encourage a rebirth of the corruption between Asian governments and big business that was, according to many economists, a primary cause of the crisis in these countries.

Which of the following most weakens the senators' argument?

(A) The aid will economically and politically strengthen those worst hit by the crisis, labourers and the emerging middle classes, who are uniformly opposed to corruption between government and big business.

(B) Some economists believe that corruption was but one of many causes of the Asian economic crisis.

(C) Many international organisations have claimed there is an alarming risk of famine and political instability in the worst hit countries.

(D) Much of the foreign aid sent to these countries in the 1970's was secretly funnelled to corporations with close personal ties to the government to support large-scale business development.

(E) The current high value of the dollar compared to the crisis countries' currencies will increase the relative value of American-provided foreign aid.

4. A group of European automobile racing enthusiasts has organised a boycott against popular motoring and motorcycling package tours of the American West. Claiming the tours' promotional literature amounts to false advertising, the racing enthusiasts argue that such tours cannot provide the "true motoring pleasure" promised by the tour companies. After all, say the racing enthusiasts, how can a European motorist experience true motoring pleasure in the United States when the American highway speed limit is so much lower than those in European countries?

Which of the following is an assumption made by the automobile racing enthusiasts staging the boycott?

(A) American motorists prefer to drive on the highway at slower speeds.

(B) The companies offering the package tours are not staffed by racing enthusiasts.

(C) Automobile drivers are more likely to drive at high speeds than are motorcyclists.

(D) Speed limits in the United States are enforced often enough to pose a serious risk that speeding motorists will be ticketed by the police.

(E) The amount of traffic on congested European highways is not so great as to limit the viable driving speed well below the posted speed limit.

Professor Kenneth M. Stampp, in the final chapters of his thorough, comprehensive study of slavery, The Peculiar Institution, convincingly explodes the myth of the "benign" plantation slave holder and argues that the greatest reason for the stubborn survival of slavery deep into the 19th century was its profitability rather than the slave holders' supposed paternal commitment to their slaves. To buttress his case, Stampp attacks two of the strongest arguments made by slave holders and their apologists. The first, the high debt levels carried by many of the great plantation owners, is claimed by those favorable to the plantation owners as proof of the financial burden shouldered by slave holders committed to caring for often unproductive slaves. But in Stampp's careful analysis of plantation account books, this high level of debt is shown to be more a sign of plantation owners' supreme confidence in their future sales and the wisdom of capital investment in clearing new lands than a symptom of inherent unprofitability. Indeed, with no shareholders to please, the slave owners were free to make the most of their businesses by taking advantage of the sizeable credit their success afforded them.

The second argument involves the substantial number of slaves supported on Virginia tobacco plantations long after these lands, exhausted by tobacco's demands on soil fertility, ceased to yield sizeable harvests. Slave holders and their apologists pointed to this phenomenon as evidence of the Virginia planters' concern for, and commitment to, their slave communities. Why else would a planter keep so many slaves on low-yielding land? But Stampp shows these same planters, far from being paternal, were encouraging the population growth of their slave communities so as to have a sizeable stock of slaves to sell in the South's internal slave trade. After the final closing of Charleston as a slave port in the early years of the 19th century, the burgeoning demand for slaves in the developing cotton belt had to be satisfied internally. The Virginia planters with their expanding surplus of slaves were ideally situated to make the most of the internal trade in their "product". And so they did, reaping rich gains by separating families and breaking apart tight-knit slave communities.

5. The author's primary purpose in this passage is to:

(A) assert that slaveholders often lost money through financial mismanagement

(B) defend the actions of the Virginia planters in the face of the loss of fertility of their tobacco lands

(C) critique a point of view in favor of the slaveholders by supporting a scholarly work.

(D) question the financial benefits of slavery.

(E) demonstrate the wisdom of carrying sizeable debt loads when that debt is invested in capital improvements.

6. According to the author, which of the following best explains the Virginia planters' willingness to support large numbers of slaves on low-yielding tobacco plantations?

(A) Tobacco farming is highly labour intensive and so required comparatively many slaves per acre of tilled land.

(B) The close of Charleston as a slave port cut the Virginia planters off from their established export slave markets.

(C) The Virginia planters enjoyed separating slave families and dismantling slave communities.

(D) The Virginia planters were concerned for their slaves' welfare and were therefore willing to subsidise a surplus in labour.

(E) The Virginia planters saw their slaves as a valuable commodity in high demand in the developing Cotton Belt.

RESULTS

OK, that wasn't so bad was it? I guess now you want to find out how well you did. The answers are:

Quantitative

1. D   2. B   3. D   4. E   5. C   6. E

Verbal

1. C   2. D   3. A   4. D   5. C   6. E

As we will explain later in this chapter, the Computer Adaptive Test uses an algorithm to calculate your score, and based on where you are in the Math or Verbal section, the right or wrong answers that you gave will push your GMAT score higher or lower.

If you answered five or six questions correctly in either section, this is obviously a strength, and you should try to maximize this score on test day. If on the other hand you got more than two answers wrong, schools will see the comparative weakness, and you are well advised to improve these areas to get a competitive overall score.

STRATEGIES AND ADVICE

A talk-through of GMAT test day

So let's start the value-adding process by taking a look at the structure and scoring mechanism of the test. The GMAT is comprised of three timed sections totalling three and a half hours. Counting test breaks, administrative procedures and a mandatory questionnaire, expect to spend about four and a half hours at the test center. When you arrive on test day, you'll be asked to show two pieces of photo identification and read and sign a security agreement. Then you'll be ushered into the testing room and seated at a computer. The test center staff will then ask you to buckle up, and will demonstrate proper use of the oxygen mask in case the cabin loses air pressure during the math section. Just kidding.

Once you're at the computer you'll first see a menu from which you can select up to five MBA programs to receive automatically your scores. The cost for reporting scores in this way is factored into the fee, thus it is "free". If you face tight deadlines or are uncommonly confident about the score you'll receive, take advantage of this feature, and have your programs in mind before you sit the exam. Otherwise, we suggest you wait to report your scores until after you've seen the results – a simple precautionary tactic.

The next series of screens will guide you through a tutorial designed to teach you the very basic computer skills necessary to navigate the exam. Anyone who has used a point-and-click interface and a mouse will find the tutorial redundant. It's there because the test makers are obliged to ensure a fair test experience by providing for those rare test takers who are new to computers and/or completely new to the GMAT. To make sure you get the hang of navigating the test, the tutorial is not timed and you are encouraged to keep working on it until you feel ready for the real thing. If you prepare adequately in advance, you'll be free to use the tutorial phase to ready yourself in other ways.

GMAT ESSAYS
ANALYTICAL WRITING ASSESSMENT

Once the tutorial is complete, you'll begin the first section of the actual exam, the Analytical Writing Assessment (AWA). This includes two timed essays of 30 minutes each. For each essay, the computer posts a topic and a series of instructions, provides a window for typing the essay, and provides command buttons for basic text editing functions (cut, paste, undo).

AWA I: ANALYSIS OF AN ISSUE

One of the two essays is called Analysis of an Issue. The topic paragraph presents a subject for debate, and your job is to select one side and argue for it. The instructions require you to state your choice and support it by giving relevant reasons and examples. Here's a sample:

> Internet-based music distribution, in which a consumer can locate online thousands of songs to download for free, has become a lively topic of debate in recent years. Most record companies and many recording artists oppose free distribution, arguing it deprives them of their rightful income, and in so doing limits the growth potential of individual artists and the industry as a whole. On the other hand, many consumers and the high tech start-ups that have pioneered this technology claim "free" distribution is merely a symptom of problems in the industry itself. They point to inflated prices for CDs and poor selection as reasons why consumers reject traditional distribution. Furthermore, they state that the income artists lose from free distribution is more than offset by the cheaper access they have to new fans and international markets.

> Which argument do you find more convincing: that in favor of free Internet-based music distribution, or opposed? Use relevant reasons or examples (drawn from your reading, observations or personal experience) to support your choice.

KSF (Key Success Factor): frame the issue before you begin to write.

The surest, quickest way to fail this essay is to write off the topic – and you'd be surprised by how many people do! Don't touch the keyboard until you've asked yourself the same questions journalists do: What's the issue? (Downloading music off the internet for free); Who's involved? (record companies and recording artists vs. consumers and Dot Com companies); When? (now, of course); Where? (not important in this case); Why do the two sides disagree? (loss of revenue and growth potential vs. low prices, selection and cheap access to new fans and markets).

Your answers to these questions form the "boundary" for what you discuss in your essay. Don't ever stray outside! Once you've set your boundary, you're ready to respond to two more questions (and get a top score in the process): Which side do you support? And, why should the reader believe you?

AWA II: ANALYSIS OF AN ARGUMENT

The other essay is Analysis of an Argument, where you'll be asked to critique the reasoning of an argument presented in the topic paragraph, pointing out its weaknesses and suggesting ways to improve it and/or information that would help you better evaluate it. Here's a typical example:

> The following appeared as part of the quarterly financial report of a major multinational manufacturing company.

> "Despite the unexpected $100 million loss we posted for the quarter and the resulting price slump in company stock, shareholders should be bullish about the company's immediate future and use the slump as an opportunity to buy additional shares. The market as a whole, as shown by the recent performance of both the Dow Jones and the Nasdaq indexes, continues to climb and inflation is projected to stay low. Furthermore, our planned $250 million factory investment scheme will give us a manufacturing capacity greater than what our competitors currently have. Finally, the new management team has a great track record in their prior work consulting for the financial services industry. The Board expects them to return us to profitability very quickly."

> Explain how logically convincing you find this argument. In your explanation, analyze the argument's line of reasoning and its use of evidence. You should consider explaining what, if anything, would make the argument more valid or convincing, or would help you better evaluate its conclusion.

KSF: Exploit what you're given for all it's worth.

Ask yourself, What's the author's claim/point? – "Buy our stock even though it isn't performing well now". Then ask, What does the author provide as evidence to try and convince me? – "Markets are going up. Inflation is supposed to stay low. Our investment will gives us greater capacity. The new management team is awesome". These are your major points of attack when you critique the author's argument. You must therefore identify and dismantle each to earn your score – the more completely you do so, the higher your score.

NB: Either essay could be the first you'll see on test day, so read the instructions carefully and write accordingly. The test makers understand 30 minutes is a very brief time to compose and write, so the essays don't need to be very long. Aim for 300 words each. Note that you must finish the first essay before the computer will allow you to move on to the second. When you've completed both (or run out of time), you'll be given a five minute break and can leave the test room to stretch your legs.

GMAT MATH
THE QUANTITATIVE SECTION

Next comes the first of the multiple choice portions of the test, the Quantitative section. Here, you'll be given 75 minutes to respond to 37 questions testing math skills and quantitative reasoning. You will see one question on the screen at a time, and you must answer that question before the computer will allow you to move on to the next. No calculators are allowed on the GMAT, but you will have scratch paper if and when you need to calculate. Tested subject matter includes arithmetic (percents, ratios, rates), algebra, number properties (prime numbers, fractions, etc.) and geometry. These subjects are tested using two different question-types that are distributed more or less at random across the section:

- Problem Solving is the traditional multiple choice math question. Below you'll find the questions from the mini diagnostic, and strategies to give you a sense of how to succeed with this question type.
- Data Sufficiency is the most challenging math on the GMAT because it asks you not to solve a problem, but to determine whether or not it can be solved. We cover this question type in detail and help you understand how you can exploit this question type's structure to have a competitive advantage.

QUANTITATIVE QUESTION TYPE I: PROBLEM SOLVING

You know the drill for Problem Solving – read the question, set up the problem, perform the calculation and select the best response from the five listed. About half of these questions are word problems (i.e. the problems are presented in prose rather than in mathematical formulae or notation – "What does two plus two equal?" rather than "2 + 2 = ?"), and in total, you'll see about 22 Problem Solving questions in the Quantitative section. Following are a few sample questions that were used in the diagnostic, and score-building Key Success Factors:

1. Which is the closest approximation of five billion divided by 397,264?

   (A) 12.5
   (B) 1,250
   (C) 2,250
   (D) 12,500
   (E) 20,000

KSF: Avoid unnecessary work.

Speed is crucial to have a shot at a top 10% GMAT math score, but to a generation of test-takers more familiar with Palm Pilots than paper and pencil, the no-calculator clause is a time killer. Learn to approximate. Learn to avoid long, drawn-out calculations. Above all, learn to avoid doing math the "traditional" way.

In the question above, do you really want to divide anything by 397,264? No! Let's approximate 400,000 and quickly restate the question:

$5,000,000,000 / 400,000 = ?$

Cancel out the zeros and you get: 50,000 / 4 = ? = (do the math in your head!) = 12,500 = Easy points in mere seconds.

Let's look at another example:

2. A jet airplane approaching the town of Springerville, which lies at a straight line distance of six miles from Tombstone, reads on its radar a distance of six and one half miles between the airplane and Tombstone's airport at the instant the aeroplane passes directly above Springerville. At that instant, what is the airplane's altitude, in miles?

(A) 1.5

(B) 2.5

(C) 3.4

(D) 5.0

(E) 6.5

KSF: Simplify confusing problems.

GMAT word problems are often deliberately confusing, and thus challenge you to "translate" the words into diagrams, sketches, or equations – anything, in fact, that helps you get the answer quickly and cleanly. You can spot a successful translation because it will put you only a few seconds away from the solution. If you're avoiding calculations like we showed you above, you'll be using your scratch paper almost exclusively to set up problems in this way. Here's how the question looks translated as a sketch:

Aeroplane

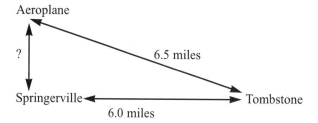

?   6.5 miles

Springerville   Tombstone

6.0 miles

If you recall your Pythagoras ($a^2 + b^2 = c^2$), you'll see that the "real" math problem is quite straightforward. Now, can you think of a short-cut that will let you find the correct answer without doing the calculations? Well the GMAT is attached to high school math, and from the multitude of right-angle triangles the ones that catch the test-maker's eye are the (3,4,5), and the (5,12,13). Just look for a ratio that is consistent with one of these two and you have usually found the correct answer.

Our last sample question is for the real pros out there:

3. For any non-prime integer q, the "proverbial" of q is the product of the largest and smallest prime numbers that divide evenly into q plus the difference of the largest and smallest prime numbers that divide evenly into q. Which of the following, if increased by five, has the greatest proverbial?

(A) 9

(B) 15

(C) 19

(D) 21

(E) 49

KSF: "Hard" GMAT math often tests your reading skills (and your composure).
Ever heard of a "proverbial"? Of course not! The GMAT test writers occasionally create "new" math concepts just to see how well you adapt to the unknown. When you see one of these Frankenstein monsters, read very carefully and take the question apart step-by-step. You can often make it even easier by focusing on the answer choices. Here's how to work it out:

Start with the question itself:
Which of the following, if increased by five, has the greatest proverbial?
Clearly, we have to add five to each answer choice before we move any further. This gives you:

(A) 9+15=14
(B) 15+5=50
(C) 19=5=24
(D) 21+5=26
(E) 49+5=54

Now let's see about this "proverbial" business:
For any non-prime integer q, the "proverbial" of q is the product of the largest and smallest prime numbers that divide evenly into q plus the difference of the largest and smallest prime numbers that divide evenly into q.

So, to find the proverbial of an answer choice, we'll need its "largest and smallest prime numbers that divide evenly into (it)" – in simpler terms, we need the largest and smallest prime factors. So let's see what we get:

(A) 14 – 2 & 7
(B) 20 – 2 & 5
(C) 24 – 2 & 3
(D) 26 – 2 & 13
(E) 54 – 2 & 3

Without going a step further, which answer choice do you think will give us the largest proverbial? You don't need to be a McKinsey partner to focus on 26 as the likely answer (and sure enough it is). Don't believe us? The full solution is below:

LPF = Largest Prime Factor   SPF = Smallest Prime Factor
Equation: proverbial = (LPFq x SPFq) + (LPFq – SPFq)

(A) 14 – 2 & 7 – (7 x 2) + (7 - 2) = proverbial of 19
(B) 20 – 2 & 5 – (5 x 2) + (5 - 2) = proverbial of 13
(C) 24 – 2 & 3 – (3 x 2) + (3 - 2) = proverbial of 7
(D) 26 – 2 & 13 – (13 x 2) + (13 - 2) = proverbial of 37
(E) 54 – 2 & 3 – (3 x 2) + (3 - 2) = proverbial of 7

Word is MIT Sloan students eat these types of questions for breakfast....

QUANTITATIVE QUESTION TYPE II: DATA SUFFICIENCY

The other question-type is the famous, dreaded, Data Sufficiency. Here, you must determine whether you have enough information to answer the question. Sometimes, but not always, the question itself provides useful but incomplete information. Once you've digested this, you then consider two additional propositions and decide if one, both or neither of them provides the additional information you need. The answer choices are standardized based on the combination of propositions needed to correctly answer the question. Data Sufficiency is very tricky for the uninitiated, but because up to 15 questions in the section are this type, your performance on Data Sufficiency will make or break your Quantitative score.

Let's see how Data Sufficiency works with the following sample question:

4. Two automobile manufacturers, Nash and Tucker, declared profits on the sales of their cars for the year 1998. Which manufacturer posted the greatest profit?

　　1. Nash's total cost per automobile is 78% of the sales price, and in 1998, it sold 250,000 automobiles.
　　2. Tucker's total cost per automobile is 85% of the sales price, and in 1998, it sold 200,000 automobiles.

(A) Statement 1 BY ITSELF is sufficient to answer the question, but statement 2 by itself is not.
(B) Statement 2 BY ITSELF is sufficient to answer the question, but statement 1 by itself is not.
(C) Statements 1 and 2 TAKEN TOGETHER are sufficient to answer the question, but NEITHER statement BY ITSELF is sufficient.
(D) Either statement BY ITSELF is sufficient to answer the question.
(E) Statements 1 and 2 TAKEN TOGETHER are NOT sufficient to answer the question. More data pertaining to the problem is necessary.

KSF: Data Sufficiency rewards a methodical approach.

Start with the question itself: what do we want to know? Answer: which manufacturer posted the greatest profit.

So we need information about both Nash's and Tucker's profits, right? Now look at Statement 1 BY ITSELF.
Nash's total cost per automobile is 78% of the sales price, and in 1998, it sold 250,000 automobiles.

Does this tell you anything about Tucker's profit? No. So Statement 1 BY ITSELF is not sufficient. What answer choices can you eliminate? The first and the fourth.

(A) Statement 1 BY ITSELF is sufficient to answer the question, but statement 2 by itself is not.
(B) Statement 2 BY ITSELF is sufficient to answer the question, but statement 1 by itself is not.
(C) Statements 1 and 2 TAKEN TOGETHER are sufficient to answer the question, but NEITHER statement BY ITSELF is sufficient.
(D) Either statement BY ITSELF is sufficient to answer the question.
(E) Statements 1 and 2 TAKEN TOGETHER are NOT sufficient to answer the question. More data pertaining to the problem is necessary.

Now let's repeat the process looking at Statement 2 BY ITSELF.
Tucker's total cost per automobile is 85% of the sales price, and in 1998, it sold 200,000 automobiles.

There is no information here about Nash. So Statement 2 BY ITSELF is not sufficient. We can now cancel the second choice.

- (A) Statement 1 BY ITSELF is sufficient to answer the question, but statement 2 by itself is not.
- (B) Statement 2 BY ITSELF is sufficient to answer the question, but statement 1 by itself is not.
- (C) tatements 1 and 2 TAKEN TOGETHER are sufficient to answer the question, but NEITHER statement BY ITSELF is sufficient.
- (D) Either statement BY ITSELF is sufficient to answer the question.
- (E) Statements 1 and 2 TAKEN TOGETHER are NOT sufficient to answer the question. More data pertaining to the problem is necessary.

What's left? We have to look at Statements 1 and 2 TAKEN TOGETHER.
Nash's total cost per automobile is 78% of the sales price, and in 1998, it sold 250,000 automobiles AND Tucker's total cost per automobile is 85% of the sales price, and in 1998, it sold 200,000 automobiles.

Read carefully. The statements give us a relationship between cost and sales price for each company, but can we calculate actual figures for profit? No, because we don't have any real numbers to work with. Can we compare these relationships directly? Only if the sales prices are the same, and this we don't know! Statements 1 and 2 TAKEN TOGETHER are therefore not sufficient. Cancel out the third answer choice.

- (A) Statement 1 BY ITSELF is sufficient to answer the question, but statement 2 by itself is not.
- (B) Statement 2 BY ITSELF is sufficient to answer the question, but statement 1 by itself is not.
- (C) Statements 1 and 2 TAKEN TOGETHER are sufficient to answer the question, but NEITHER statement BY ITSELF is sufficient.
- (D) Either statement BY ITSELF is sufficient to answer the question.
- (E) Statements 1 and 2 TAKEN TOGETHER are NOT sufficient to answer the question. More data pertaining to the problem is necessary.

By elimination, we know the last answer choice must be the correct response. By now, you might be thinking that Data Sufficiency is a long, slow, painful process. But like any method, the more you practice, the faster you get. Let's look at a second example:

5. Is the integer x an even number?
      1. x/3 is greater than 1
      2. x has only two factors

- (A) Statement 1 BY ITSELF is sufficient to answer the question, but statement 2 by itself is not.
- (B) Statement 2 BY ITSELF is sufficient to answer the question, but statement 1 by itself is not.
- (C) Statements 1 and 2 TAKEN TOGETHER are sufficient to answer the question, but NEITHER statement BY ITSELF is sufficient.
- (D) Either statement BY ITSELF is sufficient to answer the question.
- (E) Statements 1 and 2 TAKEN TOGETHER are NOT sufficient to answer the question. More data pertaining to the problem is necessary.

KSF: When a question asks Yes or No, a No is just as good as a Yes.
Start with the question itself. "Is X equal to 2, 4, 6...?" Well, if someone tells you X = 2, then the

answer is easy. You could say "Yes", and you would have enough information to answer the question. But if someone tells you X = 3, the answer is still easy. You'd say "No" and you'd still have enough information to answer the question. A statement is insufficient if you can't decide between Yes and No!

Now check out Statement 1. "X/3 is greater than 1". Simplify this to read, "X is greater than 3". So what? X can be 4 (even) or it can be 5 (odd). Statement 1 BY ITSELF is not sufficient to answer the question. Eliminate the first and the fourth answer choices.

On to Statement 2: "X has only two factors". Hey, this is the definition of a prime number! What are some simple primes? 2, 3, 5, 7... So X can be 2 (even) or it can be 3 (odd). Statement 2 BY ITSELF is not sufficient to answer the question. Toss out the second answer choice.

Last step: look at Statements 1 and 2 together. If X is both greater than 3 and prime, what does X have to be? ODD. Does this give you enough information to answer the question, "Is the integer X an even number?" SURE, because you have enough information to answer NO. The third answer choice is the correct response.

Questions that play with the idea of Yes and No (like the question above) are a particularly tricky challenge that the GMAT uses to separate top scorers from TOP 20 wannabees. The following is a second tricky Data Sufficiency question type. Try working through it before reading the explanation below.

6. What is the value of x?

    1. $y(x^2-9)=0$

    2. y does not equal zero

(A) Statement 1 BY ITSELF is sufficient to answer the question, but statement 2 by itself is not.

(B) Statement 2 BY ITSELF is sufficient to answer the question, but statement 1 by itself is not.

(C) Statements 1 and 2 TAKEN TOGETHER are sufficient to answer the question, but NEITHER statement BY ITSELF is sufficient.

(D) Either statement BY ITSELF is sufficient to answer the question.

(E) Statements 1 and 2 TAKEN TOGETHER are NOT sufficient to answer the question. More data pertaining to the problem is necessary.

KSF: One and only one value for X is sufficient.
Data sufficiency questions testing algebra often check to see if you know the difference between "solvability" and "sufficiency". Let's run through the method.
The question: X = ? No tricks here (or so it seems).

Statement 1: $y(x^2 - 9) = 0$
This is one equation with two unknowns. There is thus no way to solve for X. Statement 1 BY ITSELF is not sufficient.

Statement 2: Y doesn't equal zero.
So what. This doesn't tell us anything BY ITSELF about X. Statement 2 is not sufficient.

Statements 1 and 2 TAKEN TOGETHER:
If $y(x^2-9) = 0$ and y doesn't equal zero, then $(x^2 - 9)$ must equal zero. You can solve for X and so Statements 1 and 2 TAKEN TOGETHER are sufficient. The third answer choice is the correct response. Right?

Wrong.

This reasoning is why so many GMAT test-takers get their MBAs from a lesser known university and not Columbia. We know that $(x^2 - 9) = 0$, and so x = 3 OR –3. Having TWO possible values for X is insufficient for the GMAT. Statements 1 and 2 TAKEN TOGETHER are NOT sufficient. The fifth answer choice is the correct response.

GMAT ENGLISH
THE VERBAL SECTION

After you complete the Quantitative section and take a second five minute break, you'll start the final lap. The Verbal Section tests your English-language communication and reasoning skills using three different multiple choice question-types randomly distributed in roughly equal numbers across 41 questions:

- Sentence Correction questions test your ability to identify clear and correct English. You'll need a strong sense of both grammar and the stylistic conventions of quality business English to do well.

- Critical Reasoning questions challenge you to understand, evaluate and manipulate logical prose arguments. Here, you'll have to look past the words to the ideas, good or bad, presented by the author.

- Reading Comprehension questions demand that you quickly and efficiently grasp a challenging passage. To succeed, you'll need to be able to locate facts, trace an author's train of logic, and map the structure of a text – all in a matter of minutes.

As with the Quantitative Section, you'll have 75 minutes for the Verbal Section. Following are explanations, examples and Key Success Factors (KSFs) for each question type.

VERBAL QUESTION-TYPE I: SENTENCE CORRECTION
Sentence Correction questions present a usually knotty sentence with all or a portion underlined. The answer choices present five versions of the underlined portion and your task is to select the best. Note that the first answer choice always repeats the underlined portion of the original sentence. Many believe this question-type tests only grammar and the conventions of Standard Written English. This is not entirely true. You'll need a strong grasp of proper style and a taste for clarity in writing to do well.

1. Like many marriages between Hollywood celebrities, <u>grave difficulties in mergers between well-known companies are often experienced due to jealousy over which partner will receive more attention</u>, both within the partnership and from the outside public.

(A) grave difficulties in mergers between well-known companies are often experienced due to jealousy over which partner will receive more attention.

(B) grave difficulties in well-known company mergers are often experienced due to jealousy over which partner will receive more attention.

(C) mergers between well-known companies often experience grave difficulties due to jealousy over which partner will receive more attention.

(D) mergers between well-known companies often have been experiencing grave difficulties due to jealousy over which partner will receive more attention.

(E) well-known company mergers often have been experiencing grave difficulties due to jealousy over which partner will receive more attention.

KSF: Focus on the answer choices and cancel, cancel, cancel.

Sentence Correction is the most "math-like" question type in Verbal - speed is of the essence, and the best way to gain speed is to exploit the answer choices. The answer set above presents a typical structure. Notice how two choices start with "grave difficulties" and the other three discuss "mergers". This is the GMAT's way of asking you to make an executive decision.

(A) **grave difficulties** in mergers between well-known companies are often experienced due to jealousy over which partner will receive more attention.

(B) **grave difficulties** in well-known company mergers are often experienced due to jealousy over which partner will receive more attention.

(C) **mergers between well-known companies** often experience grave difficulties due to jealousy over which partner will receive more attention.

(D) **mergers between well-known companies** often have been experiencing grave difficulties due to jealousy over which partner will receive more attention.

(E) **well-known company mergers** often have been experiencing grave difficulties due to jealousy over which partner will receive more attention.

What do you need to make that decision? Go back to the original sentence and reread the correction portion. What does the word "Like" signal? A comparison, that's right. What are we comparing? "Marriages" and "Mergers". And so what should, logically, be the first noun mentioned in the answer choice? "Mergers"! Cancel the first and second answer choices.

(A) grave difficulties in mergers between well-known companies are often experienced due to jealousy over which partner will receive more attention.

(B) grave difficulties in well-known company mergers are often experienced due to jealousy over which partner will receive more attention.

But don't stop there. Another comparison shows another key difference:

(C) **mergers between well-known companies** often experience grave difficulties due to jealousy over which partner will receive more attention.

(D) **mergers between well-known companies** often have been experiencing grave difficulties due to jealousy over which partner will receive more attention.

(E) **well-known company mergers** often have been experiencing grave difficulties due to jealousy over which partner will receive more attention

What sounds best tied to "Like marriages between Hollywood celebrities…"? If you said one of the first two choices, then you understand the GMAT grammar principle of parallel structure ("marriages between" is like "mergers between", get it?). Cancel the last choice and compare again.

(C) mergers between well-known companies often **experience** grave difficulties due to jealousy over which partner will receive more attention.

(D) mergers between well-known companies often **have been experiencing** grave difficulties due to jealousy over which partner will receive more attention.

(E) well-known company mergers often have been experiencing grave difficulties due to jealousy over which partner will receive more attention.

Do busy executives have time to read "have been experiencing"? Is it grammatically correct? "No" on both counts. Cancel the choice and by elimination, you have the right answer.

Admittedly, that was a pretty easy question. If you're feeling Shakespearean (or simply lucky), try the following.

2. Each and every one a Nobel Laureate, Toni Morrison, William Faulkner, Albert Camus and Gunther Grass, these writers' novels have been sharp social critiques and have been seeking ways to create new spaces wherein communities can probe societal ills and lay the basis for social healing to take place.

(A) Each and every one a Nobel Laureate, Toni Morrison, William Faulkner, Albert Camus and Gunther Grass, these writers' novels have been sharp social critiques and have been seeking ways to create new spaces wherein communities can probe societal ills and lay the basis for social healing to take place.

(B) Each and every one a Nobel Laureate, Toni Morrison, William Faulkner, Albert Camus and Gunther Grass, they have been sharp social critics in their novels and seekers of ways to create new spaces in their writings wherein communities can probe societal ills and lay the basis for social healing to take place.

(C) Toni Morrison, William Faulkner, Albert Camus and Gunther Grass, each and every one a Nobel Laureate, these writers have been sharp social critics in their novels and have been seeking ways to create new spaces in their writings wherein communities can probe societal ills and lay the basis for social healing to take place.

(D) The novels of Nobel Laureates, Toni Morrison, William Faulkner, Albert Camus and Gunther Grass, sharply criticize society and seek to create new spaces wherein communities can probe societal ills and lay the basis for social healing to take place.

(E) Communities can probe societal ills and lay the basis for social healing to take place in Nobel Laureates', Toni Morrison, William Faulkner, Albert Camus and Gunther Grass, novels sharply critical of society and seeking to create new spaces.

KSF: The GMAT likes its Sentence Correction SHORT, SHARP and SIMPLE.

So when in doubt or under time pressure, go for the shorter choices. In the question above, which choices are the shortest? The last two. Let's compare them. Read anything awkward?

(D) The novels of Nobel Laureates, Toni Morrison, William Faulkner, Albert Camus and Gunther Grass, sharply criticize society and seek to create new spaces wherein communities can probe societal ills and lay the basis for social healing to take place.

(E) Communities can probe societal ills and lay the basis for social healing to take place in Nobel Laureates', Toni Morrison, William Faulkner, Albert Camus and Gunther Grass, **novels sharply critical of society and seeking to create new spaces**.

The entire last answer choice is awkward, but the bold text is particularly bad. Notice that your ear, and not your grammatical knowledge, was all you needed to spot a problem. Cancel that choice. Now, do you really want to invest time in the other, long, long choices, or does the fourth sound good? If you said it sounds good, you're not only right, but you've also saved yourself valuable time for later questions. That's smart test-taking!

Incidentally, the first three answer choices are wrong because they each have an unnecessary phrase, "each and every one...." As we said above, the GMAT likes its Sentence Correction downsized.

VERBAL QUESTION-TYPE II: CRITICAL REASONING

A second question-type is Critical Reasoning. You'll be asked to understand, analyze and manipulate a text-based logical argument. Typical questions ask you to identify: an argument's conclusion and evidence, an assumption made by the author, an addition to the argument that would either strengthen it or weaken it, or even an additional statement that can be inferred from the argument. The level of English is advanced, so expect plenty of tough vocabulary, be it in the opening text (the "stimulus"), the assigned task (the "question stem") or the answer choices. The correct answer is the one that best fulfils the task presented in the question stem. Think of Critical Reasoning as the verbal analogue to Data Sufficiency. Both test your reasoning and judgement.

3. Some advisors to the American President urge that next year's Federal budget include sizeable provisions for foreign aid to the Asian countries worst hit by the economic crisis. A number of American senators, however, have vowed to vote down this measure saying a large influx of American funds will only encourage a rebirth of the corruption between Asian governments and big business that was, according to many economists, a primary cause of the crisis in these countries.

Which of the following most weakens the senators' argument?
   (A) The aid will economically and politically strengthen those worst hit by the crisis, labourers and the emerging middle classes, who are uniformly opposed to corruption between government and big business.
   (B) Some economists believe that corruption was but one of many causes of the Asian economic crisis.
   (C) Many international organizations have claimed there is an alarming risk of famine and political instability in the worst hit countries.
   (D) Much of the foreign aid sent to these countries in the 1970's was secretly funnelled to corporations with close personal ties to the government to support large-scale business development.
   (E) The current high value of the dollar compared to the crisis countries' currencies will increase the relative value of American-provided foreign aid.

KSF: Read first, identify your boundaries second, and only then reason!

Remember our discussion of subject "boundaries" in the AWA section above? Both Critical Reasoning and Reading Comprehension constantly ask test-takers to locate and respect the boundaries set by a text. In a Critical Reasoning question, the very first boundary is the question stem itself:

Which of the following most weakens the senators' argument?

Well, what's the senators' argument? Check out the highlighted text below:

Some advisors to the American President urge that next year's Federal budget include sizeable provisions for foreign aid to the Asian countries worst hit by the economic crisis. A number of American senators, however, have vowed to vote down this measure, saying a large influx of American funds will only encourage a rebirth of the corruption between Asian governments and big business that was, according to many economists, a primary cause of the crisis in these countries.

Since we want to weaken their argument, the correct answer choice must attack the senators' reasoning. Which answer choices discuss corruption? Cancel those that don't.

(A) The aid will economically and politically strengthen those worst hit by the crisis, laborers and the emerging middle classes, who are uniformly opposed to corruption between government and big business

(B) Some economists believe that corruption was but one of many causes of the Asian economic crisis.

(C) Many international organizations have claimed there is an alarming risk of famine and political instability in the worst hit countries.

(D) Much of the foreign aid sent to these countries in the 1970's was secretly funnelled to corporations with close personal ties to the government to support large-scale business development.

(E) The current high value of the dollar compared to the crisis countries' currencies will increase the relative value of American-provided foreign aid.

Of the remaining choices, only one will weaken the senators' argument. The others must either strengthen it or remain neutral. Let's look at the first:

(A) The aid will economically and politically strengthen those worst hit by the crisis, laborers and the emerging middle classes, who are uniformly opposed to corruption between government and big business.

If the aid helps people opposed to corruption, than the senators are wrong. You needn't go further. This is the right answer.

Now let's try another question:

4. A group of European automobile racing enthusiasts has organized a boycott against popular motoring and motorcycling package tours of the American West. Claiming the tours' promotional literature amounts to false advertising, the racing enthusiasts argue that such tours cannot provide the "true motoring pleasure" promised by the tour companies. After all, say the racing enthusiasts, how can a European motorist experience true motoring pleasure in the United States when the American highway speed limit is so much lower than those in European countries?

Which of the following is an assumption made by the automobile racing enthusiasts staging the boycott?

(A) American motorists prefer to drive on the highway at slower speeds.

(B) The companies offering the package tours are not staffed by racing enthusiasts.

(C) Automobile drivers are more likely to drive at high speeds than are motorcyclists.

(D) Speed limits in the United States are enforced often enough to pose a serious risk that speeding motorists will be ticketed by the police.

(E) The amount of traffic on congested European highways is not so great as to limit the viable driving speed well below the posted speed limit.

KSF: Memorize this – an ASSUMPTION is the unstated but necessary logical link between an author's conclusion and evidence.
The question above asks for "an assumption made by" the speed racers on boycott. To find their assumption, we first need to go into the text to locate their **conclusion** and **evidence**.

A group of European automobile racing enthusiasts has organised a boycott against popular motoring and motorcycling package tours of the American West. Claiming the tours' promotional literature amounts to false advertising, the racing enthusiasts argue that **such tours cannot provide the "true motoring pleasure" promised by the tour companies**. After all, say the racing enthusiasts, how can a European motorist experience true motoring pleasure in the United States when the American highway speed limit is so much lower than those in European countries?

Stated more simply, "Europeans can't get true motoring pleasure from the tours because the American highway speed limit is too low". Hmmm... Readers devoted to "real motoring pleasure" probably already see an assumption involving speed limits. The rest of us can look again at the answer choices.

(A) American motorists prefer to drive on the highway at slower speeds.

(B) The companies offering the package tours are not staffed by racing enthusiasts.

(C) Automobile drivers are more likely to drive at high speeds than are motorcyclists.

(D) Speed limits in the United States are enforced often enough to pose a serious risk that speeding motorists will be ticketed by the police.

(E) The amount of traffic on congested European highways is not so great as to limit the viable driving speed well below the posted speed limit.

Since an assumption is a necessary part of the argument, the right answer must be true for the Europeans' argument to be valid. Which answer matches the criteria? The fourth! Speed limits are meaningless if not enforced by the cops, therefore enforcement is necessary for the low American speed limits to take away from Europeans' driving pleasure.

By this point you're probably asking yourself if an MBA is really worth Critical Reasoning. Hey, be thankful! The test for would-be lawyers (the LSAT) includes 50 Critical Reasoning questions....

VERBAL QUESTION-TYPE III: READING COMPREHENSION

Reading Comprehension rounds out the Verbal question-types. When you face these questions, the computer screen will post a text of 200 to 300 words on the left side of the screen. You must use the text (and your reading skills) to answer the three to five questions that appear, one at a time, on the right side of the screen. Once you have finished the questions for a text, you won't see that text again. Rather, later in the section, you'll be given a new text and set of questions.

The goal of this question type is to see how well you can digest a lot of new and challenging information presented in a prose format. Imagine you're a consultant new to a case. Your boss drops a load of industry reports on your desk and asks you to go through them to get the key details and arguments for your first meeting with the client... in an hour's time. You'll need to be a very efficient, discerning reader!

The texts themselves are drawn from obscure academic journals in the fields of business, the sciences and the humanities/social sciences. However, you won't need any specialized knowledge of the subjects to do well – all the information needed to answer correctly is in the text itself. Here's a particularly difficult example:

Professor Kenneth M. Stampp, in the final chapters of his thorough, comprehensive study of slavery, The Peculiar Institution, convincingly explodes the myth of the "benign" plantation slave holder and argues that the greatest reason for the stubborn survival of slavery deep into the 19th century was its profitability rather than the slave holders' supposed paternal commitment to their slaves. To buttress his case, Stampp attacks two of the strongest arguments made by slave holders and their apologists. The first, the high debt levels carried by many of the great plantation owners, is claimed by those favorable to the plantation owners as proof of the financial burden shouldered by slave holders committed to caring for often unproductive slaves. But in Stampp's careful analysis of plantation account books, this high level of debt is shown to be more a sign of plantation owners' supreme confidence in their future sales and the wisdom of capital investment in clearing new lands than a symptom of inherent unprofitability. Indeed, with no shareholders to please, the slave owners were free to make the most of their businesses by taking advantage of the sizeable credit their success afforded them.

The second argument involves the substantial numbers of slaves supported on Virginia tobacco plantations long after these lands, exhausted by tobacco's demands on soil fertility, ceased to yield sizeable harvests. Slave holders and their apologists pointed to this phenomenon as evidence of the Virginia planters' concern for, and commitment to, their slave communities. Why else would a planter keep so many slaves on low-yielding land? But Stampp shows these same planters, far from being paternal, were encouraging the population growth of their slave communities so as to have a sizeable stock of slaves to sell in the South's internal slave trade. After the final closing of Charleston as a slave port in the early years of the 19th century, the burgeoning demand for slaves in the developing cotton belt had to be satisfied internally. The Virginia planters with their expanding surplus of slaves were ideally situated to make the most of the internal trade in their "product". And so they did, reaping rich gains by separating families and breaking apart tight-knit slave communities.

Time management is an enormous challenge in Reading Comprehension. To have enough time for the questions and not sacrifice time elsewhere in the Verbal Section, you'll need to be able to get the gist of the passage in only two or three minutes. This may seem crazy compared to the amount of detail in a passage like the one above, but it is actually a much more productive, successful strategy than trying to swallow all the facts in a text. The reason for this leads to our first Key Success Factor:

KSF: in the GMAT Reading Comprehension, THINK GLOBAL.

The GMAT test-makers want to see if you understand *how*, and especially *why*, authors develop their arguments in prose. As a result, what an author *says* is much less important than what an author *does*. Furthermore, what one line of a text does is much less important than what a paragraph, or the whole text, accomplishes. We're talking structure here, rather than content. And reading for a text's global structure is crucial to Reading Comprehension. Take a look at the following, classic GMAT "THINK GLOBAL" question:

5. The author's primary purpose in this passage is to:
  (A) assert that slaveholders often lost money through financial mismanagement.
  (B) defend the actions of the Virginia planters in the face of the loss of fertility of their tobacco lands.
  (C) critique a point of view in favor of the slaveholders by supporting a scholarly work.
  (D) question the financial benefits of slavery.
  (E) demonstrate the wisdom of carrying sizeable debt loads when that debt is invested in capital improvements.

If we're going to find the "primary purpose" of the entire passage, where should we look? Common sense (and a little knowledge of standard GMAT practices) says to check the beginning of the passage. Here it is:

Professor Kenneth M. Stampp, in the final chapters of his thorough, comprehensive study of slavery, The Peculiar Institution, convincingly explodes the myth of the "benign" plantation slave holder and argues that the greatest reason for the stubborn survival of slavery deep into the 19th century was its profitability rather than the slave holders' supposed paternal commitment to their slaves. To buttress his case, Stampp attacks two of the strongest arguments made by slave holders and their apologists.

Now run through your journalist's questions again. Who is the author talking about? Some musty old "Professor Kenneth M. Stampp". What does Prof. Stampp do, according to our author? He writes a book that "convincingly explodes the myth" that slavery wasn't so bad. How does Stampp explode the myth? According to the author, "Stampp attacks two of the strongest argument made by slave holders…." Does the author like Stampp's book? Sure. The author calls it a "thorough, comprehensive study." Now put this in simple terms:

"The author of the passage praises Stampp's book, saying it refutes the "myth" of the "benign slave holder". Believe it or not, we've just answered the first question above. Look at the answer choices again and choose the one that best matches our phrase above. Also, ask yourself, "What does each answer choice discuss?"

The author's primary purpose in this passage is to

(A) assert that **slaveholders often lost money** through financial mismanagement.

(B) **defend the actions of the Virginia planters** in the face of the loss of fertility of their tobacco lands.

(C) **critique a point of view** in favour of the slaveholders by **supporting a scholarly work.**

(D) **question the financial benefits** of slavery.

(E) **demonstrate the wisdom of carrying sizeable debt loads** when that debt is invested in capital improvements.

Notice how the wrong choices echo words and phrases elsewhere in the text, but don't ever really touch the author's main point. Now let's jump back into the text and try a second question.

KSF: In GMAT Reading Comprehension, ACT LOCAL.

While you can't memorize all the details in a text, you can prepare the terrain for detailed work whenever and wherever the questions demand. This means skimming through the text just well enough to note the author's key points, references, conclusions and transitions. With the text roughly mapped out, you are then prepared to "act locally" in that specific portion of the text relevant to a question. Take a look at the following question:

According to the author, which of the following best explains the Virginia planters' willingness to support large numbers of slave on low-yielding tobacco plantations?

(A) Tobacco farming is highly labor intensive and so required comparatively many slaves per acre of tilled land.

(B) The close of Charleston as a slave port cut the Virginia planters off from their established export slave markets.

(C) The Virginia planters enjoyed separating slave families and dismantling slave communities.

(D) The Virginia planters were concerned for their slaves' welfare and were therefore willing to subsidize a surplus in labor.

(E) The Virginia planters saw their slaves as a valuable commodity in high demand in the developing Cotton Belt.

Where does the author discuss the Virginia planters? In the second paragraph, reproduced below with the first reference highlighted.

The second argument involves the **substantial numbers of slaves supported on Virginia tobacco plantations long after these lands, exhausted by tobacco's demands on soil fertility, ceased to yield sizeable harvests**. Slave holders and their apologists pointed to this phenomenon as evidence of the Virginia planters' concern for, and commitment to, their slave communities. Why else would a planter keep so many slaves on low-yielding land? But Stampp shows these same planters, far from being paternal, were encouraging the population growth of their slave communities so as to have a sizeable stock of slaves to sell in the South's internal slave trade. After the final closing of Charleston as a slave port in the early years of the 19th century, the burgeoning demand for slaves in the developing cotton belt had to be satisfied internally. The Virginia planters with their expanding surplus of slaves were ideally situated to make the most of the internal trade in their "product". And so they did, reaping rich gains by separating families and breaking apart tight-knit slave communities.

So, the question asks why Virginia planters would keep slaves even when the land couldn't support sufficient crops. One reason is highlighted below. Is it the correct one?

The second argument involves the substantial numbers of slaves supported on Virginia tobacco plantations long after these lands, exhausted by tobacco's demands on soil fertility, ceased to yield sizeable harvests. **Slave holders and their apologists pointed to this phenomenon as evidence of the Virginia planters' concern for, and commitment to, their slave communities**. Why else would a planter keep so many slaves on low-yielding land? But Stampp shows these same planters, far from being paternal, were encouraging the population growth of their slave communities so as to have a sizeable stock of slaves to sell in the South's internal slave trade. After the final closing of Charleston as a slave port in the early years of the 19th century, the burgeoning demand for slaves in the developing cotton belt had to be satisfied internally. The Virginia planters with their expanding surplus of slaves were ideally situated to make the most of the internal trade in their "product". And so they did, reaping rich gains by separating families and breaking apart tight-knit slave communities.

No. This is a classic GMAT trap. The question says, "According to the author…" but whose point of view is in bold above? The slave holders and their apologists. Rather than fall for this point-of-view trap, work further through the text and look for the author's view point.

The second argument involves the substantial numbers of slaves supported on Virginia tobacco plantations long after these lands, exhausted by tobacco's demands on soil fertility, ceased to yield sizeable harvests. Slave holders and their apologists pointed to this phenomenon as evidence of the Virginia planter's concern for, and commitment to, their slave communities. Why else would a planter keep so many slaves on low-yielding land? But Stampp shows these same planters, far from being paternal, were encouraging the population growth of their slave communities so as to have a sizeable stock of slaves to sell in the South's internal slave trade. After the final closing of Charleston as a slave port in the early years of the 19th century, **the burgeoning demand for slaves in the developing cotton belt had to be satisfied internally. The Virginia planters with their expanding surplus of slaves were ideally situated to make the most of the internal trade in their "product". And so they did, reaping rich gains by separating families and breaking apart tight-knit slave communities**.

Now that we've got the right portion of the text, we can find the answer choice that best matches it.

According to the author, which of the following best explains the Virginia planters willingness to support large numbers of slaves on low-yielding tobacco plantations?

(A) Tobacco farming is highly labor intensive and so required comparatively many slaves per acre of tilled land.

(B) The close of Charleston as a slave port cut the Virginia planters off from their established export slave markets.

(C) The Virginia planters enjoyed separating slave families and dismantling slave communities.

(D) The Virginia planters were concerned for their slaves' welfare and were therefore willing to subsidize a surplus in labor.

(E) The Virginia planters saw their slaves as a valuable commodity in high demand in the developing Cotton Belt.

Verbal final note: As with Quantitative, Verbal question types are mixed randomly (except for the questions clumped together with a Reading Comprehension text) so you'll have to switch gears quickly from one to another. And given the difficult vocabulary presented throughout the section, answering all 41 questions in 75 minutes is quite a challenge.

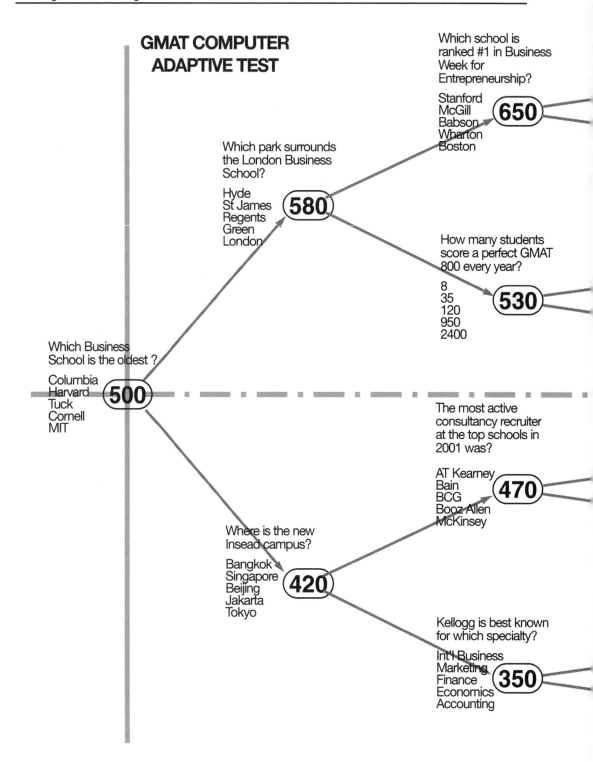

GMAT COMPUTER ADAPTIVE TEST

Which school is ranked #1 in Business Week for Entrepreneurship?

Stanford
McGill
Babson
Wharton
Boston

650

Which park surrounds the London Business School?

Hyde
St James
Regents
Green
London

580

How many students score a perfect GMAT 800 every year?

8
35
120
950
2400

530

Which Business School is the oldest ?

Columbia
Harvard
Tuck
Cornell
MIT

500

The most active consultancy recruiter at the top schools in 2001 was?

AT Kearney
Bain
BCG
Booz Allen
McKinsey

470

Where is the new Insead campus?

Bangkok
Singapore
Beijing
Jakarta
Tokyo

420

Kellogg is best known for which specialty?

Int'l Business
Marketing
Finance
Economics
Accounting

350

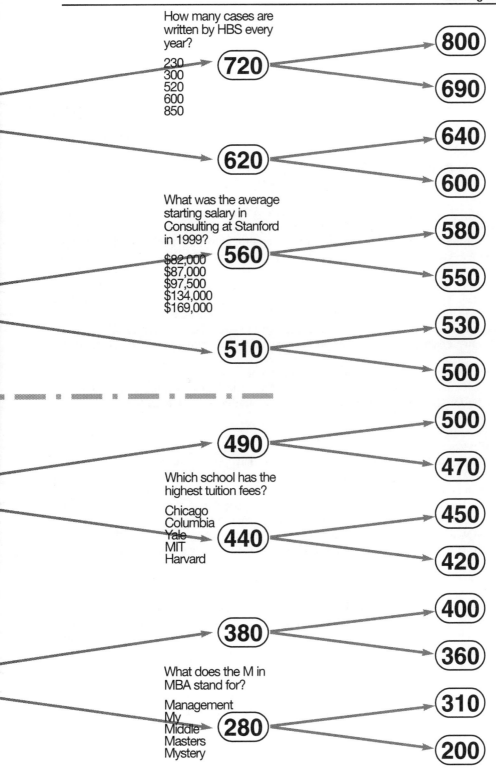

How many cases are
written by HBS every
year?

230
300
520
600
850

720

800
690

620

640
600

What was the average
starting salary in
Consulting at Stanford
in 1999?

$82,000
$87,000
$97,500
$134,000
$169,000

560

580
550

510

530
500

490

500
470

Which school has the
highest tuition fees?

Chicago
Columbia
Yale
MIT
Harvard

440

450
420

380

400
360

What does the M in
MBA stand for?

Management
My
Middle
Masters
Mystery

280

310
200

SCORING THE TEST
No means no; Yes means five years

Once you've finished the Verbal section the test is complete, but you'll have one last question to answer. The computer will ask, "Do you wish to see your score?" If you click on "yes" (twice to be exact) you'll see your Quantitative, Verbal and Combined scores. Such a quick turnaround should not be surprising – think of it as instant gratification. But as with other forms of instant gratification, the effects are long lasting. Your results go into the ETS databank, where they will stay for five years. Each time you send a score report to a business school, all results during the past five years will appear on your report. There's no way to hide a poor test result!

If you don't reach your target score, you can take another GMAT as of the next calendar month. Keep in mind that most of the top programs will consider the higher of two GMAT scores. Some will even consider a third set of results. But none of the top programs will take seriously a strong score that shows on a report next to three, four or more weak scores.

If you decide you don't wish to see your score, click on "no" and the computer will cancel your results and your performance will not be logged in the ETS databank. Your record will show you took the test, but no school will ever know how you did. Neither will you – it is impossible to cancel the exam once you've seen your scores. Because the exam is expensive and you'll be (hopefully) well prepared when you take it, you probably shouldn't cancel your score unless your exam becomes a clear disaster.

The scoring mechanism and strategies to make the most of it

So much for the administration and structure of the GMAT. The GMAT's sophisticated scoring mechanism may be far from the scoring standards you're familiar with, but understanding it is crucial to your success.

And now the CAT part...

To begin with, the multiple choice sections, Quantitative and Verbal, are adaptive (hence the acronym GMAT CAT, Computer Adaptive Test). The first question you see in each section is "pegged" at the 50th percentile, i.e. 50% of test takers are expected to get this question incorrect. If you answer correctly, the computer follows up with a more difficult question, pegged at a higher percentile, as demonstrated by the diagram on the previous page. An incorrect answer means the following question will be "easier" or pegged at a lower percentile. As you navigate through the section, your score is continually adjusted up and down as you get questions right and wrong. Wherever you end up at the end of a section becomes your final score. A great score, say 95th percentile, thus means that the questions you reached at the end of the section were so hard, 95% of test takers were expected to get them incorrect. How do the test makers know what difficulty level to assign individual questions? Well, they use you and all other GMAT test takers as laboratory rats. When you take the exam, about seven of the 37 Quantitative and ten of the 41 Verbal questions you face will be new, "non-scored" questions, distributed at random. Your responses to these questions do not count toward your score in any way, but they do contribute to a statistical sample used to determine the real difficulty level. Once the sample is large enough to be valid, the questions are folded into the real test question pool. For you on test day, this means close to 25% of the questions you face promise absolutely no return on your time investment – if you could identify them, you might as well guess on these questions immediately and save some precious minutes. The catch, of course, is that the non-scored questions aren't identified and look just like the real thing. You'll have to assume each question is probably real.

Educational imperialism I

The philosophy behind the CAT scoring method is based on two assumptions. The first is that you possess a stable, objectively verifiable skill level that can be determined through testing. Thus, the test makers have designed the CAT program as a sophisticated search mechanism, one that continually adjusts and refines its assessment of you until it pinpoints your level just right. If the computer does its job well, by the end of the section you'll be at a level where a small change in difficulty up or down results in, respectively, an incorrect or correct response.

But this is an ambitious goal given the small data sample it draws from you – that is, your responses to only 37 Quantitative and 41 Verbal questions. As a result of this small sample size and the wide range of difficulty included in the test, the computer must act quickly, within the first five to ten questions, to get a rough approximation of your score. It then "saves" the rest of the test to refine and verify your level. For test takers, the implications are immense, so tattoo the following KSF on the inside of your eyelids.

GLOBAL KSF: Not all questions promise the same return on your time investment, so prioritize!
During those first five to ten questions, the computer adjusts your score in big jumps as it tries to approximate your level. Getting that first question right can earn you from 50 to 100 points straight away. Conversely, an incorrect response to question #1 can drop your score an equal amount. With each additional question, the score movement diminishes as the computer zeros in on your proper score. By the end of the exam, each individual question moves your score very, very little.

So where are you going to focus your time and energies? Up front, of course. You should consider spending up to three minutes per question (on the first five or so) if needed to make sure you get off to a strong start. This isn't the place to make a stupid calculation error or misread a question! Take your time, double-check your work, and be prepared for the questions to get very difficult, very quickly, if you get the first few correct. If you start with six or seven correct answers in a row, you'll find yourself in the 700 score range before you complete the first ten.

Educational imperialism II

The second scoring assumption is that the famous bell curve is an accurate, valid representation of the distribution of skill levels across the GMAT test-taking population. Thus, the GMAT is designed and managed to produce a bell curve-shaped distribution of scores across the overall scale (200 – 800) and the Quantitative and Verbal scales (both 0 – 60). This is also why scores are coupled with percentile levels. A 500 is roughly pegged at the 50th percentile, a 650 at the 90th percentile, and a 750 and above at above the 99th percentile. As you can see from the big jump in percentiles from a 500 to a 650, a little movement in the middle of the score range has a huge effect. Movement at the upper limit of the range has proportionally less of an effect. Regardless, behind the percentages lie thousands of real people whose scores are constantly compared. In short, our story of Alain, Matt and the Bear is the story of the bell curve.

For top MBA candidates, the bell curve is also relevant to the separate Quantitative and Verbal scores. Don't expect Wharton to let you near one of their finance classes with a Quantitative score much below 40, even if your Verbal score is a perfect 60 and your overall score quite high. Although programs differ in their score expectations, a safe goal is to clear 40 for both sections (90% territory). If you have a finance or engineering background, you should push yourself to reach at least 45 on the Quantitative section.

GLOBAL KSF: Finish the test, even if you have to guess.
Some people needlessly fall victim to bell curve dynamics. For instance, some believe a good strategy is to do the first 10 questions or so, (taking care to get them right, of course) and then quit the test. It's the Michael Jordan "go out early and on top" syndrome. It DOES NOT WORK.

Others take the logic of our preceding KSF too far. They reason that since each question offers a diminishing return, the strategy applied to the first questions should be used on every question - i.e. you should never move on to the next question without having a satisfactory response to the current question. These people invariably get hung up on tough questions early in the test and rarely get past question 25 or 30. They also rarely get good scores. This "perfectionist" strategy DOES NOT WORK.

These strategies fail to account for the unanswered question penalty built into the test. The bell curve statistics are set based on the complete number of questions answered over the full 75 minutes per section. If you run out of time or don't complete the full sample, the computer assumes you were testing at a level above your "true" one and drops your score accordingly. The penalty is a stiff one too. The computer assumes each unanswered question is wrong, and then adds a further penalty on top of that. Fail to answer the last 10 or so questions on each section, and you'll see your score drop over 100 points. Try explaining that to Kellogg!

The upshot is that guessing is better than not completing the test. Once the clock drops below five minutes left in each section, be very, very careful about where you are and how much time you have left. Even better, consider guessing strategically at various stages of the exam so as to set a good pace for yourself – spending five minutes on a question early essentially means sacrificing at least two questions later in the exam. Ask yourself, "Is it worth it?" and "Am I managing my time well?"

Even the AWA gets the treatment
Scoring on the AWA (the essays, remember?) is very different and even sports a human element. Furthermore, the AWA score is reported separately and has no bearing on the all important 200 – 800 combined score. Once you complete your test, your essays speed out through the ETS network in two different directions. One set of essays is processed by computer software designed to evaluate your writing according to pre-programmed criteria. The computer will then assign each essay a score on a scale of 0 – 6. The other set of essays is emailed to a professional grader, usually an English professor from some minor university, who swiftly reads and scores your work using the same scale and criteria. If the computer and human grader differ greatly in their assessments, a second human is brought into the mix to referee and make the final call. The final step is to average all four scores (two for each essay) and round the result to the nearest half point. This becomes the AWA score included on the score report sent to your programs. In addition, copies of your essays are also sent.

Score distribution again follows the bell curve with the 50th percentile located between a 4.0 and a 4.5. Thus, for non-native English speakers, scores of at least 4.0 are perfectly acceptable and a 5.0 or better represents a superlative effort. There is some debate about the significance of the AWA in the admissions process. In theory, the score and essays provide admissions committees with valuable information about your communication skills – information surely useful when comparing two candidates who are otherwise similar. The AWA essays also give admissions officers a point of reference if they doubt the authorship of a candidate's admissions essays.

In practice however, admissions officers have little time to sift through thousands of AWA essays, and the score itself is less important to than the combined score. Nevertheless, a very high score is likely to be noticed…as will a very low one. Best to take the AWA seriously and embrace it as yet another opportunity to show how great a candidate you are. At the very least, a 4.0 or better shows you communicate more effectively in writing than about half of the people taking the test.

GLOBAL KSF: for great GMAT test takers, the exam is an opportunity to implement a strategy developed long before test day.

This should come as no surprise. Rather, it is the logical culmination of all the KSFs in this chapter. A good strategy will address optimal time management, question prioritisation, approach to the essays, even the proper use of scratch paper. Above all, it will give you the confidence and poise for test day that comes from being intelligently well-prepared. A Top 20 program demands, and deserves, nothing less.

A difficult issue: cultural bias

For better or worse, non-Americans often believe they face a cultural handicap on the GMAT. It's a contentious issue. ETS has invested sizeable sums of money to make their exams as culturally "blind" as possible. And of course each year, the top business schools sport incoming classes stuffed with non-American members of the "Over 700 GMAT club". But in some ways, cultural bias is inescapable. Language is an obvious factor. Speakers of native "American" should logically hold an advantage, even over speakers of the British English. Another advantage is that Americans prepare and take GMAT-style multiple choice exams at several stages of their academic career. For them, the GMAT holds few surprises.

What is this worth? Some admissions officers have actually developed and applied scaling to offset cultural bias, e.g. a 620 for a Danish test taker might be considered equal to a 650 for an American. But this is by no means universal. And for a school like Stanford, with many, many candidates to choose from, it's meaningless.

In fact, given the intense competition just among Europeans, the most constructive approach might well be to abandon altogether the concept of cultural bias. After all, once at HBS you'll no longer think in those terms, you'll be thinking "cultural adaptation" instead. Well, why not start now? The better you culturally adapt to the GMAT, the better you'll be able to leverage your own cultural strengths… and the more of a competitive advantage you'll enjoy. Here are your starting points:

- Be aware of your culture's educational roots: intellectually, you're largely a product of the school system in which you were educated. To excel, you've had to acquire knowledge, skills, work habits and values that may be quite different from those rewarded by the GMAT. In mathematics, there are less than 10 problems for an exam lasting as long as the entire GMAT – hardly comparable to the GMAT's own 37 problems in 75 minutes.
So perform a SWOT analysis of your own educational background. What habits and values made someone successful? How fully have you adopted them? What are the Strengths, Weaknesses, Opportunities and Threats that come with each vis-à-vis the GMAT? This alone will give you a big head start.

- Be aware of the classic American curriculum: the GMAT's math and grammar content has been developed based on the standard American high school curriculum. Naturally, the concepts it tests, and more importantly, the keys to a quick and correct response, will vary somewhat from your own schooling. Ever heard of a 5:12:13 right triangle? Your American competitors learned it in high school, and the concept is tested constantly on the GMAT.

But don't panic. It's pretty easy to review all the standard GMAT math and grammar concepts. Keep in mind however, the differences from your own knowledge base. Maintain a journal or log of these differences and review them often. On test day, you don't want to forget something all the Americans know by heart.

Incidentally, remember our second problem solving question above? It was based on a right triangle with a hypotenuse of 6.5, a leg of length 6, and a leg of unknown length. You probably set it up as $x^2 + 6^2 = 6.5^2$. Solving for X would take some time without a calculator, right? Not if you saw that x:6:6.5 is proportional to 5:12:13, a set of integer values that fits perfectly the Pythagorean Theorem. Applying the proportion makes it easy to solve for x: x = 2.5 and you've answered the question in seconds without calculating.

- Be GMAT aware: as you wade back into math and English to prepare yourself for the test, you'll be tempted to fall back into a classic "student" frame of mind, just like you had in university and high school. Don't! The GMAT is a unique creature, and as we've already seen, it has its own Key Success Factors. Put more brutally, a score of 700 has very little to do with how much math and English you've learned. It has everything to do with how many questions (and their location) you get correct on test day. In classic American fashion, the GMAT isn't about what you know, it's about what you can do. This is perhaps the biggest adjustment to make.

- Be self-aware: culture-based arguments are fine if we're educators or sociologists researching the testing industry. But the GMAT is about you above all. Your strategy, how you implement, and what adjustments you make, should all be based on a deep understanding of your personal strengths and weaknesses. Be honest with yourself about your problem areas and work on them. Just as importantly, know where you're good. After all, a 700 is built on your strengths rather than your weaknesses. In what subject areas will your 700 come from?

HOW BEST TO PREPARE

We hope this chapter has convinced you of the need to prepare for the GMAT… and the rewards for doing it well. For a lucky few, that preparation will involve just a practice test or two before going on to score a 750 on the real thing. Most people, however, will have to invest a fair number of hours at home with self-study books and software, at a preparation school, or with a private instructor before they feel confident they can post the score they want. Here are the minimum steps to take in your preparation:

1. Carefully read the GMAT Bulletin front to back.
2. Research your schools' average incoming GMAT scores to get a feel for your target score (this book has all the answers!).
3. Take a reputable practice test before scheduling the real thing. You'll need a baseline score from

which to gauge the amount of time you'll need to invest in preparation, and your strengths and weaknesses. Nearly all GMAT prep books include full-length tests. Some test centers offer free mock GMATs.

4. Based on this diagnostic test (and perhaps in consultation with a GMAT pro) plot out your own plan of study and training.
5. Even if your practice test score was a perfect 800, make certain you do at least some training on computer to familiarize yourself with the CAT interface and timing.
6. Schedule your preparation so that it won't conflict with your application essay writing. Some "intensive" preparation programs offer great returns in only a week or two of work, and so you might be tempted to put off your prep until, say, December before your January deadline. Try to avoid procrastinating. Your GMAT score will be good for five years, so why not start now and get it out of the way?

Once you've done the above, take a look at the gap between your practice test score and your target score. If there is no gap, or you exceeded your target score, then congratulations! You're ready to take the test right away.

If there is a gap, spend some time meditating on the choice between self-study using one or more of the many GMAT test preparation books on the market, and guided study in a test preparation center. Below, we discuss Strengths and Weaknesses of each approach, and the qualities to look for in a good product. We also list some of the key titles/centers on the market.

(1) GREAT GMAT PREPARATION: BOOKS

In terms of size, weight, and overall sex appeal, a typical GMAT preparation book is about the same as a first year MBA accounting text. What a horrible creature! However, few prospective MBAs escape using one of these mega-page monsters, and like Beauty and the Beast, many successful applicants eventually learn to love their long-time preparation companions. So close your eyes and take a deep breath; it's not that bad....

Strengths

- Ready when you are – Busy young professionals such as yourself often don't have regular schedules. The best thing about a book is that it can adapt to your time demands, no matter how crazy.
- Go where you go – Books are portable. Next time you go on a business trip, take a look to see how many young professionals are cranking out GMAT questions in their economy class seats (those in first class already have their MBAs).
- Concise review – Nearly all of the math and grammar concepts routinely tested on the GMAT can be (and are) well covered in the subject review sections of preparation books. If you've had a solid, balanced education, this will be all the review you need.
- Plenty of practice – Most prep books offer hundreds of practice questions.
- Software – Most prep books now offer CD ROMs with training exercises and practice tests that help you master the GMAT CAT interface. Some of these CD ROMS are quite sophisticated.
- Cheap (relatively), of course!

Weaknesses

- Can't talk back – Books can tell you when you've missed a question, but they can't explain why you, personally, keep missing a particular question type. This lack of personal feedback is a crucial issue that can make the difference between a 50 point score improvement and one of a 100 points or more.

- More knowledge than process – Books are great at reviewing the laws of algebra or the rules for using a particular verb tense. They are much weaker, however, at explaining how to save time on the GMAT by applying strategies and methods to specific question types. As a result, test-takers who prepared using books often learn a lot without necessarily increasing their scores. Remember, the GMAT isn't about what you know; it's about what you can do!
- A bandage rather than deep surgery – If you have a serious weakness in your math educational background, your verbal skills, or your test-taking techniques and composure, a book simply won't have the resources you'll need. Be honest with yourself here.
- Not culturally sensitive – Most preparation books are written for the North American market and make no effort to explain to test-takers from other countries where their competitive (dis)advantages lie. As we've already discussed, we believe these cultural issues can account for many points.

Making the Difference
- Number of questions – The real value of a test prep book is in the practice questions, not the math and grammar review. Check to see how many questions are in the book. Also, compare the questions to those you'll find in the GMAT Bulletin. Are they similar in style, language and difficulty?
- Depth of the software – A good CD ROM should offer more that just an onscreen version of the paper text. Look for features that tie in directly with the CAT.
- Quality of the explanations – A good test prep book won't just explain a right answer. It will explain why the other choices are wrong, and what you can do to get the right answer in as little time as possible. So when you're shopping for books, check out the explanations and ask yourself, "Are these things going to help me, or are they just padding?"

GMAT PREPARATION BOOKS
The following titles represent the best of the material available for the GMAT.

Official Guide for GMAT Review (10th Ed) ETS Books, software at www.gmac.com
List Price: $24.95 Paperback June 2000
Published by the makers of the test, the much needed update of this book has plenty of practice questions and you can download free testing software from the website.

GMAT 2000-2001 Kaplan Book & Cd-Rom
List Price: $37.00 Paperback - 371 pages March 2000
Excellent software with lots of practice questions and explanations. The book provides solid content review for the test as well as strategies for time management. The verbal section could use reinforcement.

Cracking the GMAT 2001 TPR Book & Cd-Rom
List Price: $34.95 Paperback - 432 pages June 2000
The Princeton review tends to focus on the tricks and techniques to help you score higher on test day. Good simulation software, though the book could use more sample questions.

GMAT Prep Course : 2000　　Nova　　　　　　　Book & Cd-Rom
List Price: $29.95　　　　　　Paperback - 608 pages　August 2000
Recent GMAT publisher, producing solid material, though not the strongest software on the market.

Everything You Need to Score High on the GMAT　　Arco　　　　　　Book & Cd Rom
List Price: $16.95　　　　　　Paperback - 580 pages　July 1999
Arco has a good reputation for writing challenging questions for the test.

GMAT : Answers to the Real Essay Questions Arco　　　　　Book
List Price: $14.95　　　　　　Paperback - 320 pages　January 2000
If you're concerned about the Analytical Writing Assessment, this book provides sample answers to all 230 essays on the GMAT.

How to Prepare for the GMAT　　Barrons　　　　Book & CD-Rom
List Price: to be announced　　　Hardback　　　　January 2001
Barrons have been editing test prep books for many years, and the 12th edition is much needed to update their current range of titles.

The Unofficial Guide to the GMAT Cat　IDG　　　　　Book &CD Rom
List Price: $19.95　　　　　　Paperback - 528 pages　November 1999
Despite a few errors, the book has a good question bank, and the software simulates the real test very well.

(2) GREAT GMAT PREPARATION: PREPARATION CENTERS

Okay, we hear you asking yourself, "Do I really have to go back to school just to prepare to go back to school?" And we agree it sounds not only bizarre, but also downright painful. But hey, no pain, no gain. You only get one shot at Stanford's Graduate School of Business, so how badly do you want it?

Strengths
- Personalized feedback – A good training center will help you understand where your individual strengths and weaknesses are and how you can work to improve to get the score you want to go to the school of your choice. Get the picture?
- More than one explanation – A good GMAT prep course will make certain you understand key concepts and strategies by explaining them in different ways, and by reinforcing them at different times. This variety and repetition is a key part of the learning process, and explains why centers routinely post better results than mere training books.
- Methods and strategies – The established centers have over the years acquired vast stores of GMAT "secrets" that will help you understand the test and use appropriate strategies and methods to gain a higher score. In fact, it is these "knowledge assets" that have made companies such as Kaplan so successful.
- Proprietary material – Along with the methods, a good center will provide more practice tests and questions than you will likely have time for. Furthermore, they should offer sophisticated CD ROM and computer training facilities. Don't underestimate the value of a few extra practice tests!
- Motivation – Quality training is as much about motivation as about knowledge or strategies. A good center can provide the kind of atmosphere and personal support you might need to get the most out of yourself.

Weaknesses
- Variable quality – The rising popularity of the MBA has led to a number of new entrants in the field of test preparation. Some of these companies haven't the resources or experience to offer substantial study materials or a truly well-conceived course taught by trained teachers. In fact, some do little more than talk students through an off-the-shelf test prep book. So check carefully. Does the center have its own materials? How experienced are the teachers? A quality center will have nothing to hide!
- Commitment required – No matter how good the course or the instructor, only you can take the actual test. And so if you're going to get your money's worth from a center, you must be prepared to open up your schedule, go to class, and yes, even do your homework. If you simply don't have the time or energy, a training center might not be for you.
- Expensive – Whether it's a one-on-one program over 3 days, or a group course running for 5 to 9 weeks, you're probably looking at close to $1,000 in tuition to prepare for the GMAT. That's a considerable investment, so check out the courses to see if the return they offer is justified. For that kind of money you should get a well-designed course that can be personalized to your needs, professors who know their stuff and know how to teach, and genuine computer adaptive testing. Find out if the school has testimonies from previous students, indicating their score improvements. Not just one or two students, but lots of students, confirming that the program worked for them. And before you write the check, take a free practice test to find out your level. You could be closer to your goals than you think. What did we say? Oh yeah, no pain, no gain! Then again, the typical signing bonus of, say, a Chicago graduate is about 40 times the cost of a GMAT training course. Not a bad return on investment…

Making the Difference
- Quality and amount of material – A poor center will offer you lots of promises and a rather thin workbook. A good center will back up its promises with thick books full of thousands of well-written questions and clear explanations. Be a smart comparison shopper.
- Teachers – A good teacher can make the difference between a 600 and a 700 on the GMAT. Ask for referrals about teachers at the centers you're considering. Look for testimonials from former students. Talk to your friends who have taken courses. Check to see that the center you're considering trains its teachers.
- Flexibility to meet your needs – Can your center accommodate your busy business travel schedule? Can it offer a course built around the one week of vacation you plan to take in August? Can it offer you extra hours one-on-one with a teacher to discuss your weaknesses and study plan? These service issues are key sources of differentiation, so ask about them before you sign up for a course.
- Student atmosphere – A quality center will have room enough for all the students, and offer sufficient access to computers and other study aids. Further, the atmosphere will be positive and motivating. Again, ask around among your friends and former students to get a feel for what a particular center is offering.
- More than the GMAT – Finally, a great center will do more than train you for the GMAT. It will help you with the entire admissions process by serving as an information resource, a place for special events and business school presentations, and site where you can pursue your MBA admissions goals with like-minded people. After all, the GMAT is important only within the context of the overall admissions game. A good center will recognize that fact and live up to it.

TOEFL
Test Of English as a Foreign Language

Creator	Education and Testing Services
Address	TOEFL Educational Testing Services PO Box 6103 Princeton, New Jersey 08541-6103
Telephone	1 (800) GO-TOEFL
Website	www.toefl.org
E-mail	toefl@ets.org

about the test

Format	Computer Adaptive Test
Length	Two and a half hours Listening Grammar Reading 1 essay x 30 mins
Scoring	0 - 300 points 0 - 6 points for essays
Score Reporting	Results range given on test day Official record sent to schools within 2 weeks

the registration process

Registration Dossier	By mail or downloadable from ETS web-site
Schedules & Deadlines	Year round Monday - Friday, first 3 weeks of every month, and second Saturday of every month Register at least 48 hours before test
Test center Locations	Sylvan Prometric Centers in all major cities a
Tuition fees	$110 in 2001

average scores in the top MBAs

TOEFL scores	2000 **264 (627)**

THE TOEFL
INTRODUCTION

If you haven't completed your secondary or university studies in an English-speaking institution, you will probably have to take the Test of English as a Foreign Language.

Luckily, TOEFL scoring is built around computer adaptive principles similar to those on the GMAT, so you'll be wrestling the same type of animal. However, don't take the similarities too far. For instance, reading comprehension on the TOEFL is very different from what we saw for the GMAT. And that's just the beginning....

A different test for a different purpose

In fact the greatest difference is one of purpose. The GMAT was originally designed for native English speakers (Americans specifically) headed for American business schools, whereas the TOEFL is designed to test the language proficiency of non-Anglophones who intend to study any subject at any level of the American university system. GMAT test-takers share similar goals – HBS, six-figure salaries, leather office chairs and lots of business class miles – while TOEFL people are as diverse as the world itself. Whether they want to study Italian opera at Julliard, ancient Chinese literature at Princeton, or underwater basket weaving at Bubba State, they all take the TOEFL. Even people with superb, beautiful, nay, Shakespearean English, have to take the TOEFL. You might be a fluent English-speaker, have a British spouse, work in an English-speaking environment, and spend evey weekend down your local Irish pub, but you still need a TOEFL. The only way you can be exempt from the TOEFL is to prove you have done your secondary (high school) or university studies completely in English. Otherwise you'll have to take the TOEFL.

KSF: Get used to the types of standardized questions asked on the TOEFL so you can anticipate them.

But the wide variety and large number of test takers can work to your advantage. Remember, this is a standardized test, and so you'll have a limited number of variables to prepare. True, you won't have any contact with a real person to show off the fancy idioms you learned on your last trip to the US, nor will you have a chance to argue that, well, actually you've heard your cousin in Texas say it that way. You will only have four answer choices to choose from. And you may not agree with any of them! So, you'll need to learn what the test writers want to hear (which frankly, sometimes may not reflect everyday spoken English). They pull their questions from a specific pool comprising a limited number of grammar points and listening, reading, and writing question types. If you know what these are, you'll be able to anticipate them and answer them correctly. But don't expect to get them all right. Not even native English speakers can do that!

TOEFL Organization

Let's check out the nuts and bolts of the test. There are four major sections: Listening, Structure (grammar), Reading and Writing which last a total of 2.5 to 3 hours. However, as with the GMAT, you can expect to spend more than that at the test site – count on about 4.5 hours. The test site is the same as for GMAT, and so are the registration and scheduling procedures. Here's the overall breakdown of the test:

The TOEFL is scored on a scale from 0 – 300, though you may have heard about scores in the 600s. Don't be alarmed. These "TOEFL on steroids" scores refer to the old pre-CAT scale (used before July, 1998) which was 200 - 677. Some people still quote on that scale, so it's a good idea to have a TOEFL Bulletin which has a score concordance table. In general, on the "newer" scale, an average score would be 213 (550). More competitive scores should be above 250 (600), which indeed are the scores requested by the top MBA programs.

Section	# Qs.	Length	Format	Question Types
Listening	30 or 50	40 or 60 mins	Adaptive	Short Conversations Long Conversations Talks
Structure	20 or 25	15 or 20 mins	Adaptive	Fill-Ins Error Recognition
Reading	44 or 60	70 or 90 mins	Non Adaptive	One Best Answer Click on Text Insert Sentence
Writing	1	30 mins	Non Adaptive	Given Topic

TOEFL SAMPLE QUESTIONS

So now that you've aced the GMAT, what about your level on the TOEFL? The mini-diagnostic below is presented in the way that you would see questions on the computer screen, though we have had to include the tapescript for the Listening Comprehension section.

LISTENING SECTION

Short Conversations

On the computer screen you will see:

On the recording you will hear:

Woman: Do you want to go to the game later?

Man: I'll say

You will then see and hear the question before the answer choices appear.

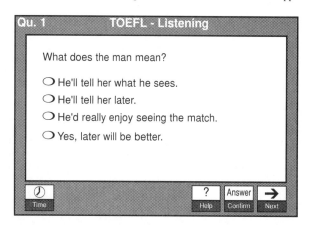

After you click on **Next** and **Confirm Answer**, the next conversation will be presented.

Long Conversations/Talks

Now you will hear a longer conversation or talk:

On the recording you will hear:

> *Welcome everyone, and my best wishes for a good semester. We've made a couple of changes in our registration procedure and I want to make everyone aware of them. First, as always, seniors and juniors get preference in signing up for any elective course. But now, those seniors and juniors on the Dean's Honor Roll, a 3.5 G.P.A. or higher, will get preference over their lower scoring classmates. We want to reward academic excellence. Second, the one week add or drop period has been extended to two weeks to give you more time to sample courses and make informed decisions. After this time frame, you'll need special permission from my office and the professor for any changes. You'll need good reasons to get my permission. Lastly, and this is very important, anyone who has not made satisfactory arrangements for the payment of tuition will not be allowed to register for classes. Class spots are for tuition paying students only. And there is one final announcement. Scholarship students must now receive a 3.2 or higher rather than the old 3.0 in order to retain their scholarships. If they do not, the scholarship will be replaced with a loan package that is repayable upon graduation.*

After the talk, the first question will be presented:

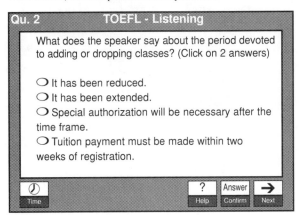

After you click on **Next** and **Confirm Answer**, the next conversation will be presented.

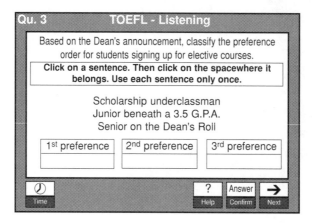

To choose your answers, click on a sentence, and then click on the space where it belongs. As you do this, each sentence will appear in the square you have selected. After you click on **Next** and **Confirm Answer**, the next conversation will be presented.

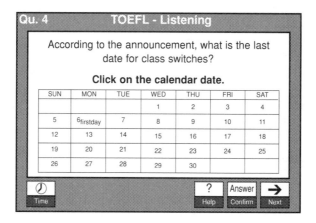

To choose your answer, you will click on the box. As you do this the box will become highlighted.

STRUCTURE

Fill-Ins

On the computer screen you will see:

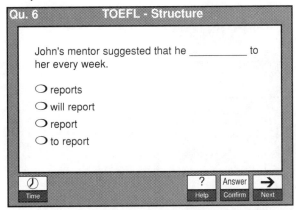

Clicking on a choice darkens the oval. After you click on **Next** and **Confirm Answer**, the next question will be presented.

Error Recognition

On the computer screen you will see

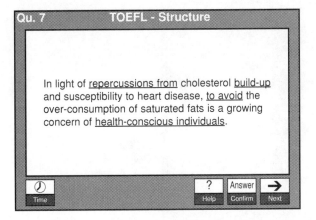

Clicking on an underlined word or phrase will darken it. After you click on **Next** and **Confirm Answer**, the next conversation will be presented.

READING COMPREHENSION

In the reading section, you are first given the chance to read the passage. As the length of the reading passage often exceeds the size of the computer screen you will use the scrollbar to view the rest of the passage. When you have finished reading the passage, you click on **Proceed**, and the questions will be presented.

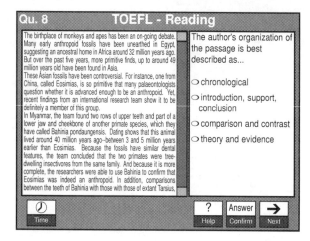

Clicking on a choice darkens the oval. After you click on **Next** and **Confirm Answer**, the next question will be presented.

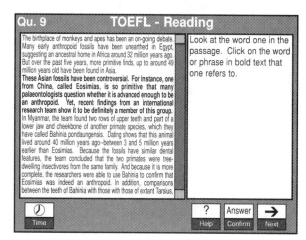

To answer you can click on any part of the word or phrase in the passage. Another question type asks you to click on a sentence in the passage:

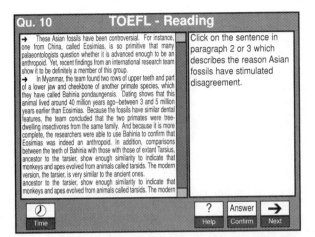

To answer some questions, you click on a square to add a sentence to the passage where you think it best belongs.

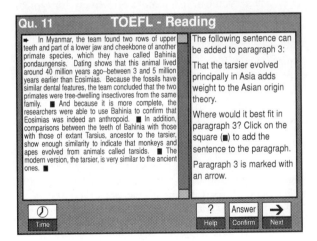

STRATEGIES AND ADVICE

The test in detail

You'll notice that the first two sections, Listening and Structure, are computer adaptive. So all the principles you learned for GMAT CAT scoring apply here as well: earlier questions count for more, unanswered questions have hefty penalties, etc. The Reading section, on the other hand, is not adaptive. Every question is worth the same. Furthermore, you don't have to answer a question to be able to move on to the next, so you can skip around if you want. The Writing section can either be done by hand or typed into the computer using an American keyboard (as with the GMAT AWA). Before we get into specific strategies, let's look at the types of questions you'll be faced with in each section.

(Are you) Listening (?)

The Listening Section has two parts: Part A: Short Conversations and Part B: Long Conversations and Talks. You'll work through this section at the test computer, wearing a pair of earphones (you can adjust the volume) and staring at a silly photo on the screen. The conversations are always between a man and a woman with a third voice chiming in to ask a question on what was said and present the answer choices. You'll point and click on the answer choice you believe is best. Listening Section questions may be daunting at first because the conversations are never repeated - either you get it the first time or you're lost. But actually, the types of questions asked are surprisingly similar. If you know what might be asked, you can listen more effectively for typical information.

For example, you will undoubtedly hear the following question on your TOEFL test: "What are the man and woman discussing?" This is a typical Main Idea question, a major testing point in Listening. You can anticipate these questions by training yourself to quickly summarize the passage in your head before answering the questions. Short Conversations, in particular, have lots of questions like "What does the man mean?" which require you to paraphrase what you heard. Think of these questions not just as memory exercises – they first and foremost test your vocabulary.

Throughout the Short and Long Conversations, the test writers will try to confuse you by using decoys or traps in the answer choices. For example, words like "dry" and "try" may sound alike, but using one instead of the other would completely change the meaning of a conversation. Finally, specific American-style idiomatic vocabulary, such as "how come", "isn't it though", etc. is used constantly.
KSF: Exposing yourself to a lot of typical TOEFL passages will help you acquire these oft-tested expressions.

Talks are academic lectures with a "professor" speaking on a particular subject that can last up to a couple minutes. Here, the TOEFL strays from reality in that you are not allowed to take notes, even though in a typical classroom, you would. Therefore, you need to learn to take notes in your head.

KSF: After a particular talk, take a second to summarize the beginning, middle, and end of the talk.
This will help you enormously when the questions come around and the passage is farther away in your memory. This may sound easy, but takes practice to master.

The major listening skills tested in Talks and Long Conversations include:
- being able to paraphrase what you heard
- identifying the main idea
- sorting out the time and sequence of events in the passage
- remembering specific facts and inferences
- identifying the tone or attitude of the speakers

You will see several different formats of questions which all test the above principles. Some may seem bizarre at first, but with practice you'll learn to answer them quickly. The most common format is "One Best Answer" or typical multiple choice with four possibilities to choose from. You'll also see a few "Two Best Answers" where you'll click on two answers instead of one. "Matching" requires you to put pieces of information into given categories. "Graphic Element" questions give you a picture of something like a map or diagram and you must click on the part asked about. All these question formats require only pointing and clicking skills, but you should nonetheless practice each kind well before test day. ETS offers a short tutorial CD in the TOEFL Bulletin which is well worth the time to master the different question formats.

(Decon)Structure

Structure is the TOEFL's fancy word for grammar. To determine your mastery of it, the test-makers want to know if you can identify both correct and incorrect grammatical forms. Therefore, you'll see two question formats mixed together in this section: Fill-ins and Error Recognition. Fill-ins give you a sentence with a portion missing, followed by four possible choices. You need to choose the correct one to fill in the blank. Error Recognition questions give you a complete sentence with four different parts underlined. One of the underlined parts is grammatically incorrect. You need to highlight the incorrect part.

Remember that this is a standardized test, so a limited number of grammar points are used. And they may not necessarily be what you learned in school - especially if you learned British English. *KSF: Focus your time on the high-yield grammar points - those that will most effectively maximize your score.*

Reading

TOEFL Reading is not the same as GMAT Reading Comprehension. Some even find it a picnic in comparison. Three main reading skills are tested.
- First, TOEFL Reading tests what specific facts are mentioned in the passage, as well as what is not mentioned. The typical format is the good old "One Best Answer". An effective strategy is to make a "road map" of the passage right away so that you can find the answers more efficiently. Certain skills such as skimming and scanning will help you more efficiently establish this map.
- Second, they test you on what certain pronouns, like "its" or 'their', refer to in specific parts of the text. You'll be asked to highlight the specific reference right in the passage.
- Finally, they'll ask what inferences can be made from certain information. This skill is usually tested by the "One Best Answer" format, although there is a strange permutation called "Insert a Sentence", in which you are given a new sentence and asked to click on the spot in the passage you think it will best fit. This one can be particularly challenging since it relies on favorite "road sign words" to give orientation.

Even though you can skip around the TOEFL Reading section, don't unless you've had a lot of practice. It's too easy to not notice that you've left something blank, leading to needlessly wasted points.

Writing

To wind up our introduction to the TOEFL, you'll be relieved to hear that TOEFL Writing is not as challenging as the GMAT AWA. In TOEFL Writing, the test makers don't really care how original your thoughts are - they just want to see that you can structure them according to the American Formula (think the Coca Cola secret formula!). The TOEFL Writing Formula is much more basic and direct than those for Analysis of an Issue or Argument. You basically need to supply about 300 words in the following tight structure:

- Paragraph 1: Introduction Sentence and Thesis Statement (what you think and the 2 or 3 reasons you will use to justify it)
- Paragraph 2: Your first reason with a couple of examples to illustrate it
- Paragraph 3: Your second reason with a couple of examples to illustrate it
- Optional Paragraph: Your third reason with a couple of examples to illustrate it
- Paragraph 4 or 5: Conclusion - or restatement of your Thesis Statement

Be careful to stick to this style since more open-ended styles will definitely bring down your score. If you manage to do this with very few mistakes and using varied syntactical structures, you can approach the high score of 6. It's important to decide whether you will type the essay or hand write it. If your handwriting is abysmal, by all means type it. The correctors give each essay just two minutes, so if they're struggling to decipher your penmanship, they're more likely to be brutal.

SCORING THE TEST

Counting by numbers

In the global economy we're all supposed to master the mysteries of English, but how do you really know if your understanding of the idioms and prepositions that keep the language schools in business is going to be enough for the schools? The TOEFL has played the role of the World English Test for the past 20 years or more, and despite its academic over-emphasis for the world of business, provides a quantified assessment of your level for the business schools. Once again the final question on the screen is going to be, "Do you wish to see your score?" Clicking on "yes" will reveal scores for each section of the test, and a range for your overall score. The range is due to the fact that the essays have to be sent to Princeton, where they will be corrected and integrated into the grammar score. You might for example see a scoring range from 225 to 250, which will be precised once the essay has been corrected. Within two weeks the official final score will be mailed to you.

Scores are valid for two years, and if you didn't get the score you were looking for you can take the test a month later. The TOEFL doesn't carry the same threat as the GMAT of taking the test too many times, and the idea of improving your level of English over a period of months or years with subsequent increases in your TOEFL score will not worry the admissions officers.

The scores on the doors

Business Week and US News & Report have never reported average TOEFL scores at the top business schools. The schools content themselves to indicate minimum requirements on the test to satisfy English language requirements. As such it is probably fair to conclude that obtaining the school minimums is sufficient, and an extra ten points on the TOEFL does not carry the same weight as an extra ten points on the GMAT. However, do at least achieve the minimum score, or schools will expect you to take the test again. Arguing with a school representative that the three years spent working in London should exempt you or excuse the missing three points on the test will not work. Your time would be better spent brushing up on your English and hitting 250+.

HOW BEST TO PREPARE

If you're wondering how to juggle your time between preparing for the tests, writing the essays, and following up on your letters of recommendation you may wonder where to find the time for preparing the TOEFL. The first step is to take a practice test. Far more than with the GMAT you may find that the years spent watching Woody Allen movies and nightclubbing in London have better prepared you for the test than you realize.

However, unless you are confident of a truly fluent English level, I would buy yourself a book or download software that offers the chance to take at least one or two full-length tests, just to make sure that there are no surprises on test day.

If your initial TOEFL level is considerably lower than the scores required by the schools, it is not just a course that you should be considering to improve your strategies for the test, but a comprehensive review of your English skills.Though this might seem like a daunting prospect, you will be rewarded not only by a higher score, but also the confidence and ability to avoid disappointment during the first weeks at the business school.

TOEFL PREPARATION BOOKS

The following titles represent the best of the material available for the TOEFL.

TOEFL POWERPREP® Software   ETS   CD-Rom
List Price: $29.95   May 2000
Published by the makers of the test, lots of practice questions, but no explanations to help you prepare for test day.

TOEFL CBT   Kaplan   Book & Cd-Rom
List Price: $34.95   Paperback - 544 pages   January 1999
Comprehensive review of the test. The software has two computer based tests, and provides great analysis of strengths and weaknesses.

How to Prepare for the TOEFL   Barrons   Book & audio CDs
List Price: $34.95   Paperback - 660 pages   September 1999
One of the best selling titles for the test, with good grammar review and many practice questions. Desperately needs software for computer-based tests.

TOEFL Success 2001   Peterson's   Book & Cassette
List Price: $29.95   Paperback - 580 pages   July 2000
Three practice tests, though not on the computer. Lots of mini-lessons to help you review.

Prepare for TOEFL Test 2000 Edition   Arco   Book & Cd-Rom
List Price: $16.95   Paperback - 437 pages   July 1999
Arco is very strong in reviewing the grammar section of the test.

TOEFL Grammar Workbook   Arco   Book
List Price: $11.95   Paperback - 256 pages   January 2000
A very helpful book to help you understand the Grammar of the TOEFL with good diagnostic
exercise.

Getting the MBA Admissions Edge

Getting the

BERKELEY

Admissions
Edge

Haas
School of Business

Address	Haas School of Business University of California, Berkeley 440 Student Services Bldg. #1902 Berkeley, CA 94720-10902
Telephone	(1) 510-642-1405
Website	haas.berkeley.edu
E-mail	mbaadms@haas.berkeley.edu

about the school

Founded	1898
Tuition Fees	$21,242 (out-of-state)
Some Famous Alumni	Donald Fisher (CEO, The Gap); Paul Hazen (CEO, Wells Fargo); W. Michael Rosenthal (Former Treasury Secretary); Robert A. Lutz (Former Joint President, Chrysler); Jorge Montoya (President, Procter & Gamble, South America)

the application

Application File	Submitted online or downloadable from website
Application Deadlines	early November mid-December early February mid-March
App. File Elements	• 3 essays (+ 1 optional) • 2 letters of recommendation • transcripts • GMAT (and TOEFL, if applicable) • résumé • interview, by invitation

rankings

Publication	Business Week						US News & World						Financial Times		
General Ranking	90	92	94	96	98	00	94	96	98	99	00	01	99	00	01
	18	**18**	**19**	**13**	**16**	**18**	**12**	**10**	**10**	**14**	**10**	**7**	**14**	**12**	**14**

before the MBA

# applicants	3,265
# applicants accepted	473
# applicants entering	238
% women students	30%
% international students	35%
# countries represented	29

Age (years)

mean	27
median	28
range	23 - 40

Education pre-MBA

Humanities and Social Sciences	28%
Engineering	19%
Business/Economics	41%
Others	12%

Professional Experience

avg. years work experience	5

Field of Work

Consulting	23%
Banking	18%
Marketing	15%
High-Tech	9%
Project Management	7%
General Management	6%
Engineering	6%
Non-profit	6%
Public Sector	4%

Average salary upon entry	$49 000

GMAT

average of all students	688

GPA

average	3.45
range	2.7 - 4.0

after the MBA	**School Total**
# companies recruiting on campus	114
Main career choices	
Consulting	32%
Software/High-tech	31%
Investment banking	20%
Consumer products	4%
Education/Government	4%
Others	9%
Function	
Consulting	35%
Finance	28%
Marketing	18%
Corporate/Business Development	4%
General Management	3%
Strategic/Business planning	3%
Others	9%
Geographical location	
North America	75%
Cenral and South America	4%
Europe	7%
Asia	12%
Salary (source: Financial Times 2001)	
Avg. salary three years after graduation	$126,780
Alumni	
# alumni in the world (MBA)	8 000
# cities with an alumni association	35

Top 10 employers

1. A.T. Kearney
2. Accenture
3. Bank of America
4. Booz, Allen & Hamilton
5. Ford Motors Company
6. Hewlett-Packard
7. Intel
8. McKinsey & Co.
9. Microsoft
10. Mitchell Madison

author

Name A. DEBANE

Consultant with Booz Allen in London.
Previously with Alstom for 4 years in Taiwan and Malaysia.

School specifics
BERKELEY

INTRODUCTION

The business school of the Univerity of Berkeley goes by the name of Haas. Founded in 1898, Haas is the second oldest business school in the United States. The school, which owes its name to the Haas family (of Levi's company fame), is situated in a new complex on Berkeley's campus, not far from San Francisco. Haas's mission is to figure among the top world-class business schools by offering an exceptional scholastic and social environment. Today, Haas draws its reputation from a number of strengths:

- Berkeley's prestige: founded in 1868, the University of California at Berkeley - or simply "Berkeley" - is one of the oldest universities on the west coast. It now has 31,000 students and is a world reference in the field of science (Biology and Nuclear Physics), Computers and Economics. The school has a plethora of Nobel Prize-winning professors. At Berkeley, doing a few lengths at the pool may mean sharing the same water as four Nobel prize winners, if that's the stuff of your dreams. On the other hand, as one of the centers of the hippie movement in the sixties, Berkeley still has a slightly marginal side to it, even if that's not apparent in the business school.

- Its teaching excellence: Haas has a long-standing tradition in research, and most of the professors are involved in research and management consultancy. Students directly benefit from the experience of the professors at Haas, as well as those from Berkeley's other schools. Lastly, "The California Management Review", a reference in management research, is published at Haas.

- The proximity of Silicon Valley: this and the dynamism of the San Francisco region (the Bay area) offer a privileged setting for finding openings in the information industries. If you want to redirect your career towards high-tech, Haas can offer you exceptional opportunities.

With 240 students admitted every year, the MBA program is one of the smallest business schools. Because of its small size and of the successful applicants' profile, students tend to be very supportive of each other. Generally, the administration and the professors encourage student initiatives, for example, the organization of seminars or courses on students' particular interests. The administration recognizes this central role of the students as being one of the particular characteristics of the MBA program.

THE DEAN'S VISION

Laura D'Andrea Tyson (the only woman Dean in the top 25 business schools) took the reins at Haas in 1998. The school has recently announced that as of January 2002 she would be leaving Haas to take over as Dean at the London Business School.

The guiding principles that Dr. Tyson established for Haas have shaped the current program, and will no doubt continue to be observed by her successor. Capitalizing on two of the school's chief assets - the small size of the MBA program and the excellence of its faculty - Dr. Tyson sought to further professionalize the MBA in order to better meet the needs of students and recruitment officers alike. In concrete terms, she articulated initiatives designed to realize this goal:

Increase interaction with Silicon Valley:
Silicon Valley's proximity offers Haas interaction opportunities with some of the most dynamic companies in the world: speakers at the school, summer courses, professional openings. These links will continue to be created and strengthened.
A course on information technology already features among the core courses. The annual seminar organized by the MBA students on management in high-tech companies takes place in the heart of Silicon Valley. This seminar brings together managers from Silicon Valley and professors and students from Haas who debate subjects such as the openings for high-tech

industry or e-business. At the career center (a careers service linked in with companies), employees have been hired to follow the Silicon Valley companies and to offer more openings for students. Haas has also been forging more links with other departments of Berkeley University (such as the Computer Science and Information and Management Systems Departments) or other research centers in order to offer more specific and applied courses: for example, the product development course followed by Engineering students involves a project generally centered on new computer applications.

Increase resources for the partnership program

Haas attributes increasing importance to business partnerships: around 10% of last year's in-take went to small, promising companies in Silicon Valley (start-ups) or to feeder companies for entrepreneurial activities (venture capital, etc.).

According to outgoing Dean Tyson, the program must better reflect the students' interests by investing more resources in this area. The activities which would benefit from this redeployment are the annual Best Business Creation Plan competition, "the incubator" and the Company Relations Office, which would receive additional personnel. The incubator provides support to MBA students who want to start a company. Haas puts at their disposal a space fitted with computer equipment, where they can exchange ideas with peers or professionals (venture capitalists, the press, other companies, etc.) and can develop, or put the finishing touches on, their entrepreneurial projects. In the same way, new classes centered around entrepreneurial activities and leadership should be added over the coming semesters.

Galvanize the career center (the Company Relations Office)

The ratio of the number of job offers per student is among the lowest among the prestigious business schools. One explanation for this is that many graduates choose to go it alone, and so in effect receive offers only from themselves. Haas also suffers from the small size of its program and its reduced student pool: if the traditional destinies of MBA students (consultancy and investment banking) and those in which Haas has a solid reputation (high-tech, and real estate) attract recruitment officers, other work opportunities don't come through the career center. Only 125 companies went to Haas last year in order to recruit MBA students. Haas' recent fall from its ranking among the top MBAs is largely explained by these statistics. The career center's reform is therefore at the heart of the administration's priorities. The appointment of three "account managers" to keep tracks on the recruitment officers in each professional sector has already enabled considerable progress to be made in the level of service given to students and companies alike.

Promotion of Haas' image

The last part of Dr. Tyson's strategy for Haas consisted of an unprecedented, concerted effort in media publicity: recruitment officers, economic players, etc. Haas will continue to organize further media events such as the visit paid by Alan Greenspan, the president of the US Federal Bank. Furthermore, Dr. Tyson's reputation as former chief economic advisor to Bill Clinton has undoubtedly helped improve the school's cachet.

THE SCHOOL YEAR

As well as the traditional two-year MBA program, Haas offers other programs such as the "evening MBA" and identical training courses or specializations (generally over three years):
- Law with Berkeley's Boalt Law School
- Asian Studies (for students speaking an Asiatic language fluently)
- Health Services Management

These specialization courses are followed by only a very small number of students, practically all American. Indeed, they are a better preparation for the (essentially legal) intricacies of the American market. The Asian studies program is followed by some Americans wanting to work in Asia and who wish to be more knowledgeable beforehand about Asiatic cultures. It holds little interest for Asian students themselves, who already have the cultural groundwork. Potential students should think very hard about the cost of an extra year studying at Berkeley before applying for this program.

The presentation which follows only concerns the traditional two-year MBA program.

TIMETABLE AND CURRICULUM
The MBA is organized in the following way:

Mid Aug – Mid Dec	Mid Jan – Mid May	June - August	Mid Aug – Mid Dec	Mid Jan – Mid May
1st semester	2nd semester		3rd semester	4th semester
Required Curriculum	Required Curriculum and some Electives	Internship/vacation	Electives and 2 Required Courses	Electives
1st year			2nd year	

The MBA is awarded at the end of a two-year program. Each year is divided into two semesters: the first (fall semester) runs from the end of August to mid-December, and the second (spring semester) from mid-January to the end of May. In the summer between the two years, students generally do an eight to twelve-week internship. The MBA is awarded after a minimum of 56 course units have been earned. A total of 32 compulsory units make up the core curriculum.

Before the first semester, two-week courses are offered in Publicity and Mathematics. Depending on the looks of your application, the administration might suggest you take one or both. Officially, it's a refresher program, but above all it's an opportunity to get to know other students before the start of the new semester, or to find accommodation, a car, etc. These courses don't count toward the MBA. In my opinion, you won't be missing much if you don't attend them.

The Core Curriculum

The pedagogical aim of the core curriculum is to bring students up to par in the fundamental disciplines. The core curriculum's compulsory units are concentrated primarily during the first two semesters so that the students can devote the majority of the second year to electives.

In the first semester, a total of 17 units
- Statistics and Quantitative Methods (3)
- Communication (2)
- Microeconomics (3)
- Financial Accounting (general accounting) (2)
- Finance (3)
- Organizational Behavior (3)
- Professional Skills (1) (the use of computers, introduction to presentation techniques, etc.)

In the second semester, a total of 11.5 units
- Macroeconomics (3)
- Managerial Accounting (analytical) (2)
- Operation Management (industrial operations, analysis and process studies, logistics, etc.)
- Marketing (3)
- Information Technology (1)
- Special topics (0.5) (a two-day symposium organized by second year students)

In the third semester, a total of 3 units
- Business Ethics (1)
- Business and Public Policy (2)

In the fourth semester, a total of 0.5 units
- Special topics (0.5) (a two-day symposium organized by second year students)

If you have in-depth knowledge of one (or several) course(s) on the core curriculum topics, you can get them waived if you pass a written waiver exam at the beginning of the semester. The school will actively encourage you to take this exam, especially if you have a significant amount of professional experience in this field. This way, an expert accountant won't have to take a basic accounting course. If you've done financial studies at university level, I recommend in particular that you get Financial Accounting waived as well as Finance in the first semester and Managerial Accounting in the second.

The first semester workload is fairly heavy, with 17 course units; this leaves little space for free time or for other courses. At the very least you will have to sacrifice all of either Saturday or Sunday, as well as much of your free time and evenings during the week, particularly if you don't have any business training. Many students face challenges with courses in statistics and math.

In this first semester, the program is divided into four "cohorts" of 60 students who will take the same courses throughout the semester. To decide who's put where, the school's administration takes care to mix foreign students with Americans students, men with women, engineers with non-engineers, etc.

One of the characteristics of Haas' core curriculum is the inclusion in the first semester of a course on written and spoken expression, which helps develop skills in oral presentation that will prove vital not only during the course of the MBA but eventually in the workplace as well.

Over the first two semesters, I was particularly impressed with the way the various core courses all fit together: professors from different fields get together weekly to ensure that the content of one lesson makes an appearance in another. For example, over the first semester, results forecasting techniques (an Accounting lesson) were directly applied to a company evaluation (a Finance lesson).

The second semester wraps up the bulk of the core curriculum content. Students can then decide upon their own timetables for each course. The cohort system set up in the first semester disappears and students can select their own schedules. Students also start to specialize in the second semester by choosing electives.

The Electives

In addition to the 32 core curriculum units, students must take at least 24 elective courses. Each year Haas offers more than 300 different electives. Each student can take as many course as he/she likes, depending on his/her particular professional or personal interests.

Officially, you can take electives from the beginning of the first semester, but the bulk of the core curriculum workload is very dissuasive. Moreover, many electives (especially in Finance) require having passed certain core courses. You can reasonably expect to take one or two electives at the start of the second semester.

In addition to the electives offered at Haas, your MBA enrollment opens the doors, for free, to every undergraduate course and to many graduate courses in the other schools on Berkeley's campus. The possibilities are almost endless: Art, History, Science, Psychology, Economics, etc. Many MBA students use this opportunity to learn a language or to improve one. However, only a limited number of courses outside Haas can count towards the total 56 units required for the MBA.

By focusing your electives around certain specialities, you can, in addition to the MBA, get some "certificates" attesting to your interest in:
- Global Management
- Entrepreneurship
- Management of Technology
- Health Management

In my opinion, the "certificates" have a limited use in the job market. They can, however, serve to demonstrate your intention to use the MBA for a career change.

Lastly, students can, with back-up from the teaching staff and the school's administration, set up electives (student-initiated classes) on more unusual subjects which reflect a private interest. These classes generally bring together a series of presentations from professors and/or professionals. Recent examples include Business in China, The Wine Industry, or Business in Japan, which begins with a three-week presentation given by a professor on the Japanese business milieu and continues throughout the semester with speakers from the professional world contacted by the students who organize the course. The students behind the courses develop relationships with the professionals in the field, and with the professors who back their intiatives.

THE COURSES – WHAT'S HOT... WHAT'S NOT

The table below compares the degree of student satisfaction with expectations for the various courses, both core and elective, offered at Haas:

	Below Expectations	In Line With Expectations	Above Expectations	Outstanding
Accounting	8%	48%	24%	20%
Finance: Corporate Finance	8%	29%	29%	33%
Finance: Capital Markets	0%	36%	43%	21%
Economy	0%	16%	28%	56%
Entrepreneurship	7%	20%	20%	53%
Ethics	13%	44%	38%	6%
High-tech/Information Technologies	18%	23%	23%	36%
Human Ressources	6%	31%	44%	19%
Marketing	9%	13%	43%	35%
Leadership	6%	29%	29%	35%
Operation Management	5%	33%	48%	14%
Organization Behavior	12%	38%	31%	19%
Strategy	10%	5%	15%	70%

First of all, it's important to note the very high level of general satisfaction: all the courses have – at the very least – met 80% of students' expectations. That's not really surprising and reflects the excellence of the teaching, the teaching staff and the quality of the interaction between students and professors at Haas.

The courses that students were most satisfied with were Strategy, Economics, and Entrepreneurship, where more than half of students stated that the respective course was exceptional. The honours go to Strategy with 70% of students rating this course as exceptional! The results are a little less enthusiastic about courses such as High-Tech or Information Technologies, because students have very different expectations depending on their professional experience and knowledge of industry.

The ten most popular electives at Haas are:
- International Finance
- Branding
- Corporate Finance
- Managing New Product Development
- High-Tech Marketing
- Negotiation
- Entrepreneurship
- Competitive and Corporate Strategy
- Internet Strategy
- International Business Developement

The courses most in demand correspond with Haas' strong points, which are Marketing and Entrepreneurship, especially in the Internet and High-Tech milieu. The real estate courses don't feature in these rankings because they draw only a small proportion of students.

In spite of the excellence of the teaching and of the general level of satisfaction, some students specializing in Finance or trickier financial techniques (Market Options) were not entirely satisfied with the range of electives run by the school. To a certain extent, the small size of the program doesn't allow the school to offer certain very specific courses. As a last point, I think Haas hasn't sufficiently capitalized on its international setting and doesn't offer enough courses directed towards this area (see the International Side, below).

TEACHING METHODS

The teaching methods include lectures (about 30%), case studies (about 50%) and group projects (20%). This seems to provide a good mix between theory and practice, whereas certain other business schools are sometimes criticized for focusing excessively on one method, whether case study (Harvard) or lecture (Kellogg). Students are expected to have read in detail (and possibly to have discussed) the chapters, articles or case studies before the class. During the case studies, the professor deals with the most difficult points and coordinates the discussions by referring to the students' knowledge and experience. Class numbers (limited to 60 students or less) and the arrangement of the classrooms into "mini-lecture rooms" creates an atmosphere that invites discussion. With the exception of a few professors who bombard students with surprise questions ("cold calls"), the discussions' style is very open. The professors don't push students into separate camps, but attempt rather to put the various arguments into perspective.

Learning outside of class: one of Haas' characteristics is to set up numerous support material/aids to help learning in the subjects taught. In addition to ensuring office hours, during which professors make themselves available to students, and weekly review sessions, conducted by an assistant professor or a doctoral student, the school has set up a mentor system. The idea is simple: if you need help in a given subject, you can call upon a "mentor" for $5 an hour. The mentors are second year MBA students (with professional experience in the field) or doctoral candidates, and receive $15 an hour. The difference is subsidized by the school.

THE GRADING SYSTEM

The system is resembles that in undergraduate programs, with a letter grade corresponding to a certain number of points (i.e., A+ (4.0), A (4.0), A- (3.7), B+ (3.4), etc.). The average of all the numerical marks in a term is used to calculate the Grade Point Average. Each student must have a GPA of 3.0 to receive the MBA. 99.8% of entering students come out the other side with their MBA. Each student's marks are calculated by balancing exam results (about 40%), projects/homework (about 45%) and contribution in class (about 15%). Unlike other schools, the marking system is not excessively competitive. The grades are based on level of mastery of the subject, rather than the relative perfomance of each student (as is the case with the "forced curve", illustrated in the Harvard chapter). If everyone masters the subject, then no one fails! Contrary to the reputation of many business schools, there is not a competitive atmosphere. Grades are considered confidential, and it is forbidden to reveal them to potential employers. The only advantage of being top of the class is its usefulness in obtaining study grants. There is no "best student of the year"-type competition, even if this is officially recognized at the end of the MBA.

GROUP WORK

An important part of the work is done in groups, since practically every core course and a number of electives have a group project element. In the first semester the groups are often selected by the professors who are careful to mix up students according to where they are from, their professional experience, etc. Numerous projects offer the opportunity to put into practice the group work techniques taught in the OB (Organizational Behavior) course. At the end of this first semester, each student thus has the opportunity to forge numerous links and friendships (going beyong the simple "How are you doing?"). The group projects and the many social events play a crucial role in the creation of a real community atmosphere in the school.

Haas stresses the importance of group work as a simulation tool for the business world. In companies, more and more decisions are made in groups, and increasing cooperation is required between companies, particularly in the areas of joint venture, outsourcing and supply chain management.

The extensive recourse to group projects certainly enables one to develop the essential qualities of leadership and communication skills. However, a certain weariness sets in after these two years due to the nearly complete use of group projects. There are some subjects (eg, Economics, Statistics, certain Finance courses, etc) in which the added value of group work is fairly low, but it will nevertheless be done in teams.

THE TEACHERS

Berkeley's and Haas' reputations attract numerous applicants for professorial positions. Haas can therefore feel free to choose its professors from the most famous in their fields.

The small size and culture of the program helps with student/professor interaction, which goes well beyond the end of each class. Most of them get involved in social or cultural activities, or support student projects throughout the year.

The standard of teaching and the interaction with the professors is one of Haas' strong points. Unlike many other MBAs where the core courses are the daily grind of the young professors, teaching the core curriculum at Haas is proof of professionalism and excellence and there is lively competition between professors. Students benefit from the best professors right from the word go, something which is rarely the case at other MBA programs. At Haas, the professors are accessible and take a real interest in their students.

The professors talk about their research and sometimes offer specific lessons on very specific themes, such as the energy markets. Some professors also get MBA students involved in their research or in the writing of books or articles. Students can also do research on a theme of their choice, upon agreement from the school's administration and a professor. This research work counts towards the MBA.

The most famous and well-liked professors at Haas are:
- David Aaker (Marketing, Branding) is a world reference (10 books published) in the field of management and of brand strategy. Calling largely on case studies (including many international cases), Professor Aaker's courses enable you to gauge the importance and

complexity of problems connected with brands. Professor Aaker is a master in the art of leading particularly lively and empassioned discussions. Recently, some MBA students were lucky enough to contribute to the writing of his latest book.

- Richard Lyons is one of the best-loved Haas professors, despite the rather unsexy reputation of International Finance. Shedding light on contemporary problems using economic theories, Professor Lyons captivates the attention of his students regarding these highly tricky issues. As well as speaking fluent French, writing songs, and singing them at the annual talent show, Richard Lyons is always ready to humiliate his students on the squash court.
- Carl Shapiro (Strategy and High-Tech) is an authority on the management of high-tech companies. Besides his courses at Haas and consultancy tasks in Silicon Valley, Carl Shapiro is co-author with Hal Varian (Dean of the School of Information and Management Systems at Berkeley) of a benchmark work in the world of high-tech and Internet business (Information Rules: A Strategic Guide to the Network Economy).
- Andrew K. Rose (Macro-Economy) is a favorite at Haas. When he's not teaching and running the Journal of International Economics, Professor Rose goes around the world helping dangerously sick central banks during financial crises.

Keeping hold of Haas' best professors is a subject of constant news: UC Berkeley fixed a ceiling on the salary of on-campus professors. Haas tries as much as possible to compensate for the gap between this minimum and their market value (very much higher) by calling upon its own funds. However, Haas sometimes has difficulty keeping up with the rise in salaries and a certain number of professors admit being tempted by other schools having more resources at their disposal (Stanford is less than an hour and a half's drive away…)

THE INTERNATIONAL SIDE

With 33% of students coming from abroad, Haas is one of the most "international" of the American universities. A third of foreign students come from Asia, a third from Latin America and a third from Europe. If this diversity has obvious advantages, the school, in my opinion, doesn't fully exploit the potential of these international students. The core curriculum makes scant reference to international issues, and electives going in-depth on international matters are few. International questions seem to be perceived as secondary to domestic issues. The relatively high proportion of foreign students earns the school its reputation for internationalism, but I was disappointed by the choice and content of the courses in this area.

Haas maintains an impressive international exchange program with 16 MBA programs in 7 languages (English, French, German, Italian, Japanese, Spanish and Portuguese), for example the London Business School, Bocconi or ISA. The exchanges take place in the autumn semester of the second year (third semester).

The strongest of the international initiatives is probably the IBD (International Business Development) program. This consists of a semester of courses on the specific nature of international business and a three-week consulting internship (with a group of four to five MBAs) abroad. Most students are enthusiastic about the personal and professional development opportunities of this program. Teams have recently gone off to Bangladesh, China, South America or Europe for local companies or for multinationals such as Motorola.

Haas has achieved great success amongst Asian students thanks to the proximity of the Pacific Ocean (Pacific Rim) and the presence of large Asian communities (Japanese, Chinese, Korean) in California. The environment at Haas reflects this orientation towards the Pacific: a two-week trip to Asia (the 'Pac-Rim trip') is organized every year after Christmas. A number of professors are of Asian origin or have worked in Asia.

COMPUTER FACILITIES – IT SYSTEM

The new building was designed with the importance of computers in mind: all tables are equipped with electrical outlets and a connection to the school's server. Computers are situated in many of the school's public areas, so you can check your e-mail or surf on the net between lessons.

The use of computers is central to life at Haas: the computer center is, after the central courtyard, the school's second nerve centre. Each professor keeps a web page for his course which offers extra information on his lessons (documents or extra links, marked work, etc.). The computer resources are considerable: all computers are linked up to a reference system in Haas'and Berkeley's library (one of the biggest in the world) and the school subscribes to on-line news search services. All students have free access to these services. This resource is enormously useful, allowing you to obtain key information quickly and conveniently. For example, within minutes you can find all the articles that have appeared in the regional and world press on the financing of new business projects around the globe.

THE ENTREPRENEUR'S CORNER

The school has made a concerted effort to back entrepreneurs by setting up the "Incubator". This program makes available to MBA students and students from other US Berkeley schools (Computer Science and Engineering) an area fitted with computer equipment to help generate interest between different disciplines in the university world and professionals (venture capitalists, professionals offering services, etc.). From this exchange of skills and ideas, business concepts grow which can be tested and improved upon by using other students, venture-capital companies, Silicon Valley professionals, and so forth, as guinea pigs. The Incubator gives great flexibility, provides the opportunity to make quality contacts, and engenders confidence in professional situations. A certain number of MBA students from the class of 2001 launched themselves into entrepreurship, having been through the Incubator at one time or another. The Wall Street Journal congratulated this initiative as a world first among business schools.

The school takes advantage of its proximity to Silicon Valley by offering a vast choice of electives in relevant fields, such as:
- Entrepreneurship: requires students to carry out an entrepreneurial project and create a business plan that must be submitted to venture capital companies for assessment.
- New Product Management: assembles students from the Business and Engineering Schools.
- Strategic Information Technologies: a top-to-toe assessment of technology and potential applications.

Students also benefit from the many group projects built into the lessons, which are less specific to entrepreneurship so as to test and refine its concepts. For example, the market research project allows you to gauge a product's potential on a target, consider branding possibilities and develop a concept or a brand image, etc.

In this way, two MBA students from the class of 1999, tested and developed a site (www.reality.com, to make real-estate transactions easier) while studying at Haas. Even before finishing their MBA, they had raised money from venture capital companies, and launched their start-up.

A competition for best business plan (for which about 80 teams compete) is organized every year to evaluate the various projects. This initiative is financed for the most part by high-tech and venture capital companies, which also have their place on the jury. As well as a reputation enabling them to raise money more easily in the future, the winning team receives $50,000 if it takes the plunge with its project.

Generally, Haas provides an excellent environment for all types of entrepreneurial projects, especially those linked with high-tech business. The cooperative spirit of students, the enthusiasm of professors, the many group projects and the proximity of Silicon Valley are an ideal launch pad for building and setting up a project.

SAN FRANCISCO AND THE BAY AREA

The University of Berkeley is on a campus on the side of a hill. On a fine day (San Francisco is renowned for its fog which invades the city in the afternoon), you can admire the Golden Gate Bridge and the skyscrapers of San Francisco. A delight to see, even after two years...

Berkeley is a half hour away from San Francisco, the second most popular holiday destination in the United States. San Francisco offers big city dynamism while retaining a little something of its own, in addition to providing a good quality of life. Wandering up and down its steep streets, you can lose yourself in Chinatown and the Italian neighborhood in North Beach. The temperature is pleasant year-round. Lake Tahoe's ski slopes are only four hours' drive away and the bay on the Pacific Ocean is a paradise for sailers and surfers. Locals and tourists alike are often to be found hiking or wine tasting in the neighboring hills of Marin and Sonoma counties.

HOUSING

Most students live on or near the campus. Several options are possible:
- University residence halls: The advantages are its proximity, a contract signed semester-by-semester, the relatively low price (about $600 a month) and the very diverse graduate community (MBA, law, science, etc.). On the other hand, on-campus dining facilities offer average quality meals (to be polite) at set times, and the rooms are too cramped. If you plan to live on campus, you should reserve a place long before the semester begins.
- Sharing an apartment/house: Berkeley is built almost entirely out of houses and owners either rent the whole house or a room in the house. Prices vary (from $500 to $1100), depending on where it is, the quality of the building, whether it has a bay view, etc. The school's administration keeps a list of MBA students interested in sharing rented accomodation.

Berkeley has a fairly extensive mass transport network, consisting of buses and a subway, the BART, which provides transport to San Francisco.

SOCIAL LIFE

The school likes to think of itself as a community. Not as a hippie community, which reigned in this area 30 years ago, but rather as a community whose way of thinking and culture is based on the cooperation and eagerness to help each other which exists between students, professors and the school administration.

The way applicants are selected reflects this culture, which stresses the importance of the applicant being willing to participate. As a former Haas MBA student told me: "the best part of my program was the other students. I was worried my colleagues would be MBA stereotypes – extremely competitive, selfish and only interested in money. It's not like that here because, although everyone has high aspirations, you don't feel that competitive mentality." The small size of the program and the organization of the student body into 60-person cohorts in the first semester gives you the chance to build a real affinity with people, and relationships which will last well beyond the program.

Working in teams becomes an art in the Organizational Behavior course right from the word go in the first semester. At Haas, being a "team player" carries more weight than being someone with a good technical mind or being a brilliant individualist.

The two years at Haas are characterized by an intense social life. The clubs bring students together around professional interests (consulting, high-tech, etc.), social interests (Women In Leadership), or geographical interests (Pacific Rim, Europe, etc.) and numerous events (lectures, recruitment evenings, etc.). Throughout the two years, clubs bring the students together in an informal way (generally with a beer) or during the talent show, where everyone can shine (or make fools of themselves!) on stage in front of the rest of the school. These points of contact even extend to the professors and to the program's administration.

But this intense social life is equally open to the outside world with initiatives such as the Bay Outreach Project, which, since 1990, unites students, companies and the school administration for the benefit of underprivileged communities in the San Francisco bay area. East Bay Outreach proposes three types of project work: tutoring high school students; offering classes in Business or Economics in local high schools; and lastly, advising small businesses. MBA students play a major role in this program, which is financed in partnership with large businesses.

The Haas mentality offers students an exceptional work environment and allows them to build solid relationships with a great number of their fellow students. It's more geared to certain professions (marketing, high-tech, and jobs where leadership figures highly) than to jobs requiring more individualistic ways of thinking (such as investment banking). Some recruitment officers criticize Haas students for their lack of aggressiveness!

TUITION COSTS

Haas is the only state school presented in this book. Tuition costs are consequently lower than those of private schools:
- $21,242 a year for non-residents of California
- $10,504 a year for residents of California.

The status of resident of California can be obtained by any American citizen after a year in California, if he/she shows they intend to stay there (by doing, for example, the summer internship there).

Estimate of the various expenses for a student (alone) at Berkeley:

Overall cost of the MBA (2 years): Out-of-state	In US $
Tuition Fees	42,484
Books, supplies	4,000
Personal (computer, etc)	5,192
Room & Board	22,516
Transportation, etc.	2,396
TOTAL	76,520

Payment of the MBA tuition costs entitles you to various services at Berkeley: the library, health center, and sports facilities, which include swimming pools, tennis courts, squash courts, several omnisport halls, an athletics track and weight rooms.

All students have the chance to significantly reduce their tuition costs by teaching classes as a GSI (Graduate Student Instructor) to undergraduates. The subjects most generally taught by MBA students are: Finance, Accounting, Marketing, Economics and Languages. These positions are relatively easy to pick up and numerous MBA students work as GSIs starting in their second semester.

As a rule, the small size of the program and the relatively small donations from alumni (compared with other MBAs) limits the financial resources available to the school. This means that Haas only offers $2,000,000 a year in fellowships/scholarships, which works out as an average of $4,200 per student.

STUDENT VIEWS

On the program:

The case studies directly illustrate the course concepts. That said, the quality of the discussions depends largely on the professors' ability to lead them and to bring in all the different points of view.

The way the MBAs are ranked penalizes schools seeking to be a little different or where entrepreneurship is promoted, which is the case for Haas. In my opinion, Haas provides an excellent quality-price ratio and is worth much more than its present ranking.

The small size of the program creates an ideal environment for learning. I felt motivated by my professors and by other students. The way groups work together was exploited well: there is very much a healthy competitive atmosphere among students, without it turning into all-out war. By the end of my MBA, I'd learned a great deal.

On the students:

Here, you make friends for life. The different nationalities tend to mix together well. In almost every country in the world there's someone ready to open their door to me!

Haas has more international students from more diverse professional backgrounds than the other big MBAs. This gives a wider perspective to things, and is very much felt in class discussions.

On the professors:

The professors make themselves very available to students and helped me analyze my career options and decide upon my career choices. Haas' professors have an excellent reputation in the academic and professional world.

The professors' experience in consulting e-business companies opened my eyes to new professional horizons.

On the surroundings:

San Francisco and Silicon Valley...this is where most of the technology which will decide our future will be developed. So why not get five years ahead of the game, starting today?

On the school's reach:

I expected Haas' alumni networks to be highly structured and organized, but there's a lot to be done before we're up there with the other top business schools, at least as far as overseas is concerned.

The admissions application
BERKELEY

INTRODUCTION

The application to Haas is composed of the following elements:
- 2 letters of recommendation
- GMAT scores (and TOEFL scores, if applicable)
- Undergraduate transcripts
- 12 open questions (requiring answers of only a few lines)
- 3 essays (+1 optional essay)
- Mathematics proficiency requirement: an estimate of your own level in mathematics and your aptitude to following the most analytical of all MBAs (statistics, operation management, etc.)

Through your application, Haas makes a real effort to get a picture of your personality, particularly via the essays and numerous open questions. One of the main purposes of the application is to determine whether you will fit in with the school's environment and culture.

Before launching into the application, you must decide upon a strategy for presenting yourself. This preliminary step will allow you to properly position yourself and to provide a structure to the various elements of your application.

In order to do this, you must at the very least have some clear and justified answers to the following questions:

- What are my mid- and long-term professional goals?
  How would an MBA enable me to achieve them?
- Why do it at Haas?
- What are the strengths that will enable me to succeed? In what circumstances have I shown my abilities and what impact did I have on my environment (professional, social, personal, etc)?
- What have I done that is meaningful in my life?
- In what situations have I been a part of a team and in what other situations have I been a leader?
- How would the person who knows me best describe me?
- What do I feel passionate about? Why? What does this say about my personality?
- What are my weaknesses? All schools ask this question - prepare a constructive reply.

Once this "systems check" has been done, you must find a strategy to describe these elements of your personality in the various sections of the application form (the essays, open questions, references, etc.). It's important to note that the Haas application form offers the peculiarity of containing, in addition to the essay, a battery of open questions intended to get to know you better. It's your chance to show the whole gamut of qualities that you identified earlier on.

One piece of advice that could seem a little obvious, but needs to be said: when checking over your application, make sure that your application is written and presented in a professional manner:

- Avoid spelling mistakes and grammar errors which can make reading an application difficult.
- Check also that there is no confusion nor incoherence in your application, in particular regarding dates and the job descriptions (titles, responsibilities, etc.). Make sure your references are consistent with the contents of your essays/open questions.
- Have a good argumentary method: make sure that your arguments flow from one to the next. Don't attempt to show your intellectual ability through complex reasoning; get to the point as quickly as possible.

This rereading should not, however, involve rewriting the substance of your application. Your personality is one of the main elements of your application to Haas and any alteration may make the application neutral and dull.

THE GMAT

Here is a review of the results achieved on the GMAT by students recently admitted to Haas:

	GMAT	TOEFL
average	688	267
deviation	+/- 52	+/- 25
range	590 - 780	253 - 287

The GMAT is an essential element in the evaluation of an applicant, and schools attach great importance to the test for two good reasons: it allows the school to compare applicants from different backgrounds according to the same numerical scale; moreover, the average GMAT score is taken into account in the various business school rankings.

At Haas, the GMAT is a deciding element in your application. Along with your undergraduate grades, your score on the GMAT determines your "academic ability". Although everyone refuses to compare it to an IQ test, the GMAT implicitly provides the school with an indication of your ability to follow the MBA courses. The seductive power of figures, I suppose…

As a rule, the GMAT's math section (quantitative) doesn't pose much of a problem for applicants with a business or engineering background. Depending on your previous education, the English (verbal) section can seem complicated or relatively simple.

As a last point, the GMAT alone will not tip the balance between getting in and not getting in. It's just another part of your application: I was told that an applicant with a 780 on GMAT hadn't been accepted recently. That said, according to Fran Hill, former Admissions Director, Haas gives places to students with "very low" GMAT scores if other elements in the application (motivation, maturity, etc…) demonstrate an exceptional personality. Your GMAT perfomance will be all the more important in the final decision if you have come out of a little known or unorthodox education establishment or if you have a below average school record.

Preparation for the GMAT

In order to properly prepare for the GMAT, I strongly advise you to take specialized lessons. I took a 9 week course with Princeton Review which enabled me to improve my GMAT by 120 points. The course allows you to acquire the necessary reflexes to finish the various sections in the allotted time, while at the same time minimizing mistakes. It furnishes you with standard models, strategies, and advice for the writing of the GMAT essays. Princeton Review allows you to benefit from their research on the GMAT: what are the most common questions, the trick questions, the strategies in case you get stuck when faced with a question. The teachers were very thorough and they knew their subject backwards and forwards.

This type of training can seem expensive: console yourself by telling yourself that it's only a tiny fraction of the cost of an MBA and an infinitesimal fraction of an MBA graduate's salary. In short, if you really want to give yourself a serious shot at getting onto one of the best MBA programs, this type of preparation seems to me to be an indispensable investment.

Another piece of advice: practice, practice, practice. Put yourself under exam conditions and do different tests. You can redo the same test (for example, the verbal sections only) every three weeks. With the appearance of computer technology in the administration of the GMAT, from now on it's possible to take the test at very reduced time intervals. An abnormally high score in a set of results is probably a bit of luck. A program such as Princeton Review or Kaplan will help you to judge your potential and your room for improvement.

THE TOEFL

International applicants must also submit scores for this test. If you have university-level English, you don't have to worry about the getting a good TOEFL score. You should nonetheless prepare the test by a taking a mock TOEFL, if only to put yourself under exam conditions. There are cassettes on the market which are perfectly suited to this type of exercise. According to Fran Hill, former Director of Admissions at Haas, the TOEFL is above all an administrative formality.

THE ESSAYS

As well as the traditional essays in MBA applications, the Hass application carries a dozen open questions which require shorter and simpler answers than the essays, like for example: "Which is your favourite author?"

A FEW TIPS FOR WRITING STRONG ESSAYS

Use your own style

An employee in the admissions office reads dozens of essays every day. Your style must strike a different note than those of the other applicants. As a foreigner, you have a different personality for the reader to appreciate. Haas expects foreign applicants to bring diversity to the program and not conformism.

Be professional and structured

Don't get your reader lost in overcomplicated reasoning. Set out from the very first paragraph your main idea or the goal of your essay. As a rule, Americans prefer reasoning which gets straight to the point. Use directness in your phrasing as much as possible. The word limit in the questions and essays is not set in stone, but if you go past the limit, it must be because you have something fantastic to say.

Figures, figures, figures

For business schools, all performance is measurable, each one of your successes must be accompanied, if possible, by a result expressed in figures. Your résumé should be packed full of figures, and it's up to you to find the numbers which will cast you in the best light.

Be enthusiastic and engaging

Dynamism, enthusiasm and the ability to "shake things up" are the essential qualities for getting into Haas. The admissions office will place enormous emphasis on your essays to gauge whether Haas is the right environment for you. Don't be shy about your successes if you want to get ahead of the nine other applicants (reminder: 9 out of 10 applicants are rejected).

Seduce your reader

The best leaders are those who are liked by their subordinates. At the end of your essay, the reader should be thinking: "well, there's someone I'd like to work with, dine with or talk with for an hour". Be adorable, spotlight your charisma and your ability to influence others. Be funny without, however, taking the risk of shocking your reader.

WHAT HAAS IS LOOKING FOR IN YOUR ESSAYS

Whether it be in essay or in question form, the goal is the same: to grasp your personality, to gauge whether Haas is the right environment for you and what you can bring to Haas.

On finishing reading your application, the admissions office fills out a grid to evaluate your character traits and what you can bring to the school. Given the profile sought after by Haas, you should have identified at least one situation or anecdote illustrating each of the following qualities:

- Professional excellence: your efficiency at work, your professional motivation, your ability to keep to professional commitments by calling upon creative solutions, if necessary.
- Academic excellence: you are able to show what your education has enabled you to do and why that's important for you.
- Leadership qualities: your aptitude to change an organization, to organize or supervise a team.
- The "teamplayer" quality – your ability to work in a team, your sense of responsibilities.
- Communication skills: your social skills and your ability to draw individuals round a project or common goal.
- A sense of ethics: your ability to measure the impact of your decisions on the various vested interests in the company.

EXAMPLES AND COMMENTARIES OF SOME OPEN QUESTIONS FOR HAAS

The questions require a short answer (often just a few lines). The diversity of the questions allows the admissions office to grasp the wealth of your personality as well as your openness of mind, whereas the essays enable them to gauge your organization of thought and your charisma on paper. If all the questions are very simple, your answers can (and must) reveal a lot of information about your personality. Have your answers read by many friends, so as to check how your answers can be interpreted. What would a psychologist think when reading what you put?

What leisure-time activities do you enjoy?

The aim of this question is to better understand what motivates you, and the personality traits which are reflected in this activity.

Show how different you are from the other applicants, what you get from these activities, what makes you run "that extra mile". If you feel very passionate about a very original activity, don't hesitate sharing it with admissions. Your force of feeling must be contagious (in a few lines, if possible…) It's also the opportunity to show qualities such as perseverance and the search for perfection. For example, explain how long you have been doing this activity, how you came to love it so and what you get out of it from a professional or personal point of view.

> *During my studies in chemistry, I was always attracted by the technicalities of photography and later spent years and hundreds of film rolls to better understand the intricate relationship between colors, exposure and light. When I attented a photograph convention, I saw some pictures from Rwanda and understood that photography was much more than light and chemicals. The photography techniques I had been relentlessly working on became tools to express emotions and feelings and to communicate with others. Through dedicated work, I was able to master a new and powerful communication tool which opened endless opportunities to express myself.*

Who is your favorite author?

More than the author's name, what seems to interest the admissions office is why this is your favorite author. Don't necessarily look for an author known to the admissions office. In my opinion, it's in your interest to bring diversity into play by choosing, for example, an author with whom you share a strong opinion, who was able to brilliantly describe an experience similar to your own or who may have served as inspiration in crucial moments of your life. It could also be the moment to show how an author or a philosopher has inspired you when confronted with an ethical problem.

What is your most valued tangible possession? What is your most valuable intangible possession?

The goal is to understand what values are dear to you and why. According to the admissions director, you must go further than the basic value of things, to explain why you are attached to an object and what that says about you. Show how this "possession" has a higher value for you because it represents, for example, the finishing post of a long slog of personal investment (time or will power).

Briefly explain what prompts your best efforts

This question basically translates as: What motivated you and why? What do you personally get out of it?

Show where you draw upon your motivation and how it enables you to get others caught up and carried along by it. Try to be very general and "grandiose" with replies like: "improving the living environment" or "learning", nevertheless providing concrete examples. Don't fall into the trap of describing your effort because this question is really asking you about what motivates your efforts. A very "Berkeley" answer would be:

Learning is definitely what drives my efforts and gives me energy to work harder. I consider myself lucky to have had a number of opportunities and would feel guilty not to take advantage of them. Ultimately, I believe that learning is central to my values because it enables me to communicate with more insights, more depth and more passion with a larger number of people around me.

Briefly state what you view as your most significant accomplishment

Normally an essay, at Haas it's a "short question". Here you have to describe (within the limited space of a few lines) this accomplishment and why you consider it important. Whatever you do, don't waste time boasting about your merits nor describing what you did. Try and leave behind the professional cliché. It's not the absolute value of your accomplishment that counts, but the effort and perseverance which it required of you. Even if every year Olympic champions make their appearance at Haas, you can write about a sporting "accomplishment" (for example, that of a team where you had a leader's role) and about the effort you made to achieve this goal. To what extent did you surpass yourself (if you had to surmount a handicap)? If possible, express your "accomplishment" as a number.

In 1990, I lead a group of 25 students from my school and set up a program to give free reading and writing classes to adults. Over three years, we gave over 900 free classes to 150 people in various locations throughout the country. I view this as my most significant accomplishment because I efficiently managed a committed group of both students and teachers in the program. Besides the organization, I view this as my most significant accomplishment, because, through our hard team work and dedication, we gave 150 adults more opportunities within our society.

What do you view as a particular strength of yours? What do you view as a particular weakness? Would friends and family share your view?

A typical question, at least for the first half. If writing about strengths generally poses no problem at all, you should be equally able to recognize your weaknesses with the same amount of ease… An elegant way of getting out of this one is to recognize you have a weakness, say how you became aware of it, and how you push yourself to be rid of it. There are, however, some weaknesses to avoid in an application to Haas, such as lack of ethics, lack of analytical ability or initiative. Also avoid clichéd replies such as:"I am such a perfectionist and expect so much from my subordinates, that I put huge pressure on their performance".

The second part refers to the interactions that you have with friends and family. Make it clear in what circumstances your friends or the members of your family have been able to gauge your strengths and weaknesses. For Fran Hill, former Admissions Director at Haas, to have an opinion on the way you are perceived by your family and friends reveals a certain maturity and self-criticism. The way you are perceived should not therefore be very different from your own analysis and should rather serve to complement it.

I believe my particular strength is an open attitude to new opportunities and an ability to have an impact on an organization. For instance, our company typically used to have short term relations with our suppliers based on price discussions only. When I started my job as sales manager, I first analyzed the suppliers market and identified longterm partnership opportunities with our suppliers. Thanks to these relationships, we have been able to save over $2.5 million in development costs and dramatically improve the quality of our products.

My particular weakness is my lack of patience in explaining the same thing over and over again when people are not paying attention. I can easily understand that I need to repeat myself if I am not understood, but I expect others to pay full attention when interacting. Having become aware of this reaction, I have worked hard to identify those times when I should be more open and receptive. I also try to be aware of my audience and adapt my language and tone when necessary. For instance, in a recent meeting with the supply department I went over the same topic from different angles and distributed written information to ensure that my explanations were better understood.

Getting my friends', relatives' or colleagues' opinions on my character is critical to me: it helps me to better understand how I am perceived and how I can improve my position in the firm. At work, it also gives me a benchmark for future performances. I am therefore confident my relatives and colleagues would share this view.

If you had four extra hours a day (i.e. a 28-hour day), what would you do with them?
This question enables the admissions office to judge what your values are, and what effort you are prepared to devote to get what you hold dear. This question also gives you the opportunity to express your creativity (think beyond the context of work) and your humor.

Don't put four hours more sleep (everyone thinks of putting this, but you can't) or four hours more work (no one will be believe you). Suggest rather some new activity, explaining why it's important for you (whilst not forgetting to mention why you don't start now, starting today).

Mathematics proficiency requirement
Put down your score on the GMAT quantitative section (if it's decent enough) and show that the level of mathematics has been high in your previous education.

EXAMPLES AND COMMENTARIES OF ESSAYS FOR HAAS

The unexamined life is not worth living – Socrates, the apology by Plato

The point of this essay:
In this essay your maturity can be determined, as well as your level of self-criticism because it encourages you to present certain experiences in your life.

Tips for this essay:
Don't try to impress the reader with your knowledge of Greek philosophy if you don't have very much; one recent Director of Admissions had nine years of Ancient Greek behind her…

There are numerous ways of approaching this question. You could, for example, choose an important moment in your life where you were made to take a crucial decision: show why this decision was important; what the motivation was behind this decision. What lessons did you draw from it? And what if you had to do it again? How does this decision reflect your personality and your values?

Sample Essay:

You can, for example, analyze why you accepted your current position (rather than any other), what you get from your work and what your motivations and work satisfations are.

What do you like about your job? What do you dislike? If you were promoted to a senior management position, what changes, if any, would you make to your former position to address your dissatisfaction?

The point of this essay:

To gauge your professional maturity, your aptitude to suggest changes in a professional organization and your abilities to initiate these changes, thus assessing your leadership skills.

Tips for this essay:

Don't hesitate to set up parallels between the positive and negative aspects of your work: "Although my position in the international sales network gives me tremendous exposure to our clients, I often feel my involvement in the decision process is limited".

The second question calls upon your leadership qualities and on your ability to introduce change in a company. I suggest the following plan:
- Identification of the problem (where does your discontent come from)
- Analysis of the situation: how is it a problem in the organization?
- Set out your solution
- Expected results of your solution (figures, if possible…)
- What's stopping you from making this recommendation today?
- What will be the resistance to change within in the company? If there is any, how do you count on solving this problem?

Sample Essay:

Typically, our company launches new products and concepts three months behind our competitors. This results in poor image of products, lack of motivation in our sales force and only 15% market share. The bottom line is that we could be making $25 million more with our products.

Currently, our sales force incentive system is based only on individual sales. Although it ensures that our sales force is aggressive and motivated, key information about customer behavior is not reported to the highest level and product design teams.

If I were in a senior management position in the organization, I would put into place an incentive system for the sales force to report emerging changes in consumer behavior. Providing an adequate reward system, sales people would probably be happy to discuss with product development teams and could certainly bring valuable suggestions to the table.

However, this program would take a change of mentality of the sales force from short term to longer term. This change would be facilitated if, in the early stages of the new incentive programs, large rewards were given to new information reported by the sales force. This will set an obvious example to be followed by other sales representatives.

Another example: the setting up of a formal system of communication between two entities (production and sales) whose objectives can be different.

Describe an ethical dilemma you have experienced and discuss how you handled the situation

The point of this essay:

To see the way you approach ethical problems and consider the role of business in society.

Tips for this essay:

Students' level of ethics are considered essential for maintaining the cohesion, culture and spirit which characterizes the school. It is therefore imperative to show maturity and thoughtfulness in this area. Ethical problems also allow the admissions office to measure a level of trust because it sometimes takes courage to come out with our values.

In the analysis of a problem, I would suggest the following plan:

- Presentation of the situation
- Set out the dilemma: what are the possible choices and their consequences?
- Analysis of the 'stakeholders': to whom am I responsible (in the largest sense of the word: to my employer, my colleagues, my friends and family, etc…) How are these people affected by my decision?
- Why did I take this decision?
- And if I could go back and change it? Consequences of my decision on the previously identified parties. Why am I satisfied with this decision?

Sample Essay:

While working in sales on an assignment abroad, I once faced an ethical dilemma: I could secure an export market by providing a commission to a local official or simply let the opportunity go away. For our company, it was a substantial market (5% of our annual exports) and if I had accepted the market, I would have exceeded my own annual objectives by over 30%. On the other hand, if I refused, our main competitor had a unique chance to break into a market where we were traditionally strong. My superior gave little advice in my choice and clearly stated that he did not want to know how I was proceeding as long as I was meeting my sales objectives. Bribery was quite common in this country and even considered by many as a part of business culture… We certainly did not want to go into expensive and probably useless litigation.

Taking into account my personal interests, the company policy and the impact on the company's reputation, I decided that it was not appropriate to pay such a commission. As expected, we lost this market opportunity. It was illegal, but also would have introduced disreputable behavior in the organization. In the long run, it would have harmed the company, the client, my position and the reputation of the company in the market place.

Please discuss your intermediate and professional long-term goals and why you want an MBA at this point in your career. In what ways do you think an MBA degree will help you achieve these goals? What do you want from an MBA program and why have you chosen the Haas School?

The point of this essay:

The question is evaluating the maturity of your decision to apply and your motivation to do an MBA. How can an MBA allow you to achieve this long term objective? It's the million dollar question not to get wrong. You need to be clear, show that you think things through and that you are motivated.

Tips for this essay:

At this point in the application your arguments should be coming to you easily. All you have to do is to present them in a direct, simple and structured manner.

- Indicate what your long term goal is, and what has influenced you in the realization of this goal. Be sure of yourself (even if there's a 95% chance you might change your mind during the MBA, with the application form, it's better to show self-confidence and determination).
- Show how its not just "your latest idea". What is the tangible proof of your seriousness?
- Compose a progress chart (which includes an MBA from Haas) which will enable you to achieve this goal. Show how the MBA from Haas is indispensable to you.
- In a progression plan, bring into play Haas' specific characteristics (the team work, the international perspective, the interaction with other students, the professors, etc…) in order to show that you have really looked at this. Link up Haas' specific characteristics with your career plan. For example: "Located in one of the most dynamic markets in the United States and with its wide pool of international students, Haas provides the best environment for my goal of international management in high-tech companies".

The optional essay: Please provide a statement concerning your personal history, background, and influences on your intellectual development. This statement should include educational and cultural opportunities (or lack of them), social and economic disadvantages that you may have had to overcome and the ways in which these experiences have affected you.

This essay is intended first and foremost for applicants for the graduate opportunity fellowships. Answer only if what you put can enlighten the admissions office about the extra effort that you've made in your life to equal (and surpass) your colleagues, classmates, etc.

LETTERS
OF RECOMMENDATION

You need two letters of recommendation for Haas. You can submit more, but this is only advisable if the supplementary references shed a radically new light on your personality. Generally, don't bog down your application with superfluous or repetitive imformation.

GENERAL ADVICE

Whom to choose?

It seems to me to be indispensable that at least one of the letters of recommendation be written by your boss. If you work in a big organization, it's better to ask your immediate boss (with whom you have daily contact) rather than trying to impress with a recommendation signed by a big director. You can give yourself more latitude when choosing the second reference. As a rule, it's advisable to choose the latter in the professional sphere, unless you have an exceptional extra-professional experience which illustrates the qualities particularly sought after by Haas. Recommendations from your former teachers boasting your intellectual capacities are therefore out: your "transcripts" (undergraduate grades) should speak for themselves.

Here are a few ideas for finding this "second reference":
- A client who you have personally followed and that you have helped in an exceptional way.
- Someone in charge of a project in which you took part. This is the opportunity to stress the values connected with working in a team.
- More generally, anyone with whom you've had frequent professional contact and who can shed light on your performance from a different perspective than that of the first reference. You had the opportunity, for example, of working with an expert quality control officer for solving a problem about a production team that you were supervising.

A reference with an MBA from Haas or from another prestigious university or who works for a large firm will probably be a plus for your application. This person can express his/her qualified opinion on your ability to follow an MBA program because they represent a point of reference for the Admissions office.

"Coach" your reference

The goal of the letters of recommendation is to measure your impact on an organization (i.e. your leadership potential) and your ability to fit into a team (team skills) in a professional environment. This is the only part of the application that comes from a third party (if you don't count the transcripts) and it must shed light which complements and remains coherent with the rest of the application. The admissions officers spend a lot of energy trying to grasp the applicant's personality through the letters of recommendation. I therefore advise you to work ahead of the actual writing of the letters of recommendation in order to enlighten your references and to "motivate" in the writing of the precious document:
- Explain why you are applying for an MBA place. Set out the profiles and qualities sought after by the school.
- Make sure that the letter of recommendation is written in a professional style. Ideally, the writer

could get the letter proofread for style and grammar.

- To put you on a level playing field with writers for other applicants, who may be gushing with praise about their recommendees, your writer shouldn't be hampered by any false modesty…
- The qualities described in the letter of recommendation must be supported by examples. Give a few examples of situations where you have shown these qualities, in order to point the reader in the right direction.
- You must check with the writer that the information mentioned doesn't sit awkwardly with the rest of the application (for example, dates, job description and responsibilities, etc.)

QUESTIONS ASKED IN THE HAAS LETTERS OF RECOMMENDATION

In practical terms, the letter of recommendation is an information card made up of open questions and an applicant assessment grid (similar to the one featured in the Harvard letters of recommendation section). The referee is asked to leave his contact number.

The difficulty of this exercise lies in the painting of a favourable picture of the applicant, whilst maintaining a certain balance between praise and credibility. The reference should therefore be nuanced and highlight the qualities sought after by Haas: team spirit, the ability to solve complex problems, a taste for initiative and the desire to think big. The letter of recommendation must describe and illustrate these qualities but also bring out the applicant's potential for rising up towards senior management positions.

The assessment grid

As far as possible, only use the "exceptional", "outstanding" and "very good" boxes (except for one of the qualities) - that should show a sufficiently balanced profile. Don't fall victim to excessive praise: according to the director of admissions at Haas, many assessment grids come back with ticks only in "exceptional" and a few in "outstanding". This automatically discredits the letter's contents. It'll be up to your referee to present a balanced profile.

The open questions

The general tone of the letter of recommendation must be dynamic and enthusiastic; you mustn't be frightened of superlatives such as "outstanding", "exceptional", "amazing", "first class", etc. Below are the main elements of the letter:

- Presentation of the referee, duration and quality of the interaction between the applicant and the writer.
- Comparison of the applicant with a reference group (other young engineers taken from your school, other young recruits selected from a pool, etc.) For example: "Among the 20 young project engineers I have worked with in the past five years, Michael is, by far, the brightest and most efficient. For instance, …"
- The applicant's major strengths: illustrate each one of them by one or several concrete examples. Include without fail the "interpersonal skills", that is to say the capacity you have to communicate and to build useful relationships. Illustrate how these strengths have enabled you to achieve results and, if possible, give these results expressed in figures (time or costs saved, new opportunities created, etc.).
- The applicant's weaknesses: to make sure of the reference's credibility, a few weaknesses must be identified and discussed with the support of examples. Here the weaknesses have to be recognized, but something positive can be gleaned from them. For example, your referee could stress the efforts you have made to correct these weaknesses. You must avoid weaknesses like

lack of ethics or of leadership, which put your application directly in the 'out-tray'. Your referee can equally cite weaknesses linked to lack of experience, which can be compensated for by... an MBA from Haas.

In his marketing job, Paul focuses too much of his attention on the technical specifications of the product and tends to forget the broader picture and the benefits that customers are seeking from our organization. However, given his ability to learn and his open-minded attitude, I am confident that with a solid business education, such as the Haas MBA, he will understand where the priorities are and be able to manage broad marketing programs more effectively.

This argument allows you to "sell" the utility of an MBA, but it must be careful not to go too far, because it makes it sound like a contrived answer.

THE INTERVIEW

Interviews are only held at Haas. If you're passing through the area around San Francisco, you can make an appointment with the admissions office for an interview. That will allow you to show how motivated you are and to make sure that Haas fits your objectives and expectations.

Typically, the "interviewers" are second year MBA students, and only have your résumé at their disposal. At the end of the interview, a report is made, based on the folowing criteria:

- Professional attitude
- Presence
- Self-confidence
- Communication skills
- Professional goals
- Why Haas? (motivation)
- Would you like to have the applicant in your class?
- What would be the personal and professional advantages of having the applicant as an alumnus/alumna?
- How would a professional recruitment officer assess this interview?
- General evaluation of the applicant's performance.

Seduce!
The interview's goal is not to put you under pressure, but to get you to speak (once again...) about your motivations and aptitudes. You have to go much further than just a simple presentation: you must be able to establish a friendly contact and to get yourself liked throughout the interview.

Be professional
The interview style must nevertheless stay professional: arrive ahead of time. It goes without saying, wear a suit, even if your interviewer shows up in short trousers and tennis shoes...

Be well-informed

Be ready to ask questions while showing that you are well-informed about Berkeley and Haas (by rereading the presentation of the school in this chapter, for example). Visit the school's website (http://www.haas.berkeley.edu) before your visit, in order to be abreast of the latest news (for example, the latest articles in the press which mention Haas). You should also get hold of a copy of the student weekly "Haasweek" (or online: http://www.haasweek.com).

In general, interviews asked for by applicants make an excellent impression for your application; better still, if you've travelled from foreign parts. Make the most of your brief visit to Haas by getting involved in the Haas Visitation Program (HVP) and showing more of your motivation and interest for the program.

The Haas Visitation Program is run by MBA students and offers you the opportunity to attend a class and to ask students all the questions you want, without it being passed on to the admissions office. You can make an appointment on any day when there are classes (from Tuesday to Friday) and attend practically all of them. If possible, avoid the ends of semesters (exams coming up) or too technical lessons (Statistics, Market Research, and Financial Specialities). Choose rather the most reputed professors and/or the livelier lessons (Marketing, Economics or Strategy).

INTERVIEW WITH THE ADMISSIONS DIRECTOR

Interview with Fran Hill, former Director of Admissions at Haas:

Whom reads the application dossiers?
We have three permanent admissions professionals (a director and two associate directors of admissions) and hire external evaluators during the cycle according to the workload. Admissions officers are not members of the faculty, student or alumni bodies.

What criteria distinguish a good applicant?
We are looking for applicants with excellent academic records, who are well qualified to study here. We are after students who have had the best learning opportunities in their country and have succeeded in the top institutions in their country. We seek candidates who value education and academic achievement, since Haas is part of one of the leading universities in the world.

We also like to see applicants with substantive work experience. The average age of our student body is 28 years which reflects the five years of work experience, on average, our students bring to the classroom. This average age and years of work experience is slightly higher than at other schools. We value candidates with strong career focus who demonstrate a thoughtful approach to their career development beyond considerations of job title or compensation.

Finally, we seek creative, resourceful, proactive applicants with strong interpersonal skills. Successful applications are very closely linked to how well an applicant expresses his or her personality on paper and communicates a real insight into his or her character and motivations.

What is the screening process?
We screen students country-by-country. For instance, we will review all applications from any one European country together, so that we can compare the candidates inside a homogeneous pool. I would like to point out that, unlike many other business schools, we use the same admission rate for international and domestic students. International students represent roughly one third of our applicants, one third of our admits, and one third of our student body.

How important is the GMAT in the admissions process?
We use the GMAT in our selection process, keeping in mind that the GMAT is not a measure of intellect. I have found little correlation between GMAT scores and grades of MBA students at Haas, especially as regards international students. There is a cultural bias associated with the GMAT so we tend to feel the GMAT has less importance for international applicants than for American students. There are other problems associated with the GMAT - it is a coachable test, which tends to give an advantage to those with the money and/or the time for extensive test preparation. The TOEFL is required by the Berkeley graduate division but is not viewed as a reliable measure of English proficiency in our admissions reviews.

What is the minimum GMAT acceptable?

There is no such thing as a minimum acceptable GMAT score. Again, the GMAT assessment is only one component of our admissions assessment and a low GMAT score can be compensated by other attributes of the applicant. For instance, this year, we have admitted a student with a very low GMAT score, but we found in his file an excellent academic background and a great personality, so clearly his low GMAT was not decisive in our admissions review.

What are the "do's" and "don't's" for the essays?

Through the essays, we want to get a sense of the personality of the applicant. We like to see applicants with a strong interest in Berkeley and the Haas School who can readily communicate a genuine insight into their character and motivations. We like to see people who are proactive, and results oriented. We value evidence of a thoughtful approach to career planning and meaningful discussion of an applicant's agenda for personal and professional growth. As for the "don't's" of application essays, avoid simple narratives or "cold" essays that fail to provide a genuine personal insight.

Is there a word limit for essays?

We give minimum and maximum word limits, but these are really just suggestions. We hope to avoid superficial thinking or glib attention to the questions we pose, but we also do not want to read essays that are too long, especially if the extra verbiage does not add value or significance. If an essay exceeds the word limit, it ought to be thoughtful, substantive, and interesting.

What are the "do's" and "don't's" for the letters of recommendation?

We use letters of recommendation to get an insight from a third party who knows an applicant in a professional context. We like to read letters from managers who really appreciate the applicant's contributions to the work effort and who are willing to spend time and effort to discuss the applicant's strengths and weaknesses. I recognize that letters of recommendations are not common in some countries, so there is definitely a cultural bias to take into account when assessing international applications. For example, American managers tend to rank applicant work performance excessively, with most tick marks in the 'exceptional' column and a token one or two ticks in the 'outstanding' column. Managers from many other countries rarely rank candidates so consistently highly, especially on those grids. On the other hand, I recently reviewed a letter of recommendation from a Korean manager who clearly took considerable effort to communicate his positive impressions about a candidate. His English was very limited, but his letter was a very strong and compelling endorsement. We like to see letters that convey appreciation and enthusiasm for a candidate.

What other schools do you see as Haas' direct competitors?

Stanford, Columbia, Wharton, Harvard, MIT, UCLA… All top institutions with a strong academic tradition.

What part does luck play in the selection process?

A very small part, I believe. We have an experienced admissions team in the MBA program and a large, world-class pool of applicants. Our graduation rate is above 99% and our graduates are in great demand throughout the world.

Getting the
CHICAGO
Admissions Edge

Chicago
Graduate School of Business

Address   Chicago Graduate School of Business
1101 East 58th Street
Chicago IL 60637 USA

Telephone   (1) 773-702-7369

Website   www.gsb.uchicago.edu

E-mail   admissions@gsb.uchicago.edu

about the school

Founded	1898
Tuition Fees	$30,500
Some Famous Alumni	Philip Purcell (Chairman & CEO, Morgan Stanley); Karen Katen (Exec. VP, Pfizer Pharmaceuticals); James Kilts (President, CEO Gillette); Jerry Levin (Chairman & CEO, Sunbeam); Kathryn Conner Gould (Partner, Foundation Capital)

the application

Application File	By mail or downloadable from website
Application Deadlines	Deadline dates same for September &January 1st round: early Nov. 2nd round: early January 3rd round: early March
App. File Elements	• 3 essays • 2 letters of recommendation • transcripts • GMAT (and TOEFL, if applicable) • résumé • interview recommended

rankings

Publication	Business Week						US News & World						Financial Times		
General Ranking	90	92	94	96	98	00	94	96	98	99	00	01	99	00	01
	2	**2**	**3**	**8**	**3**	**10**	**6**	**6**	**6**	**6**	**6**	**9**	**6**	**6**	**4**

before the MBA

# applicants per year	3,871
# applicants entering each year	487
% women students	26%
% minority students	6%
% international students	31%

Age (years)

mean	28.6
range	23 - 51

Education pre-MBA

Business	37%
Engineering	31%
Economics	15%
Social Sciences	8%
Humanities	7%
Other	22%

Professional experience

avg. years work experience	4.7
avg. starting salary (base)	$88,671

GMAT

average	684
median	630-740

GPA

average	3.4
range	2.83 - 3.85

after the MBA	School total
Main career choices	
Consulting	35%
Financial Services	42%
Technology	11%
Other	12%
Function	
Finance/Accounting	50%
Consulting	33%
Marketing	9%
Other	8%
Geographical location	
North America	88%
Asia	6%
Europe	5%
Central and South America	1%
Salary (source: Financial Times 2001)	
Avg. salary three years after graduation	$ 157,872
Alumni	
# alumni in the world (MBA)	34,444
# cities with an alumni association	60

Top 10 employers

1. McKinsey
2. Lehman Brothers Inc.
3. Booz, Allen & Hamilton
4. Goldman Sachs
5. Merrill Lynch
6. Accenture
7. Chase Manhattan
8. Boston Consulting Group
9. Bain & Company
10. Morgan Stanley Dean Witter

author

Name   S. de LONGEAUX

Summer internship with Bain.
Previously with Andersen Consulting in Paris and Dallas.

author

Name   C. OLBRECHTS

Joined Net Fund Europe, a venture capital firm.
Summer internship with Merrill Lynch in London.
Previously with Andersen Consulting in Brussels.

School specifics
CHICAGO

INTRODUCTION

Chicago is a university that very clearly focuses on research. For example, free-market theory was developed there by the famous "Chicago School" which has become one of the defining features of the university. Even today, many important discussions on the balance of the markets and "behavioral science" take place on campus.

The students benefit from this ingrained research culture through the quality of the professors as much as from the content of the courses. Indeed, they can attend classes with internationally renowned professors, notably five Nobel Prize winners for Economics, including George Stigler ('82), Merton Miller ('90), Ronald Coase ('91) and Robert Fogel ('93). In addition to the full-time professors, numerous high-caliber visiting professors come to Chicago for a year or two in order to benefit from the exceptional research conditions. In sum, the content of the courses is always on the cutting edge of their respective fields and enables students to orientate themselves towards careers with considerable analytical content, financial as much as strategic (commercial banks, consultancy, research, etc.).

The pedagogy is also influenced by this culture. Chicago attaches less importance than other universities to case studies. About 35% of the curriculum is on case studies, but more significant is the 35% on lectures and 30% on lab work (courses lasting one or two terms where students form a team to solve a specific problem of a "real" company). For example, the courses with technical content such as accounting or statistics are taught exclusively through lectures. The most demanding courses (especially finance) are also taught in a traditional way (through lectures), probably because their innovative content hasn't yet have been illustrated through real situations in case studies. We'll return to the advantages and disadvantages of this method in this chapter's section on teaching methods.

Chicago also sets itself apart from other business schools by offering complete flexibility in its curriculum. The school takes into consideration that post-graduates know what they're looking for in an MBA and have no desire to relearn what they already handle perfectly well. This means that students can very quickly specialize in the area that will be of particular use in their future careers. Not merely confined to the curriculum, this philosophy is a major driving force of Chicago GSB as a whole. For example, it's one of the few schools to allow individual professors to choose their own pedagogical methodologies. This means that, for the same subject, some professors will opt for case studies, while others may find lectures more appropriate.

Chicago isn't for everybody. For some, Chicago is the number-one choice as much for the teaching methods as for the flexibility of the curriculum. For others, Chicago shouldn't even be considered. In my opinion, Chicago is for students who have a clear idea of where they're going, are ready to take the next step in their chosen discipline, and want to be challenged with the theories of tomorrow.

To conclude this introduction, it should be stressed that the school is in full flux. Shaken by its sharp drop in its 1996 Business Week ratings, largely due to student discontent, Chicago had to take a sharp look at itself. Students had complained about the curriculum, judging the school to be too monolithic and too orientated towards finance, training people exclusively to be commercial bankers. Dean Hamada was the initiator of Chicago's *aggiornamento*. Without turning its back on its financial focus, the school reworked its curriculum by beefing up the departments of Entrepreneurship, Marketing, General Management and Strategy. Over the past few years, these departments have therefore benefited from the initiatives of reputable professors (e.g., Professor Kaplan for Entrepreneurship) and the arrival of new high-flying professors (e.g., Professor McGill from Northwestern for Marketing). The number of courses available in these subjects has also increased considerably. Finally, Chicago took several recruitment initiatives to increase the number of companies recruiting on campus as well as to improve the assistance provided to students in their job hunts in marketing and general management, or more generally in e-business companies. The results of these various initiatives were immediate, and in 1998 Chicago shot back up to number 3 in the general Business Week rankings. However, another drop in 2000 – to number 10 – means that more changes are likely in store.

THE DEAN'S VISION

This interview with Dean Bob Hamada was conducted by Sebastien de Longeaux and Cedric Olbrechts.

What is the mission of Chicago?

The Chicago GSB mission is to create cutting-edge business knowledge and disseminate it widely to the right audience. The research here is seminal. It is not an accident that our faculty received five Nobel Prizes. We are striving to develop seminal cutting-edge research. We then want to distribute and teach the results of this research. The audience includes the business world, the students and the research world.

Could you describe the teaching methods practiced at Chicago?

Chicago GSB is not 100% pure in its dogma of teaching. The Chicago approach teaches students to use analytical methods and conceptual tools from Economics, Statistics, Behavioral Sciences and other academic disciplines to solve complex business problems. Here again, the school believes in the free market. The faculty members follow a curriculum but have a lot of freedom to innovate in terms of teaching and pedagogy. This has led, for example, to the creation of the "Lab classes" in the early 1970s. Chicago GSB was the first business school to implement this way of teaching. Currently, about 35% of the classes are lecture based, 35% case based and 30% seminars and labs. Our goal is to give flexibility and choice. There is considerable flexibility for the faculty in designing an individual course of study and flexibility for the student to choose his/her classes and his/her instructors: more than half of the courses required for graduation consist of electives.

It seems that the Chicago curriculum gives more emphasis to Entrepreneurship, Marketing and General Management and slightly less to Finance. What is your opinion on this?

Over the past decades, Chicago GSB has developed a very strong knowledge in Finance, Economics and Accounting. Several of the most basic ideas guiding corporate and academic finance during the past 40 years have originated at the GSB. Among these are the theory of Capital Market Efficiency and the Modigliani–Miller Models of dividend policy and Capital Structure Choice. The Capital Asset Pricing Model (CAPM) has been embellished and extended at the GSB. This effort has been also recompensed in the corporate world by prominent alumni such as Philipp Purcell, CEO Morgan Stanley Dean Witter, John Corzine, ex-CEO Goldman Sachs or Joel Stern from Stern, Stewart & Company.

In the eighties, we wanted to show the world how we also excel in other fields such as General Management, Marketing and Entrepreneurship. We wanted our image to project this broader range of skills and capabilities. We formed teams to develop cutting-edge materials in these areas based on our strong Economics research. In General Management, the team includes Ron Burt (Sociology), Dick Thaler (Behavioral Science) and Robert Gertner (Economics). In Marketing, we have attracted some of the best scholars of their generations such as Sanjay Dhar, Ann McGill and Pradeep Chintagunta. In Entrepreneurship, we have developed a complete curriculum with a set of 19 classes with instructors such as Steve Kaplan, James Schrager, Toby Stuart and Austan

Gooldsbee. More recently, we have expanded our curriculum, introducing such courses as E-Business Strategies, Strategy and Entrepreneurship in the Information Economy to complement our more traditional courses. However, these initiatives do not mean that we are less focused on Finance! Accounting and Finance remain the intellectual powerhouses of the school. Our research and our professors are still ranked at the top of the Finance world. We demonstrated that we could be good in more than a few fields!

Sometimes people think that Chicago is too individualistic and that teamwork is not emphasized enough. Others argue that the school is too quantitative. What do you think?
Yes, it is true that Chicago is an analytical school. We believe in the power of the analytic mind to solve complex problems and we educate students to have a strong analytical spirit. By analytic spirit, I mean both quantitative and qualitative skills. Are we an individualistic school? Remember that we believe in free market for students as well as for teachers. The flexibility of our program allows individuals to make their own choice and to prepare themselves early on in their career. The great advantage that we provide is the ability for a student to prioritize classes in order to be the best prepared for his/her internship and later on for his/her full-time job. Chicago is therefore for people who know what they want and who are looking for this possibility of flexibility. Each student is different and is therefore less likely to team up with the same people all year long. We recognized this issue and the importance of teamwork. We have developed the cohort system for the first quarter as well as the LEAD program. This is our answer to balance the benefits of both worlds. Grouping students for the entire year would be much easier for us, but does not fit with our philosophy.

What are the efforts to keep Chicago at the forefront of global management education?
We opened facilities in Barcelona in 1992 and we now have 84 students graduating each year in an 18-month program. We launched the Singapore campus in September 2000. With this global program, the Chicago GSB has been at the forefront of exporting the North American model of business education to other parts of the globe. These international developments are very exciting for everybody at Chicago. They makes Chicago a global institution. The students for example can benefit from an extended Alumni network and international research and classes. These international facilities bring a lot of international collaboration to realize our mission of developing cutting-edge research.

Do you have any advice for future potential candidates?
At the Chicago GSB, we are offering people an internationally recognized education that appeals to people mature enough to develop their own curriculum and who have a strong analytical sense to develop and use the cutting-edge research acquired.

THE SCHOOL YEAR

Chicago does not offer a one-year intensive program (unlike Northwestern or INSEAD). That said, the school offers flexibility in the organization of the curriculum. Some students have, for example, spread their second year over two years (six terms) so as to have time for the setting up of a company. As a rule, students have five years to get their degree. The table below therefore shows only the traditional curriculum, which can be adapted to individual needs.

	Jun-Aug	Sept-mid Dec	Jan - end Mar	Apr-Jun	Jun-Sept	Sept-Dec	Jan-Mar	Apr-Jun
September entry (510 students)		1st term LEAD	2nd term	3rd term	Internship / vacation	4th term	5th term	6th term
IMBA entry*	IMBA classes	1st term LEAD	2nd term	3rd term	Internship / vacation	4th term	5th term	6th term

The IMBA includes an extra term (usually the summer following the first year) in which students take courses on international management. The other aspect of this program is the opportunity for IMBA students to spend a term at a partner university abroad. The IMBA involves about 60 students, which represents 10% of the student population.

As noted in the introduction, Chicago distinguishes itself by the great flexibility of its curriculum. Only one course is compulsory in the first term (LEAD). After that, the MBA student has a great deal of freedom to build his or her academic program, selecting from:
i) various courses among the required subjects (Marketing, Finance, General Management)
ii) electives from among 150 courses offered at the Business School, not counting those available in other departments (Economics, Languages, Law, Political Science... and even Medicine!).

To obtain the MBA, the student must take 21 courses, each 10 weeks long, which consist of:
- 1 compulsory leadership course: LEAD.
- 3 courses from the "foundation" subjects: Microeconomics, Accounting, Statistics and Strategy (bear in mind that Chicago offers several courses at various levels in each subject).
- 4 courses from the six "basic knowledge" subjects: Finance, Human Resources, Macroeconomics, Analytical Accounting, Marketing and Production (again, various courses and levels).
- 2 courses from "General Management" subjects: Strategy and Organizational Behavior.
- 11 electives in subjects of your choice.

So, students can (and should!) build their own curriculum. With the exception of LEAD, which must be taken in the first semester, everyone can take the courses they want in the term they want. The good thing about this flexibility is that you can prioritize the subjects that will be of most use for job interviews. For consulting, for example, students must follow the Marketing and Strategy courses during the two first terms in order to prepare themselves for the summer training courses which usually end up being on case studies.

Curriculum

Foundation: your choice of three courses from the "foundation" subjects: Microeconomics, Accounting, Statistics and Strategy.

As their titles suggest, these "foundation" courses are at the heart of the curriculum at Chicago. These three compulsory subjects (Microeconomics, Accounting and Statistics) provide students with the principles they will need very early on. For each subject, different levels of courses are offered, allowing students to choose depending on their interests and their level. They must choose one of these courses from the three subjects in order to satisfy the school's requirements:

- Microeconomics (seven courses at all levels offered). These go from introductory courses in microeconomics (the subject's theories) to advanced courses in the theory of games.
- Financial Accounting (seven courses at all levels offered): Financial Analysis I and II, Taxes, Analysis of Financial States, etc.
- Statistics (an introductory course or any other course in statistics). These go from Business Statistics to more advanced courses such as Financial Series Analysis or Data Analysis.

Breadth Requirement: you choice of four courses from six "basic knowledge" subjects.

Breadth is intended to provide students with the necessary knowledge base in different functional activities in business. Students must take one course in at least four of the six following subjects:

- Financial Management (four courses at different levels offered).
- Human Resources (four courses in relatively different areas offered).
- Macroeconomics (seven courses in relatively different areas offered).
- Analytical Accounting (two courses at different levels offered).
- Marketing (three courses at different levels offered).
- Production and Operations (two courses at different levels offered).

General Management: your choice of two courses.

The General Management courses deal with the concepts and techniques essential for efficiently managing an organization. These courses are taught from the point of view of a company manager analyzing the problems usually faced by executive committees. The student must choose a course from the group of courses offered in each of the following areas:

- Strategy (three courses in relatively different subject areas).
- Organizational Behavior (four courses in relatively different areas are offered).

Electives: your choice of 11 courses.

The electives enable students to focus on the subjects they are most interested in. You can choose from among the courses offered at the Graduate School of Business or from those offered by any of the other departments, the most sought-after being law and political science. These 11 other courses can be taken in the field of your choice in order to get "grouping", and are selected from the following list: Accounting, Econometrics and Statistics, Economics, Entrepreneurship, Finance, Analytical Finance, General Management, Human Resources, International Affairs, Managerial and Organizational Behavior, Marketing, Production and Operations, and Strategy. The groupings preferred by students are usually Finance with Entrepreneurship (which includes Internet strategy) and Strategy. In theory, you have to take four or five courses in a discipline to get a grouping and, on average, students take two groupings before getting their degree. I should emphasize that in each subject, the school offers a range of courses with various levels of difficulty. The student's goal is to never have to retake (and pay for) a subject which he can already handle with ease. For example, if a student already knows statistics, he can avoid wasting his time on the introductory course and take a course in Advanced Econometrics.

You've probably understood by now that there isn't a typical curriculum or timetable at Chicago. All students take the courses and choose the level of difficulty they deem useful for their professional development and the business activity they envisage doing after their MBA. The advantage, which we have already looked at, is the ability to specialize and to take very advanced courses very early on in subjects which interest you (without, however, totally abandoning fundamental subjects like Marketing and Strategy). The disadvantage is that it's very difficult to generate a sense of camaraderie among the students who entered in the same year. This is why the administration has created the notion of the "cohort" for first year students. Upon arrival at the school, students are assigned to one of the eight 60-student cohorts with which they'll take the LEAD course as well as one of the foundation courses. The idea is interesting but has its limitations as taking two 10-weeks long courses isn't really enough to create a "family" atmosphere.

THE COURSES – WHAT'S HOT... WHAT'S NOT

Below are the results of a survey of Chicago GSB students as to whether the courses met their expectations. Let's be clear about the fact that these assessment tables are not comparable between schools: the survey aims to measure satisfaction against expectations and obviously, student expectations vary between schools.

	Below Expectations	In line with expectations	Above Expectations	Outstanding
Microeconomics	0%	21%	54%	25%
Macroeconomics	6%	10%	21%	63%
Leadership	16%	15%	42%	27%
General Management	12%	25%	33%	30%
Operations / Production management	38%	25%	28%	9%
Marketing	5%	12%	62%	21%
Entrepreneurship	0%	11%	32%	57%
International Business	26%	41%	18%	15%
Financial Accounting	3%	16%	29%	52%
Managerial Accounting	26%	44%	19%	11%
Corporate finance	4%	28%	58%	10%
Financial Management	8%	14%	46%	32%
Statistics	18%	38%	32%	12%
Human Resources	40%	34%	16%	10%
Organization behavior	26%	38%	28%	8%

It's important to notice that students who go to Chicago often already have some financial knowledge and their expectations of the level of the Finance courses are very high. It's not surprising to see that the favourite courses are those which combine Finance with another subject such as Entrepreneurship or Internet. Our survey also reveals that students attach a great deal of importance to the teacher. The preferred professors are Steve Kaplan (Entrepreneurial Finance and Private Equity), Robert Vishny (Cases in Financial Management), Judy Chevalier (Competitive Strategy) and Austan Goolsbee (Strategy and Entrepreneurship in the Information Economy).

As is the case everywhere, there are good teachers, less good teachers and the stars. The advantage of a flexible curriculum is that each student can take the course and the professor of his or her choice. Requests for each course are handled via an online course stock exchange system (true to its faith in market forces, Chicago was the first to instigate this practice) ensuring perfect equality among the students.

The finance courses at Chicago are renowned for their excellence, and rightly so. Eugene Fama preaches the efficiency of the free market and subsequent theories developed on the idea; Richard Thaler deals with Behavioral Finance while Nobel Prize winners Fogel and Miller focus more on macroeconomic subjects.

I also recommend the courses in Organizational Behavior and Entrepreneurship (with renowned professors such as Steve Kaplan and James Schrager). In my opinion, the Strategy and Marketing departments, despite recent efforts, are still too weak and should be improved. It's interesting to note that Chicago now offers several courses in e-business and internet strategy outside of the more traditional entrepreneurship classes. It's still too early to assess the quality of this new area of concentration, but professors teaching these new courses hint that the school takes the subject very seriously.

TEACHING METHODS

As we've noted in the introduction, Chicago uses a mixture of lectures, case studies and other highly specific teaching methods such as the labs. In a given lab session, there is no lesson, strictly speaking. Students work in teams on real business problems, or on scenarios designed by the professor. In the labs, the professor plays the role of coach and consultant. Course 711, entitled "New Venture and Small Enterprise Lab", is one of the most sought-after. In this course, teams of three to five students work with start-ups or with Chicago's small businesses. Over the 10-week course, students act as consultants on a well-defined project and do regular presentations for their client. In this way the company benefits from free consulting and the students from the opportunity of putting into practice the theories learned in the classroom. Two of the many other lab courses are Lab in New Product and Strategy Development (709 – 710) and Private Equity Lab (714).

Lectures are used for learning basic technical ideas (Accounting, Statistics and Investment) so that students can quickly master principles that will form the basis of future discussions. However, this doesn't mean you work on your own. In fact, in most cases students must work together and submit the results of a group effort. Another thing worth mentioning is that lectures are also used for very advanced research courses where there aren't any case studies. In fact, in the intermediate-level courses, the case studies are intended to apply and to challenge the principles taught in the introductory courses.

In lecture courses, the professor usually explains a theory, with the support of slides and hand-outs, and illustrates it with the help of a practical exercise (which students often have to prepare before the lecture). The lectures are interactive; students are entirely free to ask questions if they don't understand, or to launch into a more far-reaching discussion on the subject.

The advantages:
- In my opinion, some subjects aren't suited to case studies (Basic Accounting, Statistics and Advanced Market Finance). In these subjects you learn more, in general, from the professor than from the students, and it would be safe to say that they don't lend themselves to discussion, since they're pretty much set in stone (who can or would want to contest an accountancy rule or a statistic theorem, and what's more, what would the other students get out of it?). This doesn't mean that class participation isn't encouraged - on the contrary - but it isn't the main focus of the course.
- The case study is reserved for intermediate-level courses. Students have mastered the basic principles (taught in the lectures) and are now able to apply them to case studies. They've got a solid foundation which will allow them to take part in more advanced and more enriching discussions. This is essential at Chicago because of the flexible curriculum: a case study in an introductory course where all the students are beginners would lead to a sterile discussion and would probably be a disaster.
- To quote Chicago's "official" argument which appears in the application form: "Get a case study right and you master the details, understand the principles and you master the world."

The disadvantages:
- The case study develops qualities of oral expression. If it's your weak point, Chicago will give you fewer opportunities than other universities in this area.

We must now bring up the delicate subject of Chicago and its reputation as a so-called "quantitative" school. For some, this reputation can be intimidating. If it's true that some courses are quantitative, you shouldn't be frightened by them for the following reasons:
- Since the curriculum is flexible, students don't have to take courses they think are beyond them.
- Whatever they say, the business world is built first and foremost on figures and someone who's not used to working with them should find these courses very useful for the next stage in his or her career... so you might as well start at Chicago!

THE GRADING SYSTEM
As with most MBAs, a certain amount of competitiveness exists at Chicago. On the one hand, this competitiveness comes from the students themselves, who are on the whole very competitive by nature, and, on the other hand, because some companies ask for students' GPAs at job interviews (investment banks and consulting firms in particular).

The grading system below is identical across all the courses:

Grade	Grade distribution
A or 4.0	Top 15-25% (top students: 15 to 25 %)
B or 3.0	Middle 70-75%
C or 2.0	Bottom 10% (bottom students: 10 %)

This is the "forced curve" system (see chapter on Harvard for a more on this), which doesn't evaluate students' absolute mastery of a subject, but rather their knowledge relative to that of the other students (the professor fixes the class average at 3.25). So for each exam, there will always be some students who get As and Bs and who get Cs. This means that even if you really know how to handle yourself in the subject, you're still going to end up with a B if 90% of students have mastered it better than you have.

Students who get a GPA of 3.5 for term's work will be lucky enough to see their names on the Dean's list at the end of each term and, more importantly, can put their GPA on their CV. Students who stockpile too many C's can, in theory, be asked to leave. But, to my knowledge, in my two years at Chicago, nobody left due to a lack of satisfactory results.

The opportunity for companies to ask a student his average (grade disclosure) isn't all that easy (many business schools ask companies not to ask their students this question) and it's the subject of hot debate among Chicago's students. The debate revolves around the following arguments:

Advantages of grade disclosure:
- For professors: the guarantee that each student will bend over backwards to do his or her best. Students benefit, too, because it guarantees quality class participation.
- For students, the grade point average is seen as something fairer than the GMAT in terms of graded, objective assessment by a potential employer. And you can see why they might think that, given that the GPA reflects one or two years of study and efforts in very diverse subjects, whereas the GMAT (the average score being very high at Chicago) is a single grade on one three-hour multiple-choice exam testing very specific, though questionable qualities.

Disadvantages of the grade disclosure:
- Stress in the first year.
- Team spirit is harder to generate.

GROUP WORK
In the rankings, teamwork usually follows assessments of individual performance at Chicago. Despite there being tons of team work opportunities (practically all classes offer students the chance to do group work), the professors look more at the quality of the work produced than at how well the group works. The result: students opt for efficiency and divide the work between them rather than meeting up for group work sessions. Our respective work experiences shows us that this actually seems to be what consultants and investment banks think of as group work. Rarely will you see in these jobs (where time is at a premium) a team meticulously discussing individual elements of a project. Work is handed out in advance and meetings give everyone a chance to pool their efforts and to discuss the projects' really crucial issues. This organization only works if the team members trust each other. The way you work as a team in Chicago is a good training experience, not only for learning how to turn out quality work, but also for trusting your teammates.

THE TEACHERS
The Chicago faculty is very diverse. Numerous professors come from other departments in the university such as Economics and Sociology and apply their knowledge to the world of business. Emphasis is placed on research and on time devoted to the courses and to the students. The

professors are judged on two criteria: firstly, the quality and quantity of their publications, and secondly on student evaluations. Their research work in no way affects the professors' availability outside of class. However, the teaching staff prefer to see students during office hours. Lastly, even though the majority of professors share their progress in their research with students, as far as I know they rarely give students the opportunity to take an active role in their research work.

GSB Chicago publishes the *Journal of Accounting Research* - one of the most reputable academic financial publications - as well as *Capital Ideas*. The faculty sends articles on a very regular basis to various international research journals such as the *Journal of Finance*.

Many faculty members have professional activities outside of the Business School. Some, such as Zonis or Nobel prize winners Miller and Fogel, spend their time rushing round the world giving lectures or handing out advice to various governments. Others are actively involved in company management, be it in multinationals or in Internet start-ups (Steve Kaplan belongs to the board of directors of many start-ups around Chicago and allows his students to benefit from his experience through the study of concrete examples).

THE INTERNATIONAL SIDE

Around 20% of the student population come from countries outside of North America. The countries with the largest contingents are China, Japan, Korea and Brazil. Among the Europeans, the Belgians top the list. There is an exchange program between the Catholic University at Louvain and Chicago, enabling Belgian students who already have suitable professional experience to get their MBA in 16 courses instead of 21. A similar program exists with the London School of Economics. Also, every year students from HEC and ESSEC and from Spanish universitites come to spend a term at Chicago as part of their curriculum. After a few years professional experience, they also have the same opportunity to return to Chicago to complete their MBA in 16 courses instead of 21, providing their application is approved.

Chicago also offers an IMBA program (International MBA) which offers the possibility of an exchange semester in a foreign university, and of specializing in courses oriented towards international problems. This program involves 50 to 60 students. To be admitted to the program, students must have had lengthy and high quality international experience. This exclusiveness affords the group members a significant cohesion, which is apparent in their many trips and experiences abroad. The program starts at the beginning of summer (June) and not in September like the standard MBA. To get the IMBA diploma, students must demonstrate knowledge of a foreign language, follow certain "international" courses, and previous study or work for at least four months abroad.

Finally, as part of its international strategy, Chicago has recently opened a campus in Barcelona and has recently opened another one in Singapore. The curriculum on these foreign campuses is generally designed to meet the needs of slightly older professionals (the average age is over 30 in Barcelona) who can't and don't want to take two sabbatical years to be students again. The courses are given one week every month. This system allows students to maintain their professional activity (at least 75%) while studying for an MBA. The courses are identical to those on the Chicago campus and are given by the same professors. The only difference is that the course list is smaller. To make up for this, these students can go to Chicago for a term and take courses of their choice at at no additional charge. This is how I met an alumnus of the program, a consultant with Mercer in

Paris, who had come to spend three months at Chicago to complete his training. He was very positive about his experience in Barcelona and recommends the program to those who don't want to become full-time students again. That said, for full-time students, the opening of the Barcelona and Singapore campuses doesn't change a thing. As I was told, you can't take courses there as a full-time student (not even an IMBA). Though the change is gradual, the positive impact of this expansion should make itself felt in the long term. It should expand the alumni network and help boost recognition of the university in European and Asian professional circles. To conclude this topic, it should be noted that nearly all the students at Barcelona are sponsored by their employers.

COMPUTER FACILITIES – IT SYSTEMS

Chicago is very well-organized in terms of online resources. As at most business schools, you can look up data on former or current students, choose your courses, directly download study aids from the relevant professor's site, look for information, or even plan your job interviews.

Two of these online initiatives are particularly worth mentioning: the Career Services site and the research tools. The Career Services site allows you to view, modify and post your résumé in the school's database, look up various resources relevant to a field of work, and even identify alumni who has worked in a specific area. The online research tools make available numerous databases from institutions around the world; some of these aren't even accessible in investment banks or consulting companies.

As for the computer labs, they're too small and the equipment is inadequate for the number of students. From time to time you have to wait (at peak times before exams, for example) to get a computer. This lack of space should be sorted out with the inauguration of the new building in 2003. If you don't already have a computer, purchasing a laptop could be a worthwhile investment. It's be a real godsend with group work. One last thing: you can hook up your computer in any study room and get access to the web and do your e-mail.

ALUMNI SERVICES

For the past few years, Chicago has had a professional service group devoted entirely to alumni. This department's task is to help alumni, for free, with their plans and career decisions. Based in the Gleacher center (the city-center campus), it offers all the advantages of a private placement firm. A former student can seek advice for negotiating his salary, have an individually tailored career consultation, or even use the service as a head-hunter to find his or her next job.

THE ENTREPRENEUR'S CORNER

For many years now, the University of Chicago's GSB has been teaching future entrepreneurs to launch, finance and manage their own companies, and during that period:

- many alumni and current students have become successful entrepreneurs.
- the quality of the courses was rewarded by being ranked as Business Week's best entrepreneurship professors: Chicago's business school alone was able to count 2 professors, Steve Kaplan and James Schrager, among the top six.

These trump cards in entrepreneurship were firmly established through the foundation of the GSB Entrepreneurship Program, which joins together the Entrepreneurial and Venture Capital initiatives under one roof.

The other factors to mention are:

- The New Venture Challenge (NVC): a business plan contest ($45,000 worth of prizes) which students take part in. The business plans are assessed by a panel composed of venture capitalists, bankers, consultants and members of the academic staff. Numerous start-ups are created after the competition.
- New Venture and Private Equity (see our description of "lab courses" under "Curriculum").
- Kauffman Summer Internships in Entrepreneurial and Private Equity Firms: every year, the Kauffman Center for Entrepreneurial Leadership gives about 10 grants to students who want to do their summer training course in a Private Equity firm or a start-up. The Entrepreneur and Venture Capital Student Association: this organizes many activities (lectures, trips to Silicon Valley, etc). Trips are organized in December at the end of the first term. It includes visits to high-tech companies, a job fair, cocktails with alumni, and lectures on private equity and venture capital. It's very popular and is the best way to get excellent contacts if you're interested in high-tech, dot.coms or capital-risk.

Apart from this, around 20 courses are offered to students wanting to know more about high-tech strategy and small companies, including Entrepreneurial Finance, Internet Strategy, and Private Equity.

LIFE AT CHICAGO

CHICAGO

Chicago has, for all intents and purposes, erased its bad reputation as a gangster city (despite the lingering memory of Al Capone). On the hit-parade of risky cities, the Windy City ranks only seventeenth, far behind Washington and Los Angeles.

Go-getting and dynamic, today Chicago is often referred to as the "second city", and it could easily be dubbed the architectural capital of the world. In fact, a fire in 1871 devastated the whole city, but made way for the construction of Chicago's first skyscraper, situated in the Loop district. Due to the sheer audacity of its recent constructions, Chicago remains true to its tradition as a forerunner in architecture, with the Sears Tower, the Amoco building, etc.

Chicago also boasts immense cultural resources: the international reputation of its symphony orchestra and its museums, situated just beside the lake, house wonderful collections. So Chicago is like a little New York, a little more provincial, but a lot more liveable. Its location on Lake Michigan allows for numerous sporting and cultural activities, including swimming, biking, sailing, and jogging.

THE CAMPUS

The University of Chicago Business School uses two main buildings: one in Hyde Park, in the south of Chicago, and one downtown, the Gleacher Center. The university campus is a collection of neogothic buildings surrounding a beautiful square. The area in which the campus is situated, Hyde Park, is pleasant, but the surrounding neighborhoods have a reputation of being somewhat run-down and unsafe. Hyde Park, however, is very green with a lot of parks, and offers the possibility for sports. The proximity of the lake means that you can take a dip (during the summer months of course!), go bike riding or rollerblading. Students can choose to take their courses on the Hyde Park campus or at the Gleacher Center. The choice is generally made for you by your schedule. For the most part, the GSB administration is at Hyde Park.

Being a little short on space, the business school is planning a move in 2003 two blocks away on the present campus to a new complex which is cuurently under construction (with an $80 million budget). The new space will allow the GSB to have all its departments under one roof.

HOUSING

Most students live either on the Hyde Park campus, or in one of Chicago's nicest (and liveliest) neighborhoods, Lincoln Park, in the north of the city (in which case you need a car). Many who live in Hyde Park for their first year get together and move up north for their second year. They take the majority of their classes on the downtown campus to avoid long trips and to take full advantage of downtown Chicago.

On campus:

- University accommodation. For low-budget unmarried students, there is International House, which offers cheap rooms ($400/mo). The university also offers a range of very reasonable one, two or three-room apartments on campus for around $700/mo.

- High-rises. There are several high-rise apartment complexes near the campus. The most popular isRegents Park, which offers one-room apartments ($800/mo) or two-room apartments ($1000/mo) with a superb view over the lake, club, indoor swimming-pool, etc.

The new business school complex slated for completion in 2003 will also include affordable luxury apartments. The aim is to keep as many students as possible on the Hyde Park campus in order to help reorganize social events there.

In the city:

The most popular neighborhhoods are Lincoln Park, Bucktown and Wrigleyville. Prices vary but tend to be higher than those on campus. Some university shuttle buses take you downtown, but I think it's pretty essential to have a car.

SOCIAL LIFE

Chicago has a long-suffering image as an austere university. Being situated south of the downtown area, where bars are scarce, it's true that the campus does nothing to promote a busy social life. The curriculum's flexibility, which in some ways prevents a sense of community from forming, doesn't help matters. Nevertheless, the GSB administration has taken some pretty effective measures to help promote networking. Friday afternoons are your chance to live it up at a free barbecue thrown by the university, with the favorite beer of one of the professors which he personally serves. Lots of other social events punctuate the university year: the semi-formal, held in the university museum; the winter formal, in one of Chicago's chicest hotels; and a night cruise party on Lake Michigan.

Students didn't wait to be asked by the administration to create their own networking events. Be they meetings organized by the various clubs (the most popular being the TNDC, Thursday Night Drinking Club) or the parties organized by foreign student organizations (the most infamous being the Belgian Halloween party). There are activities for all tastes. If you know how to take advantage of the system, you'll have an excellent time.

As far as Chicago is concerned, it's a city that offers you almost unlimited evening possibilities. Students happily go out together on Friday or Saturday nights to listen to jazz or blues in downtown bars, about 15 minutes by car from the campus.

Finally, every week the university invites students to listen to a guest lecturer. Among others, we had the chance to hear Jim Clark (founder of Netscape and of the company formerly known as Silicon Graphics, now SGI) and Thomas Jermoluk (CEO Excite@Home).

As with all MBAs, costs are considerable. Costs for the academic year 2001-2002 were:

Overall costs for the MBA (two years)	In US $
Tuition Fees	61,000
Miscellaneous costs (including health insurance)	3,282
Books	3,000
Food	9,900
Housing	14,000-20,000
Personal	4,000
Transportation	4,000
TOTAL	97,882-103,882

It is important to mention that the flexibility of the Chicago program enables many students to do several particularly well-paid training courses or to work part-time. A Chicago student must take 21 courses to get the degree. He or she has a maximum of five years to complete his or her studies. Though the vast majority of students don't take that much time, sometimes there are advantages to taking the opportunity to do one, two or even three extra training courses over the course of your studies at Chicago. The reasons for this are varied: some need to test out several industries to be sure about their final choice; others group their courses over fewer terms in order to start work or to develop a business which just can't wait.

And another thing: there are various ways to finance an MBA:
- Grants offered by the school: the GSB offers grants based on the student's academic excellence and leadership skills. The majority of grants are offered to first-year students. The selection process takes place in January.
- Loans: The Financial Aid Office administers student loans at competitive rates.

STUDENT VIEWS

I chose to come to Chicago because no other top MBA school offers so much academic flexibility. For example, I've taken several French classes as part of my MBA. These were real classes, not watered down versions for MBAs who are taking a full load of business courses. Chicago also let me skip some courses that would have been part of the mandatory core at most other schools. So instead of spending time (and money!) studying things I knew backwards and forwards from my previous work experience or that I had mastered as an undergraduate, I have been able to take courses that are more interesting to me. Next year, I plan to take an acting class to practice projecting exactly the kind of image I want to project at any given time. Only Chicago gives people with this kind of intellectual curiosity the room to explore, and its one of its greatest strengths.

The IMBA program is phenomenal, thanks to the quality and the highly international profile of the students, the trips to other continents, and the cohesion of this small group of 50-60 people.

The admissions application

CHICAGO

INTRODUCTION

Filling out the various application forms is a long and detailed task, requiring you to handle five very different things:
- Preparing for the GMAT and taking it.
- Contacting the people you've chosen to write your letters of recommendation, giving them at least four weeks notice in order to write them.
- Contacting your various schools and universities for your transcripts. Expect a wait of at least two weeks (some schools are more efficient than others in this respect).
- Filling out the application and writing the three essays.
- Making an appointment for the mandatory interview which will be conducted in your city (if possible) or on campus.

Ideally, all these things must be done before the months of September to November in order to send off the applications in time for the first or second application round (for Chicago: beginning of November and end of January). You'll realize very soon that the three-month timeframe can be very tight when you take into account all the people and institutions involved in the procedure. It is essential that you effectively deal with all the tasks you must attend to. If you opt to take them on one after the other, you run the risk of missing the application deadlines.

In my opinion, a good application must give a coherent picture of the applicant. For example, it would be inappropriate to explain in an essay that you like to work alone if your references fall over themselves with praise for your team spirit! In addition, it is essential to keep in mind what each admissions office is looking for in an applicant: their potential. The more or less concealed ambition of each institution is to place the greatest number of alumni in the very tight circle of senior managers and CEOs in the world's major companies of today and tomorrow. To do this, it must start by choosing applicants with potential and ambition and that is precisely what they are trying to deduce from your application.

Finally, the application must be tailored to each school. The various universities, especially at this level, operate in an extremely competitive market and each highlights what makes it different from the rest - its specific qualities and its strengths. You must use these points and prove through the essays and the letters of recommendation that your personality is perfectly adapted to the characteristics of the school. In addition to a careful reading of this book, it is advised that you attend the information meetings that the schools organize in each city in the United States and abroad during the first term. To receive the list of the meetings for all the MBAs, you can contact the World MBA Tour at www.topmba.com. For meetings specifically on Chicago, consult the admission office's website at www.gsb.uchicago.edu.

THE GMAT

The GMAT is unavoidable. For me, and certainly for many others, this exam was the most uninspiring part of the application. But it is absolutely essential to get a good score to stay in the running. That said, everyone, with a little effort, can get a satisfactory score.

	GMAT	TOEFL
average	684	273
deviation	+/- 30	+/- 10
range of scores	610 to 740	253 to 297

In preparing for the GMAT, I think it is best to go step by step. Start by doing a mock exam on paper or on computer, "cold" – without having done any preparation. To do this, get hold of one of the practice exam CD-ROMs published by specialist organizations such as Kaplan or the Princeton Review. Your score will give you an idea of the work you'll need to produce to get a worthwhile score. If you get a good score (over 650 at your first attempt), a few hours of revision should be enough to reach a score over 700. If such is the case, there's no point in devoting too much time to the GMAT. Get it under your belt quickly, and then concentrate on your potential weaknesses. If you're well under 600, you've got work to do.

There are many private companies that offer specific preparation for GMAT. The best known are Kaplan and the Princeton Review. For the tidy sum of around $1,000, these companies take charge of your preparation for cramming the math and verbal sections. You'll also have the opportunity to take several mock tests in the same conditions as those for the official exam. Here are my personal views of the advantages and disadvantages of these training programs:

Advantages:
- They make you revise the tests by giving you a very precise and strict study program.
- The revision methods are so meticulous that their helping hand should not be underestimated.
- The teachers know the types of questions inside out and exactly what's expected of the applicants. They can explain in specific detail which points are important to focus on and which can be left alone.
- Each of these companies has developed a specific methodology which is entirely geared toward the end result (they claim to be able to improve your score by on average 120 points). The teacher's goal is to increase as much as he or she can your chances of getting the right answer on all types of question. From memory methods to tricks for doing mental calculations more quickly, all approachs are called upon to increase your success rate. The content of the classes is not always academic, but it works.

Disadvantages
- The cost.
- The average level of the students is not always very high. If this is the case, ask to have private lessons instead of normal sessions. With a bit of luck, the company will comply.

Conclusion: only turn to one of these companies if your starting score is not satisfactory. It may be that a simple review of math theorems (algebra, geometry) and of English grammar will be enough to rapidly increase your score. If so, buying a test prep book will easily do the trick. If after a few hours of hard work you're still stuck below 600-650, you probably need a leg up, and Kaplan or the Princeton Review can definitely make all the difference.

For international applicants, TOEFL scores must also be submitted with the application. It is not a difficult test. With a little listening aptitude and some basic knowledge of English grammar, the pass mark of 600 (the minimum required) is easily obtained. A good cramming book and a few films in English should do it. I don't think the admissions distinguishes between a 620 and a 670 on the TOEFL. Therefore, to get a score of 620 or above is essential.

THE ESSAYS

A FEW GENERAL TIPS FOR WRITING STRONG ESSAYS

Writing essays can be a somewhat disarming exercise. Faced with the empty page, you can really start to wonder what you can talk about.

There are some general rules to follow:

- Keep to the format provided as well as the number of words.
- Answer the question specifically, avoiding extra verbage.
- Write in grammatically impeccable English.
- Be yourself.

I think the best way of going about this is to write the essays yourself without trying to guess what the school is looking for. Once the essay is written, waste no time in having it read by the appropriate people (teachers, alumni, parents, friends, etc.). Be patient. You'll probably have to rewrite the original document 20 times before producing a satisfactory result.

WHAT CHICAGO IS LOOKING FOR IN YOUR ESSAYS

Once again, generally speaking, Chicago is not looking exclusively for leaders or for applicants with a given personality. Chicago appreciates balanced and well-rounded personalities. If you're a born leader, don't pass up your chance to state your successes, but nevertheless remember to show your analytical ability, your ability to work in a team, etc. in your essays. The admissions committee refuses to be more precise and name the three or four principal qualities that they're looking for in an application. Nevertheless, I'm going to stick my neck out and list the following qualities:

- An analytical mind, because Chicago believes in the power of analysis to solve business problems
- Leadership, because Chicago, like every school, aims to build business leaders.
- Diversity of experience. I was surprised to see that the vast majority of students had had some sort of international experience before doing their MBA. That can't just be coincidence.

Chicago asks for three essays to be written, plus an extra one for IMBA applicants. I've listed below a few examples taken from the most recently submitted applications.

The list of essay questions:

- Why are you seeking an MBA or IMBA from the University of Chicago Graduate School of Business? What do you hope to experience and contribute? What are your plans and goals after you receive your degree?
- Ten years from now, an alumnus/a from Chicago calls you on the phone. Where will the phone ring, what will you be doing, and what wisdom will you be able to impart to them?
- If you were to bury five items, to be dug up in 250 years, that best describe you and your accomplishments, what would those items be and why?
- If you could be any age for the rest of your life, what age would you be and why?
- If you could receive any award, who would present it and for what reason would it be given?
- For IMBA only: describe a recent international issue or event that has had a negative effect on the business or economic climate of a particular region of the world. How would you address this issue? What are the implications of your approach?

EXAMPLES AND COMMENTARIES OF ESSAYS FOR CHICAGO

Why are you seeking an MBA or IMBA from the University of Chicago Graduate School of Business? What do you hope to experience and contribute? What are your plans and goals after you receive your degree?

The point of the essay:

The first essay in any business school's application usually asks you to explain why you are applying to that particular institution. Even if your reasons for doing an MBA are somewhat general, your interest in Chicago must be specified with the greatest possible precision. Don't think it's enough just to cite the the the school's ranking, its reputation, and your certitude of receiving a good education and a good career served to you on a platter. Those are examples of overly general reasons that can be used in any application, and the schools don't like that. This essay gives you the opportunity to demonstrate that you are familiar with the unique traits of Chicago GSB and know what it can offer you and that it fits right in with your goals. Beyond that, the essay of 750 words absolutely must achieve the following objectives:

- explain the coherence of your professional career up to the present.
- show that you are ambitious but realistic.
- explain your career objectives and showing that they can't be achieved without an MBA.
- demonstrate that you know what Chicago can SPECIFICALLY offer you (you have looked into the question and met some people) and that you need this curriculum to achieve your professional objectives.
- explain how your professional or personal experiences in the past will enable you to offer something to Chicago life, demonstrating that you are aware of the fact that the program's success depends as much on the interaction between the students as on the quality of the curriculum.

Tips for the essay:

You must prove in 750 words that you are going to flourish at Hyde Park and that those two years at Chicago are going to bring you more than anywhere else could. It's not asking much. Here's a bit of advice which I hope will be useful to you when you come to writing the essay:

- Avoid writing a standard essay for all the schools, merely adapting it to the specific nature of each school. In general, the result is an impersonal essay which doesn't answer the question "Why Chicago" at all well.
- Give details that prove that you know the school. In the example essay presented below, the writer shows that she knows certain professors and mentions her visit to the school, which is excellent. ("...this was evident in my conversations with students and in the classes I attended. The quality of professors like Steven Kaplan and James Schrager contributes significantly to the high academic level of the Entrepreneurship program...").
- Be concise, direct and coherent. You must get the largest number of messages across possible to go with the rest of the application. In our example, the applicant chose to clearly focus his application on the "Entrepreneurship" aspect. It would have been at odds with his application if he had mentioned the strength of the Finance department in this essay.
- Don't be afraid to devote at least a paragraph to your contribution to the community over the coming two years and then as an alumni. By the way, it's a very good excuse to bring out your leadership qualities and to describe your initiatives in students associations, charitable associations, etc.

- Have your essays read by someone, perhaps by more than one person who knows the procedure and is capable of giving you constructive criticism. It's a difficult exercise and your first draft will certainly not be the final version.
- Consider your work finished when everyone is in agreement. Not before.

Sample Essay:

I would like to set up my own business. I believe that the University of Chicago Graduate School of Business is uniquely positioned to provide me with the high quality interdisciplinary business education I am looking for. In order to build, run, and grow a business successfully, there are skills that are difficult to obtain while working for a large multinational. I am looking to build on my experience with a Chicago MBA with a focus on entrepreneurship and international business. I have visited the School and I am convinced that, in addition to one of the best MBA programs in the world, it offers an enriching, friendly environment in which to grow both personally and professionally. Of particular interest to me is the strength of the School's entrepreneurial curriculum: The School offers a challenging and enriching environment for entrepreneurs and this was evident in my conversations with students and in the classes I attended. The quality of professors like Steven Kaplan and James Schrager contributes significantly to the high academic level of the entrepreneurship program. Moreover, combining this program with the IMBA offers skills needed to pursue entrepreneurial efforts across national borders as would be the case with me. Finally, working towards an MBA at the University of Chicago will enable me to integrate and investigate the Chicago market. This is a key point for me because I want to start my business in a larger urban center and Chicago would offer an ideal location for assessing demand and targeting potential clients for my project.

I feel confident that I can make significant contributions to the School's social and academic life. My international education and my career as an international consultant and auditor have provided me with a broad perspective of world affairs and business, albeit within a specific industry. Most of my professional experience has been with Accor, a global and prestigious group and a world leader in the hospitality and tourism industries. My role was international and, over a five year period, helped me develop a rigorous approach to business problems as well as enhance my communications skills and leadership abilities. I have recently (last June) been offered a position within Accor as project manager in the conception of our brand new global reservation & revenue management system. The project is high profile, innovative and strategic for the group as a whole and has provided me with extraordinary insight into how technology is driving our businesses.

Even in earlier days, I knew I wanted to create my own business. Going into business for myself will provide me with the freedom to put into action my own ideas, the responsibility that comes with being in control of my own destiny and that of others and, hopefully, the financial rewards of business success. Perhaps the single most attractive part of running my own business is the creative part – coming up with the ideas, putting them to work and watching them develop. Upon graduation from college, I spent several months in Bavaria trying to set up a business with a fellow student from Haiti. The business idea was to import and sell inexpensive Haitian paintings. The venture was unsuccessful mostly because it met with insufficient demand. I returned home looking for work with the intention to acquire some solid, general business experience and try again.

My entrepreneurial thoughts never left me: over the last couple of years my ideas have been taking shape toward capitalizing on one of my hobbies – wine tasting. The business proposition is to develop a chain of wine-tasting centers throughout the United States and potentially worldwide. The target market for these wine-tasting sessions would be primarily corporate networking events, and, perhaps, individuals and restaurant owners. I firmly believe this is a business with high potential in many countries and would like to pursue it following my graduation. The numerous business conferences and related events in the US may be initially more receptive to wine tasting than individuals and probably easier to market to. Although I have yet to carry-out in-depth market research (I am hoping to do this locally in Chicago!), I am convinced that there is a market gap in offering a consistent, high quality product aimed primarily toward the corporate market.

The two other essays

The other essays pose surprising questions and vary from year to year. The second year students choose the questions. There's no point in analyzing each past question in detail. So we're going to analyze the group together and then provide some different examples.

The point of these essays:

To give you the opportunity to bring out your true personality. Up to this point, the whole application is supposed to have provided a rather complete and objective picture of your professional qualities. These essays will add something new to the picture. It's your opportunity for self-assessment in a different light, of showing originality, and finally of including remarks on your personal values (what do you consider important in life, etc.). There is, of course, no right anwser to these questions.

Tips for these essays:

* Be yourself and try to prove that you are something besides a top student. In my opinion, the best essays are those that show creativity and humor (if it's appropriate, a humorous essay can go over really well).
* Make a real effort of introspection and reveal your personality as honestly as possible. But don't feel you have to be an open book about everything. If your dream holiday is to spend six months on a desert island in the arms of a top model, avoid being too honest! Think about the impression you want to give of yourself.
* Once again, have your essays read as many times as possible by as many people as possible who are qualified to do so. Once you're immersed in your work, it's difficult to gauge its quality.
* Be careful with style. A well-written essay is important.

Since the questions change constantly, there's no need here to remark in detail on the questions of the previous years. That said, I think it's important to include a few examples written by students from the past two years, in order to give you an idea of what's expected.

Sample essays:

1. If you could be any age for the rest of your life, what age would you be and why?

In order to take a firm stand on such a question, I must view all the other years of my existence with a slight edge of dissatisfaction. However, at the dawn of my fourth decade, I found the question challenging and the answer could only largely depend on future suppositions and past and present feelings. My choice goes toward the near future, my thirtieth birthday, because I prefer the thrill of hope to the paralysis of nostalgia. Furthermore, I consider this age a period of feasibility and project completion. Indeed, at thirty, one enjoys the freedom of an adult life but still has the energy and enthusiasm of the young. The frustration felt during the early twenties with its' "I wish I could" is foregone yet the power of the "will" is still strongly present. Thirty is therefore the age where opportunities can be transformed into present achievements.

This statement, of course, is a simplification of what I hold to be true. Great achievements can certainly be realized at an earlier stage of life (I envision the nodding approval of Mozart, composer of some of his first masterpieces before his tenth birthday). I consider such achievements, however, not so much final realizations or sources of immense pride as springboards to go further and progress in life. Herein lies the beauty of the age of thirty. Nothing is impossible or written in stone. An easy objection to this statement is the uncertainty fundamentally linked to this age of transition. However, I have come to understand and appreciate the fertile link between uncertainty and achievement.

2. If you had the opportunity to take the vacation of a lifetime, with whom and where would you spend it? Describe your dream vacation in detail.

Jean-Baptiste Debret, my guide and friend on this trip, was a 19th century painter and is in surprisingly good health for someone who has been dead for over a century! Off we go to a dream world where people resemble the weather in their openness, warmth and demeanor: Brazil! Jean-Baptiste never ceases to be amazed at how much - yet how little - has changed since his exile to Brazil from post-Napoleonic France. Turmoil is ever present as is the diversity: mulattoes, people of European descent, native Americans, Asians give rise to an ethically varied, yet integrated, society.

In Salvador de Bahia, the music is everywhere, proclaiming African and Portuguese origins. The samba and the bossa nova remind me of my childhood in Africa, with the added flavor of the New World. People of all colors are singing, dancing and improvising by using garbage cans as drums. Jean-Baptiste explains that the intensity of life here is something that has always been present. On our way to Rio de Janeiro, a group of boys stop playing soccer and come to greet us. Our proximity prompts Jean-Baptiste into a history lesson: when Napoleon drove out the royals in 1807, Rio became the seat of the Portuguese government. When, following Napoleon's fall, the Portuguese legislature tried to return Brazil to colonial status, nationalists proclaimed the country's independence in 1822, making him a Brazilian.

At the Maracanã stadium, people from a samba school practice year-round for the Carnival. The joie de vivre is evident: Jean-Baptiste explains that living the moment enables Brazilians to embrace tomorrow with a rare optimism. So much is new: soccer, the mania with television soap operas and Formula 1 races were not around in his day. Yet, in a strange way, they remain ways in which this diverse, multicultural world draws together, in a way that reminds Jean-Baptiste how these people came together when they decided they were Brazilian, rather than a colony of a European power. It is this diversity that strengthens this nation and, perhaps, the world as a whole.

3. If you had $10 million to give away, where would you give it?

I would use the $10 million to help shape the financial system in sub-Saharan Africa. This is a part of the world where I spent most of my childhood and has always been close to my heart. Throughout the region, even the poorest locals save some money; however, individual savings levels are generally too low to provide a profit incentive to western banks or other private sector institutions. Consequently, local entrepreneurs make small investments (e.g., buy a pushcart or a stall) but are unable to invest in anything more sizable. The mobilization of local savings would enable them to have access to more sizeable loans, resulting in the creation of larger concerns and in accelerated development.

I would aim to use the $10 million as seed capital to set up small, local "savings cooperatives." About 10% of the funds would be reserved by the cooperatives for training locals in market research, *creating business plans, obtaining finance from the cooperatives, book-keeping and, generally, operating an efficient business and turning a profit. Loans will be granted only to borrowers who attend the business training sessions. The cooperatives ensure that the chances of success of the businesses are evaluated accurately based on the cooperatives' knowledge of the local socioeconomic conditions and a close relationship with their clients. Social and peer pressure from the community ensures that funds are used for the intended purpose, and are not diverted for private use.*

In the 19th century, this type of cooperative association enabled the development of rural areas in Western Europe. This approach to development took into account the specific cultural, economic and human aspects of the local environment to arrive at innovative solutions. It can work again and should be given a chance.

4. If you could receive any award, who would present it and for what reason would it be given?

The award I would receive would be entitled "Award for Enlightened Citizen" and would be created to celebrate people who spent their lives trying to understand the world and themselves through continual intellectual dissatisfaction. This award would be created in memory of such well-rounded thinkers as Thomas Jefferson and would celebrate humanism. Such an award would commemorate the selected individual's accomplishments in life. However, I imagine this recognition more as a celebration of a certain attitude than that of a specific accomplishment.

The persons bestowing me with the award are unknown to me because they do not yet exist. They are citizens of tomorrow's world at a time when I will be reduced to mere memory. Therefore, the award would sanction achievements whose greatness lie in their durability. By receiving an award in the future, I would avoid any ephemeral recognition that might fade away with time. I realize that this award is too general to exist and the accomplishment too elusive to be remembered. I am, however, convinced that at the twilight of my life I would personally be able to recognize whether I deserved such an award or not. If, in reality, I were ever to receive this merit, it would certainly be the greatest source of personal happiness.

LETTERS
OF RECOMMENDATION

Number of letters of recommendation needed for Chicago: 2

GENERAL ADVICE

As with any application, the letter of recommendation is a key element. The references must not only be extremely positive, they must also project an image of the applicant that fits with the rest of the application. Some references may be tempted to ask you to write the letter and will content themselves with first copying it out on official company letterhead and then signing it. It's absolutely essential to avoid this trap. First, the letter will probably be a lot more impersonal and thereby fail to succeed. Second, the people in charge of assessing references may recognize your style. If this happens, the letter loses all its worth and will weigh against your application in the final decision.

1) Choose the right people

Choosing the right people is crucial. The letters should preferably come from people representing different phases of your professional life. For example, good choices are a manager for whom you worked early on in your career, and a manager or colleague with whom you have worked more recently. The second letter is essential. Even if it poses problems of a conflict of interest ("I'm saying that I want to leave my job without knowing if I'll be accepted to school"), it is essential to include a letter from your last employer. In my view, you take little risk in asking for a reference for the following reasons:

- You want to go off to study again and not join the competition.
- To not be selected on your first attempt is nothing to be ashamed of given the very selective nature of the procedure.
- If you're accepted, you leave the company for 24 months, and not necessarily for good. In a word, everything depends on the way you go about your request. With a little diplomacy, everything will go smoothly.

Finally, I reiterate the same advice given over and over in every discussion on the subject. You must choose people with whom you've worked directly, and who hold positions with substantial responsibilities. Basically, that means you should avoid choosing your office mate ("same role, same responsibilities and, to top it off, we get along well!") but also avoid choosing the company's managing director whom you know through someone else. Ideally, the letter must convey your professional qualities with that personal touch. I think a manager one or two levels above you is probably the best-placed person for this.

2) The content: give out the right vibes

Although it's not a good thing to write your own letters, that doesn't mean that you should give their authors free reign to put down whatever they like. If the person accepts to write you a reference, make it clear to him or her the type of message that you want to sent to the admissions office. Without going to the point of writing it yourself, it is sometimes useful to write the basic outline of the letter together and to agree on the various key points which will structure it.

THE LETTER OF RECOMMENDATION FOR CHICAGO

Chicago does not require any particular format from referees beyond that of the table below, which they'll need to fill in. In my opinion, a good reference should begin by explaining the nature of the relationship between the recommender and the applicant. Then, certain key subjects must be dealt with. From talking with the staff in the admission's office, I came up with the following list:

- Ability to work in a team.
- Analytical skills.
- Leadership.

The following letter is only an example. Its structure seems to me, however, to be excellent. The writer begins by explaining in detail the nature of his relationship with the applicant. Then, the letter deals with four separate subjects:

- The applicant's professional responsibilities and the qualities which have enabled him to succeed. Note that the writer avoids generalizations such as: "Jane is an excellent leader". On the contrary, each remark is very specific and set in context in order to guarantee its credibility.
- Weaknesses. I think it's useful to take on this subject, because if well-phrased, it can become the highest of compliments. In this particular case, the weaknesses are simply points for improvement, which shows that the applicant is both self-aware and ambitious.
- Career development. As I've already stressed, the admissions committee is looking for applicants with potential. The best way to gauge this is to look at how the applicant has developed in the past. That is why it's essential that the writer stresses your recent achievements. In our example, this paragraph demonstrates that the applicant developed fully and that he has that famous, highly-sought "potential".
- The last point deals with the applicant's future. The writer expresses his entire confidence. Not only does the applicant possess the required qualities to succeed in his present responsibilities, but these very qualities will enable him to go further: ("In ten years, I believe Jane… is likely to be one of my partners… I see her as very successful in whatever she takes on"). As a last point, I think it is very good that the writer explicitly states that he is ready to discuss the applicant's case and includes his contact number. In my opinion, it is a sign of sincerity and of his or her dedication to help the applicant.

Example:

I have known Jane for two years as a consultant with Accenture. The foundation of our relationship is based on our interaction in various client engagements in which we have both been involved over the past two years. During that period, Jane has held a significant role on our development team and we have had multiple interaction throughout the process. I have also received continuous feedback on Jane's work results and capabilites from Associate Partners and Managers who she reports to. She has continuously demonstrated deep expertise in the functional areas of finance and account receivables. This was most evident as she helped to lead an effort to match our client's business process requirements with their application software requirement in these areas. I have found her to excel at analytical problem solving using very logical and thorough thought processes to get to the right conclusion. She is consistently focused, is very capable of working in diverse environments and has exceeded all expectations as a team player. She is creative in her solution development, but very practical in ensuring realistic business objectives are met.

I consider Jane's developmental needs as only continuing paths from the experiences that she has already gained. If any weaknesses exist, either in character or ability, I am not aware of them, nor are they represented in her work history, which I have reviewed. In discussions with Jane, she would like to have more understanding of broad and global issues which I have assured her will come with time. Though I do not necessarily consider this a weakness, I am certain that this is an area she would like to continue to focus on, both through her educational and business experiences in the future.

In the timeframe that I have known Jane, the most significant changes that I have seen in her development have come in two areas. Firstly, she has gone from focusing virtually all her attention on the Account Receivals and Credit functions to gaining a much broader exposure to all of the finance processes. This exposure has significantly increased her business and industry acumen and has allowed her a better perspective of the key indicators driving our client's decision. Secondly, Jane has taken some supervisory responsibility in the development of the solution and has excelled at managing not only the quality and timeless of her own deliverable, but also those of several others on her team.

In ten years, I believe Jane will be working in a consulting company, hopefully Accenture, and is likely be one of my partners. Because of her interest and analytical capabilities, I could easily see her working in our strategy practice where she could help clients with such complex problems as divestitures and M&A. Given her breadth of skills, her intellect and her intellect potential, I see her as very successful in whatever she takes on. And, lastly, I see Jane as hard-working and honest, dedicated to doing the right things to help an organization grow and prosper.

As a partner for Andersen Consulting, I have the pleasure of making contact with many young professionals. Almost all of these individuals are highly motivated, honest, enthusiastic over-achievers. In my honest view, Jane certainly fits into an elite percentage at the top of all our professionals. I believe that you would find her to be a great asset to the MBA program of the University of Chicago and sincerely believe that she would benefit from its educational processes. If I can provide any additional information on Jane's behalf or be of assistance in any way, please do not hesitate to call. My phone number is xxxxxx.

The recommender must also fill in a small table similar to the one featured in the Harvard Letters of recommendation section. Once again, in the interest of credibility, putting "outstanding" in each of the categories must be avoided. Nobody's perfect! In discussing your strategy with your recommender, think about what messages you want to convey to the admission committee. Don't forget that your application must be coherent. I think you should get "outstanding" in the categories corresponding to the qualities you've put special emphasis on in your essays and in the references. Lastly, even though you're not perfect, you don't have major faults (Chicago is looking for "well-rounded" personalities). Avoid, then, having any "fair"s or lower. Similarly, don't have too many "good"s. To my mind, a good table must have three "outstanding"s (any more, and you dilute your message), a majority of "excellent"s and perhaps one or two "good"s but no more.

Conclusion:
Chicago, unlike some other universities, isn't obsessed with a particular aspect of your personality (like for example leadership ability). Chicago is looking for balanced, well-rounded personalities with potential, and the main goal of your recommendations will be to bring out these qualities. The more specific, personal and rich in examples the letter of recommendation, the more effective it will be.

THE INTERVIEW

The interview is a more or less obligatory step for getting in to Chicago. 99% of admitted students have had an interview. This interview enables the school to gauge your motivation, your ability to express yourself orally, and to see if your personality fits with that of students who blossom at Chicago. So don't forget to ask for an interview at least five weeks before the application deadline. You'll have the choice of going to the campus, or of having your interview with an alumnus in the town where you live. The only advantage of going to the campus is the possibility of visiting where you'll be studying, meeting other students and sitting in on one or two classes. Apparently, going there won't give you any other competitive edge. The interviewer on campus is either a second year student or a member of the admissions office. The 45-minute interview is to get to know you better as well as to shed some light on certain aspects of your application. To have a successful interview, do your best to be yourself and make a point of stressing your motivation particularly for Chicago by mentioning the specific characteristics of the school. The interviewer must, in the space of 45 minutes, judge your motivation for doing an MBA at Chicago as well as the coherence of your application. So, expect the conversation to revolve around the following questions or themes:

- Why an MBA at Chicago?
- Explain your professional career. If you've changed job, what motivated this decision?
- Talk about your initiatives (clubs, etc.) outside work. Expect to spend a few minutes on the subject, the idea being for the interviewer to distinguish between those who are truly active and those who are trying to bluff it.
- Explain your undergraduate record, especially if there are dips.

The last 10 minutes of the interview are generally reserved for questions asked by the applicant. It's the opportunity to show once more that you know the school and that you have done your homework. Good questions to ask can be fairly general or more specific. For example:
- What are the school's strong points and the points to improve?
- Can you summarize in a sentence or two the personality of the students at Chicago?
- Can you talk to me about the "management labs" (type of course specific to Chicago – cf. the section on the school)?

INTERVIEW WITH THE ADMISSIONS DIRECTOR

This interview with Associate Dean Don Martin was conducted by Sebastien de Longeaux.

Who reads the application forms? How many people review them? How much time is spent per application?

An application is read three times before a decision is made. The first reader is a first year, full-time MBA student, who is a member of the Dean's Student Admissions Committee (DSAC). DSAC members are trained thoroughly in the evaluation process, and take their responsibility very seriously. The Admissions staff values the input of our students in evaluating applications, since those admitted will ultimately be fellow students and alumni with our current students. The second read is completed by a member of the Admissions Staff - Associate Director or Assistant Director. Second readers do their evaluations without knowing what first readers recommended on the same applications. Carol Swanberg, our Director of Admissions, does a final read, and also reviews the evaluations and recommendations of both earlier readers. At that point a decision is made. It takes approximately one hour for first and second readers to read and evaluate each application. Carol spends between 30 and 40 minutes evaluating each candidate.

What is the process? Is there a sort of preliminary filter in three categories like "Yes/Maybe/No" and then only the first category is really thoroughly read?

There is not initial filtering process. Every completed application is evaluated equally according to the process I have just described.

What are the criteria of evaluation of a good candidate?

We evaluate eight components of each application: essays, work experience, recommendation letters, community service, interview, motivation to attend Chicago, academic profile, and level of professionalism demonstrated by the applicant in all of our interactions with him/her. These are not in rank order in any way whatsoever.

What qualities would you like to see more of in candidates?

In truth, the quality of our applicants is outstanding! It makes our decisions extremely difficult. All I can say here is: "Applicants, keep up the good work!"

How important is the GMAT?

As mentioned in my answer for your previuous question, the GMAT is part of an applicant's academic profile, which is one of eight components of each application. Due to the range of GMAT scores represented in our incoming classes each year, I believe we definitely support our statement that the GMAT is not more or less important than any other part of an application.

If someone takes the GMAT many times, will you take the highest score or the average of the scores?

We take the highest score.

What are the "do's" and "don't's" for essays ?
DO:
   - Do answer the question asked
   - Do so in the number of words specified
   - Do make sure the right essay goes to the right school
DON'T:
   - Don't answer a question the way you think we want you to
   - There are no right and wrong answers
   - We are not asking trick questions

How do you recommend that students differentiate themselves from the pack?
The best way to differentiate yourself is simply to be yourself. Tell us what we ask - let us get to know you as you really are. Being fake is easily detected, and is the biggest detriment to being admitted.

What makes a good letter of recommendation?
One that is candid and comes from someone who really knows the applicant, and does not paint the applicant as truly outstanding in everything. We are not looking for perfection, but motivation, progress, and professional growth.

What is the function of the interview in the selection process?
The interview serves two purposes at Chicago: 1) It allows us to meet in person the individual who's written information we've already received or will soon be receiving. It helps us "lift the person off the paper", and see them in a person-to-person context; 2) It equally allows the applicant to meet the school in person, and evaluate its "personality". In other words, it's a marketing opportunity for both the applicant and Chicago. With that in mind, we stress to our interviewers that interviews are conversations, not interrogations.

Does the interviewer have access to the application form of the interviewee ahead of the interview?
No - this is done deliberately so that the interviewer will not be biased in any way before conducting the interview.

What other MBA schools do you consider as direct competitors to your MBA program? Why?
Based on information that we receive from those who are admitted, but choose to attend elsewhere, our primary competitors are Wharton, Harvard, and Stanford. My sense is that applicants have some ideas as to their top choice MBA school before starting the application process. As they go through the application process, they become better acquainted with their options, and upon being admitted and interacting with each school, they end up deciding which school best suits their goals/needs.

Given that some companies (Mckinsey & Co. and Goldman Sachs, for instance) seem to be traditional 'feeders' for your MBA program, how is an applicant from one of these firms viewed against other applicants in the pool?
There is not preferential treatment of applicants, period.

Is there a 'rolling' admission cycle or 'rounds' of admission?
There are three rounds. The purpose of having rounds is that of distributing the number of applications that are read by the Admissions Committee into more manageable groups.

Is this better to apply at the early rounds?

There is no advantage from our end in applying for any round. Perhaps the advantage to the applicant is that the earlier they apply, the earlier they receive a decision. Our advice is to make sure the application is the best it can be, regardless of when it is sent.

Some people say that the middle round is the best since the first round is too early because the school is afraid to give away too many places, and the last round is too late because the school might have already given away a lot of places in the earlier rounds?

No - please refer to the answer to previous questions.

What does the school expect in particular from international students?

We expect the same from our international students as we do from our U.S. citizens: a strong sense of personal motivation, and participation in both the academic and social life of our community.
Our advice is the same to all applicants: 1) do your homework in investigating those MBA programs on your list; 2) make sure to follow directions in the application process; 3) be yourself and 4) try to relax and enjoy the process.

Are there unofficial quotas per country?

No. If we have more outstanding applicants from a certain country in a given year, it is very likely that more of those applicants will be admitted. Chicago has no cut-offs or quotas of any kind. At the same time, we do try and recruit a diverse applicant pool, so that we'll have the opportunity of choosing students from diverse cultures and backgrounds. So far, we have been very successful in that endeavor.

Does the school tolerate that international students may have a lower GMAT score (if so, what is the gap?)

In recent years international students have done equally well on the GMAT when compared with their U.S. counterparts.

Last question, what is the part of luck in the application process?

Wow! That is a good question. My guess is that in the end, it's 90% work on the part of the applicant, with 10% luck thrown in.

Getting the
COLUMBIA
Admissions Edge

Columbia
Business School

Address	Columbia Graduate School of Business
	Uris Hall, Room 216
	3022 Broadway
	New-York NY 10027-6902 USA
Telephone	(1) 212-854-1961 - (1) 212-662-6754 (fax)
Website	www.gsb.columbia.edu
E-mail	apply@claven.gsb.columbia.edu

about the school

Founded	1916
Tuition Fees	$29,168
Some Famous Alumni	Warren Buffet (Chairman, Berkshire Hathaway) ; Benjamin Rosen (Chairman Emeritus, Compaq Computer Corp.); Henry Kravis (Founding Partner, Kohlberg Kravis Roberts & Co.); Rochelle Lazarus (Chairman & CEO, Ogilvy & Mather Worldwide); Sidney Taurel (Chairman, President & CEO, Eli Lilly & Co.); Michael Gould (CEO, Bloomingdale's)

the application

Application File	By mail, telephone or downloadable from website
Application Deadlines	April 20: September Term October 15: Early Decision October 1: January Term March 1: Int'l Applicants
App. File Elements	• 5 essays • 2 letters of recommendation • GPA • GMAT (and TOEFL, if applicable) • résumé

rankings

Publication	Business Week						US News & World						Financial Times		
General Ranking	90	92	94	96	98	00	94	96	98	99	00	01	99	00	01
	9	**9**	**8**	**6**	**6**	**7**	**11**	**8**	**3**	**7**	**6**	**6**	**2**	**5**	**5**

before the MBA

# applicants per year	5,637
# applicants accepted per year	704
# applicants entering per year	489
% women students	37%
% minority students	23%
% international students	27%
# countries represented	50

Age (years)	
average	27

Education pre-MBA	
Economics	28%
Humanities and Social Sciences	27%
Business	19%
Engineering	13%
Pure Science and Math	10%
Other	3%

Professional experience	
avg. years work experience	4

GMAT	
average	704
range	610-740

TOEFL	
minimum accepted score - computer	260
minimum accepted score - paper	610

GPA	3.45
average	

after the MBA

	School total
# companies recruiting on campus	589

Main Career Choice	
Investment Banking	38%
Consulting	22%
Financial Services	17%
Manufacturing	12%
New Media/Internet	5%
Nonprofit/Government	1%
Retail	1%
Telecommunication	1%

Function	
Financial Services	49%
Consulting	24%
Marketing	9%
Entrepreneur/Owner	5%
Finance (Corporations)	4%
General Management	3%
Real Estate	2%

Geographical location	
North America	88%
Europe	6%
Asia and Australia	4%
Central and South America	2%

Salary (source: Financial Times 2001)	
Avg. salary three years after graduation	$157,775

Alumni	
# alumni in the world (MBA)	over 25,000
# cities with an alumni association	37

Top 10 employers

1.	Goldman Sachs	6.	Citigroup
2.	Morgan Stanley	7.	Booz, Allen & Hamilton
3.	McKinsey & Co.	8.	J.P. Morgan
4.	Lehman Brothers	9.	Merrill Lynch
5.	American Express	10.	Donaldson, Lufkin, & Jenrette

author

Name   A. BOUREGHDA

Consultant at AT Kearney.
Previously spent three years with Deutsche Bank as a trader.

School specifics
COLUMBIA

INTRODUCTION

The continuous growth of the American economy in the late 1990s coincided with increased demand for MBA programs. Columbia Business School greatly benefited from this favorable situation, with a 100% rise in the number of its candidates between 1991 and 1999. In 2001 applications were still strong, with 5,637 applications for only approximately 480 spots. Another factor worth noting is that Columbia is the American business school that consistently recruits the highest percentage of women; during the last admissions process, they represented 37% of the entering class.

Founded in 1754, Columbia University is one of the oldest universities in the United States and the largest in the city of New York. The campus, which hosts 20,000 students every year, is a reflection of the city itself: picturesque, international, and dynamic. The university is a research hub, renowned world-wide in the fields of medicine, physical sciences, and economic sciences; since the beginning of the twentieth century, 54 Nobel Prizes have been awarded either to professors or to former students of Columbia.

In 1999, more than 600 American and foreign companies visited the campus in order to recruit students there from the Business School. Traditionally, recruitment at the school was reserved for

Wall Street Banks. Today, the majority of the students leaving with their MBAs opt for careers in finance and consulting, and the school is attracting more and more entrepreneurs. The statistics confirm this trend: 10% of the graduates of the class of 1999 pursued their own businesses upon finishing school, compared to only 3% in 1994.

Considered one of Columbia's chief assets, its alumni network numbers over 25,000 individuals active in 40 countries across the world, among them Warren Buffet (President of Berkshire Hathaway Inc.) and Benjamin Rosen (Chairman of Compaq Computer Corporation).

THE DEAN'S VISION

If there is any one man to whom Columbia owes its present fame, it's none other than Dean Meyer Feldberg, whose devoted goal is to make Columbia "the best Business School in the world." Since his arrival as head of the school in 1989, Columbia has steadily progressed in the rankings that different magazines compile each year. When you ask this atypical dean to describe his school, he doesn't hesitate to use his famous quote: "Columbia is the quintessential Business Schools in the quintessential city".

In his long-term development plan, Meyer Feldberg wants first of all to capitalize on the traditional assets of the school, which are its excellence in teaching Finance, the international dimension of the program, and of course, its location in the heart of New York City. The Dean is also perfectly aware of Columbia's weaknesses and gaps in comparison to its principal competitors. In this text, he sets several objectives:

- To develop the so-called weak departments. Columbia has the reputation of preparing students mainly for careers in Finance and in Management. To change this image, the Dean intends to concentrate his efforts on recruiting professors renowned in other disciplines and to ensure that the curriculum constantly evolves by developing courses corresponding to the expectations of the students.

- To increase connections and interaction with businesses. Meyer Feldberg himself regularly solicits renowned professionals to come to Columbia to lead courses and conferences. In addition, several Finance courses are taught by Wall Street experts. Presently, the Dean is particularly looking to strengthen ties with the sector of new technology located in New York's Silicon Alley.

- To improve campus facilities. The school has long been criticized for its dilapidated state and the limited capacity of its equipment. The Dean resolved part of the problem by the January 1999 opening of a second ultra-modern building on campus, which is shared with the Law

School, and the recently completed renovation of Uris Hall, the main building of the school. Finally, the school is considering a construction project for housing destined solely for Business School students.

- To enhance alumni connections and use this as a tool to promote the school, particularly in geographic zones where it is less well-known.

THE SCHOOL YEAR

Columbia Business School offers two periods of entry for its MBA program: each year, around 480 students enter the school in September and 180 in January. The table below lays out the typical schedule for each of these three options:

1st Year			2nd Year		
Sept - Dec	Jan - May	May - Aug	Sept - Dec	Jan - May	May - Aug
Core course		Internship and/or vacation	Electives	Electives	
	Core course				
		Core course			Electives

At orientation in the beginning of the program, the school proposes a one-week Math Camp. In this useful course, the professors review basic scientific concepts, such as derivative calculus, integrals, etc. For registered students, Math Camp is more of a chance to meet other newcomers than an actual review session. These are solid courses, nevertheless, and students prefer to meet up in the evenings or hang out during the week rather than do extra work outside of class.

The program of study is normally based on four semesters, each one twelve weeks long. At Columbia, the semesters tend to be around two weeks shorter than at most other schools, which makes for a particularly intense rhythm. A certain number of credits is attributed for each course. In order to get his/her degree, a student must complete a total of 60 credits, which means a typical semester of five courses. With the approval of the Vice Dean it is possible to earn your MBA in three semesters rather than four, but this would call for a rather heavy courseload. The large majority of students stop coursework during the summer in order to do an 8-12 week internship. Although this is not a requirement, it is a definite advantage when interviewing during the second year.

The January and May sessions are usually aimed at candidates who have either had a thorough professional experience or who are sponsored by a company. Ordinarily, students complete the program without interruption. Some students in the January session choose to do a summer internship which delays graduation by one semester. However, the search for an internship should begin shortly after starting at Columbia. Lastly, the January session is not recommended if you intend to do a summer internship.

It has often been noted that students from the January and May sessions usually form a more bonded group just from the fact that the numbers are smaller. During the second year, they encounter students from the September session in their elective courses.

Columbia Business School also offers Dual Degrees, associated with a dozen other schools and institutes within the University (Architecture, Law, Journalism, Applied Sciences, etc.). However, few Business School students are enrolled in other programs, probably because the Business School itself offers such a wide variety of courses each semester. The standard tuition allows a student to take up to 21 courses in all during the two-year MBA program. This allows students to benefit as much as possible from what the school has to offer.

1ST YEAR: CORE CURRICULUM

The Core Curriculum for first-year students usually consists of about ten to fifteen courses, some of which meet for a partial term. These classes last 1 hour and 20 minutes each and meet twice a week from Monday through Thursday with review sessions every Friday.

First Semester:
- Managerial Statistics.
- Accounting I (reading and understanding accounting and financial assessments).
- Corporate Finance (financial performance and development).
- Managerial Economics (Micro-Economics).
- Marketing.

Second Semester:
- Decision Models (introduction to mathematical decision-aid models, use of computer tools).
- Accounting II (Core course on the concepts of Cost Accounting).
- Leading and Managing in Organizations (concepts and theory on managing an enterprise).
- Operations Management (operational organization of enterprises).
- Strategic Management of the Enterprise (strategic choices of organizations, course based on case studies).

Students may be exempt from one or more courses of the Core Curriculum either by exam or by request to the Vice-Dean. I advise consulting the professor before requesting exemption, in order to see a detailed syllabus. In fact, the concepts taught in the course and the approach toward teaching them can prove equally valuable. All the same, if you are sure you do not wish to take the required courses, don't hesitate to ask for exemption. Around 10% of the student body seeks exemption from at least one of the Core courses. Once exempt, a student can enroll in any elective course as long as space is available and it's at the beginning of his/her program at Columbia.

From the beginning, students from the same graduating class are divided into "clusters" of about 60 people each. During the first and second semesters, students take all of their Core Curriculum courses with their cluster. This system was inaugurated a couple of years ago with the goal of reinforcing cohesiveness among students and to create a bond in view of the second year.

One of the requirements of the Core Curriculum is to do an Integrative Project in groups. Students put the knowledge that they acquired in their Finance, Accounting, Marketing, and Micro-Economic classes to good use in order to analyze the company of their choice. Given the difficulty of the task proposed, it is recommended to select a company in a relatively precise sector or market. My group thought a long time before finally going with Hannaford Brothers Co., a regional company in the sector of mass distribution within the United States.

From the first day of class through the rest of the semester, professors advise students on all aspects of their projects: choosing a company, compiling research materials, allocating tasks, editing, etc. The essential piece of advice is to force yourself to work on all aspects of the project, concentrating particularly on the financial value of the enterprise since this will be the best preparation for the final exam in the course Corporate Finance. The Integrative Project, which is a direct application of the concepts studied in class, carries little value in terms of teaching; on the other hand, it is extremely enriching in terms of organization and time management. In fact, the completion of the project demands a lot of cooperation among its group members. In addition to this, it's difficult to spend a consistent amount of time on the project in the beginning, since it's not until the end of the semester that students are able to acquire all the tools and facts necessary for its completion.

All in all, the workload during the first year is pretty heavy. In most subjects, individual or group work is to be handed in every week, in addition to an average of two case studies per week. During the first semester, the workload is more demanding due to the Integrative Project. Outside of class, students spend about four to five hours per day on homework during the week and one whole day during the weekend. This is of course an average estimate which varies according to the work pace and goals of each individual.

2ND YEAR: ELECTIVES

The second year is made up entirely of elective courses which are grouped by department: Accounting, Finance, Management, Marketing, etc. In total, one hundred different courses are offered each semester, except for in the summer, when the number and the diversity of the courses are reduced. The more specific/specialized electives are taught only one semester per year. Registration for electives is done by telephone about one month before the semester concerned. It's worth noting that access to certain courses and professors is sometimes difficult, even if the Registrar's Office does its best to satisfy as many students as possible at the beginning of the semester.

Business School students can select up to two classes taught in others schools within the university. There are several courses at the School of International and Public Affairs and at the Law School that are particularly good. In addition to offering the possibility of spending a semester abroad through exchange programs with other business schools, Columbia has recently finalized a deal with Haas/Berkeley which offers supplementary opportunities to students interested in a career in media or hi-tech.

As far as the amount of coursework goes, the second year is generally less intense than the first year. During the third semester, students dedicate a lot of their time to the job search: presentations of different enterprises, gathering information, editing cover letters, interviews on and off campus, etc. For this reason it's better to be careful and reserve the more difficult courses for the last semester, unless your future is already set for after your MBA.

THE COURSES - WHAT'S HOT... WHAT'S NOT

Columbia is reputed for its teaching standards in Finance. This department alone accounts for almost forty different courses and seminars taught each year. In my opinion, the elective courses not to miss are Advanced Corporate Finance (with Laurie Hodrick) and Capital Markets and Investments (with John Donaldson). It's best to take these two courses as soon as possible in the program since they provide a strong foundation for most of the other Finance courses. I also recommend the courses Security Analysis and Valuation and Financial Statements (with Michael Kirschenheiter) for students who wish to pursue a career in investment banking.

Two of the most popular courses at Columbia are two Management courses. The first, Turnaround Management, is an application of the concepts of accounting, finance, and management taught in the MBA program. This course is almost entirely based on one case study, and is one that demands the most work out of all the courses taught at Columbia. The second, Economics of Strategic Behavior, is taught by a well-known figure at Columbia (Bruce Greenwald) and considers the dynamics and factors of success in the strategies of enterprises.

The course that I liked the least is part of the Core Curriculum, Operations Management. In my opinion, certain concepts that are taught are interesting, but the course needs to be reorganized in order for it to be more enriching.

As far as electives are concerned, certain seminars are of little interest, both in the subject matter itself and in the teaching quality. To help students in choosing their classes, the Office of the Registrar publishes the evaluations of each course and professor from the previous semester. Try not to overlook this reference since it can prove to be particularly useful in avoiding unpleasant surprises during registration. Take note that a couple of the specialized Finance seminars, such as Initial Public Offerings and Corporate Shareholder Value, are taught in collaboration with professionals from investment banks (Merrill Lynch/Morgan Stanley). The table below represents the level of student satisfaction in twenty of the most fundamental courses. The evaluation and the score given is only a reflection of the course itself and not of the professor. The results provided are based on a survey administered to a cross-section of about 95 European students.

	Below Expectations	In line with Expectations	Above Expectations	Outstanding
Accounting I & II	4%	31%	43%	22%
Advanced Corporate Finance	7%	15%	38%	40%
Capital Markets	10%	24%	49%	17%
Corporate Finance	0%	20%	47%	33%
Debt Markets	12%	21%	39%	28%
Decision Models	2%	12%	45%	41%
Economics of Strategic Behavior	4%	8%	31%	57%
Entrepreneurial Finance	14%	59%	25%	2%
The Global Economic Environment	8%	57%	31%	4%
Introduction to Venturing	12%	37%	38%	13
Leading and Managing in Organizations	44%	25%	27%	4%
Managerial Economics	13%	51%	25%	11%
Managerial Negotiations	6%	28%	43%	23%
Marketing	39%	37%	21%	3%
Operations Management	38%	40%	22%	0%
Security Analysis	7%	25%	42%	26%
Strategic Management of the Enterprise	36%	34%	26%	4%
Turnaround Management	0%	6%	42%	52%

TEACHING METHODS

Teaching methods vary significantly depending upon the professor and the type of course. Overall, though, you can estimate that about 40% of the program's instruction will be based on case studies, 40% on lectures, and 20% on group projects. Case studies require considerable preparation (on average, about three to five hours worth when there aren't any documents to write). This is a point upon which professors strongly insist on active class participation from everyone during the presentation of case studies.

On the whole, Columbia professors make themselves very available to their students. They are easily accessible outside of class during their weekly office hours as well as by telephone. Interaction with students can also take place on the Internet where each professor maintains a web page which allows students to consult the syllabus, download files, or correspond by e-mail.

Students who encounter difficulties in a class have the chance to attend review sessions every Friday. For the Core Curriculum courses, they can also benefit from several specific free courses each semester. The school also covers the costs of tutoring.

As is the case with most MBA programs, learning at Columbia also comes from the multiple debates and conferences that are organized by the school. Each week, students can attend meetings with prestigious guest speakers from a variety of professional fields. In 1998, for example, Sandy Warner, CEO of JP Morgan, Bill Gates and Warren Buffet visited the campus.

THE GRADING SYSTEM

For all courses, the grading system adopted by Columbia is the following: H (Honors), HP (High Pass), P (Pass), LP (Low Pass), F (Fail). The first year of the program moves forward in a relatively competitive atmosphere. There are two explanations for this:

1) Grades are calculated by a forced curve (each student is evaluated in comparison to the rest of the class):

Grade	Distribution (% of the class)
H	15 – 20 %
HP	40 – 45 %
P	35 – 40 %
LP and F	0 – 5 %

2) During the interview period, which takes place at the beginning of the second year, recruiters, particularly those from investment banks, give interviewing priority to those students who made Deans List and Beta Gamma Sigma Honor Society, in reference to their positive results from the first year.

Any students who gets an F in a class must take the course a second time; however, professors rarely give this grade. Acquiring several F's throughout the period of the curriculum will lead to automatic expulsion from the program. In practice, this almost never happens.

In each class, the professor explains from the very start the criteria that will be considered in giving final grades (class participation, case studies, final exam grades, etc.) as well as the relative scale for each of these criteria. Typically, class participation is the most important criteria in the Management and Marketing classes, whereas the final exam grade carries the most weight in the Finance and Accounting courses.

GROUP WORK

At Columbia, as with most business schools, MBA programs are first and foremost an experience in working in groups. In about 80% of the courses taught, students are asked at one point or another to work in groups. This method of teaching allows the professor to maintain a cohesive spirit in a relatively competitive setting. Students soon become aware of the importance of team work while working on the Integrative Project (IP). For this project, teams are designated by the Office of the Registrar based on profile, professional experience and the geographic origin of the students. The IP constitutes a unique opportunity during the course of a student's academic career, working with people that the student often doesn't know at the beginning of the program. With a few rare exceptions, students are intelligent enough to make this experience a success. I personally really appreciated the human enrichment that this experience offered me. Forcing myself to work with people that were very different from me was not always easy, but putting together our knowledge and ideas contributed to the personal development of each one of us.

Throughout the program, the importance of teamwork depends on the type of course. As a general rule of thumb, Management and Marketing courses require a major project and case studies that are to be done in groups. Naturally, students have the tendency to organize themselves with people from their old cluster when they have the possibility to choose their own groups. For the more technical classes, such as Accounting and Statistics, students voluntarily work in groups to prepare work that is to be handed in individually.

THE TEACHERS

The teaching staff at Columbia is composed of 110 tenured professors and the same number of associate professors. Half of them have lived or worked abroad. A lot of them continue to practice consulting for organizations such as the FED, the International Monetary Fund, or Morgan Stanley Dean Witter (the school has had privileged relations with this bank for several years now). All full-time professors devote part of their time to the research and editing of articles for specialized magazines, and they share the fruits of their labor in their courses. In Finance, for example, Professor Beim's course, Emerging Financial Markets, is almost entirely based on concepts that have recently been elaborated at Columbia in the fields of risk evaluation in emerging countries. Among the school's most renowned professors, you'll find Bruce Greenwald (Economics of Strategic Behavior), Laurie Hodrick (Advanced Corporate Finance), Robert Botempo (Leading and Managing Organizations), Larry Selden (Debt Markets), and David Beim (Corporate Finance).

With just a few exceptions, professors are very devoted to their students. I have also found all of the professors to have a great sense of humor. To cite just one example, one day a professor came to class dressed as a cowboy in presenting a case study on the production of beef in Midwest.

The teaching staff educates and assists students, but not always on information pertinent to the working world. This is why, in 1977, the school established the Executive in Residence Program: a dozen practicing or retired executives advise students about career choices after graduating with their MBA. These individuals, who have all had at least 20 years of experience in their field, are very useful for obtaining information often difficult to find through traditional channels. When they are able, they often help students by providing the names of contacts in companies. The requests for interviews are relatively high in the beginning of the second year, right before the recruitment period. My advice is to meet one of the members of the program in the middle of the first year, while the schedule still allows some reflection about career options. Among the Executives in Residence presently active, three have made careers in investment banking, two in capital risk, one in consulting, one in the tobacco industry, etc.

THE INTERNATIONAL SIDE

Without doubt, one of Columbia's greatest assets is the ethnic diversity of its students and of its teaching staff. In developing itself abroad, the school has looked primarily towards Europe and South America. Openness and recruiting abroad have long been rooted in the spirit of Columbia. Of last year's students, 31% were not of American origin. In addition to that, many of the Americans who enroll in the school do so after a prolonged experience abroad. This diversity is reflected daily in class discussions, group work, and campus life. For various reasons, international students tend to congregate together and mingle less naturally with the American students. In my opinion, this is a mistake that American and international students alike should avoid, for business school provides a unique opportunity to encounter individuals with diverse backgrounds.

In addition to recruiting abroad, the school initiated an exchange program with its counterparts abroad in 1991 as part of its development strategy. Starting in the second year, students have the option of spending an academic semester in one of 21 business schools world-wide that have signed an agreement with Columbia. Among these institutions, you'll see names like the London Business School and the Institut Supérieur des Affaires (ISA/HEC).

THE ENTREPRENEUR'S CORNER

Since the boom of the Internet and the financial success brought about by certain start-ups, an increasing number of students have become involved in the creation and development of their own businesses after leaving Columbia (and sometimes even during their course study). The Entrepreneurship department at Columbia offers about 20 different courses and seminars each year. This program, which is well aware of the evolution and expectations of the student body, includes courses specialized in the field of modern technology in addition to financial courses. Among the most popular courses are:

- Introduction to Venturing
- Managing Growth
- Managing Innovation
- Venture Capital
- Entrepreneurship and the Internet Economy
- Entrepreneurial Finance

For the 1999-2000 academic year, a seminar entitled "Entrepreneurship Incubator" was added to the curriculum; it provides students the opportunity to finalize the execution of their company projects and, to provide the insider perspective, experts from outside the school examine the business plans and assist the students in their projects' initial phases. The school just recently sealed an agreement with Berkeley/Haas in order to permit several students each year to spend a semester near the Silicon Valley and thus to take advantage of the opportunities on the spot.

Outside of Columbia, there are many opportunities to get involved in the world of start-ups:
- Each year, a competition granting an award of 5,000 dollars is open to students of the school for the selection of the best business plan ("The Lorne Weil Business Plan Competition"). The jury is comprised of entrepreneurs and professionals in the capital-risk industry who choose the winner in accordance with a series of fairly precise criteria, such as feasibility, innovation and the eventual returns on the investment.
- The Eugene Lang Entrepreneurial Initiative Fund grants financing for anywhere from 50,000 to 250,000 dollars to students who present an enticing business plan.The participants also benefit from the profuse advice of one or more "Faculty Advisors" as well as from the professional relations with members of the "Fund Advisory Panel". Selection for the distribution of the financing is done in two parts: a first selection is carried out by members of a jury composed of members of the University, as well as of the "Fund Advisory Panel". The decision to invest in one or more projects is then reviewed by the board.
- The Venture Capital Club and the Private Equity Club organize the best business plan competition as well as "The Annual Principal Investing Forum". In November of 1999, the Internet Business Group organized its first conference day with companies from Silicon Alley ("Silicon Alley Uptown 1999"). This club equally sponsored a discussion panel at the time of the Internet Conference at Stern (New York University), then collaborated with Columbia Business School on the Boston "Cyberposium". Finally, the Columbia

Entrepreneurs Organization, The High Tech Club and The Media Management Association frequently organize presentations and meetings with professionals and Alumni.

- Beyond the specific knowledge acquired in class, Columbia also presents excellent opportunities for students to meet their future associates. The diversity of the student population makes it an ideal aquarium where all posts and almost all industries are represented.

Silicon Alley

The term Silicon Alley refers to the Silicon Valley of the East Coast, an area to the south of 41st Street in Manhattan, where you will find most of the 2,500 companies in the new media industry that are accounted for in New York. It deals with anything concerning:

- development, marketing, distribution and the transfer of text destined for the Web.
- e-commerce (companies whose principal sales are through the Internet).
- the creation and the development of software or of tools (design, illustration) which serve a site.
- service enterprises whose clients belong to one of the preceding categories (public relations firms and Internet advertising agencies).

LIFE AT COLUMBIA

NEW YORK

"The Big Apple isn't a city, it's an experience". Woody Allen

Choosing to do an MBA at Columbia is choosing to live in one of the most fantastic cities in the world. New York, which proclaims itself to be the "capital of the world", certainly knows how to let passions run wild like no other city. Urban jungle or Cultural Eden, the city is sometimes overwhelming due to its gigantic size, and casts a spell by its diversity and its incredible energy. From the Upper West Side to the East Village, the city is a patchwork of neighborhoods that each cultivates its own identity. New York is a city of all cultures, all ethnicities, all types of music. Styles and new trends are born and die here. Manhattan boasts more than 10,000 restaurants, hundreds of jazz clubs, theaters, cinemas, boutiques. At the heart of the city, Central Park is an immense oasis of greenery, the daily meeting place of rollerbladers and joggers. Spending a couple of hours there allows you to forget the city's non-stop stress and sometimes exhausting pace. As far as professions are concerned, New York offers opportunities unrivaled by other big economic capitals: the city is of course the seat of more than 3,000 multinational companies, banks, and financial institutions, but it also leads in the industries of media, telecommunications, computers, pharmacy, etc.

THE CAMPUS

Columbia University is located on the Upper West Side of Manhattan, sandwiched between Harlem to the North and the East River to the East. The North border of Central Park is about a dozen blocks from the University. The surroundings of the University's campus tend to provide a direct reflection of the city itself, in that the clichés and images which used to give it a bad reputation are no longer true.

The University is located on the subway line that serves all of West Manhattan, the North Bronx, down to the financial district and Wall Street in the South. The campus is a mix of buildings of both Italian Renaissance style and also of more modern structures, with spacious grass and red brick paths linking the buildings together. Uris Hall, the main building of the Business School, is situated near the heart of the campus, behind the impressive central library. Since January of 1999, the school has benefited from a second brand-new building that it shares with the Law School. Columbia students have numerous sports facilities at their disposal right on campus.

HOUSING

Columbia University possesses a large housing complex in the Upper West Side of Manhattan. At the beginning of each school year, the Business School reserves a set number of apartments in the immediate surroundings of the campus. These apartments, either individual studios or large flats to share with roommates, are generally in good condition and are rented at prices 20-30% lower than market value.

For those who wish to live off-campus, don't forget that New York is an extremely expensive city. Rent has been on the rise for the past few years and is consistently pricey. Therefore, you must expect to pay at least $1,300 a month for a studio in the Upper West Side ($1,500 downtown),to which you must add a real estate agent commission, which is unavoidable in New York. Otherwise, even when you have a sufficient budget, finding an apartment still remains difficult as the difference between the offer and the going price can be great. By visiting the University website, you can check advertisements for renting a room or an apartment in town. These offers, which are reserved for Columbia students, present the advantage of saving on real estate fees. As a last resort, consult the numerous ads posted throughout the school and in the University's neighborhood.

SOCIAL LIFE

Campus life is very present at Columbia. The large majority of the students are members of at least one of the 90 cultural, athletic, professional and other associations sponsored by the School. The most popular clubs are The Investment Banking Association, The Management Consulting Association, The Internet Business Group and Women in Business. Among their various activities, these clubs regularly organize meetings with professionals of the field and are responsible for transmitting résumés to the different interested enterprises.

At the busiest time of the year, nearly 1,500 students are present at the school. Happy Hour is a weekly event that unites students, and sometimes professors of the school, after classes every Thursday. At the beginning of the program, Happy Hour will be the occasion to get to know students from your classes and others with whom you don't normally have class. Each year, students, professors, and alumni are united together for a ball organized in a prestigious spot in Manhattan. Another activity worth mentioning is The Follies, a theatrical presentation given at the end of the year by students from the Business School. Lastly, several different Study Trips are organized by the students during vacations. Last year, the different destinations that were proposed were South Africa, Brazil, China, etc.

TUITION COSTS

For the 2001-2002 school year, the tuition rose to $29,168 per year, making Columbia one of the most expensive business schools in the world. Over the course of the past five years, tuition has seen a regular increase of between 3 and 5% per year. For the projected budget, it is best to anticipate a similar increase between the first and second year:

Tuition Fees for 2 years ($)	58,336
Housing:	
# studio on campus	16,000 - 21,000
# studio in town	25,000 - 43,000
Health Insurance	3,156
Books, supplies	3,000
Computer, software	3,500
TOTAL	83,992-110,992

The distribution of merit scholarships is limited, and only those applying for September admission are eligible (interested students must present their candidature before January 15 following their entrance into Columbia). On the other hand, it is easier to land a Teaching Assistant (TA) position starting during the second semester, with the condition that you have received a solid grade in the course and have asked the professor concerned.

Generally speaking, the more quantitative the course, the less of a demand there is for the position. The TA positions are relatively well-paid, but the workload can be quite demanding. The pay depends on the type of course being taught, the number of sections in the course, as well as the number of students registered. For a class in the Core Curriculum, you can count on about $2,000 per semester.

The work consists of correcting written assignments and exams, and of giving a one and half hour review session once a week. Other than Teaching Assistant positions, any student having received a good grade in a class could consider giving tutorials to other students within the realms of the school's Tutoring Program.

Another financing option to consider is sponsorship by a company as part of your signing bonus (about $25,000 on average in 2001). More and more companies are also proposing reimbursement for all or part of tuition costs.

The following quotations represent opinions from recent Columbia Business School graduates:

The School is strongly oriented towards Investment Banking and Management Consulting. Other areas of focus tend to fall between the cracks with career resources. The Administration is often lacking in responsiveness and the policies needed to deal with students. My business school experience has been excellent. I think this is in large part due to the range and years of working experience I had before coming to CBS. This experience enabled me to be a better contributor in classes, team projects and the recruiting process. I highly recommend that people wishing to go to business school have at least five years working experience - they'll get so much more out of the program.

Job hunting at Columbia is easy if you are interested in Wall Street or Consulting. Large marketing companies also come to Columbia. In any other area, the student must put in much more effort. Columbia has come a long way over the past couple of years. It has managed to maintain leadership status in Finance, General Management and International Business while greatly improving offerings in Real Estate Management, Media and Communications Management, and Entrepreneurship. Having graduated as a Marketing major and interacted with a large portion of the Marketing faculty, I also feel that this department is strong, though underrated. Columbia is a great school if you want to go into finance or consulting. There needs to be a greater emphasis on other disciplines if Columbia truly wants to be a well-rounded school. They must do this not just by offering more courses in other areas, but also by improving the quality of professors in areas other than Finance, where most of the star faculty still reside. Also, the majority of the high-powered guest speakers are CEOs of Wall Street firms, and the speaker selection therefore needs to be diversified.

The admissions application

COLUMBIA

INTRODUCTION

The following items are to be included in the application file:
- Completed application forms
- Detailed background information concerning professional, extra-curricular and extra-professional experience
- Transcripts (originals)
- GMAT scores (and TOEFL scores, if applicable)
- Two letters of recommendation
- Four mandatory essays and one optional essay.
- Interview, on invitation

The application deadlines are as follows:
- April 20: September Term
- October 15: Early Decision
- October 1: January Term
- March 1: International Applicants

The application will be carefully considered once the file is complete. The Admissions Committee may then decide to invite the candidate for an interview; according to the student's choice, the interview will take place either with an alumnus who lives in the same geographical region, or directly on campus. The Committee meets regularly to review files and make final decisions (selection is made on a rolling admissions basis). Count on about 12 weeks from the time your file is complete before getting notified of acceptance or rejection.

Given the considerable rise in the number of applicants over the past several years, it is strongly advised to submit your application well before the actual deadline. Not long ago, the school proposed an option which allows for the file to be reviewed within 8-10 weeks (early decision). This option only concerns those applicants who are applying for September admission, and the application must be submitted by October 15 of the previous year. If the student is accepted, a non-refundable payment of $2,500 will be required in order to reserve his/her place in the program. This alternative was envisioned for those students who have chosen the Columbia MBA program as their first choice.

On the application, the candidate must be specific about the admissions session of his/her choice. The school does not authorize students admitted into a certain semester to change starting dates (except under extenuating circumstances). On the other hand, when there are no more available places for September admission, the school may propose that an eligible student start in the January session instead.

One last detail about the admissions process: exceptional candidates with no professional experience may apply, but their acceptance will be deferred by two years. They should take advantage of this period to evolve in a professional environment before taking on their MBA at Columbia.

THE GMAT

With test scores, the applicant has some room to play around in order to increase his/her chances of getting in. The chart below provides data on GMAT scores for Columbia students.

During the past few years, the continual rise in the number of applicants has been accompanied by a noticeable increase on the average score obtained on the GMAT (704 for the class entering in 2001). 80% of this class received a score between 610 and 740. This statistic is much more pertinent than the average score in trying to evaluate your chances of getting accepted; you should shoot for obtaining a score within this range. A lower score will not systematically eliminate your

	GMAT	TOEFL
Average	704	273
Deviation	32	15
Range	610 to 740	253 to 293

chances of getting accepted if your application presents other assets, such as significant professional experience and excellent letters of recommendation. In any event, you mustn't make the mistake of expecting a high score alone to guarantee your acceptance into Columbia; it is important to apply yourself in all the content of your application.

When an applicant takes the GMAT several times, the Admissions Committee only considers the best scores. A candidate is allowed to take the GMAT as many as two or three times since many are inadequately prepared the first time. On the other hand, taking the GMAT more than three times without substantial improvement will notably harm your candidacy. My advice is to take the test a maximum of twice, allowing for a long preparation period beforehand.

In my case, I took the exam twice: a first time without extensive preparation, a second time 3 years later after having followed a specific preparation for two months at the Kaplan Institute. The GMAT is an exam which tests not only mathematical and verbal reasoning, but also speed and reflexes. One of the advantages of preparing with Kaplan is that it teaches precise tips for developing an efficient strategy for exam day.

For international students from countries in which English is not an official language, the minimum TOEFL score for admission to Columbia is 253 points, with a minimum of 25 correct answers in each of the three test sections. International students whose undergraduate diploma was granted in an English speaking country are exempt from this test. If you are in doubt as to whether you must take this test, you should consult the Admissions Department.

THE ESSAYS

The essays are of average importance in the admissions process in comparison to the other elements of the file: all the same, you mustn't neglect them if you want to keep every chance possible of getting accepted. Through the essays, the Admissions Committee is looking above all to understand the applicant's character, as well as to gauge his/her ability to express and organize his/her ideas.

A FEW TIPS FOR WRITING STRONG ESSAYS

Some essay topics appear on all business school applications, while others touch upon the same themes but with a different approach. The Directors of Admissions are perfectly aware that a person applying to different schools will inevitably be tempted to reuse the same essays for several applications. For a student who proceeds in this way, the main risk is of reducing the impact of the essays if the Admissions Committee decides that they are too general or worse, if they don't precisely answer the question being asked. It is therefore highly important to craft appropriate responses for each program you apply to; this will also help you display your motivation.

Each essay should reveal a new aspect of the applicant's personality or path. Before jumping into the writing, it is essential to have an organized vision of the content of the essays and to have thought about the overall approach for each one: the ideas to be developed, the style to adopt, the structure, etc. In this way, the body of the essays will constitute a homogeneous and cohesive text.

Finally, it is recommended to have your essays re-read by at least two different people. They should critique the content as much as the form.

To summarize, here is a brief list of tips before setting out to write your essays:
On the *content*:
- Carefully answer the question being asked.
- Understand the meaning of your sentences and the words that you use. The essay writing process is also an exercise in communication in which you should persuade the reader.
- Don't be repetitive. Each sentence should contribute a new element to the elaboration of your ideas.
- Choose topics that touch you personally.
- Give concrete examples rather than general affirmations.
- Be sincere. The Admissions Committee quickly picks up on false situations in the text.

On the *form*:
- Express yourself in a positive manner: state what you have done and not what you haven't.
- Use transitions between paragraphs.
- Opt for short sentences and a clear and concise style.
- To avoid being unclear, favor the active voice rather than the passive voice.

WHAT COLUMBIA IS LOOKING FOR IN YOUR ESSAYS

Essay topics have remained the same for the past three years. Applicants must write four essays and have the option of writing an additional one. Essays 1 through 3 are mandatory; you can choose between number 4a and 4b.

1) What are your career goals? How will an MBA help you achieve these goals? Why are you applying to Columbia Business School?

2) In reviewing the last five years, describe one or two accomplishments in which you demonstrated leadership.

3) Discuss a non-academic personal failure. In what way were you disappointed in yourself? What did you learn from the experience?

4a) Discuss your involvement in a community or extracurricular organization. Include an explanation of how you became involved in the organization, and how you help(ed) the organization meet its goals?

4b) Columbia Business School is a diverse environment. Please discuss a life experience of yours that shows how you will contribute to the class.

(Optional) Is there any additional information that you wish to provide to the Committee?

The essays provide supplementary information which allow the Admissions Committee to better judge whether a candidate possesses the qualities to succeed at Columbia and beyond. The principal qualities being looked for are, in order of importance: a sense of leadership and initiative, motivation, the ability to adapt, and an open mind.

EXAMPLES AND COMMENTARIES OF ESSAYS FOR COLUMBIA

1) What are your career goals? How will an MBA help you achieve these goals? Why are you applying to Columbia Business School? (Limit 1000 words)
The point of this essay:
The Admissions Committee is looking to evaluate to what extent the MBA program at Columbia is compatible with the career goals of the applicant.

Tips for the essay:
Beyond the courses and contacts, an MBA offers major opportunities to build strategic career plans, both long and short-term. A student who has not acquired sufficient professional maturity will not get the most out of this experience. After all, since two years of Business School represent a considerable investment of time and money, it is in the interest of neither the applicant nor the school to admit a person who does not have relatively concrete career goals. Thus, a candidate is strong if he or she has defined clear and realistic goals for the pursuit of his/her career. The emphasis is on making persuasive arguments that highlight your motivation for taking on an MBA.

However, the actual answers to these questions are less important than the manner in which you answer them. A great number of MBAs don't follow through on the career goals espoused in their admissions essay; the Admissions Committee, and everyone else at business school, fully expects that your career plans will change frequently over the course of your MBA. What is most important is that you make it clear that you've thought a great deal about why you want to attend business school, and Columbia in particular. This essay topic is designed to force you to move beyond simplistic explanations such as "I want to change my career." Those who successfully map out goals beyond school, and compellingly describe the intended path, display crucial logic, planning, and communication skills. Those who don't show themselves to be not too serious about the endeavor.

You may find yourself hard-pressed to come up with answer to "Why Columbia?" that isn't readily available in the most standard admissions brochure. It's okay if your reasons are common, as long as the way in which they apply to your "story" is unique. That said, an overly vague answer based solely on the reputation of the school is not sufficient. To formulate an effective response, you must research the school through various channels: the chapter on Columbia in this book, alumni, specialized reviews, MBA Fairs such as the World MBA Tour, etc. In light of this information, the candidate will force him/herself to identify and evaluate the relationship between his/her objectives and the nature of Columbia's MBA program: course offerings, location, job offers post-graduation, etc.

Sample Essay 1

During the summer following college graduation, I took a leap toward my lifelong goal of building my own business. I knew that in October, I would begin working on Social Security reform. So, from June through September, I established a catering business called Creative Catering. I designed and implemented a positive cash flow business plan. I ran the business from home, I catered parties including weekly dinners for 12 and cocktail parties for more than 300, and I netted $15,000 on an investment of $3,000.

I found being an entrepreneur to be as satisfying as I had hoped, and I was encouraged that I can develop a lifetime of entrepreneurial ventures. This summer, I will run Creative Catering again. I have already designed a more formalized business plan - through which I expect net revenue that will pay for my first year of business school.

I have learned substantial skills from projects such as Economic Security 2000, the Jefferson Awards and Creative Catering (see Essay 2). I have profited from working with individuals from all backgrounds, income levels, and races. I have learned how to market products, ideas and individuals. I have worked directly with innovators in business, politics, the media, and the non-profit world and garnered tremendous insight into how leaders lead and the successful succeed. Through Economic Security 2000, I have experienced the creation of a public sector business from scratch, taking an idea and helping build it into a successful organization with a $1 million annual operating budget.

Columbia adds a new dimension and steep learning curve. An individual at a less competive business school recently told me he had gone there to be a "big fish in a little pond". By contrast, I view business school as an opportunity to be a vacuum cleaner and to learn from those around me, faculty and peers alike.

Columbia provides the skills I need to build successful entrepreneurial ventures with classroom studies as the basis for financial analysis, business planning, and management skills, and project development and internships to put those skills to use. Columbia's location in New York City, where I grew up, provides the chance to be surrounded by the most established and entrepreneurial business leaders in the United States.

In business school, I expect to find the next challenge and develop the ones after that. Whether I work in the public or private sector, as an entrepreneur or a corporate executive, I hope to widen my scope of understanding so that I can be creative, challenged, and proud of my work. I want always to enjoy what I do and to pursue excellence. Eventually, I hope to do these things as the head of my own business, and two years at Columbia will give me the unequaled opportunity to explore others' experiences and fields of interest, while also learning skills for business success.

Sample Essay 2:

I joined Deutsche Bank in November 1993 as a junior swaps trader. During a three-month training period, I ran the portfolio along with my direct supervisor. I gained much autonomy during 1994, and in January 1995, wanting to broaden my knowledge of derivatives, I took advantage of an opportunity to develop the activity on the interest rates option products. Over the last three years, this work experience has helped me to improve my skills in terms of creativity, organization and flexibility in a stressful working environment.

Today I realize that my current job responsibilities and long term career objectives have come to a crossroads. I want to stay involved in the financial services and banking industries but now want to turn my career to global management and strategy consulting. I would first like to acquire broad-based experience as a generalist in strategic advisory services by serving companies in a consulting capacity: helping them to define and analyze complex business issues, improving their financial performance from a strategic perspective, developing solutions and implementing changes. Consequently, I hope to increase my expertise in key areas such as mergers and acquisitions. On a human relationship basis, I expect from my future professional activities to rapidly hold team management responsibilities. My previous education has not adequately prepared me for a direct change into these areas. For this reason, I feel I am at a stage in my career where an MBA degree would develop my business skills, accelerate my professional development and help me to aim credibly for top levels of management.

To define what the future holds is always very difficult. Yet Deutsche Bank Senior Management put this question to my boss and myself every year requesting projections and results forecasts for the upcoming years. It is relatively easy to foresee what will happen in the short term, but unpredictable circumstances and situation changes may interfere with not only individual but also long-term collective plans. There is only one aspect of the economy, however, of which I am certain: continued globalization of markets is inevitable and the next generation of managers must be flexible, multicultural and capable of working in any environment. My two years at Columbia will enhance my quantitative, cultural and social skills and enable me more effectively to face the challenges of global competition. This experience will be an invaluable opportunity to see the world from many different perspectives and learn how to resolve conflicts that may arise during my career. No less importantly, my time at Columbia will provide me with the academic and theoretical business background that I did not receive in my training as an Engineer.

Columbia's strong reputation and close ties with the business world, the high quality teaching and the location in New York are the initial reasons for my application. An international capital for finance, New York offers more advantages for the development of my career. I am also enthusiastic about the prospect of spending two or more years in a city which incorporates a social and cultural life that very few other cities do.

Finally, as I want to remain involved and continue to benefit from my association with the school after graduation, I am not indifferent to the international character and the size of Columbia's alumni network.

2) In reviewing the last five years, describe one or two accomplishments in which you demonstrated leadership. (Limit 500 words)

The point of the essay:
Leadership and initiative are the two qualities most sought after in a candidate. This essay must convince the Admissions Committee of your ability to make decisions and to assume responsibility in a professional setting.

Tips for the essay:
For this essay it is suitable to write on subjects that are very important to you, in order to be as convincing as possible. The Committee particularly appreciates responses involving management

or the framework of a team. Applicants who have at least one professional experience at their disposal are encouraged to relate this experience. If you haven't had much management experience in larger organizations, you may find it difficult to come up with professional examples. But you don't have to lead a formal team to display leadership. Think of times when you convinced others to follow a certain course of action, or when you boldly chose not to follow a path recommended to you. You might also draw from your experience in sports, clubs, etc. In any event, it is important to clearly explain the situation, the means and actions utilized, and the end result. Quantify your achievements when possible (improvement of the profitability, cost reduction, etc.) to better illustrate the impact of your decisions.

Sample Essay:

In April 1997, I was hired as Director of Communications for the 25th Anniversary of the Jefferson Awards, which was co-chaired by U.S. Senators Tom Daschle and Trent Lott. The Awards – America's Nobel Prize for Public Service – were founded by Jacqueline Kennedy Onassis and Senator Robert Taft, Jr. to recognize outstanding public service by national figures and local "unsung heroes".

The Board of Senators, including four U.S. Senators, Julian Bond, Bill Donaldson, Teresa Heinz, and John Seigenthaler, set a high standard for their newest employee. The organization had received little national media due to its "good news story" focus and non-"media-friendly" materials. I was responsible for finding new hooks, creating a re-focused media strategy, for marketing, fund-raising, event planning (including round-table discussions and a dinner for 500) and material design, which included writing a 100+ page program with letters signed by U.S. Presidents Ford, Carter, Bush, and Clinton.

The short time frame, as with any campaign, required I take off running and sprint all the way. My success lies in those I assembled, including Lesley Stahl, Michael Keaton, Ethel Kennedy, Jesse Jackson, and Alan Greenspan; each event's fluidity; the media generated, including coverage from C-Span, CBS, NBC, Associated Press, Gannett, Scripps-Howard and "Hardball with Chris Matthews"; the resulting materials; and finally in the long-term media and fund-raising strategies I developed.

Economic Security 2000 is a non-partisan organization, founded in 1995 by Sam Beard to restructure Social Security. When I graduated from college, Sam Beard had just finished writing Restoring Hope in America: The Social Security Solution. *The book outlined a Social Security Administration-approved economic model to add individual savings accounts to Social Security and to open up real wealth and savings to all working Americans. He asked me to help him build a national grassroots campaign as a catalyst for Social Security reform.*

Two years later, ES 2000 has ten employees, tens of thousands of volunteers and chapters in 26 states and 66 cities. We have built a $1 million-a-year nonprofit business and are on our way to being a $2.5 million-a-year operation.

At first, my role in building a new organization was broad. I crisscrossed the United States, giving speeches and meeting with political, business and community leaders. I wrote our materials, honed our message and developed our communications strategy. I targeted specific segments of the population, such as women, minorities, seniors, and college students, did the necessary research and economic analysis and created materials that showed each population cohort how change would benefit them.

As we added an executive director and other staff, I concentrated principally on media. I wrote dozens of opinion editorials for Sam Beard, published in periodicals including The Boston Globe, Newsday, The San Francisco Examiner, The Atlanta Constitution, and The Miami Herald. My work was recognized by features in ELLE, Glamour, and Working Woman magazines; in a public service announcement for Lifetime Television for Women; and in other editorial mentions.

3) Discuss a non-academic personal failure. In what way were you disappointed in yourself? What did you learn from the experience? (Limit 500 words)

The point of the essay:

What the Committee is looking for here is not to judge the seriousness of a failure, but rather to evaluate the ability of the candidate to analyze and learn from his/her mistakes. This quality constitutes another asset that a good manager must possess.

Tips for the essay:

At first, this essay seems difficult to approach given the apprehension that an applicant can legitimately encounter in evoking a failure in an admissions application. To feel reassured, the candidate should keep in mind that all of his/her competitors must also confront the same question. The essay will become advantageously easier for the candidate if he/she approaches the topic with honesty and demonstrates insight in the analysis and lessons that he/she was able to draw upon from his/her failure. Without doubt, on the last part of the question, use as much effort as possible to produce an incisive response essay that leaves a good impression on the reader.

It's tempting to pick an extremely small offense, e.g. the time you kicked the ball out of bounds. But no failure is too big for this essay – provided that you compellingly communicate what you learned, and describe how you intend to avoid the same mistake in the future. Perhaps more than any other essay, this one offers the opportunity to show your heart, and to display your sense of perspective regarding the world around you. One mistake to avoid is to try to relativize the reason for the downfall or to describe a near-defeat; otherwise, the Committee will have difficulty understanding why you've never experienced a real personal defeat in your entire life.

Sample Essay 1:

When the incoming message screen on my computer lit up, it appeared that my months of hard work had finally paid off. Open 24 Hours Dance Company, of which I am the manager and a member, had been invited to perform in an international competition outside of Paris .

We were to join a dozen other dance companies, from France, Spain, and Belgium on an outdoor dance competition under the stars in the courtyard of France's oldest Gothic cathedral, performing before a large audience and an international panel of ten judges. I requested details from the Festival's organizers - the site location, stage configuration, lighting facilities, and availability of dressing rooms and rehearsal space. Since the Festival was in its tenth year, it did not occur to me, however, to question the competency or history of its organizers. That omission resulted in a snowballing series of events which made our Paris tour an artistic disaster.

From the moment my company glided on board the plane to the Festival, nothing went right. Even the heavens conspired against us. As we stepped onto the stage, the rain began pouring down, the power went out, and the audience ran for cover. We were upset but not dismayed, because the Festival organizers had informed me that in the event of rain the competition would be held the following evening, with an alternate (indoor) venue also available if the rain continued. It turned out that they had failed to make any such provisions; after much confusion, they finally advised us that the competition would resume the next morning in a gymnasium. However, the judges had not been told there would be a rain date and almost all had left, as had several of the dance companies; and there was no audience at all. The final blow: it was not a competition; the three remaining judges were local dance teachers against whose own students we were competing.

I was humiliated. I had led seven dancers three thousand miles to compete in an empty gymnasium before a fixed panel of judges. I had jumped at the chance of having the Company perform in an international festival in Europe, but I did not research the Festival nor ask appropriate questions. Instead I was blinded by the stars under which we were supposed to perform. Before committing to such a major undertaking, I should have utilized the resources available to me as an administrator of a major national and international arts organization, as well as through my own international network from having danced in France and the United States. With some judicious inquiry, I would have found out that the Festival had a checkered history, at best, and that we would have been wise to decline the invitation. This unhappy incident has not affected my enthusiasm for professional challenges, but I have become more deeply aware of my need to temper it with careful research and a healthy touch of skepticism.

Essay 2:

I have been a keen piano player since I was five years old. Throughout my school years I had easy access to teachers, practice rooms and a schedule that had openings in it for such activities as piano practice. My college years also left me with time during the week to carry on, though not so regularly, taking piano lessons and practiing. Where I feel I have failed is in the time since entering professional life: I have not found time to continue piano lessons and get down to some serious practice. I believe I did not manage this for one main reason: I did not make time, I let day to day routine prevent me from doing things that really mattered to me even though I knew I would regret it - and I know today, although I am getting organized, I will not be able to make up for lost time.

Reflecting on this realization has taught me a fundamental precept for life: define priorities, place them in a hierarchy, and once this order of importance is clear, do what you have to do to uphold your choice. What I did was define what was important, but fail to follow through. I did not handle my free time appropriately and it has shown me that it is too easy and very dangerous to allow things to go on as they will: it invariably leads to many regrets. I strongly believe now that one has to grab hold of life and not gently float along with the tide, for as a result one often misses out on many things that may be important or even fundamental. The real lesson is that one should always try to shape one's destiny, and take matters into one's own hands; be a doer of things, not an observer, an actor in one's life, not a spectator.

Columbia Business School is a diverse environment. Please discuss a life experience of yours that shows how you will contribute to the class. (Limit 250 words)

The point of the essay:

Through this essay, The Admissions Committee would like to know what makes you different from the rest of the candidates, aside from your professional or academic profile.

Tips for the essay:

The description of the profile of incoming students that is given by the Director of Admissions in his welcoming speech shows the diversity of present experiences. For instance, in my class there was an Olympic swimming champion, a former member of the FBI, a graduate of the New York Music Conservatory, etc. Given the diversity and the uniformly high caliber of the student body, it might seem impossible to come up with a convincing response as to what you can add to the Columbia community that nobody else can. But a strong answer often lies, quite simply, in the unique qualities that make you who you are. Candidates who have followed a more traditional career path can relay an original experience or anecdote from their life. Think of an event when you displayed your own particular brand of genius – how you found your way out of a cave in South America, how you organized a potluck wedding – and describe how that same quality will enable you to do special things at business school. A real passion for music, cinema, or architecture is also a trait that the Admissions Committee appreciates, and could indicate your intention of creating a club.

Sample Essay 1:

Six years ago, while reading William Faulkner's Absalom, Absalom!, I realized that literature texts are essentially complex systems: they are collections of variables – theme, structure, word choice, style – with hundreds of different relationships functioning at any given moment. At the same time I recognized the systematics of literature, I was advancing from linear algebra to advanced calculus in college. I briefly considered declaring a double major in English and mathematics. Both disciplines required the ability to assess a problem from as many different angles as possible, weighing subtle connections in order to ferret out the best route to a satisfactory resolution. Both deal, in essence, with understanding and manipulating systems. Ultimately, I decided not to double major, but my sense of the similarity between English and Mathematics has remained.

I approach Columbia Business School from an industry that I feel is underrepresented there, and my experience in book publishing is perhaps the most obvious element I intend to contribute to Columbia's diverse mix. More tangibly, I offer a qualitative mind that thinks in quantitative ways. I have the ability to communicate with eloquence and insight, and at the same time draw connections across vast seas of information. In college, I analyzed texts through the same lens that I now apply to the "Money and Investing" section of the Wall Street Journal. That unusual perspective on the way that data sets – literature texts and numerical matrices, cultural trends and profit and loss analyses – mimic each other is the greatest asset I intend to bring with me into the Columbia Business School community.

Sample Essay 2:

My experience of a two month internship in Austria and especially, studying in the U.K. for several years, as a foreign student in a new, alien environment, has taught me the importance of holding on to one's roots while assimilating the best of the new environment/culture and growing from the experience. I can share this with other students who have perhaps not had the experience of living and studying abroad, nor felt yet culture shock when confronted with a very different environment.

I am also an individual with strong interests in music, literature, and cuisine. These I can share and develop in Columbia's multicultural environment, which is ideal for discussion and exchange and in which one can learn from and with others. I would like, for example, to found a gourmet club or perhaps a wine tasting club, where each person could bring a different cultural approach to food and drink, and we could share knowledge, experiences, compare tastes and learn more through confrontation with other cultures.

Every individual has lived through similar experiences at some stage of his or her life, but has reacted in a unique way; the sum of these experiences, like so many stones, build the community. I, with my experiences, propose to be a keystone to that building, with my multilingual abilities to communicate serving as cement.

LETTERS OF RECOMMENDATION

Numbers of letters of recommendation needed for Columbia: **2**

GENERAL ADVICE

The letters of recommendation allow the Admissions Committee to better understand the character and competence of an applicant though the testimony of other parties. Linda Meehan, Director of the Board of Admissions at Columbia Business School, stresses the importance of these aspects of the application process. On the recommendation form, the evaluator has the choice of either filling in a questionnaire provided in the application packet or of drafting a more traditional letter. Two types of questionnaires are available depending upon the nature of the recommendation: professional or academic. A dozen questions relate to the strengths and weaknesses of the candidate, his/her motivation, maturity, and more precisely, on his/her professional and/or academic competence. For candidates who have been active in the professional world for more than six months, it is strongly suggested that they provide a letter of recommendation issued by their immediate superior. Sometimes, it can be a bit delicate or even impossible to ask this person. In this case, you should ask your former employer or a colleague from work, not forgetting to explain the reasons for this choice on your application. Applicants who have recently graduated must get at least one letter from an internship supervisor. The second can come from an undergraduate professor.

Do not hesitate to warn the person whom you're requesting to write the letter of the importance of their task. Choosing a colleague from work that you esteem professionally does not guarantee a good letter. You must also be certain that he/she will dedicate sufficient time and effort to draft an efficient letter. Clearly, the letter must be written in grammatically correct English and typed. Finally, please note that the title or professional activity of the person you choose has little impact on the evaluation of the letter. Letters of recommendation are strictly confidential, which means that applicants do not take part in drawing them up. On the other hand, it could be useful to indicate to the evaluators what the Admissions Committee typically expects to see in a good letter of recommendation. Below you will find several of the key questions asked in Columbia's application packet, with an interpretation as well as some sample answers.

FIVE QUESTIONS FOR THE COLUMBIA LETTERS OF RECOMMENDATION

1) Provide a short list of adjectives which describe the applicant's strengths.

The point of the question:
Each year, the Admissions Committee strives to compose the most diverse group possible. In addition to academic profile and professional experience, the Committee is looking for intrinsic qualities in the applicant that will allow him/her to integrate and succeed in the program.

Tips for the questions:
If there exists no one set student profile that the Committee has in mind, one thing that all selected applicants do have in common is that they have demonstrated the qualities of

management, among these, leadership ability and strong motivation. It is therefore necessary to insist upon this point both in the answer to this question as well as throughout the whole letter. Finally, the person writing the letter should not hesitate to use superlatives where they are appropriate!

Example:

> *Decision-maker, strong-minded, dynamic, highly motivated, quick, top writing and interpersonal skills, ability to adapt to unexpected circumstances, strong analytical skills.*

2) Comment on the applicant's ability to work with others, including superiors, peers and subordinates. Would you enjoy working for the applicant?

The point of the question:

Around 40% of your time will be devoted to working in groups, case studies, or projects. Under these conditions, the Admissions Committee wants to be convinced of your ability to work as a team member. The goal of the second part of the question is to assess your professional maturity and your leadership qualities as the head of a team.

Tips for the questions:

Applicants who have not demonstrated these specific aptitudes have little chance of getting in. So you must be particularly convincing in answering this question.

Example:

> *I might say that Jane has built a pleasant relationship with our company and myself through her great communication skills and open-mindedness. She has consistently made powerful contributions to the team. I would definitely enjoy working for her as she certainly has the will, drive and potential to become an effective and inspiring upper-level manager.*

3) In what way could the applicant improve professionally? - OR - What aspect of the applicant would you most like to change?

The point of these questions:

In relation to this question, the Admissions Committee is looking to find out your weaknesses. For the person who is writing the letter of recommendation, it is easier to answer the question objectively with the way it is formulated here, rather than to directly elaborate on your weaknesses.

Tips for the questions:

Certain faults or gaps of character, for example, an average ability to communicate, will irretrievably penalize your candidacy. Whatever the weaknesses may be, ideally, the evaluator should conclude by stating that you are making every effort possible to improve yourself.

Example

> *Jane is sometimes too direct in her talks and her attitude towards her colleagues. As she is aware of her weakness, Jane has been improving in this area through his capacity to draw lessons from experience.*

4) How well has the applicant made use of available opportunities? Consider his or her initiative, curiosity and motivation.

The point of the question:

The Dean of Columbia regularly affirms that its students are one of its assets, due to their dynamism and their initiative. From this point of view, the Admissions Committee expects each selected applicant to play an active role in school life during their two years of attendance.

Tips for the questions:

Here, too general of an answer risks not being sufficient enough for the Committee. A brief anecdote or a well-chosen example drawn from your academic or professional activities will be much more appropriate.

Example:

Motivation is Jane's greatest asset. Curiosity leads her to cope with the situation when the available opportunities prove insufficient (through her sense of initiative).

5) Comment on the applicant's business ethics.

The point of the question:

Ethics is a particularly sensitive and dominant topic at Columbia. All students sign the Code of Integrity upon acceptance by which they commit themselves to prove their total integrity in their university work. The school wants to be sure that it is understood that any violation of this code will result in the expulsion of the offender.

Tips for the questions:

As with the meaning of teamwork, the candidate must imperatively have demonstrated trials of complete integrity in their undergraduate work and in their professional life as well, in order to maximize their chances of getting in.

Example:

Her strict family upbringing has won her profound respect of such necessary qualities as honesty and integrity which constantly appeared during her activity with us.

THE INTERVIEW

Each year, the Admissions Committee invites approximately 50% of the candidates to an interview. Between 15% and 20% of interviewed applicants will actually get in, whereas a minority of candidates will get admitted without having had an interview.

The interview takes place either on campus with a director of the Board of Admissions or in your geographical region with an alumnus of Columbia. Without doubt, choosing to come to New York for the interview demonstrates motivation. An interview with an alumnus will certainly be more convenient, but I think that it risks having less of a direct impact with the Admissions Committee even if officially there is no difference.

An applicant who chooses to be interviewed in his or her home area chooses an interviewer from a list of three alumni of the school. These graduates are selected at random among alumni who volunteer and live in the same region as the candidate. The only information about the interviewer that will be provided to you is their year of graduation from Columbia.

The goal of the interview is to clear up certain points about the applicant's file, such as his/her intentions and career plans for after the MBA. Your interviewer may spend more time trying to see what motivated you to make a certain decision rather than delving into all the details of your professional and personal history. He or she will also attempt to gauge your conversational skills and your articulateness. Class participation being an omnipresent aspect of the program, the Admissions Committee wants to be assured that you will be able to contribute strongly.

The interview, which lasts for approximately one hour, takes place in two parts: in the first part, the interviewer asks a series of questions which will enable him to understand why you want to pursue an MBA at Columbia. These questions are drafted by the Admissions Committee and are identical for all applicants. They are relatively standard and should not surprise you if you have read over your assays well before going to your interview. You can expect to be asked:

- Why do you want to do an MBA at this point in your career? Why at Columbia?
- What career path do you plan to take upon graduating from Columbia? Why?
- Give an example either from your professional life or some other some other occasion where you directed a project.
- What will you contribute to the campus community?
- How do you plan to finance your studies?

In the second part, the applicant is called upon to ask questions about Columbia. At this point in the application process, your interviewer expects you to ask questions based on your knowledge of Columbia rather than on your ignorance of it. You must avoid asking general questions about the admissions procedure, especially since the alumni will not give you any information that you don't already know. On the other hand, this interview represents the perfect time to show your interest in the program of study, in the teaching methodology, or in the life on campus. For example:

- What are the key courses one should take?
- Is there any advice for the quickest possible integration into the core of the school?
- What mistakes should one avoid in order to get the most out of the experience?
- What was perception did you have about Columbia upon your graduation?

- Are there any other career prospects besides investment banks and consulting firms?

Afterwards, the interviewer goes over his interview report, gives it a score on a scale of 1 to 4, then transfers this information to the Admissions Committee in New York.

INTERVIEW WITH COLUMBIA'S ADMISSIONS DIRECTOR

Interview with Linda Meehan, Director of Admissions at Columbia Business School.

Could you first tell us about the application review process?

Applications are reviewed on a rolling basis. Once completed, each application is thoroughly read by three members of the Admissions Committee. Sometimes, the Committee requires the assistance of one of our Executives-in-Residence when the background or the profile of a candidate is not familiar. It takes approximately 10 to 14 weeks for the Committee to process an application and make a decision.

What makes a good candidate stand out from the pool of applicants?

We are looking for motivation, solid work experience and proven leadership qualities in or outside the work environment. We are looking for interesting diverse applicants. More and more of our applicants come with stronger credentials, and that allows us to be more selective.

The difficulty when you look at the numbers is that there are always exceptions to everything. You look at people with a wide range of backgrounds and experiences, so not everybody looks the same. But the application pool and competitiveness have increased. Standards have changed quite significantly. More scrutiny is called for to differentiate between both a greater number of applicants and a higher quality of them. I have been here for four or five years, and over that time I have seen the application pool change quite drastically. The students that we are admitting now are obviously different than five years ago. Admittance really depends on the pool and how you stand up to the competition..

How would you rank admissions factors, highest to lowest, in order of importance: GMAT, grades, recommendations, essay, interview, work experience?

Work experience is first, and part of that would be the recommendations as a subset. Then I would put GMAT and grades, lumped together, because you are competing against a pool of applicants. After you have assessed that an applicant can fit in, you need to see how they stack up against their colleagues. Then comes the personal interview because personal characteristics set you apart as well.

However, ranking these numerically makes me feel uneasy because uniqueness and background may offset how we weigh quantitative scores. Rather than putting them in order I would put work experience and recommendations as the most important factors because if they're not there, then nothing else matters. We deny people with 800 GMATs and we deny lots of people who have 700 GMATs. Someone with phenomenal work experience and accompanying recommendations puts herself in a strong position for review.

As a school known for its strength in finance, does Columbia place a lot of importance on a candidate's quantitative background, such as the GMAT or grades?

We are without a doubt a quantitative program, and we don't deny that. Quantitative scores are important to us. We want to make sure that the student can get through our program. The best way we have of evaluating that is through the GMAT, specifically its quantitative piece. Not everybody took calculus in college, and it is no longer a prerequisite for admission. So if you don't have the mathematical background, how can we assess it? Well, the answer is: we use the GMAT.

What are the chances of being admitted off the waiting list?

They are quite good because many of candidates are on there not because they are not viable candidates or that they are not competitive, but because we can't see the whole pool. There are some people who are carried over because they choose to be. And we ask them, "are you willing to stay on to the bitter end?" Few will be accepted into the program who are wait listed closer to the deadline. It's really a matter of how many people decide not to show up on the first day of class. Historically, there have been a few people that haven't shown up, but that's a small minority.

Do you encourage rejected applicants to re-apply?

We do encourage some applicants to reapply. Some are rejected and receive a letter that is fairly specific. We try and give as much feedback as we can. But we logistically just cannot get back to everyone. Rejected applicants may request feedback in writing. We then will try to reach them with another letter or with verbal feedback.

Which other business schools do you consider as direct competitors with your MBA program? Why?

The schools with which we most often compete for students are Harvard and Wharton. These offer the same quantitative program and attract the same pool of applicants.

How big a role does luck play in the application process?

The numbers speak by themselves: 7,200 applications received in 1999 for 670 places. You can pick and choose more carefully than, say, when you have 2,500 applications, when the quality and quantity is not as high. You will diminish the part of luck by focusing on the school you want to be at.

Getting the
HARVARD
Admissions
Edge

Harvard
Business School

Address	Harvard Business School Soldiers Field Boston, MA 02163
Telephone	(1) 617-495-6127
Website	www.hbs.edu/mba
E-mail	admissions@hbs.edu

about the school

Founded	1908
Tuiton Fees	$30,050
Some Famous Alumni	George W. Bush (US President); Elaine Chao (US Secretary of Labor); Scott Cook (Chairman of Executive Committee, Intuit); Louis Gerstner (CEO, IBM); Meg Whitman (President & CEO, eBay); James Wolfensohn (Pres., The World Bank Group); Robert-Louis Dreyfus (CEO, Adidas - Solomon AG); Pamela Thomas - Graham (Pres. & CEO, CNBC) Michael Bloomberg (Founder, Bloomberg Financial Markets)

the application

Application Dossier	By mail, telephone or downloadable from website
Application Deadlines	late October early January early March
Dossier Elements	• 5 essays + 1 optional • 3 written references • Academic Transcripts • GMAT (and TOEFL, if applicable) • résumé • interview on invitation

rankings

Publication	Business Week						US News & World						Financial Times		
General Ranking	90	92	94	96	98	00	94	96	98	99	00	01	99	00	01
	3	3	5	4	5	3	3	5	1	2	1	2	1	1	2

before the MBA — class of 2003

	class of 2003
# applicants	8,893
# applicants entering	880
% women students	34%
% married students	21%
% minority students	20%
% international students	34%
# countries represented	69
Age (years)	
median	27
range	21 - 44
Education pre-MBA	
Humanities & Social Sciences	45%
Engineering	30%
Business	20%
Other	5%
Professional experience	
avg. years work experience	4
Field of work	
Industry	26%
Consulting	21%
Investment banking	14%
Other	39%
GMAT	
average	703

after the MBA

class of 2000

avg. job offers per student	3.95

Main career choices

Financial Services (Investment Banking, Venture Capital/Private Equity)	34%
Consulting	24%
High Tech (Internet, Hardware, Software, & Telecom Companies)	21%
Other	21%

Function

Finance - Professional Services	28%
Consulting	23%
General Management	13%
Business Development/Strategic Planning	12%
Entrepreneurship	12%
Marketing	10%
Other	2%

Geographical location

North America	86%
Europe	8%
Asia/South Pacific	3%
Canada and Mexico	1%
Other	2%

Salary

median total compensation at graduation	$130,000

Top 10 employers

1. McKinsey & Co.
2. Bain
3. Goldman & Sachs
4. Siebel
5. Boston Consulting Group
6. Lehman Brothers
7. Monitor
8. Deloitte
9. Microsoft
10. Apax Partners

author

Name   A. DE MENDONCA

His early career was in brand management at Procter & Gamble. He recently graduated from the Harvard Business School, spending his summer internship at McKinsey. He is currently leading an internet project in Europe.

School specifics

HARVARD

INTRODUCTION

This chapter details the specifics of the Harvard MBA. The goal is twofold: 1) to help you decide if this school corresponds to your personality and future projects, and 2) for those who have already decided to apply, to help you adapt your application to the Harvard profile.

In my opinion, the quality of Harvard courses as well as career possibilities are the same as those of its principal rivals (Stanford and Wharton, and INSEAD in Europe). In each school, professors are world-renowned, students are chosen after a highly competitive admissions process, and companies fall head over heels to employ graduates. However, Harvard has known better than other schools how to cultivate the myth surrounding itself. Since the beginning of the century, the school has been the breeding ground for the business elite (close to 20% of Fortune 500 company executives are Harvard graduates), dynamic entrepreneurs, and even the presidents of certain countries (Vincent Fox, recently elected president of Mexico). More than any other school, Harvard has become a symbol of success. The old red brick buildings, the peaceful calm of wandering alleyways and the numerous statues honoring famous alumni seem to come right out of a movie set.

This myth fascinates and awakens the desires of nearly 8,500 young professionals each year who compete to come and spend a couple of years at Harvard. More than at any other school, companies go out of their way to hire Harvard Business School MBAs and the salary packages (salary + bonus + tuition reimbursement) of the last graduating class hit a record high ($145,000!). A Harvard MBA opens the door to the largest business club in the world. The alumni network is generally very active not only in the States (72 clubs) but also in most countries (50 clubs abroad and nearly 7,000 alumni in Europe). The Harvard network is probably the biggest strength of the school. This will be an invaluable resource for your entire career: from your first months on campus you have access to the Alumni Advisory Network (nearly 35,000 alumni who give students advice on their professional field, their responsibilities, or on the company they work for). In the years following, the network will be a unique source of information, contacts and opportunities for your professional success.

The Harvard MBA offers a general business education during which all courses are approached from the General Management perspective - learning to look through the eyes of the CEO, whether at a major multinational corporation, or a new start-up with full growth potential. For example, the goal is not for you to become a technical specialist in finance, but to understand financial problems so that you are able to direct a company's overall management. Harvard also distinguishes itself by its teaching methods, particularly with its nearly exclusive use of case studies, in which learning occurs via class discussions of real-life examples.

THE DEAN'S VISION

Interview with Dean Kim Clark was conducted by Alain de Mendonca.

What is the mission of the Harvard Business School (HBS)?
The HBS mission is to educate leaders who will have the ability to change the world around them, be it in large corporations, start-ups, or non-profit organizations. In this capacity, HBS aims to build knowledge not only by emphasis on theory in the classroom, but also by putting these practices into action. In addition, our curriculum is an integral part of a truly transforming experience that stimulates not only intellectual growth, but also personal growth. I use the word "transforming" here deliberately. When I speak with our alumni, I hear over and over again how deeply they were transformed by HBS.

Could you describe the teaching methods practiced at HBS?
The HBS classroom is an amazing place to be. Though demanding, it is also fun, which creates an interesting dynamic. HBS utilizes a variety of teaching methods, but our hallmark technique is the case study method, which successfully blends analysis with practical application. Our goal is to create an environment where students learn how to tackle difficult problems through group discussion and probing which result in a much deeper understanding of the issue than could have been achieved individually. Students learn what it feels like to exercise judgment, make decisions, and take responsibility. In so doing, they sharpen skills like effective communication through the use of persuasion, synthesis, and adaptation.

It seems that HBS is increasingly more focused on Entrepreneurship and a bit less on General Management. What is your opinion on this?
HBS has, for many years, been focused on teaching General Management. This commitment has not changed and will not change. In the past, General Management described the study of administrations of large, complex, and relatively stable businesses. Today, General Management also encompasses the study of large and small enterprises and of those who shape them. In addition, HBS is now making sure that a strong educational commitment is made to study General Management from the perspective of an entrepreneur. In other words, HBS is broadening its portfolio of research and education in regards to General Management. While we have always had a history of research in and teaching of Entrepreneurship, today, we feel that an entrepreneurial perspective on General Management is just as important. So, much of what HBS has learned about Entrepreneurship can also be applied to large corporations and vice versa.

Sometimes people comment that HBS is too individualistic and that teamwork is not emphasized enough.
We do put a lot of value on teamwork since strong leaders must develop proficiency in their abilities to work effectively with others. In fact, an integral part of the HBS experience is participation in group projects and study groups that are formed by students to prepare cases. However, we are aware that business leaders must also take responsibility for their own of projects. They are part of the team but they act as individuals to carry out business initiatives.

The bottom line is that companies value and reward the ability to lead and to get things done. This is also true for entrepreneurial ventures. The HBS focus on both teamwork and individual responsibility help students to become effective and recognized leaders in the business world.

What do you think of a 1-year MBA program?
I want to make sure that we are comparing apples with apples. I am aware that some institutions offer students an MBA diploma after only 1 year. However, the diploma is only one part of the equation. Indeed, I am convinced that these students do not have the same transformational experience as with a 2-year program. Again, we consider that this 2-year experience strongly stimulates intellectual and personal growth of our students (that could not be achieved in a 1-year MBA program).

Do you plan to increase class size over the coming years?
Today, HBS has the largest class size of all leading MBAs with about 900 students admitted per year. Class size has doubled over the past 40 years. We would like to have the opportunity to offer our education to a higher number of students. Yet, we have some physical constraints like classroom space. Over the coming years, little by little, we will find a way to increase the number of students admitted to our program.

Could you say a little bit about international projects at HBS?
In the sixties and seventies, HBS devoted resources to help European institutions like INSEAD or IMD develop their MBA and Executive programs. We are pleased that these institutions have now become full-fledged programs. Just like Asia and South America, Europe is part of HBS's global initiative. It's an initiative that aims to expand the scope of our educational programs and enrich our collaborations with alumni, academia, and business leaders throughout the world. We will not be in Europe and other regions as a satellite MBA program (n.b.: INSEAD has opened an MBA center in Singapore), since we consider our unique situation and facilities in Boston a vital part of our MBA's transformational experience.

Instead, one of the primary charges of this global initiative is the establishment of research centers in key regions of the world. These centers will enable HBS to expand research and case study writing on a global scale. One immediate benefit is that our MBA students will study more and more international cases. These cases yield key insights about business practice of all the major regions of the world. For example, you do not carry out a privatization the same way in Italy as you do in the US. In January 1999, we opened our first center in Hong Kong. Shortly, more centers will be opened in South America (Buenos Aires) and Europe (not yet determined). Once we have built an outstanding knowledge capital of business in Europe, we plan to be more active in Executive programs across Europe in a similar capacity.

Do you have any advice for candidates?
The admission process is highly selective since more than 8000 individuals apply for about 900 places. We are looking for people who have very strong leadership potential like the ability to initiate projects and lead people to accomplish objectives. We want to determine evidence of this leadership potential in applicants through a careful look at their academic performance, work experience, community service, and extracurricular activities. We hope that our graduates will go forward as outstanding leaders in business and in the community as well.

THE SCHOOL YEAR

The table below lays out the studies at Harvard. The Required Curriculum (two semesters) corresponds to mandatory core courses and the Elective Curriculum (two semesters) corresponds to the period during which the student can choose his or her classes.

Program	end Aug - mid Dec	Jan - end May	Jun - Sept	Sept - Dec	Jan - Jun
September Entry (600 students)	1st term Required Curriculum	2nd term Required Curriculum	Internship and/or Vacation	3rd term Elective Curriculum	4rd term Elective Curriculum
	1st year			2nd year	

Previously, there had been two possibilities for doing the Harvard MBA. The September entry (called "September cohort") and the January entry ("January cohort"). However, the school recently decided to eliminate the January program.

THE FIRST YEAR: THE CORE COURSEWORK (REQUIRED CURRICULUM)
The core curriculum is the foundation of business education. It is composed of four parts:

Foundations I (three weeks):
The objective is to give students the basic knowledge essential for the first semester of classes. The principle courses are Quantitative Methods (statistics), Basic Accounting, Applied Personal Skills (individual organization methods and teamwork), Creating Modern Capitalism (a study of the economic history of the major capitalist countries), Business Ethics, and Career Development, where the aim is to help students reflect on and choose career paths that best correspond to their personality.

The First Semester:
After the three weeks of Foundations, the serious stuff starts! Students are divided into sections of 80 people. These sections will last for all of the first and second semester courses. You will take all of your classes with the same group of 80 people in the same classroom.
The course takes place from Monday to Friday, starting early in the morning (8:30 am) and ending around 2:00 pm. But it's not as if you have the rest of the day free, because you have to prepare your case studies. For the first semester, the afternoons and evenings are very often entirely devoted to the numerous readings and preparation of case studies, which will be discussed in the following section.

The main courses for the first semester are:
- Financial Management and Reporting
- Finance I (investment decisions, calculating NPV, assessing a company, etc.)
- Marketing
- Leadership and Organizational Behavior (a study of key leadership qualities)
- Technology and Operation Management (a class on the principles of operational organization)

The first semester is undoubtedly the hardest and most stressful of the entire academic program. You need to adapt to new teaching methods, make new friends, and come to grips with a grading system that encourages intense competition. Nights are short and it is often necessary to work on the weekend. On the good side of things, the classes on Leadership and Technology and Operation Management are truly fascinating.

Foundations II:

Two weeks are devoted to additional essential courses aimed at giving students the material they need for the 2nd semester of classes. The main courses are: Macro-economics, Principles of Negotiation and Social Enterprise.

The Second Semester:

- Finance II
- Negotiation
- Business Government & International Economy (a study of the economic development models of a number of countries)
- Entrepreneurial Management
- Strategy

This semester is generally less stressful - provided you got good grades during the first semester! The courses on Business Government and International Economy are stellar and the classes on Finance are very well done - especially for neophytes. The Entrepreneurial Management class has just been added to the Required Curriculum, which is an indication of the growing interest in entrepreneurship. The great diversity in the case studies exposes students to many of the different challenges they may face as entrepreneurs (fundraising, management of steady growth, organizational problems, acquisition of another start-up, etc.).

One of the particularities of the Harvard program is that students cannot waive first-year classes even if they have already worked in those areas. The disadvantage here is the inconvenience of slogging through course material you may already be familiar with. On the other hand, there are two big advantages: first, there is always the opportunity to learn new things as professors manage to run their classes on two levels (simplified discussions for newcomers and in-depth discussions for students with experience); second, the case study teaching method at Harvard amounts to discussions between students led by the professor. During these discussions, the presence of students with experience in the subject area is invaluable because they are able to share their experiences and to explain hard-to-understand subtleties to others. Along the same lines, students who are experts in one area are often novices in another, and here they receive the help of other students in turn. In other words, the inability to waive classes ensures that the skills of students better complement one another as much as possible.

THE SECOND YEAR: ELECTIVES (THE ELECTIVE CURRICULUM)

The second year (the third and fourth semesters) is exciting because you pick and choose your own course schedule. You can therefore devote yourself to material that interests you and to looking for the job of your dreams, or to writing a business plan. You have to take at least five electives per semester among a choice of 90 possible classes. The quality of electives varies, but most are at a very high level. Since the best electives are the most popular, the school has devised a bidding system where the students classify their courses by order of preference and participate in a computerized lottery which has the ambitious goal of maximizing student satisfaction by matching student preferences with the number of available spaces in each course. Each student finds that he or she usually gets into some of the best courses, and a few that are a little less popular. Moreover, you also have the possibility of taking some of your electives at MIT, the Harvard Kennedy School (Political Science), or at Harvard Law School.

If you would like more experience putting your knowledge into practice, you have the option of doing a field study. These projects can count for up to 30% of your credits for the second year. These projects are, therefore, far from being trivial and there are a number of ways to go about it:

- Writing a business plan for the creation of a start-up.
- Analysis of a particular sector of business activity (e.g. an analysis of venture capital in Europe).
- A real-life project with an organization or team to solve a problematic situation at a company that has been contacted for the occasion, or else at a number of very major companies, from multinationals to start-ups, that directly propose projects to the school.
- A research project in collaboration with a professor.

More than 60% of students choose to undertake a field study that is carried out in small teams (three to six) with a professor designated as advisor. Every 15 days, the team meets with the professor, and he or she provides feedback and perhaps even some contacts. The professor is also in charge of the grading, which is understood to be collective so that it will ensure real group effort.

For those of you who want to create your own company, these field studies are an opportunity for developing your business plan during your academic studies. Thus up to 30% of your second year credits can be devoted to this unbelievably monumental task of writing a business plan. For budding entrepreneurs, the ideal plan is to take some electives on entrepreneurship (Entrepreneurship Finance, Entrepreneurship Marketing, Starting New Ventures, etc.) and to then to devote your field studies to writing a business plan. This is what I did during my second year and it was extremely educational because I applied what I learned in my morning classes to my business plan which I worked on in the afternoons and evenings.

THE COURSES - WHAT'S HOT...WHAT'S NOT
Some classes are outstanding, others less so, if only in relative terms. It is always tricky to give quantified evaluations of the courses - how do you best determine the best criteria for evaluation? My feeling is that the most useful criterion is the level of student satisfaction in relation to their expectations. In effect, students are "consumers" who have invested both time and money to come to learn, and thus have very specific expectations.

Below are the results of a survey of students regarding their levels of satisfaction in relation to their expectations.

% recent graduates from Harvard Business School	Below Expectations	In Line With Expectations	Above Expectations	Outstanding
Corporate Strategy	43%	28%	23%	8%
Leadership	5%	23%	30%	42%
Operations	9%	19%	60%	12%
Marketing	56%	28%	14%	2%
Entrepreneurship	0%	31%	31%	38%
International economy	13%	10%	48%	30%
Capital Markets	0%	15%	46%	38%
Corporate finance	13%	33%	40%	13%
Accounting	17%	57%	26%	0%
Human Resources	0%	57%	43%	0%
Negotiations	24%	41%	29%	6%
Business Ethics	18%	34%	34%	13%

Some explanations:

- I want to emphasize that this evaluation table is not easily comparable with other schools. As the survey measures satisfaction compared to expectations, it's quite clear that students from different schools have different expectations. For example, Harvard is reputed for its General Management education. Students no doubt have higher levels of expectation and are quite severe in their appraisal if the reality of these courses falls short of what they expected. In comparison, Northwestern is better known for its courses on Marketing than on General Management. Kellogg students are therefore perhaps less severe in their judgement if the General Management courses are not outstanding, but they'll be very critical towards the Marketing courses.

- It also seems reasonable to believe that a professor is a key element in the satisfaction level of students. In order to avoid a bias based on a particular professor, I have asked students from all the sections to obtain results across the faculty.

In general, the fields in which Harvard offers the best courses are Entrepreneurship, Leadership, International Economy, Corporate Finance, Market Finance, Organizational Operations and Business Ethics. On the other hand, Harvard is not so strong in the areas of Marketing and Corporate Strategy.

Harvard is renowned for its training in General Management, but there aren't any specific courses on General Management! In fact, General Management is developed more through the other courses (Finance, Accounting, Marketing, Operations, etc.) where the approach to the subject material is always from the perspective of a General Manager. For example, the purpose of an Accounting class is not for you to learn all of the subtle mechanics of accounting, but for you to understand the ways in which accounting can help a general manager make good decisions. This General Manager approach to solving functional problems (finance, marketing, operations, etc.) enables students to develop great reflexes.

Harvard prioritizes a generalist approach, whereas most of the other schools place more emphasis on technical aspects. In concrete terms, this means that class discussions focus more on cases studies to apply theoretical concepts than on technical calculations, which are rarely the subject of attention. During my internship at McKinsey, my conversations with other MBA students (Chicago, Wharton) left me thinking that these schools give a lot more attention to calculating technical answers. This is not to say that you will not do spreadsheets at Harvard. It's just that there are a lot fewer than at other schools. The strength or weakness of the Harvard approach? It's hard to say because there are no precise studies on the question. But to give just one anecdote, Harvard MBAs are often the butt of jokes from other schools: "Harvard MBAs are poets who don't know how to count!". Inversely, Harvard MBAs can be snobs about being general experts as opposed to mere technicians (for general strategy questions, you need a Harvard grad and for calculations, take a Wharton grad).

TEACHING METHODS:

What makes Harvard special is its almost exclusive use of case studies. Invented at Harvard nearly 60 years ago, the case study method was rapidly adopted by the majority of other business schools. This has even become a profit-making activity because Harvard generates and sells cases to other schools! More than 6000 institutions across the world buy case studies from Harvard. Nevertheless, Harvard remains the only business school to exclusively use case studies. The majority of other schools use both case studies and lectures.

The case study describes a company's given situation (and its surrounding market). The goal is to use this information in order to resolve a given problem (marketing, finance, strategy, etc.). When preparing the case, you need to analyze and recommend strategies and a plan of action. In fact, case studies are similar to role-plays in which you are placed in a given situation and you need to make the best decision possible.

The preparation for case studies is done individually at home or with the help of a study group. While you are preparing the case, you have to analyze it, recommend strategies and design a plan of action. You usually have to spend about one hour to really understand the company's issues, and then at least one hour to prepare responses to the questions posed, which will serve as the basis for class discussion. Doing the preparation is one area the study groups are a way of lightening the workload by dividing the tasks up among several people. After the first semester the preparation time is much faster because students are broken in, so the nights start to get longer again!

For more technical matters (finance, accounting), the professor will have assigned theoretical readings in specialized textbooks. He or she also may put some practice exercises up on the school intranet. For example, for a financial case that deals with the Net Present Value of investment, the professor will assign 20 or so pages to read and four or five calculation exercises.

The solution to the case is done in class (nearly one and a half hours per case in an auditorium of 80 students). At the beginning of class, the professor calls on a student (a cold call) to "open the case." In the space of 10 to 15 minutes, the student needs to communicate, in a structured way, his analysis and recommended strategies. The "cold call" is never a relaxed affair because you need to be able to explain your ideas off the bat in front of 80 people. After this opening into the material, the professor opens up the discussion to the rest of the class ("So, do you agree with Matt's analysis and recommendation for this case?..."). Students throw themselves into the discussion supporting or refuting the analysis presented at the beginning of class. Class discussion takes place in an organized manner because i) students raise their hands cautiously and it is the professor who gives them the floor and, ii) students listen attentively to one another and the discussion progresses in a very constructive way. In addition to ensuring equal "air-time" for students, the role of the professor is to i) ask certain questions to fully explore the discussion ii) introduce as necessary certain frameworks and theories and, iii) conclude the case study in the last 5 to 10 minutes with a wrap-up of the main arguments, and provide his or her own opinion.In my own experience, I found this method to be effective, though it has both pros and cons.

Advantages of exclusively using case studies:

- The essential point of the case study is to simulate a real situation so that the student envisions himself as the person in a company responsible for making a decision on a given topic (organization, finance, marketing, strategy). This is similar to role-playing games in which the goal is to diagnose a company's problem and propose strategies and a plan of action. This is the big difference between case studies and lecture courses, where students are passive because they don't have the opportunity to express themselves. Besides, it is often the case that the protagonists of the case help the class and explain the decisions they made and their results (for example, Jay Walker, CEO of Priceline.com, came in order to explain the way he implemented his concept of "name your price," not only for airline tickets, but also for purchasing food products.
- The progression of a class discussion of a case study is: 1) to start from the company's actual situation, 2) to prepare and discuss in class the relevance of different strategic options, and 3) to walk away from the discussion with certain general principles that apply to a variety of situations. I find this way of learning much more natural because we work with concrete examples and infer the theories (learning "from the bottom up"). This way of learning differs quite a bit from lecture classes where the theories are often taught and examples are given only to support the theories ("top down").
- For more those who are somewhat intoverted or who are accustomed to lecture classes, the case method is not always easy to get used to. But the intensive practice of discussing cases does prove to be a rare opportunity to practice and perfect the art of public speaking.
- Given that the case study is a group discussion during which students exchange their opinions on a given case, the opportunity for student diversity to express itself is evident. Depending on their pre-MBA studies, native countries, and personal experiences, certain students always bring new and fascinating ways of seeing and understanding a problem. On one occasion during a discussion on operational organization, a former American army officer explained the organization principles behind introducing and managing US spies in North Korea!
- Case studies are based on preparation efforts, in which you need to read 20 to 30 pages of rather dense information. Very quickly, students learn how to read effectively and to know the difference between important information and details. This skill of synthesizing large amounts of important information is an extremely useful reflex because no matter what job you choose after your MBA, you will be forever reading reports and internal notes and making or participating in decisions based on them.
- Lastly, a student will analyze over 500 cases during the course of his or her studies: from Intel's strategies for launching new products, and General Motors' acquisition strategy in Europe, to taking a look at Amazon.com's organizational problems due to its strong growth. Since each case is a company situation with a functional problem to analyze, it's almost as if you were confronted with more than 500 real situations where you are asked to make certain decisions. You can therefore imagine yourself in a real business environment.

The disadvantages of exclusively using case studies:

- For learning specific skills (e.g., finance or accounting), the professor assigns readings from textbooks on those topics so that the discussions of the case studies are used for applying these skills. Therefore, learning specialized skills often remains the fruit of individual labor. Regrettably, these skills and concepts aren't always easy to grasp, so it's unfortunate that it's not possible to ask the professor about them before using them to resolve a case study.

- As we have already seen, the case study is based on deep analysis of a highly detailed company case. Consequently, if you haven't read the case, you'll get nothing out of the class discussion, which is not true of a lecture class, because the professor draws out the theories through discussing it with the students.

- Given that writing a case is the result of investigative efforts from the perspective of a company and/or a manager, brand new case studies that cover all the most recent global economic developments are not immediately available to students. For example, the school had to write a lot of cases on the new economy (internet). Therefore, I regret that during my first year, there were relatively few cases dealing with internet issues.

- Class participation counts for 50% of the final grade: the professor grades you on how often you speak as much for the quality of what you say. Therefore, it is not surprising that students force themselves to participate as much as possible (the infamous "air-time"), and this is sometimes counter-productive. In effect, it may be tempting to make simple remarks that are redundant, against the flow of the discussion, or sometimes to be confined to articulating facts already mentioned in the case without adding anything of real value. So, if the professor isn't already well-versed in the art of group discussion, this can make things become very chaotic.

THE GRADING SYSTEM

The Harvard MBA has a reputation for being competitive, and this is especially true during the first year. This is due, in part, to the large number of students who are admitted after distinguishing themselves within selective academic and professional environments in the world. Most students have therefore developed a competitive attitude. Once at Harvard, the grading system contributes to maintaining this competitive spirit. For the large majority of classes, the grading scale is as follows:

Grade	Distribution of grades
I	Top 15-20% (15 to 20 % top students)
II	Middle 70-75%
III	Bottom 10% (10 % bottom students)

This system is called the "forced curve" because grades are not based on an overall understanding and mastery of the subject matter, but rather in relation to how well other students have done. For each test, there will always be students in category I and in III. This means that even if you have learned the subject matter well... you could fail if 90% of the students have learned it better than you have.

Category I
The students who accumulate the largest number of Grade I's will be officially distinguished with Honors and/or as Baker Scholars. The advantages amount to having the Dean smile at you and putting this distinction on your resumé. But aside from impressing friends and family, I am not really convinced that having "honors" gives you an advantage when looking for a job. The MBA diploma from Harvard is already so well known, that having honors is just the icing on the cake.

Category III
Students who accumulate the largest number of grade III's are reviewed by the Academic Performance Committee. The Committee studies these students on a case-by-case basis in order to understand each student's particular difficulties (personal problems, language problems for international students, etc.). After deliberating, the Committee will usually ask the student to finish his studies in three rather than two years. Being expelled is rare (1 to 2% each year).

With the "forced curve" system, you need to not only understand the course material of each class, but understand it better than the vast majority of other students, if your hope to have a grade I. You'll have to understand it just a bit better than most if you hope to avoid a grade III. This system infuses students with a certain competitive spirit. Don't be disheartened with this because competition is not always a bad thing. There can be strong benefits to competition if it is well-channelled.

The *advantages* of this grading system are the following:
- The assurance that every students is compelled to give it his all. This is even more important considering that the teaching method at Harvard is based on students' class participation. You also have the assurance that students benefit in class from the experience of others and from their opinions.

The *disadvantages:*
- There is a certain amount of stress because the first grades are not given out until December. In the meantime, you have no idea if you are going to be in category I or III. Other students are rarely lightweights, so it is hard to tell if you are doing better than they are.
- No one is ever going to stab you in the back (i.e. let the air out of your tires or steal your photocopies on the way to class), so don't go away thinking that Harvard is a den of wolves! The competitive grading system does, however, tend to diminish a bit the tendency to help one another out.

As a general rule, final grades are generally based nearly 50% on class participation and the rest depends on written exams (nearly 35-40% for the final exam and 10-15% for the midterm).

It's important to note that the students have voted for grade non-disclosure, which means that grades are not made available to companies that recruit for internships for jobs. The school is very strict in respecting this rule and companies won't ask you any questions about your grades in interviews.

GROUP WORK
It should be pointed out that group work is not the strong point of the venerable institution that is Harvard. The opportunities for group work are not enormous and the emphasis is clearly on

individual performance. This is a huge difference between Harvard and other schools such as Northwestern where the team seems to be the driving force behind every activity. The few opportunities that there are to work as a team are:

- The "study group," in which 4 to 8 students join up to prepare the endless number of cases in the first year. The groups are formed by choice or by chance, according to whom you meet during the first few weeks of classes. Each member of a study group has to prepare some cases in detail, which means analyzing and writing a summary for the other group members. In the morning, all the group members meet to quickly discuss their different notes for each case. So the heavy burden of preparing for the case studies is lightened a bit because only one student prepares the case in detail so the others are content with just reading the case and very briefly analyzing it. The study group is not true teamwork in the genuine sense, rather it's just a way of dividing up work among students in same group.

- The field study in the second year: nearly 60% of students choose to do such a project (see the section on the courses). It's more about real teamwork, where the students have to devise a plan of action together, divide up the various tasks, but also discuss their conclusions and formulate their report.

THE TEACHERS

The school has nearly 220 permanent professors. Needless to say, the majority of professors are eminent figures in their respective fields. In general, professors' time is divided between students, research and, frequently, consulting for companies. Most professors have already written several books and write regularly for the largest and most respected economic newspapers such as The Wall Street Journal, The Financial Times, Business Week and of course the Harvard Business Review! A large number of professors have professional experience, so their courses reflect real-life economic situations.

The most well known professors are Nobel Prize winner Robert Merton (Market Finance), Michael Porter (Corporate Strategy), Bill Sahlman (Entrepreneurial Finance), Andre Perold (Investment Management), Nitin Nohria (Leadership), Pulitzer Prize winner Thomas McGraw (Theory on Modern Capitalism), Linda Hill (Leadership), Thomas Eisenmann (Internet), Jason Rottenberg (Business and Government International Economy), and Joe Lassiter (Entrepreneurship Marketing). Courses with star professors are often mind-blowing not only because the subject matter is fascinating, but because these professors have perfectly mastered the art of leading group discussions.

A teaching staff with a worldwide reputation is not always an advantage. One price to pay is that professors are often busy. They will never refuse to meet with you, but you will always get the sense that their time is too precious for them to be able to delve into the depths of class discussions or student projects. This is of course a generalization, and there are many exceptions.

THE INTERNATIONAL SIDE

With-one third of its students coming from abroad, Harvard is on a par with other MBAs. This diversity is evident in just a sampling of student clubs, such as the European Clubs, Africa Club or South Asia Club. Aside from students' home countries, an international angle is added to the program by studying international cases, such as those on non-American companies or on the international strategies of American companies. Contrary to other MBAs, Harvard does not offer the possibility of a semester abroad or the possibility of doing a joint degree with a specialized international program such as the Lauder Institute at Wharton. My opinion is that Harvard could make an effort to make its MBA more international. However, the feeling of being in an international environment is already quite present since daily interaction with students from around the globe offers plenty of opportunities for cultural exchanges.

COMPUTER FACILITIES - IT SYSTEM

The school has recently made huge progress in order to make up for lost ground in this area, and it now has cutting-edge technology. Every student should equip himself/herself with a laptop in order to benefit from a number of different possibilities:

- On-line class schedules and assignments
- Downloading certain class readings
- Server space for student websites
- On-line internship and job announcements
- Free access to the school's database (as powerful as those at major consulting companies and investment banks) for online research
- A list of the email addresses of all Harvard alumni. This is particularly useful for finding former students who now work in a company or a sector which interests you
- A life-long email account which makes it easier to network with alumni.

THE ENTREPRENEUR'S CORNER

Whether it is Harvard or one of the other schools presented in this book, I strongly recommend an MBA education for anyone interested in becoming an entrepreneur. Before doing an MBA, I asked myself if an MBA was really necessary for an entrepreneur. Today, here is my opinion: how could an MBA be unsuitable for an entrepreneur, who will eventually handle every aspect of a business (marketing, finance, organization, strategy, etc.), and at the same time be suitable for big businesses where employees are responsible for only one function (marketing or finance or strategy, etc.) and never have to be alone if they don't know enough? From my perspective, it is the entrepreneur who has to learn it all, because from the start, and often all on his own, he/she has to make all of the decisions in all those areas. Besides, the statistics belie the contrary: Harvard is a real conduit for entrepreneurship since between 30 and 40% of graduates declare themselves as self-employed within 15 years after graduation.

Harvard offers a number of possibilities for preparing to become an entrepreneur:
- A range of electives covering a range of problems: Entrepreneurial Finance (how to manage the finances of a start-up and notably how to raise funds), Entrepreneurial Marketing (how to manage the aspects of marketing that apply to a start-up), Venture Capital (understanding the world of Venture Capital). It should also be pointed out that you have the right to subscribe to the E-Lab of the MIT MBA (five minutes from Harvard). The Entrepreneur Laboratory enables you to work one day a week in a young start-up in Boston. This is a unique opportunity for you to learn from experience (see a description in the chapter on MIT).
- Contact with the most dynamic entrepreneurs. First of all, there is a weekly on-campus event during which young entrepreneurs share their successes and generously give out advice to budding entrepreneurs. Second, each year students organize the West Trek where nearly 300 Harvard students go to Silicon Valley for a week to meet the region's high tech companies.
- The Harvard Business Plan Contest. This contest has become one of the biggest moments at Harvard. Each year, nearly fifty teams made up of several MBA students develop and polish a business plan for creating a company. The jury is made up of the biggest American names in Venture Capital, the best professors of the school's Entrepreneurship Department and high-flying entrepreneurs. The jury holds a number of interviews to test out the project, which amounts to a rare opportunity to improve different aspects of the business plan. For the four project laureates, this is a guarantee that the phone will be ringing off the hook with calls from twenty companies wanting to invest funds in the project!
- The Cyberposium is a conference bringing together numerous major players in new technologies: venture capitalists, entrepreneurs, computer service providers, etc. It's an unique occasion to make contacts for a job or for your own future start-up.

LIFE AT HARVARD

BOSTON

Boston is definitely one of the prettiest and most pleasant cities in the United States. It is the country's historic birthplace, with numerous monuments commemorating those who liberated the colonies from the British yoke. A number of neighborhoods have old European charm with their winding streets and brick houses. In addition, you feel safe in Boston.

For weekends, the possibilities for getaways are numerous. You have easy access to the some of the East Coast's most fashionable beach resort areas, such as Cape Cod, Newport or Martha's Vineyard. There's Vermont for those who ski or hike, and of course there's something for everyone in New York City (three hours from Boston by car or train).

As far as money goes, take note that Boston is a rich town. Historically, it was a financial center and was home to the first mutual fund companies (for example, it's the headquarters of Fidelity). Boston and its surrounding areas are also very well known for new technologies with the famous Route 88, which abounds with computer start-ups swarming with hundreds of MIT engineers.

In general, Boston and its surrounding area are one of the student capitals of the US. The city has nearly 20,000 students from prestigious schools such as Harvard, MIT, Tufts and Wellesley College. The town is generally quite lively and there are plenty of places for going out. Harvard is located in Cambridge, which is 15 minutes from Boston by car. Cambridge is at once a rich Boston suburb, and also a student neighborhood, with the campuses of both Harvard and MIT.

THE CAMPUS

With close to 30 buildings, the Harvard Business School is one of the few schools to have a separate campus for its MBA and Executive Programs. Most other MBA programs share the campus with other university programs (Law, Humanities, Engineering, etc.).

The Harvard campus has a grand beauty all its own: the old red brick buildings are covered with green ivy, squirrels jump from branch to branch and the library looks like something out a movie, with its numerous study carrells and paintings of stern-faced professors.

The Business School campus offers a first-rate sports facility: four outdoor tennis courts, a luxury fitness club (with Jacuzzi and sauna!), 10 squash courts, basketball courts, access to a rowing club. You have no excuse not to break into a sweat!

HOUSING

There are three main possibilities:
- Living on campus; the school offers 1,500 on-campus rooms. The comfort level varies and ranges from small student bedrooms with communal bathroom (around $700/month) to duplex apartments with terrace and child-care ($1,700/month).

- Renting an apartment in Cambridge, but rents are rather high.
- Renting an apartment in the center of Boston for those who want to avoid having their life taken over by being a student. You should count on about 15-20 minutes in the morning for getting to campus (by car or subway).

SOCIAL LIFE

From the third week on, students are all divided into sections of 80. Students will take all of their classes for the first year with this same group of 80 people and all in the same room! The section is the basis for the social fabric at Harvard. You will brunch with them, you will grab a beer with them on the night of the Super Bowl, you will go to Cancun together for Easter vacation, and after you graduate, they will become your privileged professional network! This is a distinctive trait of Harvard, in comparison to other MBAs where the division between sections is much less significant. Harvard has a reputation for the tight bonds among its alumni, and sections are, in part, the basis for these ties.

Outside of sections, like all other respectable MBAs, Harvard has a lot of student clubs (59 in total). The clubs are organized around special interests (e.g. Oil & Gas, for those interested in the petroleum industry), geographic interests (e.g. the European Club for those who want to work in Europe), or side interests (e.g. the Soccer club for fanatics of the game).

The social life is also marked by numerous balls or "formals." A long-standing tradition, these balls are the occasion to bring out your tuxedo (rented, of course!) and to go strut about Boston's luxury hotels smoking a cigar. There are generally six or seven balls per year.

Last but not least, well-known personalities appear day-in and day-out to give lectures at Harvard. This is a unique opportunity to listen to the wise words of the big wigs and possibly to try your luck at approaching them for a job. Not only do the big names of the American economy appear: Michael Dell, Georges Soros, Jeff Bezos, but also those from other continents like Rupert Murdoch, Richard Branson, Jean-Marie Messier (Vivendi), Thomas Middelhoff (Bertelsmann), and Jean-Claude Trichet (Banque de France).

TUITION COSTS

As with all MBA programs, the costs soon add up:

Overall cost of the MBA (two years)	In US $
Tuition Fees	60,100
Housing	10,000 to 25,000
TOTAL	70,100 to 85,100

As far as money goes, don't count on working as a Teaching Assistant, as the workload for your student courses is intense. However, three other interesting possibilities exist for making ends meet:

- Each year, Harvard Business School receives several donations from former students wanting to testify to their later successes! With its financial capacities, Harvard is able to distribute a large number of fellowships to MBA students who need them. On average, students who ask for financial aid receive nearly $15,000 over the two years (about 50% of students receive fellowships). Aid is given to American students as well as to international students, with no discrimination between the two since the only criterion is financial need. To my knowledge, Harvard offers more fellowships to its students than any other program.

- Harvard has also established a student loan program in partnership with Citibank. This is a unique program that only Harvard offers. The big advantage of this is the possibility of receiving a loan without having collateral (Harvard itself guarantees the loan). The Citibank loans are sufficient to cover all tuition fees, and offer a competitive interest rate and no fees.

- In every country, the Harvard Alumni Club offers aid to students who have been admitted to the school. The number of scholarships and their amounts varies according to the country.

"I had had a very traditional educational background: a business degree, then national service, followed by three years in a company abroad, with diverse responsibilities in marketing and sales. At Harvard, I could share my own experiences, and benefit considerably through my contact with other students. Hoping to re-focus my career on new media, I was easily able to find an interesting internship in film in Los Angeles, followed by another internship in an internet company in London, mainly thanks to the Harvard network. Having thus built-up my résumé, that left second year for me to add on the finishing touches by doing a company project along with other students with the support of an ultra-qualified professor - a dream come true!"

"An MBA? OK. But why a Harvard MBA? Harvard really does have advantages. Among them, the two most enduring are the brand name of the school and its alumni.

The brand name:
The level of instantaneous, world-wide recognition of Harvard is simply unbeatable! Harvard's reputation will open a lot of doors for you. However, this privilege usually comes with high expectations of students (for what you get paid, one expects you to be worth it). For example, it already happened once during one HBS student's summer internship, he was cold-called by a VP during his training to respond to this request: "For this most difficult question, our friend from HBS can give us the answer!" Every privilege comes with its inconveniences and responsibilities.

The alumni:
The alumni have proven to be an invaluable resource in terms of contacts and various kinds of information that only circulate between alumni. Once again, the name Harvard can open doors. The Harvard MBA now is home to nearly 900 students, which makes it the biggest MBA class. Thanks to this mass effect, the number of alumni is therefore the highest of all business schools. So you will have lots of luck meeting alumni often throughout your career, or even just on the street! For example, you know that due to the size of the classes at HBS (900 students vs. 400 at Stanford), there are more Harvard MBAs going to Silicon Valley than Stanford MBAs (in absolute terms, of course). In addition to being an extremely vast network, it is also exceptionally close-knit. Having made a fortune, some Harvard alumni can afford to give several tens of millions of dollars to the Business School. These traditions help explain why there is a certain internal code of ethics at HBS that makes the Harvard network one of the most solid. Alumni have the impression that they've been privileged to attend this institution, and have a sense of obligation to it.

The campus clearly facilitates a more intense camaraderie than in other MBA programs where the campus is less central to the students' lives. In addition to having very close friends all over the world, you can also have high-level contacts in several countries: all you have to do is look at the online database to get all the contacts you need wherever you go. So, by introducing yourself properly, you can be welcomed by Harvard alumni everywhere, be introduced or recommended, save time, and find good business partners and investors. After a little time, you'll surely forget the cases... but not the friends."

"Contrary to what some people think, Harvard is not competitive. To start with a statistic: some 99.9% of students who enroll in the school get their MBA, and most in two years. Some take what amounts to one or a few years sabbatical between the two years in order to devote themselves to personal projects (start-ups or others). The only existing competition is for people motivated to get "honors," which, as the name indicates, only results in an honorary title at the end since there's no class ranking at graduation. Some students may resent the pressure due to the forced curve grading system. But it's a pressure that students, for the most part, put themselves under and it doesn't transform the exams into a competition. In fact, quite the contrary: the level of mutual assistance and solidarity is really high, because the goal is to create team spirit in the sections and a network for the future that the students are well aware of. For example, the primary stated objective of my section was to ensure that everyone would return for their second year (an objective that was ultimately not achieved because one of my classmates stayed in Singapore, where he established an internet start-up). We identified which students in my section were experts in fields that were taught (Accounting and Finance, in particular), and organized review sessions before exams. On the school level, an informal group called "Team 2000" was established for exchanging assignments and revision notes. In brief, it was the best."

"Here are a few thoughts on my first year at Harvard:
* *Some professors, especially in the first year classes, are somewhat disappointing.*
* *The academics (that means courses, exams, etc.) only make up 10% of the entire experience. The real richness comes from the 100,000 things that are going on around the school.*
* *Harvard cultivates an atmosphere of quasi-military style elitism the places the Code of Honor above everything else. Budding anarchists need not apply.*
* *Harvard is without a doubt one if the best places in the world to learn to create your own company. A Harvard MBA gives you access to essential resources for a successful start-up: training, contacts, advice and capital.*
* *The summer internship is a unique opportunity to discover a new industry. In addition, an internship in a given sector will give you much more credibility if you want to look for a job in that industry afterwards.*
* *If you are a normal person, your professional career path is going to change 100% every three months, as you are exposed to new opportunities along the way. Go with an open mind and leave your preconceived notions aside.*
* *At HBS, "networking is king." Your classmates as well as the tens of thousands of active alumni constitute the best access to jobs imaginable. Whatever your field, whatever your skills, along the way you will always find an HBS alum nearby to help you. Though I was skeptical at first, I have tested it several times (for both my summer and my full-time job searches) and I can now say IT WORKS!"*

"The field study is one of the unique aspects of the second year curriculum at Harvard.
The case study method is based on the concept of learning by practice, all contained in a single hour and a half discussion with 80 other students. During the second year, there is the opportunity to push this concept of learning by practice a little further: the field study. A special feature of Harvard, a field study is a real-life case study by a team of two to six students lasting an entire semester or for the whole second year, all supervised by a professor. The field study is done instead

of one of the five required second year courses and students are evaluated based on a final presentation given at the end of the semester.

There are two kinds of field studies. The first option is to form teams that play the role of consultant to a company to resolve a strategy or marketing problem, or to do new market studies. The second option is to write a business plan. Many budding entrepreneurs choose this option in order to compete in the business plan contest, which allows access to money from venture capitalists and entrance in the Nasdaq six months later, with an anticipated pay off as angel investor after three years! The field study offers several advantages. Above all, the team benefits from the supervision of a well-connected HBS professor who can open a lot of doors. The Baker Library has an impressive collection of market studies online (that would cost you several thousands of dollars outside of HBS), and other resources that would be terrible to pass up. In the market study stage, the HBS name and the alumni database open an impressive number of doors that become very useful contacts for the next stage. One benefits from the network and the support, all the while avoiding the workload of an extra course.

The field studies represent a big workload, which often proves to be more considerable that the work for a normal course. Many teams find themselves up to their necks in work the last month if they haven't been doing their work regularly. A lot of discipline is necessary to meet this challenge".

"HBS teaches you to set priorities. Some people focus on academics, others on attending all guest speaker events, others on meeting people, others on preparing their start-up, others on seeking their dream job, and so on. It is obvious that one cannot do all these activities at the same time. Therefore, you are forced to i) set clear objectives BEFORE starting the MBA program; and ii) more importantly, discipline yourself to stay true to your priorities on a daily basis (since the huge variety of activities is always tempting).

Furthermore, one learns to prioritize between "networking" and "building relationships". Think hard about whether you want to invest your precious spare time in more general, superficial networking, or in building fewer but deeper life-long friendships. Again, making a conscious decision is key. At the same time, striking a balance is very important to enjoying your time at business school. Many students get so caught up in school work that they forget their hobbies which are essential in order to keep a healthy balance during the program. People who continued doing sports, music or whatever their passion may be, were happier and did better in the long run."

The admissions application
HARVARD

INTRODUCTION

The Harvard admissions application requires:
- 3 letters of recommendation.
- Transcripts from your previous schools and universities.
- GMAT and TOEFL scores.
- 5 required essays and 1 optional essay.
- An information sheet (a highly detailed CV).
- An interview only upon invitation by the school after an initial selection - only 15% of applicants are offered the chance to have an interview.

There are three time periods in which to apply. The deadlines are typically early November (answer early January), early January (answer mid-March) and early March (answer mid-May). The admissions decisions are made around these three periods. This means that all the applications sent before a given deadline are evaluated at the same time.

Harvard holds the record for the number of applicants since each year more than 8,000 candidates apply for close to 900 places. Even so, the first selection is not made by the school; it's made by yourself. In effect, it's you who makes the decision to apply, or else you disqualify yourself right away. Put aside any pre-conceived ideas, even if your GMAT score isn't outstanding or your academic record is less than spectacular - you should just give it a chance. Every year there are a number of surprises: those who on paper have an ideal profile but are not even offered an interview, and those whose record is seemingly modest but are offered a place on the program. Honors, grades obtained during at university and the GMAT score do not seem to count as much as a leadership potential that you have shown through your experience.

THE GMAT

Below are the average GMAT (and TOEFL) results obtained by students recently admitted to Harvard.

	GMAT	TOEFL
average	690	273
deviation	+/- 40	+/- 18
range of scores	600 to 750	253 to 297

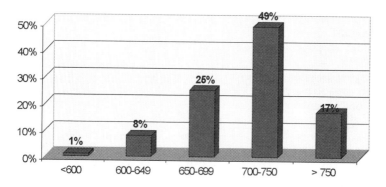

Distribution of GMAT scores for all admitted students

Just as for the all the major business schools, the average GMAT score at Harvard has consistently risen in recent years. That is due to the substantial growth in the number of candidates who are applying to MBAs.

In general, the GMAT is the MBA applicant's nightmare. Apart from the few candidates who obtain outstanding scores (more than 700), most candidates bang their heads against the wall over their GMAT scores. I encourage you to not get obsessed with having the "perfect score" and to not discourage yourself or write yourself out of the race because of your GMAT score. Rather than getting fixed on the average score, it is in your interests to think about the deviation from this average or the range of accepted GMAT scores (520 – 800 for the school overall).

My paragraph about the average scores will maybe reassure those among you who have a score in the 630-640 range or there about. But, I can hear those among you that haven't gotten to the 630-640 range asking yourselves if you should retake the GMAT! I can't give you a pragmatic answer. Above all, do not retake the GMAT unless you are certain to raise your score significantly (the Admissions Committee will hardly be impressed with a score that goes up merely 30 points!). Moreover, try to estimate how strong your candidature is overall: if you already have solid professional experience, striking essays and outstanding letters of recommendation, it is not necessarily advantageous to retake the GMAT.

Serious candidates take several trial runs in order to prepare themselves for the GMAT. But which tricks make the differences?

Cram intelligently!

The GMAT is better mastered with practice than with cramming. I encourage you to not only do lots of practice exercises but to do them in an effective manner. For my part, I made flashcards for the trickiest questions. Upon finishing a series of practice exercises most of us are eager to know our total score. It is certainly less pleasant to look at the your mistakes in detail. Yet having a good understanding of the underlying principles of a question (theorems, rules and formulas…) is essential to your success because questions are never asked in exactly the same manner.

Time yourself!

Don't underestimate the fact that the GMAT is above all an exercise in speed. The questions are rarely "technically" difficult: the math level on the GMAT would be the equivalent of 11th grade (remember Thales, Pythagoras, powers, square roots, etc.). The difference between an excellent score and a good score is the speed with which you are able to respond to the questions. While you are doing all of your practice exercises, you should time yourself and simulate the conditions of the real test, and stop yourself even if you haven't finished in the allotted time.

I insist on timing yourself because it's important for you to develop the "sixth sense" that recognizes precisely how much time is passing. The majority of candidates (your rivals) take a number of practice tests, but few of them force themselves to practice under exam conditions. I know that you might feel a bit stupid with a stopwatch around your neck, but it's worth it!

Organizations that prepare for the GMAT

A number of organizations exist that will give you the keys to the GMAT. The best known among them is Kaplan. Such classes are generally costly, but offer several advantages. Above all, they re-teach you mathematical principles and grammatical rules. In addition, they give you "tricks of the trade" which help you save time. Beyond this, the cost of the classes is also a good mean of forcing yourself to work regularly on the GMAT (the preparation process is long, and your worst enemy is lost motivation!). Finally, these classes are generally a chance to meet other candidates - this could maybe be the occasion to exchange pointers on admissions applications.

THE ESSAYS

Harvard is the school that asks for the most essays (5 mandatory plus one optional) with word limits for each response (generally 300 words). The high number of required essays indicates their importance. The emphasis on the essays is probably linked to the particularities of Harvard's admissions process: a preliminary selection based on the application (around 20% of those admitted) and a second selection after interviews (the majority of those interviewed are admitted). This admissions process differs from that of Harvard's counterparts, such as Northwestern, at which the selection is made in one single round, with all of the information in the application and an interview (which is offered to all students). In other words, Harvard does not have all of the substantive information provided by an interview when making its initial selection. To make up for this, the school requires a large number of essays.

I encourage you to fine-tune your essays for Harvard more than for any other school. You are surely aware that there is no way for you to change your academic record nor even your professional experience. On the other hand, I am not convinced that the GMAT and educational background are the deciding factors in the Harvard application. It seems that once you have demonstrated that you have the minimum academic ability required, various scores and grades are only a marginal factor in the selection process. However, you have complete freedom to write good (or bad) essays, and these are the deciding factors for your admission. Tell yourself that the large majority of Harvard candidates all have good work experience, decent scores on the GMAT and very good letters of recommendation. The essays are the key element that make the difference. Don't mess up - it's in the essays that you need to invest your time!

A FEW TIPS FOR WRITING STRONG ESSAYS

1. Introspection

Before beginning the long and painstaking process of writing each essay, I strongly encourage you to take a bit of time out for yourself. No, I don't mean that you should hide out on a small Greek island far from the rest of the world, but more so that you should take the time to go through a process of self-reflection.

Most importantly, the idea is for you to take the time out to think about the reasons motivating you to do an MBA and to conclude what you will get out of it. On the other hand, considering what doing an MBA is going to cost you, not only the financial and professional implications (from interrupting your career), but also the consequences for your social and personal life.

After this first stage of reflection (the cost-benefit analysis), I encourage you to reflect on your leadership style and skills. You have to understand that Harvard's primary selection criterion is the leadership potential that the Admissions office sees in you. So it makes sense the you should start thinking about your leadership potential. Don't worry if you have not officially been a team leader or responsible for a department. The Admissions Office is aware that your professional experience is limited and that you might not have had the opportunity to be in an official leadership position. But it is waiting to see that you have been in "unofficial" leadership situations, such as being responsible for a project in which you collaborated with or supervised other individuals. Once you have come up with such a situation, I encourage you to analyze it to better understand exactly how you lead the project (Were objectives clearly established? How did you determine your objectives? How did you communicate them to others? What techniques did you use to motivate people? How did you follow along with the evolution of the project?)

Above all, this self-reflection may seem like a waste of time, but you will gain from it mature thinking and generate a wealth of examples and situations. Play the game, because this introspection is indispensable for you to be able to talk about and reflect on your personal experiences. It's this reflection that is going to make your essays stand out and the Admissions Committee will reward your mature thinking. It's obviously hardly worth mentioning that the worst thing you can do is to copy someone else's essays.

Beyond the final goal of being admitted into an MBA, I find that it's healthy to put aside the time to take stock of your professional experience and what sense you are trying to give to your life by your choice of careers. Start thinking about this as soon as possible because you will be asking yourself such questions throughout your MBA.

2. The strategy of Positioning

Writing the essays really seems to be an exercise in marketing in the sense that the image that you communicate through your essays has to make you stand out from other candidates. Most candidates have similar experiences (there is a plethora of consultants, bankers, marketing executives and so on who apply each year). This means you will talk about more or less the same things! It is critical, therefore, that you come up with a specific positioning in order to distinguish yourself. For those among you who are not familiar with the concept of positioning, the idea is to make your personality stand out by choosing a few distinctive qualities. These qualities can be your distinguishing factors, areas of expertise or your passionate interests. You need to be on the lookout for building up these themes throughout your entire application (during the essays, letters, and résumé). The positioning of a candidate should be summed up in three or four chosen themes. Here are a few examples of positioning:

- In my case, my positioning was centered around my sense of initiative (multiple examples of times that I have initiated and lead team projects), and my marketing expertise (nearly five years, three of which I worked on major consumer products for Procter & Gamble and Kraft).
- One of my colleagues (who was among all of the consultants), chose to position himself around the theme of "multiculturalism" (he had grown up in two countries, done his military service in a third and spoke around four languages). He also emphasized his "analytical abilities" (he has always been fascinated by numbers and their rigorous interpretation), and his "sensitivity" (15 years of piano and a recent passion for painting).
- Another of my colleagues, who was an auditor in a large company, had as his themes: Europe (he worked in Brussels on many European problems), his academic excellence (over the years, he had received numerous honors and academic prizes), and finally his generosity in helping others (he was a tutor for kids in underprivileged communities and had worked for humanitarian projects in Africa).

Positioning isn't helpful unless it enables you to show that you are what the consumer wants (here the consumer is the school because it chooses!). Be careful, because having a theme is not the goal in itself. A theme only makes sense insofar as it enables you to forcefully express your skills that the school is looking for (leadership potential for Harvard). For example, if one of the themes you choose is multiculturalism, don't hesitate to show that your knowledge of other cultures has permitted you to refine your ability to listen to others or even to form a solid value system which guides you during ambiguous situations - these are the qualities of a leader.

3. Don't forget the results.

For most of the Harvard essays, you are asked to describe and analyze your actions (example: "Describe your three most substantial accomplishments and why you view them as such" or "How have you helped a group to change?"). For this type of essay, it is absolutely indispensable that you talk about the results you attained. For example, if you explain that you have led a radical change in your department, do not forget to discuss precisely what the results of your actions were. On this point, I encourage you to not only indicate your results numerically (with "hard data" such as the figures on increased sales) but also the human results (the "soft data" such as a better working environment). It is important that you show that you know how to "make the numbers", but not to the detriment of others!

4. Form and format

Respecting certain rules about the form of your essays is important because if you do not follow the given guidelines you will distinguish yourself from others, but not to your benefit!

- Respect the word limit: an Admissions Officer explained to me that the number of words per essay is not counted. Readers look only to see if the essay seems to be more or less within the guidelines; they are not, therefore, going to realize that your essay is 10% over the word limit. However, if you go way past the limit (more than 20% over) this will be noticed and held against you because it will be perceived as an inability to synthesize your ideas in a limited amount of space.
- Your essay should be well structured and concise. Get right to the point and do so in a very structured manner. Use linking words to indicate your different ideas (First, Second, Third, etc.) and to show the logic of your argument (therefore, but, yet, on the other hand).
- Regarding formatting: Double space your text. It is also recommended that you recopy the essay question wording before answering it. Finally, you need to indicate your name in the footer on every page (for example: John Smith - Candidate for the Harvard Business School Class entering 2002).

WHAT HARVARD IS LOOKING FOR IN YOUR ESSAYS:

I have gathered a list of questions Harvard has asked over the last four years. It is important to remember that the questions change little between years. In four years there have been 11 different questions (meaning that on average only two change a year).

A list of essay questions:

- Please describe your most significant leadership experience. Feel free to draw on work experiences, extracurricular activities, or your personal interactions, describing a period of formal or informal leadership. Please focus less on the specific situation and more about what caused you to be effective.
- Recognizing that successful leaders are able to learn from failure, describe a situation in which you failed. Why did you fail?
- While recognizing that no day is typical, please describe a representative workday.
- What specifically have you done to help a group or an organization change?
- Describe a situation when your values and/or beliefs were challenged. What did you do, and why?
- What are you career aspirations and why? How will you get there?

- Describe a teacher/mentor you admire and explain why you admire him/her. How have you incorporated what you have learned from this individual in your life?
- Describe your three most substantial accomplishments and explain why you view them as such?
- Describe an internal conflict (or difficult decision) that you have faced. How did you resolve the situation? What did you learn from this?
- What do you enjoy and what do you dislike about your current job? Why?
- What could you do to be an even more effective member of your organization?

Studying the themes of the essay questions will give you an excellent indication of what the schools are looking to know about candidates. In other words, you can deduce which qualities are necessary to be admitted to the school. For Harvard, you can figure out that one of the primary qualities being sought is leadership. This should come as no surprise since the very first words of the school's brochure state: "Harvard Business School educates general managers: individuals who possess the talent to lead and the capacity to learn throughout their lives" (Kim Clark, Dean). Other brochure sections go even further, revealing the magic secret to being admitted into Harvard: "Harvard Business School students share key ideas with others and an orientation to purposeful action" or further still "In keeping with its commitment to educating leaders, Harvard assesses each applicant's potential to lead effectively."

If you think these statements serve only to decorate pretty marble plaques on the campus walls, then there's a large chance that your essays will miss the mark and have little of the "Harvard spirit." Of course, I realize lofty words often seem empty and that they are too general and hardly original. If these phrases are general, then its because if is difficult to define leadership precisely. There exist innumerable different leadership styles and the effectiveness of one style depends on its appropriateness for a particular context (country, work environment, employee profiles...) The school cannot allow itself to define precisely what it means by this, which is by definition, general.

To be admitted into Harvard is to demonstrate your leadership potential as it relates to past experiences where you used a particular style or method of leadership that was effective for a given context. Obviously, there exist almost as many different leadership styles as possible contexts. A strong applicant will be able to make a distinction between the ubiquitous, everyday leadership styles and the those common to most great leaders. Reading over the essay questions already gives you good hints on the essential traits of leadership:

- The humility and capacity to analyze and learn from mistakes.
- A strong value system that resolves ethical dilemmas. The course on leadership during the first year at Harvard analyzes in detail other capacities of great leaders.
- The ability to define and communicate an appropriate vision (objectives and strategies). In defining their vision, leaders need to be able to analyze the available quantitative and qualitative information and come up with a big picture vision.
- Be determined to reach fixed goals and to motivate employees to attain these objectives, which means knowing how to listen to and dialogue with others.
- Train others to help them meet their goals.

EXAMPLES AND COMMENTARIES OF ESSAYS FOR HARVARD

In this part, I review certain classic Harvard essay questions, For each essay I look at what the Admissions Committee is trying to find out about the candidate, with recommendations for the content. There is an example of either one of my essays, or that of another Harvard graduate.

Please describe your most significant leadership experience. Feel free to draw upon work experiences, extracurricular activities or your personal interactions, describing a period of formal or informal leadership. Please focus less on the specific situation and more on what caused you to be effective (300 words).

The point of this essay:

To estimate your leadership potential using the story and analysis of your most significant leadership experience. This is surely one of the most important essays on the application.

Tips for the essay:

- Choose an experience during which you were clearly identified as the leader and initiated the majority of decisions and your impact manifested itself. Certain candidates make the mistake of not distinguishing themselves enough because they are afraid of appearing individualistic. Do not make this mistake because the Admissions Committee is looking to clearly identify the role you played. This does not mean that the rest of the work of the team should go by unmentioned. The idea is more to show how you have led a team than to show how you have been a team player.

- Answering this question well means placing less of an emphasis on the description of your leadership experience than on the explanation of the reasons for your success. The school seems to evaluate the importance of your accomplishments in the context of your responsibilities as it is impossible to compare the situation in one application to another (it's hard to say if being the President of your school's sports team has more value than being the head of a military unit). On the other hand, it is possible to compare the methods used to lead a group or project (for example: did the candidate define objectives? How were these objectives defined? What methods were used to motivate the group to achieve these objectives?) It is therefore important to clearly explain the leadership methods you used.

- In order to make your successes and the relevance of your leadership methods stand out, it is important for you to identify the difficulties you encountered. For example, one of my friends at Harvard was responsible for rapidly overhauling the selling methods of a sales team. He took the time to explain that doing so was not easy because of the following: i) he was new in the department, ii) he lacked experience in the industrial sector and iii) the sales team members were, for the most part, old hands who felt they had nothing to learn from a spring chicken! This concise explanation of the context of his accomplishments, permitted the relevance of his leadership techniques and the value of his success to really stand out.

Example

As Region V Chair/National Executive Board member for the National Society of Black Engineers (NSBE), my philosophy regarding leadership is simply to focus on helping those within the organization to succeed. I believe that when individuals within an organization are successful, the organization itself will inevitably become successful, as well. As a leader, I focused on the development of my colleagues and believed that everyone has the potential to create impact within an organization.

First, I focused on developing my executive board members using a "hands-off" approach to managing individuals. Board members set their own expectations and performance targets that they would later be held accountable for achieving. They also had the opportunity to redefine the role of their positions and establish a foundation that future board members could follow. For instance, Rashad, the Region V Telecommunications Chair, envisioned an Internet Web site that served as a complete information center for NSBE members. By leveraging corporate resources, Rashad created Region V's first Web site during his term. In addition, Rashad created and implemented the NSBE's First Webmaster Top Ten Chapter

Home Page Contest to encourage chapters across the organization to take advantage of the Internet opportunity. Rashad was recognized as a telecommunications pioneer within NSBE and later matriculated to a national NSBE position.

Second, I believed that everyone has the potential to create impact within an organization. Kenneth, who was a junior at Texas A&M University, served as my Texas Zone representative. His role was to monitor the activities of chapters within his zone. He felt that he was having minimal impact so I encouraged him to think of innovative ways to expand his reach. After several discussions, we implemented the Texas Zone's first zone meeting. The zone meeting, sponsored by Kodak, was a tremendous success.

In summary, I believe that an organization is as successful as the individuals within the organization. As a leader, I focused on developing my colleagues and helping people create impact within the organization.

What are your career aspirations and why? How will you get there? (300 word limit)

The point of the essay:

To test i) the maturity of your thinking about your career objectives (what do you want to do and why) and, ii) your strategy for achieving your goals and, particularly, why a Harvard MBA will help you. If your response to this essay question is not convincing, the Admissions Office is going to think that you are not really focused enough to do an MBA!

Tips for the essay:

- You need to give a long-term vision of your professional goals. If your objective is to work in investment banking for a few years in order to be able to transition into working in the financial executive of a large multinational, then you need to indicate your difference goals, long and short term.
- Do not confuse means and ends. Do not just say that you would like to do an MBA in order to have a global understanding of how a company runs or that you want to develop a specialty in a particular area (finance). It is not the means that enable you to arrive at your goals. The most important thing to do is to explain the ways in which the means (an MBA) will enable you to reach your goals. For example, instead of saying that you would like to do an MBA in order to understand a company in its entirety, you need to say that having an overall understanding of a company thanks to the education you will receive from an MBA (the means), will enable you become an excellent consultant (the ends).
- It is essential to explain the basis for your motivation behind your professional goals. Most candidates detail their objectives and their strategies for reaching them, but only very superficially explain the reasons behind their career choice. To illustrate this point, the first essay below clearly lays out the reasons that motivate my desire to be an entrepreneur, which are: i) my desire for independence, and ii) my willingness to deal with being faced with global challenges (in strategy, finance and organization).
- If you say that the Harvard MBA is part of your strategy for arriving at your goals, then you must show the ways in which the specific qualities of the Harvard MBA will get you there. To do that, you need to be well informed about the points that distinguish Harvard from Stanford, Wharton and Insead. Do not say that you hope to enter Harvard because it offers an excellent business education - this is true for all the schools described in this book!

Sample Essay 1

I strongly aspire to start a business of my own. This is clearly driven more by an in-depth self-assessment that allows me to identify my entrepreneurial potential than the revelation of a ready-to-develop business idea.

While president of the Junior Enterprise as an undergraduate, I realized that pursuing an entrepreneurial idea is a unique opportunity to face global challenges that address organizational, functional and human issues. In a large corporation, such a high-stimulating exposure is only made possible after having made one's way to upper management. My increasing frustration with Procter & Gamble's centralized structure has further confirmed my belief that business ownership is a key element to my professional and, more importantly, my personal fulfillment.

Currently, however, I do not feel that I possess enough theoretical or practical knowledge, which are crucial prerequisites of being a successful entrepreneur. Hence, Harvard Business School's commitment to forming the leading entrepreneurs of the future is of great interest to me.

Firstly, the Required Curriculum as well as the wide range of Electives relating to entrepreneurship will provide me with a strong foundation for understanding the variety of issues that entrepreneurs face. It will be important for me to focus a great deal of attention on finance and strategic planning, two areas that interest me because I have not been very exposed to these fields through my professional experiences. Secondly, I had the opportunity to meet Harvard students who explained that the Harvard Business Plan was a unique opportunity to stimulate and help Harvard students to mature a business plan and then uncover financing. Thirdly, I value Harvard's unrivaled Alumni network that may serve as a sounding board to my business idea or provide me with an up-to-date perspective on specific areas.

Last but not least, Harvard is said to be an incubator for great ideas. Hence, it is likely to be the very location that will generate the business idea that will launch my business adventure!

Sample Essay 2

I envision developing a technology-based company that leverages the raw talents of Jamaicans, creates opportunities for Jamaicans, and serves as a beacon for other technology companies to invest in Jamaica's development. Even though my family relocated to America 15 years ago, I visit the island frequently to maintain my connection with family and friends. Over the years, I have witnessed a drastic shift in Jamaica's economy. The value of the Jamaican dollar has declined, jobs are scarce, and the island imports much more products than it exports. Inflation has risen 669% between 1990 and 1996. From several discussions with family and friends, I recognize that the situation is intensifying. Unless the island transforms its approach to economic development, Jamaica will continue to struggle in the global economy. Many years ago, education was a sure path to success in Jamaica. That's no longer the case. For instance, a close friend from preparatory school recently graduated from Case College in Kingston, Jamaica. Since graduation, Keisha has lived with her mother because she is unable to find a job. Ironically, only a portion of the many talented students in Jamaica attend high school because of financial constraints. An even smaller portion complete university studies. Even the highly educated encounter difficulties in finding jobs.

I am always amazed by Jamaicans' raw talent and ingenuity amidst dire circumstances. I have observed men with less than a high school education and no formal training rebuild old radios that people have discarded. I've seen them create stringed instruments from pieces of bamboo. My vision is to establish a technology-based company (e.g., a computer manufacturing company) that would leverage the raw talents of Jamaicans, create opportunities for Jamaicans, and serve as a beacon for other technology companies to invest in Jamaica's development. Companies like Microsoft in Seattle, Washington, and WorldCom in Jackson, Mississippi, have reshaped communities by providing opportunities to local residents. Several years ago in Barbados, the government focused on creating a market attractive to technology-based companies. Companies like Intel established production facilities in Barbados that were extraordinarily efficient and productive.

To fulfill my vision, I need the best education and business training, and a global network of people interested and knowledgeable about business, especially in developing economies. HBS provides these crucial elements.

What do you enjoy and what do you dislike about your current job? Why? (300 word limit)

The point of the essay:

To measure the level of your reflection about your professional life, and the coherence of your future projects in relation to this reflection.

Tips for the essay:

- To answer this question well, it is critical to say "what" but also to say "why." The majority of candidates are satisfied with saying "I like X, Y and Z and I don't like W and V" and they forget to analyze what they are saying "I like X because... and I do not like W because..." For example, in Sample Essay 1 below, I explain that I like marketing because it has a central role that enables me to understand the internal workings of a company.
- This essay ought to correspond with your essay about your career plans since your opinion about your work generally impacts your career plans. It would be logical for your future career plans to reflect what both satisfies you in your work today and what you find unsatisfactory. So make sure there is coherence among all your different essays (the Admissions Office constantly stresses that all the elements of the application must represent a coherent whole). In the essay below, I write that while working as a marketing associate, my source of satisfaction was the opportunity to handle multi-faceted problems (marketing is the crossroads between other departments). In another part of the essay, I comment on the difficulty of my dependence on the heavy hierarchy of Procter and Gamble. This is coherent with my essays about my professional aspirations where I explain that I would like to be an entrepreneur. An entrepreneur is constantly confronted with global problems (finance, sales, strategies etc.) but is very independent and responsible for his decisions. In Sample Essay 2, the author explains that he it is important to him that his company encourages its employees to be well-rounded individuals who develop their personal interestes. This comment plays off his essay on a personal failure (page 325), in which he recounts how he learned that he needed to invest time and effort in his personal as well as his academic and professional life.

Sample Essay 1

Overall, I have very much enjoyed my three years spent in Procter & Gamble's marketing department. The first reason is the marketing department's function which is very central and allows me to understand the interactive relations between the main departments (R&D, Finance, Sales). For instance, I am currently coordinating a multifunctional team to launch a new product initiative.

My position offers me a unique observatory from which to understand the mix of functions that allows an organization to generate superior product value for consumers.

Secondly, I value Procter & Gamble as a highly stimulating environment which allows me to effectively develop my interpersonal skills and marketing expertise. It is a competitive place staffed with demanding employees. I truly believe that competition pushes everyone to learn how to give their best. Although competitive, P&G is not a cut-throat organization and thus, permits me to learn through everyday business discussions with skilled peers.

Lastly, Procter & Gamble is a powerful corporation which can dedicate additional resources behind newly identified business opportunities. For instance, last year I ran a quantitative analysis demonstrating that the endorsement of Tide by clothing brands significantly drives purchase intention. As no money was left in our budget, I was extremely motivated when Management, based on my analysis, allocated additional funds that allowed me to further develop partnerships with clothes brands.

On the other hand, I sometimes feel frustrated by the decision process at Central Headquarters. My disappointment does not stem from a loss of authority at local level but from the absence of communication of the rationales that support these decisions. Indeed, I found it hard to implement a decision without knowing the business rationales. I had to assume that these decisions were the balance of conflicting long and short term objectives. I would be even more effective if I was informed of these perspectives, as I could then fully understand how my work fits into the greater whole.

Sample Essay 2

As a business analyst at McKinsey, I enjoy my many opportunities to develop my business skills. However, it has sometimes been difficult to balance professional growth with personal aspirations.

McKinsey provides a challenging work environment where I can develop my leadership and problem-solving skills. The experience provides exposure to a range of business issues from a general management perspective and rigorous business analytics. On a strategy study with a printing client, we reshaped the way senior managers viewed paper procurement based on my supplier selection analysis and Profit & Loss analysis for a major business unit which included 3-year projection targets. From a personal perspective, McKinsey encourages consultants to pursue their own interests outside the firm (e.g., Berlitz French courses) and within the firm (e.g., accessing Firm resources). As a result, I have been able to speak to my French and African college friends in their native languages. In addition, I have company resources to develop a concrete perspective on my future career aspirations. I have met wonderful people at work who are genuinely interested in helping me succeed at McKinsey and beyond.

On the other hand, the work at McKinsey is demanding and standards are high. On a pro bono study, I completed client work while on vacation because the team established aggressive deadlines for completing the current phase of the study. While I have enjoyed the challenge, often it has required long hours to meet the challenge. Whether I am working in-town or out-of-town, most of my weekdays require 16-hour days or longer. Therefore, it is virtually impossible to schedule events with friends during the week. I have missed events like dinner and movies because of my intense work load. Such activities are enjoyed primarily on weekends.

Even though balancing both personal and professional lives at McKinsey is challenging, McKinsey provides me with exciting opportunities to develop business skills. The sacrifices that I am making now are an investment in myself and my ability to accomplish my career aspirations in the future.

What specifically have you done to help a group or organization change? (300 words)

The point of the essay:

To measure your leadership aptitude, because one of the biggest qualities of a leader is his ability to manage difficult changes in his or her organization.

Tips for the essay:

- Certain candidates often have trouble finding past experiences that enable them to respond to this question. You do not need to have been the person in charge of overhauling the computer network for a large multinational in order to answer this question. For example, it is enough to have initiated changes within a small team (even without having been the leader) or to have consulted on a restructuring project or a merger or acquisition. You ought to be able to find plenty of examples since nearly every company in every sector has had to undergo major changes in the last few years in order to keep up with a rapidly evolving economy.
- During the first year at Harvard, students learn certain rules for managing changes. If you have naturally followed some of these rules during your own experience, then you are on the right path!

The rules are:

a) analyze the context in order to take the time to figure out the most effective method for facilitating the changes (this can be true in both individual and group circumstances).

b) identify influential individuals and communicate your plans to them. In order to have their support, it is wise to share part of your analysis of the situation with them in order for them to understand the reasons for the changes.

c) communicate to the other employees in a reasonable, yet emotionally inspirational way. For example, if a supervisor has to accept the necessity of automating some of the company's production tasks, the rational approach consists of explaining the statistical analysis that motivated this change. That will allow you to convince the more practical-minded employees. For the others, you have to trigger an emotional reaction such as the company can't be left by the wayside by it's mean competitors (it's almost like a kind of company egocentrism) because the company has a tradition of uninterrupted success (pride).

d) reassure employees because it is part of human nature to be afraid of change (the unknown). The reasons for this fear can be many. People are not generally afraid of not being up to par, but rather of loosing their power. Solutions exist according to the particular character of the situation (for example, to appease the fear of not being good enough, it is a worthwhile idea to train employees in their new responsibilities).

Sample Essay

In my first assignment with A.T. Kearney, I was acting as a facilitator to help my client's organization achieve durable savings in sourcing expenses. This meant entirely changing the manner in which the purchasing department interacted with its suppliers.

Firstly, I made it clear to everyone that the purchasing VP was leading the project and that I was merely a facilitator. This way, he felt much less threatened and this gave me a chance to win his trust. Furthermore the fact that the project leader belonged to the organization gave a lot more credibility to the whole initiative.

Next, I aimed to help the purchasing VP to set goals for the organization and means of attaining those goals. Together, we audited the performance of his organization and, through competitive benchmarking, set ambitious but realistic goals. He had a very clear perception of the supplier market and I provided the methodology for change management. I made him accept the degree of uncertainty inherent to any change. Moreover, I helped him define a vision for his organization, mobilize his people around this vision, and also give them a chance to participate to and to enrich this vision. As an "external eye," I was in a way catalyzing the change by bringing a sense of urgency which, in turn, led to a need for radical change. Furthermore, I was directly overseeing the implementation of the "quick and easy" improvements required to keep the people motivated.

The tangible outcome of this project was 20% savings on purchasing expenses. But the more important part is the degree to which we have aided people in the client's organization in appropriating the project. There is no doubt that all parties believed in the project and that the change we have fostered will be a lasting one.

Recognizing that successful leaders are able to learn from failure, describe a situation in which you failed. (100 words) Why did you fail? (200 words)

The point of the question:
This question tests your ability to learn from mistakes, your willingness to recognize your errors (humility) and your analytical capacities (understanding your mistakes). This ability to learn from your mistakes is one of the essential qualities of leadership.

Tips for the essay:
- Responding well to this question involves a description of an error (100 words) and an explanation (200 words). Some candidates attach too much importance to the description and not enough to their explanation. Be careful then to follow the guidelines given here.
- It is appropriate to explain what you learned from a particular circumstance but more importantly to discuss what were the general lessons that you were able to use later on in other situations. For example, the essay below describes how the applicant sacrificed his personal life to his academic goals. As he points out in the essay's conclusion, through reflection on this oversight he has learned to strike a balance between personal and professional commitments.
- Last but not least, be genuine. Talk about a situation in which you really did make a mistake. Failures can be of particular value if you can explain how they inspired positive change. Avoid stating failures that aren't really failures (for example, "I really wish I hadn't been ranked 24th in my school!").

Sample Essay

As a college student, I was extremely focused on maintaining a high GPA and being involved in many extracurricular activities. My motivation was to be the best student at LSU. However, my professional motivations were at the expense of my personal life. Since most of my time was spent focusing on my undergraduate life, a much smaller portion of my time was spent with my parents, and most importantly, my little brother. My normal daily schedule involved leaving home for campus at 4:00 a.m. to begin studying and returning home at 11:00 p.m. for dinner and rest. My days were consumed with studying and being involved in several campus initiatives. I rarely ate evening dinner with the family. I considered this a failure because I placed my personal success secondary to my professional success. As a result, I partially missed the most crucial years of my brother's young life.

In retrospect, I have learned that there must be a balance between professional and personal success. Even though I have high professional goals, those goals must not be accomplished at the expense of my strong spiritual foundation and ties with family members. I failed because I did a poor job of placing my priorities. Even though I realized that my family is most important in my life, I was consumed with my undergraduate success. I thrived in the classroom and in my extracurricular endeavors because I passionately strove to be the best in my competitors' eyes. Nonetheless, I also wanted to be the best in my family's eyes. Being from a impoverished family, I acknowledged the sacrifices that my parents made for me. This created additional pressures to build on what my parents had achieve. Unfortunately, I neglected the one dimension of my parents' success that I hope to achieve - to provide a loving and nurturing environment for my family which requires spending quality time with the people that I care about the most.

To truly be successful, I had to define what success meant to me. Only then would there be a personal and professional balance in my life. Life will always have pressures but by establishing the correct hierarchy of priorities, I can be successful in all aspects of my life.

Describe your three most substantial accomplishments.

The point of the essay:
Be able to identify your most significant accomplishments in order to determine whether or not you are a high achiever, and in which areas.

Tips for the essay:
- Don't be modest! The advice is the same for the letters of recommendation; you should be clear about your successes and show your failures to your advantage. You don't have to be afraid of being arrogant, and don't hesitate to mention that you were the finest tennis player in your town, or a concert-level pianist, or that the analysis you provided while working on a project proved to be highly perceptive, or that you achieved the best regional sales figures in your division.
- Try to outline achievements in both your professional and personal life. Furthermore, make sure that the nature of your achievements varies. On the one hand, you may have had "quantitative successes" (market share, profits, sales), and on the other hand you have more "qualitative results" (helping underprivileged children with their learning, or being the first in one's family to earn a college degree - see essay below).

Sample Essay

My three most substantial accomplishments are graduating from college, expanding the reach of the NSBE's Region V Scholarship and Awards Program, and saving the lives of oil rig workers.

Graduating from LSU was a personal accomplishment because I fulfilled my parents' dream of obtaining a college degree. Although my parents do not have bachelor's degrees, they taught me that education, hard work, and persistence line the path to success. In 1982, my parents lived in Jamaica and dreamed of a better life for their children. They risked a great deal – two stable jobs, a car, and a beautiful home in one of Jamaica's finest neighborhoods. They had a vision of a limitless future for their children in America. So, with only $150 in their pocket, they relocated the family to Baton Rouge, Louisiana. Once in America, my parents worked full-time and attended community college. As a child, I remember Mom's daily routine. She worked at a nursing home about three miles from our apartment, and walked to and from work six days a week. On weekdays, she attended evening classes at Delta Community College to obtain her degree. I remember many nights waking up at one or two in the morning to see my mother studying her course material. All the hard work, persistence, and sacrifice was for the pursuit of a better future for our family. This experience instilled in me the confidence, motivation, and strength to not only graduate from LSU, but also graduate with honors.

As NSBE Region V Scholarship & Awards Committee Chair, I expanded the reach of the scholarship program that provided financial support and recognition to outstanding college students across our 11-state region. Prior to taking office, the program participation was between eight and 10 students annually. The Scholarship and Awards Packet needed customized applications for each award, detailed criteria for the award categories, summaries of corporate sponsors, and a publisher to produce the booklets. In addition, a communication gap existed in the implementation process. Therefore, I distributed monthly newsletters promoting the benefits of the program and the impact that the program has on the organization. By revamping the packet and developing an implementation plan for the program, the participation skyrocketed to more than 250 participants during my term in office. Not only was the program successful that year, but it also laid the foundation for new committee chairs to develop the program further. Today, the program has expanded to include high school students and graduate school students. In addition, more corporate sponsors have entered Region V's Awards Program. The program also has served as a model that other regions followed in the development of their awards programs. Most importantly, more students are being rewarded for their undergraduate accomplishments in areas of academics, leadership, and community service.

I was able to make a difference in an unusual environment – ARCO's off-shore oil rig. Oil rigs are dangerous places. The workers on oil rigs, called roustabouts, are renegades and fear nothing. The danger is what makes the job exciting for them. On a day that I'll never forget Bull, an 18-year old bull rider from Texas, directed a crane operator unloading a ship's cargo. I was watching from the edge of the platform when suddenly, Bull disappeared. He fell though a well slot to the lower deck 40 feet below. Others have fallen to their deaths, but Bull survived. Although the roustabouts were upset, they accepted the hazards as a part of the job. However, I refused to accept this as the status quo. I took the initiative to design well slot safety covers that now are used extensively in the field. No one asked me to do it. But, I knew it had to be done. In retrospect, what began as a near tragedy ended with a positive outcome – a safer environment for oil rig workers. To this day, I feel a sense of fulfillment thinking about the fact that there is one less hazard facing the brave men and women who work in this field.

Graduating from college, expanding the reach of the NSBE's Region V Scholarship and Awards Program, and saving the lives of oil rig workers are my three most significant accomplishment. They are the stepping stones to many more accomplishments in the future.

Describe a teacher/mentor you admire and explain why you admire him/her. How have you incorporated what you have learned from this individual in your life? (400 word limit)

The point of the essay :

To understand you better through an understanding of the reasons you have for admiring somebody.

Tips for the essay:

- Don't force yourself to find someone world-renowned or a famous personality. The admissions committee is looking for individuals able to articulate what's led them to where they are today, because with such self-awareness they will strongly contribute to the program and will be able to use the school's resources to help them refine their future path.
- You don't have to choose someone who comes from the world of business. You can choose a figure from the world of politics or art, a member of your family or a former professor. You might learn as much from Mike Tyson as you can from Alan Greenspan or President Kennedy.

- The important part of this essay is not who you admire but, moreover, your reasons for admiring this person. Indicate clearly why you admire someone. In the example given below, this international applicant chose a political figure fom European history, Charles de Gaulle. He explains clearly that the reason for his choice is the vision, leadership and courage that this general and former president used in leading France through World War II. Not only do you need to highlight the qualities you admire in a person, but you need to choose qualities of great leaders (which is what the school is looking for). Avoid telling the school that you admire someone because of their ability to recite poetry or their culture, but rather focus on their leadership qualities such as the ability to inspire others, the ability to communicate and persuade, or a refined sense of strategy.

- Finally, it is crucial to underline what this admiration has taught you for your own way of life, as opposed to a simple groupie! Admiration is great provided that it teaches us to achieve greater things ourselves. Therefore you should give tangible examples of successes that result from the things you have learnt from others.

Sample Essay

My mentor is Charles de Gaulle, the late French President. I admire him for several reasons:

- De Gaulle was a visionary: he always had a clear vision of events, whether in war time or during his days as a statesman. Most importantly, he had the courage to shape France according to his vision, whatever the difficulties.

- He was an entrepreneur. During WWII, he built an extraordinary political and diplomatic network, he designed from scratch a new overseas French government which swiftly seized power in France in 1944, he launched the reconstruction effort, and introduced a new Constitution still in force today. This entrepreneurial spirit was backed by an uncommon ability to understand and analyse the trends that shaped both the world and France.

- De Gaulle was a true leader. In June 1940, he went to Great-Britain with nothing except his own will and courage. In five years, he had managed to gain respect from the Allies, to share his vision with tens of thousands of soldiers, to be chosen by the French people and to lay the foundations of the modernization of France. From a political point of view, De Gaulle was criticized when in power but is widely respected in France today, even by his political adversaries.

- De Gaulle was an innovator. Throughout his years in power (during the war, and from 1958 to 1969), he has laid the foundations of everything that made modern France: social reforms (including the founding of the social security system), infrastructure and transport programs, national defense goals and equipment, and reshaping government and state relations.

I have learned from De Gaulle's life that everything is possible provided that you have faith, courage, and some sense of leadership to share your vision with enough people to make it live. This is what I try to apply in my personal and professional life. In particular, setting up the strategy, organization and marketing tools of my division when it was set up in 1992 was a very demanding task for which nearly everything had to be created. Since then, managing the division development in a very dynamic and competitive environment has been a constant challenge requiring a strong drive to succeed and some sort of entrepreneurship spirit. In this context, De Gaulle's own history is a model and an always inspiring and motivating force to me.

What could you do to be an even more effective member of your organization? (200 word limit)

The point of the essay:

It's a sneaky way of finding out a little more about your weaknesses, especially to test:

i) your willingness to recognize your weaknesses (humility and maturity),

ii) your capacity for analysis of your own performance, and

iii) to sound out if you are lacking in certain leadership qualities.

Tips for the essay:

- Avoid weaknesses connected to central leadership qualities (communication, strategic analysis, capacity to movitate, self-confidence, etc.). Also avoid strengths disguised as weaknesses such as being a perfectionist. The ideal is to recognize a real weakness, but one that is marginal in relation to major leadership qualities. Some good examples are: poor time management, an over-specialized skill set (like engineering) since you haven't had a general business education.
- Try to choose weaknesses that an MBA education will allow you to fix. That's also a clever way to qualify your decision to apply. For example, if you are an engineer and your lack of knowledge of business culture is interfering with your understanding of certain challenges and problems at your company, an MBA will be a unique chance for your to acquire this knowledge and significantly improve your performance.

Sample Essay 1

My bi-annual merit reviews and regular promotions indicate that I am an appreciated member of my organization. Still there are several aspects I need to tackle. Among them efficient time management, especially related to meetings, is an area I should improve. A recent article in a business magazine described inefficiencies due to meeting-mania as common in high technology firms. I spend over half of my time in technical, planning, or managerial meetings. Some I must attend do not require my full participation; others could be limited to short one to one conversations. In addition many meetings address too many topics at once or are not well prepared. To gain time and efficiency, in the future I will only accept invitations with advanced notice of the agenda. Moreover, for meetings I organize, I will set an agenda and enforce time limits on each item.

More generally, I am now increasingly facing decisions beyond the technical domains with which I am familiar and for which I need an understanding of finance, marketing, and business strategy. I read on these topics and attend part-time classes. Although I learn through experience, deepening and integrating broader business knowledge is a necessity. This is my main reason for applying to Business School.

Sample Essay 2

To maintain its current rate of client service requests, McKinsey needs to increase the number of consultants while maintaining its high recruiting standards. McKinsey's challenge is that the availability of potential consultants through the traditional recruiting channels is limited. To identify more talented candidates, McKinsey must expand its recruiting initiatives beyond its current channels. As a McKinsey consultant, I can leverage my background and interests to identify potential candidates.

To grow and identify talented candidates, we must recognize that there are bright students who attended schools other than those in McKinsey's core recruiting locations (e.g., Harvard, Princeton, Stanford). Being from a non-core school (Louisiana State University), I realize that resources like NSBE can be used to find talented students who meet McKinsey's quality standards. NSBE student members represent hundreds of schools in North America and have diverse backgrounds, experiences, and interests.

As a McKinsey consultant, I can help identify exceptional students within organizations who have interests in general management opportunities but who have not explored management consulting opportunities. For example, as leader of the NSBE Business Analyst Recruiting Team, I help establish McKinsey initiatives that allow us to bring non-traditional candidates into the recruiting pipeline via NSBE and the National Black MBA Association conferences. Non-traditional candidates can not only meet McKinsey's high recruiting standards but also add a new dimension of diversity to the company.

As McKinsey employees, we support non-traditional recruiting initiatives to help the business grow while maintaining its current talent standards. To foster the holistic efforts of the company, we use our own backgrounds and experiences to help create the prosperous environment that we enjoy working in.

Optional essay: Is there any other information that you believe would be helpful to the board in understanding you better and in considering your application? Please be concise.

The point of the essay :

To give the applicant the chance to address issues that have not been covered in the previous questions. The Admissions Committee wants to be sure that they have all the necessary information before deciding your fate.

Tips for the essay:

- Firstly, I recommend you to make the most of this open mike (it's a luxury - very few other schools offer the chance). Though writing nothing will not take points away, it certainly won't help you get any extra! Tell yourself that the majority of candidates use this essay. The idea is to talk about an important subject that you haven't been able to address elsewhere in the dossier. The success of the essay depends on your ability to bring out enlightening new material about yourself. My advice is to take examples that strengthen your positioning. If for example you have positioned yourself as the open-minded and determined entrepreneur, it would be wise to use this essay to i) describe a travel around the world that you organized for a group of friends or ii) explain that you have consistently worked throughout school to pay for your studies.

- You could also use this essay to pre-empt certain questions about your personality or career path, for example: i) if you did not ask your immediate boss for a letter of recommendation, or ii) if there are controversial aspects in your past experience (see example on the applicant working in the highly contentious nuclear industry), or iii) to further justify some of your weaknesses (an example below is of a candidate who explains why his school grades were not outstanding).

- Finally, this essay can be used to emphasize your intense motivation to apply to Harvard. In the essay below, the candidate doesn't hesitate to highlight his two campus visits to HBS and his several conversations with students. That reassures the Admissions Office of the applicant's determination, and shows him employing every method possible to get admitted (this is a leadership quality).

a) Examples of essays to reinforce the candidates positioning of openness and determination.

Extensive Travel Experience:

As a child, I did not have the opportunity to grow up in different countries. It was only after saving money through part-time jobs that I had the means to start traveling. Since then, I have taken advantage of every possible travel opportunity to visit 31 countries on five continents. As part of my service with the army, for instance, I was one of the 3,000 students annually selected, based on academic and extra-curricular activities, to work in a multinational corporation abroad.

My extensive travel experience has enriched my knowledge of foreign culture and provided me with a different perspective in viewing my own environment. For instance, facing a problem in a new situation, I put aside my preconceived notions to make sure I make sound judgments.

Competitive Sport:

Tennis has been a strong passion of mine since childhood. The point is not to display my tournament trophies or to offer tennis lessons at Harvard Business School. Tennis is worth mentioning for me because I have gained a strong self-confidence through high-level competition. At the biggest tournaments, I have felt that a positive mind and determined spirit were the key elements of my success.

Life Values:

Although I now have a good standard of living, I have learned in the past to work hard in order to afford my hobbies. While a teenager, I worked summers to afford my tennis equipment for tournament competition. Then, later, I had to give private Math lessons in the evenings to fund my passion for travelling. Therefore, I am, today, in a good position to measure values such as self-fulfillment, work or freedom.

b) Example of an essay to reinforce the candidate's positioning of leadership and benevolence.

In question 6, I was torn between writing about my karate accomplishments and about my very special experience when performing at a home for disabled children with 'the Snappers' (the a capella music group I founded). Since question 6 b) asked for the most substantial accomplishments, I decided to write about the former. However, had the question asked for the most satisfying or fulfilling accomplishment, I would have chosen the following: my a capella group, 'The Snappers'. We are already used to singing under emotional circumstances such as at the AIDS home, several hospitals and retirement homes, but one concert by far exceeded all of our previous experiences – the one at the home for the disabled children. Although many of these children were not able to applaud or voice their appreciation, the radiation of the joy in their faces, their gleaming eyes, their expression of excitement and surprise cannot be described. For the whole a capella group, but particularly for me as the organizer, this has certainly be the most memorable, most satisfying experience/accomplishment in my life. That night, knowing that we have given those children something they will never forget, we left the home with such an amount an happiness that these feelings will stay with for the rest of our lives.

Example of an essay to anticipate questions about a student's career path

Since the Nuclear Industry is highly controversial, I would like to clarify what my involvement means to me. First, I would like to emphasize that I work in the civilian nuclear industry. My initial attraction to this industry was to participate in defining the energy sources for the 21st century, which I believe to be a crucial issue. At the time, the controversy did not deter me; on the contrary, it aroused my curiosity - I wanted to see for myself. Today, I am able to weigh the pro's and con's of this means of producing electricity. I am not convinced of its efficiency with respect to its drawbacks.

Although reactors' safety levels have steadily increased, we still do not know exactly how radiation affects workers or what to do with nuclear waste. My job, testing new safety systems in nuclear power stations, is often performed under intense pressure from the utility, anxious to start its plant. The slightest mistake could signal disaster. This environment has helped me to coordinate exceptional team organization, rigor, efficiency and calm. I have matured tremendously by working in this industry.

Example of an essay to demonstrate a candidate's motivation

Upon my two visits at the university's campus in February 1996 with Gregory Deldick (HBS graduate in 1997) and November 1997 John Boschetto (currently at HBS), I was very impressed and motivated by the community of students and professors I met and discussed with. I believe I have acquired a good understanding of the type of personality that the Admissions Board is looking for in considering an application. My personal and professional profile, as well as the variety of experiences I have presented reveal well the characteristics of my personality: my ability to learn from others, my leadership skills and my sense of ethics and responsibility.

While I hope that you will find these characteristics attractive, I think that they will enable me to enhance the experience of other Harvard students and to make a significant contribution to Harvard Business School.

THE LETTERS OF RECOMMENDATION

Numbers of letters of recommendation needed for Harvard: 3

The letters of recommendation are far from being an administrative formality and you have to give them as much attention as the other parts of the application. Think about what your objectives are, and take the time to carefully explain your approach to the people who write your letters. The school leaves the choice of who writes your letters up to you. It is, however, absolutely necessary to have one or two of the letters come from individuals who have worked with you professionally.

GENERAL ADVICE

Choose people close to you rather than big names at your company:
This advice is written and repeated in all the MBA guides and not even Harvard breaks the rule. Some candidates feel obliged to have well known individuals recommend them because they think Harvard prefers well connected candidates. The school actually places very little importance on the notoriety of the person who recommends you. So don't look to have the president of the company or your consulting firm's founding partner write your recommendation unless this person really does know you well. Rather look for people who have spent enough time working with you to be able to give an account of who you really are.

Highlight different aspects of your leadership ability:
Try to choose people who each shed a different light on each of your qualities. It doesn't help much to have three people from your company each say, in a slightly different way, that you have a wonderful talent for analyzing situations. Above all, Harvard is looking for signs of your leadership ability. So don't hesitate to have each one of your letters speak about a different aspect of your qualities as a leader. For example, have your first letter, from a former professor, describe your ability to motivate the students belonging to student association X. A second letter, written by your first boss, will emphasize that your data analysis defined new goals and objectives for department Y. Finally, a third letter from another employer can discuss your natural talent as a mentor, which enables those who work under you to develop their talents.

Don't be too modest... especially for Harvard:
Emphasize your achievements. For example, if you were at the head of your class, or if you are one of the top performers at work, encourage the person writing your letter to focus on these qualities. Competition for places at Harvard is intense. Tell yourself that other candidates' letters of recommendation will be full of superlatives, like the one written for one of my classmates: "I am pleased to write this letter of recommendation for Mr. X to attend Harvard Business School. I can report that Mr. X is in the top 5% of business people I have ever had the pleasure to know".

Letters of recommendation for Harvard include an additional graph where candidates must be graded on 14 different qualities:

	No information	Below average (Bottom third)	Average (Middle third)	Good (Top third)	Excellent (Top 15 %)	Outstanding (Top 5%)
Integrity						
Leadership potential						
Sensitivity to others						
Self-confidence						
Personal maturity						
Professional maturity						
Imagination & creativity						
Motivation						
Intellectual ability						
Analytical ability						
Quantitative ability						
Organization skills						
Teamwork skills						
Oral expression						

Inform the person who is recommending you that, if you are truly strong in one of these areas, that they should not hesitate to check off the box titled "outstanding" rather than modifying it for fear of seeming to give "the hard sell."

A bit of emotion!
Letters of recommendation are usually rather dull because they simply list qualities (in the best case scenario) as proven facts. Don't hesitate to encourage the person who recommends you to have free reign with his or her emotions. It's not supposed to be like a romance, but the people who have to read 300 letters of recommendation each day will surely be sensitive to a few more personal touches. So encourage your recommenders to adopt a personal style rather than a cold and impersonal tone like in an administrative report.

Avoid technical jargon:
Don't forget to be aware that the people who recommend you must not lapse into the technical jargon of your professional field. The admissions office staff at Harvard are not all familiar with the syntactic subtleties of the business world. Therefore, the letters of recommendation have to refer to your role by using simple terms. If need be (if you work in a specialized field), it may be wise to take the time to explain the basic aspects of your responsibilities.

Demonstration by example:
Now, after reading the above advice, you're convinced that it is appropriate to have a few superlatives in your recommendation, so read carefully what follows. It is essential that the person recommending you for your talents provide a demonstration of your being exceptional. The more the person is convinced of this, the more the proof must be relevant. If you are described as the best marketing person in your company, but the letter of recommendation doesn't provide any tangible proof... well, then the praise for you will turn against you! Superlatives and high praise therefore have to be used with caution. At the same time, you have to ask yourself what exactly constitutes relevant proof? Americans attach a lot of importance to facts and figures because they are often

better indicators than kind words. So it's important that your sucesses be quantifiable. For example: if you are recommended as the best engineer in a company's R&D division, a good proof would be that you found the new formula for product Y that led to a growth in sales by +Z% in the space of XX months. If you are recommended as one of the best consultants at firm X, a good proof would be that your analytical efforts on mission Y were critical for opening up immense opportunities for reductions in costs (XXX dollars would be X% of the budget of...). From the reported savings, the directors of company YYY (one of the oldest clients of your company) indicated that the report was one of the best that had been compiled in the past five years.

QUESTIONS ASKED IN THE HARVARD LETTERS OF RECOMMENDATION
The letter of recommendation is made up of a number of open-ended questions about the candidate. Below is an analysis of some of the key questions.

a) How long have you known the applicant and in what connection? Please comment on the frequency and context of your interactions.

The point of the question:
To know the nature and frequency of your contact with the person writing your recommendation. The Admissions Committee is checking to make sure that your recommender knows you well enough to give a good account of who you are.

Tips:
- As noted earlier in this section, do not have someone famous who doesn't know you write your recommendation because the Admissions Committee will see through this.
- It's essential that the recommender precisely describe his hierarchical relationship to you, the type of work that you've done for him or her, and the nature and frequency of your interactions.

Example:
I have known Alan throughout the time he has been working at Procter & Gamble (almost three years). I participated in his recruitment. Then, Alan worked for me as Assistant Brand Manager for eighteen months. We had daily meetings on his various projects including TV advertising development, business analysis and production planning. After, he was promoted to work on another brand. However, I kept being informed of Alan's performance since I am a member of the Management Committee, which reviews Assistant's performance every six months.

b) What do you consider the applicant's talents and strengths?

The point of the question:
To discover what qualities others see in you. The school pays particular attention to your leadership ability, since this is the quality Harvard most seeks in its applications.

Tips:
- Bring to the forefront different aspects of your leadership potential.
- Your recommender should not feel obliged to be modest (see above).
- Your recommender should mention whom he or she is comparing you to (ex: the other engineers in the research department or the other junior consultants at company X).
- Your recommender needs to give brief examples for each of the qualities he or she mentions.

Example:
Compared to the other Assistant Brand Managers, Alain has proved to be one of our most brilliant

elements. Alan possesses outstanding leadership skills: he has charisma and spontaneously comes up with visionary ideas (eg: he proposed a partnership between Ariel detergent and a major soccer team to enhance Ariel's strategic benefit of superior stain removal). I have also been impressed by his superior analytical skill, which enables him to sort through complex data and to think through alternatives (eg: he performed an exhaustive analysis of various image surveys and made key recommendations for the strategic positioning of the brand).

c) What do you consider to be the applicant's weaknesses or developmental needs?
d) In what development areas has the applicant changed most over time?

The point of these two questions:
i) To find out where your weaknesses are, ii) to see if you are humble enough to learn from your weaknesses and iii) to test the objectivity of your recommender (if your recommender doesn't see any weaknesses in you, then he will hardly come across as being objective!).

Tips:
- These questions are always a bit tricky because it is never easy to discuss somebody's weak areas. Avoid: i) weaknesses that are too strong (example: a bad handle on human relations… has a hard time being a leader because he has difficulty working with others), and ii) weaknesses that don't hold true either because everyone uses them or because they are just strengths disguised as weaknesses (example: being a perfectionist, which translates as a weakness for wanting to do things too well!). The margin for error here is tight.
- Your willingness to learn and progress should come through again and again. The admissions committee is looking for candidates who are to humble enough to recognize their mistakes and tenacious enough to surpass them.

Example:
Alan has a tendency to be too conceptual and wordy while communicating ideas. His communication style was not straightforward enough. He has worked hard on this area. He requested that I give him on-going feedback on his memos and meetings. He has now become a truly effective speaker who makes crystal clear presentations. During numerous meetings, I have checked that he can now express his ideas in a way that builds commitment to them.

e) What will this individual be doing in 10 years? Why?

The point of the question:
i) to measure your potential according to the level of future success others expect you to have, and ii) to test the coherence between your own aspirations and what others see you achieving.

Tips:
- Whatever the professional domain, make sure that you are presented as a future leader (eg: one of the leading vice-presidents in the industry or the partner of a consulting firm or bank). The schools are looking to recruit students who are going to speak well for them later on!
- Your essays will probably outline your long-term professional goals. It's important for your letters of recommendation not to contradict the professional objectives you describe later on in your essays. It would be unfortunate, for example, for a letter of recommendation to say that you are perceived as having the potential to become Chairman of the Board because you have the political savvy necessary to succeed in a big multinational, when, at the same time, your essays talk about how you would like to get involved with a start-up company in order to escape the internal politicking of big corporations!

THE INTERVIEW

Contrary to certain of its direct competitors, such as Northwestern, Harvard does not automatically offer the possibility of an interview. Interviews are conducted only upon invitation by the school. Each year, the Office of Admissions "invites" somewhere between 15% to 20% of candidates to interview. Of this 15% to 20%, more than half are finally accepted to Harvard. There also exists a percentage of applicants who are admitted directly into the school without an interview. These are the exceptional applications, about which the Admissions Committee has absolutely no doubt. On average, only 20% of students are admitted this way; 80% (myself included) have to go through an interview in order to get their ticket into Harvard.

Interviews generally last an hour. You can choose to have your interview in Boston with someone connected to the Admissions Office or elsewhere with Harvard Alumni. It is difficult to say if one of these options is better than another. Travelling to Boston for an interview shows that you are really motivated and gives you the chance to speak with students on campus to fine-tune your preparation. On the other hand, the inconveniences of this approach are i) cost and time of travel, and ii) the style of interviewers from the Admissions Committee, which is generally more formal than that of Alumni representatives.

I won't insult your intelligence by going over the basic rules of interviewing such as being well dressed, smiling, and demonstrating familiarity with the school. This certainly is neither your first interview nor your last. Being given an interview is a sign that you have already made it through four-fifths of the admissions process. It would be a shame for you to stop there!

1. Work on your weaknesses
Given that an interview is not given until after your application has been filtered through the first round, the Admissions Committee has already made a preliminary judgement about your application. If you are given an interview, it means that the Admissions Committee thought you were an interesting candidate, but that there are still a few points about which they'd like to have more information. It seems that the Admissions Committee passes on such questions to "interviewers," whose role it is to clarify these points during the interview. In addition to these pointers, the "interviewer" has access to general information about you (your personal statement and résumé). He does not, however, have access to your essays, your letters of recommendation nor your transcript.

Now that you know a little bit more about the inner-workings of the Harvard interview, don't miss the chance to make the most of it. Read and reread your application, putting yourself in the place of one of the members of the Admissions Committee, and try to identify the places in your application where you would like to have more information. For example, one of my friends received many questions about his ability to work in a team. The Admissions Committee had probably identified a dark cloud over his team spirit, and the interview was used to sound out this problem. So work on your cloudy areas!

2. Try to inform yourself about the person who will interview you
If you have an interview with a Harvard alum, I encourage you to find out about this person.

Try to get hold of a copy of the Harvard Business School Alumni Directory. It is often helpful to know in what area the person who will be interviewing you works in. This will enable you to anticipate the precision of certain questions. Obviously, if you work in the same sector as your interviewer, you risk having harder and more precise questions about your professional activity.

3. Take charge of the interview

"Classic" interview techniques hold true for Harvard. Strong candidates are those who guide the conversation without even having their interviewer realize it! To do this, the technique used is "windows": you answer the question asked, but in doing so, guide your answer so that you can briefly refer to another subject (open a window). Having done this, it is probable that your interviewer will take note of the reference and ask you about it. You can then answer the question while opening up yet another window… and so on and so forth… you guide the line of questioning without him realizing you are doing so. This is not always easy since the interviewer probably has fixed objectives before the interview.

4. Prepare for the questions

An interview is usually made up a few standard questions (which can be anticipated in advance) and a few specific questions depending on the personality of your interviewer (unforeseeable). In general, there are a set number of standard questions. Going on the principle that it is naturally impossible to prepare the questions that are unforeseeable, I encourage you to be very well prepared to answer the standard ones; you will be more at ease when expressing yourself during your interview.

Interviews for MBA admissions have their pool of standard question types (eg: what motivates you to do an MBA and why Harvard? What are your plans after school?) At Harvard, you are likely to receive a number of questions about i) your leadership ability, so sought-after by the school (eg: describe a project during which you lead a group), and ii) your ability to get on with others, due to the school's use of "case studies" where students work together amongst themselves under a professor's supervision (eg: How will you contribute to discussions in class?). For my own interview, I made a list of responses for about 30 standard questions. Everyone has his or her own method, but be prepared, because you have to maximize the points you get from the standard questions so you will be able to afford to loose a few on the unpredictable ones!

5. Repeat yourself until you're exhausted

The key to success is not only thinking ahead of time about your responses to the standard questions but also practicing communicating your answers. The miracle of success is none other than mock interviews. Try having interviews with former MBA students or at least with colleagues at work or friends. One of the best known professors at Harvard describes three levels of preparation for candidates:

- The "stammerer": the candidate is vaguely prepared for the content and form of the conversation. The only advantage of this level is that the candidate seems spontaneous.
- The "recording": the candidate is prepared for both the content and the form...but not well enough to not give the impression of sounding like a tape recorder.

- The "actor": the candidate is so well prepared for the content and the form of the interview that he is able to concentrate on interacting with the interviewer, who doesn't even realize that the conversation is prepared!

Studies show that the worst thing that can happen to you is to fall into category 2 and that the best is to be the "actor" (category 3). For once you can use your practice interviews to reach the point where you're no longer pre-occupied with finding your words and more able to interact with your environment.

6. Prepare intelligent questions

After having to answer numerous questions, you can be sure that your interviewer is going to give you the opportunity to ask one or two questions. Don't leave anything up to chance and prepare several questions in advance. Avoid sugar-coated questions (example: How did your Harvard diploma help you in your brilliant career?) In general, your interviewer will detect such flattery. Try to find questions that are pertinent and related to your professional plans. My favorite questions were: what are the strengths and weaknesses of the teaching methods at Harvard? Which courses have been the most useful in your professional life up to now? How do you think the Harvard MBA program has changed since you were a student there? Is an MBA really necessary to be an entrepreneur?

Last but not least, to state the obvious: be relaxed! I haven't yet mentioned the word "stress" in regards to the interview. Alumni representatives and those responsible to the Admissions Office have enough insight to know that you don't get much out of a stressed interview. Don't forget that the person interviewing you is also an "ambassador" who is looking to polish rather than tarnish the school's image.

INTERVIEW WITH THE ADMISSIONS DIRECTOR

Interview with Kirsten Moss, Admissions Director of Harvard Business School:

Who reads the application forms (faculty? alumni? students? MBA Admission officers?)
Primarily MBA Admissions Officers read the applications although some faculty may also provide perspective. All Admissions Board members have their MBAs.

How many people read them? How much time is spent per application?
The Board may have as many as 15 people. The time varies per application. An admitted candidate will most likely be read by four to five people.

What are the criteria of evaluation of a good candidate? (if the school is looking for leadership and academic excellence, please specify what leadership means to you.)
We are looking for people who will help our community reach our mission - to develop outstanding business leaders who will contribute to the well being of society. Instructional methods used in the Program rely on a dynamic exchange of ideas among faculty and students. To ensure the depth and richness of group learning, we try to select a class composed of people who possess high ethical standards and academic competence; diverse work experiences, backgrounds, and personal attributes; as well as a commitment to a managerial career.

The criteria we seek include:
- Leadership potential and past demonstration of leadership experience: there are many kinds of leaders, however, we look for evidence of being able to set a vision, motivate others to follow, and accomplish results. No matter what their academic and professional background they have an ability to demonstrate those kinds of capabilities.
- Pursuit of excellence: our best candidates are committed to excellence no matter what their interests.

- Academic ability: to be considered for admission, a candidate must provide academic transcripts, a Graduate Management Admissions Test (GMAT) score and, for most international applicants, a Test of English as a Foreign Language (TOEFL) score. The MBA Program requires students to master new concepts and techniques quickly to profit fully from their educational experience. Quantitative analytical aptitude is a prerequisite to successful participation in the Program and candidates should provide evidence of that aptitude in their applications.
- Personal Characteristics: we look for candidates who have the highest ethical standards and feel that leading is a responsibility.

What qualities would you like to see more of in candidates?
Commitment to ideals, passion to make a difference, creativity, entrepreneurship. Successful applicants are able to demonstrate how they have shaped a team or organization, and how they have had an impact in their community.

How important is the GMAT in the HBS application?

The GMAT is just one of many data points we consider. We do not promote our average GMAT score. In not doing so, the Admissions Board hopes that all applicants will recognize the following: that the range of GMAT scores is very broad, that there is no "minimum" score requirement, and that the GMAT is just one piece of data among the many used to evaluate an application.

If someone takes the GMAT many times, will you take the highest score or the average of the scores?

We take the highest score. Do bear in mind that all of your scores will be reported on the score report sent to us by ETS, but that the Board will focus on the score you indicate on page 2 of the application.

What are the "do's" and "don't's" for essays?

Tell us about you as a person – about what you care about and why you have made the choices you have made. If we don't read about the "real" you, your application won't stand out from the pack. Please write about how you accomplished things not just what you have accomplished. Don't be afraid to describe your dreams because we are looking for people who have the passion and commitment to make a difference in the world.

It is also important to identify your role and the contribution you made within a project, deal, or perhaps the launch of a product. Often candidates explain what a team or group did without explaining about their individual role.

What makes a good letter of recommendation?

Choose someone who has worked with you closely and can really tell us what is unique about how you shine. We're focusing on people who are going to change the world. Good letters of recommendation help us to identify that potential.

What is the role of the interview in the selection process? (If the answer to this question is that HBS wants to evaluate the 'fit' with the school, please make sure you specify what are the criterion for fit). What kind of information will an interview give you that you will not get from an applicant's essays?

Every interview is unique based on issues we identify from reading the application. Before an applicant comes for an interview - by invitation only - their folder will have been read three times through. Readers will raise issues on which they want to probe more deeply, and that are specific to that particular application. It may be something described in an essay that we need to further understand. It may be why this person has made the choices they have in regard to their career. It may be hearing more about a community activity that they've been involved in and getting more details.

What other MBA schools do you consider as direct competitors to your MBA program? Why?

We believe schools do offer different experiences and it is the responsibility of the applicant to identify which program most closely meets their needs.

Is it better to apply for the early rounds?

It's better to apply in the first two rounds. Although the Admissions Board will give the same careful consideration to all applicants, applying in the earlier rounds will give you time to address the following issues:

International students may need additional time to arrange for their visa and funding and to work on their English proficiency. Some students may be required to complete preliminary course work prior to their enrollment. Many deadlines for outside (non-HBS) fellowships are in early spring. Only students who have been accepted are eligible for these fellowships. Financial Aid decisions are made on a rolling basis. Knowledge of your financial aid award may help you make important decisions. Housing decisions are also made on a rolling basis. The lottery for the Harvard Real Estate apartments is generally held in mid-April. You must have been admitted to participate in the lottery.

What does the school particularly expect from international students? Does the school tolerate that they may have a lower GMAT score?

International students need to be able to speak fluently due to our use of the case method. They really must be able to "think" in English to keep up with a quickly moving conversation. We expect that those students who do not speak English as a native language may not score as well on the GMAT, especially on the verbal portion. We take that into consideration as we review a candidate's academic capabilities.

Last question, what role does luck play in the application process?

I recommend students apply to several schools because evaluating applicants is an art not a science. Different schools have different cultures and criteria, and one candidate may "read" better by one Admissions Committee versus another – even though the candidate is strong.

Getting
the
INSEAD
Admissions
Edge

INSEAD

Address	INSEAD Boulevard de Constance 77305 Fontainebleau Cedex France
Telephone	(33) 1-60-72-40-05
Website	www.insead.edu/mba
E-mail	mba.info@insead.edu

about the school

Founded	1959
Tuition Fees	35,500 Euros
Some Famous Alumni	Kevin Ryan (CEO, Doubleclick Inc.); Helen Alexander (President, The Economist Group); Lindsay Owen-Jones (CEO, L'Oréal); Per Johan Kaufmann (CEO, France Printemps); Yves Carcelle (President, Fashion, LVMH); Claude Brunet (CEO, Groupe Ford France)

the application

Application File	By mail or downloadable from website; via embark.com
Application Deadlines	February 1 - September entry July 1 - January entry
App. File Elements	• 6 essays • 2 letters of recommendation • transcripts • GMAT and TOEFL • résumé • a "job description"

rankings

Publication	Business Week	US News & World	Financial Times
General Ranking	*First year of int'l rankings 94 96 98 00 01* **not applicable 1**	96 97 98 99 00 01 **not applicable**	99 00 01 **11 8 7**

before the MBA

# applicants per year	3,500 approx.
# applicants accepted per year	975
# applicants entering per year	750
% women students	24%
% international students	90%
# countries represented	66

Age (years)

average	29
range	23 - 39

Education pre-MBA

Engineering	32%
Business	21%
Economics	14%
Arts/Other	13%
Law/Politics	11%
Sciences	9%

Professional experience

avg. years work experience	5

Field of work

Industry	46%
Consulting	26%
Finance	19%
Other	9%

GMAT

average	690
range	580 - 790

TOEFL

minimum	260
range	260 - 300

after the MBA	School total
avg. job offers per student	3
# companies recruiting on campus	150
Main career choices	
Consulting	43%
Finance	26%
Industry/Other	26%
New Economy	5%
Function	
Consulting	51%
Finance	20%
Corporate Planning	10%
Entrepreneurship/Other	9%
General Management	6%
Marketing	4%
Geographical location	
Western Europe	74%
North America	8%
Asia Pacific	6%
Central & South America, Middle East, Africa	5%
Central and Eastern Europe	4%
Salary	
avg. salary at graduation	$110,000
Alumni	
# alumni worldwide (MBA)	12,000
# cities with alumni association	50

Top 10 employers

1.	McKinsey & Co.	6.	Lehman Brothers
2.	Boston Consulting Group	7.	Merrill Lynch
3.	A.T. Kearney	8.	Morgan Stanley Dean Witter
4.	Bain & Co.	9.	Eli Lilly and Company
5.	Booz, Allen & Hamilton	10.	L'Oréal

authors

| Name | R. CZUWAK |

Consultant at McKinsey in Poland for two years.
Joined the McKinsey Paris office after graduation.

authors

| Name | JESSICA JENSEN |

Consultant at Boston Consulting Group in L.A..

School specifics

INSEAD

INTRODUCTION

Heading to France for your MBA is decidedly different from diving into the heart of Silicon Valley at Stanford, or discovering the delights of New York while at Columbia. The goal of this chapter is not to promote INSEAD, but rather to give you a maximum amount of information so you can judge whether what the school has to offer complies with your needs.

Reasons for pursuing an MBA can be broken down into three categories whose relative importance will vary among candidates: academic teaching, new career opportunities, and a rich human experience.

INSEAD's geographical location is an important factor in deciding whether to apply. The program also differs significantly from that of other business schools in terms of its duration (one year). However, opportunities and courseload are not fundamentally different from those offered by other MBAs. Therefore, deciding whether to consider INSEAD should be easy, given its distinctive traits; in other words, everyone usually knows whether he or she wants to pursue an MBA in the United States or abroad, and whether to study for one or two years.

In reality, there are many other criteria, much more subtle, which I would like to point out in a clear and realistic manner in order to help you make your choice, and, if your decision is already made, to help you prepare a solid, well-documented application dossier.

Finally, this chapter will have served its purpose if you start to appreciate what a one-year MBA can mean -- or, better yet, if you can already picture yourself in the shoes of a student sitting in a gigantic amphitheater, on the first day of class, listening to the various welcoming speeches and necessary information, thinking about what's waiting for him/her in the forthcoming year.

Even though it is expensive and a lot of work, a year in an MBA program should be seen not as a year-long sacrifice, but as a year's investment in advancing your career. Before being difficult, laborious and costly, it should be a great time - a time to learn, meet new people, and be in a dynamic environment. The year presents a great challenge to succeed, and to vie to be among the winners of exciting intellectual competitions. Other events to anticipate: frantic job hunting (concluded by wonderful successes), making friends and rediscovering the pleasures of student life (especially going out toward the end of the year, even on a "school night"); tennis games on Tuesday at four p.m., poker from ten p.m. til the wee hours of the morning, and many other activities which may or may not be so dazzling. But if those mentioned so far don't leave you cold, then continue to follow the guide.

INSEAD's first class was held in 1959, and had 52 students. Today, there are about 700 students split up into different programs which finish at six month intervals: September to June and January to December. The school has also developed a program for Executives (program lasting several weeks and designed for managers) which in principle is a supplementary activity, but which is gaining in notoriety. The total number of INSEAD alumni is 11,500, by far the largest European business school, and in terms of alumni, competitve with many U.S. programs.

INSEAD has opened another campus in Singapore with the motto "one school, two campuses". The program type will be the same as that in Fontainebleau with regards to courseload, teaching staff, and profile of accepted students, and INSEAD are aiming to accept 150 in January 2002 with the first September intake also in 2002. The first class started in January 2000 with 45 students. The recent crisis in that region of the world has not tempered the will of the school's directors who feel that the need for managers will stay the same. This opening will offer the possibility for students in Europe or in Asia to complete part of their studies on the other campus. (for more on applying to the Singapore campus, see the 'Admissions Application' section of this chapter.)

Furthermore, beginning in 2002, a new alliance with Wharton will allow INSEAD MBA students to spend a portion of their program at this venerable institution. A summer period at Wharton West, San Francisco will offer specially designed electives, which will be open 50/50 to Wharton and INSEAD students and staffed by faculty from both schools. INSEAD students will also be able to take elective courses at Wharton in Philadelphia during periods 4 and 5 of their MBA, and to use facilities of the Wharton Career Management Services during this time.

THE SCHOOL YEAR

INSEAD offers an intense MBA: one year as opposed to the traditional two, which can be completed from September to June or from January to December, with a summer break in the second case. The year is broken down into five periods of about six weeks, each one ending with exams plus a break for a few days. Students taking the January to December option have a summer break of seven weeks. About 40% of the students use this time to take part in an internship.

Below is the course schedule for INSEAD:

	Period 1	Period 2	Period 3		Period 4	Period 5
September entry	September – October	November - December	January – February	→	March – April	May - June
January entry	January – February	March - April	May – June	Summer: Internship or Vacation	September – October	November - December
Classes	Managerial Behavior Applied Statistics Financial Accounting Prices and Markets Marketing Management I	Managing Organizations Management Accounting and Control Production and Operations Management Finance I Marketing Management II	Finance II Corporate Strategy Economic Analysis + 2 elective courses		Industrial Policy and International Competitiveness International Political Analysis + 2 elective courses	3 elective courses
				Job search		

The choice between the September class and the January class depends mainly on the professional projects of the student and the timeline for completing them: only those who start in January have the possibility of doing an internship (during the summer); on the other hand, the school year lasts a full twelve months instead of ten. The chances of getting in are independent of the choice made on this level (when an applicant is seen as being interesting, but there is no more room in the class requested, the school offers entry into the next class, four or eight months later).

Concerning which class is more pleasurable to attend, some prefer the September class, believing that the greatest amount of work is concentrated during fall and winter, while the academic pressure in spring gives way to an enhanced social life (see "Life at INSEAD", below). However, others say that this is true for January entry as well; and the entire debate is irrelevant for Singapore.

Finally, the fact that the MBA lasts just one year has its advantages and disadvantages with regards to other MBA programs. The major advantages are financial and professional:
- The cost is naturally about half of what it is for a two-year MBA.
- The duration of an MBA is not considered as a criterion in itself in terms of job offers. While those who recruit are of course interested in the quality of the school and their preferences

concerning one MBA over another, their offers do not change because one program was completed in one year and another in two years, other than the fact that the signing bonus may be less because it is in part destined to help pay off school fees. So for example, offers made by consulting companies are standard; they may be adjusted for the former position of the graduate, or for the market value of the diploma, but not for the number of months spent on campus.

- After a year of studies, certain students (at least among those at INSEAD) felt ready to leave the world of studies to resume professional life, and earn a living. Personally, after a year, I felt as though I had accomplished what I had set out to do and was happy to go on to something else.

The major inconveniences are due to the speed at which everything happens:

- On the very first day, we were told that ten months later, when the diplomas were handed out, we'd find ourselves asking how it all went by so quickly and where the school year went. This prediction was dead right. The great haste of the program raises some questions about whether you are taking enough time to seriously reflect upon your career choices (the first job offers come up about five or six months after the school year starts).
- Some students who are really interested in going into certain academic studies in more depth, to do research for instance, may not find all that they are looking for in a ten-month period.
- The same argument goes for entrepreneurs who need time to develop their project and study the market without abandoning their classes.

However, it is certain that the accelerated nature of the curriculum does not at all hamper the richness of social life, both during and after the year at INSEAD. When you see your classmates after graduation, they won't seem like casual acquaintances, but instead like people known under intense circumstances.

CURRICULUM

Before the school year begins, INSEAD offers an optional pre-term course in Math. Designed for "students from a non-mathematical background who feel they could benefit from a review of mathematics and statistics", this course revisits basic concepts such as the fundamentals of calculus.

As the table above shows, there are normally five courses per period. The required curriculum is as follows:

- Marketing and Strategy: Marketing Management I and II, Strategic Management
- Finance: Finance I and II, Financial Accounting, Management Accounting and Control
- Management/Human Resources: Managerial Behavior, Managing Organizations
- Economy: Prices and Markets (Microeconomics), Economic Analysis, Industrial Policy and International Competitiveness
- Quantitative sciences: Applied Statistics, Production and Operations Management
- Other: International Political Analysis

Each course lasts a total of about sixteen hours. It is possible to forgo a course by taking an equivalency test, which can be useful for those who have already studied or worked in the field of a course offered. For other courses however, such as Marketing or Managing Organizations, no equivalency test is offered. The official reason is that these are courses which are fundamental and essential to the study of an MBA. In reality, it is possible that equivalency could be obtained by those with no professional experience in marketing or managing organization, but possessing good common sense, as there is no hard and fast technical data to be learned in them. One would then have to raise the question of the ability of marketing or strategy exams to adequately gauge one's level of knowledge, which the administration may feel is a taboo subject.

Other than these core courses there is the elective curriculum for periods three, four and five. Most of these delve more deeply into the subjects described above (for example: Financial Statement Analysis—equivalent to Financial Analysis, a course on options, Advanced Economics, Information Technology for Managers, Brand Management, etc.). New areas have also been added. In addition, there are electives such as "Entrepreneurship" (New Ventures, Financing Entrepreneurial Ventures, Family Firms, etc.) and "IT Technology" (Cyber Entrepreneurship, Electronic Commerce, etc.). Other elective courses allow for more generalized learning: Negotiation Analysis, probably one of the best courses, which offers extremely interesting negotiation models and simulations; or other courses on reflection in business which give rise to very enriching debates: The Ethical Dilemma (one of the rare courses taught by a French professor, Henri-Claude de Bettignies) or Strategy, Innovation and Corporate Governance.

The Fontainebleau class is broken up into four sections of about 75 students each. The class at the Singapore campus consists of two similar sections. That may seem like a lot, but you will learn your classmates' names and faces very quickly. Of course sub-groups form rather quickly. Right from the start, social events are organized in order to heighten the feeling of camaraderie (especially the "section parties", occasional dinners voluntarily organized by randomly selected groups of students.)

TEACHING METHODS

Case studies serve as the basis for most classes, so the teaching methods here hardly differ from the American MBAs. Most courses are in the form of discussion forums (in particular courses in marketing or strategy, where about 80% of the course material is given in this format, as opposed to about 20% lecture). This method does require preliminary preparation: nearly every course includes a case which must be studied beforehand, which usually takes one to two hours of work, and requires reading articles and other works (one hour on average). The advantage of this method is that it accelerates the progression of the course: with the basic knowledge already acquired, it is easier to go more in depth more quickly.

Also, this method encourages student participation, which is of course received very positively, and can represent anywhere from 10% to 30% of the final grade of a class. The risk is that sometimes the discussions can turn into "talk shows" where individuals try to take center stage. The key factor to avoiding this scenario is the professor's ability to lead, control and structure the debate. When case-study discussions are led well, they can be extremely enriching.

For some courses, lectures are held, which are slightly closer to the European tradition. This is the case for subjects that intrinsically require this type of teaching: Finance, for example, is taught almost entirely by lecture.

One professor (Eric Noreen, Management Accounting) has an intermediary method which works very well. He structures the class by asking multiple choice questions which the students then vote on. The

professor gives the answer when voting is completed. Each student must follow what's going on and participate intelligently, because who wouldn't be just a little ashamed of voting for wrong answers? Typically, classes are broken down in the following way (especially for Marketing or Strategy):
- 30% lecture
- 40% in-class case study discussions
- 30% work/group projects

THE GRADING SYSTEM
- Each course usually ends with a final exam (on average, 50% of the final grade),
- Reports, exercises, mid term exams (on average, 20% to 30% of the final grade),
- Class participation (on average, 20 - 30% of the final grade)

A part of the grade concerning reports and exercises constitutes group work and is therefore graded collectively.

Next, you receive a grade based on your placement:
- 4 - top 17% (1/6)
- 3 - upper middle 33% (1/ 3)
- 2 - lower middle 33 % (1/ 3)
- 1 - lower 17% (1/6)

In order to graduate, you must have an average of at least 2. This system therefore does not encourage you to be among the last (an average below 2 means you must repeat the year, or much less often, be expelled) and pushes you to give the best of yourself if you want to be at the head of the class. In theory, it is possible for the entire class to graduate. In practice, there are always some who will repeat the year and a (very) few people who drop out (generally, these are people who thought they would be taking a sabbatical but discover they were wrong).

Grades are confidential and distributed individually. Students who are above a 3.25 average are on the Dean's list, which is published and posted.

During some job interviews, students are asked for their grade point averages. This is especially true for companies recruiting in offices in London or in the United States (for example, GE Capital asked one student for his grades at INSEAD, his GMAT score and even his grades as an undergraduate). The person interviewed is free to disclose his grades or not, and can, if he wishes, authorize the school to provide the company with a copy of his grades. For most French companies, and most foreign companies recruiting for France, this question is only very rarely asked.

GROUP WORK
Group work is an essential part of the teaching methods at INSEAD. Right from the start, the four groups of 75 are broken down into sub-groups of five to seven people. These sub-groups remain together for four months, after which they are broken up and new sub-groups are formed. In both cases, they are formed for maximum diversity (professional, geographic, etc.). A considerable amount of time is spent in these sub-groups, as each course will include at least one group project, usually requiring several dozen hours of work (distributed among the sub-group), as well as various preparations for case studies and exercises.

Generally speaking, group work creates intense relationships which can be positive in nature (the group becomes close-knit through intensive, efficient work in the first months), or negative (when the extreme diversity leads to explosive contacts that must also be handled - which of course is part of the learning process). Indeed, an important part of the grading (between 20% and 60%, depending on the course) comes from the group work (and is therefore shared among all members). In addition, at the end of the first period, when the first grades have been handed out, students help out peers who have found themselves in difficult situations.

Most of the groups I saw kept in great contact after the first six months, or even after the INSEAD experience was finished. Working in groups also gives you the chance to meet people with radically different backgrounds. In my group, for example, there were an entrepreneur who had been working in Brazil, a Filipino consultant, a Canadian accountant, and a British engineer.

The group dynamics require that each person brings his personal knowledge; thus, group work represents a great chance to compare your own abilities to those of others and to find out what you're good at, and what you're best letting others do.

THE TEACHERS

There are about 145 full-time professors at INSEAD. In general, they are very good and the students I interviewed on this subject were quite satisfied: there are the "stars", and then the many very good professors -- but there are also a few lame ducks.

How is it that there are "lame ducks"? Most likely, the rapid growth in the number of students is partially responsible. Furthermore, some young professors are simply lacking in the experience necessary to satisfy the high standards of the MBA student. Out of the 25 to 35 professors who you may have, there are only one or two, maybe three, who are disappointing.

Luckily, there are also brilliant professors, and you'd never want to miss a class. The best of them are usually those who teach elective courses; they have often written the case studies themselves, and present the results of their research. For example, a negotiation professor, Ingemar Dierickx, a strategy professor, Karel Cool, a corporate governance professor, Mary O'Sullivan, and a statistics professor, Anil Gaba, make an extremely interesting time of it, despite the austerity of the subject matter. Professors are generally available to meet with students by appointment. However, it is rare that a professor will participate in the social life of the school. It is regrettable that some among this category of brilliant teachers are more inclined to teach executive seminars than the MBA courses.

THE INTERNATIONAL SIDE

The students come from very diverse geographic locations: there are usually about 50 nationalities represented. 10-12% come from North America, 20% from Asia or Australia, 8-10% from England, 8-10% French, 5-7% German and 8-10% from Eastern Europe. Geographic diversity is a reality, even though there is a majority of European students. No one nationality makes up more than 10% of the population. Social life at INSEAD will allow you to make the best of this composition, thanks in part to the National Weeks (week long periods centered on a geographic theme and organized by those coming from the area in question).

It must also be noted that the Fontainebleau campus is not French (nor is the Singapore campus particularly "Singaporean".) It is very often that you will hear a foreign student saying that he came to improve his French, whereas that same foreign student will probably leave the experience with the same level of French or worse. Indeed, a student spends his whole life on campus (working or taking advantage of the social life) and nothing happens in French. Because of this, whether we like it or not, INSEAD is an island unto itself, completely disconnected from the surrounding world of Fontainebleau. The only time you can be immersed in the French language is during shopping trips or perhaps some visits you may organize.

With the opening of the second campus, the percentage of Asian students in Fontainebleau will likely decrease. However, the Fontainebleau INSEAD site has not necessarily become more American and/or European because the exchange of professors and students between the two campuses is possible (and encouraged). It is possible to spend part of the school year in Fontainebleau and part of it in Singapore. The elective courses with themes relevant to Asia (Business in China, Strategies for Asia Pacific, Business in India, etc.) will be maintained on both campuses, although naturally will be concentrated more in Singapore.

INSEAD is often seen as being an MBA program which is more European than it is international. This is partly true, given that the majority of students are European. North American students who participate in the program often have a specific tie with a European country (having spent a part of their professional career there, or wanting to settle down there). About 10% of students come from the Middle East and Africa. Most job offers are for positions in Europe, and, to a lesser degree, in Asia; INSEAD has a very weak competitive position with the United States, for obvious reasons. However, the school's stature in the U.S. may well begin to increase as a result of its recently inaugurated partnership with Wharton.

THE WORKLOAD

The workload is particularly heavy during the first two or three periods. The grading system, based on the "forced curve", encourages you to work hard (see section on the Harvard Grading System for an explanation and summary of the principal advantages and disadvantages of this system). As a result, the first six-week period is particularly intense; since no one is able to judge their relative levels of competence, everyone must work extremely hard. The second period allows you to settle for what you obtained in the first period or make up for what you lost. Generally, the pressure eases off after that, which does not mean, however, that you can afford to be idle. You must still put a lot of energy into the classes, and then the job hunting begins.

There are many opportunities to meet with prospective employers at the school itself. The large, traditional recruiters (consulting groups, banks, some industrial companies) hold interviews on campus: for one and a half months, over 200 companies come to recruit at the school (the number of on-campus interviews is estimated at 8,940). They make their selections out of the "Profile Book" (a catalogue of CVs). Cover letters are only necessary for those who wish to obtain interviews with companies who have not specifically asked for them. In the case of more specific searches (for example, a job position in telecommunications), the process is of course more complex and takes a longer time because it includes the traditional cover letter and going to interviews, often in London or other foreign cities. In any case, academic pressure, along with that of the job search, make for a speedy year and little time for extra-curricular activities.

COMPUTER FACILITIES – IT SYSTEM

The school is equipped with a good number of computers and each student is given an e-mail address (firstname.lastname@insead.edu). Each professor has his or her own website, and course preparation is often taken care of by consulting or interacting with it: you can get complementary reading and Excel spread sheets for case study preparation, or you may participate in discussion forums for classes or debates that take up where real-time discussions left off.

Nevertheless, it is well known that INSEAD's computer infrastructure is lacking in comparison with the number of students. At peak times (breaks between courses, for example) it is difficult to find an available computer. In addition to that, many other services could be offered on the computers (schedules to be downloaded on a Palm Pilot, for example) It is recommended to have a laptop computer (just about everyone has one), but it is more a question of convenience than necessity as the work can be done on the school computers.

THE ENTREPRENEUR'S CORNER

There are several elective courses which deal with the creation of companies:
- Financing Entrepreneurial Ventures
- Realizing Entrepreneurial Potential
- Starting and Growing Entrepreneurial Enterprises
- Family Firms
- New Ventures
- Managing Creativity

Most of these courses are useful to students who already have an entrepreneurial project in mind before starting, or one that develops during the time spent at INSEAD. They then have the possibility of dedicating a lot of time to their idea and of benefitting from the experience and the contacts with professors who teach these electives. In the second half of the school year, schedules are more flexible, because more time is spent on job interviews. So, during the last two periods, it is possible to take three or four elective courses, which take up about four or five hours a week in class time, of which some are specifically oriented around entrepreneurship. However, it is necessary to put this into perspective with two-year MBAs which allow more time to be dedicated to this type of project.

Research for questions concerning the financing of a project promotes a certain synergy with the rest of the class. One classmate spoke of the usefulness of a course in helping him to decide whether or not he would take up the family business. Another student developing a start-up project made, through one of his courses, a contact in another start-up which he joined following the completion of the MBA.

Experience also shows that many a would-be entrepreneur falls prey to the temptation of more classic job offers, made by consulting firms or banks interested in this profile. The debt created due to enrollment in an MBA no doubt plays a certain role in this choice. In addition, ambitions to create a business on the internet are often spoken of openly with recruiters, who are more and more willing to accept a free option from students: the job offer is good for a certain number of months, allowing the candidate to launch a project and nurture it during its early stages. At the end of a predetermined period of time, he can choose whether to join the company or continue with his venture.

But on a more general level, the question of the usefulness of an MBA for someone with a specific project and who already knows something about finance, accounting, etc. can be less striking. The great entrepreneurs may not need it; if they have a good idea to be exploited, if they know the basic techniques of business and know how to surround themselves with the right specialists, they won't necessarily have the time to spend a year or two studying, while their potential market is evolving.

LIFE AT INSEAD

PARIS AND FONTAINEBLEAU

Fontainebleau is about 40 miles from Paris (usually less than an hour by car). I won't take time in relating the cultural advantages of the city of Paris here, as the list would be too long. It is good to know, however, that students often take short trips into Paris, during the week, or on the weekend, usually in spontaneously organized groups. For example trips to the Opera are often organized by interested students (likewise, trips to night clubs for the night birds!). The list of good bars and restaurants is virtually endless. A guide to the best places has been created by students and passed on from class to class, evolving with the students' tastes and the city itself. It is unfortunate, however, that the school does not provide a system by which trips and events in the city are organized (brochures, reservations) to help students who don't know Paris or don't speak French.

Fontainebleau is a small town with a lot of charm, thanks in part to its wonderful château. It is surrounded by a forest which is heralded as being the lungs of Paris. Much of the student housing is in or around the Fontainebleau forest. It gives you the opportunity to go hiking, horseback riding, walking, etc. The surrounding area is also very pretty, thanks to charming villages near the forest (Barbizon, Moret) which served as an inspiration to impressionist painters (Jean-François Millet, Alfred Sisley, and Camille Corot, among others) and the châteaux which are worth a visit, like Vaux-le-Vicomte.

HOUSING

A year at INSEAD can also give you a chance to have some very fine housing. If you take care of it relatively early (four to six months in advance) and are not opposed to shared housing, you can rent large houses or even châteaux. These places are rented to students from year to year. The prices are not exorbitant ($330 to $600 per month, not including fees). A real-estate agency (Thévin-Cadeau, accessible through the INSEAD website) takes care of the management of some of these places, but the best are found by word-of-mouth. Another way is to obtain a "Profile Book" (available on campus), to see the addresses of those already living there in order to make contacts. I could recommend, just to give you an example, the Château de Montmélian, the domaine de Bois-le-Vent, or the domaine du Vivier.

It is also possible to live on campus, but few students opt for this choice because it is not necessarily less expensive (at least $330 per month for a studio), has no charm and it is more difficult to invite guests.

SOCIAL LIFE

The social life at INSEAD is very rich, with cultural weeks, evenings and dinner parties.

Cultural weeks give students of different nationalities the chance to present different aspects of their cultures...and to organize fantastic parties! They go on all year long (but not every week!). For example, Scandinavian, Italian and Japanese cultural weeks are renowned in the INSEAD festive calendar. Each usually includes the opportunity to sample traditional cuisine, watch films, and attend conferences or demonstrations (of national dances, for example), with a final night party in one of the châteaux of the area.

Two formals (one in the winter, one in the summer) are also important aspects of the social experience. The summer formal is also a time for former classes to come back for a reunion (normally after one, five and twenty years). The inaugural summer ball in Singapore took place in 2000 atop Fort Canning.

INSEAD does not have student associations based on culture, economy or other interests. This is simply due to a lack of time: the activities described above take up all available time. So for example, those who are involved in sports must organize themselves independently and form their own groups. This happens easily enough: you can send an e-mail to the entire class, and you'll always be able to find someone with whom to go up to Paris or horseback riding. There are also tennis courts and a swimming pool next to the campus. That being said, the INSEAD MBA rugby team consistently wins gold at the World MBA Championships.

The cultural and intellectual diversity of the students is of course highly enriching. Debates involving, say, someone having worked in a humanitarian association in Africa, a London banker, and a journalist, can be very invigorating. Be aware, however, of one weak point: women are somewhat underrepresented (usually about 25% of the class).

TUITION COSTS

$40,000 is a realistic and relatively comfortable budget for someone who is alone. Other than tuition, the above amount includes all extraneous expenses, including a used car. You must take into consideration lost earnings during this period. You mustn't count on the possibility of earning money while you study: there won't be time, outside of the possible summer internship (don't count on a lot of money for that either) for the January class. There are some scholarships awarded, however rare, mainly to students coming from Eastern Europe.

Given the fact that INSEAD only lasts one year, the cost is much less than that of American schools. The major expenses are as follows:

Overall cost of the MBA	In US $
Tuition Fees	32,000
Books, supplies	1500
Housing	4300 to 8600
TOTAL	37,800 to 42,100

STUDENT VIEWS

For me, business school was the key to getting out of the narrow investment field that I was in. I felt I didn't know what questions to ask, but after a whirlwind 10 months at INSEAD, I have a broad appreciation of all the different components of a business and I know where to start with the questions.

I went to INSEAD because in such a fast-moving economy, and aged nearly 30, I was not keen to spend two years in school. What I got was a fantastically international environment (50 nationalities with no group representing more than 15% of the total). It felt like my colleagues had, between them, worked virtually everywhere on earth in every industry. I loved the emphasis on internationalism, multiculturalism and multilingualism. We studied hard, but the environment never felt competitive or in any way hostile. Teaching quality was mixed with some excellent professors and some weak ones. Study materials were up to date with many New Economy issues addressed in courses such as Microeconomics, Industry and Competitiveness Analysis and High-Tech Strategy. Course papers and individual study projects gave plenty of opportunity to explore areas of interest.

I enjoyed living in a beautiful farmhouse in one of the villages, and on a regular basis discussing study and philosophy with my Singaporean and Indian housemates until the early hours. For me, the living arrangements cemented the spirit of mutual learning. The quality of life was high: watching the leaves of the Fontainebleau forest change through the full circle of colors on my drive into school, fine food and wine, dinner parties, Paris for clubbing, excellent château parties… plus the huge range of extra-curricular activities to be squeezed in.

At recruiting time, I was happy to be able to interview with different companies in different sectors. I had not realized that quite so many companies would be interested in us! The MBA, the school reputation, and the alumni network really have been effective in getting me through many doors.

All in all, it was the most intense year of my life, and although it was difficult at times, I can only look back on it with joy - grateful for all the experiences that I had and for all of the friends that I made."

Simon J., class of 2000

My decision to go to business school was admittedly a difficult one. At the age of 30 having studied business administration and having worked for six years in multinational companies renowned for their good training, my decision to go to INSEAD was actually driven by the desire to take a break. What INSEAD really meant for me was much more than a break. It was like opening the windows and letting new fresh air in. INSEAD makes one go through a process in which you eventually realize how narrow-minded ones interests actually were. The mixture of people, the international touch and the enthusiasm of some professors makes you realize that there are many more interesting areas than one might have thought. While in most cases this leads people to a stage of confusion about which professional field to choose, this is a highly enriching experience. From a social point of view, the alumni network is very impressive. Beyond giving you the possibility to make great friends, INSEAD offers you a network that really works. During the MBA, all the alumni I contacted had the time to offer advice. Back in the working world, I was also impressed by how quickly I could turn these contacts into real business opportunities. Thanks to INSEAD, I found a job that perfectly fits my "real" needs. Without INSEAD I am certain that I would not have realized that these are my needs and I would probably have blindly followed my pre-programmed corporate career. INSEAD is an eye-opener.

Albertos S., class of 2000

INSEAD was a great move for me in every possible way. After several years working abroad in transport engineering, I wanted to move back to France and take a job with increased responsibilities in a different sector. I did this after spending a year in the States working for an American bank, and then returning to France with some great work experience under my belt, and a top-class CV. I have since joined the founding team of an extremely promising internet start-up. The additional skills that I was able to bring to the team I owe largely to INSEAD (in terms of experience, credibility, contacts, etc.). From a financial perspective, I have already been able to make up the investment I initially made. I regard the time I spent at Fontainebleau as exceptional both in terms of my personal development and the quality of life.

Pierre K., class of 1999

When I entered INSEAD, my way of thinking was greatly influenced by the big corporate company culture to which I had been exposed for the past five years. My experience at INSEAD enabled me to tackle business questions from a different angle, and to appreciate different cultures. On the academic front, I was able to develop my understanding in the areas of strategic planning and finance. Beyond the quality of the teaching, if I had to pick out one thing which I particularly appreciated, it would have to be the cultural weeks (national theme weeks organized by students from a range of different countries). These weeks often brought about unexpected yet enthusiastic cooperation between politically-opposed nations, with the aim of promoting knowledge and understanding between cultures.

Bernard G., class of 1999

Overall, the INSEAD experience was very good, although it presented several drawbacks due to the short duration of the program. I do not think that the condensed duration was an issue except for the fact that during the last four months, a great deal of the time was spent on recruiting activities, taking precious time away from the most interesting classes. Probably the most important restult of the program was the very strong alumni network, especially in Europe, where almost every key company had an INSEAD alumnus occupying a key position. Socially, life at INSEAD could not be better; this experience was enhanced by the campus design which encouraged the convergence of activities on a few central locations.

Andrés B., class of 2000

The admissions application
INSEAD

INTRODUCTION

The INSEAD admission process is a two-step procedure, including the application and the interview, organized in the following way:

- Pre-selection of applications (around 3,500 before, 1,500 after). This is carried out by four members of the Admissions Office.
- Interviews (normally two per candidate). The interviews are held with alumni in their respective countries. They give their recommendation, without consultation of the Admissions Office.
- Final decision, based on the initial evaluation of the Admissions Office and the recommendations of the interviewers, made by the committee which includes the members of the Admissions Office, professors, and former students (other than those who hold the interviews.)

The admission application is in English. It includes:

- Two letters of recommendation.
- A formal résumé (diplomas, professional activities, international experience, languages, other activities and interests, GMAT scores, and TOEFL scores, if applicable).

- A Job description (containing two 20-line pieces about the nature of the position you had before the MBA, the progression of your career and what you accomplished).

6 essays based on the following questions:
- Description of the personality of the candidate (strengths, weaknesses, etc.).
- Successes.
- The description of a failure (the way in which it was overcome, the lessons learned, etc.).
- Career objectives.
- International experience (the description of a culture shock, the reasons for going abroad).
- One essay with an open question letting the candidate write about whatever he likes.

INSEAD requires that you speak three languages, at least by the time school is over. Knowing three already when you arrive is therefore an advantage. Those for whom this is not the case will have to study a third language during their school year (usually Spanish, German or French in Fontainebleau; with additional languages available in Singapore). In reality, you needn't be worried: everyone knows it is impossible to master a language during a school year at INSEAD, but you'll at least have the opportunity to get the basics of another language.

It is extremely rare that the Admissions Office of INSEAD changes its mind concerning a refused application, even if the candidate presents his application again, with new elements which may have come about after the initial rejection. In some cases, INSEAD may ask you to improve on certain elements of your application.

It is a good idea to start the procedure fairly early: 85% of the candidates send in their applications within the last two months before the deadline (February 1st for the September class and July 15th for the January class). You should start your application process (signing up for the GMAT, ordering applications, etc.) about a year before classes actually begin.

As for applying to the Singapore versus the Fontainebleau campus, applications are made centrally for both of them, with the option to check a box indicating preference. INSEAD considers each aplication to be to the school as a whole, and will try to accomodate a student's choice of campus and start date. The admissions criteria for both campuses are identical. Students can also spend part of their MBA on both campuses, although this is subject to balanced demand existing in either direction.

One last detail about the admissions procedure: exceptional candidates that have no professional experience can still apply, but will have their acceptance deferred by two years. They should take advantage of this period to evolve in a professional environment before taking on their MBA at INSEAD.

THE GMAT

The GMAT requires some preparation, especially for people who are not that keen on Mathematics -- not that the difficulty level is that great (the requisite skills don't surpass what is taught at the beginning of high school) but the speed at which you answer the questions or the ability to calculate in your head are factors not to be ignored.

A proper preparation will include the use of test books or computer programs (it may be useful to take the test at least once on a computer, as that will be the case during the real thing). These tools should be sufficient to prepare you well - I cannot judge the potential usefulness of test preparation centers because I did not go through one; most of my classmates did not use them either.

In the case of a preparation through books and/or computer programs, an important factor is time: as is the case for all tests, it is much more beneficial to start preparing well in advance at a moderate pace instead of trying to cram at the last minute.

The computer versions of the GMAT (and the TOEFL, for international applicants) are designed so that they adjust the difficulty of the questions based on the number you get right in the first ten or fifteen that you answer. The computer then automatically gives you a set of questions more or less difficult, the value of each correct response changing in function with the difficulty of the questions asked. In that way, you may get a higher score in a difficult section with some wrong answers than you do in an easier section where you get them all right.

The average GMAT score for the September 2001 entering class was 685. Depending on the year, the average may be from 660 to 700, with a tendency to go toward the higher numbers in recent years. The latest classes have been closer to 700 than to 660, and may even go beyond that high average. It seems that the average score of European applicants is slightly higher than that of the the rest of the applicant pool. This is not due to their superior intelligence of Europeans, which would be absurd to suggest, but because European candidates historically do very well on the qualititative section, and also because INSEAD requires of them higher scores in order to make up for their slight lack of international edge relative to other candidates.

According to Myriam Pérignon, the Admissions Director, the importance of the GMAT must be put in perspective: it is but one element among others. There is no required minimum and it is weighted with the other criteria (age, schooling, mother tongue, etc.). This is the reason why there is a large variation in GMAT scores (less than 600 to 800).

For applicants coming from a country where English is not an official language, the TOEFL (Test of English as a Foreign Language) is a requirement. The TOEFL is easy enough for those who have worked hard on English during their studies and who haven't forgotten too much of it. There is therefore no major advice to give other than practicing it a few times with one of the books which are sold and that provide corrected test examples. The minimum grade required is 260 out of 300.

THE ESSAYS

The essays constitute a very important part of the application. I have heard of students with excellent profiles - good diplomas, strong GMAT scores - who were refused acceptance to the school; they confessed to making mediocre attempts on the essays. However, it is true that the essay questions are not particularly original and are not always a great source of inspiration.

A FEW TIPS FOR WRITING STRONG ESSAYS

Since the questions are fairly open, a good approach is firstly to define what exactly is going to be the subject and therefore the goal message you are trying to put across to the reader:

1) What aspects of your personality do you want to bring out in an essay?
   Two types of characteristics can be mentioned here:
   - General "required" characteristics: those present in every good manager (ability to work in groups, ambition, etc.) that must appear and are in accordance with what INSEAD expects of a candidate;
   - Two or three more original characteristics which are unique to the candidate (for example, projects in "exotic" countries, humanitarian work, etc.) You can refer to the "positioning" section of the Harvard chapter for more insight on this particular issue.

2) What are the examples or anecdotes which show this?

3) Does this description correspond sufficiently to INSEAD's criteria? There are four axes of criteria: past academic performance, international motivation and cultural openness, managerial potential and the personality of the candidate (see above, in the admission process). There is of course no standard discourse to go by, but there are certain essential qualities that should not be ignored: the readers should be left in no doubt as to the capacity of the essay writer to work in groups, exude ambition, etc.

4) What do you want to emphasize, given these criteria?

If this first level of work is well structured, then there should be a series of examples or anecdotes which will compliment to the story you are trying to tell. They will serve to strengthen the message you are trying to convey. Have colleagues read them over - it is a great opportunity to clarify your ideas, and also to make sure there are no grammatical errors.

And finally, to what degree can you really sell yourself? The American tradition encourages writing where the ego is present; Asians on the contrary tend to adopt a more modest approach. According to Myriam Pérignon, these cultural biases are taken into account. From my experience and from that of some of my classmates, modesty and fear of presumption are to be banished, so don't hesitate to claim successes as your own, even if you may point out that there were others involved who helped out. Using the first person is also very much accepted. So for example, concerning professional success, don't be afraid to show you're proud.

WHAT INSEAD IS LOOKING FOR IN YOUR ESSAYS

The following is a list of INSEAD's essay topics (these questions may change occasionally):
- Give a candid description of yourself, stressing the personal characteristics you feel to be your strengths and weaknesses and the main factors which have influenced your personal development. (30 lines)
- Describe what you believe to be your two most substantial accomplishments to date, explaining why you view them as such. (30 lines)
- Describe a situation taken from school, business, civil or military life, where you did not meet your personal objectives, and discuss what you learnt from this experience. (20 lines)
- Discuss your career goals, and explain how an MBA will contribute to achieving these goals. Why are you applying to INSEAD and what means of ensuring your personal and professional development are you seriously considering as an alternative to INSEAD? (40 lines)
- Is there anything that you have not mentioned in the above essays that you would like the Admissions Committee to know? (15 lines)

From these essays, INSEAD is trying to gauge the following four aspects of your profile:
- *International motivation and cultural openness:* In looking at the French-speaking students in my class, this criterion seems extremely important, as the majority had spent a number of years abroad. Myriam Pérignon, the Admissions Director, specifies nevertheless that "international motivation" does not necessarily have to mean "international experience". As for being open to other cultures, this is more or less essential, considering the diversity of backgrounds represented at the school.
- *Managerial potential:* The recruiters look specifically at past professional successes, taking into consideration the age of the candidate. One's actual position in the company is less important than one's evolution within it.
- *"Character":* The application gives a glimpse of the overall profile of the candidate via lists of extra-professional activities and interests, as well as the essays. A classic essay question is concerned with professional projects and how the candidate plans to use the MBA to further his or her career. The standard answer mentions some entrepreneurial project, often invented for the purposes of getting into the school. Myriam Pérignon notes, however, that responses that are less specific in terms of projects but strong in terms of sincerity can be just as valid; a candidate who confesses that he or she in uncertain about future projects can be acceptable (for example "I don't yet know the exact shape my career path will take, but I am counting on an MBA to help me orient my goals..."). Interviews also present a perfect opportunity to present the less quantifiable aspects of your background and intentions.
- *Past academic performance:* This criterion does not mean that INSEAD will only consider candidates who have come out of a top-notch university. The GMAT also counts. The average GMAT score for the entering class of 2001 was 685.

EXAMPLES AND COMMENTARIES OF ESSAYS FOR INSEAD

In this section, I will review the different INSEAD essay topics. For each topic, I will analyze what the admissions committee is seeking from your essay, give advice for writing the essay and provide examples of successful essays.

Give a candid description of yourself, stressing the personal characteristics you feel to be your strengths and weaknesses and the main factors which have influenced your personal development. (30 lines)

The point of this essay:

To give a general description of the candidate, which will serve as an introduction.

Tips for the essay:

As is the case for all open-ended questions, this essay can give a great advantage to the candidate, in the same way that it can give him a great disadvantage. The answer to this question should be relatively simple once your basic message has been well defined. The example below gives a possible response.

Sample Essay:

I was born and raised in Kansas, in the heart of America's farmland. Kansans are generally known to be hard working, honest, and warm-hearted, but also a bit provincial. I am extremely grateful that I was raised there. My first 15 years in Kansas, and the loving tutelage of my two generous parents, played a great part in making me who I am. I like to think I am warm and welcoming, quick to laugh, and eager to get to know people. I shoot "straight from the hip"— in fact, I can be excessively honest at times. I ask questions when I do not understand. These are fairly common traits of a Kansan, and I am proud to have most of them.

However, living in Kansas can leave a person thinking that most people are middle-class, white, and Christian. I have been extraordinarily fortunate to be able to travel and live abroad at several points in my life, and I credit those experiences with broadening my perspective. My parents took me with them around Europe during my earliest years, showing me that people ate different food, spoke different languages, and did not all look the same. Later in my life, I lived in Japan for a total of three years. I also lived and worked with refugees in a small town in West Africa for six months during my senior year of college. Along this winding path of wanderlust, I have witnessed some of the great diversity of human experience—from the ultra-modern convenience of Tokyo, to the chronic malaria and poverty of rural Africa. Living and traveling abroad has given me a voracious appetite for different experiences—living in radically different places, surrounded by different kinds of people. I also believe that my experiences living abroad among diverse groups of people have made me flexible, understanding of difference in thought and behavior.

Perhaps most importantly, living abroad has made me enormously thankful for the abundance of resources and opportunities to which I have had access throughout my life. I can see one negative effect this international education has had on me: I can be somewhat intolerant of people who do not feel a sense of gratitude for what they have or a need to give something back to their community. I carry around an awareness of my great fortune, and I believe that I have to do something significant in my life to help more people enjoy that good fortune.

The following is an example of a more structured approach (by bullet points), all the while keeping in line with the same fundamental characteristics.

Overall I see myself as a person who is 1) ambitious to continuously develop, 2) eager to change things and look for new challenges, and 3) social and humorous enough to enjoy life even in difficult situations.

My key strengths are:

- *Leadership: founder and president of the biggest junior enterprise in Switzerland.*
- *Determination to succeed: even when confronted with difficult situations, I focus on the opportunities rather than the limitations. Working at ABC, I developed a turnaround plan that resulted in a market share growth from 16% to 25% within eight months.*
- *Team effectiveness with my management, my subordinates or colleagues: at ABC, I had seven*

assistants working for me from whom I consistently got positive feedback on my coaching capabilities. The formal feedback from colleagues in other functions supports the fact that I am adding value in teams.

My key weaknesses are:
- *Demanding on people: when I am determined to achieve something I have the tendency to be very demanding with the people working for me. When this happens too repeatedly it can generate frustrations even though the business results are achieved in faster times.*
- *Neglect details: while focusing on the bigger picture is one of my strengths, I tend to give too little attention to the detail. For example, I did not know all the details of the songs I was going to record on CD with my a cappella group. As a result, all the group lost time in the recording studio and I could not sing all the songs.*

There are four factors that have influenced my personal development:
- *My parents who encouraged me to always make important decisions on my own and motivated me to try out new things.*
- *My international experience gained from living in different cities and from my ambitious friends I had there. This allowed me to develop my team effectiveness within multicultural environments.*
- *My early inter-personal experiences working with persons in a non-profit environment (as president of a junior enterprise and a cappella singer). Here I learned to demand a maximum from myself and colleagues even though there was no monetary incentive.*
- *My professional work experience in marketing at ABC over five years. Here I learned to succeed in a corporate environment including leading multifunctional teams and developing direct reports.*

Describe what you believe to be your two most substantial accomplishments to date, explaining why you view them as such. (30 lines)

The point of the essay:
Show that the candidate knows how to take initiative and succeed in his projects.

Tips for the essay:
This question gives you a chance to show what you have accomplished in the professional field (necessary) and eventually, a personal or academic success. For each issue you should "help" the reader see the strong points relative to your success: perseverance, ambition, intellectual abilities, etc. (every major quality except that of being humble!) Also, you should be able to show tangible results (numbers: the number of persons managed, cost reduction, progression in sales...).

Sample Essay:
I believe my most substantial professional achievement has been to act as a "cultural emissary" between the U.S. and Japan. Prior to becoming a consultant, I lived in Japan for three years, and studied the language and culture for over 15 years. While living in Japan, I had hundreds of opportunities to sit with Japanese people and have lengthy conversations with them about their and my own perceptions about Americans. It was astounding how many Japanese I spoke with who thought that all Americans brandished guns around their homes and neighborhoods, and believed that America was on the verge of a race war. I was able to share with many Japanese a more complex understanding of America and Americans. Then I came home to the U.S., only to find that

I would have as many opportunities in my own country to share an alternative perspective on the people of Japan. Once anyone I met learned that I had lived in Japan and spoke the language, they overwhelmed me with a torrent of views on what makes the Japanese "tick." It never ceased to amaze me how little information people required to formulate their negative opinions of the Japanese. I was able to share my own experience of living with Japanese people. I even had the opportunity to work with noted Japan scholar Ulrike Schaede, helping her to write a book about Japanese government-business collaboration, Cooperative Capitalism. It has given me great satisfaction to be able to try to wear off some of the hard edges of peoples' opinions on both sides of the Pacific.

My second major accomplishment has been my ability to infuse my business career with my zeal for community service. Shortly after joining BCG, a group of us within the company decided that we needed to create a formalized mechanism for orchestrating our pro bono and other community involvement efforts. Thus, I became a founding member of our office's Community Involvement Committee. Over the past two years, I have played a leadership role in catalyzing community service on the part of our 70 person staff. In 1999 I worked for four months on a pro bono case for a childrens' charity, and have been active in the selection of BCG's pro bono client for the year 2000. I have organized BCG's monthly participation in the Reading to Kids program, which brings volunteers to read in English to Spanish-speaking elementary school children in schools in downtown L.A. I have also lead two BCG teams in the American Cancer Society's Making Strides Against Breast Cancer Walks, raising over $3000 for breast cancer research. Working to juggle my heavy client-service commitments with my community activities is a great source of pride and happiness for me.

Describe a situation taken from school, business, civil or military life where you did not meet your personal objectives, and discuss what you learned from this experience. (20 lines)

The point of the essay:
Show your ability to accept a failure and your ability to learn from it.

Tips for the essay:
The learning aspect of the failure is to be very much favored in this essay, such as what you learned and how what you learned will help you have greater success in the future (for example, a failure to get a certain job meant having to go for another company which ended up meaning something important for new career goals which hadn't previously been taken into account, such as going for an MBA) This question will also offer you the possibility of toning down some of the non-stop positive declarations which are necessary for the rest of the application, but that can also be seen as dehumanizing the experience if not for the fact that you can show your ability to see failure in yourself and integrate it into your positive experiences.

Sample Essay:
While working as a research fellow for the Japanese government in Tokyo in 1995, I learned of an academic essay contest for people working in the Development Economics field. As I was researching Japanese foreign aid to Africa at the time, I became very interested in entering the contest. The contest consisted of submitting a 30-page paper, in Japanese. I had already been working on a text in English, and so I decided to shorten it a bit and translate it into Japanese. I thought this would be the perfect test of my ability as a researcher, and as a foreign "expert" in the Japanese language. Well, as you have no doubt already surmised, I received a nondescript postcard in the mail informing me that I did not win the contest. I was very disappointed with myself. I had to take stock of the situation and assess what I had done wrong. After considerable mental self-flagellation, I finally concluded that the competition was

fierce: I was up against many fine academics, most or all of whom where native speakers of Japanese. I acknowledged that I had probably had inflated expectations for my own success. However, I also reflected that the only way I could ever hope to succeed at anything would be to work very hard and always decide to compete, even while accepting the risk of failure. This attitude lead me to attempt a career in management consulting, in spite of having virtually no business experience prior to joining BCG. I was extremely unsure of whether or not I would be able to perform well enough to succeed at BCG, but the experience has been more challenging and rewarding than I could have imagined.

Discuss your career goals, and explain how an MBA will contribute to achieving these goals. Why are you applying to INSEAD and what means of ensuring your personal and professional development are you seriously considering as an alternative to INSEAD? (40 lines)

The point of the essay:

To test and understand the candidate's motivation for an MBA and the coherence with his career objectives.

Tips for the essay:

The answer given most often for this type of question is "I want to be an entrepreneur"... which can work, if we are to judge by the example given below, which comes from a student who was accepted to the school. However, it is not necessary to show in this response that you have specific career goals which have been reflected upon for a long time; that might give the impression of projects which, as of today, are not highly credible (as if it were too ordinary to say that you wish to start a career in a consulting company or an investment bank, which is in fact what happens for one half and one quarter of the students respectively...).

So then, the major advice here is to be sincere. It is well known and not a problem that many MBA students, at the time when they start the program, do not know what they want to be doing when they get out of the school. Yet even still, Myriam Pérignon has stated that very few candidates dare make this kind of "confession". But one of the points of doing an MBA can be to help in this type of decision making. So you shouldn't be afraid to say that for you (if indeed it is the case), an MBA is the occasion to take a break from the professional world and take a look at what may be the next step.

For candidates who really do have entrepreneurial projects, this essay constitutes the perfect place to share them. In this case, it will be necessary to delineate the advantages the MBA will furnish you to carry your project through (by elective courses, new contacts, etc.). There is more information which specifically treats these goals in the section in this book entitled "The Entrepreneur's Corner".

To answer the portion of the questions dealing with alternatives to INSEAD, feel free to name other eventual schools which have been considered. A good answer may state, however, that INSEAD is the preferred school.

Sample Essay:

As possible alternatives to INSEAD, I could transfer to another office [of my present company], in a different country, or pursue an MBA at another institution, such as Harvard, Stanford or Kellogg. However, INSEAD is clearly my first choice: I hope to add my own mark to INSEAD by my involvement during the MBA program, and, in the longer term, by contributing actively to the alumni community.

It is also possible to reaffirm a professional project as being an alternative to the MBA:

Should I not get accepted at INSEAD, I would consider joining a top consulting company. This would give me the possibility to learn how a professional consulting company is run in order to prepare for my first business idea. Also it would allow me to better define where there are opportunities in the area of offering marketing services.

Sample Essay:

My career vision is to become a successful entrepreneur. This will allow me to leverage my leadership skills and my experience in founding an organization. I have two business ideas that I want to pursue consecutively.

Firstly, I want to found a consulting company specialized in ABC, in order to build on my knowledge acquired at XYZ. The idea is to offer these services to small and mid-size companies not having the resources and experience to have a professional marketing department. My second business project is based on a non-profit idea. I want to pursue the latter at the age of 45-50. By then, I will have proven to myself that I can successfully build up a profit-oriented business and I will have achieved a certain financial independence. This second business idea is to create... Specifically, ...

While I believe to have already acquired valuable experience in founding an organization and applying in-depth marketing knowledge, I see three areas in which I can profit from an MBA education to best achieve my career goals. Firstly, it will broaden my view beyond the functional expertise I have acquired in marketing. Secondly, the MBA will allow me to learn more about entrepreneurship from some of the best known and experienced professors worldwide and from the continuous analysis of business cases. Thirdly, it gives me the opportunity to broaden my cultural as well as my business horizons via the intensive interaction with my fellow students. I consider the latter of upmost importance having spent 5 years at XYZ, a company with a very strong corporate culture in which there is a tendency to focus on internal company learnings.

I am applying to INSEAD because I have gained the certainty from talks with a variety of INSEAD alumni that this school is the best option to achieve all the above mentioned goals. I am intending to visit all the entrepreneurial courses available.

This example also shows a classic way of constructing a response around a specific question, which consists of citing the qualities that INSEAD is known for having (the teachers, the alumni network, the international aspect reinforced by the campus opening in Singapore, the advantages of a one year MBA, etc. - these arguments can easily be found in the school's brochure). It will help to show that you are interested in INSEAD and have reflected on the coherence of your expectations with what you know the school has to offer.

Another classmate used this question as a platform to discuss his ambitions in terms of commitment to a political association and so he briefly presented his ideas in the realm of ethics and developing countries. He was hoping that INSEAD would allow him to study in greater depth on certain theoretical questions, and give him the opportunity to think about and work on certain broad themes (NB: upon finishing, he accepted a position in a investment bank in London. Perhaps he should have presented himself as a very pragmatic ideologue.)

I further believe that professional success is more meaningful if it is not only an individual achievement but also useful for society. For this reason, my goal is to be able to contribute to society through a number of possible ways. (...), I want to be strongly involved in the debates on economic or even political issues that shape our world. After graduating, I intend to dedicate the time necessary to be involved in associations that promote ideas in which I believe. This implies that I need to gain enough experience and knowledge to be able to analyze, understand, and make an impact on changes in society. I am convinced that INSEAD can provide some of these tools and knowledge that will be critical in the future. For instance, one of the proposed courses, International Political Analysis, enables participants to get a better understanding of such issues as global management and the relationship between politics and business.

What you should get out of this example is that you need not be afraid to show your convictions and even expound upon them whole-heartedly, as long as it is done well.

Job description essays

Other than the personality questions, two essays describing the candidate's work will be required:

- *1. Please give a detailed description of your job, including the nature of the work, your major responsibilities, the employees under your supervision, the size of the budget, the number of clients/products and the results achieved. (20 lines)*
- *2. Please describe the evolution of your career with your present employer. (15 lines)*

These questions are perhaps simpler in that they require no introspection. It is necessary to indicate a sufficient number of objective examples which will allow the results to be judged or quantified (for example: the budget managed, internal evaluations, size of the team managed, etc.). The progression of the career is of course an important element (the key to the second question is the word "evolution"); it is necessary to illustrate the rungs on your professional ladder, growing responsibilities, etc.

Is there anything that you have not mentioned in the above essays that you would like the Admissions Committee to know? (15 lines) (This question is in fact optional.)

If you answer this question, you must be certain that either you are truly giving new information that has not been covered in any of the previous sections of the application, or to give you the chance to point something out about yourself which has not already been covered:

I am certain I can make a special contribution to class discussions, to study groups and to individual interactions because of my unique perspective and leadership experiences I have gathered in XYZ.

But while the open-ended questions really offer a good chance for those who have something with real impact to add, it will be a trap for everyone else. If you feel as though everything worthwhile has already been stated, this last essay will only serve to dilute the intensity of the message you are trying to convey. If you do not have a particularly luminous bit of information to provide, it is okay to not answer this question.

LETTERS OF RECOMMENDATION

Numbers of letters of recommendation needed for INSEAD: **2**

GENERAL ADVICE

The recommendation includes an evaluation chart of the candidate along with open questions regarding his or her strengths and weaknesses and leadership ability (which must be demonstrated through concrete examples). The letters must be written by individuals who have known the candidate for a fairly long time, preferably in a professional setting.

These letters of recommendation must be considered as added selling techniques in the application and not the opportunity to show evaluations or give feedback concerning the weaknesses and doubts of the candidate in order for him to improve his capabilities (the famous "room for improvement"). Indeed, the candidate should never even see the letters because the person who writes the letter must send it directly to the Admissions Board of INSEAD who will evaluate it in comparison with all the other highly complimentary letters they will have received. So be sure to tell the people who write your letters so they don't misinterpret its goal!

THE QUESTIONS ASKED IN THE LETTERS OF RECOMMENDATION

There are three question groups: those concerning the relationship between the candidate and the person recommending, a classification of the candidate's qualities, and six open questions.

How long have you known the candidate? Define your relationship with the candidate and the circumstances in which you met.

In this question, the person writing the recommendation must give a very precise answer as to the length of time he or she has known the candidate, and how often he or she was in contact/worked with the candidate. The duration and frequency of the relationship are important factors in establishing the importance of the person recommending, more so than his or her level of prestige.

One of the myths concerning letters of recommendation is that, for those able to get big-name contacts to write them, INSEAD will be at their feet. Of course, if the president of a major company has worked with a candidate, and can speak about the circumstances with any depth and precision, that can certainly be of help (though it is rare for a vice-president to apply for an MBA) If, on the other hand, this very important person has had only briefly contact with the candidate, it is not worth the time he or she will spend writing it. The questions call for specific answers that can only be given by people who are in close contact with the candidate. It is therefore typical to ask for your supervisor or another colleague or manager (possibly a former one); and of course you have to be confident about your relationship so you can be sure they will write you a decent recommendation!

How do you rate the candidate on the following criteria

You are not expected to have in this table all of the "outstanding" or "very good" boxes checked. It is more usual to find "spikes" of competence coupled with other categories in which one could expect a need for improvement. Quite simply, certain characteristics are favored by INSEAD, whereas others are deemed less important. These are areas that can be developed during the course of the school year.

	Outstanding Top 2%	Very good Top 10%	Above average Top 25%	Average Top 50%	Below average Bottom 50%	Unobserved
Competence in his/ her field						
Professionalism						
Focus on the task at hand						
Creativity and resourcefulness						
Intellectual curiosity						
Energy and drive						
Personal integrity						
Ability to work in a team						
Organisational ability						
Oral communications skills						
Written communication skills						

Finally, the results of the table must correspond to what is included in the letters themselves.

The other open questions on the candidate

The questions are as follows (and they do not change from one year to the next):

- Comment on the candidate's career progress to date and his/her career focus.
- What do you consider to be the candidate's major strengths? Comment on the factors that distinguish the candidate from other individuals at his/her level.
- What do you consider to be the candidate's major weaknesses? Comment on his/her focus to improve them.
- Describe any situations or incidents based on first-hand experience which illustrate the candidate's sense of purpose and maturity.
- Comment on the candidate's potential for senior management. Describe an occasion you may have had to observe the candidate's leadership role.
- Describe the candidate's interpersonal skills. Comment on his/her ability to establish and maintain relationships, sensitivity to others, self-confidence, attitude, etc. Specifically comment on the candidate's behavior or skills in a group setting/team environment.

Through the numerous concrete examples requested, the questions show just how much the writer of the letter must know the candidate and needs to have observed him or her in a professional setting. The answers to the questions concerning the candidate's capabilities must be highly complimentary; you must not forget that this will be the case for all top-notch applications.

It is of course very difficult to get a hold of former letters of recommendation, but according to the experiences of some of my classmates, the questions which call for remarks concerning the candidate's capabilities (typically: "candidate's potential for senior management", "the candidate's major strengths") were among the best opportunities to sell a candidate. Strengths spoken of here carry a lot of weight because they come from a third party.

The third question - on weaknesses - is not a trick question, unless the weaknesses constitute specifically what INSEAD is trying to avoid. Generally speaking, however, they help give a tone of sincerity which might otherwise not seem credible because it is too complimentary. They can also indicate how the MBA itself will be useful to the candidate, like, for example, certain theoretical disciplines.

The point of the last question ("Describe the candidate's interpersonal skills") is specifically designed to make sure that, through personality and ability to relate to others, the candidate will work well with those in his class to make it a better place, during the MBA and when they become fellow alumni.

THE INTERVIEW

About 1500 candidates (out of an initial pool of about 3500 applicants) will usually have two interviews with alumni who live in the candidate's city. Even though the interview is the last step in the admissions process, it only constitutes one of the criteria for admission; in other words, the opinion of your final interviewer is not decisive to your application, contrary to some job interviews in which selection is made from interview to interview. The interviewer's opinion is submitted to the jury which considers it, as well as the other selection criteria.

All interviewers receive the same briefing and instructions. They do not have access to the application (essays, for example). The structure of the interview can vary widely: some are very friendly and finish off with typical alumni advice ("I recommend such and such a place to live", for example) whereas others try to test the motivation and aptitude of the candidate in a more challenging way. I was told that for one candidate, the first interview went well, but the second went very poorly so he was invited to have a third. The interviewers are instructed to gauge the applicants' aptitude with foreign languages, so don't to be surprised if he or she starts to speak to you in a language other than English. My interview started in English, switched to Spanish halfway through, and finished in French!

The interviewer must of course try to gauge the candidate's level of motivation. So it is necessary to know about the school, the classes, life at Fontainebleau, etc. - all information which can be found in this book!

The main questions are fairly typical:
- Why INSEAD?
- In what way has your professional career up until now been a success?
- What are you expecting from INSEAD? (they are usually looking for answers which mention hopes of advancing your career, academic learning, social life at the school, etc.).
- What are your major qualities and faults? (NB: the interviewer does not have your application, and so has not read your essays. However, the committee can verify whether or not they are in accordance with your interview answers.).

Getting the KELLOGG Admissions Edge

The School	Before the MBA	After the MBA

Kellogg
School of Management

Address	Kellogg School of Management Northwestern University 2001 Sheridan Road Donald P. Jacobs Center Evanston IL 60208-2001
Telephone	1 (847) 491-3300
Website	www.kellogg.nwu.edu
E-mail	mbaadmissions@kellogg.nwu.edu

about the school

Founded	1908
Tuition Fees	$30,255
Some Famous Alumni	Christopher Galvin (CEO, Motorola); Philip Marineau (CEO, Levi's); Colleen Coggins (CEO, Johnson and Johnson); Betsy Holden (CEO, Kraft Foods)

the application

Application File	By mail or downloadable from website
Application Deadlines	mid-November mid-January mid-March
App. File Elements	• 6 essays of 1-2 pages • 1 letter of recommendation • transcripts • GMAT (and TOEFL, if applicable) • résumé • interview

rankings

publication	Business Week							US News & World						Financial Times		
General Ranking	88	90	92	94	96	98	00	94	96	98	99	00	01	99	00	01
	1	1	1	2	3	2	2	5	4	6	2	5	3	7	7	9

| The School | Before the MBA | After the MBA |

before the MBA

# applicants per year	6,039
# applicants accepted per year	900
# applicants entering per year	620
% women students	32%
% married students	38%
% international students	33%
# countries represented	60

Age (years)	
average	28

Education pre-MBA	
Business	22%
Economics	20%
Engineering/Sciences	27%
Social Sciences/Humanities	31%

Professional experience	
avg. years work experience	4.6

GMAT	
average	700

TOEFL	
average	273

GPA	
average	3.5

after the MBA	School total
avg. job offers per student	3
# companies recruiting on campus	325
Main career choices	
Manufacturing	25%
Consulting	39%
E-Commerce	8%
Investment Banking	15%
Other	13%
Function	
Consulting	39%
Marketing	18%
Investment Banking	15%
Other Finance	12%
Business Development/Strategic Planning	11%
Other	5%
Geographical location	
North America	87%
South and Central America	3%
Europe	6%
Asia	4%
Salary (source: Financial Times 2001)	
avg. salary three years after graduation	$134,341
Alumni	
# alumni in the world (MBA)	over 40,000
# cities with alumni association	85

Top 10 employers

1. McKinsey & Co.
2. The Boston Consulting Group
3. Bain & Company
4. Goldman, Sachs & Co.
5. Mercer Management Consulting
6. Booz-Allen & Hamilton
7. Lehman Brothers
8. Siebel Systems
9. Hewlitt-Packard Company
10. Merrill Lynch

author

Name   J. F. DIEUDONNE

Completed his internship Gap.com in San Francisco.
Previously with Marks and Spencer in London, and
before that, Vivendi in Ethiopia.

School specifics

KELLOGG

INTRODUCTION

Founded in 1908, the School of Management of Northwestern University is situated in Evanston, a wealthy suburb of Chicago. In 1979, the Kellogg Foundation, funded by the son of the founder of Kellogg's Cereals, donated $10 million to the school. In appreciation for this generosity the school was renamed the J.L. Kellogg Graduate School of Management, in 1999 the Kellogg Graduate School of Management, and in 2001, the Kellogg School of Management. Today, Kellogg offers three MBA programs: the classic two-year program (480 students), the accelerated one-year program (80 students), and the 2-year MM (Master of Management in Manufacturing), in association with the McCormick School of Engineering of Northwestern University (55 students).

The changes instituted by Donald P. Jacobs (Dean since 1975) have propelled Kellogg to the top rank of American business schools. From 1985 to 2000, the Wall Street Journal named Kellogg the number one business school, just as Business Week did in 1988, 1990 and 1992. Each year, Kellogg continues to innovate and improve its program as well as its infrastructures and student services. For example, the school has recently introduced new courses which integrate the latest innovations in the world of economics (courses in E-Commerce and Technology Management). In addition, the school has invested almost $40 million in the construction of an ultra-modern, which was recently inaugurated. Kellogg is constantly looking to hire professors at the top of their profession; for example, Oprah Winfrey, one of the biggest stars of television talk shows, teaches a course in Dynamics of Leadership.

Kellogg has become one of the major business schools for General Management (ranked No.2 behind Harvard in Business Week for this area). It remains also the world reference in marketing. This reputation rests as much on its teamwork approach (a key component of marketing functions) as on the quality of the courses and professors. Kellogg has also rapidly improved the reputation of its Finance and Entrepreneurship Departments. In the area of technology, Kellogg is on the cutting edge of the e-business revolution and is certainly one of the best business schools for high-tech marketing.

These favorable rankings, along with an excellent academic and professional reputation, have allowed Kellogg to improve its selectivity, to recruit world-famous professors and to increase its international standing. Its alumni are very active, not only in the United States, but in many other countries (over 39,000 alumni in 85 countries). Kellogg regularly welcomes impressive guest lecturers.

Kellogg students are considered to be well-rounded team players. Kellogg emphasizes the personal and professional development and blossoming of its students. Extra-curricular activities are an integral part of the MBA experience at Kellogg. The group work facilitates student interaction and develops a spirit of collaboration. There is also a strong "Kellogg spirit" evident at the school. In this academic and cooperative environment, students can develop strong self-confidence, receive an excellent education, and have access to the best companies in the world.

Kellogg does not necessarily look for candidates having a "top of the class" profile or coming from the most prestigious backgrounds. In 1999, for example, the 627 entering students came from 265 different undergraduate schools. The most important requirements are to have a strong personality, a clear vision of the world and of one's objectives, a good academic profile (GPA, GMAT) and excellent reasons for doing an MBA at Kellogg.

THE DEAN'S VISION

Interview with Donald P. Jacobs, Dean of the Kellogg School of Management.

Could you talk about Kellogg's strategic initiatives?

Kellogg had a strategy that we launched in the late 1970s, a strategy that we hoped would take the school from a good second-tier school to the best there is. That strategy, as you know, worked and was implemented much more quickly than we thought. So by the early 1990s, there was concern about what to do next. We had developed a learning organization where the curriculum would be routinely redesigned. There was no need for the Dean to interfere. So we chose what we thought were the three major initiatives to maintain the school's momentum going into the new Millenium.

Number One was to bring Kellogg to the global stage: globalization of the student body, curriculum and school reputation. Second was to place greater emphasis on entrepreneurship in our courses, because an increasing number of people trained for management are going to be doing entrepreneurial tasks rather than purely going to work for an existing corporation. If you look, you'll see that there has been a dramatic change in the viewpoint of students at management schools, away from becoming a cog in the wheel of a major organization to starting their own businesses. Moreover, people work in a more entrepreneurial fashion, even if they do work for large businesses. The third initiative was to make the latest information technology available in our teaching methods and classrooms. The world has changed dramatically. The traditional models of business have been completely altered by the increase in the capability and power of information technology.

We developed strategies to work on these three initiatives. On the globalization front, we changed the curriculum. A major curriculum change was to provide courses that took 350 of our students for a major educational experience. We have developed alliances with a number of schools around the world. Our goal was to have an alliance with a school in a number of regions. Our stated goal was that the sun would never set on Kellogg. Any minute of the day, seven days a week, 24 hours a day, there would be someone around the world studying for a Kellogg degree. So, we have a Middle-Eastern program, a European program and we have programs in Hong Kong and Bangkok. We have an initiative in China, and we are currently helping to start a new business school in India in partnership with the Wharton School.

With information technology, we think we have done a fantastic job. In a very short period of time, we have introduced a new major in e-commerce. Also, we have hundreds of executives coming to learn e-commerce at the Allen Center, our Executive Conference Center. We have worked with several dozen companies to develop their e-commerce strategy, and many of our students have started their own companies. Our students published a book on e-commerce from papers written for an e-commerce course (Techventure class) last year. It was published in book and CD-ROM form and has impressed even senior executives.

What makes Kellogg unique?

Our first initiative is to choose our students by determining whether or not they can work with other people. We are not training loners; we are training people to be managers. Managers work with people, so a lot of the work here is done in groups. To do this we started to interview all applicants. When we first started interviewing, this was unheard of in business schools; now of course other schools have followed.

We also emphasized research capability in the faculty we hired. To assure that their research was rooted in the real world we built the executive center (the Allen Center) to bring executives on campus. This was the first time that had been done in such large numbers by any school. We now have 6,000 executives coming to our campus every year for training and education. That means our research-based faculty can try out their research on executives, on campus, before they take that information into the classroom. We have developed a methodology for bringing new material back into the classroom very quickly. It makes a great difference.

So what makes us unique is the way we choose our students and the kind of people we have here. It is the way we choose faculty and the way we develop our curriculum. The traditional school is very slow to change curriculum, so the curriculum gets out of date. Then there has to be a massive change. We change curriculum continuously. Also, we have a large number of new experimental courses every year, and that affects the school positively. It is an engine for change.

THE SCHOOL YEAR

CURRICULUM

The MBA in one year (four quarters)

The accelerated one-year MBA program runs from June to June in four quarters. Kellogg is the only big American business school offering such a flexible program aimed specifically at those students who have a very definite and clear professional goal. Limited to 80 students, it is very international (about 45% from outside the USA). A minimum of 15 courses is needed for graduation with only one required course (in strategy). The rest consists of elective courses.

A recent graduate of the one-year MBA comments: "The one-year program is aimed at those candidates who are particularly motivated by an international environment (25 nationalities among 80 students). It offers a program of choice and the same opportunities for employment as the six-quarter program. However, I recommend this program to people wanting to stay in the same sector of activity."

The two-year MBA program in six quarters

The program is composed of 2 x 3 quarters (fall, winter and spring) and there is only one starting time - September of each year.

A minimum of 23 courses is required for graduation:
- 9 "core courses" (required courses from a common-core syllabus; it's possible to be exempted from certain courses - see the next chapter).
- 14 electives to be chosen from 166 courses offered by Kellogg.

THE FIRST YEAR:

	Sept - Dec Fall	Jan - end Mar Winter	End Mar - Jun Spring	Mid Jun - Sept
1st year	1st term Required curriculum	2nd term Required curriculum	3rd term Elective curriculum	Internship
2nd year	1st term Elective curriculum	2nd term Elective curriculum	3rd term Elective curriculum	

The core courses are taken during the three quarters of the first year. The major courses are

First quarter (fall)
- Managerial Decision Analysis (Probability)
- Accounting for Decision Making (Financial Accounting)
- Business Strategy
- Strategies for Managing Organizations (Organizational Behavior)

Second quarter (winter) and Third quarter (spring)
The student is free to choose the sequence of courses each semester according to his/her priorities, as long as the following courses are included:
- Statistical Methods for Management Decisions (Advanced Statistics)
- Finance 1
- Microeconomics Analysis
- Marketing 1
- Operations Management
- 3-4 electives

The Kellogg program is characterized by its flexibility. In fact, it is possible to be exempted from certain required courses. To get this "waiver" you must be able to show either that you have already covered the material in your previous studies (send your transcripts and description of the course from your school), or that you are well acquainted with the subject because of your profession. If you don't receive the waiver automatically, you can also take an exam to try to show that you have the level required to bypass the course in question.

About 50% of students are exempted from at least one of the nine core courses. If you obtain waivers of core courses, you can take electives from the first quarter (a minimum of 3 courses and maximum of 5 courses a semester). However, the workload is heavy during the first and second semesters (mostly because of the search for the summer internship and the interviews in February and March). It is better to take only 4 courses during these semesters.

During the first quarter of the first year, the students are divided into eight sections of 65 each. These smaller groups encourage closer relationships among their members. For the following two quarters (winter, spring), the students follow their own program, the only obligation being to take the rest of the required core courses during the first year. Students are free, therefore, to choose the courses, the professors and the hours for the five core courses that remain. For example, a student could take three electives and one required course during the second quarter; then the three required courses the last quarter. The idea is to let the students define their own sequence of courses and manage their program according to their academic priorities and professional goals.

The second year
In the second year, you individualize your program by choosing at least 14 electives. Kellogg offers 166 electives, which means a lot of choice. However, the most popular courses, such as Entrepreneurial Finance, Management Communications and Tech Marketing, are sometimes difficult to get into. Entry into these courses is based, in general, on a bidding system. If your goal is a job in finance, you will specialize in this area by taking most of your courses in, and thus majoring, in Finance. More than 95% of the students gain more than two majors. The most popular are Marketing, Finance, and International Business.

Kellogg is particularly attentive to student demand and can very quickly create a new course -- more than 50 new courses have been introduced since 1996. In the space of just a few months, the school established a new major in e-commerce comprised of 5 new courses. Kellogg is constantly innovating to keep its program up-to-date.

THE COURSES - WHAT'S HOT... WHAT'S NOT

The following table shows how 25 students rated the quality of the content of the main courses (satisfaction compared to expectations). The survey does not cover all the courses, but it does give a general idea of how students evaluate the offerings:

	Student Satisfaction based on expectations			
	% recent Kellogg students			
	Below Expectations	In Line With Expectations	Above Expectations	Outstanding
Finance	5%	21%	32%	42%
Marketing	12%	41%	24%	24%
Decision Sciences	14%	52%	29%	5%
Management Strategy	0%	29%	14%	57%
Managerial Economics	21%	21%	21%	36%
Organizational Behavior	13%	35%	39%	13%
E-commerce	9%	0%	36%	55%
Entrepreneurship	0%	13%	25%	63%
Accounting	5%	15%	45%	35%

As with all the other charts in this book, it's important to remember that it is impossible to compare the evaluation tables of different schools. The survey aims to measure the satisfaction given by the different courses compared to the expectations of the students. Obviously, expectations differ from one school to another. To take one example, Harvard is well known for its general management courses. The students, therefore, have high expectations and criticize harshly if the courses don't satisfy them. Kellogg is better known for its Marketing courses than for General Management; therefore, Kellogg students are less critical if the General Management courses are not excellent, but they are much more demanding of the Marketing courses.

E-commerce and Entrepreneurship

Kellogg offers 16 courses covering a large variety of disciplines:
- Marketing: Technology Marketing, Internet Marketing
- Finance: Entrepreneurial Finance
- Logistics: Logistics and Supply Chain Management
- Technology: TechVenture
- Strategy: Models and Processes, Strategic Management of Technology and Innovation

It is important to carefully consider the sequence of courses. Here is an example of a sequence: 1) Fundamentals of Technology & E-Commerce, 2) Internet Marketing, 3) TechVenture and 4) Entrepreneurship and New Venture Training to finalize your business plan. TechVenture provides a class of 150 students with a basic understanding of the creation, development and evolution of the new technologies and their impact on the economic world. This course combines concepts and practical research (conferences, participation of the contributors, research projects, and a week-long stay in Silicon Valley).

The quality of the Finance and Accounting courses at Kellogg is in constant progression. The school has increased the number of quantitative courses in recent years and has just created a new major, Analytic Finance, in addition to the classic major Finance. Kellogg has a complete program of courses in market finance and company finance (more than 40 courses in all). These courses are always practical in their approach; for example, in the course Investment Banking the first 30 minutes are devoted to the analysis of economic data and different indexes as well as to a detailed analysis of the current state of the companies. The faculty is of the highest level, in particular Dr. Rogers (Entrepreneurial Finance), Dr. Marciano (Financial Decisions), Dr. Peterson, (Finance II), and Dr. Revsine (Financial Reporting and Analysis).

Given Kellogg's reputation in the area of marketing, the expectations of the students are very high. The survey below shows how the quality of the courses meets expectations. The strong points of the Marketing Department are:
- the quality of the faculty
- the existence of very specific electives that cover all aspects of marketing; thus the course "Promotion of Sales and Distribution" (Dr. Blattberg) uses sophisticated statistical tools evaluating the efficiency of different elements of the marketing mix from the point of view of the distributors and manufacturers. The course Models of Consumer Behavior (Dr. Calder) explores the psychological aspects of consumers' purchasing decisions.
- the involvement of top marketing professionals

By the end, the holder of a major in Marketing from Kellogg has mastered every element of the marketing mix and possesses solid analytical tools and a sense of consumer psychology. In addition, this graduate will have met numerous professionals in his field and will often keep in contact with professors who are doing the latest and most important research in their fields.

Kellogg recognizes more than other business schools the importance and value of the discipline Organizational Behavior. The school offers more than 25 courses covering all aspects of organization and the management of human resources.

TEACHING METHODS

At Kellogg, the pedagogical method rests on a scholarly mix of case study and lectures but also on simulation and "field study". Thus, the school marries theory and practice. The professors decide the best teaching method based on their personal styles and the requirements of the course.
- Lecture: 30%
- Case study: 30%
- Group Projects, Consulting Reports, Independent Study: 40%

THE GRADING SYSTEM

As with most undergraduate programs, exams are marked on a scale of 100 points and given a letter grade. The grade depends on the level of the students: generally, the best 30% of students have an A, the next 60% a B, and 10% a C. The letter grades are then given a numerical value on the scale of 1.0 to 4.0 (4 corresponds to an A) to calculate grade point average. At the end of the year, students with high marks can make the Dean's List, a distinction that impresses recruiters, especially those from banks and consulting firms.

Grades are based on class participation, the mid-term exam, the final exam and group projects or a paper. The school year is composed of 3 semesters of 10 weeks each. The regularity of the exams is unflagging. For every course there is a mid-term exam at the sixth week and a final exam in the tenth week.

Grades are not usually asked for by recruiters during interviews, although many companies in consulting and investment banking ask for your first semester grades (or to see your GMAT score!). These grades are therefore important, and an atmosphere of competition often surrounds them.

GROUP WORK

It is important to underline the importance of "teamwork", the great speciality of Kellogg. From the first course, the professors will assign you to a group (4-5 students). You can compose your own groups in the second year and in certain courses the first year. Students spend on average two hours each course working in groups on different projects.

An example is the course Organizational Behavior, in which the students work in groups of five on a project called Senior Manager Case Analysis. They interview two senior managers about their professional experience and analyze their method and style of management. Students are free to contact managers of their choice. Each group is responsible for the planning and structure of the final report (15 pages). The first work of the group is always tedious because the members have to determine how the team will function (sharing of tasks, establishing deadlines etc.). All the time, you are learning bit by bit how to work as a team and maximize the resources and abilities of each member.

The interaction with the other students is one of the most important dimensions of your MBA experience: you are constantly stimulated and challenged intellectually in class, but also outside of school (in your team, in the clubs, in your contact with other students) in an atmosphere of cooperation.

Advantages of working in groups:
- Sharing and discussing ideas (intellectual stimulation)
- Learning to work in a team, to listen others, to argue and to explain ideas clearly and concisely (and sometimes to manage crisis situations!)
- Meeting other students, some of whom will become friends

Disadvantages
- Cliques can form (and cause tension in the group)
- Compromises must be accepted (frustration at not being able to reach agreement)
- Occasionally, it wastes time (the meeting syndrome)

THE TEACHERS

There are, in all, 156 permanent professors and 50 visiting faculty. Kellogg is known for its Marketing department. This reputation cannot be denied; the courses in Marketing are excellent. The best-known professor is the "star" Dr. Kotler, outstanding in his field. Dr. Mohanbir Sawhney, guru of high-tech marketing (Electronic Commerce and Technology) writes regularly for business journals and is famous for his expertise. In finance, Steve Rogers (Entrepreneurial Finance) is also a star at the school and has been named by Business Week as one of the 10 best professors of Entrepreneurship in the USA. In strategy, Dr. Besanko (author of the work *Economics of Strategy*) is a highly regarded economist. These professors are in great demand by the students.

The professors are evaluated regularly by the students. They dread this process because a bad grade can have an adverse effect on their professional careers. This feedback is important because it helps continuously improve the quality of teaching.

THE INTERNATIONAL SIDE

The flags of 40 nations hang in the Atrium, in the heart of the Kellogg building, symbolizing the importance accorded to the international composition of the student body. The emphasis put on internationalism is characterized by:

- an increase in the number of foreign students (from 16% in 1992 to 33% in 1999).
- the introduction of numerous courses focusing on international aspects (example: Intercultural Aspects of International Management, International Technology Management).
- the creation, in 1989, of the course GIM-Global Initiatives in Management (www.kellogg.nwu.edu/gim/), which focuses on the study of a country's industry. Managed by the students, this program brings together several courses and includes a two-week field study. This year, more than 350 students participated in 15 GIM courses, (example of subjects: Marketing Eco-tourism in Costa Rica and China E-Economy Overview). Emmanuel Hemmerle (second year): "During the GIM trip to India in February, 1999, we met Ratan Tata (the boss of the group Tata), the Minister of Finance, the Secretary of State for Finances, the Minister of Culture, the Minister of Education, and some of us were invited to a religious ceremony in the presence of the President and Prime Minister."
- an exchange program with schools in 10 foreign countries (LBS in Great Britain, IESE in Spain, HEC ISA in France) for a semester.

THE ENTREPRENEUR'S CORNER

The Entrepreneur Department is becoming increasingly important at Kellogg. Last year, more that 20% of the students launched their own start-ups or created their own companies upon finishing school. Kellogg offers numerous courses on the subject as the following examples show:

- Entrepreneurship and New Venture Formulation
- Managing Entrepreneurial Growth
- Entrepreneurial Leadership
- Business Law for Entrepreneurs
- Entrepreneurial Finance
- Kellogg TechVenture

Many students have created their companies during their two years of studies at Kellogg (for example, the site EthnicGrover, launched by two Kellogg students; the founders of Garden.com and Ubid are also from Kellogg). The courses cover all aspects of creation of a company including the Business Plan to convince venture capitalists to invest.

Among the students there is a real creative and entrepreneurial energy which is channelled and structured by the courses, the presentations of successful alumni, the many conferences on campus, including a Digital Frontier conference and the different clubs (Entrepreneurship and Venture Capital Club, High Tech Club). There is also an "incubator" for start-ups situated near Kellogg, the Evanston Research Park, where the students have the opportunity to work on concrete projects and launch new companies.

LIFE AT KELLOGG

CHICAGO

Chicago is a town full of resources (the third largest in the USA) whose dynamism is manifested by the exuberance and modernity of its architecture, its numerous museums (the Art Institute, the Field Museum, etc.), and its nightlife, (bars, jazz clubs). Chicago is also famous for its many sports teams (including, of course, the legendary Bulls). It is also one of the biggest economic centers in the U.S., and several multinationals are headquartered there (Andersen, Motorola, McDonalds, Kraft Foods, AT Kearney). Overall, Chicago is a very pleasant city, especially in summer, when it is possible to sail on the vast Lake Michigan, or to run, bike, and barbecue along its shores.

THE CAMPUS

Kellogg is situated in Evanston (Illinois), a suburb about 8 miles north of dowtown Chicago. It is a wealthy and pleasant neighborhood. The Northwestern University campus offers first-class sporting facilities including a remarkable indoor sports center. Evanston is a small town of 74,000 inhabitants, very quiet and safe. A metro takes you from Evanston to Chicago in 35 minutes. A taxi takes 20 minutes.

HOUSING

Full-time MBA students study at Leverone/Anderson Hall, a modern building in the middle of the Northwestern University campus. The school offers Kellogg students without children the possibility of living at McManus, a residence characterized by:
- its proximity to campus (5 minutes by foot).
- 300 furnished or unfurnished apartments, with 50 reserved for couples.
- a gym, a computer room, laundry room etc.
- apartments recently renovated (bathrooms/kitchens) and connected to NWU's network, making it possible to surf the web 24 hours a day.
- prices ranging from about $600 to $950 a month for a studio or two-bedroom apartment.

If you choose an apartment off campus, in Evanston, the prices are higher ($900-$1500 for a two-bedroom apartment). It is more economical to share a house with other students.

SOCIAL LIFE

Kellogg is distinguished from other schools by the importance of social life to the MBA experience; (the 1300 students participate in one way or another in the social life of the school). In fact, one of the specialties of Kellogg is the autonomy of the students. The administration lets the students manage the clubs themselves, as well as the conferences (see below) and the GIM trips. Kellogg's administration is always ready to consider suggestions on improving all aspects of the school (infrastructure, computers). This approach creates a certain dynamic and adds another dimension to the MBA program because, while maintaining academic rigor, the school encourages the students to take initiatives and to discover new fields. This is what students feel, at the end of their studies, has had an impact on their life at the school. The Graduate Management Association (GMA) oversees the more than 60 different clubs. To see a complete list of these clubs, go to www.kellogg.nwu.edu/club/club (most of the clubs have web sites). There are 10 business and international culture clubs, 20 professional clubs, 12 religious, social and community clubs, and 24 sports, leisure and arts clubs. Most students belong to several. The challenge is to manage all the activities offered each day; you learn to juggle the presentations, workshops, club meetings, speakers -- in short, you become a real expert at time management!

In addition, seven conferences are organized by the students each year. To give an example, the program for this year is as follows:

November
Business of Healthcare Conference - www.kellogg.nwu.edu/confer/tbohc/Welcome.html
    This annual event focuses on the latest developments in the healthcare industry.
Real Estate Conference - www.kellogg.nwu.edu/student/club/realestate/
    This conference aims to answer questions and study developments in the field of real estate over the course of various debates around a central theme.

January
Digital Frontier Conference - www.digitalfrontier.org/
    The Digital Frontier Conference is the oldest (since 1994) and most important high-tech conference organized by the American business schools. It brings together 700 participants, including company directors, technology gurus, entrepreneurs and venture capitalists. It is organized by and for students. Recent themes include "Surviving the Digital Storm" and "Leading the Evolution of E-Business". Joe Galli (COO of Amazon.com), Kevin Rollins (Vice Chairman of Dell Computer), George Shaheen (former President and CEO of the former Webvan, and former CEO of Accenture (then Andersen Consulting), and Jay Walker (Vice Chairman and founder of Priceline.com) have recently been present.

February
Marketing Conference - www.kellogg.nwu.edu/confer/mktg00.html
    Aimed at students, alumni, businesses and members of the Chicago community, this forum provides an excellent opportunity to acquire advanced marketing skills, discuss current developments and find out about career prospects in marketing.

Global Business Conference - www.kellogg.nwu.edu/confer/global99.htm
    The aim of this event is to discuss and analyze worldwide geopolitical, economic and technological changes and to study the foreseeable consequences on business management.

April
MMM Manufacturing Conference - www.mmmconference.org/
    This conference deals with strategic and operational questions currently facing the field of manufacturing. Professionals and professors present techniques and approaches used by the world's most competitive companies.

TUITION COSTS

The total cost of an MBA is very high. At Kellogg, it will run you about $92,000 and, as with starting salaries, it is constantly increasing. However, the return on investment is more than positive in the long run. The MBA is an investment that is profitable in terms of salary and career. The average starting salary of an MBA graduate from Kellogg is $92,000, not counting bonuses. With signing bonus, compensation approaches $120,000 (Business Week, 2001).

Of course, the cost of the two years at Kellogg will vary according to the type of housing and the standard of living chosen by the individual student.

Total cost of Six-Quarter MBA (2 years)	In US $
Tuition fees	60,500
Books, supplies	3,000
Computer materials	3,500
Housing	27,000
Cost of living (food, transport...)	11,500
TOTAL	105,500

Financial Aid

Kellogg has made loans available to students at favorable interest rates, which protects against the risk of change and offers another source of financing. The amount of the loan is based on the needs of the individual student.

STUDENT VIEWS

The following comments reflect the opinions of some 1999 graduates of the Kellogg MBA:

Kellogg's strong points:
- *Very good program in General Management (ranked second after Harvard by Business Week)*
- *"Cooperative" atmosphere - the people who come to Kellogg are the coolest and nicest*
- *Extensive alumni network (over 40,000 alumni)*
- *Dynamic curriculum (constant improvement of courses, infrastructure, etc.)*
- *Reputation (arguably the second most renowned school after Harvard)*
- *Environment: Chicago is a great town*

Kellogg's strong points:
- *Teamwork: you really learn how to work together and to be effective as a group. This is vital in marketing where it's important to capitalize on the abilities of each person to advance a project..*
- *General quality of the courses: the fact that you grade the professors (in mid-term to give suggestions; at the end of the term to give an official grade) is not strange there.*

Kellogg's strong points
- *Extra-curricular activities extremely well-developed thanks to the autonomy granted to students. They are organized into many clubs, not only to enrich the social life at Kellogg, but to entice onto campus top ranked companies and personalities.*
- *The culture of flexibility that leads to permanent and rapid adaptation of the program to the new challenges of business; for example, in the areas of entrepreneurship and information technology.*
- *Access to the professors: unparalleled*

I The admissions I application
KELLOGG
I

INTRODUCTION

The Kellogg application file consists of:
- GMAT scores (and TOEFL, if applicable)
- 6 essays (1-2 pages each)
- 1 Letter of Recommendation.
- a detailed Résumé
- an Interview
- Transcripts from previous schools

To maximize your chances of admission, apply for the first round and send the complete file before the middle of November. Decisions are made as the files are received. You can also send your files by the Internet ("online application").

Kellogg is the only major American business school where you can apply to do an MBA in one year (see the paragraph on the four quarters program in "School Specifics" section of this chapter). This program is recommended for candidates who have a definite professional goal in mind. You are asked to state in the application exactly which program you want to apply for.

THE GMAT

The GMAT is often the first step in the preparation of the MBA application. Your results will determine the level of business school you can hope to be admitted to. Over the last few years, the average score has increased enormously.

GMAT	TOEFL
700	273
45	15
610 to 760	253 to 287

Given the increased average, a score below 600 strongly diminishes your chances of being admitted to Kellogg. In fact, as the graph below indicates, only 2% of those admitted have a score below 600.

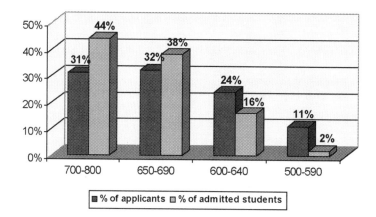

If you retake the GMAT, Kellogg takes the highest score. Personally, I took the GMAT three times and my score progressed from 570 to 680. In all cases, if you retake the GMAT, you need a "jump" of 50 points to have any significant impact on your application.

THE PREPARATION

Taking the GMAT without a preparation course often leads to catastrophic results. Without preparation, I had a score of 490 on my first practice test. It is always possible to prepare on your own by buying books on the subject, but it is strongly recommended to register at a special center. I took the course at Kaplan. The cost is not negligible, but having a good score increases your chance tenfold of being admitted to the best MBA.

For the quantitative part, I recommend that you plan a strategy of attack for the questions. Review all grammar rules, analyze the recurring questions and keep a list of all difficult questions
(cf. Examples of revision lists below).

Verbal

Subject - Verb Agreement

List of conjunctions followed by the singular form:

anyone, anything, each, everyone, everything, no one, none of, nothing,

what, whatever, whoever, along with, with, as well as, in addition to, accompanied by, together with, as much as,

None of these trades **requires** a college education

Steve, **along** with his oldest brothers, **is** going to...

The prime minister, **as well as** his press secretary, **was** late.

List of nouns followed by the singular form:

jury, committee, audience, crowd, class, troop, family, couple, majority, system, athletics, economics, mathematics, physics,

statistics, measles, news, the US, the audience, citrus, politics, the amount, the majority, series, staff, variety, class, band, team

The jury IS currently making its decision

Three years/Three days IS a long time

Economics really **IS** his strong point

Math

Water Added (WA)

Ex : How many liters of water must be added to **3 liters** of a **20% alcohol solution**

in order to obtain a **15% alcohol solution**?

Vol O = original quantity of water

% salt original,   % salt final

Wa = liters of water to be added

FORMULA : $Wa = \dfrac{\% \text{ salt original} * \text{Vol O}}{\% \text{ salt final}} - \text{Vol O}$

APPLICATION : $Wa = \dfrac{20\% * 3L}{15\%} - 3 = \dfrac{3/5}{15/100} - 3 = 4 - 3 = 1$

Wa : quantity of water to be added= **1 liter**

Water Evaporated

Ex : A **24 liter mixture of alcohol and water** is **8% alcohol**.

How many gallons of water must be evaborated in order to obtain a **12 % solution**?

We = Vol O - (% salt original *Vol O)*% salt final

APPLICATION : We =24 - 8%*24 = 192/100 - 24= 8 liters
                            12%   12/100

We= quantity of water to be evaporated=**8 liters**

STRATEGY AND TIMING

Test minus 3 months

- Register at a test preparation center and begin to familiarize yourself with the test.
- Take a practice test.
- Get motivated and set an ambitious goal (+600).

After the first practice test you can quickly assess your level. If you have less than 500 on the first practice test, you have some work ahead of you and three months is not too long to gain 100 points. If you have between 520 and 600, two months should be enough to raise your score to more than 600. If your score the first time is more than 600 (yes, it happens!), a month of revision should be enough to get up to 700.

Test minus 2 months

- Follow the course at the test prep center.
- Analyze your method of comprehension and assimilation (making lists, keeping a notebook) each one has a method, but the important thing is to analyze your errors and note them if possible. You should understand the strategy for attacking each type of question.

The whole of the second month should be devoted to reviewing math and grammar basics and to taking the practice tests. The advantage of the GMAT CAT (on the computer) is that you can choose the date when you want to take the test. However, be sure to contact the Graduate Management Admission Council (GMAC on the web site www.gmat.org/gmat) several weeks in advance to get the date you want, especially if it's on a weekend.

Test minus 1 month

You need to spend the last 4 weeks cramming intensively and taking practice tests. You can either do the tests at home on the CD-ROM supplied by the preparation center (complete test) or work on specific parts of the test at the center to improve your weak points. The center offers many supplementary tests as well as a series of specific questions classed by category. I worked a lot at home thanks to the CD-ROM, (which gives you the score and level) and I did practice tests at the center on my weak points (the verbal part, especially Reading Comprehension). If you do not practice the test on CD-ROM, don't forget to time yourself.

D-Day

Feel ready and confident. The advantage of the new format GMAT is that it gives you a score at the end of the test, which lets you get on with your MBA application process.

THE ESSAYS

Writing the essays is often the most difficult part of the application process. It involves a thorough analysis of your motivation, your character, and your vision of the future and of the world around you. You should not underestimate the time necessary to write the essays (1-3 months) and I advise you to begin just after finishing the GMAT. You should stand out from the other students and show how you are going to adapt to the pedagogical method at Kellogg (teamwork).

A FEW TIPS FOR WRITING STRONG ESSAYS

Before starting, it is useful to think about the questions below (see table). It's important to fill out this grid in order to define the aspects of your candidature and to structure your ideas. Then you can come back to the grill regularly during the writing to check the coherence of your ideas (have you dealt with all the themes in the different essays?).

- Personal background
  What is your country of origin, your family environment and in what ways have these influenced your personality?
- Career history
  What are the reasons for and the chronology of your professional choices?
- Academic history
  What are the reasons for and the chronology of your academic choices? Why an engineering school? A business school...etc?
- Values
  How would you define your values? How do you participate in your community?
- Strong and weak points
  What are your successes/failures, academic or professional?
- Motivations
  What is this training going to bring to you, both personally and professionally?
- Why Kellogg?
  Describe specifically what attracts you about the Kellogg MBA.
- Career plans
  What are your professional goals after the MBA (be specific about the industry, the area) and why?

1. Identify the obstacles and quantify your impact on your professional environment

To capture the interest of the reader, you must explain how you have succeeded to overcome the obstacles and what you have learned from that. This idea of the "lesson" you learned is important in the essays because the school wants to understand your personality and your commitment to go all the way to realizing your ambitions.

2. Emphasize your experience of working in teams

For Kellogg, it is important to show that in your professional and personal life you have been able to work with groups and participate in community life (humanitarian associations, volunteer groups, etc.). In effect, Kellogg wants students who fit the profile of "people who are committed to teamwork and to giving back to the community".

3. Show your personality

The essays demand a real self-reflection. You must put your cards on the table, unveil your values, your ideas, your aspirations. To communicate authentically, I suggest that you recount the experiences that have marked you, the lessons you have drawn from these experiences and the ways in which they have transformed you. The essays should also highlight your results and what still needs to be accomplished for you to attain your goals.

4. Answer the questions

It is imperative to answer the question completely and precisely. For example, the first essay, "Briefly assess your career progress to date. Elaborate on your future career plans and your motivation for pursuing a graduate degree at Kellogg", includes four questions (1. Career progression, 2. Professional goals, 3. Why an MBA now? and 4. Why Kellogg?). The secret is to balance your essay (divide into 4 quarters). In addition, I advise you to write a dynamic first paragraph.

5. Pay attention to the format

Keep your essays short (two pages per essay maximum, because the selection committee must read more than 24,000!). Be aggressive in the style and content (use active verbs like "manage", "execute", "implement", etc.). Limit each paragraph to one strong idea supported by concrete examples. In effect, you must illustrate and quantify whatever you claim (% savings, $$ in additional sales). Don't be discouraged: you will rewrite your essays on average five times before the final result!

I recommend that you read *Essays that Worked for Business Schools: 35 Essays from Successful Applications to the Nation's Top Business Schools* by Boykin Curry and *Graduate Admission Essays: What Works, What Doesn't, and Why* by Donald Asher.

WHAT KELLOGG IS LOOKING FOR IN YOUR ESSAYS

List of essay questions from the last three years

- Briefly assess your career progress to date. Elaborate on your future career plans and your motivation for pursuing a graduate degree at Kellogg.
- Each of our applicants is unique. Describe how your background, values, and non-work related activities will enhance the experiences of other Kellogg students.
- You have been selected as a member of the Kellogg Admissions Committee. Please provide a brief evaluative assessment of your file.
- Complete three of the following six questions or statements:

    A Through the course of your life, what would you identify as your most valued accomplishment?

    B Outside of work I enjoy…

    C Describe a situation that forced you to re-evaluate a personal belief.

    D Describe your most significant contribution to an organization or individual.

    E Be your own career counselor. What aspects of your personality or background present the greatest obstacle(s) to achieving your goals?

    F I wish the Admissions Committee had asked me…

In the essays, the school is trying to understand the following elements of your personality:

Questions	Essay objectives	Qualities looked for
Essay 1	What is the career history of the candidate? Why does he/she want to do an MBA and why at Kellogg? Will he/she profit from the Kellogg experience?	Maturity. Professional ambition
Essay 2	Will he/she integrate into the group and contribute to the school life?	Teamplayer, adaptability
Essay 3	How is he/she better than another? Does he/she have a good profile? Does he/she know how to sell and to convince?	Humility, ambition. Force of character
Essay 4 (3 questions of choice)	What other aspects of his candidature have not been revealed in the first 3 essays? What is his/her potential after the MBA?	Potential Leadership

Reading the essay questions (see below) gives a good idea of the aptitude necessary to be a good teamplayer. To understand the notion of working in a team is particularly important for each Kellogg applicant. A team could be defined as a group of people interacting to achieve a common goal. That implies a sharing of tasks and the convergence of the efforts of each member of the team. This definition brings out two essential characteristics of a group:
- A common goal: it is essential to precisely define the objective to be attained and to make sure that all the members of the team understand it.
- The convergence of the efforts of each member: it concerns the individual contributions and the interaction between the members of the team. In this sense, the team is a fragile system, whose total energy depends on the individuals who comprise it and the quality of the interaction between them.

For a group to work well, the following qualities are essential:
- Leadership: to assure that the team does not miss its objective and to motivate the members to give their best to attain the goal.
- Knowledge of the other members: in order to understand the abilities of each one and how to best utilize them.
- A capacity for organization: define the role of each one, the method of exchange between the members as well as the different timing.
- Communication: to present and to share your analyses and recommendations clearly and constructively (for example, by diagrams and tables).
- Active listening: understand the arguments of the other team members.

EXAMPLES AND COMMENTS ON KELLOGG ESSAYS

In this part, I review some Kellogg essays. For each one, I specify what the committee is looking for (essay objectives) and give advice as well as sample essays.

1. Briefly assess your career progress to date. Elaborate on your future career plans and your motivation for pursuing a graduate degree at Kellogg.

The point of the essay:

To evaluate the coherence of your professional goals and your motivation for doing an MBA at Kellogg. The school is looking for mature candidates who can really contribute to this experience while profiting from it. Furthermore, I am convinced that they are looking for candidates who nurture ambitious projects, not necessarily aspiring to be CEO of a multinational. The idea is to select students who are going to make a name for themselves in the sector they choose whether it be a multinational, a start-up, or even a humanitarian organization.

Tips for the essay:

It is important to structure your essay in the following order:
- Explain your professional choices
- Illustrate your maturity (eg: you have attained a plateau in your career)
- Define your future professional goals
- Show your ambition, while still being realistic (not easy)
- Explain what an MBA is going to do for your career
- Analyze your motivation for doing the Kellogg MBA (discuss the specifics of Kellogg)

Sample Essay:

I made my first career decision at 16 in high school. After an introduction to economics, I opted to go into business, rather than into engineering or medicine. At 19, I became aware of an important shortcoming: my lack of English proficiency. I took a second initiative: to find a student job in the U.S. These fundamental decisions have shaped my educational and career experiences: undergraduate studies in Commerce at the University of Paris Dauphine, summer jobs in the U.S., officer in the French army, research associate at INSEAD, account executive with Yoplait and Nextel in the U.S.

When I was a student at Dauphine, I became a great admirer of Sam Walton and Wal-Mart. I decided to major in Marketing and became increasingly interested in retailing, sales and negotiation. I spent four summers in the U.S. to learn English and the American way of doing business. I worked as a waiter in Maine and as a trip leader in the East and West coasts. While discovering the U.S., I started to dream about settling there.

After graduating, I was drafted and decided to join the Reserve Officer School. I chose this demanding training to get the opportunity to lead sections of other draftees. I was recognized for my service as a Lieutenant with the rare Distinguished Service Award. I then accepted an offer at INSEAD to work with a professor on a consulting project for Carrefour. The job dealt with marketing in retailing and I wrote a case study on Carrefour's strategy. Working at INSEAD allowed me to learn more about MBAs. Rather than moving into consulting, I wanted a sales career in a fast moving consumer goods sector with strong brand orientation. I was hired by Yoplait to fight a store war to increase market share among retailers' shelf space. It was tough and I had never been in such a competitive environment. Nevertheless, after one year I was able to achieve an 11% sales growth in this 0% growing market.

In September 1997, my wife had the possibility to start her Ph.D. studies at Kellogg. I seized that opportunity to finally enter the U.S. business market and left my career at Yoplait. After settling in Evanston in November I accepted a position as Account Executive at Nextel. I was attracted by telecommunications, one of the fastest growing industries worldwide. After being focused on sales and fully involved in the field, I want to make a career move to a broader strategic position in marketing. I want to take on the responsibility of a brand manager evolving in a multinational environment, a job that requires people skills, adaptability, and the exposure to different business cultures. I was amazed by the incredible potential of telecommunications and would like to stay in that industry.

I decided to apply to Kellogg's Master of Management program because I feel that it correlates well with my previous experience and career aspirations. First of all, Kellogg is the top school in marketing. I have acquired the necessary strong field experience and the understanding of customers. I want to join Kellogg to take stock of my achievements to date, and to learn what is needed to grow from sales to marketing. Secondly, Kellogg's top MM emphasizes general business. I need to broaden my perspective with entrepreneurship, organization, strategy and finance for my goal of getting to senior line management. I am hungry for a dynamic educational program, where I will get the "big picture" of business. Thirdly, Kellogg values teamwork. I believe that it is in group situations that I learn the most, that I contribute the most to others, and naturally give the best of myself. My motivation for Kellogg is also to join exceptional fellow students with whom we can create an entrepreneurial dynamic and share our business backgrounds, motivations and visions.

2. Each of our applicants is unique. Describe how your background, values, and non-work related activities will enhance the experiences of other Kellogg students.

The point of this essay:

To better define your personality (value system, personal aspirations) in order to evaluate how you would integrate and contribute to the academic and social life of the school. Kellogg also tries to measure the depth of your involvement in your community. The idea of "giving back to the community" is very important at Kellogg, and this essay should explain your experiences in this area. Kellogg is looking for people who are involved and active and know how to take the initiative in school clubs and who will have a passion to share their expertise with other students. This is definitely the most important essay for Kellogg.

Tips for the essay:

- Explain your behavior in groups and your passion for teamwork (speak about your experience as project leader, for example, and the satisfaction this brought; show your passion for managing people if you have had this experience)
- Describe what you can bring to the class and the social life of the school. It's a good idea to discuss your extra-curricular activities, to tell how you have helped someone (as a member of a humanitarian association) and what initiatives and responsibilities you took, as well as their impact on your environment.

Sample Essay:

Being Swiss with a strong appetite for group activities and an experience in the army as a platoon leader will help me contribute to Kellogg in a unique way. Switzerland is a small country with a long history, strong culture and regional specificity. I take a special pride in the latter principle. Swiss people have an acute sense of fraternity. When I came back to Switzerland in December 1998 after almost two years in the U.S., I went to visit my grandmother for two days in the south of Switzerland. She had organized a huge lunch with our close and extended family. There were 50 of us in total. We started lunch at 1pm and only got out after dinner at 1am the next morning. We spent 12 hours eating, drinking, talking, singing, and just enjoying being gathered together. I am not saying that I am going to organize 12 hour lunches with other students at the business school, however, I will definitely share my Swiss culture, roots and vision to build strong relationships and fraternal camaraderie with my fellow students at Kellogg.

I enjoy team playing and especially coaching groups. When I started college in 1989, I decided to take on a new challenging sport. I was 19 and wanted to run my first marathon! When I was a kid, my father used to say: "Sport is the school of life. If you want to win and succeed, you have to work hard, prepare well and believe in long-term efforts." I went to the University Sport Center and surprisingly discovered that there was no running team. My first and only question at that moment was: what do I need to do to create one? Ten minutes later, I was President of the first running association, with... one runner! After a great deal of going around on campus, distributing flyers and convincing students, I recruited 10 people daring enough to challenge themselves in the marathon. For six months, we trained, motivated and pushed each other to work towards our common objective: crossing the finish line. From being novices, we became runners and in April 1990, after 26 miles in the streets, we were marathoners! I approach life and build my relationships the same way. In all the groups I will get involved with at Kellogg, I will invest myself to make sure we achieve our common goals. Thanks to my ability to understand and cope with different personalities, I will be able to see what is needed to enhance teamwork.

In 1995, when drafted for a year in the Swiss military service, I opted for officer training and applied to the Reserve Officer School. I became Second Lieutenant and led five different sections of 40 drafted soldiers each. Leading a section taught me a great deal about group dynamics, managing people and human responsibility. I had the opportunity to meet people I had never encountered before: many did not have schooling, some were even illiterate, some did not have any family and others were awaiting prison sentences in civil trials. This was the best lesson of humility I ever had in my life. I realized how lucky I was to have my family and my degree. One week, I had to command a section of 30 soldiers in a training exercise. Four soldiers in the section were particularly undisciplined. I took the risk of giving each of them the responsibility of a small section of six soldiers. The result was incredible: they were positively demanding to their soldiers and became fantastic leaders committed to the goal I had given them. We achieved an outstanding training. I learned in the army how people in difficulty can hold back the rest of the group. Most importantly, however, I realized that giving responsibilities to these same individuals and asking them to take initiatives could make them become the main pillars of the sections. At Kellogg, I expect to face similar challenges and find myself sometimes in difficulty. I will rely on fellow students as much as they will be able to rely on me to take initiatives and responsibilities to focus on the task at hand.

3. You have been selected as a member of the Kellogg Admissions Committee. Please provide a brief evaluative assessment of your file.

The point of this essay:

To show your ability to stand back and view your application from the larger perspective: indicate what distinguishes you from the other candidates.

Tips for the essay:

To present your profile most favorably, you are advised to show that in addition to your academic and professional qualities, you have successfully managed projects in other domains (the idea of "success patterns": you succeed in everything you undertake, thus setting up a virtual cycle of success). Once again, it's important to convince the admissions officer that you meet more than the minimum criteria for admission. Insist, therefore, on the original aspects of your career path and explain how these can enrich the other students.

Sample Essay:

When evaluating Kellogg applicants, I am naturally looking for evidence of sustained academic excellence, professional achievement and interesting human qualities. This file satisfies these criteria but also scores highly on two other counts which I wish to comment on more fully. First, is the unusually developed international focus of the applicant. From the French Indian Ocean island of Réunion, the applicant spent one year in the United States as a 15-year-old exchange student and chose to pursue bilingual undergraduate business studies in mainland France, learning equally about the French and Anglo-Saxon business environments. During this time he spent a 10-month internship in Canada working on a marketing project on behalf of Air France. After graduation, he spent 16 months in East Africa, managing materials and labor on two civil engineering projects. On his return, he was hired by Marks & Spencer, quickly moving to the London head office where he has been working as Financial Controller since November 1997.

Both the quality and quantity of his international work experience stand out. Over the past five years, he has worked for three different companies in different industries and functions. He has specialized in Finance but has also had some exposure to Marketing. He has experience of several different cultures and ways of doing business. In Canada, participating in the launch of an important marketing campaign and monitoring its success for Air France enabled him to see how a marketing idea translated into concrete results, producing additional sales, prestige and a positive image. His work experience in Ethiopia/Eritrea was more operational. He had to manage the day to day operations and deal with local constraints. This challenging experience in a third world country has taught him to become flexible, organized and determined. His work experience at M&S, in France and the United Kingdom, was more quantitative and analytical. Being in a Financial Control department, he has acquired a good framework for analyzing the profitability of a business and understanding strategic issues such as globalization.

Second, is the applicant's ability to take on responsibility, produce results and demonstrate his sense of commitment. For example, in Ethiopia, after a successful first project, Vivendi put him in charge of a much bigger contract ($ 75 million) in a neighboring country. This, too, came in on time and within budget. At M&S after 12 months in the company, he successfully implemented the migration of the European Financial Control Function from Paris to the UK head office. As a result, M&S promoted him twice in two years, from grade 8A to 8 then 7 between May 1996 and August 1998 (twice the usual speed of promotion).

Through his work and travel experiences, he has enriched his culture and developed an open-minded character, inquisitive nature and leadership and teamwork abilities. In the past five years, he has spent three years outside France in five different countries. In addition, his international exposures have developed his flexibility to change and adapt to a new environment quickly. His extracurricular activities and experiences prove that he interacts well with others, seeking more than just superficial contact with people and striving to develop long term relationships. In short, he has acquired a truly international background. These two distinctive features when taken together with the record of demonstrated achievements both inside and outside the classroom (GPA, GMAT, the creation of a humanitarian association) add up to an exciting profile and a very competitive application.

The 4th essay

You have to respond to *three* questions from *six* choices. I suggest choosing the three questions that will best show your abilities and will complete the first three essays.

4A. Though the course of your life, what would you identify as your most valued accomplishment?

The point of this essay:

To evaluate your greatest success (personal or professional) in order to compare your capacities with those of the other candidates. Having managed a humanitarian association in India or having won a ski championship, for example, would be more impressive than having participated in a marathon.

Tips for the essay:

This question is common to all the schools. I reiterate the same advice all applicants need to remember.

- Explain why you have chosen this example
- Don't be modest
- Show the difficulties you have met and how you overcame them
- Quantify your results

Sample Essay:

Personal accomplishments can come from all over, even professional situations. Such is the case for me. In 1994, I left a prestigious job at a world-renowned tobacco company to become the marketing manager of a small and declining company that produces automobile fluids. The company was in a mess and unless it could be turned around quickly, it was destined to disappear. The challenge was both daunting and thrilling and I decided to go after it. I quickly understood that the company would survive only if it adopted drastic measures. It needed to completely change its business strategy and marketing position. Moreover, the employees, many of them lifelong, would have to completely change the way they worked.

By personally defining, encouraging and implementing a new and ambitious business strategy, I was able to play an exceptional role in the development and recovery of the company. I brought a new vision and perspective to the company and provided it with radical and unexpected solutions. I took the company's commodity product and re-positioned it to a more upscale market. It is now considered the top-of-the-line automobile fluid. I also created a full range of innovative new complementary products such as non toxic antifreezes, long life coolants and defreezing windscreen washers. These innovations were possible thanks to strategic partnerships I initiated and developed with international players on our market. My actions completely challenged the company's philosophy, organization and results. They forced management to take tremendous risks. Today, the company has become a market leader. After four years, it has recovered and even increased its turnover by 10 million francs.

In 1997, the president of our country selected our small company as being among the most innovative in the country and invited us to join him on an official trip to Brazil. Perhaps most important was that, at the age of 27, not only did I contribute to saving a company from failure and turning it into a success, I managed to do so while saving most of the employees' jobs.

The experience confirmed my belief that even in manufacturing industries, human intelligence adds more value than products and machines. There is always a lesson to be learned from adversity. It can usually lead to success, if you really persevere. This is a lesson I learned early in life and one I try to apply every step of the way.

4. B. Outside of work, I enjoy...

The point of the essay:

To evaluate your passions and hobbies to better understand your extra-professional qualities.

Tips for this essay:

I advise you to use this question to tell of an original activity (sport, hobby, religion,etc.) which will highlight another facet of your personality and which will complete your other essays. It is important to explain why you got started in this activity and what you have gained from it (introspection, will to win…). Show your competitive spirit, (taking on challenges), your curiosity and your openness to the world.

Sample Essay:

During my military service, I took the opportunity to learn how to play the game of "Go". I always liked games, especially strategy games, and I had been told that "Go" was one of the most famous games. I liked the idea of learning how to play an Asian game, which was typical of the Asian way of thinking. I bought a copy of "Go", read the rules and tried to play with a friend: what we did was a mere tick-tack-toe game, with no particular interest. I could not believe this was the game taught to Asian Kings to help them rule their countries… I decided to go deeper into this question.

When I bought a "Go" book, I discovered that besides the simple rules of the game, playing the game of "Go" was a real art. This introductory book for beginners really made me love the game: I looked for the "Go" association, and attended "Go" classes. I have now been playing the game of "Go" for seven years, and I really love the game and its philosophy. As in everyday life and business, you need to measure influence, assess the global picture, seize initiative, avoid jealousy and greed, assess relative strengths, build more than your opponent does. Playing the game of "Go" is a real lesson about life and yourself.

4 C. Describe a situation that forced you to re-evaluate a personal belief.

The point of this essay:

To evaluate your ability to question yourself and be critical of yourself.

Tips for the essay:

Expose a personal situation that marked you and had an impact on your outlook on life. The secret of this essay is to really explain how and why you had to examine your beliefs. It must also show the impact this situation (or event) had on your personality, how it has changed you and your vision of the world.

Sample Essay:

My East Africa experience forced me to examine some previously unchallenged beliefs I held about the Third World. Prior to my time in Ethiopia and Eritrea, I tended to believe that helping such countries was mainly a question of transferring money and resources to them from the rich industrialized world. My experience in two of the poorest countries in the world has changed my perspective. Twice the size of Britain, Ethiopia has a population of 57 million, trapped in conditions of medieval poverty. The country's recent history has been grim and bloody. It took years of civil war before the Ethiopian People's Revolutionary Democratic front succeeded in taking power from Mengistu Haile Mariam, the Marxist dictator who ran the country from 1973 to 1991. Even today, the country is still among the poorest countries in the world and heavily dependent on donations and the IMF to revive its economy. Giving such a country the right aid is far from simple. I now realize that poorly thought out aid can cause as many problems as it cures. Little positive can be achieved by foreign aid unless it is delivered with a very clearly detailed understanding of the local inhabitants' real needs, traditions and aspirations. My first hand experience of the Third World also led me to re-evaluate my attitude towards others. I have, I hope, learned to become much more open-minded and flexible, recognizing that diversity is a factor of personal enrichment. I have also realized how one's own cultural background can shape one's perception of the world around one. To be able to adapt in a new environment, I have also learnt to put aside preconceived ideas and absorb as much as possible of the local environment.

4 D. Describe your most significant contribution to an organization or individual.

The point of this essay:

To evaluate your capacity to take initiatives and your "commitment", your determination to go all the way in defense of your ideas or convictions.

Tips for the essay:

It is important to analyze the method you have utilized and to quantify the impact of your initiatives. You should explain your approach to solving complex problems (of organizations, people, operations) and emphasize your ability to successfully lead a project to the end. Illustrate your leadership qualities (leading a team, managing a project) and demonstrate your "drive" towards self-improvement.

Sample Essay:

Working sixteen months in Ethiopia and Eritrea when I was 23, dealing with the local authorities and managing up to 600 local employees, was my most valued accomplishment.

First, when I arrived in Addis-Ababa in September 1994 for Vivendi, my assignment was to set up an administrative office and manage the day-to-day operations of two road construction projects (contract of $ 6 M in Ethiopia and $ 75 M in Eritrea). Every day brought fresh problems and challenges. One of my duties was to deal with the local authorities (tax, customs, and banks...), a task made exceedingly difficult by the local bureaucracy and corruption. For example, we had great difficulties obtaining the release of our materials from customs. I regularly had to intervene personally and meet the customs authority and negotiate the release of our materials. By being persuasive and determined, I managed to convince the authority to clear our goods within an agreed timescale. Another example of the problems I encountered when dealing with the local government arose in Eritrea. The Eritrea employment agency systematically refused to give Vivendi work permits for Ethiopians, as there was great political tension between the two countries. I had to negotiate for several days with the local employment agency to persuade them that we were looking for the best skilled employees. To my great relief, I succeeded.

My second accomplishment in Eritrea was to set up an entire administrative center on a base camp in the desert and learn how to manage local employees. In Eritrea, the scale of operation expanded rapidly with the number of local employees increasing to 600 in just five months. As administrative and accounting manager, I supervised all the administrative aspects of this project, dealing with day to day operations, recruiting hundreds of local employees, contacting all the local authorities and setting up efficient communication with the Addis-Ababa office.

LETTERS OF RECOMMENDATION

GENERAL ADVICE

Kellogg requires only one letter of recommendation. Since the interview is mandatory, Kellogg considers one letter to be sufficient. As Michele Rogers, Director of Admissions says, "Generally, we use the career progress survey (letter of recommendation) as just another piece of the puzzle for us to understand the applicant's background". You are strongly advised to choose a person you can trust from your company who has worked with you and knows you well. It is important to take the time to explain exactly why you want to do an MBA. You should not write the letter yourself, but you may offer some things that might help, for example, a list of your strong points, or a profile of the MBA you are applying for. I suggest also that you give your recommender your essays, whether they are finished or not, in order to have some continuity between the letter and the essays. You could also give him/her your evaluations from the Human Resources Department of your employer. These give a good overview of your strengths and weaknesses. The recommendation letter should be short and concise (two pages maximum) and written in English. It should also give specific and quantifiable examples to demonstrate your personal and professional qualities.

Planning for the recommendation letter

April:
- Think about a person who could recommend you.
- Prepare a list of your strengths and weaknesses, motivations, etc.

September:
- Arrange an interview with your recommender and explain that you are preparing an MBA application.
- Brief your recommender on the contents of the questions and give an idea of the responses.

October:
- Contact him or her again and give more information if necessary.

November:
- Pick up your letter of recommendation.

QUESTIONS ASKED IN THE LETTER OF RECOMMENDATION

Below is a study of the questions Kellogg asks in the letters.

1 What are the three areas of the candidate's professional character that have improved the most in the time you have known him or her?

The objective:

To evaluate your capacity for training and progress. The school is looking for candidates with the ability to improve and grow as needed.

Advice:

The question considers your rate of progression. There are three cases:
1) A weakness that you have eliminated (from weak to normal).
2) An area where your performance was average and you have improved (from normal to strong).

3) A weakness which has become a strength (use this in moderation if you want to retain your credibility!). For an example of this last case, I remember a friend who had a reputation for his inability to manage his time efficiently. In just eight months he had made such good progress that he was asked to organize a course in "time management" for other colleagues!

- The recommender should illustrate with specific examples each of the three areas in which the candidate has made strong progress.
- In a general way, the letter should make apparent your determination and your continuous improvement. Ideally, it should show that you are not one who persists in his/her errors, but that, on the contrary, you know how to recover quickly, you listen to others in order to improve yourself almost methodically.

Sample Response:

There are many facets the applicant has developed since I have known him. However, the three key elements I would highlight are:

- Judgement of when to be assertive and when to adopt a less challenging manner. Although a naturally likeable individual, the applicant has an inquisitive mind which can lead him to pursue lines of questioning which may be interpreted by certain types of individuals as challenging. However, over the last year the applicant has become much more aware of his personal impact and has learned to judge the situation more effectively.

- Self-starter status and initiative. Given the fluid nature of the reporting structure for Continental Europe, the applicant has demonstrated many times his ability to operate in the interests of the business in the absence of management direction. Many of his peers and colleagues would have failed to tackle these hurdles.

- Bridge-building outside of finance. Although the applicant's skills have always been recognized within the finance group they have recently been recognized by the operational areas of the business. This has lead to an environment where the applicant is being expected to operate as a quasi-consultant. This has resulted in a change in the mental attitude of the applicant from one of "cost centre" to "service centre". Many of his peers have still to grasp this change in culture.

2. What do you perceive to be the applicant's weakness?

The objective:
To assess the nature of your weaknesses and your ability to work on them. The school probably wants to eliminate candidates with incapacitating weaknesses, like the inability to work in a group or a lack of leadership ability.

Advice:
This question is very much like the preceding one. In bringing up your weaknesses, your recommender must also show how you have been able to overcome them. The idea of constant self-improvement is very important because it shows your desire to surmount handicaps and weaknesses.

Your recommender can show, for example, your progress in "communication skills" or "analytical skills". The reader wants to see a rapid curve of progress in two or three weaknesses (maximum), which will prove your ability to recover and improve.

3. Please address the following components of the candidate's character. Cite specific examples where possible.

	Abilities evaluated	Details
A	Intellectual ability	Analytical skills, communication creativity, curiosity
B	Career performance	Relative to others in the industry
C	Career focus	Clarity of post-degree plans
D	Interpersonal skills	Maturity, listening skills, sense of humor, sincerity, concern for others
E	Leadership potential	Initiative, contribution beyond expected responsabilities

The objective:
To better discern the different dimensions of your personality, notably your academic potential (can you follow the program?) and professional potential (will you be a business leader after the MBA?).

Advice:
In dealing with the above five questions, the recommender must highlight your intrinsic qualities (intellectual faculties, ability to listen, assurance and persuasive abilities). By giving specific professional examples, he shows, point by point, not only your drive to constantly improve, but that you are distinguished from the other candidates by your multiple talents within the company. It is a good idea for your recommender to evoke your leadership abilities (example: project leader), your capacity to adapt in difficult environments (example: a project abroad), and your ambition (coherence in career choices and rapid promotion).

THE INTERVIEW

An interview is required at Kellogg (unlike at many other schools). In the admission brochure, you can read "By interviewing every applicant, we identify those individuals who share Kellogg's fundamental principles for teamwork and involvement outside of work and class." More precisely, the goal of the interview is "to assess an applicant's maturity, interpersonal skills, professional and personal experiences, career focus and motivation". The interview weighs heavily in the evaluation of your candidature to Kellogg.

All candidates can ask to have an interview before or after having sent in the application file. Your interviewer does not have access to your file: he is testing your communication skills and will question you about your professional projects and your motivation for doing an MBA at Kellogg.

Before choosing the date you want, it is best to contact the admissions office early. The busiest period is from September to December. I advise you to contact admissions at least two months in advance of the date you want. I also advise you to do the interview on campus to show your motivation and to visit the school. It is not required to have it on campus: it's possible to do the interview with an alumnus in any part of the world.

Finally, I advise you to do the interview just after writing your essays. You will have all your strong points and arguments fresh in your memory and will thus be well prepared to communicate all the elements of your candidature during the interview.

Preparation for the interview

Start by preparing for the question types (see below), then you can practice by doing some interviews. The subjects of the questions are as follows:
- Background personal/professional
- Character strengths/weaknesses
- Current job
- Career goals/Why?
- How does an MBA integrate into your medium and long-term career plans?
- Why Kellogg?
- How do you perform in a team? Are you a team player?

For the questions about your motivation for Kellogg, I indicate below the three principal characteristics of Kellogg. Each student must adapt the strong points of the school to suit his personal and professional aspirations.

1) Emphasis on teamwork
- Group work dominates studying, classwork and social life. The team-group concept was pioneered at Kellogg

2) Quality of curriculum: balanced, innovative and flexible
- A well-rounded management education (ranked #2 in General Management in Business Week)
- A highly-rated program in Marketing and Finance
- A focus on e-commerce and technology (new Major in E-Commerce, Digital Frontier Conference...)
- Curriculum flexibility (possibility to waive some courses and over 160 electives to choose from)

3) Kellogg social life
- A good balance between work and social activities. This is the cornerstone of Kellogg's culture: "This is a school for people who like people. Backstabbing is not tolerated. Kellogg develops leaders who have the simultaneous ability of being team members."

The day of the interview

On the day of the interview, your interviewer will ask you to fill out a presentation form (name, school, GMAT, etc.). The interview is relatively short (30-45 minutes) and the secret of success rests on four factors:
- Being dynamic and enthusiastic (you must make a good impression)
- Being prepared for each of the "classic" questions
- Standing out from the other candidates (the interviewer should remember your qualities)

It is very important to show clearly how well you fit the school's profile. Kellogg is looking for students who like working in teams; you must highlight how much of a team player you are. At the interview you will be asked first of all to describe your background (personal and professional), to talk about your professional goals and to demonstrate that Kellogg is your first choice. At the end of the interview, I suggest you ask pertinent questions about the school (questions you will have prepared in advance) such as "Could you tell me more about the GIM Trip and the Digital Frontier Conference?" and "How has globalization impacted the Kellogg curriculum?"

INTERVIEW WITH THE ADMISSIONS DIRECTOR

Interview with Michele Rogers, Director of Admissions at Kellogg.

What factors are considered in admissions decisions?
1. The candidate's potential for a successful career in management. We admit poised, confident, mature, motivated individuals who carefully fashion their career plans, and who show strength in communication and leadership skills. We evaluate these characteristics using essay question responses, recommendations, assessment of work experience, leadership activities, and impressions made in evaluative interviews.
2. The candidate's academic background and promise for successful completion of the MM degree. We consider the GPA, school attended, trends in grades, difficulty of the major, etc. We examine results of the required Graduate Management Admission Test (GMAT).
3. The candidate's personal qualities - self-confidence, maturity, self expression, etc.
4. Candidates also should understand why Kellogg is different from other graduate schools. A keen interest in Kellogg is always an advantage, but Kellogg admits the strongest candidates despite stated "first choice."

Is it better to apply during the early rounds?
Yes, I recommend to apply by Jan. 15.

What is Kellogg's usual response time?
It can be anywhere from 3 to 12 weeks for a response. Our process is more like rolling admissions, we send the decision as soon as it is made. It takes time for a file to be evaluated. It goes through three pairs of hands. There is a student reader, a staff reader, and myself. If we disagree, another student reader reviews the file, and we meet. All decisions are made through a consensus.

Is it permissible for foreign students to have a lower GMAT score? If so, what concession is made?
Ther is no prescribed difference, but many international students have a lower verbal score and a higher analytical score.

If someone takes the GMAT more than once, will you take the highest score or the average of the scores?

We take the highest score. I feel comfortable using all of the pieces (GPA, GMAT, essays, transcripts, etc...) to evaluate candidates.

What are the "do's" and "don't's" for essays?

The candidate should answer the questions we ask and not offer a generic response.

How do you recommend that students differentiate themselves from the pack?

Ther is no formula for this, but those who have done something very well tend to be more interesting.

What makes a good letter of recommendation?

A letter from someone who knows and can address the candidate's work performance.

I understand that you and your office attach a lot of weight to communication skills, does that mean that the interview is considered a significant variable of your evaluation sheet?

The interview is important for two reasons:

Firstly, it answers the question: "Can the candidate effectively present himself or herself to another person?" But it's also a chance for the student to learn about our programs from someone who knows what we really offer. It is not any more important than any other aspect of the application, although it does vary in importance from candidate to candidate because different candidates have different strengths. One candidate may be incredibly charismatic and more savvy than many of his or her peers but may be weaker in another area. So that's probably a key reason why the interview is not more important than other factors.

We generally use the interview to assess fit. The reason we emphasize communication skills is because of our learning environment here. We work and learn in teams. We're looking for a person who cannot only survive the program, but thrive in it. Most of the knowledge that Kellogg students amass is garnered by noodling over information that they get from professors with other students.

What other MBA schools do you consider as direct competitors to your MBA program?

Our direct competitors are Stanford, Harvard, Wharton - based on surveys of our admits.

Given that some companies (such as McKinsey and Co. and Goldman & Sachs...) seem to be traditional "feeders" for your MBA program, how is an applicant from one of these firms viewed against other applicants in the pool?

There is no difference - the company hires the same type of candidates we seek.

Getting the MIT Admissions Edge

MIT
Sloan School of Management

Address M.I.T. Sloan School of Management
50 Memorial Drive
Cambridge MA 02142

Telephone (1) 617-253-2659

Website mitsloan.mit.edu/mba

about the school

Founded	1914
Tuition Fees	$31,200
Some Famous Alumni	**John Reid (CEO, Citicorp);** John Ridge (President, CitiBank); Michael Porter (President, E*TRADE); Carly Fiorina (President, Hewlett Packard); Gérard Pelisson (Founder, Accor); Jeff Shames (Chairman, Mass Financial Services); Xavier Fontanet (President, Essilor)

the application

Application File	Online only
Application Deadlines	late November mid-February
App. File Elements	• Cover Letter • 2 essays • 2 letters of recommendation • transcripts • GMAT • Résumé

rankings

Publication	Business Week						US News & World						Financial Times		
	90	92	94	96	98	00	94	96	98	99	00	01	99	00	01
General Ranking	**13**	**13**	**10**	**9**	**15**	**4**	**2**	**2**	**3**	**5**	**4**	**5**	**5**	**4**	**6**

The School	Before the MBA	After the MBA

before the MBA

(all figures approximate)	
# applicants per year	3,000
# candidates accepted per year	470
# candidates entering per year	350
% women students	30%
% minority students	15%
% international students	37%
# countries represented	50-60

Age (years)	
mean	28
median	27
range	23 - 41

Education pre-MBA	
Engineering	41%
Business	25%
Social Sciences	20%
Humanities	5%

Professional experience	
avg. years work experience	5

Field of work	
Consulting	33%
Financial Services	21%
Computers/Software	16%
Investment Banking	8%
E-commerce/Internet Companies	6%
Chemistry/Biotech	6%
Government/Education	5%
Others (Automative, Law, Transport, Medecine)	5%

GMAT	
average score of all students	700
median	710
range	480-800

GPA	
average	3.5

after the MBA	School total
# companies recruiting on campus	247
Main career choices	
High Tech (Biotech, Computers, E-commerce, Electronics, Telecom)	32%
Consulting	30%
Manufacturing/Technology	21%
Investment Banking	16%
Function	
Consulting	36%
Other Finance	17%
Investment Banking	12%
Marketing	12%
Business Development/Strategic Planning	10%
Operations	10%
General Management	3%
Geographical location	
North America	81%
South America	4%
Europe	7%
Asia	8%
Salary (source: school)	
avg. total compensation (at graduation)	$137,726

Top 10 employers

1. McKinsey & Co.
2. Goldman Sachs & Co.
3. Bain & Co.
4. Intel
5. Morgan Stanley Dean Witter
6. Boston Consulting Group
7. Diamond Technology Partners
8. Booz Allen & Hamilton
9. A.T. Kearny, Inc.
10. Merrill Lynch

The School	Before the MBA	After the MBA

author

Name   F. ALOISI

Second year student after internship with Bain in Milan.
Previously project manager for Alcatel and then Paribas in London.

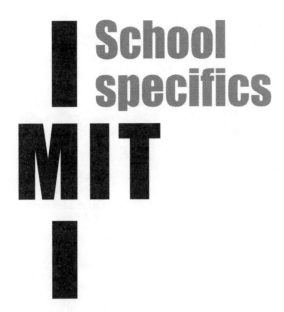

School specifics MIT

INTRODUCTION

If you want to immerse yourself in a universe of permanent innovation…
If you are ready to be exposed to cultures and approaches which are radically different…
If you want to be part of those who will create (and not just manage) the growth of tomorrow…
… then the Massachusetts Institute of Technology may be the place for you.

Today, more than ever, the Massachusetts Institute of Technology is at the forefront of innovation in general, and of information technologies in particular. Whether it be in the economic and financial sector with leading figures like Modigliani and Krugman, in the field of technology with pioneers like Negroponte, or in the scientific field, MIT is one of the most recognized universities in the world.

The alumni of Sloan, MIT's business school, are among the leaders in today's economic, industrial and political world. Counting among their ranks Carly Fiorina, who directs Hewlett Packard, the CEO of Citigroup, and the former prime minister of Israel, Sloan alumni constitute an international network which will open doors for you on all horizons, whether you're interested in business banks, venture capital, industry, consulting, or nearly any field.

As is the case for most MBAs, companies fight to recruit on campus and the simple fact of being at Sloan will systematically open doors to interviews. No more résumés sent that go unanswered. On the contrary, your answering machine will be recording messages each week from companies throughout the world who got access to your résumé and wish to meet you.

But more than that, MIT gives you solid credibility. Whether it be signing a contract with a strategic partner or raising your first round of capital, MIT gives you the unique ticket which will help in your entrepreneurial work.

You should take into account the fact that MIT is not a dream campus. The weather is not sunny all year round, the buildings are often old and outdated, and the roads are often in poor condition. The students are sometimes disappointed by the infrastructures. No sporting complex (there is one for all of MIT), no ultra-modern library, no quality IT support.

MIT's richness lies in the people who work there and their frame of mind, and not necessarily in the place itself. No marble and no chandeliers. But the generous donations recently made by former students who have become rich (Bill Porter, founder of E*TRADE, and Kenan, founder of Kenan System together donated, in the same month, over 120 million dollars to MIT) should change all that little by little.

THE DEAN'S VISION

Sloan inaugurated in 1998 Dean Richard Schmalensee, a world-renowned economist who intervened on several occasions during the Microsoft trial between October 1998 and May 1999. Dean Schmalensee contributes doubly to Sloan, bringing his talents of a visionary and his reputation as a top rate economist.

Interview with Richard Schmalensee, Dean of MIT - Sloan School of Management.

What differentiates Sloan from other MBAs?

To me, Sloan has always distinguished itself from other MBA programs through its unique position in one of the most active poles of innovation in the world: the Massachusetts Institute of Technology (of which Sloan is a part). Sloan is one of the best places to learn not only to be a leader but also to be an *innovative* leader, capable of inventing new business models, new methods of organization and new rules of the game.

How would you qualify this relationship between MIT and Sloan?

The interaction between Sloan and MIT has given rise in the past several years to an incredible number of business opportunities. Over 4000 companies throughout the world have been created by MIT alumni and each year new start-ups are born, often thanks to "50K" which contributes to interaction between Sloan and MIT. The 50K is a business plan competition organized by the Entrepreneurship Center, whose home is at Sloan, and which is open to any group of individuals including at least one student at MIT. Each year a jury selects 10 teams of finalists with a first prize of 50,000 dollars. Otherwise, there are many students at Sloan who follow Engineering or Computer Science courses as well as students at other departments who follow courses at Sloan.

What are your present projects for Sloan?

Sloan has decided to nurture the closest possible relations with the key players of the new economy. The E-Commerce Awards, whose success has been recognized the world over, bring together the major actors of the sector and put Sloan on the forefront of information technologies. In this spirit, the Sloan alumnus Bill Porter, founder of e-trade, the on-line trading site, just offered 25 million dollars for the construction of a new building. Charles Vest, president of Massachusetts Institute of Technology, has just signed a historic agreement with British prime minister Tony Blair to make MIT and Cambridge University sister schools. Cambridge is one of the high-tech poles in Great Britain, and Microsoft has concentrated its European presence there.

How open is Sloan to the international community?

Sloan is more of an international program than most other MBAs. We have students coming from over 60 countries and they represent an important percentage of the class. Sloan is proud of this diversity that stimulates exchange and helps give graduates the aptitude necessary to work internationally. Sloan benefits from a privileged position in the international community, as shown by the vitality of the MIT Club de France, run by a Sloan alumnus.

THE SCHOOL YEAR

SCHEDULE AND PROGRAM

Sloan offers one 21-month program which starts each year at the end of August. The school year is broken down into four semesters (cf. table below). All Sloan students must take a predetermined course load for the fall term (first semester). They are then free to take the courses they choose during the next three semesters. The only obligation is obtaining a minimum of 144 credits during these three semesters with a maximum of 60 credits per semester. Sloan students also have the opportunity to do a thesis (24 credits, mandatory for students who wish to obtain a Master of Science).

Below, Course schedule table for Sloan School:

	End Aug - mid Dec	Jan	Feb - May	Jun - Aug
1st year	1st term Required curriculum	IAP	2nd term Elective curriculum	Internship and/or vacation
2nd year	3rd term Elective curriculum	IAP	4th term Elective curriculum	

IAP : Independent Activity Period

The First Semester (core curriculum)

The objective of the fall semester's core curriculum, which everyone must take, is to give to all students a common base of knowledge. Some courses may be redundant for some students. Nevertheless, it allows for all students to start the curriculum at the same level.

At the beginning of the first year of the MBA, the class is divided up into 6 "cohorts" of 50 to 60 students, each of which is then sub-divided up into teams of 6 to 8 students. The administration makes certain that the teams are well varied. Nationalities are mixed, as well as professional and scholastic backgrounds. The team is an essential part of the first semester at Sloan because it will prepare the case studies and write a certain number of papers. Other than the papers, which are to be handed in by groups, Sloan invites the teams to break down the work load, which may seem somewhat heavy during the first semester. It should be noted that the first semester is the only part of the curriculum during which courses, schedules and work groups are compulsory.

The first semester starts off with a week-long orientation during which, in addition to attending to administrative formalities, students take part in different activities to help to get to know the team and to get to know more about life at Sloan, MIT and Boston in general. The newcomer's life is completely taken charge of as soon as he or she arrives. Opportunities abound for meeting second-year students, sitting in on diverse conferences and workshops, and tasting New England's famous lobster.

The courses that each Sloan MBA student must follow in the fall semester make up the core curriculum. They are the product of a permanent dialogue among the professors, the administration and the students. For this reason, they may be subject to change.; recent courses include:

- A market perspective (Economic Analysis for Business Decisions): This course looks at the basics of micro-economic analysis to be applied to decision making in a company: demand evaluation, monopoly, pricing, external forces, growth, game theories…
- A company perspective (Strategic Management): many appreciate the Strategic Management course, which is extremely useful for those who would like to go into consulting. You will study the basics of strategic analysis and apply them case by case to such companies as De Beers, Intel or American Express.
- A human perspective (Organizational Processes): Organizational Processes is a fascinating course (although it may seem overwhelming at the beginning). Its focus is an analysis of organizations and power struggles which can be generated from them. The course is paired with a field study which generally turns out to be very instructive.

Three tools, developed in three different courses, can be added to these three perspectives:

- Managerial Accounting: this course will give you all the quantitative tools you need to analyze and measure the results of a company. It is a classic course with first-rate teaching using numerous illustrative examples.
- Data, Models and Decisions: a course like you've never experienced which will introduce you to (or refresh your memory of) the basics of a large array of statistics essential to decision-making. You will come across the central limit theorem, the Monte Carlo simulations and the Poisson Distribution.
- Communication for Managers: this course will turn you into a (potential) star by giving you all the public speaking methods so you can get your message across more effectively. This class is very popular and is usually taught by professors from the Harvard Kennedy School of Government.

While the courses with more quantitative information like Economic Analysis or Data, Models & Decisions may seem old hat for those with scientific or commercial backgrounds (even though it's rare to find someone who has mastered, even after years of professional experience, the usage conditions of the central limit theorem!), they nevertheless present an opportunity to round off or to broaden your knowledge in a wide range of subjects like game theory or statistics.

Because this is the "core curriculum", you may not be excused from any of the courses, even if you feel very much at ease in one of the subjects (each year, there are many students with Ph.D.s). Take advantage of the situation to broaden your knowledge by discussing research with professors or to help your fellow students who don't share your background. Professors count on the participation of students who have specific expertise in a subject to help enrich the subject matter of the courses and make the classes more lively.

IAP: Independent Activity Period

This aspect of the MBA is unique to MIT. Every year, the month of January is consecrated to alternative courses which allow you to participate in one-month programs in the departments and subject matters of your choice. In this way, you can be introduced to new subjects (or deepen your knowledge of old ones), for example, taking a course on Java, participating in a conference cycle on biotechnology or learning how to write a business plan with a venture capitalist. But nothing stops you from using this period with no required courses for travel: for example, you may be interested in participating in the "business trip" organized by Sloan in California, which allows you to make contact with some of the stars of the West Coast, from Seattle to Silicon Valley. January is often used by students to finalize their business plans for the 50K competition (see the Entrepreneur's Corner section).

Second, Third and Fourth Semesters: The Elective Curriculum

While all MBA students at Sloan must take a required courseload for the fall semester, they are free to enroll in courses they choose during the next three semesters. However, they must obtain a minimum of 144 credits during these three semesters, which is an average of 48 credits per semester (about five courses).

Second, third and fourth semesters are slightly more relaxed. You are free to choose the courses which interest you. However, certain courses require a prerequisite, which means you must have previously taken specific courses. For example, if you want to take the Corporate Finance course, you must have taken Finance Theory during the previous semester. You can, however, bypass this obligation if you pass a short test which proves your knowledge in the field.

You can also take classes outside of Sloan ("cross registration"), whether it be in another department of MIT (many enjoy the Computer Science department's "Course VI" which includes an intensive introduction to Java, and a very popular course entitled Building and Maintaining a Professional Website). You can also take classes at the Kennedy School of Administration, Harvard Law School (you can even receive a double major in MIT Sloan/Harvard Law), and Harvard Business school. You are, however, limited to two external courses per semester. About 10% of Sloan students follow more than one class outside of Sloan.

THE COURSES - WHAT'S HOT... WHAT'S NOT

The students' expectations are very high and sometimes some individuals are disappointed by a professor whose teaching abilities do not seem to live up to his international reputation. Generally speaking, however, the classes are very well liked. (cf. poll below).

Some of the good classes at Sloan are: Finance (with internationally renowned professors like Myers, Rock or Pindyck – the specialist in Real Options), Macro-economy (Thurow, Dornbush, Rigobon and Modigliani to name but a few of the most famous), Technology Strategy and Technological Innovation (Cusumano and Henderson), Entrepreneurship (with the very popular Ken Morse and John Preston), Information Technologies (with Madnick, Malone, Brynjolfson to name but a few), Marketing (Bund, specialist in entrepreneurial marketing) and finally the must of Sloan: System Dynamics (a course which quantitatively integrates the effects of feedback into the optimization of decision-making) with Sterman. On the other hand, the lighter courses, such as Organization, Leadership and Teamwork, are less sought out.

On the opposite page are the results of a poll of recent students at MIT and their opinion of main courses. This poll should be viewed only as means of obtaining a very general idea of the popularity of MIT's courses. It does, however, reflect the excellence of the professors as well as the general satisfaction of the students.

% students	Below Expectations	In Line With Expectations	Above Expectations	Outstanding
Finance Theory	15%	45%	25%	15%
Corporate Finance	5%	25%	35%	35%
M&A Finance	5%	25%	30%	40%
Macroeconomics	20%	35%	40%	5%
Technology Strategy	15%	25%	35%	25%
Entrepreneurship Lab	35%	10%	10%	45%
New Enterprises	15%	25%	20%	40%
Entrepreneurial Marketing	35%	25%	25%	15%
Marketing	25%	25%	35%	15%
System Dynamics	5%	30%	40%	25%
Accounting	25%	50%	25%	0%
Organizational Processes	35%	40%	20%	5%
Power & Negotiation	5%	30%	40%	25%
Information Technologies	15%	45%	25%	15%

THE TEACHERS

Generally speaking, the vast majority of the professorial body at Sloan fills the double role of teaching and research, which contributes to the quality of the instruction. Last year, over 100 companies sponsored over $12 million in research at Sloan. Research is organized at Sloan by centers which bring together researchers, professors, doctors and students to conduct academic work.

The principal research centers at Sloan are:
- Center for Information Systems Research, directed by John Rockart, on the management and use of information technologies
- Finance Research Center directed by Paul Asquith and Michael Siegel, on the understanding of financial risks
- Center for Energy and Environmental Policy Research directed by Richard Schmalensee, on the understanding of energy markets and stakes
- Center for Innovation in Product Development
- Inventing the Organization of the 21st Century
- Laboratory for Financial Engineering

The professorial body on the whole is highly accessible and international figures such as Myers, Thurow or Modigliani can be reached daily. Beyond the questions which you can ask your professor, it is possible to secure a position as Teaching Assistant (TA) or Research Assistant (RA) where relations with professors can be developed. However, it is most often the case that the student must make the first step toward the professor to obtain such a position (which is, by the way, usually relatively well-paid). It is important to note that the number of positions for RA is limited and the MBA students are often in competition with the Ph.D. students (the position is quite difficult to obtain).

TEACHING METHODS

The professorial body at Sloan has adopted a mixed approach to teaching methods. Some very good courses are still in lecture format while other very good courses follow a case study format. The balance during the first semester between lectures (Data, Models & Decisions and Economic Analysis) and case study courses (Strategic Management, Organizational Processes, and Accounting to a lesser degree) is about 50/50. Throughout the second, third and fourth semesters the ratio of case study and papers (mini research) courses increases considerably (about 2/3 of your time will be spent with case studies and group research).

It is unthinkable to attend a course without having read the assigned chapters, completed the exercises and prepared the case of the day. These study habits are essential for participating in class and also for gaining as much as possible from your MBA.

Sloan has the reputation of having a very quantitative approach to education. I think that it is above all a question of point of view and of choice. Seeing as you are free to choose your courses starting second semester, you can take a Power and Negotiations course, where writing out an equation or formula is very rare, or a course like System Dynamics, or how to build and maintain a professional website where you will need to adopt a scientific method to solve different problems and participate in projects. The first semester gives you the opportunity to familiarize yourself with management's basic quantitative tools if you do not have a scientific background (Statistics, Microeconomy, Accounting). Sloan is not only for the scientific person. On the contrary, it is a meeting ground between technology and management.

THE GRADING SYSTEM

The grading system at Sloan is similar to that at most universities: 1.0=E-, 5.0=A+. Each professor is free to grade how he or she pleases. In the particular case of cross-course examinations, grades are adjusted to obtain an average and a standard deviation which are similar in all classes. The "fairness" of a test is important and consequently grading is usually generous if the corrector sees that you know your course material. A minimal effort usually obtains a C whereas a sustained and regular effort should get you a B or an A. Pass or fail is at the discretion of the professor, usually for an average below or equal to a D.

In general, a course is comprised of a mid-term exam (two months after the start of the course) and a final exam. The grade is not entirely dependant on the final exam, but on a ratio (which will vary from class to class) of the different grades obtained for participation, papers, the mid-term and the final. For example, a micro-economy course might be graded with 20% toward participation, 20% toward papers, 25% for the mid-term and 35% for the final.

Sloan still has a "disclosure policy", which means that employers can ask for the GPA (grade point average) for potential employees. A certain percentage of students feel concerned with grades and it is not rare for a student to discuss with his/her professor a grade received for an exam. But it is highly possible that in coming years the disclosure policy will be replaced by a non-disclosure policy. Finally, like most American universities, Sloan attributes honors to its best students. Students who made specific contributions to the organization of events are also rewarded by the Dean.

GROUP WORK

Group work is an integral part of the Sloan culture. The groups made up in the first semester give you the opportunity to make a first network of acquaintances and to share information and advice. The second, third and fourth semesters no longer contain such a formal organization as teams (because courses are chosen individually), but this does not mean that teamwork is no longer an important aspect of the Sloan education. It is up to the individuals to make up work groups for shared projects, for an association or for a start-up operation.

THE INTERNATIONAL SIDE

MIT is one of the most international American universities. Nearly 40% of its students are of a nationality other than American, with a majority of those being South American (Argentina, Brazil, Chile). Asians (Japan, Korea, Singapore) come in second. Europeans are slightly under-represented. This diversity is one aspect that enriches the case studies: a student who has worked in a particular company can often be found in the class which is studying that company. And generally speaking, the different approaches to a single problem can be extremely beneficial.

One very sought-after course which makes the most of the presence of many international students is International Entrepreneurship, taught by Simpson Johnson. It analyzes the opportunities for companies and entrepreneurs from an international perspective.

Sloan has many contacts with universities in other countries (notably Tsinghua University in Beijing and Cambridge University in Great Britain). Nevertheless, these exchanges more directly apply to the professors rather than give students the opportunity to spend a semester abroad.

COMPUTER FACILITIES - IT SYSTEM

Each student at Sloan is required to have a personal computer. However, Sloan makes available to students several computer rooms that offer the possibility to get a taste of fast internet connection. From your home, Sloan provides you with three hours of daily connection to internet, unless you are on campus, where you benefit from a permanent connection to the network. You also benefit from memory space on a common drive shared among your entire class (so your resources depend in part on the appetite of your fellow students). You can also host a web-site (non-commercially) on their server, web.mit.edu.

Sloan has recently made available a Virtual Campus from which you can access all information concerning classes, lectures, homework, etc, which strengthen the advantage of having internet access in your home. If you get back late Sunday night from a weekend out on the sea, a couple of clicks on Virtual Campus should keep you informed of your impending responsibilities for Monday morning. I say "should keep you informed", for the Virtual Campus has fallen pray to numerous glitches. Generally speaking, computer access at Sloan, apart from the Trading Room (see below) could use a bit of financing so as to offer somewhat more professional solutions.

But a description of computer use at Sloan would be incomplete without mentioning the Trading Room, which, in partnership with Merrill Lynch, prepares tomorrow's traders in "real-time" situations. More than twenty positions in trading (TIBCO+IPC Tradenet telephones) are synchronized with the tick-by-tick price-volume data from Reuters and Bloomberg on all financial instruments, while the Lux-Data screens post the information which comes from Wall Street. Simulations, developed with some of the largest banks (who often send their traders for training at

Sloan), allow for testing and fine-tuning of the most sophisticated pricing techniques. While the Trading Room is mainly used during numerous courses and workshops of the Sloan's Finance Track, it is in fact open 24 hours a day. Glenn Johnston, the Trading Room's manager, has some medium-term objectives for its development: "What we would love to see down the road is for our students to be able to log in and conduct trading simulations against students at other schools in real time."

THE ENTREPRENEUR'S CORNER

Entrepreneurship is becoming more and more important in the courses, life and culture of Sloan. An "entrepreneurship track" has been created to offer courses in e-commerce, marketing, and information technology, for those who wish to understand the ins and outs of the mysterious dot-com. Nearly every day you will be able to attend conferences, workshops, meetings with entrepreneurs or venture capitalists, young and old, with more or less success, but always with great experience to share. Sloan can brag about having participated in a great number of success stories. These start-ups often recruit on campus and even if you decide not to start your own company, nothing stops you from joining another start-up.

The MIT entrepreneurship center, directed by Ken Morse, is central to entrepreneurship at MIT. Ken Morse also teaches the very popular Entrepreneurship Lab, where in teams of three or four you will be put to work for one semester with one of 40 start-ups specially chosen by Ken. You will most certainly go on business trips, whether they be throughout the United States or even in Europe, working with companies who are looking to prove their concept, sell their new product or fine-tune their strategies. State of the art technologies in telecom (for example: CopperCom, Californian start-up in the voice over-DSL sector), e-commerce (for example: drugstore.com) and other sectors offer a context of behind-the-scenes developments of stimulating projects. In general, the E-lab requires a lot of free time (especially if your company is outside the Boston area). Weekends will therefore often be dedicated to it, while during the week, you will use the E-lab to organize your conference calls.

And finally, MIT would not be MIT without the 50K Club, the famous business plan competition toward which so much energy and passion is focused. Even if there are only 10 teams chosen, and three winners, there are many others who gain the attention of venture capitalists during the first-round presentations. 50K can also be the opportunity for you to get a team together around your idea or to learn about other ideas. All ten teams from last year's selection were financed. One of them, www.akamai.com, created by a Sloan student and an Applied Mathematics professor, has been particularly successful: its market value was over $1.5 billion barely a year after the results of the 50K competition, and they were able to obtain capital from Microsoft and Cisco.

LIFE AT MIT

BOSTON

Sloan is in the heart of Boston's famous Old Town, the Beacon Hill neighborhood. Just a few minutes' walk and you'll be on the bank of the Charles River, where you can sail from May to October and ice skate from January to March. You can follow the Freedom Trail, marked by a red stripe which takes you through the entire city of Boston, from Copley Square (designed in part by I.M. Pei, who conceived the Louvre Pyramids) to the Boston Common (center stage of the American Revolution), from Faneuil Hall (historic market, since renovated) to the North End (little Italy). Across from Boston is Cambridge with two university centers, MIT and Harvard. Cambridge is marked by "Mass Ave." (Massachusetts Avenue) and by the red line of the "T" (subway), which stops at the four squares: Kendall Square (MIT), Central Square, Harvard Square and Porter Square. Everything else is relatively close.

There's one last important aspect of life in Boston: its peculiar microclimate. An old saying says, "If you're not happy with the weather in Boston, wait fifteen minutes!" Which also means that if it is a beautiful morning, it may be snowing come evening time. You should also know that while it is very hot in the summer, it is very cold in the winter, and autumn and spring are both very pleasant. Autumn in New England is known for its "Indian summer", and if you are not familiar with it, it is really worth catching a glimpse of. Fall foliage is a major attraction and every year tourists come to watch the spectacle of the maple trees whose leaves go from yellow to orange to bright red and finally to brown. You can take part in "foliage trips" or go off by yourself to visit the forests of Massachusetts, Maine or upstate New York. Judicious planning is a must: hotels and bed and breakfasts may be reserved from six months up to a year in advance. Spring is also fabulous, trees' white flowers sometimes budding before the last snows have melted. But speaking of snow, don't forget that January to March is usually extremely cold and often very windy, that snow storms are a regular occurrence and for one or two days each winter, the city is literally closed down for a snow emergency; everybody just has to stay home!

HOUSING

It must be said: the hardest thing to do after getting into Sloan is finding housing at a reasonable price. The alternatives for the newcomer are on-campus housing or off-campus housing. As soon as you are accepted, Sloan will provide you with all necessary administrative information. Their goal is to give you an idea of the different types of housing available.

On-campus housing has its advantages. It's furnished, simple, less expensive (about $400 per month, all expenses included), and with a little luck, you'll have a view of the Charles River. Nevertheless, not all Sloan students are content. Some residences (especially for non-married students) are fairly isolated and far from campus. The rooms may be very small and not necessarily in the best condition. Rooms are assigned by a lottery, all information being provided before the summer of your arrival.

Off-campus housing provides the complementary advantages and disadvantages: often not furnished and expensive (expect to pay about $600 per month while sharing a two or three-bedroom apartment). On the other hand, some apartments/houses in Cambridge, Beacon Hill or Back Bay are very charming and can even be very close to campus.

SOCIAL LIFE

The social life of the typical Sloan student is organized around a weekly ritual: the Consumer-Function or C-Function which takes place on Thursday evenings. C-Functions are evenings organized by second year Sloan students, on or off campus, usually by theme, and usually very successful. These evenings are mainly sponsored, but an annual fee is required for those who would like to participate.

While evenings and nights are usually filled with readings for courses and by the different Functions, lunch time is usually consecrated to clubs. In exchange for an annual fee, you can join a club and once a week attend luncheons, discussion groups or presentations given by outside members, often of great quality (presidents of large companies, venture capitalists, financial analysts, entrepreneurs). The clubs are yet another way to meet other students, share your passions or strengthen your connections with potential employers. The major clubs are: the Media & Technology Club, the Venture Capital Club, the Management Consulting Club, the Finance Club, the Marketing Club, etc.

Almost every sport is represented and can be practiced: sailing (with the MIT Boat Club on the Charles River or in the Boston Port), football, swimming, tennis, squash, hockey. All year long sporting activities are organized among the MBA students.

TUITION COSTS

MIT is expensive and there is little financial aid. In 2001-2, it cost about $31,200 per year in tuition and fees (in some cases these fees can be tax deductible). To this you must add the exorbitant price of books and photocopies (about $700).

Total cost of the MBA (2 years)	In US $
Tuition fees	62,400
Books, supplies	3,000
Computer and software	3,000
Housing	7500 (on campus) to 25 000
TOTAL	75,900 to 93,400

Starting in second semester or more likely starting second year, you can hope to obtain a position as a Teaching Assistant (TA) or even as a Research Assistant (RA). In exchange for a number of hours agreed upon with your professor, you can receive a monthly salary and a reduction in tuition. But you mustn't depend on that to cover your costs; MIT will ask for a declaration of your resources to be able to pay for your two years at Sloan.

Finally, do not forget that the signing bonus with your post-MBA job is generally very high and often enough to pay off a year's tuition and fees all at once.

STUDENT VIEWS

The bottom line: the people at MIT Sloan are one of the best parts of the program. Invite someone to lunch, introduce yourself to a second-year student, or hang out in the lobby.

Thomas M., MBA 1999

Whether it be for opening doors in the business world, becoming immersed in entrepreneurial culture, perfecting your finance skills or discovering or widening your knowledge in IT, MIT offers everything you wish for and more.

Isabelle D., MBA 1999

An MBA, and the Sloan School MBA in particular, represents a huge investment in terms of time and money. I recommend that you think hard before leaving your job, your career and your city, as you may not necessarily need an MBA if you are already in the fast-track stream of your business.

John H., MBA 2000

The greatest strength of the Sloan School is its excellent academic curriculum. It is particularly strong in addressing the challenges posed by the globalization of the economy, and educational visits are organized to every corner of the world. The School is characterized by its quantitative approach, owing to its links with MIT, and its general spirit of cooperation and teamwork.

David V., MBA 2000

The MBA program at the MIT Sloan School of Management is unique in many respects. From its strong quantitative reputation and excellent teaching to its international flavor and charming location, MIT manages to differentiate itself effectively from the other top 10 schools. MIT is particularly special in that it is a mecca for top faculty talent.

Mark B., MBA 1999

The admissions application
MIT

INTRODUCTION

Successfully filling out an admissions application is the first step in getting accepted to MIT. A botched application, or one that is simply not taken seriously, will most likely ruin your chances. An application for Sloan includes:

- 1 Cover Letter
- 2 Letters of Recommendation
- Transcripts of your grades and diplomas
- GMAT
- 2 essays (out of 4 topics)
- Résumé

The application must be obtained and completed online (http://mitsloan.mit.edu/mba); there is no paper application. The Sloan candidate has two periods during which he can apply: end of November (response given in February) and mid-February (response given by mid-April). While it is true that there are more candidates for the second round than there are for the first, the percentage of candidates accepted in each round stays roughly the same. It is therefore not necessary to prefer one application period to another if you want to increase your chances of getting in. And no matter when you submit your application, courses will start at the end of August following the application's submission -- Sloan has only one session per year. Deferments of enrollment are not granted if you are accepted and decide not to attend. However, reapplicants have an expedited process of reapplication .

THE GMAT

The GMAT is a must and you will not escape it. Much literature is available on how to prepare for this test, so I will leave that job to the professors who can teach it to you! I personally did not sign up for courses a GMAT preparation course, but I did look at several collections of previous tests. I strongly advise against taking the GMAT without at least familiarizing yourself with the type of test and questions which will be asked. Even if the questions sometimes seem easy, there are a lot of them, and a little practice is necessary.

The average GMAT score at Sloan is fairly high (consistently over 700). But remember, this is only an average -- see the graph below for the range scores from the most recent entering class. It does not mean that you have no chance with a GMAT score of 610. I will say it over and over again: the essential key to your admissions application is to give an impression of coherence and overall strength. Don't panic if you don't reach the tip-top scores of the GMAT; no one will hold it against you! Nevertheless, it is certain that poor results can seriously handicap you; the admission board has admitted to occasionally carrying out a first level screening by eliminating applicants with low GMAT scores (less than 600). So don't hesitate to re-prepare for the test, and to retake it if necessary.

	GMAT
average	700
deviation	+/- 30
range of scores	480 to 800

A note for international applicants: Sloan does not require the TOEFL, feeling that the verbal portion of the GMAT is already a very good indicator of the level of English of the candidate.

THE ESSAYS

A FEW TIPS FOR WRITING STRONG ESSAYS

1. Apply yourself

The Sloan School of Management, as with most MBA programs, attaches considerable importance to the essays. The amount of time and attention you spend on them will be apparent to the reader. Neglected format, spelling errors or poor style will all contribute to narrowing your chances of getting in. It is absolutely essential to pay close attention to writing the essays. Unless you have a lot of free time, it is important to concentrate your efforts on a limited number of universities so you can be concentrated on a limited number of essays. There is a French proverb that roughly translates as: "He who hugs too often kisses poorly", and this applies just as well to filling out admissions applications.

The essays are all the more important for Sloan, as the school does not always offer interviews and thus the essays might be the only part of the application in which you are given the opportunity to show your personality. Furthermore, as most candidates have good GMAT scores and very complimentary letters of recommendation, it is that much more essential to stand out in these essays and to give the reader the conviction that you are an ideal candidate.

2. Be convinced to be convincing

As I have already pointed out, to create a successful application it is indispensable that you be convinced that Sloan interests you and that you are able to get in. To achieve this, it can be helpful to ask a certain number of questions:

- What will two years in Cambridge bring me? (New skills? A new network? An opportunity to change careers? Increased credibility? Access to the American work market? Knowledge of the American technological/business world? etc.)
- What are these two years in Cambridge going to cost me? (What is your "opportunity cost" to come to Sloan when you consider lost salary? What is your "opportunity cost" to come to Sloan in terms of career opportunities for your current work? What is the familial/sentimental cost of coming to Cambridge?).
- What can I bring to Sloan? (What is it about my education and professional experience that give me the specific skills and motivations which may enrich my entourage? Am I ready to share my time with others?)

I advise you to think about the overall coherence of your application. There is nothing worse than seemingly contradicting yourself when answering questions! It can be worth it to take the time to isolate yourself and write down on a piece of paper, just for you, the reasons for your choice and what you are expecting. This paper (which you can reread two years later) must be able to clarify your objectives and motivations. It is important to have a clear head when you start writing your essays.

3. Be sincere in order to be consistent

In your answers, do not focus on any preconceived notion on what Sloan expects. It seems to me that Sloan prefers candidates who are sincere and dedicated to those who create a character based on qualities that are often devoid of meaning. The worst you can do is give the impression of playing a role which is not your own. If you want to do an MBA because you want to change your career and start a new life as an entrepreneur, write it! As long as you will be able to show by way of your application that this choice is in sync with your qualities, your chances will be great. As for me, I had made information technologies and their impact on the industry my primary positioning. But this is not a must, far from it! Others were able to emphasize an entrepreneurial image (cf. a friend who organized the purchase and turnaround of a bankrupt company), an ability to adapt to diverse cultures (another friend who had studied in a foreign country and worked in a third) or expertise in the financial realm.

4. "Fun, entertaining, exciting"
The advice from the admission board can be summarized in three words "fun" (to read), "entertaining", and "exciting". Put yourself in their shoes! Over 3,000 applications on average are read by the professionals of the admission board.

5. The rules of style to follow
Once again, stay with the same page set-up: twelve-point characters, a space between non-indented paragraphs. Give as much breathing room as possible, and make sure the argumentation is clear from the first so the reader is not forced to go over the document three times before understanding your prose. Essays must not be longer than one page. The number of words/pages is not counted but try not to go beyond that for the simple reason that those are the orders. Take the time to reread and have your essays proofread a sufficient number of times to eliminate any trace of grammatical or spelling errors. Rewrite the questions. Don't hesitate to use tabs and other bullet points, which are very much appreciated, to clarify your arguments. Put your name at the bottom of each page.

WHAT MIT IS LOOKING FOR IN YOUR ESSAYS
You must write two essays (out of four essay choices). All but one of the essay topics on the MIT application were modified for admission into the 2002-2003 school year. The current essay topics are:

1. What is an important lesson that you have learned in life? How did you come to learn this lesson? How will you apply this lesson in your future career?
2. Sloan is a very diverse place with over 60 countries represented. What will you bring to this diverse community? What do you expect to gain from the environment?
3. At Sloan we view leadership as "making things happen." Tell us about a time when you made something important happen. What did you learn about yourself from this experience?
4. Describe a situation where you introduced and/or managed change in an organization. Tell us how you influenced others in an organization (business, school, extracurricular activity) and comment on the professional and/or personal attributes you used to do that and how these attributes (and others) might be important in the attainment of your career goals. How do you expect to further the development of these attributes at the MIT Sloan School of Management?

The above questions give you an excellent indication that Sloan is looking for the following:
(1) the ability to adapt, and, among other things, learn from your mistakes;
(2) the ability to undertake and organize;
(3) the ability to succeed and have an impact on one's environment.

To understand the frame of mind necessary to writing these essays, I advise you to look through the Sloan website (http://mitsloan.mit.edu). In general, the answers must be honest and simple. They must reflect your reasons for applying and their relation to your personal and professional goals. In short, there are no bad objectives ("I hope to change careers" is a perfectly valid motivation).

EXAMPLES AND COMMENTARIES OF ESSAYS FOR MIT

Below, I examine the essay topics that MIT has used in the most recent application rounds. Although you will be responding to different questions, you will find that the themes that you are asked to address bear much in common with these recent topics. Thus, for each essay, I will analyze what the admissions office is looking for and provide advice on the writing and an example of my essays or those of another recent graduate. Once again, I must stress the importance of being sincere and conistent rather than trying to fit some preconceived notion of what MIT wants. To achieve this, you must get some perspective on your professional and personal path before you begin writing.

Discuss the effect that an increasingly global economy may have on your future responsibilities as a manager, both generally and as regards your chosen field, and what you hope to learn at MIT to enable you to meet this challenge.

The point of the essay:
Evaluate your ability to integrate into your career a more global vision of the economy (have you thought about how your work in your sector will be transformed by the changes brought about by increased globalization? What are the challenges you think you will come across in your career on the dawn of third millenium?)

Tips for the essay:
This question is for those who prefer a more global and economic study than a local or technical viewpoint (see the following question). However, when answering this question, don't hesitate to take specific examples from your work experience. You can certainly use other sources of information to elaborate your points, such as examples from the current economy.

Finally, you must show how you may foresee MIT as an aid to facing these challenges. Once again, use these essays to show that you have obtained specific information concerning courses and professors at MIT.

Sample Essays

I have already had the opportunity to measure the effects of an increasing global economy through the international aspects of my current position. Most of my projects include the involvement of several multinational contractors, engineering, consultants and industries, each of them developing business operations around the world. In the future, as a manager in a multinational, I will have to coordinate several functions executed in different countries by people from different cultures. This coordination job is becoming more complex as new markets are emerging, such as the Eastern European countries and Asia.

The business environment is becoming more competitive, as accessibility to other markets is facilitated. The communication and the information flaws are improved. New technologies are transferred more rapidly, so that new products have to be developed in a shorter amount of time and innovation provides a competitive advantage. This requires the companies and their leaders to permanently adapt themselves to the changing market conditions.

In a global environment, the sizes of all economic agents are expanding, for instance through mergers and acquisitions. So, negotiation with the counterparts is getting more difficult as their negotiating power is also greater. A growing strategy has to be adopted by more and more companies.

An MBA at MIT will address these issues. It will broaden my international perspective and allow me to study and live with people who mostly originate from countries from around the world. The international dimension of MIT's community is clearly one of its main qualities. A lot of faculties participate in research abroad and teach their international experience to the students, which confirms the School's commitment to address international issues in its curriculum, like Prof. Simon Johnson in International Entreprenreunership. The School offers many internationally focused courses, such as International trade & Competition and International Management."

And last but not least, the Sloan School undoubtedly attracts one of the most diverse student bodies among the leading U.S. business schools. The opportunity to converse daily with students from diverse backgrounds and perspectives contributes significantly to the MBA experience and will help me understand different ways to approach the same problem.

Discuss your views regarding the management of technological change as a vital skill for future managers, what impact technological change has had on your chosen career field, and how study at MIT will prepare you to face these challenges.

The point of the essay:
- Evaluate your ability to integrate technological changes into your everyday work. MIT wants to be considered as a university of innovation and places a great deal of importance on having students and individuals who are capable of innovating and understanding some technological revolutions which have changed the rules of the game.
- Understand what you are looking for from MIT.

Tips for the essay:
- As you can see, a recurrent theme in the questions posed is "change management". MIT in general and Sloan in particular would like to be considered as the place of reference concerning creation and management of change. Existing "business models" are studied so as to understand how those mechanisms can be circumvented or modified, in general through the implementation of new technologies. It can therefore be stated that you will be confronted with a dynamic model at Sloan rather than with a static vision of management. This dynamic approach must be reflected in your essays.
- This question holds both a theoretical aspect (discuss your views), a practical aspect (what impact change has had on your choices) and an aspect of personal conviction (how study will prepare you to face these challenges). I advise you to treat each of these parts separately.
- Concerning form, it is a good idea to divide your response into three parts by using, for example, bullet points, which are fondly looked upon in the US. Be fairly personal right off the bat and use the first person. It will give a more personal and sincere aspect to your essay. Emphasize your ideas, your convictions, your choices and your experiences: "Through my work experience, during which I had to face innovation issues that I will describe, I have been convinced that…"
- You must remember that the reader prefers having your point of view rather than a description of your job or your titles. It is difficult for the admission boards to evaluate and compare different job titles.
- Finally, take advantage of Sloan's web site to help you understand what the courses can offer you. Be convincing, and, if one course in particular interests you, mention it. You can read a description of the different online courses at their site (*http://www.mitsloan.mit.edu/course/electives.html*). Talk about the seminar "Planning and Managing Change", explain how the course "Introduction to Managing the Innovation Process" will help you manage the process of innovation in a company.

Sample Essay
One example I had experienced of the importance of technological change is in banks. Banks seem in fact to have realized that new technologies could be a major key to their success. Over 40% of our trading floor in London was occupied by IT employees, developing software, databases and

improving telecommunications. Technological change has become an issue as important as finance itself and bankers are starting to take it into account.

Productivity and quality improvements were in the hands of those who could identify a new technology, have it accepted by the group, and implement it. This involved technological knowledge to understand and assess innovative alternatives, human and leadership skills to have the changes accepted, and day-to-day management ability to implement them.

I am convinced that an education at Sloan will give me the tools to better assess strategic and technological alternatives and to understand how strategic, technological and organizational changes can be carried out. Receiving a cutting edge competency, through classes such as Rebecca Henderson's Technology Strategy, in the analysis of business problems in general, and of technological innovation in particular, will give me an exceptional chance to understand and to face the challenges of corporate and entrepreneurial innovation strategies.

Describe a situation where you introduced and/or managed change in an organization. Tell us how you influenced others in an organization (business, school, extracurricular activity) and comment on the professional and/or personal attributes you used to do this, and how these attributes (and others) might be important to the attainment of your career goals. How do you expect the Sloan School to further the development of these attributes?

The point of the essay:
Evaluate your ability to introduce and manage change.
Understand what you expect of MIT.

Tips for the essay:
- Again, do not focus on the importance of your professional situation, rather, prepare yourself to give concrete and precise examples by emphasizing your method more than you do your responsibilities.
- If possible, coordinate your examples with the letters of recommendation, for two reasons: it convinces the reader of the truth of what is put forth; and it reinforces your argumentation for your reader by twice discussing a single theme.
- Separate in a logical way the different abilities (subject knowledge, analytical qualities, listening skills, organizational and leadership qualities) and show how they have helped you or were lacking during the implementation of this change. It can be an industrial problem which you have resolved, but, as the questions suggest, do not choose accomplishments you have carried out alone. What's important is being able to look at these situations with hindsight so as to better analyze how you were successful.
- Typical tools which are helpful (but are not absolute necessities) in "change management" are capabilities in negotiation (understand just how much your colleagues are willing to change, convince a team of the validity of your methods by identifying opinion leaders, etc), the ability to implement structures of adequate motivation, to control and to discipline, to lead, etc.

Sample Essay:
Having been at X for two years, I have the enormous advantage of being able to participate very closely in a fundamental change in the organization of the department where I work. The management has decided to switch from a traditional structure (in specialized groups) to a modern structure in multi-functional teams or "flow teams". In the old structure, the production of machines needed the implication of several different functions, each fulfilled by one group leader. The new

structure makes the multi-functional team responsible for the whole production process. It is an empowerment process of the team members who should organize themselves the activities of the autonomous team. My function as a project leader then becomes the leading function in the team.

I have to use my personality and my leadership skills, such as diplomacy, reasoning and expertise, to make things change. This has resulted in excellent customer service, reduced average delivery time (by some 10%) and lower costs.

Both changes were successful for two main reasons which I consider fundamental for the attainment of my career goals: (1) firstly, both changes involved high technical competence and needed a strong capacity of communication and common language between me and the outside scientific community; (2) secondly, changes were accepted by the final users who I always associated with the decision process. They felt ownership of the change and made all that was possible to successfully implement it.

What I retain from this experience is that I should always have clear objectives, be very motivated and work hard to reach them. It is also absolutely essential to be able to work in a team and to know how to motivate my peers or subordinates. I believe my ability to work in a team and to communicate with people, combined with my capacity to analyze issues (I always put the key issues in perspective) helped me to organize the prospecting and negotiate sponsorship with companies. MIT will directly develop my interpersonal skills, for instance through courses in Communication and Negotiation and Conflict Management. Discussions, group projects and presentations will also contribute to improving these qualities, enhanced by the renowned Sloan college environment with its emphasis on teamwork.

Managing change in organization requires increased expertise, i.e. one must consider problems from a larger perspective: the subject experience opened my mind to other business functions which were new for me. The kind of daily problems I have had to solve since then cover new fields and non-technical matters, such as business strategy, human resources management, marketing, finance and accounting. I can learn these subjects "on the job" but only in a non-structured way, with luck and over a long period of time. An MBA will supplement my work experience and intensely prepare me and expose me to other business functions also required to run a successful business.

I expect the Sloan School to help me enhance my capacity to work intensively in a team and with people of different frames of mind. So far, I have worked with people who have had the same engineering background as myself. I am attracted by Sloan's International student body and the wide range of backgrounds one can find there. For my part, I hope I will contribute actively to the enhancement of the Sloan environment.

If we had met you five years ago and then met you again today, how would we say that you have changed? Include specific examples that characterize your development.

The point of the essay:
Evaluate your ability to change, adapt, and progress. The economical environment has changed a lot over the last five years. The purpose of this question is to understand how you have repositioned yourself and adapted in this continually evolving environment.

Tips for the essay:
- Show how you have identified and overcome your weaknesses (for example, through listening skills).
- Show how you were able to set objectives and obtain them (for example, thanks to being obstinate).

- Show how you have been able to adapt and react to change (for example, although you studied industrial chemistry, you decided to change sectors for ecological reasons, to be in phase with current environmental concerns).
- You may take the opportunity here to show that although you knew how to adapt and be "flexible", your values and ethics have not changed.

Sample Essay:

From 1989 until 1992, I spent most of my holidays working in a youth center. As a staff member, I worked with people who were much older than I was at the time and was in charge of organizing holiday activities for the teenagers such as four-day hikes in the mountains, and working as a ski instructor. I was in charge of a group of ten people who were just slightly younger than me and I was often in a situation where I had to explain to my group our scheduled activities. Although shy at first, I had to improve my speeches. Today, I feel totally at ease when I have to speak publicly. Recently, I had to make a presentation to one of our major clients, in a strategic meeting where the top managers were present. I think I did it successfully. In May, I will go to Atlanta. I am confident that I will succeed.

I believe I have made a dramatic improvement in my leadership skills and my sense of responsibility in the past five years. This year, I organized the prospecting of companies to find sponsors for my end-of-study trip. During my first academic year, in the position of team leader, I conducted a study with 14 colleagues on the employment situation of engineers in my region. I learned about most of the difficulties involved in team work and how to manage teams. I have always felt comfortable working in a team and have acquired a real appreciation for working with people from different cultures, backgrounds and with different frames of mind.

Over the past five years, I have had a "strategic" thought about my career, though my goal has not changed a lot. I want to make a considerable contribution to the success of my company and be an active member of society. I feel I need to react to my environment rather that to sustain it. So far, every time I have had the opportunity to do things voluntarily, I have done so. Moreover, I have tried to create opportunities and have not hesitated in the face of challenges or change. In my second year at a top Engineering School, I was required to complete significant project work, and proposed and co-founded a new project, Central Transaction, a student stock exchange investment club.

THE LETTERS OF RECOMMENDATION

Number of letters of recommendation for MIT Sloan: 2

It is essential to understand the importance that the schools place on the letters of recommendation and to know how to take advantage of this fact when filling out an application.

GENERAL ADVICE

The admissions bureau of Sloan is not looking for an impersonal letter from a prestigious person and it is not looking for a biased listing of qualities and superlatives. A letter of recommendation should be a sincere, well-argued demonstration of your qualities.

To achieve this, choose someone who knows you personally (i.e. someone who knows your qualities) and professionally (i.e. someone who has been able to see what you have accomplished). A letter of recommendation requires time and attention. Take that into consideration when you decide who you want to ask. It is better to choose your manager who knows you well than the president of your company who has only who has only seen you twice. Take the time to explain what you need from this letter and its importance in your admission application.

It is important that the letters of recommendation correspond to the rest of your application and that they illustrate the qualities and different achievements which you have decided to concentrate on. So it's up to you to choose the right individuals! For example, you can alternate the letter of a university professor who discusses your analytical capabilities (which is important in the eyes of the Sloan admissions bureau) with someone who will explain your leadership skills (organization, innovation, etc.). A general rule is that you should not underestimate your achievements. Without being arrogant, it is important to point out your qualities and illustrate them faithfully.

THE QUESTIONS ASKED IN THE MIT LETTERS OF RECOMMENDATION:

The letters of recommendation for Sloan consist of *four* questions:

How does the candidate stand out from others in a similar capacity?
The point of the question:
To see which of your qualities are particularly noticed by your entourage. It is not so much a question of verifying that you have one of the qualities judged essential (the diversity of the students admitted to Sloan shows that there is no one acceptance profile at Sloan) as it is a question of seeing how you have taken advantage of your skills to obtain hard results.

Tips:
More specifically, it is important that the letters shed light on your personality("ability to motivate", "analytical skills", "motivation and leadership in pushing the project", etc.) which correlates with the examples then given by the person writing the letter.

Standard formulae such as "I rank X among the top 5% students I ever had" (in the case of a former professor), or "If X were available I would offer him/her a permanent position" (in the case of a former employer or client) are also appreciated.

Example:

"His capacity to listen to other actors regardless of their hierarchical positions, from the chairman to the workers, demonstrated a real sense of leadership and adaptation."

B) Which of the candidate's professional or personal characteristics would you change?
The point of this second question:

First of all to check whether or not the person who writes the letter knows you well (and therefore whether or not the first response is credible), and also to better understand your weak points and make certain they have a more complete image of you.

Tips:

This question can be more difficult. It is of course dangerous to put "he doesn't know how to work in a team!" but it can be taken badly if the person writing the response is not capable of giving at least one example of a credible weakness. It is ideal to have weaknesses which can be helped or that can somehow be considered as an advantage (too stubborn, too quick to compromise, shy, etc). It is also appropriate for there to be proof given that you are working on these weaknesses.

C) Describe a specific project that the candidate led or otherwise where he/she played an important role. What were his/her contributions? Was the project successful?
The point of this question:

To illustrate not only your qualities but also the results which you have achieved during your professional activities. The school is looking to see that you are a doer, someone able to put ideas into action and get results.

Tips:

This question must create an image which is coherent with the rest of the admission application. Your skills at taking initiative and putting your initiative to work (i.e. making an impact) will be studied closely. Do not hesitate, when requesting a letter of recommendation, to sit down with the person and select the project(s) to be illustrated in this letter. This will also be useful to him/her, who perhaps does not remember the details of a specific project quite so well as you.

Example:

Augustin was really the leader on this project by collecting relevant information, helping other more senior team members to precisely define the content, structuring in a coherent manner all the actions, and organizing an effective follow-up and reporting of results. The result was that the project was successfully implemented. Augustin's ability to work ahead of the problems has helped the company to avoid many costly difficulties.

D) What have been the candidate's key accomplishments in the past 18 months?
The point of this question:

To make the commentary of the person writing the letter relate to who you are today. Your current character profile is what interests MIT the most, and for this reason the admissions bureau wants to know the professional results you have obtained in the last 18 months.

Tips:

This question is curious because although it is appropriate for your current employer, it may seem strange to your former university professor. This question must be taken advantage of to broaden the response to the previous question, to be in conjunction with your performances as a whole. "Apart from this project, John was involved in several other tasks where his accomplishments were key".

If the person writing the letter has no ties to your current professional activities, a standard type sentence like "there is little doubt that he/she has excelled in what he/she is doing" can reasonably save you on this one.

Example:

After her studies at X, Emily joined one of the most prestigious investment banks. There is little I can say about her accomplishments there, since our contacts have become fewer. However, given the highly elastic nature of her curriculum, there is little doubt that she has excelled in what she is doing.

THE INTERVIEW

For a long time, and contrary to most other universities, Sloan required no interview. Sloan now interviews all candidates being considered for admission. The interviews are only by invitation from the admission board. However, that does not mean that, if you are in the Boston area in the month of February, you should not go by the admission office to let them know you are there, ask some questions, and even sit in on a class or two. Statistical information concerning Sloan's interview practices is not yet readily available. A little more than half of all candidates will be interviewed; the rest of the entrants bypass this stage thanks to a coherent application with motivations and goals which are in accordance with the Sloan culture.

Interviews last about 45 minutes. You will receive an invitation by e-mail to discuss topics including Sloan MBA programs, your background and work experience. Interviews are one-on-one, i.e. you will meet a single representative of the university, generally a member of the admission board, whose name will be communicated to you. Your invitation will specify a series of possible dates and places for your interview. Another possibility is to come to the campus in Cambridge. If you are not familiar with the campus and wish to meet students, it's a good opportunity to kill two birds with one stone.

Ask questions

The interview is not an interrogation. You must do what is necessary to make this a dialogue and ask questions yourself. However, do not ask questions just to impress. Do not repeat the school's brochure. Be sincere and concentrate on what has motivated you to apply to the school. If you are worried about your spouse who is going to follow you and therefore has to quit their job, say it! Last year, a candidate whose wife worked for an important law firm mentioned that he was worried about finding work for her. The director of the admission board told him of Sloan's policy to find work, when possible, for the students' spouses. The young woman now works in one of the departments at MIT.

Be a good communicator

One essential criterion by which you will be judged is your ability to communicate. Be clear and concise. With short sentences! Use the first person to communicate your own opinion. And above all, listen! If you give the impression of being a prerecorded tape, you will probably not be convincing. Answer questions in a precise manner and if you do not understand the exact meaning of a sentence, ask to have it repeated!

Be cultivated

It is of course important to have a very good knowledge of the economic environment in which you live. Regular reading of the *Financial Times* (or of the *Wall Street Journal*) can help you understand both the actors and the dynamics of the economic world. Knowing that AOL has bought TimeWarner is not enough. Sloan will require you to know the logic behind this acquisition as well as its mechanisms and the implications on the rest of the industry. Be smart!

Emphasize the qualities by which Sloan defines itself

Sloan means hard work. You must convince your interviewer that you are a hard-working person. Use examples taken from your professional experiences to prove it. Sloan also requires a lot of initiative. So you must convince your interviewer that you are a self-starter. Remember that your interviewer has most likely not read your application. So he does not know who you are! You must convince him/her that you are made for Sloan and that Sloan is made for you.

Be yourself

There's nothing worse for an interviewer than to have the impression that he/she is talking with an actor. So be relaxed, cheerful, alert. Show the interviewer that you are ready to go and that it is the good time to take a two year break in your career.

THE COVER LETTER

THE MINDSET

The first thing Sloan will ask you to do is to write a professional cover letter addressed to the admission board and which presents the main reasons why you are applying to Sloan. The cover letter is what the admission board will read first. Its purpose is to give the reader an overall view of your application as well as an impression of coherence, intelligence and motivation. I invite you to apply yourself! It is the cornerstone on which everything else in your application is built: essays, letters of recommendation, grades and your curriculum. It is in this cover letter that you will be required to make the overall application coherent, solid and attractive to the admission board.

FORMAT

One to two pages maximum, ten point characters minimum, and spaces between paragraphs that are not indented. Make the logic of your argumentation crystal clear so the reader is not forced to go over your prose three times before understanding it. Put in a subject (Re: Cover letter for Jean M.'s application to MIT Sloan School of Management), an address and a date along with the person to whom it is written (c/o: Members of the Admission Board).

CONTENTS AND EXAMPLES

Be self-confident. The cover letter is not the best place to share your failures or even your doubts. The cover letter is your "elevator speech" (a short discourse which succinctly presents the relevant aspects of your project, in the time it takes to go up the elevator to the highest floor in a skyscrape). The cover letter must tackle two important themes. It must: 1) give an idea of who you are to the committee; and 2) explain the reasons why you are applying to MIT.

1. Who you are

It is up to you to organize the text. My suggestion is to start off with your professional and academic background in a few paragraphs. Do not hesitate to emphasize what has distinguished you from others during your academic history. In sum, American admission boards generally prefer the leader in a second rate university than the someone in last place in a top school.

... In June 1991, I obtained my high school degree with highest honors from a competetive-entry magnet school. At University of X, I studied engineering and graduated magna cum laude. My undergraduate studies contributed to providing me with excellent quantitative and analytical skills. My graduation with honors demonstrates my ability to learn quickly and thoroughly.

In the same way, concentrate more on your role in a company than on an emphatic description of the company itself. Your title should come from your curriculum! Apply yourself toward emphasizing what you have learned and accomplished during your career.

Today, as a project leader at X, I am actively participating in a fundamental change in the organization of my department, whose main feature is the creation of multi-functional teams.

I spent a year in a $20m data storage company where I was given the responsibility of upgrading the production process for the launch of a new product. Effective time, cost and team management were indispensable to achieve the needed technological changes.

Do not limit yourself to your diplomas and to your work. Many other activities can be important to talk about: sports, music and social or political activities are part of the image that you wish to present to the reader.

It is undoubtedly during my sailing activities that my leadership abilities are most appreciated. As trainer in one of the foremost sailing school in Boston, I learned to share my passion with friends and other people who do not know each other before the cruise. To live on a sailboat requires not only technical knowledge of how to use wind forces, materials or weather forecast, but also leadership and interpersonal skills to manage the crew, coordinate its activities and prevent conflicts in difficult environmental conditions.

2. Reasons for applying to MIT

Next, you must explain your motivations and the reasons why you wish to be accepted to MIT. That can mean general course study offered as well as specific skill that you wish to acquire.

1) In order to treat adequately the broad and complex strategic issues that corporate level managers are facing, I have become aware that on top of my engineering studies, I need to make a success of three new challenges: acquiring deep functional knowledge in an industrial perspective, developing general management skills and learning to apply them in an international environment. Studying an MBA program at MIT will perfect these needs.

The first challenge is to acquire deep functional knowledge in an industrial perspective. Through my Engineering studies, I have already acquired an excellent level of quantitative skills and technological knowledge. I am now successfully using these skills in my job. But my career will be best supported by further developing specific areas. I choose the Sloan School principally because of its commitment to link technology and management.

The second challenge is to develop general management skills and to address cross-functional issues. I am interested in general management and business strategy because I always consider problems in a broad context, and look for long term solutions. It is essential for a general manager to consider the many different functions of the business when solving problems. Another very important aspect is to be able to anticipate future complex problems, as an experienced sailor can do with the wind directions and velocity. The Sloan MBA program studies numerous cases of different companies in different environments, showing how their competitiveness can be improved by efeectively managing decisions.

The third challenge is to apply deep functional knowledge and general management skills in an international environment. I have special interest in international management thanks to the influence of the international aspects of my current position. The Sloan renowned international focus will adequately fit my professional aspirations.

2) I believe this is an exciting time to be a student at the MIT Sloan School of Management. Technological changes have affected almost every field and created challenges and opportunities. The Sloan School is for me the best place, where technology and management intersect in a highly productive environment, and where I can get the best preparation for leadership positions in a changing business environment.

Prove your motivation by mentioning what you have done to learn about Sloan (meeting with alumni, telephone conversation with a professor, visit to the campus...)

I have gathered information through the Sloan Evenings in the city where I live. I have also had precious discussions with Mr. Gerard Pedraglio and Prof. David Znaty, two Sloan alumni. I am particularly attracted by your Strategic Information Technology course. I am also interested in the international dimensions of Management, partly due to my multicultural past: since I have had to adjust to many new cultures throughout my life, I have acquired a real appreciation for the difficulties involved in working with people with different frames of mind.

Remember that in one sense, MIT is also choosing you based not only on what you can get from Sloan but what Sloan can get from you. Your personal qualities, experience and your energy are all advantages to the eyes of the admission board, for they will contribute to what makes Sloan an attractive choice for candidates in the years to come. So take the time to mention what you think you may bring to MIT and show that you are not only coming to take. This is all the more important when we consider that MIT places a great deal of importance on exchanges among students.

I am strongly convinced that the diversity of my accomplishments -- considerable foreign experience, especially though my current work, extensive experience with sailing,, and my engineering studies -- will enable me to enrich the classroom discussions and the student life as much as it will enable me to benefit from others. I am sure that following your MBA program will be a very relevant and valuable experience for me. I hope you will give me the opportunity to be a member of your international student body and to contribute actively to it.

INTERVIEW WITH THE ADMISSIONS DIRECTOR

Interview with Rod Garcia, Admissions Director at MIT

Who reads the application forms?
The applications are read only by the professionals of the admission board (no former students).

What is the decision process?
A single admission officer makes a first selection so as to eliminate candidates who are either whimsical or too weak (not enough career experience, etc.) The candidates who we decide we may accept then go to the validation committee, which decides, case by case, whether or not to accept an candidate.

What are the criteria of evaluation of good candidate?
The selection committee is above all looking for candidates who are "good in their class". MIT prefers candidates who have excelled in small business rather than those who have a mediocre history in a Fortune 500 company. The board is more concerned with professional performances of the candidates (notably through letters of recommendation) than the value of their diplomas or the prestige of their company. While 60% of the accepted candidates have a "square" curriculum (i.e. an excellent university background and solid work experience in a big company), 40% of those accepted have a profile which is off the beaten path.

How important is the GMAT?
There is no official minimum but the GMAT is an important key to the pre-selection. It mustn't be forgotten that the median GMAT score at MIT is currently 710.

What are the "do's" and "don'ts" for the essays?
The essays must be agreeable and well-written. They must make the reader curious. On the other hand, the admission board is wary of botched jobs or essays which seem excessively prepared, where the personality of the candidate does not show through.

How important is it to respect the word limits for the essays?
There is no systematic counting of how long the essays should be, but the limits are given so that they will be respected.

What are the do's and don't's for letter of recommendation?
The letters of recommendation must explain the motivations for your application. The admission board must be able to understand, through reading the letter of recommendation, the reasons why you want to do an MBA. To do so, the candidate must sit down with the person who is writing the letter to explain the frame of mind of the letter. It is essential that the letters of recommendation be enthusiastic.

What is the function of the interview in the selection process?
The role of the interviews is to know more about the goals of the candidates. The candidate must prove to a member of the admission board who has not read their application that Sloan is made for them and

that they are made for Sloan. I recommend that candidates come relaxed and show that they have what it takes to come here: 1) that they are hard-working, and 2) that they are self-starters.

Is there a "rolling" admission cycle or "rounds" of admission?

Historically, 40% of candidates apply in November and 60% in February. The applications are evaluated in a comparative way and responses are sent in two blocks one to two months after each deadline. The acceptance rate is very similar (10%) for each round. It is therefore not necessary to try, at any cost, to apply in November.

What does the school particularly expect from international students?

The admission board expects a motivated, coherent and complete application. The candidate must give off an aura of success and prove that he/she has been able to contribute to his/her environment and create an impact.

Getting the NYU Admissions Edge

| The School | Before the MBA | After the MBA |

NYU
Stern School of Business

Address	Leonard N. Stern School of Business Henry Kaufman Management Center 44 West Fourth Street New-York NY 10012 USA
Telephone	(1) 212-998-0100
Website	www.stern.nyu.edu
E-mail	sternmba@stern.nyu.edu

about the school

Founded	1900
Tuition Fees	$28,685
Some Famous Alumni	Alan Greenspan (President US Federal Reserve); Richard Fuld (President, Lehman Bros); Kenneth Langore (Founder, The Home Depot)

the application

Application File	By mail or downloadable from website
Application Dossier inteviews)	December 1 (consideration for scholarhsips or off-site January 15 March 15
App. File Elements	• 3 essays • 2 letters of recommendation • transcripts • GMAT(and TOEFL, if applicable) • résumé

rankings

Publication	Business Week						US News & World						Financial Times		
General Ranking	90	92	94	96	98	00	94	96	98	99	00	01	99	00	01
	17	**15**	**16**	**14**	**13**	**13**	**17**	**13**	**14**	**13**	**14**	**12**	**17**	**13**	**10**

before the MBA

# applicants per year	4,039
# applicants entering per year	435
% women students	38%
% international students	33%
# countries represented	over 50

Age (years)

average	27.5
range	25 - 36

Education pre-MBA

Social Sciences & Humanities	39%
Engineering	29%
Business	32%

Professional experience

avg. years work experience	4.7

Field of work

Investment Banking	15%
Consulting	13%
Financial Services	11%
Commercial Banking	5%
Other	56%

GMAT

average	689
range	640-740

GPA

average	3.4
range	2.6 - 4.0

after the MBA

	School total
Main career choices	
Consulting	17%
Financial Services	8%
Investment Banking	37%
High-tech	4%
Media and Internet	6%
Other	28%
Function	
Consulting	14%
Investment Banking	29%
Other Finance	20%
Marketing	14%
Business Development/Strategic Planning	6%
General Management	3%
Others	14%
Geographical location	
North America	83%
Central and South America	1%
Europe	10%
Asia	6%
Salary (source: Financial Times)	
Avg. salary three years after graduation	$127,255
Alumni	
# alumni in the world (MBA)	over 50 000

Top 10 employers

1. Lehman Brothers
2. J.P. Morgan
3. Chase Manhattan
4. Deutsche Bank
5. McKinsey & Co.
6. Salomon Smith Barney
7. American Express
8. Bear Sterns
9. Goldman Sachs
10. Merrill Lynch

author

Name   P. SOMMELET

Investment banker with Merrill Lynch in London and Paris.
Previously with CCF Capital Markets in Paris.

School specifics

NYU

INTRODUCTION

The New York University business school has changed a lot over the last ten years. In the spirit of the city it is home to, it has adapted to the increasing globalization of the modern business world, the appearance of new technologies, and increased competition. From its beginning, NYU-Stern has been the business school of Wall Street, and was even located near Wall Street in downtown New York until the early nineties, which helps to explains its renown in the New York financial scene. Following a donation in 1988 from a former student, Leonard Stern, the administration built a brand new high-rise on Washington Square, in the heart of Manhattan's student neighborhood.

Today, under the new leadership of Dean Daly, NYU-Stern has climbed once again to the level of the other top international business schools. It's not hard to find reasons for studying at NYU-Stern:

- Its excellence in Finance: NYU-Stern has some of the best finance professors in the world. They are remarkable as much for their innovative teaching as for the relevance of their research work.
- Unique connections and opportunities throughout your studies to meet people at leading companies in their respective fields, including investment banks, consulting firms and other movers and shakers at the headquarters of major American companies based in New York.
- The atmosphere that defines the heart and soul of Manhattan is one of the most attractive

imaginable. In particular, it is home to Silicon Alley (the second highest concentration internet start-ups in the US after Silicon Valley); it is one of the world's centers for artistic creation; and its unequalled cultural diversity makes it a real melting pot of present-day life. The list of cultural attractions is endless.

- The constant modernization of the school will soon offer students a greatly enlarged and renovated high-rise, increasing space allocated for team projects.

THE DEAN'S VISION

Interview with Georges Daly, Dean of NYU-Stern School of Business.

How do you picture the school five years from today? What is your vision?
We have directed our energies and resources toward several major goals:

- Aggressively recruiting the best students and faculty.
- Expanding the frontiers of knowledge and keeping Stern's academic programs on the cutting edge.
- Dramatically increasing job opportunities for our graduates.
- Expanding and improving our facilities.

What are the most important projects you have for the school?
A $10 million gift from Henry Kaufman, Chairman of the Stern School's Board of Overseers, is underwriting a major expansion and upgrading of Stern's facilities. New and renovated space will be used almost exclusively to improve the quality of student life and will house a student lounge, a study and meeting areas.
Stern's classrooms and facilities are being equipped with the latest technological support, providing students with access to the cutting edge tools they will be using in the business world. Student services have also been enhanced through technology - course registration, grade reporting class rosters and other administrative services are now available through the World Wide Web, along with all class syllabi and teaching materials.
Furthermore, we are currently involved in the construction of a student dormitory located on 14th Street in Greenwich Village, a five-minute walk from Stern. This new building will provide housing for 120 MBA students, as well as athletic facilities, study areas and conference centers. Efforts to locate additional proximate graduate residential space are ongoing.

I have heard that you plan to redesign the MBA full-time curriculum. Can you tell me about the new curriculum? Why did you decide to change the current curriculum? What is the frequency of change of MBA curriculum?
The MBA curriculum was redesigned not because there was anything wrong with the existing program, but because we wanted to make it even better. Overall design changes were made to

create a program that was more "modular", that allowed for greater integration between courses and areas, and to incorporate a more global perspective. One specific change, for example, was to move the Strategy course, which was offered in the second year of the program, to the first semester. This change will enable students to develop a stronger strategic foundation earlier in the program and build a stronger foundation for many elective courses. By design, the new curriculum will also allow students to take courses in functional areas - Finance, Marketing, Operations Management - earlier in the program. We believe that we must continuously review all programs in our curriculum and make changes whenever needed.

What is your current focus, if any, in terms of career counseling and recruitment? What is your goal and how do you plan to reach it?
We emphasize career development and support students' goals in every way we can. Strong academic preparation, exposure to experts in various fields, intensive career counseling and interview workshops help graduate students refine their professional focus.

As a result, the number and the quality of companies recruiting on campus have increased substantially. Moreover, companies that previously came to Stern to recruit for one function are now interviewing undergraduates and MBAs for several of their divisions. In addition, new entrepreneurial companies, including Silicon Alley firms and other multimedia, Internet marketing, and software design companies are actively seeking to hire Stern graduates.

THE SCHOOL YEAR

The school year at NYU-Stern consists of two programs: the full-time MBA and the part-time MBA. The following presentation principally concerns the full-time MBA program.

The full-time MBA program is made up of slightly more than 400 students in each year's entering class; the term begins at the beginning of September. From the beginning, the full-time program's 400 students are divided into six "blocks" of about 65 students each. The division of the students by block is done by the administration which skilfully mixes nationalities, pre-MBA experiences and professional objectives to guarantee the socio-cultural diversity in each block. While these blocks remain throughout the 18 months of the MBA, their importance is seen primarily during the first semester.

NYU-Stern has adopted a four-day week for courses, from Monday to Thursday. But not so fast with the champagne, because over the first semester Fridays are often completely taken up with preparation seminars for interviews. These seminars run at an extremely high level, although they can sometimes be a little repetitive, and I urge you to follow them assiduously. Over the second semester, Fridays are often used for preparing the Integrated Strategy Exercise, which I'll explain later.

The courses themselves start after a pre-term orientation week. This week enables everyone to meet each other and to get into the swing of things with a few MBA-type exercises. The highlight of this week is a cruise around Manhattan organized for the new entering class.

THE CURRICULUM

NYU-Stern's curriculum was entirely overhauled in September 1991. Here's the schedule:

The first semester

	1st year		2nd year	
	1st term	2nd term	3rd term	4th term
	end Aug – mid Dec	mid Jan – early May	early Sept – mid Dec	mid Jan – mid May
Core Courses	Business Strategy Analysis	Business Environment	Ethics	
	Managing Organizations	Corporate Strategy		
	Understanding Fims & Markets	Integrated Strategy Exercice (ISE)		
Foundation Courses	Data Analysis Accounting			
Breadth Courses	Marketing Foundations of Finance Operations (1 to choose out of 3)	Marketing Foundations of Finance Operations (2 to choose out of 3)		
Electives		2 classes to choose	4 classes to choose	5 classes to choose

The first semester begins with an Integrated Module that is spread out over the entire first year. The goal is to give students a multifunctional vision and training for taking on the responsibilities of being a managing director or manager. It includes the following academic elements:
- Business Strategy Analysis: how a company establishes a competitive advantage.
- Managing Organization: how companies are organized, structured and managed.
- Understanding Firms & Markets: case studies of companies taken from recent news.

After the Integrated Module come the Foundations courses, which present the technical knowledge that you'll need to use both in the MBA program and throughout your career (your "toolbox"). Lastly, there are the Breadth courses, which apply information from Foundations courses to business situations (Finance, Marketing). You can take them either in the first or second semester of your first year.

You will take the Integrated Module, the Foundation courses and some Breadth courses at the same time during the first semester. Some Foundation courses are designed in such a way so that you can very quickly use them in the Breadth courses (so you'll immediately be using material from the

Data Analysis course in Finance).

During this semester, nearly all the courses are required, with the aim of leveling the playing field for all students. You will have the possibility of being exempt from the first year Foundation or Breadth courses if you can justify having had equivalent training before the MBA. Nevertheless, waiving these courses is a double edged sword: it enables you to take more electives sooner, but it gives you a heavier workload at the start of your MBA. In general, students rarely waive the core courses. They want to be able to get the best grades when it comes to the internship interviews, so they don't think twice about taking a course again even if it corresponds to their previous training. While the Foundations and Breadth courses are conducted in a very academic manner (continuous assessment, exams), they are useful in getting you to focus on the basics. In addition, they present valuable "getting to know you" opportunities.

The workload during the first semester is heavier than in any other in the MBA program, and the majority of your weekends will be devoted to schoolwork.

The second semester

Over the course of this semester, you complete the integrated module:

- Business Environment: essentially a macroeconomics course.
- Corporate Strategy: you will study how companies choose their activities and how they accomplish them; a course particularly suited for understanding multinationals and conglomerates.
- Integrated Strategy Exercise: formerly called MET (Multidisciplinary Exercise in Team-Building), to be discussed in detail below.

You take the Breadth courses that you didn't take over first semester. You will be able to take elective courses. The electives allow you to personalize your MBA by choosing a major and, if you wish, a minor. The word "major" in a given field doesn't really have any bearing on the value of your MBA, but sometimes gives you priority in registration for some very popular courses. Of the two elective courses you must choose, the school strongly advises you to choose Corporate Finance, which is absolutely fundamental. So try to fit it into your schedule as soon as possible.

The second semester workload is a little lighter than that in the first in terms of coursework, but it is considerably weighed down by the process of hunting for an internship, something which will take a lot of your time in January and February.

The third and fourth semesters

The workload during the third and fourth semesters remains very significant, but will be more in line with your particular interests and goals. These two semesters are principally geared to electives. So you are almost entirely responsible for the academic content of your MBA, and it's great!

Courses at other schools

As early as the second semester, you can take courses at one of New York University's other schools such as the Wagner School of Public Administration, the Law School, and The Real Estate Institute. Personally, I recommend you take certain courses offered by the NYU Law School, which are particularly reputable in Commercial Law.

The Integrated Strategy Exercise

One last point on the courses: the Integrated Strategy Exercise. Previously called MET (Multi-disciplinary Exercise in Team-Building), this exercise takes place at the end of the first year at NYU-Stern. Its goal is to get you to work in groups of six on a strategy theme concerning a real life company. The theme is the same for everybody, and it is mandatory. It is a competition, though the atmosphere remains very relaxed. Over the past three years, the themes have been:

- The strategy employed by the American pharmaceutical group Merck in facing the results of the company's acquisition of the treatment management company Medco.
- The strategy of Southwest Airlines, in particular its search for new domestic and international markets.
- The strategy of the New York-based bookstore Barnes & Noble, its entry into electronic business, thanks to Barnes & Noble.com, and its sparring match with Amazon.

This exercise is punctuated with several training presentations during which professors and second year MBA students give you advice on the content and shape of your work. All this is accomplished in a fairly relaxed atmosphere where the school seeks to produce very constructive contrasts and comparisons of ideas.

In the end, the final presentation takes place before a panel of about fifteen or so people made up of professionals and professors. It's much more formal than the exercises and attempts to simulate a global strategy presentation to the board of the company in question. Up to that point, this all seems very familiar territory for an MBA-type exercise. But the Integrated Strategy Exercise comes into its own when the school invites the management of the company concerned to the final presentation and when its members are invited to comment on and to assess the proposed strategies. This has sometimes meant job offers for the best teams.

Honorary prizes are awarded to the winning teams during a gala event for all the first year students, professors, administration and the company's management. This gala takes place the evening of the final presentation in a very lively atmosphere.

The part-time program

NYU-Stern's part-time program has the advantage of being geographically situated in the heart of Manhattan, in close proximity to the headquarters of many companies. Therefore there are many middle managers who do a four-year long program with the same core courses and electives as the full-time program, but spread out over a longer time period.

In general, part-time students take their courses from Mondays to Thursdays between five and ten p.m. Part-time and full-time students never share the same Foundations and Breadth courses, but occasionally share the same electives. For full-time students, taking a course open also to part-time students has advantages and disadvantages: advantages because mixing with part-time students can enable full-time students to generate contacts in companies; disadvantages because full-time students have very busy schedules and can very often only plan group work team meetings in very tight time frames. In that case, full-time students have no other choice but to be flexible.

The exchange between full-time and part-time students is often very productive in the courses they take together. For example, while doing a study on the influence of the internet on the strategy of investment bank Donaldson, Lufkin & Jenrrette, our work was greatly facilitated by the fact that a member of the group worked there part-time. On the other hand, for everything related to campus life, interaction with part-time students is very limited, and sometimes even non-existent.

THE COURSES – WHAT'S HOT... WHAT'S NOT

The table below shows the overall perceptions of courses by some recent students at NYU-Stern. This survey is not exhaustive, and there are a few possible causes for distortion. For example, in 1999, the year this survey was conducted, the Business Strategy course was received particularly poorly by students. Due to their pressure, the administration completely revised it, split it in two (Business Strategy and Corporate Strategy) and placed it at the beginning of the curriculum. It is therefore probable that this course is now better received.

Another factor likely to distort the data is the professor who gives each class. I took into account the range of the professors assigned to each course. For some, it wasn't possible: the Corporate Finance course is taught by Aswath Damodaran for 75% of students, and the very positive evaluations are a result of his teaching.

There are so many electives that it would be impossible to provide an assessment of each one of them. Those selected in the table are probably the most indispensable for your MBA.

	Below Expectations	In line with expectations	Above Expectations	Outstanding
Integrated Module, Foundation or Breadth Courses				
Business Strategy	55%	25%	20%	0%
Managing Organizations	25%	40%	25%	10%
Data Analysis	5%	20%	30%	45%
Accounting	15%	60%	25%	0%
Marketing	40%	40%	20%	0%
Foundation of Finance	10%	40%	40%	10%
Operations	15%	20%	40%	25%
Elective Courses				
Ethics	25%	50%	15%	10%
Corporate Finance	0%	0%	20%	80%
Equity Instruments	10%	20%	50%	20%
Debt Instruments	5%	20%	25%	50%
Futures & Options	15%	30%	40%	15%
Mergers & Acquisitions	10%	30%	40%	20%
Negotiations	10%	35%	45%	10%
Competitive Analysis	0%	20%	70%	10%
Competitive Marketing Strategy	0%	5%	20%	75%
E-commerce	20%	50%	30%	0%
Macro-economy	20%	25%	30%	25%
Entrepreneurship	35%	40%	25%	0%

Two points emerge from this data:

- Firstly, the electives are generally more popular than the required courses. No surprises there, given that the students choose subjects that are relevant to them. Moreover, the best professors are often specialists in their field, and they develop electives in own way, making them more interesting.

- Secondly, the Finance courses are generally well-received by students. In the other subjects, high quality courses also exist (for example, Competitive Marketing), but on the whole the quality of the courses is more uneven.

TEACHING METHODS

The teaching methods are generally a mixture of lectures, case studies and team projects. The teaching methods used, and in what proportion, vary according to the type of course. In the previous table, I have charted the various teaching methods. I separated the Foundations and Breadth courses and three types of electives to better help you see how the pedagogy is organized:

Time distribution by teaching method and class type	Foundation & Breadth Courses	Electives I Corporate Finance, Equity Valuation, Economics, Accounting	Electives II Marketing, Management, Operation, Communication	Electives III Other finance courses, statistics courses
Lectures	40%	50%	30%	60%
Case studies	40%	25%	30%	20%
Team projects	20%	25%	40%	20%

The Lectures

Lectures are generally held in rooms accommodating 60 students and last 1 hour and 20 minutes; very popular courses like Corporate Finance and Competitive Marketing require the use of larger rooms (180 people). Student participation is encouraged, though it's not usually graded.

The Case Studies

They take place in rooms holding a maximum of 60 students and last 1 hour 20 minutes. The cases are presented by a team of students. This doesn't mean that you're let off the hook from working on them, because your participation during the lecture is graded by the professor. This grade is based on the relevance of your questions and replies and can be raised with a brief written summary.

The Team Projects

These take place in rooms of 30 to 60 students, depending on the type of project. There are two kinds:

- A case study on which you're asked to do an oral presentation. The team project differs from the case study mentioned above by the fact that it demands more work and more preparation over a longer period.
- A strategic study for which you yourself must collect the data. For example, in the Business Strategy course, we were asked to select from a particular industry a very successful company and also a struggling company. Then, through a thorough and detailed study of the two companies' strategies, we pinpointed what best explained their differences in performance. This study was then used for a presentation and a written report.

How is all that organized?

Two course structures are most common, depending on the professor:

- Traditionally, the courses are made up of two weekly sessions. One is devoted to the explanation of a theory and the other to its application through a case study. This case is presented by a team and is worked on by the class as a whole, which asks questions and replies to those of the professor and the case study's presenting team.
- More recently, some profesors have developed a different structure. The first third of the semester is devoted to the presentation of the theory, the last two thirds are given over to application exercises (team projects and case studies).

Examples

Here's how three courses at NYU-Stern were organized:

THE GRADING SYSTEM

The Grade Point Average is calculated to express your overall performance. For each course you can receive grades ranging from A to C, where A corresponds to a maximum GPA level of 4.0; A- corresponds to 3.7; B+ to 3.3; B to 3.0; B- to 2.7, and so forth.

Three parts make up the final grades:

	Corporate Finance (Aswath Damodaran)	Competitive Marketing (John Czepiel and Avijit Ghosh)	Negotiation (Dale Zand)
Lecture	Throughout the term	During the first third of the term	Throughout the term
Case study	A fairly lengthy case study covering all aspects of capital budgeting. Will take up an entire weekend.	Two cases per week throughout the term, preparing for presentation and discussion session. A report to submit for each case study covered.	2 case studies per semester.
Team project	A team of 5 students chooses 5 companies from the same sector of activity and conducts a comparative analysis of their financial states. A written report is handed in.	A case to be presented as a team of 5 for 20 minutes followed by 10 minutes of questions. The follow-up for the session is devoted to a discussion involving other students. In the last 10 minutes the professor wraps up the case.	Negotiation simulations in each class + a full day session (a Saturday) simulating a real negotiation in near real-life conditions. The teams are made up of 2 to 4 people.
Tests and grades	Three 30 minute quizes (10% each) and a final exam of 1.5 hours (40%). Grading: case (10%) and group project (20%).	No test. Grading based entirely on the cases (40%) and the team project (60%).	1 final exam (60%) and grading of the two case studies (20% each). The simulation sessions aren't really graded so as to encourage risk taking.

- Written exams (mid-terms and finals)
- The cases, including your oral participation and sometimes written reports on a specific theme are graded (for example, following the Dell presentation, identify the sources of Dell's competitive advantage)

- Team projects are then used for an oral presentation and a written report.

The weight of each element depends on the course. This flexible system seemed to me to be perfectly adapted to the diversity of the subjects taught.

The grading process is done in two stages: first a grade is given based on the quality of your answers relative to a preestablished grading scale. Then, all the grades are combined and ranked in order to get a total A, B or C grade. For example, in Finance only the top 20% get As, the next-best 60% get Bs and the remaining 20% get Cs. On the whole this system often produces extremely high averages, but they have only a limited relative value. What counts is the grade expressed as A or B and hence the GPA.

Recruitment officers know all about this since they often ask students for their GPA in interviews. A GPA of 4.0 means that the student got straight As every time and so, whatever happened, he was among the top 20% in every course he took. Don't worry - even the most prestigious companies don't exclusively recruit applicants with 4.0 GPAs!

Alas, the fact that recruitment officers may ask for your grades all too often creates over-competitiveness in the first semester. As I have already stressed, it's not unusual to see accountants taking accounting courses with the sole aim of getting top grades so they can show them off to recruitment officers. This kind of thing sorts itself out over the following semesters because the electives are new for the great majority of students.

GROUP WORK

Nearly all the courses require teamwork for presentations or case studies. Constructive teamwork was for me one of the main things to learn from the MBA. It requires a degree of selflessness and personal investment to reach tangible results at the end. On the other hand, it substantially increases each person's efforts to arrive at a finished product representing the combined team effort, which surpasses any individual efforts. In most of NYU-Stern's electives, the percentage of the grade devoted to team work is over 30% and often approaches 50 or even 60%. So there's no point in hoping to get good results if you don't make the effort needed for efficient teamwork.

THE TEACHERS

What most strikes you about the teachers is their availability to the students. Most have access to their home e-mail, so you can reach them easily 24 hours a day, 7 days a week. For example, one weekend before a quiz, Aswath Damodaran received 135 e-mails (at his home) asking him various questions on Corporate Finance. He had personally answered each in the space of three hours.

Let's take a look at the most famous NYU-Stern professors:
- Aswath Damodaran teaches the Corporate Finance and the Equity Valuation courses: his classes are well-liked by both students and New York investment banks. The Corporate Finance course is truly exceptional, but will consume a large amount of your time over the second semester. Everybody agrees, there are few courses where you'll learn as much.
- The Competitive Marketing class taught by John Czepiel and Avijit Ghosh is equally a must. This class is as much based on strategy as on marketing and will work you silly on a team oral presentation.

- In the Management department, I would advise you to take Dale Zand's courses on Negotiation or Richard Friedman's on the study of organizations. The Competitive Advantage class taught by professor Massad is also exceptional.
- In the Finance department, the sky's the limit in terms of choice, as long as you don't go past the 18-credit limit per department. Take Matthew Richardson's Debt Instruments course, David Yermack's Restructuring course, Marti Subramanhyam's Futures and Options course, and Roy Smith's and Ingo Walter's Global Banking course.
- Nouriel Roubini's Micro-Economy course is really phenomenal because Professor Rubini manages to make micro-economics as exciting as a thriller. (At this writing, it is unclear whether Professor Roubini has returned to Washington or joined the President's economic staff.)

THE INTERNATIONAL SIDE

Due to its location in the heart of New York City, NYU-Stern has an MBA program that benefits from very diverse socio-cultural influences. With 33% of the student body coming from countries other than America, the school is one of the most international in the States and you can take advantage of this diversity among the faculty as well as the students to make connections with people in every corner of the world.

NYU-Stern has also developed a number of partnerships that will enable you to spend a semester at other business schools. In Europe, there are the partnerships with the London Business School, HEC-ISA in France, the Rotterdam Business School, Bocconi in Milan and ESADE in Barcelona. So there's no shortage of overseas opportunities.

On the other hand, NYU-Stern could do with improvement in the following areas:
- The school uses few cases based on non-American companies. That also goes for the Integrated Strategy Exercise subjects.
- The school must develop its notoriety among European applicants: their proportion is relatively weak compared to the proportion of Asian or South American students.

COMPUTER FACILITIES – IT SYSTEM

Although the school doesn't require you own a laptop computer, it's very strongly advised and the majority of students purchase one. The school has several computer labs with a total of 200 PCs connected to the NYU-Stern network. Laptop owners can easily reconfigure their system to gain access to the network through connection points available just about everywhere on the campus. But if you don't have a laptop, or don't want to always lug it around with you, the school can loan you one when you reserve a room for a group meeting.

In addition to the computer labs, NYU-Stern offers:
- a personalized computer account which includes: a life-long e-mail address, access to the school's database for research and data storage, and web-site hosting for student homepages.
- all Microsoft applications as well as specialized applications (mainly for the Statistics and Finance courses).
- access to laser printers.
- about twenty or so Bloomberg services (real-time financial information data) situated in the various study rooms and computer labs in the school.

All of NYU-Stern's classrooms are equipped with PCs connected to a projector system as well as with audiovisual equipment. Outside class time, access to these rooms is open, which will enable you to practice the presentations you'll be preparing in similar conditions as in the professional world.

All the school's administrative information is located on its website. You'll be able to use it to choose your courses, consult your grades, peruse résumés and student evaluations of each individual faculty member, and even to participate in selecting candidates for interviews in the recruitment process. The school has also made all students' CVs available with several sorting and filtering criteria, enabling employers to gain quick access to the applicants they are interested in.

THE ENTREPRENEUR'S CORNER

New York is, after Silicon Valley in California, one of the most dynamic places to set up an internet company. Silicon Alley (the name given to the high-tech multimedia sector in Manhattan) draws teeming swarms of start-ups. NYU-Stern is solidly up there with the elite players right in the middle of this vibrant scene by offering quality electives and through its links with Silicon Alley.

The Electives
The electives for entrepreneurs are in the Entrepreneurial Studies and Information Systems departments. To name just a few of the best, there's Electronic Commerce, Venture Capital Financing, and Entrepreneurial Finance.

Interaction with Silicon Alley
This is one of NYU-Stern's greatest strengths, and this sector is evolving so rapidly that this interaction will have a completely new face by the time you get to NYU-Stern. The school is well-represented by alumni who have set up their own businesses in this area (Concrete Media and also KnitMedia), which presents a tremendous opportunity for students. Just a few of the hi-tech and I.T. companies who've hired NYU-Stern graduates are About.com, InterWorld, Intervu and Nickelodeon Online.

In addition, some specific initiatives to encourage links between NYU-Stern and this area include:
- Annual lectures organized by the school's Technology and New Media Group (TANG) and the annual Entrepreneurial Exchange lectures are opportunities to meet Silicon Alley's bigwigs, a way of testing new start-up ideas, and a first exposure to the venture capitalists who finance new businesses.
- A series of cocktail parties called "Mixer in the Alley" organized by TANG means important meetings not only for students, but also for the managers of these young companies located a few blocks away from the school.
- The Berkeley Center for Entrepreneurial Studies organizes several events including three business plan competitions (one of which is intra-NYU-Stern), Brown Bag Lunches (informal lunches for talking with entrepreneurs) and the Entrepreneurial Training Retreat (three intensive days with professors, entrepreneurs and students devoted to studying business creation projects).
- Opportunities to participate in several events organized for big names in e-business, such as a recent visit by Bill Gates to meet with MBA students in New York (co-sponsored by the Columbia University Business School), and sponsorship of lectures by Sprint and Deutsche Telekom/France Telecom executives.

LIFE AT NYU-STERN

NEW YORK

New York is a fabulous city. You will love living in the heart of Manhattan and will very quickly get your bearings in NYU-Stern's neighborhood located among Greenwich Village, Soho and the East Village. These neighborhoods are bustling with life, night and day.

Recently, New York has become one of the safest cities in the States and you go pretty much anywhere without much risk. What strikes you most living in New York is the diversity of the neighborhoods and their inhabitants. How is it possible for so many different people to live together in such a small space? The result is dynamite! You can go from a poverty stricken area to one of the most exciting centers of American economic power, or to the international art gallery mecca - all just by going from one street to the next. There really is something for everybody and even two years won't be enough to uncover New York's many hidden faces.

Though your lifestyle will inevitably be very urban, don't go away thinking that getting out of the city is difficult. In winter, ski slopes in the Catskills are just an hour and a half away, and in summer, the most fashionable Long Island beaches are just two hours away.

Lastly, you will benefit from the cultural richness: jazz bands and world music, exhibits at MoMA (Museum of Modern Art) and the Met (Metropolitan Museum of Art), concerts at Carnegie Hall, street performers and more. Pursuing an MBA in New York is a stellar opportunity to live in New York, and the city will make your experience in business school that much more memorable.

SOCIAL LIFE

Unlike many other schools, NYU-Stern is situated in the center of a city and the limits of the campus are not very clearly defined. Though student life isn't really affected by this, the lives of students' spouses are greatly affected. Without a common meeting place, they can find themselves very isolated from one another.

NYU-Stern has many clubs that bring together students with common interests or ethnic origins. It would be tiresome to list the names all these clubs, but it's worth knowing that if you don't find a club representing your personal interests, the school will enthusiastically welcome your plans to set one up. These clubs have many purposes: to organize lectures for students and professionals based on specific themes (including a field trip to Silicon Valley over spring break); to help first-year students obtain interviews for summer internships, etc. At NYU-Stern, the interaction between these clubs and the professional world is particularly strong given the school's location. For example, the annual M&A lectures organized in the spring by the Graduate Finance Association and the NYU law school attract some of the most eminent members of the New York banking scene. Events like this exist for all fields (marketing, entrepreneurship, new media, etc.).

Twice a year the school organizes formal balls for students, professors and administrative staff. The atmosphere is usually excellent. There's also the "Beer Blast", which is held every Thursday at the school and allows everyone to talk about and keep up-to-date with the week's events (classes, exams, jobs, etc.). The Dean and many professors make frequent appearances at these Beer Blasts so they can chat with students. This informal atmosphere helps you get to know people better and often opens up important discussions among the various main players in the school. Since NYU-Stern is situated at the intersection of three of New York City's most lively neighborhoods (the East Village, Greenwich Village and Soho), the Beer Blast usually ends up continuing in nearby bars until late into the night. First thing in the morning. however, everybody's there for the team projects.

Although the school is situated in the city, it has access to very high quality sports facilities. Your student card gives you free and unlimited access to the Cole Center located right next to the school in Greenwich Village. If you play football, soccer or rugby you can play in inter-business school matches and tournaments in New York as well as in other cities.

HOUSING

Accommodation in Manhattan is no easy matter, but there are various options open to you:

- NYU-Stern offers one option open only to single students. The school rents a certain number of apartments in regular buildings, which it then offers students at unbeatable prices for Manhattan. This system has three advantages: first of all the price (less than $1000 a month); next, the quality (the apartments are generally luxurious); and lastly, the flexibility, since the school offers nine-month contracts, based on the duration of the school year. The drawback with this type of accomodation is the lack of privacy: although the apartments are fairly luxurious, they're not very big and don't provide the students with any communal space outside of their bedrooms.
- Outside of what the school offers, finding housing can be a real headache because rents and cost of living are extremely high. I think that the best solution for getting a place in Manhattan is to share an apartment with one or several other students. If your summer internship takes you out of the city, you'll have no problem at all subletting your apartment through the Student Association.

TUITION COSTS

The annual cost of tuition at NYU-Stern is set out below.

Spending for 2 years	Amount
Tuition fees	$57,370
Books	$2,500
Health Insurance	$1,800
Total	$61,670

In addition to these necessary expenses, you will be responsible for all your living expenses. To give you an idea, I have tried to itemize these living costs, but this estimate is still rough:

Expenses	Amount for 2 years	Evaluation
Tuition fees	$57,370	
Housing	$27,000	Monthly rent of $1500 for 9 months
Transport	$1,000	The New York subway pass costs $60
Daily expenses	$18,000	
Total	$103,370	

Obviously, it's a tall order (over $50,000 per year), but here are a few ways of keeping down the cost:

- Try to get a fellowship in the States, awarded by the school. To be eligible you should submit your application before January 15th and you can expect to receive a sum of money ranging from $3,500 up to total coverage of tuition fees for really exceptional applicants. About 30% of students benefit from one of these fellowships. The school's administration declined to report the average amount given to students.
- From the start of the second year, you can apply for various assistantship positions. The condition is that you must have a GPA of at least 3.0 and you usually have to have already taken the course for which you want to be assistant. You can also work for the career placement office, or another administrative office. The average pay for this type of position is $3,500 per semester. The light workload for these assistant positions makes them easy to do.
- And don't forget that you're generally paid very nicely over the ten weeks of your summer internship.

The admissions application

NYU

I

INTRODUCTION

The NYU - Stern application can be requested by mail, or downloaded from the website, and consists of:

- 3 essays
- 2 letters of recommendation
- transcripts
- GMAT scores (and TOEFL scores, if applicable)
- a detailed résumé

There are three application rounds each year: December, January and March. Candidates need to stay on top of the whole process, hunting down transcripts, keeping after their recommenders. Remember that the GMAT and the admissions essays are the two elements that can still be improved by the applicant at this stage, so it is important to allocate your time accordingly.

THE GMAT

The GMAT is an important part of your application to NYU-Stern. Here are the scores of students the 2001 entering class :

	GMAT
average	689
range of scores	590 to 750

Here's a bit of advice on how to prepare more efficiently:

What's the ideal timing?

You'll probably send in your application form between January and March of the year you want to begin your MBA. Ideally, you'll take the GMAT around September in the previous year so that you can take it again if you feel that you haven't done as well as you could have. If you plan on three months of preparation as being about right, you should get down to work in June of the year preceding your potential admission date.

What books and other materials should you use?

Preparation books do the job, but the official exams (*The Official Guide for GMAT Review, 9th ed.,* Warner Books) are only published after they're given. It's this one that you need more than any other. To supplement it you can use others, which may offer good advice and questions that are close to the real thing, but concentrate first and foremost on past exam questions.

How should you organize yourself?

You're going to have to be strict with yourself. Here's my plan of action:
- Start by doing a mock GMAT, putting yourself in exam mode (get up early, no long breaks between sections, silence, etc.).
- Depending on your first score, decide on the amount of work you're going to have to do. If you think you'll need to work a lot, set aside weekly blocks of time.
- Go over grammar rules for the syntax questions. Get into the habit of reading as much as possible - magazines such as Business Week and The Economist are highly suitable, and also have the benfit of improving your awareness of current afairs.
- At the same time, keep testing yourself with questions from past exams.
- Half-way through, do another practice GMAT test under exam conditions so you can check on your progress. Depending on the results, you can turn your undivided attention to the question types that still cause problems. Learn to recognis esuch questions, so that you do not waste an inordinate amount of time on these weakness during the real test.
- Lastly, finish your preparation with one or two practice GMATs under exam conditions. The last one should be close to your set target.

What is an acceptable score?

There is no official minimum. In theory, any score above 620 can be considered acceptable. In the event you get a lower score, but the rest of your application offers very competitive features (professional career so far, secondary studies, etc.), there's no use wasting time working on your GMAT. Bear in mind that putting together an MBA application takes time and that you should manage your time as best as you can. No point in retaking GMAT to go from 620 to 640; concentrate instead on your essays and your references. In short, retake GMAT only if you've made a mistake, and your score was significantly lower than the one you did during your preparation.

During the test

Throughout the GMAT exam period, time and stress management are as important as the material covered. Stay calm during the exam (it really is of the utmost importance!), do breathing relaxation exercises during the short pauses between sections, and eat well before the test.

Are preparation centers of any use?

In a word - yes! These centers deliver perfectly adapted preparation, providing you with preparation books and analysis of your score, and offering you strategies for each question type. They will greatly simplify the whole business, and will practically guarantee you an improvement in your score relative to your first practice test that you took with them. Finally, they will reassure you (and the importance of this should not be underestimated). I personally did the course offered by Kaplan, which enabled me to increase my GMAT score by 80 points. Beyond the simple GMAT aspect, the preparation courses are a good way of getting into contact with other applicants, to swap tips, and to keep track of your progress in relation to other applicants.

THE ESSAYS

NYU-Stern requires three essays plus a fourth optional essay. The essays make up a crucial part of the application because they give you the opportunity to present yourself and to sell yourself. At the end of the day, the rest of the application corresponds to assessments of your abilities by third parties. So this part of the application is the one I urge you to spend the most time on.

A FEW TIPS FOR WRITING STRONG ESSAYS

1. Basic format rules to stick to

The NYU-Stern application sets a limit of two pages (word limit of 500 words) per essay which is important to respect. Mary Miller, the director of NYU-Stern admissions, stresses the importance of keeping to this format in the interview which she was kind enough to give us.

If you're having trouble organizing your thoughts, try following these guidelines:
- For the introduction, start out by synthesizing your main idea or ideas.
- The body of the text is then made up of the presentation of arguments to support your ideas.

Also, don't send off your application without having your essays read by someone who can correct the final errors.

2. Preparing to sell yourself

It can't be said stressed enough that the key to an application's success is the applicant's skill in selling himself or herself. In order to do this effectively, I advise you to choose the most important events that have set the tone of your studies and your professional life, and to present them in such a way as to show a coherent whole. A successful effort to sell yourself requires, in my opinion, that you avoid two pitfalls:
- First of all, there's no need to be exhaustive and to run the whole gamut of your failures unless it's specifically asked for (beware not to go to the other end of the scale by showing yourself in an excessively favorable and unrealistic light).
- Next, you should give coherence to your career so far: demonstrate that you have been able to show flexibility and adapt yourself to your surroundings while still retaining your personal goals. The MBA is a must right now because it's the fastest road to your goals, in the best possible conditions. Be it the admissions panel or your future employers, you will be asked the question: "Are you sure you really need an MBA to reach your goals?"

3. Make the whole application coherent

Coherence must be applied on two levels:
- You are not supposed to know what exactly your recommenders have said about you, but you've certainly got a pretty good idea. You should hand the admissions panel a coherent application and should make sure that you don't contradict what was said in the recommendations.
- Coherence should also apply to the match between the school and your personality: give qualitative points in the criteria which inform your choice, such as a discussion with students, meetings with professors or former students, etc. Highlight your abilities to participate in a group, to integrate yourself into new teams and to be on top of things in every situation you are involved in.

WHAT NYU-STERN IS LOOKING FOR IN YOUR ESSAYS

Over the last four years the questions asked by NYU-Stern in its application have been the following - the first and third essay questions occur up every year, whereas the second essay question changes from one year to the next.

- Essay 1: Think about the decisions you have made that led you to your current position.
  PAST: What choices have you made that led you to your current position?
  PRESENT: Why is a Stern MBA necessary at this point of your life?
  FUTURE: What is your desired position upon graduation from the Stern School?

- Essay 2.1: It's August in the new century and you have three years of experience with the company that hired you after you earned your MBA. Layoffs, mergers and acquisitions continue to define the business climate. You have just learned that your position will be eliminated. You don't have the seniority required to severance pay or outplacement services but will receive your salary through September 15. What is your plan of action?

- Essay 2.2: As a graduate of the Stern MBA, you are a successful manager and responsible for hiring people in your department. It now appears you may have made a mistake. An employee you selected six months ago is not performing at an acceptable level. You have confronted this person reviewed performance expectations and given constructive suggestions for improvement. However, the employee's performance has not improved and you've decided this cannot continue. How will you handle the situation?

- Essay 2.3: Assume that you are planning to launch a new business venture. Write an executive summary of your business plan to present to potential investors

- Essay 3: Describe yourself to your MBA classmates (You may use any method to convey your message: words, illustrations, etc.).

- Essay 4: (Optional) Please provide any additional information that you would like to bring to the attention of the admission committee. If you are unable to submit a recommendation from a current employer, please give your reason here.

Far be it from me to claim that the school is seeking a certain type of student - even if the school claimed to do so, the diversity of the students offered a place prove otherwise. However, there are still see some salient qualities that you need to highlight:
- Your analytic skills: even if your university career or your GMAT has already demonstrated these, don't think twice about going on about your analytical abilities. NYU-Stern is a very technical MBA program, just like other schools with a reputation in finance.
- Your taste for teamwork: this is very important at NYU-Stern. Be aware of the fact that you will have a minimum of two sets of teamwork throughout the MBA. You should therefore be in a position to demonstrate the characteristics which make you a "team player" such as:
  - willingness to help others
  - aptitude in putting the group's objectives before your own
  - the ability to avoid monopolizing a group discussion
  - the ability to delegate tasks and also to effectively complete tasks assigned to you by others.
  You must demonstrate these qualities through your past experience.
- Leadership: show that you can do it. To help you highlight this in your essays, here's an extract from *The Leadership Triad,* a work written by Dale Zand, Professor of Management at NYU-Stern: "Effective leaders build productive, adaptive teams by integrating knowledge, trust, and power, guiding the teams toward common goals, employing their competence, and building mutual trust." This short quote gives a good sense of the leader's role in the modern world; refer to the book for further details. It's important to note the complementary relationship between a taste for team work and the qualities of a leader. One enables the other to reveal itself.
- Your desire to get involved: don't think of the MBA at NYU-Stern as simply being an opportunity to learn; be aware of the fact that you could also benefit other students with your knowledge and past experience.

EXAMPLES AND COMMENTARIES OF ESSAYS FOR NYU-STERN

Some of you will perhaps notice that some of the essays below breeze past the 500 word limit. The explanation lies in the fact that NYU-Stern has very recently lowered this limit. This brings home a little more the necessity to always synthesize your thoughts a little bit more.

Essay 1: Think about the decisions you have made that led you to your current position.

PAST: What choices have you made that led you to your current position?

PRESENT: Why is a Stern MBA necessary at this point of your life?

FUTURE: What is your desired position upon graduation from the Stern School?

The point of this essay:

You must show that you are "goal oriented". Here's how these qualities can be defined in four steps:

- Analyze a situation
- Set your objectives
- Set things in motion and work
- Reach your goal or learn from your failure

Don't be frightened about aiming high in your post-MBA goals because NYU-Stern is looking for ambitious students.

Tips for the essay:

- Even though the question doesn't state it explicitly, you should concentrate on your academic and professional career. The other essays will give you the opportunity to elaborate on other aspects of your personality.
- Avoid falling into the trap of merely writing a chronological description of your career. Try to organize your description around a particular theme. In the example below, the two themes that mark the writer's career were "information technologies" and "international experience." To this, the applicant adds his ability to deal with other people and for teamwork, which are particularly appropriate for an MBA candidate. The writer of the example below really gives the impression that he can't wait to throw himself into group projects and there's no shadow of a doubt that the admissions panel really values this way of thinking.
- See the MBA as an important turning point in your life and a career must. You have to make the admissions panel understand that by remaining in your present position you face a dead-end for achieving the goals you have set for yourself. In the following essay, the writer is an engineer who needs the MBA to increase his knowledge of management. This profile is fairly typical. Some other real-life examples of similar career changes are a trader wanting to move from market finance to company finance, or a product manager wanting to become a trader. All these conditions are acceptable provided they are motivated by solid reasons which are up to you to explain.
- Make them understand that you specifically want to do your MBA at NYU-Stern: spotlight how you found out about and have come to like the school. In our example, the writer refers to an information session, and I can cite other real-life examples which really show that the choice of NYU-Stern has been very seriously considered:
  - One applicant applied to NYU-Stern after meeting a representative of a consulting firm who strongly recommended the school to him.
  - Another applicant made a preliminary visit to the schools he wanted to apply to and chose

NYU-Stern, rather than the other equally prestigious schools, based on the good contact he had had with the students.

Whatever the situation, these anecdotes show the intensity of applicants' preparation.

Sample Essay

I am an international telecommunications project manager. I work for France Telecom North America (FTNA) at its New York City headquarters. When, in France, my country of origin, I entered the Orsay Scientific University for undergraduate studies in Computer Science, I had radically different career objectives. I wanted to become a researcher in Artificial Intelligence. From speech recognition to the ability to produce new knowledge from a given set of hypotheses and logical rules, there is something truly magical in a computer program that is able to reproduce intelligent processes. Yet, a research internship at the Orsay Computer Lab made me realize that, however intellectually rewarding I found research work, it would not meet a more fundamental need of mine: a craving for more action and more interaction. This realization profoundly influenced the educational and career decisions that I have made from then on, and it is at the root of my desire to pursue a career in management today.

I decided to join the National Institute of Telecommunications (INT) for my graduate studies. I went to INT to offer myself the best grounds to re-orient my career to the industry and by taste for information technologies: telecommunications was an exciting and largely unknown world after my Computer Science undergraduate studies. The choice of the INT clearly contributed to bringing me to work for France Telecom. However, to start an international career directly upon graduation from INT, it took a number of other choices and initiatives.

I started acquiring an international experience by accomplishing summer jobs abroad during my undergraduate studies. At the INT, I fine-tuned my English and Spanish language skills, I took up Japanese and participated in an international summer program taking place throughout Europe. These initiatives, along with my involvement in extra-curricular activities contributed to giving me the credentials that are often required by corporations for their international positions. Each of these individual choices therefore contributed to bringing me where I am today. During my early career at FTNA, I have made yet another choice. I accepted the cross-departmental promotion which led me to leave my position at the Management of the Information Systems department, my first position in the company, in order to take the position of Associate Manager which I currently occupy at the Global Services Support. I was motivated by the challenge of increased responsibility and the prospect of being in direct contact with France Telecom's major international customers.

In recent years, Information Technologies have led general management and technology management to converge. Awareness has risen that computers and networks do not merely concern logistics, but are also tremendous business assets. My educational background prepared me well to actively participate, within my company, in the changes that this new perspective brought about. At the Management of the Information Systems, from the design of a customers' information tracking system to the support of the communications and computing needs of the office's mobile users, my work, though grounded on technology, often had to consider and understand organizational issues. In my current position at the Global Services Support, a project leader for my departments' intranet development and manager of my company's EDI (Electronic Data Interchange) activities in the US, I have increasingly involved myself in all areas where organizational and business matters meet with information technology.

My long-term career goal is to become a general manager in an international firm in the telecom industry or in a related high-tech industry. Management and technology may converge; however, for my part, one reality remains: my knowledge in the management fields is very limited! After three years experience in the operations at FTNA, in order to progress towards my career goal, I need to complement my background in sciences and engineering with the instruction and the recognition that no other degree than a top-tier American MBA can offer me. An MBA education would enable me to understand the mechanics of the core corporate functions, to broaden my vision of the organization, and to grasp the relevant components of the economic environment, everything that general management demands.

Why Stern? Attending a Stern information session, carefully reviewing the school's program, and engaging in numerous discussions with high-ranking managers have all convinced me that the Stern MBA would be an exceptional asset for my career. Indeed, in order to gain a broader outlook and practical experience in management, I first intend to work in the management consulting field. Stern's management consulting specialization and its recognition among the world's major consulting firms, as well as the New York City business environment, perfectly bolster my aim of breaking into the management consulting field. Furthermore, I particularly value the openings that the school's strength and recognition in the fields of finance and international business would give me for my long-term career goals. Direct and enthusiast feedback from current students regarding their satisfaction with the program and faculty, as well as on the placement office's efficiency, are motivating factors in my choice of the Stern School of Business.

Finally, in pursuing an MBA, I am looking forward to discussing other business practices with my classmates and bringing my own insights to the class discussions. In that respect, I value Stern's diversity, which finds a concrete reflection in the student body as well as in the faculty composition. Through my past involvement in extra-curricular activities, my work experience, personal background and personality, I believe that I would significantly contribute to this diverse and dynamic environment. For all these reasons, I would most welcome the opportunity to do my MBA at the Stern School of Business.

Essay 2.1: It's August in the new century and you have three years of experience with the company that hired you after you earned your MBA. Layoffs, mergers and acquisitions continue to define the business climate. You have just learned that your position will be eliminated. You don't have the seniority required for severance pay or outplacement services but will receive your salary through September 15. What is your plan of action?

The point of this essay:

To understand your capacity to energize yourself into action when faced with a major difficulty.

Tips for the essay:

- Show that you have a structured way of confronting the problem: situation analysis, definition of objectives, action. Try to give yourself precise deadlines for action.
- Unlike a lot of MBA essays, this one doesn't ask you to talk about your past but to predict

your future. So be imaginative! Try to take advantage of a tendency in the surrounding economic climate which the reader could easily identify with (the impact of the internet in the market, movement of industrial concentration in various industries, new buouyancy of activity in southeast Asia, for instance). Don't forget that you're supposed to be an MBA graduate, which will enable you to have a great geographical and functional mobility.

- Show your capacity to react when faced with a major difficulty and to think big. You don't need to set yourself up as the victim. A failure is a fruitful experience if it enables you to bounce back and to draw lessons from the past. So put yourself in that frame of mind.
- Be realistic! Americans have a fairly compartmentalized vision of the professional world, except when it concerns setting up business. Therefore, different solutions are open to you. For example:

1) *Seek an opening in the same field*

Up to now, your career has evolved in such a way so that you have become a specialist in your field. You decide to stay in the same field by choosing the opportunity which seems to you to be the most attractive in this area. So, if you're a product manager at Procter & Gamble, avoid attempting to suddenly become an investment banker. The following example shows the situation of trader who uses his trading experience in order to go and develop trading activities for another bank in Eastern Europe.

Sample Essay

Today, August 4th 2002, I just lost my job in Bank X, a famous Manhattan investment bank. I decided to work in the US after my MBA. I found there the best application for the skills acquired during my years at Stern. For X, I worked on the South America Emerging Market trading desks. This job involved a great deal of travel in order to study the feasibility of profitable trading activities in these countries and as a result, I built competitive desks.

I now have to react very quickly. In order to do so, I will first draw up an assessment of my professional competences, then define the new orientation I want to give to my career, and finally decide on a plan of action.

I have three main assets on which I must rely to achieve my goal:
1. I have an MBA from a well-known school. With the integration of international studies, the MBA is more than ever the best supranational diploma.
2. I have a successful experience of trading in New York on risky markets.
3. I have trading experience in Europe.

During my MBA years, I carefully followed the integration of Europe. In 1998 the new Euro currency was officially launched in a few countries. It has developed a unified financial market. Very low interest rates have allowed the appearance of a solid growth in Europe, and the countries have earned the dividends of their efforts. Today, many other countries are trying to meet the criteria to enter Europe. Although it requires a strong commitment, they know they do not have any other choice. The time has come for me to work on the financial markets of these growing countries.

Why are Eastern Europe markets so promising? When the Eastern governments understand that their chance of economic development rests on a unified European market, they will follow the same road of integration as France or Germany, in order to meet the required macroeconomic criteria. At that time, the reactions of their domestic financial markets will be highly predictable and will allow huge profits.

Why is my profile suited to this field of work? I have an internationally recognized MBA that is a guarantee of strong quantitative skills, and the habit of working with people from diverse cultures and backgrounds. I have the leadership skills and the experience necessary to build a new department of trading. Working in an American bank on the South American financial markets taught me how a large structure was able to adapt itself to non-integrated markets. Moreover, I have already worked in an environment of financial integration. Eight years ago, the French financial system was confronted with the same dilemma and its reactions were very concise. I know how to pinpoint and rectify inefficient areas of a market, and turn them into profitable environments.

The first thing to do now is to put the above ideas together in a letter in order to show my strong motivation. I will insist on the fact that I did not lose my job because of poor performance but because of a merger. The second thing is to contact the people I know in various investment banks. I have always tried to develop contacts with other people, and the Stern Alumni Network is a great source of information. I am going to make the best out of it.

I will keep one idea in mind: transform this setback into a new chance for my career and my personal development.

2) Set up your own business

You have acquired competency in your field which you feel to be sufficiently global to enable you to launch yourself into setting up a business. Having set out your idea, be sure to be clear about how you intend to fill the roles in which your personal competency is limited. So, if you were a consultant and now decide to set up an e-business company, don't say that you could take on the technical side. Rather, show your capacity to build a good team around you and to work in that team by having chosen brilliant associates. The following example shows how the writer uses a field that he knows well, his MBA training and his network of contacts to set up a business on the basis of an original idea. Though the development objective is particularly ambitious, it is not unrealistic, and the idea seems to be new.

Sample Essay

In this essay the initial product has been replaced by The Product in order to preserve anonymity and to not interfere with the development of a business that is currently in the process of being set up.

At home, there have always been few boundaries between family life and business. My parents operate a family business. From the age of fourteen onwards, I have been interested in finding practical business solutions to a business not renowned for its practicality. I often assisted my father with the books, which introduced me to basic accounting skills, and turned my attention toward more complex financial instruments. This work relationship set the base for future collaboration between my parents and myself.

This sudden change in my professional life and the loss of my position after these three years make me realize that I want to run my own operations. I anticipate increasing involvement in the family business. In collaboration with my father, an investment banker and a NYU graduate, we recently laid down the structure of an international company.

Using the latest information technology, we plan to revolutionize the distribution of the product. Creating ventures throughout Europe, the United States, and Asia, our aim is to create a network of franchisees, gradually increasing our presence in order to establish a worldwide label. All franchisees will have access to a central database of original Products. Not only will they be able to sell the Product they purchase for their outlet, but also they will be able to offer customers any product available on our network. We see this niche as a viable market, both in terms of price and scarcity. Moreover, the Products are inherently reproducible, but the number of copies is controlled. This characteristic, native to the commodity, means that there are enough copies to generate market demand, and few enough to encourage arbitrage among the most popular works.

The development of the company has hinged on my involvement. After my father approached me with the original concept, I introduced him to a business partner, whose knowledge of finance and the telecom industry seemed relevant to the operation my father aimed to create. From initial contact onward, both acknowledged the potential synergy in their business pursuits; some months later, we committed to a legal partnership. Since then, a fourth individual has joined the nascent company; a graduate of Stern will design the database specifications, constructing a plan for the infrastructure of the network. In addition we have located a software company in India which is currently developing our operating system. My focus has now turned to attracting potential investors to provide the seed money which we require to launch operations in Europe. We plan to expand to the States and Asia within the next two years.

The development of this enterprise provides me with a profound sense of personal achievement, particularly because without my efforts to coordinate resources, the company might still be in its inception phase. The skills I acquired and improved by participating in The Stern MBA Program not only benefited me, but also my business partners. Moreover, I hope now to find some partners amongst my fellow alumni.

Essay 2.2: As a graduate of the Stern MBA, you are a successful manager and responsible for hiring people in your department. It now appears you may have made a mistake. An employee you selected six months ago is not performing at an acceptable level. You have confronted this person, reviewed performance expectations and given constructive suggestions for improvement. However, the employee's performance has not improved and you've decided this cannot continue. How will you handle the situation?

The point of this essay:

To get you to solve a people problem inside a company to gauge your methods of analysis for a given situation as well as your human qualities such as empathy.

Tips for the essay:

- You were responsible for employing someone who is not producing the expected results. So this essay asks you to find a rapid solution to a problem that directly affects you. For example, in an American investment bank, a banker may have a recruitment role as well as their job as banker. The evaluation of their performance will therefore be partly based on their success with the recruiting they have done. The main issue at hand is not about delegating the problem to a human resources department, but working closely with this department.

- The essay title wording is clear: the employee you have selected is not satisfactory. The dismissal solution must therefore be dealt with clearly in this essay. Bear in mind that in the States, dismissal is not as much a personal insult as it is in Europe. What's more, in the big picture, losing one's job is not the end of the world.
- This essay is also asking you to apply an analytical approach to a personnel problem. The example below lays the groundwork for this approach first by separating the technical qualities from behavioral qualities, and then by taking into account the surrounding picture. Without specifically referring to an evaluation grid, it's definitely this type of analysis that the writer is referring to here.
- Lastly, highlight human qualities for seeking to understand the problem: the writer of this example uses here informal discussions to truly understand the professional and personal life of the employee he has taken on. American companies often have a more paternal attitude than European companies. The Europeans often feel this attitude is hypocritical, the Americans take it for granted. So play their game!

Sample essay

There is no clear-cut answer to this problem. I have hired this person because I believed that they had the right combination of intellectual and behavioral abilities, something they have not been able to show in their work so far however. Either I really misjudged their skills (technical abilities not sufficient while personality fits, or simply unsuitable personality), or there are other factors that prevent the employee from growing in the organization (technical skills and behavior are fine).

In the case that either the individual's technical skills or personality are insufficient, I will have to admit the error I made by hiring them. If their behavior is such that they easily interact with peers and superiors, we may transfer the employee to another department which is either less demanding and/or which fits his/her personality better. If however there are no suitable opportunities for an internal transfer, or if we judge his/her personal qualities to be insufficient, we will have to fire the individual.

In the other case, after re-assurance that both their intellectual and personal skills are sufficient for the job, we have to look for other, probably external factors that prevented the employee from executing their task as required. At this stage, I am convinced that it is not useful to have a new face-to-face interview. I will arrange unofficial meetings (e.g. by having lunch or coffee together) and try and make the individual talk not immediately about their specific tasks, but rather about how they see the department and colleagues, what they think they can contribute to the company, how they see their possible evolution within the organization, and, completely differently, what they do after work. Maybe a temporary personal problem could be the reason for their weak performance. If a short-term solution is within reach, we might have some more patience with the person, nevertheless not without giving them the clear hint that their job is at stake. Alternatively, if we do not find any short term solution we will have to fire this person: since we do not have any explanation for their underperformance (intellectual and personal skills seem to be all right), transferring them to another department will most probably produce the same problems.

Essay 2.3: Assume that you are planning to launch a new business venture. Write an executive summary of your business plan to present to potential investors.

The point of this essay:

1) To gauge your ability to convince since a business plan is an exercise in sales; and 2) to sound out your "grasp of reality" in terms of objectives and the main elements of your business plan (a "grasp of reality" is one of the most important qualities of the entrepreneur).

Tips for this essay:

- The subject of this essay is recent; it stems from the growing interest of MBA graduates in launching a start-up. Indeed, there are many Americans who pursue an MBA in order to acquire the knowledge and the necessary credentials to start a business.
- This type of exercise is close to the "interview box" frequently used by consultancy firms at job interviews. The goal here is to test the method more than the business idea you develop.
- If you don't have any business ideas, invent one or get inspiration from an example that you know of simply by changing the type of product sold. What counts in this essay is not your inventive ability, but your ability to plan in a precise way what the key elements of your business are (logistics, stocking, distribution, etc.)
- The difficulty with this essay lies in the word limit (500 words). To synthesize a business plan in two pages isn't all that easy. My advice would be to use the following plan:
  1. Presentation of the business idea or of the product
  2. Use of an analytical tool like these "Five power points" in order to scan the various characteristics of your business:

     a) Suppliers' negotiating power: depends on their degree of concentration. Are the suppliers sufficiently powerful so that this could present a problem for you?

     b) Clients' negotiation power: in exactly the same way, the more your clients are concentrated, the more they can negotiate the sales conditions and reduce your profitability.

     c) Threats from new entries: is the business you plan on introducing to the market attractive for new competitors and if so, do you risk being copied? What initial investment is necessary? Are you going to submit patents? Will you have lower costs than the other businesses? Can you secure a distribution network? Will you be protected by the legal statutes?

     d) Threat of the product being phased out: might your market disappear overnight because a competitor finds a better and less expensive equivalent product?

     e) Intensity of competition: how many competitors are there at the present time in your industry? Are there ways to increase production, or is there any unused stockage space? Do you think that costs could be reduced?

  3. Positioning and marketing strategy: price, distribution, markets, type of publicity, etc.
  4. Source of competitive advantage: in short, a company has a competitive advantage over its rivals when it makes more profit from the same activities. It could come from more advanced technology, from higher employee motivation, from access to raw materials at the best price, or from a more efficient production line.
  5. What sort of team-workers are you going to build around you?
  6. What are your financial resources?
- Close your essay with a quick description of the how your business plan will become reality: how soon, how much money, in conjunction with whom?

Essay 3: Describe yourself to your MBA classmates (you may use any method to convey your message: words, illustrations, etc.).

The point of this essay:

The school is asking you to present yourself in a more personal way. This is your opportunity to highlight your team spirit.

Tips for this essay:

- Although the example below is a written text, you can easily use the other suggested modes of expression (illustrations, photos). I personally know some applicants who got in using these less traditional means.
- Even if this essay is asking you to stress the more personal aspects of your application, there's nothing stopping you from mentioning your work. As an MBA applicant, the fact that your work is one of your main centers of interest is indeed looked favorably on. In particular, don't hesitate to talk about the intellectual stimulation it gives you.
- The following example refers to a taste for travel and culture which has been realized by studying in many European countries. This shows the writer is open-minded and is used to rubbing shoulders with people from varied backgrounds. This mindset will undoubtedly be very much appreciated at NYU-Stern.

Sample Essay:

Dear student colleagues,

I have been working for over two years at the xxxxx. After a few months of analysis of fixed income products, I became an Assets & Liabilities Management analyst. In co-operation with Andersen Consulting and a Swiss Risk Management consulting firm, we set up a company-wide Assets and Liabilities Management system. Asset/Liability analysis implies assessing market (interest rate) risk for the bank as a whole (proposing overall exposure and macro-hedges), performing adequate transformation of liabilities into assets ("ride the yield curve") and simulating and developing strategies for individual banking products (balance sheet structuring).

There are two main reasons why I am recommencing my studies: on the one hand, I hope to learn management skills, on the other hand I want to broaden my basis of financial theory, and more specifically in corporate finance. After the MBA program, I plan to work in financial advising, which could range from risk management consulting to investment banking.

My educational background shows a shift from linguistic studies into engineering and finally international economics: after studying Latin/Greek at high school and one preliminary year of Mathematics (preparatory studies for a university Engineering course), I studied Commercial Engineering at university. For one term, I was an Erasmus Exchange student at the Universidad de Valencia in Spain. Thereafter, I went to the Institute of World Economics in Kiel, Germany, a German economic "think tank" which also offers a Masters program in Economic Policy. Coursework focuses on macroeconomics and financial economics. Every year, 20 to 25 students out of 10 to 15 different countries participate, about 75% of them having several years of previous work experience. Courses are taught in blocks of one to two weeks by visiting professors (among them Richard Levich and Ingo Walter from New York University).

Lots of my free time goes into travelling. Whenever possible, I try to combine travel and culture by making weekend trips with friends to Madrid, Bruges, Hamburg, etc. This way of living does not leave me a lot of time anymore for sports, which is very different from when I was a student and practiced horse-back riding, soccer and jogging. One thing, however, did not change: I am not happy if I am not busy. Or as Seneca (4 B.C. - 65 A.D.) said: "Quid illum octogina anni iuvant per inertiam exacti? Non vixit iste, sed in vita moratus est, nec mortuus est, sed diu." ("Of what use are the eighty years of that man that has been living in emptiness? Such a man has not been living but has been hanging around in life, and he has not died late, but has been dying over a long time.")

Essay 4: (Optional) Please provide any additional information that you would like to bring to the attention of the admissions committee. If you are unable to submit a recommendation from a current employer, please give your reason here.

The point of this essay:

Take on any subject that's close to your heart and that you think will be significant for NYU-Stern's admissions panel. As I've already mentioned above, I strongly advise you to get a recommendation from your present employer so you will be able to forget the second part of this essay question.

Tips for this essay:

Because this essay is optional, the first question that comes to mind is: "do I have to write it?" The reply is "yes" if you are adding something new that was not included in the three preceding essays. I think it's the right place to highlight your participation in a charitable organization, your performance in the sport you excel at, your military service experience, your gift for music, etc. The following two examples fit into this category very well:

Sample Essay

The writer shows how he proved himself in the context of a charitable event.

I would like to write about my experience in a TELETHON fund raising operation. As the Treasurer, I was in charge of raising funds from the alumni of my school and eleven other universities in the country. Thanks to my perseverance and my sense of leadership, I managed to motivate the universities for the cause and the total money raised approached the record amount of $200,000.

Sample Essay

The writer uses his military service as his first leadership experience.

I would like to mention the experience acquired during my military service. It was my first leadership experience in real life and an opportunity for me to have important responsibilities. My military service took place from January to December 1992. After three months of training, I graduated as an army officer and was placed in a situation of command. I found the experience particularly challenging because, as a young officer, I had to command experienced commissioned officers. Doing this required a mix of decision-making and collaboration. Moreover, this experience taught me that a title is not enough to develop adhesion in a group and that effective leadership must be built rather than simply stated.

THE LETTERS OF RECOMMENDATION

NYU-Stern requires 2 letters of recommendation.

GENERAL ADVICE

The requirement of letters of recommendation can seem a little strange, since a reference written by a person of your choice will in all probability be written entirely in your favor. A well put-together reference can carry a lot of weight. The people you choose must skillfully find a balance between honesty and enthusiasm, and avoid all forms of cynicism. Remarks like "through both his team spirit and his own work, X was the principal architect of the turnaround of our Korean subsidiary" won't look wildly exaggerated if they're accompanied by precise examples.

Before getting down to the nitty-gritty of NYU-Stern's questions, here are a few guidelines for searching for recommendation letter-writers, and for writing the letters:

- For NYU-Stern, you must either send a recommendation from your present employer (ideally your immediate boss), or explain why this isn't possible in the fourth, optional essay. This latter option courts danger, and so my advice is to do whatever it takes to get a recommendation from your immediate boss. But if it's really not possible, try one of your close colleagues.

- The recommendations are supposed to be written by a person of your choice and sent back to you in a sealed envelope so you can send it with the application forms. So in theory you don't have access to what's said about you. In most cases, applicants respect this procedure, but they do discuss the contents of the letter with the person writing the recommendation. This is obviously the best way of dealing with the recommendation since it assures that no positive comments about you will be left out. What's more, after many weeks of preparation, the themes important to business schools (leadership, team spirit, entrepreneurial mentality) will be more familiar to you than they will to your recommender. So it's in your interest to help your recommenders as much as possible and set them off in the right direction!

QUESTIONS ASKED IN THE NYU-STERN LETTERS OF RECOMMENDATION

1. How long have you known the applicant? In what capacity?

This is where you can really see exactly how important is to be recommended by people who know you well.

Example:

I have known Matthew for almost four years, both as a professional, as a mentor, and later as a friend. We collaborated successfully through his tenure at the firm.

2. What do you consider the applicant's outstanding talents?

Tips:

Here, spotlight one or a few adjectives expressing facets of your personality that can be supported by concrete facts. In the following example, the applicant is a "reliable team member" whose abilities shone through in a tricky situation (part of the team abandoned the project). Stress upon your recommenders the importance of solidly backing up what they say by using real life situations as examples to beef up the credibility of their remarks.

Example:

Throughout our professional collaboration, Matthew proved to be a trustworthy and reliable team member. His loyalty and integrity have been successfully tested in many critical situations. A few months into the job, five of the seven members of our team defected to a competitor. While I struggled to maintain confidence amongst my clients by visiting them across Europe, Matthew was left alone to handle all our business. Matthew was instrumental in ensuring that none of our important clients left the firm.

3. In which areas could the applicant exhibit growth or improvement?

Tips:

Here you must spotlight, in no uncertain terms, one of your weaknesses or an area you need to work on to become more effective. This weakness must be a real one and not something that could be taken as strength masquerading as a false weakness, like "Oliver's biggest weakness is that he demonstrates too much dedication to his projects." It sounds false and doesn't really count as a weakness. Your recommender shouldn't swing too wildly to the other end of the scale either and mention some really grave weakness, like "Oliver is a very capable person but he has proven to be unable to collaborate with his teammates and to share responsibilities."

Example:

The following example avoids both pitfalls:

"When he undertakes a project, Oliver wants to succeed. In some cases he prefers not to act rather than take the risk to fail. This may prevent him from 'learning by doing'. Oliver must understand that any successful learning experience involves risks of failure." Here the fault is real (excessive caution in preparation) but it's not permanent and can be corrected.

4. Please comment on your impression of the applicant's capacity for graduate work and his or her potential for a successful career in management.

Tips:

By "graduate work", the question can be taken as meaning the ability to see a project through to a successful conclusion. A lot of companies make a distinction between "graduate" and "undergraduate" level in the type of work they entrust to the people they work with. At the "undergraduate" level, even a brilliant colleague will find himself being given tasks only sporadically however complex they may be. At the "graduate" level, an employee should be capable of taking on the responsibility of a more long term project, and to carry it through to a successful conclusion while keeping his superior informed over a long time period.

Example:

Intelligent and sensible, Matthew will certainly excel in a competitive Business School environment. He has proved it many times by collaborating successfully with the MBA graduates hired by the firm. Not only are his ambitions realistic, but I am confident that once again he will deliver a quality of work beating expectations.

Hard-working and dedicated, Matthew will without doubt be able to attain a position of managerial responsibility. Matthew is determined to do what it takes to achieve his goals and has, I believe, the required abilities to successfully complete a rigorous MBA program.

| GMAT | Essays | Letters of rec. | The Interview | Admissions Director |

5. Please use this scale to rate the applicant in relation to his or her peers.

	Exceptionnal (Top 2%)	Outstanding (Top 10%)	Good (Top 1/3)	Average (Middle 1/3)	Poor (Bottom 1/3)	Unable to Judge
Leadership, Maturity, Teamwork…						

Your recommender should categorize you as either "Exceptional" or "Outstanding", or else he or she may place you in an unfavorable light. Don't forget that the scale of values for the top business schools is really biased towards the upper end, so it is imperative that you position yourself in the top 10%.

Lastly, your recommender must choose between: I strongly recommend/I recommend/I recommend with some reservations/I do not recommend. Obviously, it's better if your letter writer chooses the first of these options.

Three final points to mention about letters of recommendation for NYU-Stern:

- Your recommendation letter writers shouldn't feel confined to the form included in the NYU-Stern application. It's required, but can be accompanied by another sheet describing a particular situation or expanding more fully on what was mentioned on the form for quick-fire answers. Having talked about this with members of the admissions panel, it turns out that NYU-Stern looks favorably on any situation explained by your recommender that sheds a positive light on a particular aspect of your personality.

- You're welcome to submit a third recommendation, but it must address something new. For example, in an ideal world you would offer a recommendation from your immediate boss, another from a client, or a colleague (but not from the same circle), and lastly a third from a different activity, such as a sport in which you've reached competition level or a charitable organization.

- Recommendations from teachers are only advisable if you've worked with him or her as part of a team. Having had you as a student doesn't necessarily mean that a teacher knows you well, and the admission panel is aware of this.

THE INTERVIEW

Nearly all applicants admitted to NYU-Stern have had an interview. If your application is of interest, the school will send you a written invitation indicating that an interview with a representative of the admissions panel is the next stage in reviewing your application.

Interview on-site or interview off-site?

Normally, NYU-Stern's interview takes place at the school, which offers you the following advantages:

- Coming to New York to have an interview is proof of your motivation.
- Mary Miller and her team at the admissions office are undeniably the most qualified people to conduct interviews (so your interview has every chance of going well).
- It an opportunity to visit the school, to meet students and professors, and to sit in on some classes. If you make the trip, spend a day on the campus.
- This immersion period gives you a very good taste of what your life will be like for 18 months. It's a good way of getting to know the MBA world before taking the plunge of resigning from your present job, moving and setting yourself up in a city as disconcerting as New York.

Coming to New York for interview can be difficult for some applicants to arrange. Having an off-site interview is also possible. They are usually conducted by someone from the admissions office who moves around, grouping interviews of applicants in a given country together. Alumni conduct interviews on occasion, but it's less frequent. Be absolutely sure you have done some solid preparation if you have the interview off-site. Experience shows that people often prepare more for interviews if they travel to New York than if they do it after a day's work in their own city.

How to prepare?

The interview will last about half an hour and will have three parts:

- You present yourself (5 to 10 minutes)
- The interviewer asks you questions (15 minutes)
- You ask the interviewer questions (5 to 10 minutes)

This type of interview is what I had in New York. It follows relatively faithfully the classic job interview format. It's not guaranteed that your interview will exactly follow this structure, but in any case it's a good way to prepare.

Presenting yourself

The best way of going about things in this part of the interview is to re-use the themes that you developed in the essays. It should also follow your resume (coherence always!). This is all the more important since the person who will interview you is usually very familiar with your application for the interview because they have access to all of it.

The questions the interviewer will ask you

The following questions, or their equivalent, are often asked by the admission officers:

1. Questions about you relative to the MBA in general and to NYU-Stern in particular:
- Why at this time in your life do you think you need to go back to school to pursue an MBA?
- How did you find out about NYU-Stern?
- Why did you apply at NYU-Stern?
- What other schools did you apply to?
- What do you expect to find at NYU-Stern?
- What makes you think that the fit between NYU-Stern and yourself is going to be good?
- You have reached a certain level in your career, do you think you will easily readjust to student life?
- What contact have you had with NYU-Stern representatives and/or students?
- What would you change about the NYU-Stern admission process?

2. Questions about your professional career:
- What are your professional goals?
- Why do you want to change your career orientation?
- Are you sure you need to do an MBA to make this change?
- Have you tried to change without an MBA?

3. Questions about your personality and your life in general:
- Tell me your three most important strengths and weaknesses.
- Tell me about a situation where you experienced a failure due to a decision you made.
- Tell me about a situation where you were part of a team. How did you handle it? Was it a good experience for you and why?
- Tell me about a situation where you have been a leader. What did you learn from this situation?
- Describe a situation where you faced an ethical dilemma. How did you deal with it?
- What are your hobbies?
- Who is the person you admire the most? The least?

The questions you ask the interviewer

In my opinion, this is the most important part of the interview because it's the only one which calls for your creativity. In the first two parts, you can prepare perfect answers to the great majority of the questions you will be asked. In this last part, depending on the quality of the questions you ask, it's up to you to strike up a conversation with your interviewer. Seize the opportunity; have your questions ready; and listen to the replies so you can listen to them carefully.

Here is a list of themes on which you can base your own original questions: the professors, the school's projects (at NYU-Stern, the creation of a new building, its partnerships with international schools), student life (group work, clubs, evenings out and in, etc.), the Integrated Strategy Exercise, links with companies, etc.

During the interview

I don't need to go over pointers like arriving on time or wearing a dark suit. Here are some pieces of advice that I hope you will find useful:
1. Make sure your level of preparation is sufficient for you to be able to relax.

2. Never cut your off your interviewer; let them finish their questions.
3. Before replying, take a few seconds to organize your thoughts.
4. Unless there's a strange question, adopt the following structure for your answers:
   - restate the context
   - present the action or measures that you have taken
   - give the results of your action including, if possible, evaluations of your performance from third parties or numerical results

INTERVIEW WITH THE ADMISSIONS DIRECTOR

Interview with Mary Miller, Admissions Director at NYU-Stern School of Management.

Who reads the application forms? (Faculty?, alumni?, students?, MBA Admission officers?)
All of the above. We always have MBA admission officers read the application, but this is supplemented with current students, faculty, other administrators at Stern, and sometimes alumni.

How many people read the dossier?
The committee is composed of 20-30 people, but at least three people read/evaluate every application.

What is the process? (Is there a sort of preliminary filter in three categories like Yes/Maybe/No and then only the first category is really thoroughly read?)
The first reader can vote to interview, put them on the waiting list or reject. We invite someone to interview if we think there is potential for admission. The next steps depend on if the applicant accepts our interview invitation.

What are the criteria of evaluation of a good candidate? Please explain clearly what you mean when using generic terms, give examples if possible.
"Good" means different things to different schools. Certainly of utmost importance are the individual's academic capabilities. This is determined by undergraduate (and sometimes graduate) performance, which includes their major grade, the selectivity of the undergraduate institution and then the GMAT score. Work experience – length of time and level of responsibility. Leadership – in personal and professional life. Ability and desire to work in teams. Communication skills – excellent verbal and written. Focused and realistic career goals. Strong recommendations. Commitment and match with goals of our program.

How important is the GMAT in the admission process? Do you expect a minimum score? Once the minimum is reached, what difference in value do you put on an applicant with a GMAT at 670 and another applicant with a GMAT at 720?

There is no minimum. It is very important; assuming all other things being equal, we will admit the applicant with the higher score. However, we will never offer admission if the GMAT is high and everything else is weak.

If someone takes the GMAT many times, will you take the highest score or the average of the scores?

We take the highest score.

What are the "do's" and "don'ts" for essays?

Do use spell check, follow the word/page limit, answer the question. Don't say you want to attend XYZ school in an essay you send to us.

What are the "do's" and "don'ts" for letters of recommendation?

Don't go for title; go for substance and knowledge the recommender has of the applicant.

What is the function of the interview in the selection process? How do you measure the fit between the applicant and the school?

This is very important for Stern. We not only determine fit, we determine commitment and communication skills. It is also an opportunity to get to know the candidate in a more personal way than just through the application.

Does the interviewer have access to the application form of the interviewee ahead of the interview?

Absolutely, and also has the benefit of the comments/concerns of the first reader.

Can you communicate the evaluation grid used by the school?

No, there isn't one.

Does an applicant in the early rounds have more chance than an applicant in the later rounds?

Yes and no. The earlier we receive the application, the earlier we make the decision. By the end of the cycle we have a better idea of the class profile and if we will be admitting from the waiting list.

Some people say that the middle round is the best since the first round is too early because the school is afraid to give away too many seats, and the last round is to late because the school might have already given away a lot of seats in the earlier rounds. How would you comment on this?

We have rolling admissions, so this really doesn't apply. We admit the best candidates no matter when they apply. Candidates that we are not sure about, depending on the strength of the pool, are offered a place on the waitlist.

The admissions committe uses the "rolling admissions" method as opposed to the "round admissions" process:

- In the "round admissions" process, the total number of spaces available are distributed, evenly or unevenly depending on the school, over the three rounds. This type of process may thus make a round more or less preferable, depending on the distribution of the places between the rounds.

- In the "rolling admissions" process, such as is the case at NYU-Stern, places are distributed as and when applications from suitable candidates are received. It is therefore advantageous to the candidate to send their dossier in early. It should also be remembered that in order to be eligible for a student grant from the school, you must submit your application before January 15th. It is therefore in your interest to send it as early as possible.

Are there unofficial quotas?

No quotas; we admit qualified people, not numbers. That is why there is so much difference in the class profile each year.

Getting the
STANFORD
Admissions
Edge

Stanford
Graduate School of Business

Address	Stanford Graduate School of Business Stanford University 518 Memorial Way Stanford, CA 94305-5015
Telephone	(1) 650-723-2766
Website	www.gsb.stanford.edu/mba
E-mail	mba@gsb.stanford.edu

about the school

Founded	1925
Tuition Fees	$31,002
Some Famous Alumni	**Charles Schwab (founder & CEO, Charles Schwab & Co.);** Scott McNealy (CEO, Sun Microsystems); Vinod Khosla (co-founder, Sun Microsystems); Philip E. Knight (CEO, Nike); Kurt Lauk (Globe Capital Partners); Lorenzo Zambrano (chairman & CEO, Cemex); Jeff Bewkes (Chairman & CEO, HBO); Ann Livermore (VP & General Manager, Hewlett-Packard)

the application

Application File	Paper application: mailed on request or downloadable from website. Online application: see website.
Application Deadlines	1st round: early November 2nd round: early January 3rd round: mid-March
App. File Elements	• 2 essays (+ 1 optional) • 3 letters of recommendation • transcripts • GMAT (and TOEFL, if applicable) • résumé

rankings

Publication	Business Week						US News & World						Financial Times		
General Ranking	90	92	94	96	98	00	94	96	98	99	00	01	99	00	01
	7	7	4	7	9	11	1	1	1	1	1	1	3	3	3

The School	Before the MBA	After the MBA

before the MBA	**Class of 2002**
# applicants	5,431
# applicants entering	365
% women students	41%
% minority students	24%
% international students	29%
# countries represented	28
Age (years)	
mean	27.2
median	27
range	23 - 37
Education pre-MBA	
Applied/Natural Sciences	5.1%
Behavioral/Social Sciences	13.5%
Business/Accounting	15.4%
Economics	26.2%
Engineering/Computer Science	25.4%
Humanities	11.4%
Mathematics	3.0%
Professional experience	
avg. years work experience	4.4
median total compensation	$72,000
Industry (Top 5)	
Consulting	21.6%
Investment Banking/Brokerage	11.4%
Venture Capital	4.1%
Investment Management	4.1%
Foundations/Non-Profit Organizations	3.8%
GMAT	
average	727
range	620 - 800
TOEFL	
average	280
range	257-300

after the MBA | Class of 2000

	Class of 2000
avg. offers per student	3
# companies recruiting on campus	379
# companies in recruiting activities	1,170

Main career choices	
Management Consulting	18%
E-Commerce/Internet Services	14%
Manufacturing	14%
Venture Capital/Private Equity	14%
Entrepreneurship	10%
Investment Banking/Brokerage	9%
Other (incl. Nonprofit/Govt., Entertainment/ Media, Investment Management/Hedge Funds)	10%
Undecided	3%
Function	
Consultant	18%
Venture Capitalist/Private Equity	14%
Brand/Product/Marketing Manager	12%
Business Development/Strategic Planner	11%
Founder/Entrepreneur	10%
Investment Banker	7%
Investment Research/Portfolio Manager	4%
Other Functions (including Product Development Manager, General Manager)	13%
Undecided	11%
Geographical location	
North America	85%
Central and South America	5%
Europe	5%
Asia and Australia	4%
Middle East and Africa	1%
Salary	
Median Base Salary	$100,000
Median Total Compensation	$135,000
Alumni	
# Alumni in the world (MBA)	15,500
# Cities with alumni association	45

Top 11 employers

1. McKinsey & Co.
2. Goldman, Sachs & Co.
3*. Bain & Co.
3*. Intuit
3*. Siebel Systems, Inc.
3*. Boston Consulting Group

4. Loudcloud
5. Morgan Stanley Dean Witter
6*. Cyclone Commerce
6*. Deloitte Consulting
6*. Yahoo!

* indicates a tie

author

Name   E. MICHEL

MBA Class of 2001. Began working for the Ministry of the Environment in the Pacific before joining Accenture.

School specifics
STANFORD

INTRODUCTION

Situated at the heart of Silicon Valley, 28 miles (45 km) south of San Francisco, the Stanford Graduate School of Business (GSB) is a collection of superlatives. Notably, it is the most selective business school in the States, the most sought-after by employers and its graduates are the highest-paid; it is the most innovative, and also the most expensive. Some of these qualifiers may be questioned by our colleagues from other prestigious institutions. However, Stanford has inarguably established an exceptional place in the world of business schools.

Stanford's principal assets are:
- The emphasis placed on research, which attracts prestigious professors including: Irv Grousbeck (Entrepreneurship), James Van Horne (Finance), and Paul Romer (Economics) to name a few, and occasional lecturers such as Andrew Grove (CEO of Intel).
- The very strong synergy with Silicon Valley's network of businesses (a side note: the acronym for SUN Microsystems stands for Stanford University Network).
- Small class size and sense of community.
- A balanced approach to teaching and learning.

Stanford Graduate School of Business (GSB) was founded in 1925 by Herbert Hoover, before he was elected president of the U.S., in order to attract and retain the West Coast's most brilliant students, who were previously obliged to flee to the East to continue their studies. The school was established in the heart of Stanford University, which was then dubbed "The Farm" by students in reference to Senator Leland Stanford, who donated his farm land to set up the university. The university includes seven schools which reflect its primary areas of specialization:

- Graduate School of Business
- School of Earth Sciences
- School of Education
- School of Engineering
- School of Humanities & Sciences
- School of Law
- School of Medicine

In addition to the wide range of courses offered by Stanford GSB, either in the core curriculum or electives, it is possible to take courses in Stanford University's other schools. The school encourages taking "intellectual risks" and invites students to explore new areas to broaden their spectrum of skills. Likewise, it allows a great deal of flexibility in the selection of the academic program. For example, students can complete research projects in partnership with companies as part of their second year of study. Two programs – one in public administration and the other in international management – include courses on these themes and permit students, on a voluntary basis, to obtain a certificate in addition to their degree (about 10% of each entering class). Several events sponsored by these programs are open to all students (such as meetings with political figures, study abroad opportunities, etc.)

The grading system allows students to take initiatives within their academic program as well as in extracurricular activities. Stanford GSB makes a point of not ranking students, and of not posting grades. At graduation, the top 10% of each class is designated as Arjay Miller Scholars (in memory of one of the GSB's former deans). Likewise, the top student in each class is recognized as the Henry Ford II Scholar.

Stanford is a breeding ground for ideas and exploration is a dynamic environment and business community. Upon graduation from the business school, students find many diverse opportunities, including creating their own companies, working for start-ups with key responsibilities in management, and leading new initiatives at Fortune 500 companies. All of the major players in the business world have their eyes on Silicon Valley. Many come to study this economic miracle and hope to reproduce it elsewhere. This environment offers considerable opportunities to Stanford GSB students, regardless of career choice.

THE DEAN'S VISION

Robert L. Joss has been Dean of Stanford GSB since September 1, 1999. A former student of the business school, where he obtained his MBA and Ph.D., he made his career in banking at Wells Fargo Bank and at Westpac Banking Corporation (Australia). Most recently, he was CEO of Westpac, one of the largest banks in the Pacific, where he managed more than 33,000 employees.

"We're trying to have you leave with something in your head that will serve you for at least 30 more years. … What we're trying to do is give you a tremendous underpinning of academics, so you won't find that we're trying to tell you what's working today.

"You will find our faculty somewhat different from those in other business schools. You can read articles in the press and it seems if you can get into one business school or another you've pretty much succeeded. However, they're not all the same. You don't find other schools with Nobel Laureates on their faculties, or as many distinguished members of important groups such as the American Academy of Arts and Sciences. This means our faculty is continually searching for new ideas and research and bringing it into the classroom, not merely harvesting material that has been working for them for a number of years. That's not what will serve you. They're going to push you and challenge you with new ideas and new knowledge. You're not here so much to acquire knowledge, because we don't make it our goal to simply pack into you all the current knowledge we have available. You are here instead to make mental efforts under criticism, criticism in the best sense of the word - give and take, a critique with your peer group and also with the faculty. You are here to stretch yourself to understand what works and what doesn't.

"Stanford GSB, being an academic school, is also a school of management, and management is something I passionately believe is the world's greatest need right now. I look around the world and I see no shortage of ideas, no shortage of capital, no shortage of technology, but there is a huge shortage of management and management skill. Society needs good management institutions, public and private."

Source: Stanford GSB News and Information

THE SCHOOL YEAR

CALENDAR AND PROGRAM:

The Stanford MBA degree program lasts 18 months spread over two academic years. The first year is geared toward mastering basic management skills. The second year allows for a deepening of these skills, with the possibility of developing particular expertise according to the student's wishes.

Programs	Sept–Dec	Jan-Mar	Apr-Jun	Jun-Sept	Sept–Dec	Jan-Mar	Apr-Jun
September entry (360 students)	1st term 2nd term 3rd term Required curriculum + electives			Internship and/or vacation	4th term 5th term 6th term Elective curriculum		
	1st year			2nd year			

The structure of the degree program allows each student a lot of flexibility to shape an academic program according to his or her preferences. A system of waiver exams allows students to explore other areas of interest if they have already mastered a subject. Typically, accountants and financial professionals will be exempt from Financial Accounting, and engineers from Data and Decisions. The program is once again adapted to take into account results from faculty research, changes in the economic environment, student evaluations, etc. The particulars of all the courses need to be frequently updated as well. The school's information pack accompanying the application forms and the school's website constitute the primary sources of information for those interested in Stanford.

FIRST YEAR: THE CORE CURRICULUM
The first year allows students to develop a solid base in all the disciplines necessary for future managers. The year consists mainly of common required courses for all students in the same entering class.

Orientation
Orientation Week includes a series of events, both academic and social, which help acclimate new students to the GSB environment; there is the opportunity to meet fellow classmates, faculty, staff, and alumni. Attendance of orientation week is mandatory.
In addition, Stanford GSB offers Pre-enrollment Programs to raise students' skills to a common level before they begin the MBA:
- Quantitative: review of math basics necessary for the courses. The school also offers a review program that students may complete on their own before classes start.
- International: preparation for American student life: American administrative procedures, teaching styles at Stanford GSB, communication methods, etc. An excellent way to get settled at Stanford and to start to meet future colleagues. Students' partners are welcomed during this program.

Pre-Term

From year to year, over three weeks following Orientation, professors, students and administration develop a condensed version of the concepts, skills and techniques which require instruction before the actual event of the start of classes. For the academic year 2001-2002, the pre-term included:

- Ethics: An introduction to the principal concepts in ethics and practical application through the study of concrete case studies from the business world.
- Managing Through Mutual Agreement: Theory and practice in management through the study of the influence and reciprocal agreement by comparison of authoritarian and hierarchical approaches.
- Modeling and Analysis: Reviews intermediate/advanced modeling and spreadsheet analysis. Since Excel is a critical skill for this course, the school offers a compensatory class on the program before classes start.

The Core Curriculum

The courseloads for the three quarters of the first year are very full. Thus, except for opting out of a core curriculum course, it seems difficult (but certainly not impossible) to take an elective course to complement the official program during the first two trimesters. In the third trimester, students can choose one to two elective courses.

- The first quarter is concentrated on fundamental management skills: Accounting, Microeconomics I (foundations), Statistics, Organization, Non-Market Management (Political Economics).
- The second quarter moves toward advanced management skills: Microeconomics II, Finance, Marketing, Financial Management.
- The third quarter tackles the responsibilities of a managing director: Strategy, Organization within the Bounds of New Technologies, Human Resources Management.

Don't hesitate to surf the Stanford GSB website for detailed descriptions of all of these courses. However, don't forget that these courses are altered every year, so the courses described will have surely changed by the time you take them. The student body is divided up into sections of 66 students, the make-up of which change each trimester.

In the core curriculum, students are divided into sections of 66 students each. These relatively small groups permit a high level of interaction with professors. Students are actively encouraged to work in study groups of five or six people, either pre-assigned or chosen by those taking the class. These groups allow an intense exchange between students when they prepare case studies. They also allow students to complete projects in teams for some courses (market studies, opportunity analyses, business plans, for instance).

SECOND YEAR: ELECTIVES

Each year, about a hundred elective courses are taught at Stanford GSB. About half of the electives are added or modified in a substantial way every five years to reflect the changes in the economy and in research. Macro-Investment Analysis, Social Entrepreneurship, Managing Organization Networks and Electronic Commerce are some examples of recently added courses. In addition, students can take many courses in other divisions of Stanford (mainly within the School of Engineering, the School of Law, the School of Education and the School of Humanities and Sciences). Students therefore have a wide range of possibilities to create their academic program in the second year (in the first year, to a lesser degree).

The Stanford MBA does not require an area of specialization. Students can decide to tailor their MBA experience and can choose courses accordingly. In addition to their degree diploma, students may decide to obtain one of two existing "certificates": Global Management and Public Management. These "certificates" illustrate Stanford's desire to emphasize the globalization of the economy and its impact on managers for the former, and on the importance of management of public institutions for the latter. Typically, a large number of students demonstrate interest in these programs, though about fifty of them complete all of the coursework.

To complement the coursework, the school allows students in their second year to complete research projects called "390". These projects have to be supervised by a faculty member and must offer an educational advantage for the student. It is an excellent opportunity to apply one's knowledge and further explore a particular subject area. Many Silicon Valley companies offer themes that reflect their particular concerns.

You are also free to choose your own subject area. Between a third and a half of each entering class take advantage of this opportunity to start writing a business plan proposal, or a market forecast analysis. Some examples of recent studies:

- Children's Internet Tools: analysis of potential business opportunities: an analysis of the market for internet portals for children.
- Building a Loyal Customer Base at XXX: strategic approaches in the development of a loyal customer base
- Business Opportunities in Internet Telephone: a market forecast analysis of telephone service on the internet. These projects can be completed either individually or in groups of up to four.

THE COURSES – WHAT'S HOT... WHAT'S NOT

The core curriculum: all of these courses are required, unless you have opted out of them. Together, they cover all of the skills the Stanford GSB would like you to acquire. Each of these courses is under the responsibility of a tenured professor.

Electives: by a process of natural elimination, the worst electives don't attract enough students and are rapidly removed from the curriculum. The electives in the Entrepreneurship department, such as "Electronic Commerce" and "Entrepreneurship: Formation of New Ventures", are especially popular. The reputation of certain professors can sometimes attract too many students. Therefore, it is difficult to register for courses with professors Grousbeck (Entrepreneurship) and Van Horne (Finance) during the same trimester!

Many criteria are taken into account in course evaluations: the material, the style of teaching, the professor, the level of student participation, their expectations and the other courses offered. In addition, from one year to another, some courses disappear and others are created. Some courses are totally redesigned, so one single title can correspond to very different courses from one year to the next. Similarly, the level of satisfaction is difficult to assess. Nevertheless, on the opposite page is a table featuring the results of a poll completed by a sample of students from the entering class of 2000 at the end of their second year.

Some explanations:
- These figures are difficult to compare with other MBA programs. In effect, the students'

	Below expectations	In line with expectations	Above expectations	Outstanding
Accounting	5%	25%	35%	35%
Economic Analysis and Policy	16%	26%	32%	26%
Finance	0%	37%	11%	53%
General and Interdisciplinary	18%	12%	35%	35%
Human Resources Management	6%	24%	35%	35%
Marketing	53%	32%	5%	10%
Political Economics	21%	36%	21%	21%
Organizational Behavior	5%	35%	20%	40%
Strategic Management	6%	25%	13%	56%
Operations, Information and Technology	10%	30%	20%	40%

expectations differ widely. In addition, these figures change dramatically from one year to the next according to changes in the program, arrivals and departures of professors, and changes in student expectations. Thus one must take a great deal of precaution in interpreting the above table.

- The entering class of 2000 had a low opinion of the Marketing courses. The core Marketing course was particularly criticized and was targeted for major modifications. The school made special recruitment efforts to attract professors such as the brilliant Jennifer Aaker. This was greatly appreciated by the entering class of 2001. Thus, based on her first year, she was awarded the Distinguished Teaching Award by the students.
- Finally, the core courses are given simultaneously by several professors. So the same course may be perceived differently, according to its professor.

Really, the most important thing to remember is Stanford's great capacity not only to create new courses in response to student expectations, but to question those less appreciated.

TEACHING METHODS

The teaching methods can be generally categorized in the following way: 50% case studies, 30% lecture and 20% simulations (role plays). However, this may vary widely depending on the courses you take. In contrast to some other business schools which almost exclusively use the case study approach, the methods used are adapted according to the subject and the professor. This contributes greatly to the richness of the teaching.

THE GRADING SYSTEM

The Stanford GSB grading system rewards the values of cooperation and teamwork. Similarly, it encourages risk-taking. Students must give it their best in all of the academic disciplines as well as in their extra-curricular activities.

In concrete terms, in order to obtain your MBA, you must earn a minimum total of 100 credits. Some "certificates" like the Global Management program requires additional units, which could raise the total to 108 to 116 credits. Courses last one quarter and you can get from one to four credits from each course. Typically, a course with 20 sessions is worth four credits, and how many credits other courses are worth is determined in proportion to the number of sessions.

The grades:

H: An honors performance, typically received by 10% of the students
HP: A high pass performance.
P: An average passing performance.
LP: A passing performance, but one in the low end of the distribution of passing grades.
U: A failing or unsatisfactory performance.
EX: Exempt courses. (Does not affect grade calculations.)
The percentage of students receiving H and HP combined typically will be no more than 35% total. The percentage of students receiving H, HP and P combined typically will be no more than 75% total. The grade of U is awarded strictly on an absolute basis and is grounds for disqualification.

The school strongly recommends that students do not report their grades to anyone outside. This rule is especially well respected! Class ranking does not exist either. Only students with cumulative averages in the highest bracket – the top 10% – are recognized with the presentation of "Arjay Miller Scholar" diplomas. Other students are awarded for their extra-curricular achievements (school social activities, for example) with different titles and scholarships.

The precise inner workings of the grading system are definitely not of great interest for a potential student. However, it is important to note that with this system, the MBA program has succeeded in reconciling the need to monitor the progress of its students while at the same time encouraging them to take risks. Because the grades are not published, students can throw themselves into studies of material they are less familiar with, without being obsessed with the risk of getting mediocre grades. Thus, accountants, if they wish, may widen their field of knowledge by taking courses in Marketing or Entrepreneurship instead of their umpteenth course in Financial Reporting for Mergers. In effect, they will not be penalized for the difficulties imposed, for example, by a mediocre class rank at the end of their studies.

This grading system represents recent reforms by the administration intended to reinforce recognition of the top students while conserving the anonymity of the grades for all the students. As another example of this, a scholarship award of $25,000 was put into place to compensate the top five students at the end of the first year.

GROUP WORK

Group work is actively encouraged as part of the academic program. Different means to this end are employed:

- The administration assigns you a study group for most of the required courses. You prepare case studies and projects within this group. This practice presents an immense educational advantage of mixing people of different backgrounds, nationalities and professional experiences. What do a European new technologies consultant, an American ex-Marine officer, a New York mergers and acquisitions banker, a raw materials trader from Japan, and a sales director all have in common? They might, for example, analyze, together, the challenges presented to General Motors in the process of marketing its new series of pick-ups and detail different marketing strategies. The different areas of expertise and points of view offered by the various group members are enriching (but should I really go on raving about the merits of group work?). On the other hand, this method is particularly time-consuming and requires using a lot of diplomacy to maintain a good social atmosphere among group members.

- Grades are kept secret and students are not ranked. Students collaborate well together and this spirit of exchange and co-apprenticeship drives them to complete all of what the program asks of them.

THE TEACHERS

About 95 professors divide their time between teaching and research. Most of them are employed full-time, but some come to teach on a temporary basis for one course or one seminar (Andrew Grove, CEO of Intel and Stanford GSB lecturer, for example). The business school's reputation attracts numerous professors, and to land a position there is extremely difficult. The school accommodates renowned researchers who have been recognized by awards as prestigious as the Nobel Prize: Myron Scholes – Professor of Finance (created Black-Scholes, for the experts) or William Sharpe – Professor of Finance (devised AD-M).

Considered among the most well-respected professors are also:
- Professors Irving Grousbeck and Charles Holloway – Entrepreneurship
- Professors David Baron and David Brady – Economics and Political Science
- Professors David Kreps and Paul Romer – Economics
- Professors James Van Horne and Darrell Dufie - Finance
- Professor Jennifer Aaker - Marketing
- Professor Jeffrey Pfeffer - Organizational Behavior (or Human Resources)
- Professors William Beaver and Mary Barth - Accounting

THE INTERNATIONAL SIDE

Stanford is a markedly international community. More than one third of the students and teachers were born outside of the U.S. In 1999, 55% of the graduating class accepted jobs with an international dimension, and 20% of former students currently live outside of the U.S.

The school pays particular attention to this international orientation. This has been demonstrated on many occasions through courses and by research undertaken in this area. Though most of the courses have an international component, 20% of the electives concentrate primarily on management in an international context. Case studies frequently deal with European, Asian, or South American companies.

The Global Management Program (www.gsb.stanford.edu/gmp) concentrates most of its efforts on making the school more internationally oriented. Besides the "certificate" offered to students who wish to orient their careers toward international management, the GMP also offers numerous opportunities to students who deal with the economic realities of other countries. The Global Management Immersion Experience (GMIX) permits students to work in a region of the world that is new to them. After taking a course aimed at international issues in the first year, students can complete a summer internship abroad. These internships are followed by a research project related to this experience in cooperation with a local company.

The students themselves are also the source of many international initiatives. Several clubs (Europe, Asia, South America...) organize cultural and business meetings between students and with local economic actors. It is not uncommon to be able to meet foreign company directors at events, presentations and colloquia organized at Stanford GSB. Between trimesters, study abroad projects are organized involving the economic environment of foreign countries. Recently, groups of students have gone to Brazil, India, Thailand, Vietnam, and Scandinavia.

THE ENTREPRENEUR'S CORNER

Due to its history and its privileged location in the heart of Silicon Valley, the Stanford MBA program is strongly oriented towards entrepreneurship. In 1996, the Center for Entrepreneurial Studies was created. Under the direction of professors Holloway and Grousbeck, this center facilitates the interactions between Stanford GSB and the business community through the following activities:

- Development of research programs focusing on challenges faced by entrepreneurs in the areas of strategy, organization, and project realization.
- Updating of coursework to take into account the concerns of entrepreneurs.
- Putting entrepreneurs in contact with students.
- Providing support for student activities: entrepreneurship club, student projects and "390".

Many students develop business plans during their stay at Stanford GSB. Close to 20% of the last graduating class now work in companies with less than 50 employees. Some examples of companies created by students from that class include: PlanetPro.com (web-site hosting and production assistance), ChinaRen (internet provider in China), and Autodaq.com (business to business e-commerce).

Students can participate in different business plan competitions organized by various Silicon Valley figures (Venture Capitalists, Business Angels) and by other universities. The School of Engineering organizes several competitions such the E-challenge and Global challenge. These competitions allow students from different divisions of Stanford to meet one another and to initiate contact with investor and entrepreneur groups in Silicon Valley.

LIFE AT STANFORD

SAN FRANCISCO AND SILICON VALLEY

For those who haven't yet checked out the university, Stanford is located in Palo Alto, a small city of 60,000 residents 25 miles (48 km) south of San Francisco. Stanford is the heart and soul of Silicon Valley. This valley includes the length of the Bay Area, from north of San Francisco to San Jose (24 km/15 miles south of Palo Alto), where nearly 8,000 businesses function as the driving force behind the American and global electronics and computer technology industries. Companies as celebrated as Hewlett-Packard, Intel and Apple have were born there. Stanford University is both instigator and beneficiary of this exceptional economic environment. The very strong synergy between the neighboring industries and Stanford allows it to be at the forefront of teaching and to provide the flourishing local economy with the brains it needs.

All along Sand Hill Road to Palo Alto, hundreds of VCs (Venture Capitalists) advise and finance entrepreneurs all over the globe who come to develop their business concepts in the Valley. Millions of dollars are invested each year in new high tech companies (start-ups). These investments represent the full range of high tech businesses: computers (especially the internet), biotechnology, environmental sciences, and medical technology are especially well-represented. Most high-tech companies are represented in Silicon Valley. Similarly, many financial institutions are attracted by the investment opportunities (offices for Morgan Stanley Dean Witter and Goldman Sachs are technically on the Stanford University campus).

Stanford has the additional advantage of being in California. I wouldn't want to compete with the many authors who praise the merits of this state for being the birthplace of many cultural movements, its ideal climate, and its well-preserved wilderness. San Francisco attracts tourists from the world over for its extraordinary scenic views of its roller-coaster-like streets, coastline and breathtaking buildings. Offering museums, cultural events, bars and nightclubs, it's a city that Stanford students love to visit.

THE CAMPUS

The Stanford University campus is particularly nice to live on; the natural environment is well-preserved - a large park with eucalyptus and oak trees surrounds the buildings, to the great pleasure of joggers and squirrels. Strict construction regulations limit the height of buildings and create the harmonious combination of Hispanic mission-type architecture with more contemporary constructions.

Leisure time activities: on campus, one can participate in many cultural and athletic activities, even indoors. Several concert halls play host to events year-round. Likewise, the music, theatre and film departments sponsor various events open to all students. The seven university libraries offer an enormous choice of reference material, periodicals, newspapers and videos. All of the athletic facilities are open to students and their partners: several pools, numerous tennis courts, weight-lifting rooms, sports fields, and a well-known 18-hole golf course. Finally, the largest stadium in Northern California is on campus and accommodates high-level athletic competitions.

Services: many world-class stores are easily accessible to students at the Stanford Shopping Center. On campus, bicycle is the best means of transportation. Otherwise, there is a network of free buses covering the whole campus. Daycare centers and schools are available for children. The university hospital and Cowell Clinic, both located on campus, offer a full range of health care services. Finally, Palo Alto and the neighboring towns provide the full complement of services available for students.

HOUSING

Stanford University assures housing for all of its students for the first year of the MBA program. A lottery system assigns apartments, taking into account your preferences. In fact, according to your family situation, certain residences may be available to you and others not:

For single students:
- Schwab Residential Center: opened in 1997, it houses 280 people in two-bedroom "suites". These suites have two separate entries, two bedrooms, two bathrooms and a kitchen, which is the only room shared by the two roommates. These apartments are especially well-equipped: they are furnished, air-conditioned, and have high-speed internet connection. Computer labs, athletic facilities, study halls and rooms with stereo and video equipment are available to residents. The cost is about $700 per month (indicated on the budget below). Situated about two blocks from Stanford GSB, this luxurious center more closely resembles a professional training center than a student residence.
- The university offers other options, such as the Richard W. Lyman Graduate Residence and the Liliore Green Rains Houses. And you could be so lucky as to be paired up with Silicon Valley's next Mr. or Mrs. Packard! Finally, some housing in Escondido Village may be shared by two single students. These are small single-story buildings opening on a large tree-lined park. Schwab remains the best-liked residence on campus. Also, be sure to register in time so that you will be assured housing, though it may not necessarily be in Schwab.

For married couples without children:
- Escondido Village has several seven and 11-floor buildings available to married couples without children. The apartments consist of one bedroom, a bathroom, a living room and a small kitchen. Most of them have a large balcony, where you can have lunch, work or just sunbathe! An ambitious renovation program, completed in 2000, saw the refurbishment of a large number of these housing units.
- For couples where both are Stanford students, a few lofts are available (less than 10).

For married couples with children:
- Some small houses with two to four bedrooms are reserved. With playgrounds, bike paths, and schools nearby, the campus is a real paradise for children.

SOCIAL LIFE

The school's extra-curricular life is very intense. So the most difficult thing is to find enough time to participate in all of the activities one would like to.

Clubs: currently, there are more than sixty clubs that energize the school's social life. There are:
- professional clubs: Consulting, High-tech, Venture Capital, Marketing
- philanthropic clubs: Social Entrepreneurship, I Have a Dream (academic support for disadvantaged secondary school students.)
- athletic clubs: ski, golf, rugby, volley-ball, soccer, tennis; and clubs just for socializing: Wine Circle, Student Show.

These clubs, all student student-run, organize meetings, debates, trips, and exchanges all year long.

Social activities: lots of occasions to develop one's network of social contacts are offered: Breakfasts, Wednesday night outings, and Friday night cocktails - these are also opportunities to meet other students from outside the school.

Lectures: many speakers come to present their companies (110 companies made presentations last year), their experiences (career, industry, setting up a company), or the results of their work projects (research, studies).

Resources: the Communications department organizes a series of seminars open to students (Successful Presentations, Persuasion, Communicating with the Press). The Career Management Center (CMC) facilitates job hunting through seminars, company forums (International, Entrepreneurship), on-campus interviews (318 companies last year). In addition, the CMC helps students job hunt (advice, résumé, mock interviews). The information system at Stanford GSB provides several services to students (email, internet access, online forums and courses). Finally, the Jackson Library allows access to extensive resources: reference material, periodicals, databases.

TUITION COSTS

Stanford GSB offers a financial aid package to all of its students. It is certainly the most important point to keep in mind in your comparison of the different MBA programs you apply to. The school doesn't want financial constraints to prevent some potential students from applying or from being accepted to come to Stanford. The financing options include scholarships and loans. These are also available for international students. You need to make a careful calculation of expenses, taking into account your needs (see below), and all of your financial assets in order to evaluate Stanford's offer to you. The average scholarship award is $6,000 per year, which is far from negligible; as for loans, the interest rates are relatively high, but allow you to do a comparative analysis with your available credit sources (interest rates, repayment schedule, deductibles, guarantees, loan currency). You can of course accept the scholarship, but refuse the loans.

That said, financing your education is one of those crucial issues that you have to deal with as part of the process of obtaining an MBA at Stanford. It comes down to being a real investment in time and in money. Though a good portion of the costs incurred by your MBA are tuition fees, the total costs will largely depend on the standard of living you want to have during your two years at Stanford. In addition, if you don't want your financial situation to dictate your choice of an employer upon graduation from Stanford (i.e., if you are headed to an investment bank, it will be for love of the business, and not to pay off your debts), you have to set a realistic budget and carefully manage your expenses.

The chart below combines the figures for the academic years 1999-2000 and 2000-2001 to give an estimate of the total cost of the MBA program for two academic years of 9 months each:

	Single on Campus (Two Years)	Single off Campus (Two Years)
Tuition Fees	59,898	59,898
Living costs	26,148	32,472
Books and supplies	4,110	4,110
Transportation	1,229	2,754
Medical Insurance	1,401	1,401
Total	**$92,856**	**$100,633**
		+$712/month/child

On the basis of these figures, you should plan your own budget. To do this, here's some general advice:
- The figures presented here are not overestimates; they are used as the basis for Stanford GSB's calculations for the financial aid package it may offer you. Don't forget your additional costs such as moving, transportation, purchase of a vehicle (not absolutely necessary if you live on-campus, but useful).

- Don't forget the rate of inflation; it will certainly have an effect on tuition fees by the time you enroll. Also, if you want to take three months of vacation between the two years, you will have to finance them. A majority of students decide to complete summer internships that pay about $6,000 per month.
- The high cost of living in Silicon Valley and Palo Alto (the city that surrounds Stanford) and its environs has beaten some American records, especially in real estate costs.
- Set a budget ahead of time that allows for some extras. It would be a pity to pass up opportunities for budgetary reasons. Compared to the average salaries upon graduation, the costs remain relatively modest.

Find out via the Stanford web-site or direct email contact with the school whether a major city near you has a Stanford Business Club, or similar organization, which may have an agreement with a national bank offering low interest rate loans.

STUDENT VIEWS

The first reason I chose Stanford was because of its great weather/location. Since I'm married and my wife can't work in the U.S., a good environment was necessary for her to enjoy her life abroad. Of course I love the cooperative culture of Stanford. Unbelievably, before every exam, several students kindly post their personal notes/summary of readings for the whole class. This strong collaborative culture helped me a lot, as an international student less fluent in English than my American classmates. Moreover, Stanford students are extremely smart and filled with a strong entrepreneurial spirit. I'm sure that the network I'm building will help me in my future career. Last but not the least, Stanford owns a great golf course and we can, as students, play there for only $20.

Being at Stanford does not only mean attending one of the top MBA programs in the world, it means enjoying the two best years of your life! With every breath I take since I've been at the GSB, I'm learning something. I'm learning from my wonderful classmates, from the extremely stimulating environment of the Silicon Valley and from the top-notch professors who teach in this School. The pool of admitted students at Stanford is composed of 360 incredibly diverse and talented individuals. You will work together with an opera director and a consultant, a medical doctor and a banker, a technology pro, a marketing whiz, and many more. Each of them will help you to gain a new perspective of the world and to challenge your entrenched assumptions. Furthermore, being part of such a small class allows you to really get to know your classmates and to develop long-lasting friendships. So, if "network" means to you not only a list of names you might call upon, but also a collection of emotions and memories deep in your mind, Stanford is the place where you want to be!

What makes your experience at the GSB absolutely unique is Silicon Valley, the world's largest incubator of ideas and successes. Every day you can attend panels about the latest technology issues and venture capital trends. And if your Club wants to organize a conference, just send out a couple of emails and you can get speakers such as Jeff Bezos (Amazon.com) or Scott McNealy (Sun Microsystems). If you think these are not good enough reasons for coming to Stanford, well, make a tour to the cold and rainy East coast in January and then come here, where the sun is always shining. This is what I did one year ago, when I had to make my final decision, and... I had no more doubts!

The primary reason I chose Stanford was my respect for the alumni. Over the course of my applications to U.S. business schools, I met a number of MBAs from top-ranked schools and I realized that I would work best with those from Stanford. It seemed to me that, unlike some of the top East coast business school alums, Stanford MBA's were clearly the best team-players, had the broadest interests, and were the most "easy-going".

Consequently, I had very high expectations for my fellow students before coming to Stanford. True to form, my classmates' capabilities and friendliness have not only fulfilled, but also exceeded these expectations, and they have provided me with an enjoyable experience both in and outside the classroom.

Another reason I would recommend the Stanford GSB is that I regard studying at the forefront of the New Economy as a clear advantage for my future career. In short, the people, the opportunities and the integrated lifestyle have made the Stanford GSB a unique personal experience for me.

My career goal is to be a socially responsible entrepreneur. Going to Stanford made the most sense for me. The first factor was the high level of entrepreneurship that it fostered. The major proof of this was the strong link between Stanford and the tremendous innovation and value that was coming out of Silicon Valley. The second factor was the strong social thrust that the school had. Indeed, Stanford was one of the few B-schools that offered the possibility to get a Public Management Program certificate together with the MBA degree.

So far, my experience has been even better than I had imagined it would be. One thing that has surprised and pleased me the most has been the level of cooperation among students. For example, during quantitative exams, some people would bring extra calculators/batteries and leave them in the courtyard for anyone who might be unlucky enough to need them.

Stanford's best qualities

#1 classmates
#2 the university's environment and that of Silicon Valley
#3 the courses

The combination of these three elements make Stanford the best MBA program in the world. Just go to Wharton and try to find one student who was admitted to Stanford. There isn't a single one. In contrast, here, 80% of the people had the choice, and chose the best: between Wharton and Stanford, there's no competition. Let's look closely at each of these three characteristics that place Stanford at the top of the MBA programs.

#1 Classmates

The person who is the key to success at Stanford is the director of recruitment. He personally selects each student for each class according to their personality traits and intelligence. Each of my 360 classmates is an exceptional individual. Each small group that forms (for studying or going out together) is like a Mission Impossible team. Each person has their own unique and unusual skills and talents Even the consultants and bankers have surprising hidden talents. Every discussion with a classmate is like the experience of reading a great book.

This remarkable selection process is only possible with a relatively small class and a low admissions rate. In coming here, you will feel like you are an essential part of a singular unicellular organism, constantly being enriched and nurtured by your neighbors vibrations.

#2 The University Environment

Stanford is a global epicenter of learning. It is a community devoted to research in pursuit of truth and excellence: just take one step outside of the GSB and you will be plunged into a wonderful world of scientists, artists, literary scholars (most of them at the peak of progress in their discipline) with whom you will have interactions that will enrich you forever.

For business, welcome to the geographical area that has triggered global economic growth. The development of the internet and the New Economy originated here, under the Palo Alto sunshine. Every single café is buzzing with talk of growing companies and new technologies that are going to sweep everything else away, so get in on these conversations! Every day, prestigious speakers come to Stanford GSB's auditoriums to talk about the changing world. Students from the East Coast, with pale complexions, visit us once a year to dive into what is essentially our daily bath.

#3 The Courses

Stanford GSB is a school: so there are courses, professors, and homework. 80% of our courses are taught by professors who are exceptional in both their fields of expertise and their clarity in teaching. There are of course one or two exceptions, courses that could be a little better, but on the whole the faculty's efforts to structure the coursework to form a coherent whole is evident in each and every class. Here, teaching is by the Socratic method, and the genius of the masters consists of orienting class discussions in such a way that we can spend an hour and a half talking about an issue, each student feeling like they have learned something new.

Warning: the work is demanding and this program is not for the lazy. You will spend on average two to three hours each day studying, in addition to attending your classes. A lot of the projects are done in groups, and each person makes their own unique and inspired contributions to the topic at hand. Hard work, but the end results make it all worth it.

The admissions application
STANFORD

INTRODUCTION

The Stanford Graduate School of Business (GSB) application consists of:
- 3 letters of recommendation
- transcripts (grade reports from your previous schools)
- GMAT scores (and TOEFL scores, if applicable)
- 2 obligatory essays + 1 optional essay
- a very detailed information sheet that includes personal and professional information (similar to a detailed résumé)

There are different options for completing your application online, including word processing to application submission online. It is even possible to pay the application fee on the Internet. The first stage in your application process is to surf the school's website (www.gsb.stanford.edu/mba). This site includes all of the resources the school gives you to get to know the program better. This will give you a taste ahead of time of the technological resources used at Stanford.

There are three application rounds each year: early November, early January and early March. The school recommends applying in the first two rounds for *four* reasons:

1) It is very difficult (but not impossible) to distinguish yourself from the other candidates in the third selection round: as there are fewer places available than during the other rounds, the candidates might pay the consequences.

2) In addition, applying during the first two rounds allows you more time, once you are admitted, to think about the choice you are faced with. In effect, once you choose one of the schools to which you've been accepted, you will have to plan the finances, logistics, etc. This extra time also lessens the risk of choosing an East coast school in haste, as well as giving you a little rest before the semester begins. This is even more relevant for international students, who have to take into account the problems involved with moving to another country.

3) You can participate in a weekend program for prospective students which takes place a month after the decision date for the first two rounds. It allows you to go to the campus and to meet professors, students and members of the administration, which will then give you a more precise idea of what awaits you.

4) Finally, you can take part in the on-campus housing lottery. In fact, to be housed on-campus presents many logistical and financial advantages, and it is harder to get one of these residences if you apply for the third round.

Applying to Stanford is no small affair. The application is particularly complete and requires a lot of time, especially for editing the essays. These require that you do some real introspection. However, besides the fact that this exercise offers you an excellent opportunity to work hard on preparing for your future and on what you want to do with it, you know it's worth it in the end. A lot of applicants give up during the application process; a large part of the selection decision is made based on motivation. Be persistent until you send your application and if you get to that point, you will have already displayed a good number of the qualities the Stanford GSB admissions office is looking for.

THE GMAT

Stanford, like most MBA programs, asks you to take the GMAT, and if you are an international applicant, the TOEFL; they are mandatory. Even though the importance placed on these tests is debatable, there's no point entering into the argument for too long: you must take them. Finally, the way in which the results are used by the admissions offices will allow you to judge them as well. If you are rejected solely on the grounds of your test scores, maybe the MBA program in question doesn't deserve you!

Note that at Stanford, the average GMAT score is very high: 720. What does that mean? For one thing, that the students perform particularly well in this exam! That means that above all the school looks for students who have especially high-level analytic skills. However, the GMAT is certainly not a principal selection criterion as such. It represents the school's interest in quantitative profiles.

SOME ADVICE

1. Cram intelligently!

Signing up for a preparation course isn't mandatory, but is widely recommended, as it is an excellent way to motivate you to study. However, be careful because if you need this kind of external motivation to prepare your MBA application, it's a bad sign. What are you going to do for the essays? You can find the vast majority of advice that one would get in this type of place in the numerous very good books on the subject. Finally, don't forget that the time you spend going to these courses, you could be using to peacefully study at home (as long as your neighbors aren't particularly noisy). You can guess that I myself did not take courses. Several people I know got very good scores (over 700) without going to a test preparation center. I encourage you, however, to go take a preliminary test, free most of the time, at one of these organizations. That will allow you to get oriented and then you can choose, knowing all the facts first.

2. Take the test as early as possible

Afterwards, you will be busy with other things: essays, letters of recommendation, then finances and moving. However, these tests are valid for a limited time. So you have to plan your period of test preparation wisely. Your preparation period should immediately precede taking the tests. You will be astonished by your capacity to quickly forget grammar rules, logic, and math learned for the test. Good GMAT (and TOEFL) scores will motivate you to continue the admissions process.

3. Be careful with the math section

Applicants endowed with non-scientific backgrounds and "allergic" to numbers will have to concentrate all their efforts on this section of the test. For that, there's no miracle solution. However, you will quickly notice that certain questions frequently reoccur on the GMAT. The number of math rules one has to know is relatively limited. Focus on these and forget the rest from your previous math classes. To optimize your preparation time, concentrate on "GMAT math." It is not impossible for people with a non-scientific education to attain scores in the 700 range.

THE ESSAYS

Stanford asks for two main essays, a secondary essay, and an optional essay (see explanation below) "Is that all?" It's definitely enough! Actually, the essays are not about a pure writing exercise (the kind with a word limit, or "describe a day in your professional life"). They're more like interviews on paper from which Stanford is seeking to get the most accurate idea possible of your personality. For your part, you have one sole objective: to nail down your admission. These two essays are critical for your application. Of all the various parts of your application, it's definitely through the essays that you can differentiate yourself most clearly from the other candidates. The Stanford essays give you complete freedom to express yourself. So, in three to seven pages (the length recommended by the admissions office for each of the essays), you are going to have to sell yourself!

Length of the essays: at first, you will find that three to seven pages is very long. Above all, don't forget the practical guidelines: double-spaced and minimum 10-point font -- you have to consider the readers of your essay who also read several hundred others! As you continue writing, you will end up thinking that three to seven pages is the minimum you need to fully express yourself.

WHAT STANFORD IS LOOKING FOR IN YOUR ESSAYS

Stanford wants to get to know you better. And no, it's not more complicated that, or at least so it seems. While you are looking to be admitted to this MBA program, Stanford for its part wants to select the best candidates possible, i.e. people with a superior education, rich and diverse professional experiences, and admirable personal qualities (refer to the interview with the Director of Admissions for more details). These people contribute an important additional value to the educational process by sharing their experiences with the other students. Following their graduation, they contribute to the prestige of the program by embarking on brilliant careers.

Up to 1999, Stanford offered the two following essays:
- Each of us has been influenced by the people, events, and situations in our lives. How have these influences shaped who you are today? (Our goal is to get a sense of who you are, rather than what you have done.)
- Based on your professional experiences to date, what are your short- and long-term career goals? Why do you now wish to earn an MBA? What specific aspects of the Stanford MBA Program make it attractive to you? How will this experience help you to achieve your short- and long-term goals?

For 2000, those two essays have been replaced by the two following:
- What matters most to you, and why?
- Given your reasons for earning an MBA degree, what type of alternate preparation might you seek if formal MBA programs did not exist? (Note: The limit is eight pages. Please use Additional Information page if necessary)

To complement these, two optional essays are offered to students. "Optional" means that nothing obliges you to write them. A good number of your potential peers have been admitted without having written them. However, these essays allow you to express your interests in one of the two programs offered by Stanford GSB to supplement the MBA, i.e. the Global Management Program and the Public Management Program. Apart from any real interest you might have in one of these two programs, writing these essays allows you to highlight some of the strengths of your candidature: perhaps your background is exceptionally international, or you have a particular interest in working in the public sector. However, don't underestimate the amount of extra work you are imposing on yourself, especially since it is more than likely that you will participate in these programs once you have been admitted. You should, therefore, definitely write one of these two essays, but the context will be different: you'll no longer be writing with the sole aim of getting into the MBA program.

- GMP ESSAY: Describe your interest in global management and how you intend to use your GSB/GMP experience to prepare you to manage more effectively in the global environment. (Suggested length: 500 words) (Note: The limit is six pages.)
- PMP ESSAY: Describe your interest in public service and how you intend to use your GSB/PMP experience to help prepare you for a leadership role in public service, whether in business, government, or the non-profit sector. (Suggested length: 500 words) (Note: The limit is six pages.)

Finally, Stanford GSB offers an additional essay that allows you to add elements that might have been left out of the other essays. It would be a shame not to benefit from this opportunity to make a case for your candidature one last time, or simply to explain a point that might be a little unclear in your application. A classic example of a use for this essay is to explain mediocre grades in your academic transcripts; choose a believable explanation -- major personal problems (illness or a death, for example), exceptional performance in extra-curricular activities (President of the Student Association or of a philanthropic association), setting up a business, an unusual grading system at your school or university, etc.

However, don't waste the reader's time with stuff that doesn't add any value to your candidature. Remember that the Admissions Officer is going to read several hundred applications over the course of the year. Win the reader over, and don't bore them to death with an extra essay that doesn't contribute any new information to your application.

Essay question wording:
- If there is any other information that is critical for us to know and is not captured elsewhere (e.g., extenuating circumstances affecting academic or work performance), please feel free to include that information here. (Note: The limit is eight pages.)

A FEW TIPS FOR WRITING STRONG ESSAYS

1. Do some introspection ahead of time.
Before you get down to writing your essays, you have to know yourself very well. Take a moment to reflect on the following themes: how would you describe yourself - your personality, your strengths/weaknesses, your successes/failures? What do you want to do after getting an MBA? Don't hesitate to do this exercise on paper. Once you have done this exercise, you will have an easier time figuring out which of your personal qualities you want to stress in the essays. This pre-writing job is more difficult than it sounds. Get help from your friends.

2. Demonstrate what sets you apart.

View the essays as a one-shot opportunity to paint a vivid, unique, and truthful picture of who you are inside beneath the veneer of good grades, work experience, and letters of recommendation. I encourage applicants to not only spend the majority of their preparation time brainstorming and outlining their strategy for their essay, but to also figure out the answer to basic question, 'What makes me different as a person ? What's my unique story ?', but setting forth to try to tell a story. Think of the outlining period as a way to warm yourself up, discovering what's really there, and organizing the story of your life out in front of you – it takes time to sort through and figure out where the meat of the story begins, just like a film editor sifts through countless takes of scenes, searching for those short, choice moments where the story really gets told in as succinct and effective manner as possible.

Most of all – think of the GSB in this way : it was only after I was admitted that I finally figured out how admissions worked (later verified by Marie Mookini, former director of admissions) – that each person really does have an absolutely amazing and unique personal story to tell, whether it was being an Olympic athlete, the director of the New York Metropolitan Opera, delivering power to the remotest regions of India, or piloting F-14 Tomcat fighters. Figure out your own 'magic', and then tell your story. Honestly, clearly, vividly, and personally.

3. Tell the truth.

Be aware that this is not about inventing aspects of yourself. Try to select strengths that have been apparent throughout your professional career, your educational experiences and your non-professional activities. All these points must be backed up with concrete examples in order to be taken into account. You will be much more credible if you provide real-life examples to illustrate your claims. That having been said, sometimes you won't want to reveal only the high points of a certain experience. It is never good to pour your heart out too much over your failures, except to show how you dealt with such an experience, that you have learned from it and how you have grown from it. Giving an example that has already been referred to in one of your letters of recommendation makes your application more coherent. However, to avoid being too repetitive, present it from a slightly different angle, using it to illustrate another facet of your personality.

4. Make the most of the freedom the essay format allows.

In fact, Stanford's essay format is definitely one of the least restrictive. The school doesn't impose a word limit, though it advises you not to stretch out what you have to say in your essays to more than seven pages. The wording of the questions is brief and leaves you a lot of autonomy to structure the essay. Make this work to your advantage in adopting a structure that will allow you to best demonstrate your talents; for example, prove your strong capacity for analysis and synthesis by rigorously organizing your essay.

5. Select aspects to focus on.

Which aspects of your personality correspond to the admissions criteria (see the three criteria below)? Can you illustrate them with relevant examples? This effort is going to allow you to sketch a portrait of yourself that responds to Stanford GSB's demands

EXAMPLES AND COMMENTARIES OF ESSAYS FOR STANFORD

Each of us has been influenced by the people, events, and situations in our lives. How have these influences shaped who you are today? (Our goal is to get a sense of who you are, rather than what you have done.)

The point of this essay:
Stanford is looking to get to know who you really are through your experiences.

Tips for the essay:
- As indicated, it is important to describe yourself through your past experiences. Don't submit an exhaustive list of all your achievements, but instead use them to illustrate salient aspects of your personality.
- You are in competition with several thousand applicants. Specify how you are different and unique.
- Similarly, don't forget to explain the logic of your experiences up to the present. Even if the Admissions Officer is not convinced, it is important to prove that you can rationalize the different stages of your previous experiences.
- It is important to mention extra-curricular activities. Mention your experiences in clubs, educational or philanthropic organizations, and sports teams. Through these, you should indicate skills you have developed.

Sample Essays:
Only extracts of the essays are presented here. The complete essays are the full length recommended by Stanford.

Example: Relating unique experiences.

The logical sequence of experiences is particularly convincing.

[My parents] enrolled [my sisters and me] in Japanese Saturday school and made certain that we were as conscientious about Japanese studies as we were about our American school classes and activities. In this way, my parents always sought to blend the two cultures within our household.

I believe the culmination of this fusion was my matriculation to a university in Japan. Though ultimately the decision rested on each one of us, my parents expressed their strong desire that their daughters attend a Japanese university after high school graduation. I was ecstatic about having been accepted to Stanford University as an undergraduate and looked forward to attending in the fall of 1989, but I gave my parents' request many hours of intense consideration. The self-confidence it had taken years to build within me, my friends, and my own sense of identity were at stake in committing the crucial years of my personal development to a country whose language I was not entirely comfortable speaking and whose culture was not entirely familiar to me. However, ultimately I decided to come to Japan because I wanted to examine what it really meant to be Japanese.

Until then I had felt that I was an American trapped inside a Japanese body. My parents had educated me in the Japanese language and traditions - but not in the Japanese way of thinking. Despite their teachings, to me the Japanese were still a race of "salary-men" who could not think for themselves, and Japan was a country which could not proclaim its views or take a leading role in world politics. I came to Japan because I wanted to establish a feel for Japanese ways before making such sweeping generalizations. More importantly, I wanted to explore my roots and in doing so impart an inner existence to my outer appearance. This decision is one of the most difficult choices I have ever made. It is also a choice which I believe has made the difference between a two-dimensional American of Japanese descent and a three-dimensional, international Japanese American.

[...] My experiences have given me confidence in personal and professional relationships and instilled in me a sense of challenge. Graduating from a major university with excellent grades and working as a professional in a conservative Japanese firm have underlined the success of my journey to Japan. I have learned that fear of failure should not keep a person from tackling a task head-on, and that sometimes you have to laugh at yourself and your blunders. Because I was able to overcome the frustrations that I encountered as a foreigner in her own country of origin, I can approach people and matters today with confidence and a positive attitude.

Author: Grace Y.

Example: Demonstrating Personality

The following essay also touches on themes of multiculturalism, but uses it to address such crucial topics as significant experiences, future goals, and particularly that most elusive of attributes -- personality. As the author explains, "In sorting through my personal history and all the moments of introspective realizations along the way, I learned quite a bit about myself in trying to tie it all together. In some ways, it was like somebody asking me, 'so what have you REALLY learned about life so far ?', and getting a chance to answer that question in my own words. I wanted to demonstrate that although it seemed that I was all over the map just looking at my resume and list of professional and extra-curricular pursuits, that I indeed had a method to my madness, a master plan, a macroscopic goal in mind." .

I've always had a problem with categories. Categories, groupings, classifications – I know that these are what allow the human mind to break down complex information into digestible bits of data, allowing us to handle complicated tasks like, say, hunting down a pair of size 9 red pumps in a place as vast as the Mall of America – but to me, I've always had a problem fitting comfortably under categories, like a blanket three sizes too small on a cold night.

If you were to take snapshot glimpses at specific portions of my background, interests, or achievements, then you'd take away a different image of me each time, much like the proverbial blind men who each touched a different portion of an elephant's body, and thought that the other person was dealing with a different beast altogether. Depending on which page of my file you read, you might gather that I'm a typical tech-head, because of my engineering degree and work experience in the automotive and computer industries – except this wouldn't seem to gel with my current position as a product marketing manager. If you looked at my ethnic background and test scores, you might imagine me as yet another Asian-American bookish overachiever – but then my stage acting career and second life as a semi-pro rock star blows the "good Chinese son" image. All my life, puzzled peers and frustrated friends have asked me, "how can somebody as artistically-inclined as yourself have such an interest in the stock market?" and "what's an engineer doing starring in a musical?" and even "why can't you just settle nicely into one side of the fence?" But that's the whole point: I'm purposely trying to hopscotch between both sides of every fence, not only because I'm sincerely interested in what's on the other side, but because things are never quite as different or unrelated as people imagine.

This belief and attitude was borne out of my own personal struggle in dealing with my multi-cultural background. Now, if you ask my Mom, she'll say that all the credit for my cross-cultural abilities is due to her. Apparently, I came home one day from Pinecrest Elementary School, all sobbing and drippy-nosed, because my classmates had called me racial slurs, pointing out how "different" I was from them. I cried to my Mom about how I wished I was never born Chinese, so that I could fit in with everyone else, hoping to make her feel guilty for my not having blond hair & blue eyes. Instead, she looked at me matter-of-factly and said, "Tim, you will never 'fit in'. In America, you'll always be seen as Chinese, because of the color of your skin. So, you have two choices: you can spend you're life trying to pretend that you aren't Chinese, and forget all about things like Lunar New Year and egg rolls, replacing them with Easter Bunnies and Big Macs; or else, you can treasure your culture, and use it to become more than just a 'normal' American."

... When I won a summer fellowship to study at Japan Center Michigan Universities, I had two goals in mind: quickly bring my Japanese skills up to fluency for my professional use, and come to personal terms with the country that had so firmly affixed itself in the id of my family's subconscious. After the summer classes ended, I headed off for Hiroshima and Nagasaki. When I finally toured the atomic bomb memorial museums, I was greatly saddened by what I saw. Not only did the displays depict Japan as an undeserving victim of senseless American hostility, but at the exits, the curators encouraged visitors to write down their anti-American sentiments in a guest log. I was shocked and offended to see tourists from all over the world angrily scribbling blistering slogans such as "GOD DEM AMERICA," and "USA, NO MORE BOM!" on their way out. Equally distraught American tourists were also lashing back with pens drawn: "What about Nanking?" "The Japanese are hypocrites!" "They would have dropped the bomb too, if they had it first!"

How was I to interpret everything I had experienced over the course of my summer in Japan, which had shown no signs of the seeds of hate that had blossomed so fully in the hearts of my parents' generation? I ended up writing down all these lessons I had learned in the Hiroshima museum's guest book – 10 pages, in fact – describing my own experiences that had revealed the situation to be far more complex than "who bombed who, and who deserved it," and far more needy of compassion and understanding across both sides of the Pacific. Afterwards, when I arrived back in Michigan from my summer abroad, I found several air-mailed letters waiting for me, all stamped from Japan. It turned out that other foreign visitors had not only read my piece, but had felt moved enough to respond and offer similar sentiments. Even local Japanese visitors had written to me to express their deep regret of past events, and thank me "for exemplifying a bright hope for the future." I eventually developed these writings into a composition entitled "Walls," which won the University of Michigan's 1995 Cooley Non-fiction Essay Contest.

Now, one unexpected side-effect of my efforts at cross-disciplinary fence-hopping and cross-cultural adaptation has been enormous ambition and the belief that I should never acknowledge limits. I don't mean that I've grown a particularly swelled head or anything, but rather that I feel restless unless I'm trying to take on more and more to expand my current capabilities. I never feel as if I know enough, or have seen enough places, or studied enough subjects in school, and as a result, I often worry that I'm missing something important or not getting the most out of what's around.

Still, for all my ambitious ideological and professional motivation behind my attempts to excel at as much as I can get my hands on, there are two very, very private personal reasons behind what I do. The first one I'm a little bit embarrassed to admit, but the second would hopefully make both Mom and my great-grandfather proud. When I was in high school, I did a palm reading in Chinatown one night, just for kicks. Although I'm not usually much for superstition, I remember my heart skipping a beat when she exclaimed, "Ai-yah! Your life-line cuts off abruptly, but it runs very deep, very strong. You lead a charmed life, but how long, I cannot say..." At first, I laughed it off as nonsense, before looking for pianos falling overhead and other freak accidents with my name written on them. Yet, in a way, I approved of her reading – even if my life were to be a brief shooting star across a dark sky, then wouldn't it make the most sense to make it the brightest flash possible, leaving a silver contrail behind as an example for others?

Author: Tim Chang

A little bit of humor. But be careful not to turn your essays into a big joke!

When I started to think about how to answer this question, a million events and people I knew passed through my mind. When I was a 3-year-old child, I was reprimanded for spilling ketchup all over our white walls of the dining room. Is the shame of the ketchup incident the reason that nowadays I never put sauces on my food? Maybe. I can't say for sure.

Author: Pedro M.

Based on your professional experiences to date, what are your short- and long-term career goals? Why do you now wish to earn an MBA? What specific aspects of the Stanford MBA Program make it attractive to you? How will this experience help you to achieve your short- and long-term goals?

The point of the essay:

Stanford is looking to understand what your motivations are in doing an MBA and how you are going to be able to benefit fully from such an experience.

Tips for the essay:

- You must convince the Admissions office of your interest in completing an MBA at Stanford. The Admissions Office probably doesn't doubt your motivation for being admitted after all the efforts your have made to finish your admissions application. However, Stanford has also understand why you want to get this education. What will you learn? What are you looking for? Are you going to take full advantage of the teachings offered? Or are you just looking for a new diploma to decorate your walls?
- You have to elaborate on a career/life plan and explain how a Stanford MBA is going to allow you to best achieve your goals and reach them more quickly.
- The two essays below do a good job of demonstrating the cohesiveness of the applicants' career paths thus far and the clarity of their plans for the future. The author of the first essay explains: "Having had the chance to explain what drives me and makes me tick in the first essay, I viewed my job in this essay to demonstrate why the time for an MBA was NOW, and that the right place was Stanford. I wanted to show that all my past accomplishments had been stepping stones, one after the other, and that they had reached a culminating point for me to cross the next threshold – not just an MBA, but an MBA in the company of the world's finest ... Part of my strategy was to explain why a non-business oriented engineer/musician/actor not only fit into an MBA world, but could also

excel within it, based on personal achievements already accomplished, but also attitude, an open mind, and the willingness to work hard. ... Finally, I wanted to point out that a Stanford MBA was a means to an end – that the arc of my voyage did not terminate in Palo Alto, but would simply be boosted by my 2 year rest stop there."

Example 1

As the boundaries in our world dissolve ever more rapidly in a blur of fiber-optic lines and wireless modems, more and more companies every day are beginning to proliferate the term "globalization" throughout its hallways and meeting rooms, like some sort of secret password into the 21st Century Success Club. However, I believe that real globalization requires more than opening overseas branch offices headed by first-time expats. Leaders truly capable of thriving in the hyper-converging, international arena of high technology must possess the skills to cross not only geographic boundaries, but also categorical and disciplinary ones as well. This is exactly the kind of leader I am striving to become, drawing upon my technical training, international experience, and cross-disciplinary potential.

At the University of Michigan, I chose to major in electrical engineering – not because I was especially enamoured of triple-integral calculus theorems, or because I had violent allergic reactions to Shakespearean sonnets (actually, a well-worn volume of the Bard's collected works sits lovingly on the "VIP Shelf" of my bookcase), but because I wanted to develop an engineer's disciplined approach to information organization and problem solving. Indeed, the most valuable training I took away from my engineering courses wasn't what I learned specifically, but how *to learn.*

During my first years at college, the covers of news and business publications everywhere were coming down with the Asian Flu, as Japan vaulted itself to center stage of the world's business focus with its flawless manufacturing and gee-whiz-how'd-they-get-it-so-compact technical muscle. My professors had also taken notice; however, they also lamented the inability of American engineers to catch up, being unable to read the latest technical papers published in Japanese, and unprepared or even unwilling to investigate first-hand in the native environment overseas. This is when I realized that the tools I developed through my engineering studies could be even more powerful if complemented with Asian language skills – first capitalizing on my ethnic Chinese background and Mandarin abilities, and then augmented with fluency in Japanese.

After graduation, I was recruited by General Motors Japan to work as a chassis engineer in the anti-lock brake (ABS) development group at its Tokyo-based Asian Technical Center (ASTEC). While the multi-lingual aspect gave me the occasional brain-lock, it also allowed me to take on much more responsibility, leadership, and cross-cultural exposure than my classmates working back in the States (not to mention the chance to carry around business cards in four different languages!). I had the chance to participate in high-level business dealings from day one, and I gained valuable knowledge studying his world-class abilities to integrate engineering analysis with keen business acumen. However, I also saw that despite his tremendous technical, entrepreneurial, and leadership skills, my mentor would always face language and culture barriers in Asia, which actually cost GM the bid on several occasions. This was an obstacle I had always planned to turn into an opportunity, since my Asian face and language abilities granted me an "in" unavailable to most visiting ex-pats.

While my time at GM gave me an appreciation for the challenges of managing technology internationally, I didn't discover my own cross-functional leadership potential until I joined Gateway 2000 Japan. Two weeks after I joined the company, the director of Marketing called me into his office one morning and casually announced that he was handing the Server Launch project over to me, explaining that I was expected to launch not only a new product line, but also the infrastructure to support a whole new business unit. On the way out the door, he left me with this message of encouragement: "don't worry, Tim – I know you can pretty much do a great job at just about anything, which is why I hired you. Oh, and by the way, the last three guys who tried to launch servers failed and were fired, but don't let that bother you. Good luck!"

Because nobody was available to supervise or train me, I could only rely on my own resourcefulness and ability to learn quickly in order to understand the product, the market, and the Gateway corporate environment. Over the course of the next two months, I experienced the equivalent of several crash courses resembling the schedule from some nightmarish business school from hell...

On May 15th, 1998, Gateway 2000 Japan launched its first PC Server product, the NS-7000 Workgroup Server, right on schedule. The Server Launch media event went smooth as silk, and the press reviews all came in favorably as planned, leading to a rush of incoming phone calls for the Sales teams, and a quick jump to 2% market share. PC Market researchers announced that Gateway had surprised them all by entering the Japanese Corporate PC Market with such an aggressive strategy and strong product, especially in light of the company's relative youth in Japan and limited resources.

In climbing the near-vertical learning curves for the server launch and other projects, I've discovered that not only do I actually enjoy balancing all these different business aspects and responsibilities, but that I can also really shine when faced with such international and interdisciplinary challenges, because they are so well suited to my own skills and personality. Of course, I've also learned a great deal about my weaknesses and areas for improvement. Another lesson I've learned is that strong leadership does not always automatically mean good management: while I was able to align and motivate my most talented team members to pull off a successful launch, I didn't realize that I also needed to focus on creating robust, fool-proof processes to help average, staff-level employees to do their jobs effectively, and handle exceptions and emergencies smoothly.

This is why I feel I'm ready to take the next step, and return to school for my MBA. I'm looking to bolster my tools, abilities, and experience with a solid foundation in the fundamentals of business theory, as well as cutting-edge strategies used by other world-class international firms. If I can do so, then not only will I be able to build the credibility needed to launch more ambitious, higher-profile projects, but I'll also be able to plan and execute them more efficiently and effectively. In fact, the president of Gateway Japan agrees with my thinking, and has even offered to grant me Gateway Japan's first MBA sponsorship, because of my leadership potential. My short-term goal is to attain my MBA and return to Gateway as either the overall head of Product Marketing in Japan, or else as champion and consultant for the international regions at Gateway Global headquarters in San Diego.

Eventually, I'd like to be an international business consultant to high-tech multinationals at both the "big picture" scale and at the execution and process level of detail. Using my background in Asia, I'd like to help international companies understand the unique challenges of globalization into countries like Japan - and I most certainly feel that I'd be a valuable resource in China, as the "sleeping giant awakens to amaze the world," as Napoleon once prophesized. Because I love to think on my feet, see all the sides of an issue, identify the key trade-offs, and figure out the most efficient solution, I believe I'll make an excellent troubleshooter. Because I love to get people to work together, help them understand each other, and mediate when they have conflicts, I'm confident of my capacity as a "cultural ambassador" within the Asian arena. Because I love to learn by taking on new challenges, and then share my knowledge and experience with others, I know I'll be an effective consultant.

Author: Tim C.

Sample Essay 2:

While I have thoroughly enjoyed the leadership experiences that I have had in the Army, I knew since before I went to West Point that I would eventually return to Puerto Rico to contribute to its improvement. In the last five years, I have accomplished my goals as an Army officer of serving the nation and polishing my leadership skills. After much soul-searching, I have decided to leave the Army and become personally involved with efforts to solve Puerto Rico's social and economic problems.

My long-term goal is to be in a senior executive position with the Government Development Bank (GDB) of Puerto Rico. The purpose of the GDB is to help the Governor of Puerto Rico in designing and implementing economic policies. To accomplish this goal, I first want to gain experience as an investment banker in Puerto Rico. An MBA from Stanford and the completion of the Public Management Program (PMP), combined with my military background and multicultural perspective, would allow me to enter the investment banking arena with the purpose of eventually joining the GDB. Above all, the skills that I will learn at the Stanford Graduate School of Business will help me to better understand the underlying roots of the economic problems facing Puerto Rico and to help develop solutions for these problems in the future.

[...] In order to assume a leadership position at the GDB, I must first understand the intricacies of local and regional capital markets and how government can best help design and develop a free exchange of capital. To gain such understanding, I want to work as an investment banker in Puerto Rico. I want to learn about the needs of new companies and foreign investment coming to Puerto Rico. Specifically, I want to become involved with high-technology companies expanding operations in Puerto Rico. As an electrical engineer, I have the technical foundation that, combined with the proper business knowledge, will allow me to better understand how to develop the business climate for high-tech industries to flourish in Puerto Rico.

Author: Rafael L.

Examples: Why Stanford?

Sample Essay:

Stanford is my number one choice. It offers characteristics no other MBA can match:
The People: *Thanks to an exhaustive, very selective admission process, they combine the highest professional and intellectual standards with the friendliness and teamwork that make the experience worthwhile. A number of Stanford alumni have convinced me of this idea: Luis M., Nicolas B., and Juan Maria A.. Also current students at GSM like Zuriñe R. and Luisa A.. I also feel that making use of the Alumni Network Program will enrich my professional career and help me to find out what suits me in the world of business.*

The Location: *Silicon Valley is the center for IT, the Internet and e-commerce. Where better to be to really feel the atmosphere and even get to know some of the entrepreneurs and venture capitalists? I would love to meet the individuals responsible for Amazon.com, AOL, Cisco, E*TRADE, Pixar, WebTV, Yahoo, Kohlberg Kravis Robert. Even if not all of these firms are located in California, all those founders and leaders visited Stanford last year! I was quite impressed to learn that California is, by itself, the seventh largest economy. And, more important than that, the one with a most brilliant future.*

Entrepreneurship: *Stanford clearly excels in Entrepreneurship, thanks to its Center for Entrepreneurial Studies, its electives on Entrepreneurship and, again, its location in Silicon Valley. The Conference held this year must have been an incredible opportunity to meet some of the most successful entrepreneurs worldwide. I can't help thinking how much I would enjoy talking to Jeff Bezos, discussing his impressions on the Bertelsmann effort, and get access to his plans for the future.*

I find it very attractive that Stanford offers the Public Management Program option. A rich professional life will involve many interactions with various administrations (national governments, IMF, World Bank) and non-profit organizations.

Author: Alvaro F.

Global Focus: *To develop my potential and achieve my future ambitions, I'm seeking an environment like Stanford's Graduate School of Business to reach the Next Level. I need truly globally-thinking teachers attuned to my cross-cultural focus, and I desire the company of peers from around the world to share, challenge, and relate to my own overseas experiences in an independent setting such as the GMP. I've always been at my best under pressure, in the face of seemingly impossible odds, and though I've often swam my way from little-fish-in-a-big-pond to the very top, I crave the humbleness and competitive drive as a big-fish-in-a-cozy-tank-full-of-sharks.*
Throughout my career, I've always forged my own path, so I desire an environment that not only accepts but nurtures the pursuit of what-hasn't-been-done-before (one of my career goals is to always have a title that reads similar to my original Gateway Japan business card: "_____ Pioneer"). I'm building my own integrated approach to leadership for the 21st century, synthesizing the technical and non-technical, logical and abstract, words and numbers, and East with West. I believe that an MBA from an environment as diverse and challenging as Stanford's will ultimately allow me to achieve my goals, and become not only an example of a truly globalized leader, but also a tour guide at the door of the 21st Century Success Club!

Author: Tim C.

LETTERS OF RECOMMENDATION

Number of letters of recommendation for Stanford: **3**

The letters of recommendation constitute an important part of your admissions application, as much for the admissions office which will get three outside opinions on the applicant without having met him or her directly, as for the applicant him- or herself. In fact, getting three recent and relevant letters in time from your recommenders, who are often completely swamped, isn't always an easy thing. Also, you have every interest in monitoring the composition of these letters very closely.

GENERAL ADVICE

1. Start the process as soon as possible.

To select the best people for the job, ask them for their opinions, explain what you expect of them, follow up with those who haven't finished writing yet, and make sure the letters are sent in on time - all this takes a lot of time. All the more so since you won't be able to control all the factors involved (example of one true story: the person writing someone's letters of recommendation left for the other end of the world one week before the application deadline!). Though you can pull a few all-nighters to finish your essays on time, it will be hard to impose such strict time constraints on the people writing your recommendations, who inevitably do not have such a direct interest in your progress (although, shouldn't it be enough to want to make you happy?).

2. Select people who know you

The admissions office will make judgments based on precise facts and details. So they will not be pleased with vague statements like "an extremely brilliant person". In order to convince them, one has to indicate the relevant skills involved, specify the context, and cite concrete examples of achievements. Also, don't choose the CEO from the multinational you worked for (unless he knows you well! But then would you really need to get an MBA?). Someone close to you will undoubtedly be more willing to spend that much more time on your letter. Taking this time is necessary so that the letters represent a real effort in analysis and composition.

Finally, sometimes it's hard to ask your direct supervisor to write you a recommendation when he may not yet know that you want to leave, or is worrying about how he will ever be able to replace such a brilliant employee. So, look for someone for whom you have worked recently, but who does not have such a direct interest in whether you leave or not. (though you should avoid asking the guy on the local newsstand who has sold you your favorite paper for the past 15 years!) Stanford wants to know what you are like now, or who you have been recently (two or three years maximum). Clients or suppliers may also be good alternatives. However, use at least one person from the organization you currently work for. Stanford lets you be the sole judge of the advantages of sending in a fourth letter of recommendation. So do it only if it adds something new and valuable to your application. Don't forget that the admissions officers read several hundred applications each year. Do you really want to risk coming across as unpleasant?

3. For at least two of your three letters, choose people from your professional arena.

Above all, Stanford is looking to measure your professional success and your potential as a manager. Therefore, two, if not three, of your letters of recommendation should come from your professional environment. However, if you have had a leadership role in one of your activities outside of your professional work experience, it might be advantageous to be recommended by someone who can explain that. Balance that out with a third letter from your professional field. A letter of recommendation from one of your professors is not required, especially if he or she can't contribute anything to help determine your managerial potential.

4. The format for the letters of recommendation is more flexible than for the essays

The people who recommend you will have more latitude than you will for their writing exercise. Stanford - like all MBA programs - gives a very detailed outline of questions for structuring the letters of recommendation; however, it is entirely possible to respond with a more classic letter format without even really directly addressing all the questions one is supposed to answer. You'll have to make sure that the letter writer covered all the main points and that the evaluation grid (see details below) is also filled out and attached. This flexibility gives the people who recommend you more freedom. Be aware that other MBA programs may not be as flexible and will look down upon any deviation from the guidelines. So don't follow this practice across the board, though it may be useful for approaching potential letter writers whom you do not want to place under too many constraints.

QUESTIONS ASKED IN THE STANFORD LETTERS OF RECOMMENDATION

The letter of recommendation is made up of an evaluation grid and a series of six questions. Remind yourself that you are applying to one of the best MBA programs in the world; don't hesitate to state in what areas and skills you excel. Also, make sure that your letter writer is not underestimating you. It would not be surprising for you to be "Truly exceptional" in some areas. In truth, you may deserve to be described with a number of superlatives. The evaluation requested for is relative to other people at the same level in your company. The letter writer has to specify precisely in what capacity, and to which group he or she is comparing you.

Here are the questions to which your recommenders must respond:

	No basis for judgement	Below average	Average (Top 50%)	Good (Top 25%)	Very good (Top 10%)	Outstanding (Top 5%)	Truly Exceptional (Top 2%)
Analytical/ quantitative skills							
Initiative/ motivation ...							

1. Define your relationship to the applicant and describe the circumstances under which you have known him or her.

The point of the question:

To present the specifics of your relationship with the letter writer and to get a better idea of whether he is an appropriate person with a basis for sound judgment.

Tips for the question:

What's the hierarchical relationship? In what context? For how long? What types of interactions have the two of you had? These are the questions that have to be addressed. They will permit the reader to better discern the relevance of the letter.

Example:

I selected Erick at the beginning of 1999 to conduct the selection of an ERP package to replace the current custom system for one of the country's major [...] companies. Erick and I worked together very closely from February to August 1999.

Erick's personal contributions were:

- *designing the decision making process. He notably designed tools for analysis and comparison of three ERP packages.*
- *managing the project. He developed the planning and produced the deliverables within the deadlines and with the Board of Directors' approval. He facilitated the numerous meetings we had with the client's top executives.*
- *qualifying each package based on its strengths and risks. He took part in the negotiation with the vendors.*
- *etc.*

2. What are the applicant's greatest strengths? In what ways might you distinguish the applicant from other able individuals at his or her professional level?
3. What are the applicant's weaknesses or developmental needs? How has the applicant addressed this needs?

The point of the questions:

Through these very classic questions, Stanford wants to know how the candidate's strengths and weaknesses are perceived.

Tips for the questions:

It would be great if the strengths and weaknesses people perceive in you are in sync with those you state in your essays! That would lend credibility to your whole application. As much as possible, make sure that the different parts of your application are coherent. It would be surprising, for example, if an activity described in one of your essays does not appear on your résumé. Stanford will be particularly interested in your analytical skills, your ability to solve complex problems, to work within a team, and your entrepreneurial talents. Don't forget that the reader would like concrete examples in each area. Furthermore, in responding to Question 3, the writer shouldn't find too many weaknesses! You should have already worked on these to improve on them, or else they have to help prove that you must get an MBA! It's not necessary to have set up one's own company to be considered an entrepreneur. Haven't you taken initiative, at whatever your level in the company, to start projects, to take action (studies, problem-solving, etc)?

Example:

> *Erick demonstrated an outstanding ability to anticipate problems and assess risks. His deep analytical and project management skills efficiently contributed to the success of the project. On this assignment, Erick did not have the opportunity to manage a team, as I understand that he now does. His new assignment will certainly complete his professional training. Moreover, to reach his current goal of working in Strategic Services, he would efficiently enrich his academic and professional education with an MBA...*

4. Describe the applicant's interpersonal skills (effectiveness in establishing and maintaining relationships; working with supervisors, peers and subordinates; sensitivity to those less competent; willingness to work in a team environment; etc.).

The point of the question:

To complement the two preceding questions, Stanford would like to get your letter writer's point of view on your interpersonal skills. Teamwork is especially valued in the school. So, do you know how to work within a team? Can you adapt to being in a diverse group of international students? In brief, will you be capable of working effectively with your classmates during the MBA program, and with your colleagues? Here are the reader's concerns regarding this question.

Tips for the question:

Don't hesitate to prepare your letter writer for the task at hand. In fact, especially if you haven't worked with him for a long time, he or she may have forgotten some details of your performance. So, remind him or her of the times that seem to you to best represent your capacity for teamwork. By giving these concrete examples, you will help your letter writer, and you will allow the reader of your application to better pin you down.

To have worked in an international team is an important asset. If none of your letters mention it, don't forget to include it in one of your essays.

Example:

> *Erick worked in a very cooperative spirit with the technical team and contributed to instilling a positive working relationship with the client. Moreover, this study has been conducted during a critical phase of this project: after a poor performance during the first years of the project, we significantly improved its image thanks, to a great extent, to Erick's contribution to the success of this study...*

5. Discuss the applicant's performance in leadership roles, including specific strengths and weaknesses. If you have not had the opportunity to observe the applicant in a leadership role, please comment on his or her potential for senior-level management.

The point of the question:

Do you have what it takes to be a leader or a future manager? Stanford would like to determine, in particular, if you are a future ambassador for the Business School.

Tips:

To be able to claim that you should be admitted to Stanford, the letter has to make it utterly transparent that the answer to this question is Yes. However, don't forget that every statement has to be backed up, or else is it loses its value. You should stress above all else your experiences in team management. How many people did you supervise? In what circumstances? To what end? How did you manage to carry out a project successfully? How did you motivate your team?

Example:

> *...Erick led the overall project with very little supervision. He facilitated our meetings with the client and helped them go through the decision making process he designed. I encourage him with his MBA project and I think that he has the capability to become one of our top executives...*

6. Is there anything else about this applicant that you feel is relevant to our assessment of his or her candidacy (e.g. personal integrity, maturity, demonstrated commitment to improving the lives of others, impact and unusual accomplishments in the workplace)?

Hasn't your letter writer said it all? If the answer is yes, he or she can stop here. If not, he or she shouldn't hesitate to speak highly of your personality traits mentioned in the question: your maturity, integrity and so forth.

THE INTERVIEW

The interview is not an essential part of the Stanford selection process. Even according to the Admissions Office, you should treat your essays like interviews on paper. They are designed to obtain the same information as from traditional interviews. The advantage of this method is that it avoids basing your admission on a single half-hour interview with illustrious alumni who may not even have the qualities required for this kind of exercise. In fact, even if opinions differ on this matter, these admissions interviews can bring an element of unpredictability to the selection process. One admissions officer from a well-known East Coast business school, when recently asked about the subject, responded, "It's already a good sign to be selected for an interview!" Small consolation for the people who apply to these MBA programs, and who, after having spent long hours preparing their admissions applications, see themselves rejected after a half-hour interview!

Nonetheless, it is true that some applicants who are particularly brilliant speakers may regret not having interviews, which would permit them to distinguish themselves by this exercise.

INTERVIEW WITH THE ADMISSIONS DIRECTOR

Who reads the application forms (faculty?, alumni?, students?, MBA Admission officers?)
Professional admission staff members read the Stanford MBA applications. Neither students nor faculty read applications. All decisions on applications are made within the MBA Admissions office.

How many people read the dossiers? How much time is spent on each application?
We have six professional staff reading applications, as well as a group of two to four trained part-time evaluators. These part-time staff members have been reading files for many years, and are well calibrated. We spend anywhere from 20 - 40 minutes on a file. It depends on the length of the applicant's essays and letters of recommendation, and the complexity of the file (e.g., if the applicant has held several positions in several different firms, we take the time to understand the transitions).

What is the process? (Is there a sort of preliminary filter in three categories like Yes/Maybe/No and then only the first category is really thoroughly read?)
The reader approaches each individual file asking, "For every ten files I read, I can admit only one candidate. Will this be the one?" There are some files that are "clear admits" - exceptional academic profile, recommendation letters that are descriptive and enthusiastic about the candidate's professional accomplishments, and well-written essays that specifically address what the questions ask.

Other files are less clear-cut, e.g., the letters of reference are impressive, but the essays are not. These types of files might be kept "on hold" for another review later on to compare with other candidates with similarly unbalanced profiles.

There is absolutely no quantitative formula. This would be hard to do, because grades vary from school to school, and it is impossible to come up with a number that would fairly represent the myriad of majors and universities.

What are the criteria of evaluation of a good candidate?
The criteria are easy to define. They are academic excellence, demonstrated management potential, and "perspective" (your ideas and attitudes that you bring to the program based on the sum total of your life experiences). What is difficult to understand is their applicability to a specific case.

The Stanford Business School has a "highly selective" admissions process. What that means is that there are more qualified candidates than spaces available. Many more candidates meet the criteria than do not. Therefore, our final decisions have more to do with shaping the class with a good mix of backgrounds and talents. This is precisely where the "mystery" of admissions comes in - all decisions are made in the context of the applicant pool, which only the admissions committee sees. The "randomness" that individual applicants may see in our decision making occurs because their frame of reference is their friends, not the total applicant pool.

Because there is no formula, and because there are more qualified candidates than spaces available, there necessarily has to be an element of subjectivity (read: luck) in the application process. I always liken highly selective admissions to the Olympic Games. Congregated are the top athletes from around the world, but only a handful can win gold medals. Does that mean that the non-medal winners are any less brilliant in their athletic careers? Does that mean that if the non-medal winner had trained longer and harder, he/she would've emerged victorious? No. This is one of the hardest things for candidates to accept - that they can influence the process (i.e., spend time preparing for the GMAT; spend time thinking and writing their essays; choose their recommenders wisely), but they cannot control the outcome.

What qualities would you like to see more of in candidates?
Especially appealing to us are candidates who have both IQ and EQ (emotional intelligence) as defined by Daniel Goleman (Emotional Intelligence, Bantham 1995).
The five components of Emotional Intelligence:
- Self-awareness: the ability to recognize and understand your moods, emotions and drives, as well as their effect on others.
- Self-regulation: the propensity to suspend judgment - to think before acting.
- Motivation: the passion to work for reasons that go beyond money and status.
- Empathy: the ability to understand the emotional makeup of other people.
- Social skill: the proficiency in managing relationships and building networks.

How important is the GMAT?
The GMAT is a common measure by which to evaluate all candidates, regardless of educational background. It also is a useful predictor of performance in first-year core classes. We have admitted students with scores in the low 600s, and denied candidates with scores in the high 700s. Is the GMAT score important? By all means, yes. Does it mean that applicants with a 600 test score cannot make it through the MBA Program? Not necessarily, because one cannot underestimate the power and value of determination, discipline, and hard work.

If someone takes the GMAT many times, will you take the highest score or the average of the scores?

We would only consider the highest score.

What are the "do's" and "don't's" for essays ?

DO:

1. Answer the question asked. You need to write a unique essay for each business school you apply to as each one asks for information tailored to its program.
2. Tell us about your values and priorities.
3. Proofread the answer.

DON'T:

1. Ask someone else to write your essays if writing is not your strength. You will have to write many papers while in business school, so if your writing skills need to be improved, do so before applying to business schools.
2. Don't cut-and-paste answers from one school's essay question to another. It is obvious to admissions officers when you do this, and it shows a lack of respect to the school.

How do you recommend that students differentiate themselves from the pack?

Because Stanford does not provide interviews, the essays become the applicant's alter ego. The most common mistake applicants make is in telling too much of what they've done and not enough of who they are as people. So tell a story, and tell a story that only you can tell. Indeed, everyone loves a good story - including admissions committees. Stories have themes. Stories can be revealing. And well-written stories are evocative, creating vivid images of characters and events. That is what application essays should accomplish.

Moreover, if the details of the latest IPO the applicant has worked on or the narration of travels to faraway lands may be informative and somewhat interesting, anyone can tell those stories. Many people have travelled, many people have conducted due diligence. You should tell more about why the financial transaction was so interesting, what was learned from the team experience, how travel influenced an outlook on life. Many applicants spend too much time trying to figure out how to "market" themselves to stand out from the other six thousands applicants – a futile task, since aspiring MBAs don't know who else will be applying and what they'll be presenting. The best plan of attack is to share you with the committee in a sincere and compelling way. When the committee gets a good sense of the person who has applied, and the applicant articulates well his or her passion for management and how Stanford can help realize goals, it is easier to determine a fit between potential students and the GSB. And "fit" is what admissions is all about.

What makes a good letter of recommendation?

Detailed recommendation letters from individuals who can provide specific anecdotes about a candidate's demonstrated leadership and management potential enhance the chances of admission.

Why have the essays changed from previous years? What are the benefits of this change for the application process?

We have changed the questions in the past (not always with successful outcomes). This was another step in our quest for continuous improvement, to solicit the kind of information we would like about candidates. We are changing the questions again for admission in 2001 (especially the second) because we did not receive as complete answers to the questions as we had hoped.

Can you explain the evaluation grid used by the school?
We don't have one. Evaluating files is a very cerebral process, one in which we weave information together to create a profile of a potential student, and then weave that individual profile into the larger tapestry of the class.

What other MBA schools do you consider as direct competitors to your MBA program?
Of the candidates we admit and who choose not to enroll, Harvard is the option of choice.

Given that some companies (Mckinsey, Goldman, etc.) seem to be traditional feeders for your MBA program, how is an applicant from one of these firms viewed against other applicants in the pool?
The investment banks and consulting firms have analyst programs that are designed to provide candidates with a solid background and foundation for business school. While these candidates are attractive to us, we also want to fill the class with candidates from other professional backgrounds. Be careful with the assumption that somehow we are admitting companies to the business school, not individual candidates. We care more about a candidate's accomplishments and personal qualities than about the firm for which they work. Similarly, we care about the content of the recommendation letter, and less about the title of the person writing the letter.

Is there a "rolling" admission cycle or "rounds" of admission?
We have three application rounds. In general, it is better to apply in one of the first two rounds instead of the last round. Always apply in the round where you can confidently say that your application is your best effort. If this means applying in the final round, that is better than sending in a poorly constructed application in an earlier round. This process is very important to admission committees and to you, and it deserves your very best effort.

All schools have to make a tradeoff between the diversity of the student body and the strength of the individual candidate - which is most important? If there were 50 outstanding candidates from any one given country, would the school accept seeing its percentage of students of this nationality increase dramatically or would it refuse some of those outstanding candidates, preferring instead to take less outstanding candidates from other countries so as to maintain a certain diversity in the student body?
The question assumes that we know the entire universe of applicants at a particular point in time, when in fact we do not since we have three application periods. In fact, the percentage of candidates from a particular country can and will fluctuate based on the quality we see, and in which round they apply. For example, if a great European candidate applies in the third and final application round, and is comparable to other candidates from the same country we've already admitted, AND we have someone with a different profile who fills the gaps in our class, we might give the nod to the other person because that person helps give the class the shape and form we would like.

What does the school specifically expect from international students?
Nothing different. Everyone is held to the same standard. Most international students are

required to submit the results of the Test of English as a Foreign Language (TOEFL), but the rest of the application process is similar to that for U.S. citizens. We certainly take into account when essays in English may not be in the candidate's first language. At the same time, we need evidence that he or she has the language facility to comprehend rapidly spoken English (to ensure maximum benefit from classroom discussions), and has strong English reading skills to keep up with the volume of outside reading. The average FMAT for both internationals and non-internationals is similar, because regardless of background, all students compete in the same classroom. As such, each student needs to have the requisite skills to contribute to class discussions and group work.

Getting the

WHARTON

Admissions Edge

Wharton

Address	The Wharton School The University of Pennsylvania 3733 Spruce Street 102 Vance Hall Philadelphia, PA 19104
Telephone	(1) 215-898-6183
Website	www.wharton.upenn.edu/mba
E-mail	mba.admissions@wharton.upenn.edu

about the school

Founded	1881
Tuition Fees	$28,970
Some Famous Alumni	James Bankoff (President, Netscape); Harold McGraw (President & CEO, Mc-Graw-Hill, Inc.); Ann. McLaughlin (Chairman, The Aspen Institute); J.D. Power III (Founder & Chairman, J.D. Power & Associates); Christine Grant (Commissioner of Health & Human Services, New Jersey); Mortimer Zuckerman (Owner, U.S. News & World Report); Todd Thomson (CFO, Citigroup); Ronald Perelman (Chairman & CEO, MacAndrews & Forbes Groups)

the application

Application File	By mail or downloadable from website
Application Deadlines	Three Rounds: early November, early January, mid-March
App. File Elements	• 4 essays (+ 1 optional) • 2 letters of recommendation • Transcripts • GMAT (and TOEFL, if applicable) • résumé • Interview by invitation

rankings

Publication	Business Week					US News & World						Financial Times		
	92	94	96	98	00	96	97	98	99	00	01	99	00	01
General Ranking	4	1	1	1	1	3	3	2	3	3	4	4	2	1

before the MBA

# applicants per year	7,336
# applicants accepted per year	1,057
# applicants entering per year	785
% women students	31%
% minority students	21%
% international students	36%
% married students	30%
# countries represented	58

Age (years)	
mean	28.6
median	28.3
range	20 - 42

Education pre-MBA	
Business	15%
Economics	16%
Engineering	20%
Liberal Arts and Sciences	26%
Others	23%

Professional Experience	
avg. years work experience	4-7

GMAT	
average	703
range (middle 80% of class)	640-760

undergraduate GPA	
average	3.6
range (middle 80% of class)	3.35 - 3.9

after the MBA	Class of 2001
# companies recruiting on campus	429

Main career choices

Consulting	39.9%
Investment Banking	30.0%
High Tech/Telecom	7.8%
Investment Management	4.8%
HealthCare	2.9%
Venture Capital/Private Equity	2.3%
Other	12.3%

Function

Consulting	38.6%
Corporate Finance/Banking	20.0%
Marketing	8.1%
Private Equity/VC	4.5%
Strategic Planning	4.5%
Sales and Trading	4.5%
General Management	1.9%
Other	17.9%

Geographical location

North America	81.6%
Asia	7.4%
Europe	7.1%
Cenral and South America	2.3%
Other/not specified	1.6%

Salary (Source: Financial Times 2001)

Avg. salary three years after graduation	$162,610

Alumni

# alumni in the world (MBA)	33,913

Top 10 employers

1. McKinsey
2. Bain & Co.
3. Goldman Sachs & Co.
4. Boston Consulting Group
5. J.P. Morgan Chase & Co.
6. Credit Suisse First Boston
7. Morgan Stanley
8. Deloitte Consulting
9. Merrill Lynch
10. Accenture

author

Name   SHANA JOHNSTON

Started her career in investment banking at Chase Manhattan Bank, then worked in corporate development for Swiss Life Re & Health America. Since graduation, she has been working in the Staff Associate program at Sprint Corporation.

School specifics
WHARTON

INTRODUCTION

Ten years ago, if you had asked someone to describe Wharton, they would have stressed its strength in Finance, the competitive student body, and its production of individual contributors. Today, the reality of Wharton could not be more different.

Traditionally, Wharton has been known as a Finance school. Students today would agree that the Finance program is still very strong, but they would encourage you to examine the other programs at the school. The Marketing, Operations and Information Management, and Strategic Management Departments are just some of the other very strong departments and most students consider the overall curriculum excellent. If you like rankings, Business Week continually places Wharton in the top five over the broadest number of subject-matter categories. The breadth of strong departments improves not only the core curriculum, but also the amount and diversity of electives available to students.

The spirit of teamwork is found throughout Wharton from the Admissions Office, which carefully selects team players, to Academic Services, which assigns all students to a Learning Team for most of their first-year classes, to the numerous student-run conferences and events. If you are not a great team player when you start at Wharton, you will be when you leave.

As for the competitiveness of the student body, most students, faculty, and administration would disagree strongly with this stereotype as well. The preponderance of teamwork would not be possible if the atmosphere on campus was cut-throat and competitive. Students consistently work together on projects and their cooperation spreads outside of the classroom. During the first year, for example, cooperation is evident as classmates help one another learn new subjects, navigate the recruiting process (from seeking interviews to trading notes on offers), and locate apartments around the world for summer internships.

THE DEAN'S VISION

Patrick T. Harker was named the Wharton School's twelfth dean in February 2000. A faculty member for 15 years, Harker has held numerous leadership positions at the University of Pennsylvania, including interim dean and deputy dean. In these capacities, Harker oversaw development of the MBA program's Technology Management and E-commerce major and expanded the school's distance learning initiative. In his own words:

"Wharton's mission is to create leaders in business, in public life, and in private character. That leadership is characterized by three sets of qualities: depth and substance; inclusiveness; and passion and commitment.

Leadership is more than obtaining a position of authority. Real leaders must have depth and substance. If they do not have analytical skills, a broad, deep knowledge of business basics and the essential personal skills in communication and teamwork, they are not going to succeed.

A second characteristic is inclusion, which requires outreach and seeking the views of individuals with divergent interests and really valuing the different voices, and the gray areas between those views. Innovation is born in the cracks - in the "in between" of one idea and another. Without the quality of inclusion, leadership will ultimately fail as a result of missed opportunities.

The final set of qualities that are a hallmark of Wharton leadership is passion and commitment. Wharton leaders are individuals that truly care about serving the needs of people, about making their lives better. They have passion to make a difference. Without passion, work is reduced to routine, and eventually you wonder, "Why am I doing this?" Leaders with passion ask, "What can I do today to make a difference?" Passion is the essential raw material of success.

Wharton graduates are also leaders in their professional commitments, in the broader affairs of society, and in their communities. In today's rapidly transforming business environment, leaders cannot rest on the good name they carry or the reputation they've built from past achievements. They must continue to serve - and their service must constantly change because the world continues to change.

Wharton leaders don't just react to change - they create it."

THE SCHOOL YEAR

Wharton's academic calendar is fairly typical of MBA programs: the first year is primarily filled with required courses while the second year allows students to explore electives in their area(s) of interest. Each semester is divided into two quarters and students will find classes that last either a quarter or a semester in both the required curriculum and the electives. This schedule allows faculty flexibility in developing classes of appropriate lengths.

All students are placed into cohorts of approximately 65 students. Each cohort follows the required curriculum together, and smaller sub-groups called Learning Teams are assigned within it. Three cohorts make up a cluster, which shares the same faculty during the first year.

The Wharton curriculum is known for its focus on quantitative skills. All students are expected to be conversant in quantitative analysis and the discipline of using numbers to justify a thought process. In order to bring all students to a level playing field before classes begin, PreTerm was designed to help provide support for students without a mathematic background and as a refresher for those with more technical backgrounds.

PreTerm occurs in the August before first-year classes begin. Courses are offered in statistics, accounting, finance, and microeconomics. A calculus refresher is available for those whose memories of calculus are dim. Waiver exams are also held during this period to give students with particular experience the option to forego the corresponding requirements. Finally, PreTerm ends with a two-day leadership retreat during which Learning Teams for the first-year are announced. (For further information on Learning Teams, see "Group Work" below.)

TIMETABLE AND CURRICULUM:

Due to its focus on quantitative skills and to the varying backgrounds of its students, Wharton's curriculum allows students to cover the required material at various speeds. For example, in finance, students can choose to take a basic course that lasts a full semester, an accelerated course that covers the same material in half a semester, or (with the right credentials) waive the course entirely. Most students find these options very helpful; a course that is tailored to one's prior knowledge base helps prevent the fear of slowing down more experienced classmates, or, on the other hand, the frustration of spending too much time covering material previously mastered. This also facilitates classroom discussion, since students with less experience don't hesitate to ask questions, and those with more experience don't have to wonder whether their comments will be understood.

The chart below shows a typical first-year academic schedule:

Fall Semester						
First Quarter	Foundations of Leadership and Teamwork*	Financial Accounting*	Financial Analysis	Marketing Management : Program Design	Strategic Analysis for Management	Managerial Economics
Second Quarter	Foundations of Leadership and Teamwork*	Financial Accounting*	Operations Management: Quality and Productivity	Management of People at Work	Competetive Strategy	
Spring Semester						
Third Quarter	Field Application Process*	Management Science	Managerial Accounting	Macroeconomic Analysis and Public Policy	Government and Legal Environment of Business	
Fourth Quarter	Field Application Process*	Marketing Management Strategy	Global Strategic Management	Core Bracket Course**: -Risk and Crisis Management -Geopolitics -Innovation, Change, and Entrepreneurship -Information: Industry Structure & Competetive Advantage -Technology for Managers	Global Immersion Program (optional)	

*Full-semester course
**Choice of one of the courses

Between the first and second year, most students participate in an ten- to twelve-week internship. Upon returning to campus for their second year, students typically take a courseload of four or five courses a semester in their major area and as electives. Most students find the major requirements are not burdensome and use the credits to take electives in other areas of interest. A substantial number of students decide to purse a double major, which with a little advance planning is not too difficult.

Requirements for graduation include:
1. completing the required credits, either by taking the class or waiving it
2. 1 core bracket course
3. 5 semester credits in a major area
4. approximately 3-5 elective credits

Students need 19 credits to graduate (a credit is awarded for a full semester class, and a half-credit for a half-semester class). Elective credits can be earned by taking classes in other departments of the University of Pennsylvania, and MBA students have taken classes in everything from engineering to film studies to art history.

THE COURSES – WHAT'S HOT... WHAT'S NOT

MBA students select their courses using the "Auction System", which includes both the process of registration and the system for placing and tracking your requests. It works like this: each enrolling student is awarded a fixed number of points - an "'initial endowment" of 5,000. The "clearing price" that you'll pay for a given course is directly dependent on its popularity. Depending on the amount of courses you take, your store is "replenished" every quarter, regardless of the grade you've received.

There's a complicated system of rules governing the buying and selling of a seat in courses, explained in an 18-page, fine-print document available to enrolled students. Despite the complexity, the system is good practice for work in Finance. But most importantly, most students feel the auction is a fair mechanism for allocating classes, and there is tons of information available to help a student through the process. As the weighty student handbook explains, "The auction is intended to transform what could otherwise be a random outcome ... into a matter of choice for you."

Most students are able to use the auction system to obtain the classes they want, when they want them. And, in general, the richness of the course offerings mitigates the fear that "if I don't get *that* course, my time and money will be wasted!" Nonetheless, you ask, "What classes will suck up most of my auction points?" Historically, these are some of the classes that demand the most points:

Financial Analysis
This is a required first semester course on financial analysis, primarily focusing on publicly traded companies. If you want to learn Finance, this is the class to start you on your way. This class is not part of the auction system, since it's a required part of the curriculum; thus, you won't have to spend any points to take one of Wharton's best courses.

Information: Industry Structure and Competitive Strategy
This class is a core bracket course and usually finds itself packed to capacity. Students look at how information and industry structure can affect competitive strategy.

Entrepreneurship and Venture Initiation
This class guides students through the ins and outs of starting a company, including concept development, business plan writing and actual operation. Techniques learned in the class can also be applied to prospective members of the venture capital community.

Macroeconomic Analysis and Public Policy
Why does the stock market move when the Federal Reserve raises interest rates? Who cares? Professor Siegel packs them in for this class, but many of the other professors of this core class are equally good if not as renowned. A great basis for understanding the financial markets and government fiscal and economic policy.

Marketing Strategy
How can a company use marketing to advance its corporate strategy? How do you decide the best marketing mix and product line? This elective course digs deeper into the Marketing decision process than the core marketing classes. If you thought Wharton was just a "finance school", this is one of many courses which will change your mind.

Negotiations and Dispute Resolution

Many would argue that this is a class every MBA student should take. How else do you negotiate your signing bonus to pay off your school loans? Wharton not only has a great class, its professors are recognized as industry leaders. Companies around the world send executives to the Wharton Executive classes taught by the same professors who teach at the MBA Level. And you don't have to pay anything extra!

TEACHING METHODS

The teaching method at Wharton depends on the class and the instructor. Some courses rely heavily upon case studies, while others favor lecture and case discussion. In most cases, students will find that they are encouraged (if not required) to participate actively in classroom discussions. Even classes which do not use cases as the basis of the discussion require substantial student interaction.

THE GRADING SYSTEM

Professors are encouraged to grade students on a relative basis, although the brackets are large enough that students do not find the atmosphere overly competitive for grades. This is facilitated by the non-disclosure policy on campus that does not allow recruiters to ask students for transcripts or GPAs. Students who receive academic honors are allowed to discuss their honors during recruiting, but otherwise, discussing grades is off-limits. Job-hunting is tough enough!

The distribution of grades is as follows:

Distinguished (DS) is assigned to the top 15% of students in a course.

High Pass (HP) is assigned to the next 20% of students.

Pass (P) is assigned to the next 55%.

Qualified Credit (QC) is assigned to the bottom 10%. This grade is only used internally and does not appear on an official transcript (a P is posted in its place).

No Credit (NC) is only assigned if a student has not completed a minimum level within the course. A very small number of students receive NCs, and generally substantial attempts have been made to help the student before that point.

GROUP WORK

Group work is a central tenet of a Wharton education. Starting before classes begin and continuing through graduation, teamwork ties the school together. Faculty, administration, and students believe strongly that good team skills are essential in today's workplace, and you will be faced with numerous opportunities to explore your personal style and to observe others'.

The most intensive of these opportunities is the Learning Team. At the beginning of the first year, all students are assigned to a Learning Team of five or six students (including at least one international student and one woman). Throughout the first year, this group will work together on projects for most of the core curriculum. Since the Learning Team has no assigned leader, the team must determine in what way and under what rules they will operate in order to fulfill their tasks. While this structure provides considerable challenge, most students find it to be an invaluable skill to have mastered when they re-enter the business world of matrix management and leadership by example, rather than authority.

Teamwork does not end with the Learning Team. Students work on teams for the Field Application Project, throughout most second year classes, and on business plans and committees that invariably spring up outside of class. These bring the additional challenge of learning how to select teammates (hint: your close friends may not be the best choice) and how to juggle multiple teams (and teammates' schedules) at any given time.

THE TEACHERS

Overall the teaching faculty at Wharton is excellent. As with any institution, there are lesser faculty, but the student pipeline is active and with a little effort a student can arrange to have some fantastic professors. Information on faculty is provided by Academic Services, which makes available the student evaluations on all professors (these are filled out at the end of each class by the current students, and include information on reading load, instructors' grasp of the subject, and willingness to help students).

These evaluations are used not only by students as they consider electives but also by Academic Services to work with faculty whose scores are less than desirable. Most faculty are very flexible and eager to work with students to create a course the students find informative and enjoyable.

One of the most prestigious ways these evaluations are used is to determine the recipients of the annual teaching awards. Some of the recent winners, and their departments, include:
H. Franklin Allen, Finance
Philip G. Berger, Accounting
Eric T. Bradlow, Marketing
Michael Brandt, Finance
Stuart Diamond, Legal Studies
Neil A. Doherty, Insurance and Risk Management
Thomas J. Donaldson, Legal Studies
Gavan Fitsimons, Marketing
Michael R. Gibbons, Finance
Robert P. Inman, Finance
William S. Laufer, Legal Studies
Andrew Metrick, Finance
Jeremy Siegel, Finance
Nicolaj Siggelkow, Management
Christian Terwiesch, Operations & Information Mgmt
William Tyson, Legal Studies
Karl Ulrich, Operations and Information Management
Mike Useem, Management
Lisa Warshaw, Communication

Since the awards are based upon highest overall ratings in the year-end evaluations, professors in the core curriculum and of large sections are disproportionately represented.

This is not to undermine the talent of these faculty - just to point out that a number of faculty choose to teach only smaller sections and are hence, less likely to win a teaching award.

THE INTERNATIONAL SIDE

International students represent nearly 40% of the Wharton class. Considering the Wharton class size, this means over 300 students in any given class hail from outside the United States. This number does not include the numerous American students who have spent substantial time abroad and bring those experiences as well into the classroom.

The Wharton website provides extensive information on students' origins and recruitment efforts on the part of the Admissions Office. What is hard to gauge from the website is the richness of the international flavor that pervades the Wharton community.

Some of the international clubs on campus include the African Association, Asian, Australia/New Zealand, Canadian, Eastern European, European, Greater China, Hispanic MBA, India, Israel, Japan, Korea, Latin America, and Southeast Asia club. These do not include other cultural clubs and associations on campus, and students are always encouraged to form a new club if there is interest among other students. One of the newest and most successful events on campus is the International Cultural Show, in which students from all over the world bring a little bit of their local culture to the Philadelphia area.

Recently, Wharton announced an alliance with INSEAD to increase the cooperation between the schools and expand the global opportunities for their students (for further details, see the INSEAD chapter in this book). MBA students from both schools will be able to enroll for coursework across four campus locations worldwide (Philadelphia, California, France, Singapore) and they will be able to participate in unique and exclusive summer elective programs on Wharton's California and INSEAD's Singapore campuses. Each school is offering its career management services to participants from the partner school, enhancing the global opportunities for MBA graduates of both. Additionally, the alliance will create a new research center to raise global awareness of emerging business and societal issues.

This INSEAD alliance is on top of the numerous international opportunites that Wharton has developed around the world, including:

Exchange Programs: Exchanges are possible with schools around the world, including the Australian Graduate School of Management (Australia), Instituto de Pos-Graduacao e Pesquisa em Administracao (Brazil), London Business School (England), Institut Superieur des Affaires (ISA) (France), Institute of Business Administration at Universita Commerciale Luigi Bocconi (Italy), Keio University's Graduate School of Business Administration (Japan), Rotterdam School of Management (the Netherlands), Asian Institute of Management (the Philippines), Instituto de Estudios Superiores de la Empresa Barcelona (IESE) (Spain), Stockholm School of Economics (Sweden), Sasin Graduate Institute of Business Administration (Thailand).

Global Business Forum: The lectures, panels and interactive debates of this on-campus event address emerging business themes and opportunities in Africa, East Asia, Europe, India, and

Latin America; issues facing global organizations; and the application of technological developments in a global business environment.

Joseph H. Lauder Institute of Management and International Studies: For those with serious international education and language inclinations, Wharton offers an excellent dual-degree program with The Lauder Insitute. Students complete both the Wharton MBA and the Lauder MA in International Studies in 24 months. Lauder combines an outstanding management education with intensive exposure to a foreign country's culture, politics, economy, and language. Students may specialize in one of four areas: East Asia, Europe, Latin America or the Middle East. During the 24-month program students spend roughly 25 percent of their time abroad, beginning with a cultural immersion program prior to the start of their Wharton classes. Students are encouraged to seek an internship with a multinational company requiring extensive use of a foreign language. Lauder/Wharton students are a very diverse group with many interesting stories from opening the first "western-style" bar in Vietnam

MBA/MA program: This three-year program is offered by Wharton and the Nitze School of Advanced International Studies of The Johns Hopkins University in Washington, DC. Students have access to Washington's resources and leaders in foreign policy and international trade while they attend SAIS, which has pioneered world area studies and the integration of international politics and economics.

Global Immersion Program: This optional, half-credit course provides first-year MBA students with an in-depth exposure to international business. Five weeks of introductory lectures are followed by a four-week immersion experience in a country or region (recently China, Japan, Russia, South America, and the European Union) where students are able to directly interact with leaders in business and government.

THE ENTREPRENEUR'S CORNER

Wharton has an amazing number of resources available to the aspiring entrepreneur (or the future manager who wants to maintain an entrepreneurial spirit in a larger corporation). The most obvious resources are the courses and the faculty of the Entrepreneurial Management major. Wharton's Entrepreneurial Programs are among the largest in the world, offering more than 20 courses every year to more than 2,000 students and executives. A faculty of over 20 professors and practitioners teaches courses and guides initiatives for a range of entrepreneurs, from high school students to senior executives. From courses on writing a business plan to raising money to establishing the appropriate legal structure, the budding entrepreneur will find more courses then she will probably have time to take. Equally valuable, the faculty, whether within the major or teaching in other disciplines, are valuable resources outside as well as inside the classroom.

Outside the classroom lies a further wealth of opportunities to learn and apply what it takes to build a business. The Entrepreneurs Club is just one of many clubs on campus bringing start-up founders to campus to speak. The Tech Club and the eCommerce Club are among many others which are likely to bring successful entrepreneurs to campus. Participating in one of the many Career Development Treks can also provide an opportunity to interact with alumni and founders. The Treks are organized for cities where students are interested in pursuing job opportunities with companies which typically do not recruit on campus and are arranged around a week or weekend when students can meet with a number of companies, learn about them, and meet regional alumni. Some past cities have included Austin, Atlanta, Boston, London, Los Angeles, Miami, New York, San Francisco/Bay Area, Seattle, and Washington, D.C.

The Wharton Business Plan Competition (the "WBPC") is managed by Wharton Entrepreneurial Programs and typically draws around 200 student teams competing for over $60,000 in prizes. The competition allows students who want to start businesses to have access to: 1) more resources; 2) start-up financial capital; 3) the intellectual capital of business advisors and seasoned entrepreneurs; and 4) greater coordination of the many entrepreneurial resources available on campus and in the Philadelphia area. In addition to the competitive aspect students receive feedback from judges after each of the three phases, mentoring opportunities during the year and extracurricular workshops. As the year goes on, the WBPC aims to match students with one-on-one advisors or coaches who can provide perspective and assistance on the specific business problems or industry areas where the students need advice. There are seminars and workshops on various aspects of developing a business plan, drawing on the resources of the Wharton School, the University of Pennsylvania, the Philadelphia business community and entrepreneurial business leaders.

But enough of *my* talking about what Wharton has to offer. In the words of a student entrepreneur who took advantage of most of the resources:

"I thought it was terrific to be an entrepreneur at Wharton. Every day there was another speaker that I could listen to, that I could learn from. CEOs of Fortune 500 companies and new start-ups were constantly in the classroom telling us how they did it and what they learned from their experiences.

Wharton makes it incredibly easy to be entrepreneurial. First, the curriculum gives you the luxury of flexibility so that you can design your class schedule to meet your personal interests. For me, that meant taking ten classes in two years that were directly related to starting my business. In many of those classes, I was able to use my entrepreneurial venture as the main class project. That gave me the ability to build my business while in school, but more importantly, I obtained critical feedback on my venture from faculty and classmates. Also, Wharton has worked hard to respond to the students' interests with classes that match those interests and needs.

Second, I thought the Wharton professors were awesome. Many professors will even serve on students' advisory boards in the early stages in order to provide some additional credibility for the young companies. It is important to note that they will not do this unless they have thoroughly vetted your idea and they believe in your prospects, but nevertheless, there are always a couple of examples of this every year. I had three professors who were willing to help me on a fairly consistent basis.

Wharton also has a very active alumni network that always seems willing to lend a hand. I have taken advantage of this resource many times, and often, these people can help you find managers, investors, and customers.

Wharton also has a Small Business Development Center which I have not yet utilized, but that I understand is a terrific resource. A number of my entrepreneurial colleagues were able to obtain substantial - and free - mentoring from this team of people who are devoted to helping entrepreneurs launch their businesses.

One of the center's programs is the Venture Initiation Project (VIP), launched in spring 2001. VIP aims to make student businesses "venture ready" by providing the student teams access to a full range of the University of Pennsylvania's entrepreneurial and development resources. In addition to obtaining a professional street address and access to a fully outfitted office, VIP students gain access to the expertise of legal, personnel, accounting and marketing professionals as well as introductions to valuable funding sources with no loss of equity.

VIP complements some of the many activities sponsored by Wharton Entrepreneurial Programs that make it easier for Penn students to start a business. In fact, six student teams entered VIP after participating in the Wharton Business Plan Competition. All Penn students may apply to VIP (for more information, see http://whartonsbdc.wharton.upenn.edu/VIP.html).

Related opportunities for Penn students sponsored by Wharton Entrepreneurial Programs include the Entrepreneur in Residence program, a new course on business plan creation and paid positions as consultants at the Wharton Small Business Development Center.

Steven Woda, Class of 2001

LIFE AT WHARTON

PHILADELPHIA

Most Wharton students either love or hate Philadelphia. The students who love it point to the charm and history of the cobblestone streets, the relatively small geographical size of the downtown area, and its location in relation to the beach, the mountains, New York City, and Washington, D.C. Those who hate it point to high crime rates and the limited late night scene (compared to a city like New York).

Philadelphia is the fifth largest city in the United States with approximately 1.5 million people. At Constitution Hall in Old City Philadelphia, the U.S. Constitution was drafted and ratified, and throughout Philadelphia reminders abound of the city's central role in the country's birth. The bustling downtown area, Center City, hosts the headquarters of companies such as Cigna and PECO Energy. At the edge of the Delaware River, visitors will find numerous historic buildings recording the beginnings of America and the people who played a part in the that history.

Visitors are also likely to be drawn to Museum Row including the Rodin Museum, Philadelphia Museum of Art, and the Museum of Natural History. The Reading Terminal Market, Italian Market, Barnes Foundation, and Boathouse Row are also popular destinations. Fairmount Park, the largest in the city, is a great place to watch skullers on the Schuylkill River, go for a run, or ride bikes.

THE CAMPUS

If you are reading this, you will be able to enjoy the campus' new building. Lucky you! The former facilities were cramped and worn, but the new building will address many of the students complaints. Along with providing a much-needed update and additional space, the new building will provide many of the amenities that MBAs want – wireless network, team meeting space, auditorium for speakers, coffee area, etc. Old and new buildings alike on the Wharton campus are surrounded by the beautiful University of Pennsylvania. The historic campus is full of red brick buildings and shaded walk-ways which remind you this is an Ivy League institution. If that doesn't do it, then all of the undergrads will certainly remind you that you are not eighteen anymore!

HOUSING

Housing for Wharton students consists of a wide variety of options. Some students choose the convenience of living in West Philadelphia to be close to campus and to save some money. The majority opt for Center City with its active nightlife, bustling streets, high rise buildings or brownstones, and finally, its large concentration of other Wharton MBAs. Students with families are more likely to choose to live in the Art Museum area or in the suburbs of Philadelphia. A limited number of on-campus housing units are available, but they are typically chosen by international students who are not able to find an apartment on their own and who like dormitory living. Like most large East Coast cities, Philadelphia has its range of housing prices and styles. From a Victorian brownstone to a modern high rise to converted warehouse space, students should be able to find housing that matches both their interests and budgets.

TUITION COSTS

Wharton's tuition figures should look similar to other American MBA programs. For 2001-2002, the numbers are:

Overall costs for the MBA (two years)	In US $
Tuition Fees	$61,000
Housing	$14,000-$20,000
Books	$3,000
Food	$9,900
Personal	$4,000
Transportation	$4,000
Misc.(including health insurance)	$3,282
TOTAL	$97,882-$103,882

Wharton does provide substantial financial aid, both through assistance with government loan programs and through a school loan program called the Wharton Loan. Additional information can be found on the website.

STUDENT VIEWS

The most unique aspect of Wharton is the number of opportunities that are open to you there. There are so many interesting people with diverse backgrounds that have done incredible things before business school. In addition Wharton offers an unparalleled variety of extracurricular activities that enable everyone to contribute to the schools culture and environment. Students are as enthusiasitic about contributing to the social and extracurricular environment as they are about contributing in the classroom.

Chuck Bush, Wharton Class of 2001

When I was going through the applications process, I decided that I wanted to attend a b-school with a cooperative atmosphere, excellent instructors, a good "brand", and international focus. I also wanted to attend a school offering well-developed quantitative courses, as my previous work experience required that I learn primarily "soft" skills. I have been thrilled to find all of these qualities (and more!) at Wharton.

In my time at Wharton, I've met and become friends with many international students and have spent substantial time traveling overseas while taking part in Wharton's career treks and Global Immersion Program. Through these experiences, I've learned about some of the differences between doing business in the U.S. and in other countries and have made contacts all over the world.

In addition, Wharton's academic offerings and excellent instructors have more than met my needs, giving me the quantitative skills I felt I needed. And, the school's learning team-oriented program allowed me to be a part of a ready-made group of students in which we all supported one another both academically and on a more personal level when needed.

It's very difficult to describe all the things I've liked about Wharton in only a few sentences. The school has truly exceeded my expectations in so many ways. It's great to attend such a terrific school and to know that, given the experience and knowledge I will gain, going to b-school was definitely the right decision for me.

Shelley Knowlton, Class of 2002

One of the things that most surprised me when I started at Wharton was how down to earth everyone was. In early conversations with my classmates, everyone felt that they had been the "admissions mistake". My prior boss (and a Wharton alum) had told me that Wharton does a great job of admitting smart, talented people who know how to get the job done without a lot of pretense. From what I saw in my two years, he was absolutely right.

Shana Johnston, Class of 2001

The admissions application
WHARTON

INTRODUCTION

The application to Wharton is composed of the following elements:
- 2 letters of recommendation
- GMAT scores
- Transcripts
- 4 essays (+1 optional essay)

While considering your application to Wharton, it is important that you maintain a holistic approach. All of the pieces should tell a cohesive story – and you should try to use all of the pieces to contribute to a complete picture. For example, do not write in your essays that you love finance and then tell your interviewer that marketing is your passion. This may seem obvious, but you would be surprised at what some people say. Use each part of the application to show the different facets of who you are. The Admissions Committee admits people – not facts and figures. Bring your application to life.

Finally, be honest and be yourself. Each of the schools you will consider has a different personality and culture. During the process, it can be hard to distinguish between the schools, but I've found that people usually end up being accepted at the places where they are happiest in the end (which is not necessarily what was their first choice during the application process). By allowing yourself to shine through, you allow the Admissions Office to see your uniqueness and provide depth to your application. Don't just say what you think they want to hear. In that vein, I'm going to provide some of my thoughts on preparing an application, but do not feel you must follow them all.

THE GMAT

No one enjoys taking standardized tests, but they are a required portion of your application. There is a wealth of resources available to help you study for these and you should consider using them.

While the GMAT may not be a breaking point, it can indicate your level of desire to go to business school. If you are unhappy with your score, try to retake the exam. If you do not test well, you have at least shown that you are willing to try again and that you are serious about your application.

Below is information on the scores of the most recent entering class at Wharton:

	GMAT
average	703
middle 80%	640 to 760

Wharton will evaluate the pieces of your score as well as the total. For example, if you have a high verbal score and a low quantitative score, it is probably worth your while to study and retake the exam if you believe you can raise your quantitative score. Low would be considered anything below the 80th percentile. This is even more important for TOEFL where an applicant should show a clear understanding of English.

THE ESSAYS

A FEW TIPS FOR WRITING STRONG ESSAYS

1. *Edit your essays.*
Read through for logic, and be sure to use your computer's spelling and grammar check. This won't catch everything, but it will help.

2. *Have someone who knows you well read your essays.*
Ask them if that describes you. Is it an accurate picture? What do they NOT say? Friends and colleagues are often a good source for singling out your accomplishments, strengths, and weaknesses.

3. *Have someone who does NOT know you read your essays.*
Ask a friend of a friend. Find someone who only knows you professionally. The admissions committeee does not know you personally, so this can give you a better feeling for the tone your essays are setting for a stranger.

4. *Think before you write.*
The writing can be the easy part; deciding what you want to say can be harder. You have limited space to convey a lot of information about yourself and you should use it most effectively and efficiently.

5. *Be interesting.*
If you are naturally funny and light hearted, let some of that show in your essays. While you should certainly take the essays seriously, make sure you allow some personality to show through.

6. *Be true to yourself.*
Do not write what you think the Admissions Office wants to read if it does not accurately reflect the "real" you.

7. *Be a contributor.*
Wharton does not want to admit someone who is smart but unlikely to add to the greater community. Through your application, show what you can add to the experience of your classmates – whether that be through extracurriculars, a unique professional background, or your quirky sense of humor.

WHAT WHARTON IS LOOKING FOR IN YOUR ESSAYS

The essays are where you can provide the "how" and the "why" behind the "what" and "when" of the data forms. Before reading your essays, a reader will have looked at the data forms and your resume. Use the essays to explain the path you have taken, what you have learned along the way, and what you can offer to the Wharton community.

As part of the reworking of the application process in 2001, the essay questions have been changed. As Director of Admissions Rosemarie Martinelli explains, "The essays were changed in order to allow our candidates greater freedom to express what they think is important to the admissions committee, in addition to answering more typical questions regarding the candidate's reasons for obtaining an MBA, path, goals, and interest in the Wharton MBA." (see "Interview with the Admissions Director, below, for further information on changes to the application.)

What we therefore set out to achieve in this section is to remind you that there is no one response to each essay, but to give you tools to ensure that you are addressing the question, and thinking about it in terms that better enable the admissions committe to evaluate you for Wharton.

This is your chance to convey a sense of self – a level of self understanding that validates your previous experience whilst conveying your potential for future achievement.

You might be talking about your values – what is important to you, what are your priorities in life? Equally you can communicate your goals – what do you intend to achieve, what are your ambitions?

To be truly convincing, make sure that you provide concrete examples. When the school asks you about your strengths and weaknesses, convey each strength with a specific illustration. Telling the school, "People say that I am very creative", will not get you very far. It is only when you back up your claim that you can impress the school. "A good example of my creativity would be the investment proposal that I put together for Company X, which provided an innovative solution to ..."

It is also important at this stage to avoid lists – nobody remembers them, least of all a school handling over 7,000 applications a year. It is far more effective to limit yourself to two or three strengths, or to focus on a singular achievement, and provide a valuable insight as to what this says about you as a person.

To fully grasp this idea, and use is to your advantage in your essays, compare your résumé with your answers to the school questions. A résumé will provide dates, locations, either job titles or qualifications, and a brief description of your responsibilites:

1998-2000   Financial Analyst   Singapore
- Advised on US investment for key Asian accounts
- Averaged 12,7% return on portfolio investment

In comparison, the essay is the chance to convey the characteristics that made such an experience a success, or tells the admissions team about your personality. Why for example did you leave your US domestic comfort for an international position? Maybe it is because you love to face new challenges, and are open-minded to international business. Over the two year period you had to demonstrate multicultural sensitivity, be determined and even single-minded when negotiating with another culture. These are the stories and illustrations that bring your admissions file to life, and help you to stand out from the other applicants.

The other golden rule is to always answer the question, whether in an essay or during an interview. If the interviewer asks you about a weakness, a shrug and the answer "I don't have any weaknesses" has just had the opposite effect, and highlighted a major weakness of self awareness!"

Most candidates struggle with the dilemma of either providing an honest answer that ruins one's chances, or the rehearsed answer which leaves one looking evasive, phony, or guilty of giving yet another tired cliché. How many times have Eric Chambers and the rest of the admissions team at Wharton heard "My greatest weakness is that I'm a perfectionist, and work too hard"?

Such a candidate has obviously tried to rely on the idea of naming a fault that's not really a fault. Impatience with incompetence, might be another example. If you do try this technique, again be sure to use a real example to give the story some interest and substance.

An alternative is to provide a weakness that is actually related to others. "I get frustrated when committees or institutions fail to respond decisively or in a timely fashion. Worse though is when they avoid taking a decision, pass it on to another department or group, and then criticize how it's done."

Your answer should be in keeping with the school to which you are applying. Telling Wharton that you are a shy person, or that you don't like mathematics, would make a school renowned for its leadership training and quantitative program quite concerned. It is often better to avoid interpersonal issues, because explaining that you don't get along with people challenges the importance of the shared estudent experience on campus.

You could consider naming a real weakness, but one you're taking steps to improve. This shows that you are aware of a situation, and are taking the initiative to do something about it. Examples could include learning another language, or improving your comfort level with technology.

As The Wharton School emphasizes, there is no one right answer – just the freedom to express what you feel is important, and says something about the real you.

Essay Questions for Wharton:
- Describe how your experiences, both professional and personal, have led to your decision to pursue an MBA at the Wharton School this year. How does this decision relate to your career goals for the future?
- Describe a situation where leadership and teamwork were critical to the outcome of a project in which you were directly involved. What did you learn from the experience and how have you applied what you learned to other situations?
- Describe a personal achievement that has had a significant impact on your life. Give specific details. What did you learn from the experience? How did it help shape your understanding of yourself and the world around you?
- Please tell us something else about yourself that you feel will help the Admissions Committee know you better.
- The Admissions Committee believes the required essay topics address issues that are important in understanding your candidacy. If there are extenuating circumstances or concerns affecting your

application of which you fell the Admissions Committee should be aware, please elaborate here (e.g. your academic performance as an accurate measure of your potential, unexplained gaps in your work experience).

EXAMPLES AND COMMENTARIES OF ESSAYS FOR WHARTON

In order to get your creative juices flowing, I have analyzed each of the new questions. Since the essay questions are completely new for the year 2001, we can't offer you any examples of successful responses - the decisions haven't yet been made! However, the applicant will not find any topics that are particularly surprising, if he or she has looked at a handful of admissions applications.

My commentary is meant to make evident the crux of the questions, so that the applicant can approach the essay writing process in a more focused fashion. Where possible, I have included excerpts of relevant essays. Of course, these examples aren't meant to suggest that you should write in a similar way - on the contrary, Wharton (and all the other schools!) value originality, and the extent of possible responses is unlimited.

1. Describe how your experiences, both professional and personal, have led to your decision to pursue an MBA at the Wharton School this year. How does this decision relate to your career goals for the future?

Tips for the essay:
When considering this question, take a lesson form the school itself. The home page of the Wharton MBA website reads:

"Wharton's MBA program is considered one of the finest in the world, and is frequently cited as the most effective in preparing graduates to lead organizations in a global business environment."

Your answer to this question will indicate to the school your level of motivation, and thoughtful reflection. You need to demonstrate that in applying to their program you have done the background research, and prove, based on your personality, abilities, experience, and future goals, that Wharton is the right school for you.

Note the emphasis on leadership in the text. It is important to think in those terms, providing examples where you have taken a role of leader, or at the very least identifying your potential for leadership in the future.

This essay consists primarily of two parts – where you have been and where you are going. For this essay to be successful, the two parts should tell a coherent story and should make you interesting. Tell your story – don't expect a reader to figure it out.

The first part is targeted at understanding where you came from and where you are going. It is similar to the "Walk me through your resume" interview question. Your resume tells a reader what you did and where you did it, but it does not describe why you made the choices you made, what you liked about your work, or what you learned. This is where you can highlight rapid advancement, unusual experiences, and bring your application to life.

The second part helps the Admissions Office understand if you have really thought about going to business school, if it makes sense for you, and what you want to get out of an MBA. You should spend twice as much time thinking about this section of the essay as the first half in order to tell a compelling story. This is also where you can show your knowledge of the school and how well you think you will fit there. If you have visited campus, discuss what you liked from your visit and how you see yourself fitting in. If you haven't been able to visit, use the website, student2student, and similar resources to interact with the community and get a feel for its culture.

2. Describe a situation where leadership and teamwork were critical to the outcome of a project in which you were directly involved. What did you learn from the experience and how have you applied what you learned to other situations?

Tips for the essay:
Teamwork is essential to your experience at Wharton. All applications are read by a current student who has just spent the last year and a half working on teams with classmates – you need to show that you will not be the one student no one wants to work with. Theoretical pontificating will not cut it here. Talk about details – how did you handle an undefined project? How did you deal with a slacker on a project? How did you juggle five different projects with tight deadlines? This essay can be harder than it looks and you should DEFINITELY have other people read it before submitting it. What sounds like taking charge to you may sound like conceit and brow-beating to a third party.

This topic bears much in common with one from previous Wharton applications:
At Wharton, the Learning Team, which consists of approximately five first-year students, is often assigned group projects and class presentations. Imagine that, one year from now, your Learning Team has a marketing class assignment due at 9:00 a.m. on Monday morning. It is now 10:00 p.m. on Sunday night; time is short, tension builds and your team has reached an impasse. What role would you take in such a situation? How would you enable the team to meet your deadline?

Both questions seek to gauge the applicant's understanding of team dynamics. The biggest difference between them is that, whereas the old question required the student to use both imagination and brains to solve a hypothetical problem, the new question places a stronger emphasis on the applicant's analysis of his or her real-life experience.

In responding to this question from a previous application, one successful candidate recounted a situation with a former company:

Sample Essay:
In 1998, as a development manager, I led a team of nine that successfully redesigned a silicon product for a major airbag cushion manufacturer client of my firm.

At the outset of the project, the team was faced with two possible solutions. The first one, favored by the team's senior chemist, involved a radical change in the choice of raw materials and an expensive 6-month qualification process. The second alternative, which I supported, offered the triple benefit of higher margin, potential for immediate implementation and unchanged raw material specifications.

The senior scientist strongly opposed the second solution and over the weeks, our relationship deteriorated accordingly. To reach consensus and restore healthy team dynamics, I decided to set up a project review to evaluate each solution and pushed my team to debate the results of the evaluation. I took everybody's point of view into account, built consensus and made sure nobody felt excluded. In addition, I invited staff from other team projects to give objective piece of advice regarding the two competing solutions.

The solution that was ultimately chosen offered better product performance, lower cost and quicker time-to-market. It reflected my initial proposal, yet considerably enriched by the input of the senior scientist. Customers' productivity thus increased by 130%. As a result of this redesign, we doubled product revenues within a year and my team received the company's innovation award.

3. Describe a personal achievement that has had a significant impact on your life. Give specific details. What did you learn from the experience? How did it help shape your understanding of yourself and the world around you?

Tips for the essay:

Show the Admissions Committee what you have accomplished. Tell them how you have learned from your experiences. This essay allows you to add depth and maturity to your application. Past essays have included everything from moving to a foreign country to becoming a parent to establishing charitable organizations. So far you have presented the Committee with information about your professional background and you should use this essay to discuss who you are on a more personal level.

Relating the experience though must be coupled with what you gained from it. You should talk about the wisdom you gained from the experience. How has this made you a more interesting person? Or a more compassionate person? Or a better person?

This essay topic has remained unchanged from previous applications. The following excerpt, from a current student, shows how this particular applicant managed not only to clearly articulate his achievement, but also to analyze its effect on his professional goals and his personal outlook.

Sample Essay:

At the age of 19, as General Secretary of a non-governmental organization, I initiated and led a volunteer project that raised funds and helped students to learn Chinese and to discover China. At that time, I was pursuing a career in physics and fundamental research. This NGO experience triggered my interest for professional activities with practical projects and concrete outcomes. I consequently drastically changed my career path and seized an opportunity to work in China for a corporation. Today, I want to further develop my leadership skills in projects with broad international exposure and to work against targeted revenue goals.

When I first started to learn Chinese at the age of 13, I was eager to discover a language considered as one of the most difficult in the world. Over the years, I wanted to satisfy my desire to get immersed in the Chinese culture. At the age of 18, I applied for an intensive language program organized in Beijing by a non-profit organization founded by the Chinese teacher of my high school. The aim of this organization is to set-up intensive language programs in China for high school and undergraduate students.

This first trip to China was an exhilarating experience. There, I participated actively in community activities, helping the staff to organize weekly conducted tours around Beijing.

Back home, I joined this organization and eventually was elected General Secretary. Mid 1991, I took over the management of the fund raising activities. The latter fulfilled my ambition to get involve in volunteer projects that could help the student community to share my keen interest for China.

The major challenge I had to overcome was that most students did not have the money to go on the trip. I reflected on how to finance scholarships for the Association's next ambitious project: bringing 40 students along the 3000 miles of the Chinese silk road during the summer 1992. I surveyed all major possible sources of funding and came to the conclusion that the city government was my first target to raise funds.

In September 1991, I presented the project to the city and consequently raised a $25,000 endowment, enabling us to provide ten students with substantial scholarships...In February 1992, I set up a project team with students in order to prepare our summer trip to China...

After four months, the group was ready for the trip to China. Once there, I took a real leadership position. I had to supervise 40 students of my own age in an unusual environment. I also greatly improved my personal maturity by managing student groups in China. I learned to evolve into a leadership role with the consensus of the team, to exercise authority with care and to express empathy when necessary. I later on built on this experience when I managed people older or more skilled than me both in China and at home.

In China, I also learned to deal with uncertainty and to develop a sense of decision making under time pressure and with serious issues at stake. I overcame crisis situations such as the handling of students who needed surgery or the difficulties related to organizing travel along the Silk Road from vehicles resembling bicycles to trains and buses. This helped me to develop a high degree of responsibility towards others and a resourcefulness when facing unexpected problems.

During this NGO experience, I learned how to raise money and organize a project. I learned that I could rely on my organization skills and creativity to achieve goals that were never achieved before. I also learned how to initiate projects and take initiative within organized structures, such as associations or companies. In addition to as successful track record, I realized that my action helped students to fulfil their ambition. Two students in particular, discovered China through our program. They both work today in China; one is a teacher in Chengdu and the other is a chemist in Shanghai.

Finally, this project was a source a incredible satisfaction. I discovered that helping others to fulfill their goals brings as much satisfaction as living my own dreams. I realized how important it is to give back to my own community and to make others benefit from my own experience. Ever since, this important lesson has guided my endeavors when I undertake ambitious projects.

4. Please tell us something else about yourself that you feel will help the Admissions Committee know you better.

Tips for the essay:

What have you not discussed already that you consider important to who you are? This can be hobbies, extracurriculars in college, a leadership experience, or a defining experience. This essay is incredibly broad in order to allow you to showcase what makes you unique. That being said, you should avoid the temptation to rush and out join a club or pick up a new pasttime, in hopes of "rounding out" your profile. It is important to fit the experience or activity that you choose to highlight in this essay into the context of your overall profile - what you've studied, where you've worked, how you've spent your spare time and holidays, etcetera. By taking this broader look, you will present to the admissions committee a coherent portrait of a candidate, whom they will be able to evaluate as a whole person.

Along these lines, the sample essay below provides a remarkable example of how a candidate used her experience in the performing arts - a background somewhat atypical for an applicant to an MBA program - to show her understanding of the importance of teamwork and attention to detail in both a business school program and in business. The clarity of her parallel between dance and business convinces the reader that she has the understanding necessary to succeed in the MBA program, and the unusualness of her background distinguishes her application.

Sample Essay

Risk - an inherent ingredient of business - is also an integral part of a dancer's experience. Every time I step on stage, I put my whole being at risk, committing myself fully to the challenge of rendering a near flawless performance that will draw in the audience and communicate the magic of my art. My willingness to take both personal and professional riskes contributed significantly to my success in both my dance and arts administration careers.

Dance teaches other lessons valuabe to business: the importance of teamwork (imagine a dance company where each performer follows his or her own whims), and of painstaking attention to detail. A dance performance is an exercise in precision - a thoroughly rehearsed team, each member totally aware of and dependent upon the others to produce a coherent product. The parallels to business operations are clear.

Sharing my experiences as a professional dancer should therefore be a valuable contribution to the class as we jointly explore what makes an enterprise successful. I look forward to an intensive dialogue with the school's talented faculty and its highly talented student body. I know I will learn from my classmates and I hope they in turn will learn from me, particularly about the world of the arts and artists.

5. (Optional): The Admissions Committee believes the required essay topics address issues that are important in understanding your candidacy. If there are extenuating circumstances or concerns affecting your application of which you fell the Admissions Committee should be aware, please elaborate here (e.g. your academic performance as an accurate measure of your potential, unexplained gaps in your work experience).

This essay question is truly optional for most candidates, however candidates with unusual circumstances should consider this required. Students have written about a variety of topics in this question, but all of them should discuss what went wrong, what was learned from the experience, and how it has been remedied (if applicable). Some examples of situations you may want to discuss include:

- Several low or failing grades in college
- Overall poor performance in college
- Time off from work
- Unusual selection of recommenders

All of the above could have reasonable, logical explanations (for example an extended illness) or more worrisome ones (inability to keep a job). By explaining the situation, you can help the Admissions Committee understand what you went through and how you are a better applicant because of it.

You are also able to discuss the event in the most advantageous light. If you have taken action to remedy the problem, you should also use this opportunity to discuss it. For example, an applicant who performed poorly in college but feels she or he has matured since then, may choose to enroll in a part-time class at a local college or university to demonstrate that she now has the focus to be able to excel in school.

The bottom line is that past difficulties should not derail your application. By discussing what happened, rather than trying to ignore it and hoping no one notices, you will be improving your overall application.

LETTERS OF RECOMMENDATION

Number of letter of recommendation needed for Wharton: 2

GENERAL ADVICE

Pick someone who knows you.

While it may sound nice to have the President of your company recommend you, it may not help much if he or she can't say more than that you work at the company. The most persuasive and effective recommendation letters reveal qualities about the applicant that have not been discussed in other places. They make the applicant come alive to the reader.

The preferred letter seems to be from your immediate boss, the person you work with on a daily basis. Of course, he or she may be the last person you intended to forewarn about your project for heading to business school the following September. The school recognizes this, and will understand if it is more expedient for you to have chosen other recommenders. Nevertheless, by asking your immediate supervisor you are also making a clear statement to the school just how committed you are to the MBA project.

It is clearer from the questions asked by other business schools that it is better not to approach a professor from college for one of your recommendations. Though well-placed to describe academic achievement and class participation, they would struggle to describe your potential for senior management. If you in a doctorate program however, your academic supervisor would be a natural choice.

Other alternative recommenders could include clients and suppliers. Given that they are expected to describe the circumstances under which you have worked together, make sure to choose a professional contact with whom you have a substantial working relationship (not just selling them advertising space every six months).

In some cases your recommender may have been to business school, perhaps even to Wharton, and is well-versed with the need for a detailed letter, and well-placed to identify the qualities required of a successful student at the school.

Coach your recommenders.

Make sure they know why you are applying to business school and what you want to get from it. Ask them to include anecdotes or particular details that might be enlightening to the Admissions Committee.

Ask for specifics.

The more specific your recommenders can be, providing concrete examples of your abilities, contributions and achievements, the better the Admissions Committee will be able to understand you.

Give them time.

Writing a good letter of recommendation requires considerable time and effort. To ensure the best results, speak at length with the recommender beforehand, perhaps even taking them to lunch. Describe the process of application, your motivation for the school, and what is expected of them. This could prove invaluable for a boss or colleague from two or three years back who may appreciate the reminder of your roles and achievements during your time working together.

Try to give them six to eight weeks to complete the letter, making sure they know the deadline you are trying to meet. A phone call or e-mail in the ensuing weeks enables you to keep track of their progress, until the letter is finished, placed in the envelope with their signature on the back, and either sent directly to the school or returned to you to include in your application.

QUESTIONS ASKED IN THE WHARTON LETTERS OF RECOMMENDATION

The evaluation grid asks recommenders to rank candidates as follows:

	Truly exceptional (Top 1%)	Superior (Top 2%)	Outstanding (Top 5%)	Very Good (Top 10%)	Good (Top 25%)	Average (Top 50%)	Below Average	No basis for judgement
Analytical Skills								
Verbal Skills								
Self Discipline								
Initiative								
Integrity								
Creativity								
Maturity								
Teamwork								
Managerial Potential								
Leadership Potential								
Ability to operate effectively in cultural environments other than his/her own.								

In addition to filling out the grid, the recommender is asked to respond to the following questions, which should be answered in a separate letter and attached to the form.

1. Please tell us the peer group you have chosen to use, and free to explain any of your ratings in your evaluation.
2. Define your relationship to the applicant and describe the circumstances under which you have known him or her.
3. Comment on the applicant's personal integrity.
4. Please discuss observations you have made concerning the applicant's leadership abilities, team and/or group skills.
5. How would you describe the applicant's sense of humor (seriously)?
6. Please discuss the applicant's most salient strengths?

7. Please discuss the applicant's weaknesses. What efforts has the applicant made to address these issues?

8. If you have additional comments that you think would assist the Admissions Committee in making its decision, please add them here.

9. Your overall impression of the applicant. (same ranking scale as above).

THE INTERVIEW

The interview should be where you bring your application to life – literally. It should be considered another piece of the overall package and the same attention and energy you applied to your essays should be given to the interview. Many of the tips for essays – be yourself, be interesting, think before you speak – should also apply to the interview. On top of that, the standard decorum for any interview should be followed.

For the first time in 2001-2002, Wharton will be selecting applicants to interview rather than allowing any applicant to request an interview. This change is in response to the large volume of applicants at Wharton and a desire to provide a more fair process to all applicants. After evaluating the application, the Admissions Committee will invite selected candidates to an interview. The purpose at this point is to allow the applicant to present himself in the best possible light and to try to determine if the applicant seems to fit with the Wharton student body.

Selected applicants will have the opportunity to interview with a current student, an alumni, or an Admissions Officer. Who interviews an applicant is more a function of timing and location than anything else.

INTERVIEW WITH THE ADMISSIONS DIRECTOR

Interview with Rosemaria Martinelli, Director of MBA Admissions and Financial Aid, The Wharton School

Wharton has recently changed its application process. Can you explain the reasons for this?

The MBA market has witnessed a series of changes in recent years that have led us to re-assess how we promote the School, as well as select and retain the best candidates. Among our new initiatives is a change from rolling admissions to admissions by rounds (three), and from interview for any interested prospective student to interview by invitation after a full evaluation of their application. These changes were designed to create a more transparent and understandable admissions process, allowing our candidates to focus their time and energy on crafting the best application rather than trying to obtain an interview before submitting their application, and receive their admissions decisions on a fixed date rather than within the 8-12 week framework in rolling admissions.

Who reads the completed application?

Typically, each application is reviewed at least three times prior to the final decision. Evaluators may include a trained second-year MBA student, an associate director, the admissions committee, and the director.

Why have the essays changed from previous years? What are the benefits of this change for the application process?

The essays were changed in order to allow our candidates greater freedom to express what they think is important to the admissions committee, in addition to answering more typical questions regarding the candidates reasons for obtaining an MBA, path, goals, and interest in the Wharton MBA.

What are the "do's" and "don't's" for the essays?

Do not try to write what you think the Admissions Committee wants to hear. Describe your own experiences and motivations. Be concise, and answer the questions completely. It is always helpful to summarize the points you want to cover before you begin. Finally, let us get to know you both professionally and personally.

What are the "do"s and "don't's" for letters of recommendation? What makes a good letter of recommendation?

It is important to choose recommenders (in a professional setting) that know you well. Do not choose people based on their title or name recognition, unless they know you well. A current supervisor is preferred. I would encourage the applicant to sit down and talk with each recommender about the importance of the recommendation in their overall application. It might be helpful to discuss each of the questions with them, and provide them with examples that might be useful. Encourage your recommenders to provide detailed and honest feedback

How important is the GMAT to the admissions process? What is the minimum score you accept?

While the GMAT scores are important to measure academic ability, this is only one area of the application. There are no minimum scores, but students should be aware of the range of scores of successful applicants. It is important to present yourself well, so if you feel your score does not represent your ability, I would encourage you to retake the test again. Wharton will evaluate the highest total score.

What is the function of the interview in the selection process?

Once we have evaluated the full application, it is necessary to meet in person to assess an applicant's passion, vision, communication skills, and their overall fit within our community.

Does the interviewer have access to the application form of the interviewee ahead of the interview?

No, the interview is conducted without any prior information beyond the applicant's resume. We want each student to have a full, unbiased opportunity to present themselves and their passions to the interviewer.

What criteria distinguish a good applicant?

While accomplishments are important, describing your motivations and the lessons learned from your experiences helps to distinguish you in a very competitive applicant pool. In addition to your professional development, the Admissions Committee seeks to know you in a personal way as well: your passions, hobbies, a commitment to giving back, and being involved with one's community.

All schools have to make a tradeoff between the diversity of the student body and the strength of the individual candidate – which is most important?

Both! With such a talented applicant pool, we are able to achieve both at Wharton. Diversity at Wharton includes not only race, ethnicity, and gender, but also personal and professional backgrounds, perspectives, and ideas. Diversity is key in an educational environment. Not only will you be learning while in school, you will be teaching your professors and classmates through the sharing of your experiences.

Are there quotas by country? By background? By gender or race?

No. Wharton seeks to enroll a diverse class, including students who have diverse backgrounds, experience and perspectives. We seek to enroll a class of leaders who will be instrumental in effecting change in their professional and personal lives. Diversity in the classroom is valuable, but the final decision comes down to selecting the best students for the school regardless of their race, gender, or citizenship.

Wharton has a reputation as a very quantitative environment. What if an applicant does not have a quantitative background?

Students come from various backgrounds into the MBA program. While Wharton's curriculum is quantitatively-based, we provide opportunities for each student to gain the necessary skills through pre-term and the core curriculum to be successful at Wharton and in their professional careers. We recommend that students who have not had prior quantitative coursework in their undergraduate degree do some basic preparation for the MBA by pursuing courses in calculus, statistics, economics and finance.

How do you measure the fit between the applicant and Wharton?

We're looking for the next generation of leaders – people who want to make a difference. Being passionate, collaborative and committed to being the best you can are key elements of the Wharton community. Applicants demonstrate this by their past history, their knowledge of the Wharton program, and how they can make a contribution to this community.

What qualities would you like to see more of in candidates?

Passion and purpose, the ability to communicate a plan, and a desire to make a difference.

Wharton has a reputation as a very quantitative environment, what if an applicant does not have a quantitative background?

Students come from various backgrounds into the MBA program. While Wharton's curriculum is quantitatively-based, we provide opportunities for each student to gain the necessary skills through pre-term and the core curriculum to be successful at Wharton and in their professional careers. We recommend that students who have not had prior quantitative coursework in their undergraduate degree do some basic preparation for the MBA by pursuing courses in calculus, statistics, economics and finance.

Is it better to apply in the early rounds?

Yes, only if that applicant feels that she/he can prepare the best application in time for the earlier deadlines. This is more important than timing. If an applicant needs additional time, then he/she should take it. The last round may be a bit more difficult, because the Admissions Committee may have some limitations. I would encourage international students to apply early to have ample time to make arrangements to transition to the United States.

Do you encourage rejected applicants to re-apply?

That depends. I would encourage unsuccessful applicants to review their applications to see if they presented themselves well. Wharton offers the opportunity to obtain feedback. If you plan to reapply, I would encourage an applicant to seek out this information, and then make sure to follow that guidance.

What does the school specifically expect from international students?

The expectations are no different for our international students, except that they have a good grasp of the English language, including verbal, listening, and writing skills. Since an MBA education is a fast-paced, intensive environment, being very comfortable with the English language is a prerequisite for success.

Getting the MBA Admissions Edge

Now that you have finished reading about many of the major international business schools, you should be in an excellent position to make a start on the application dossiers for the schools of your choice.

On behalf of all the contributors and the research team who helped to compile this book, we wish you the best of luck in getting the MBA admissions edge,

Alan Mendonca   &   Matt Symonds
alain@theMBAsite.com   matt@theMBAsite.com